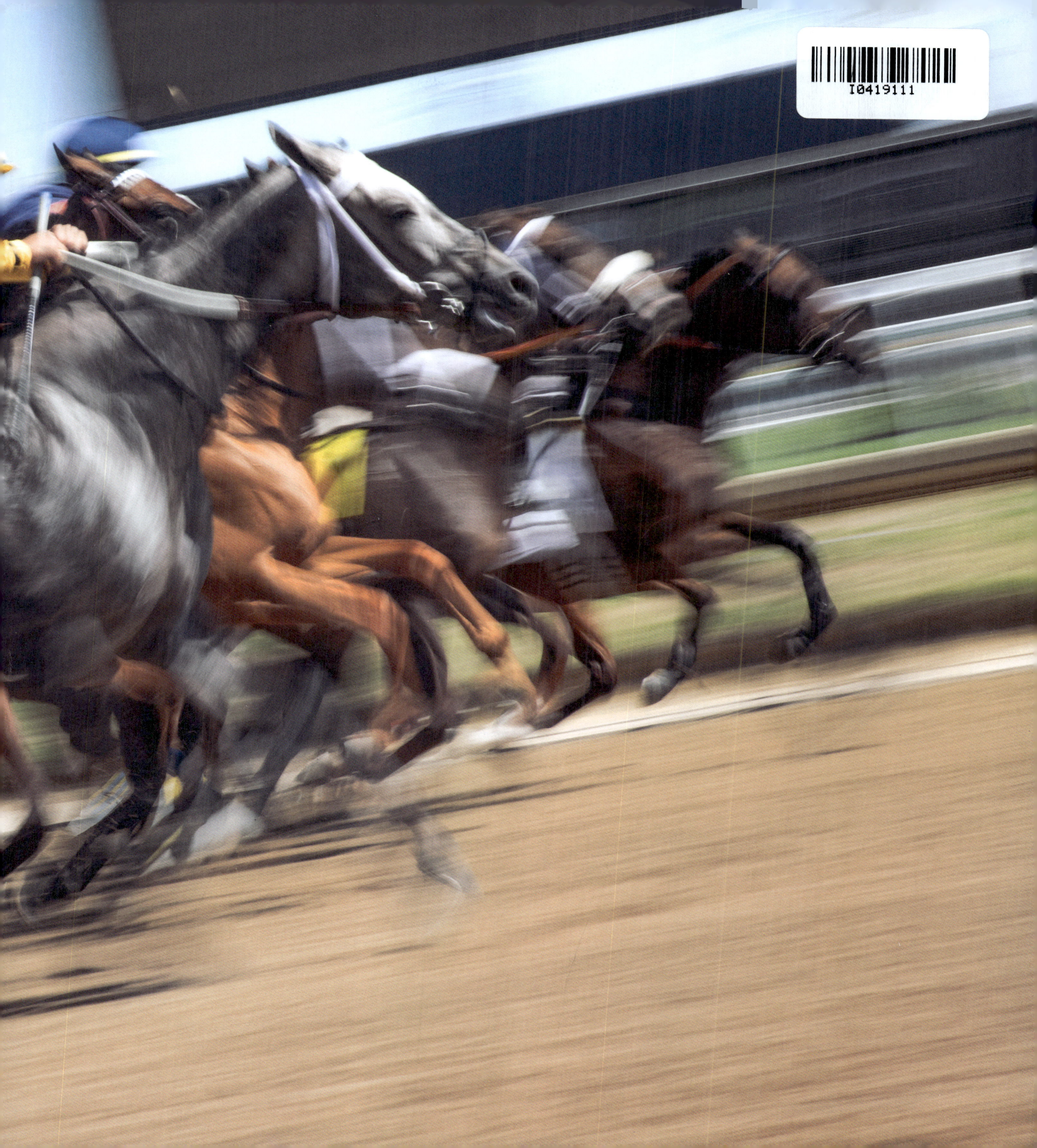

At the Derby

Photographs by
Lili Kobielski

Foreword by
Helmut Lang

At the Derby

Photographs by Lili Kobielski

Foreword by Helmut Lang

Kentucky's Grandest Celebration of Fashion

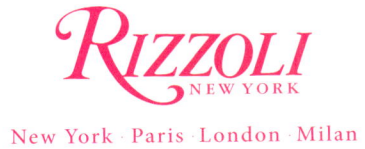

RIZZOLI
NEW YORK

New York · Paris · London · Milan

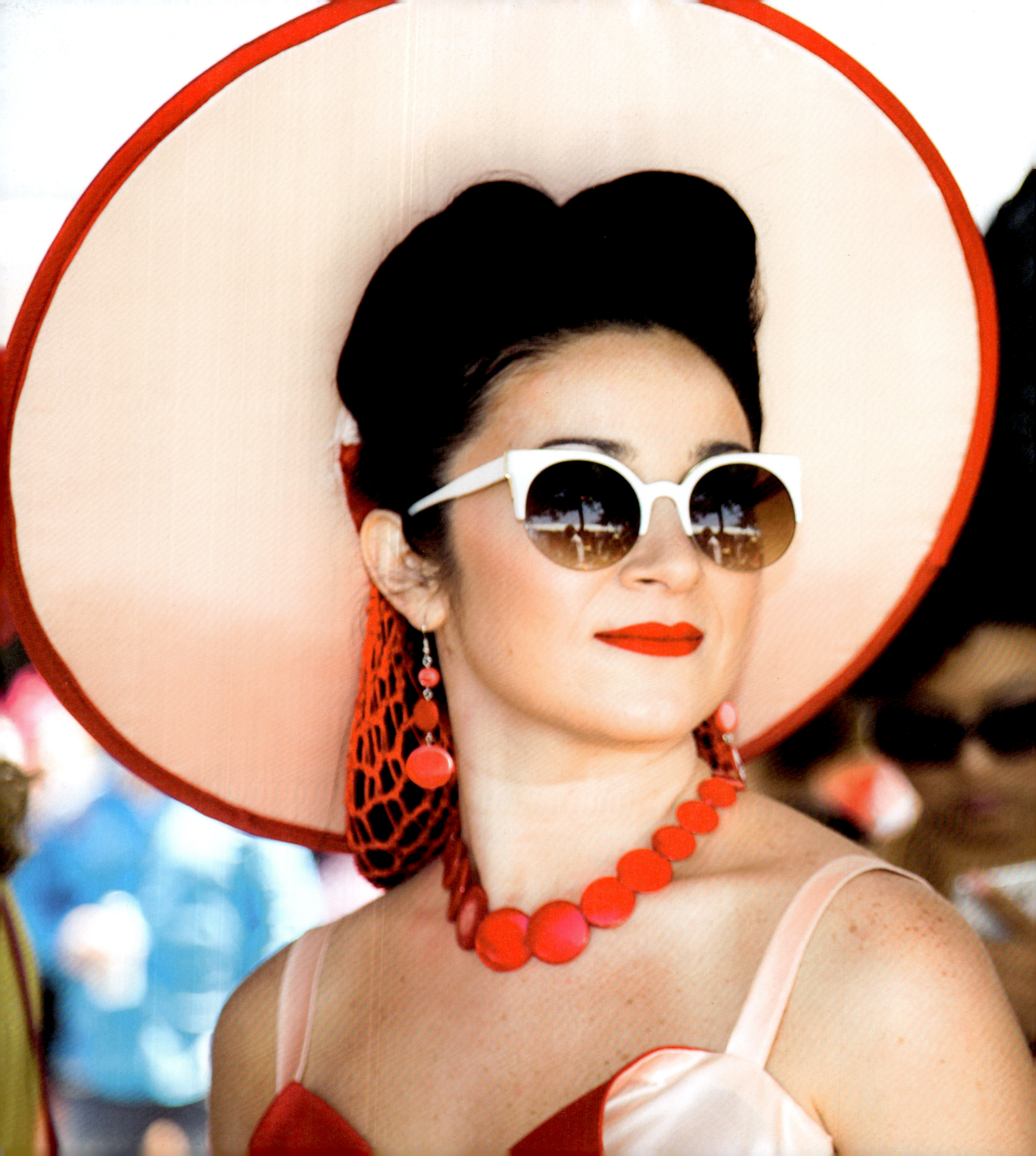

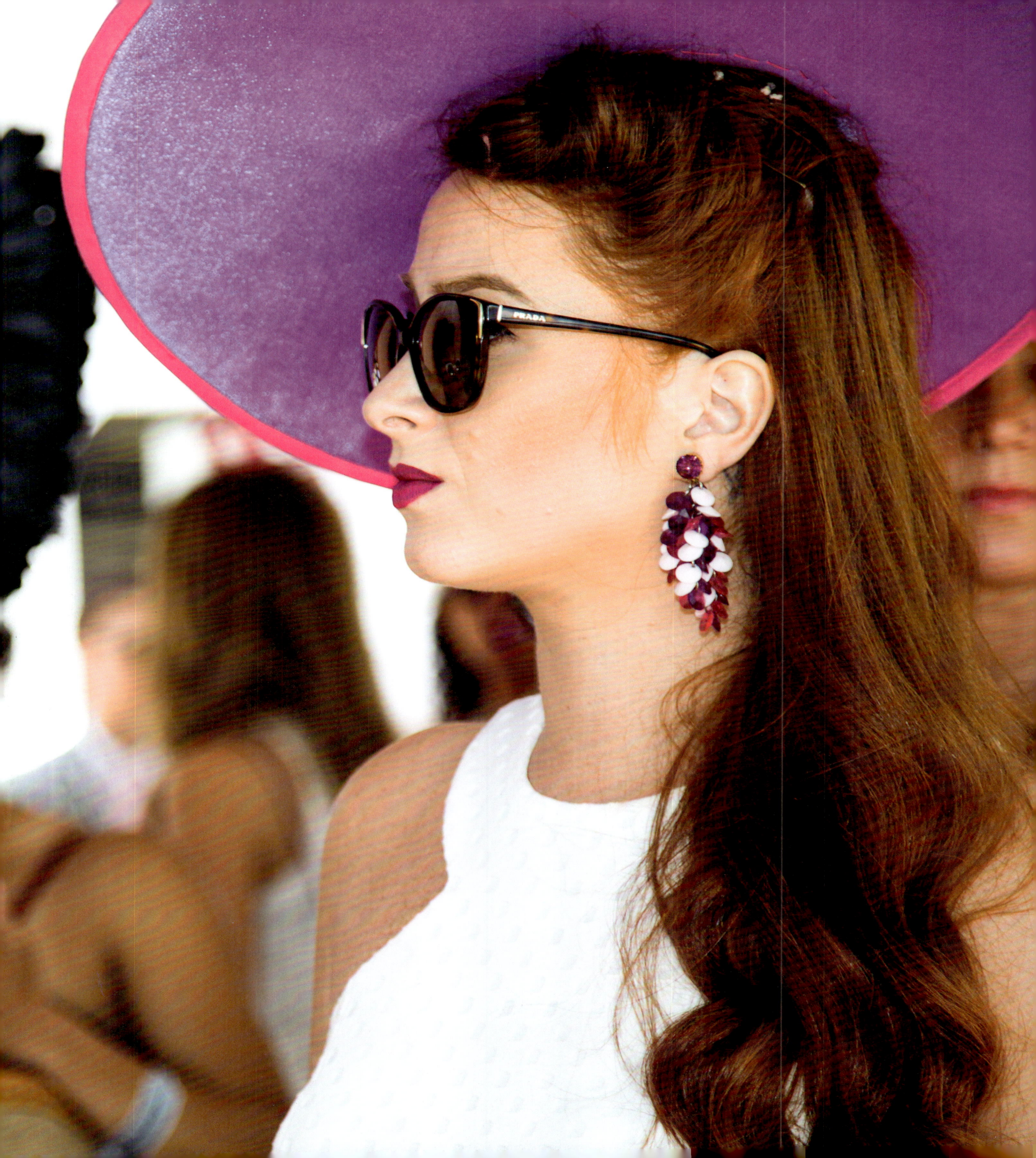

Contents

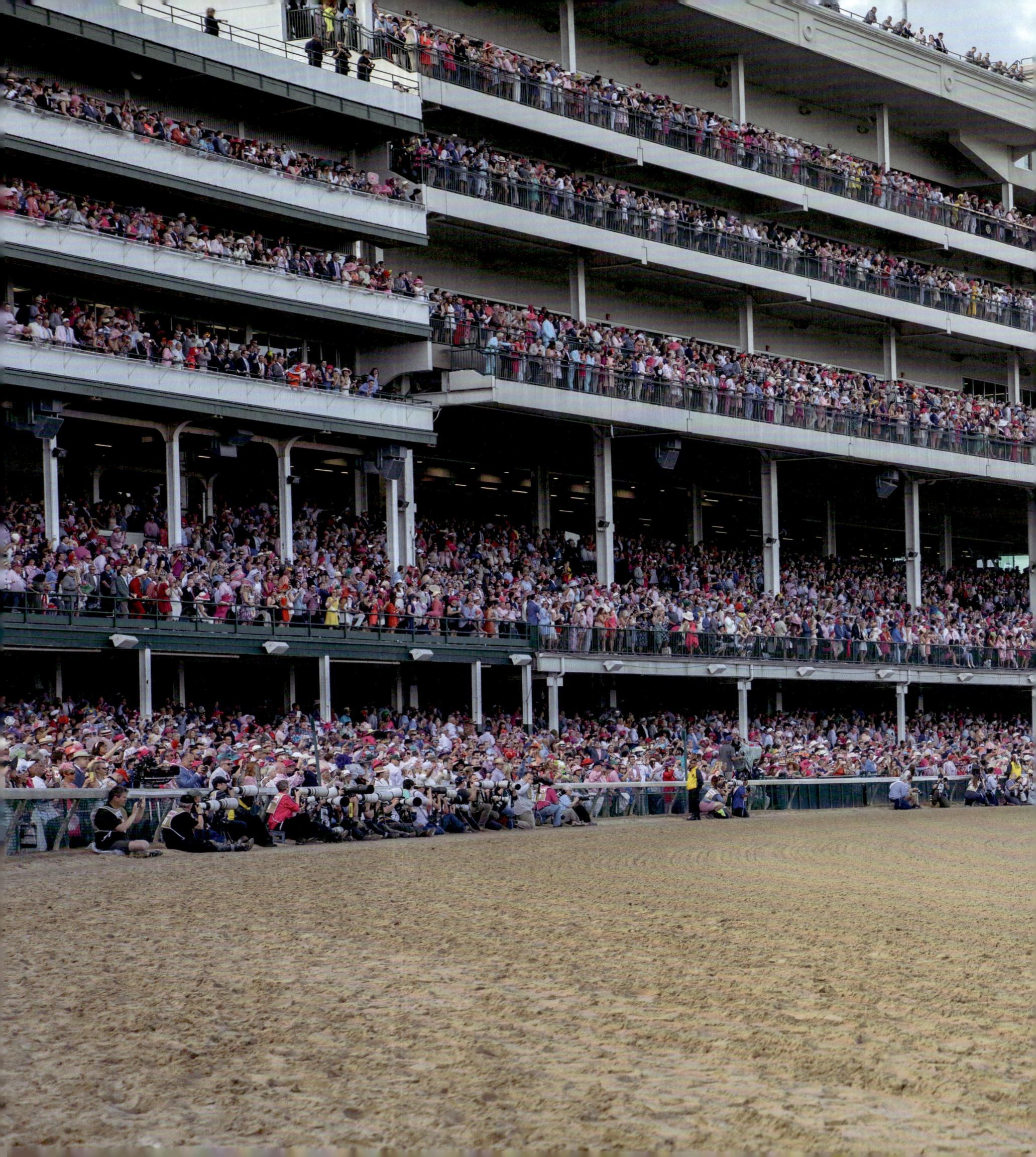

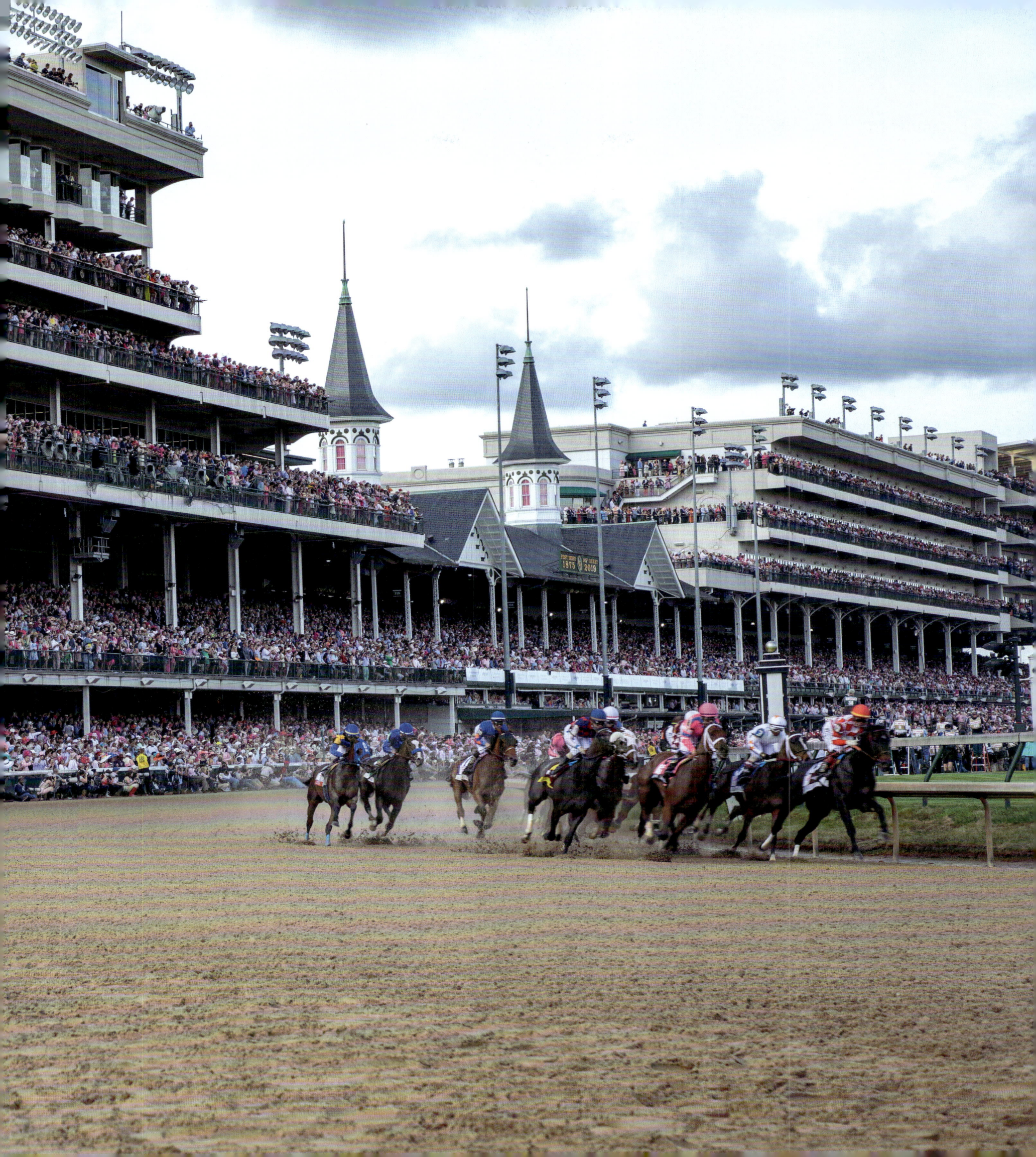

This Is Personal
by Helmut Lang

Lili's engagement is deeply rooted in a four-generational family history dedicated to horses and farming, and an inherited visual DNA.[1] Gifted with this historical imprint, Lili could ride (or was on the back of a pony) before she could properly walk, naturally cultivating her passion for horses and all life forms and allowing her to grow into her own authentic self—caring, capable, and seriously talented.

The Kentucky Derby is very American. It's a massive space, a massive crowd, the two most exciting minutes, no place where the prizes or hats are too huge. It's American capitalism at its best and worst.

Horse racing, which draws together people from as many walks of society as any sporting event, makes equals of everyone who is not a gladiator. Viewers, no matter their status, occupy the same level playing field: that of fans.

Social gatherings offer a shared experience, a place of communication, belonging, exposure, and conscious or unconscious competition, all of which are vital to the human condition.

Lili is not exploring her visual objects or found situations in a judgmental way, only for sensational purposes. There is always enough kindness for the variety of life, taste, personal presentation, and celebration seen through her lens.

Her unique mind and eye create captivating compositions that seem incredibly alive. Not just a frozen image of the moment, they unfold in the mind like short movies that seem eager to vocally communicate and engage one in a larger experience.

It's a rare gift to be able to participate in a still image that intensely.

For me, Lili always demonstrates a unique talent for combining the truth, the wondrous, the crazy and absurd, the insane, the joyful, and the beautiful in her photographs. Not settling for the obvious first impression, she creates a multi-layered story to be explored, where there is enough room for individual experience and emotion.

Like with any art, it takes on different lives once it is handed over to the public.

---

[1] Her grandmother Jennie Donaldson Beasley's horse stable, the famous Windy Hill Farm, hosted visiting dignitaries.

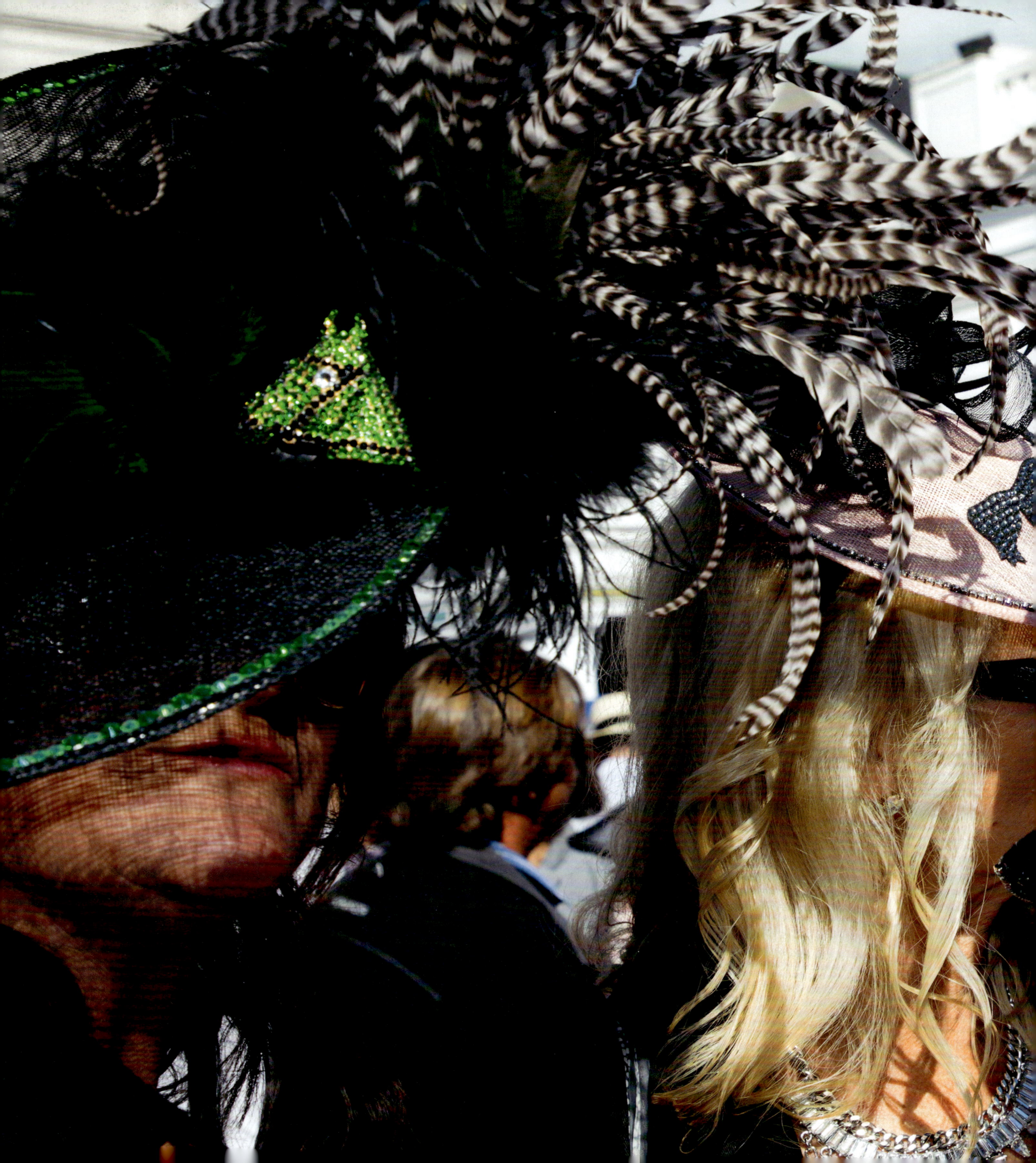

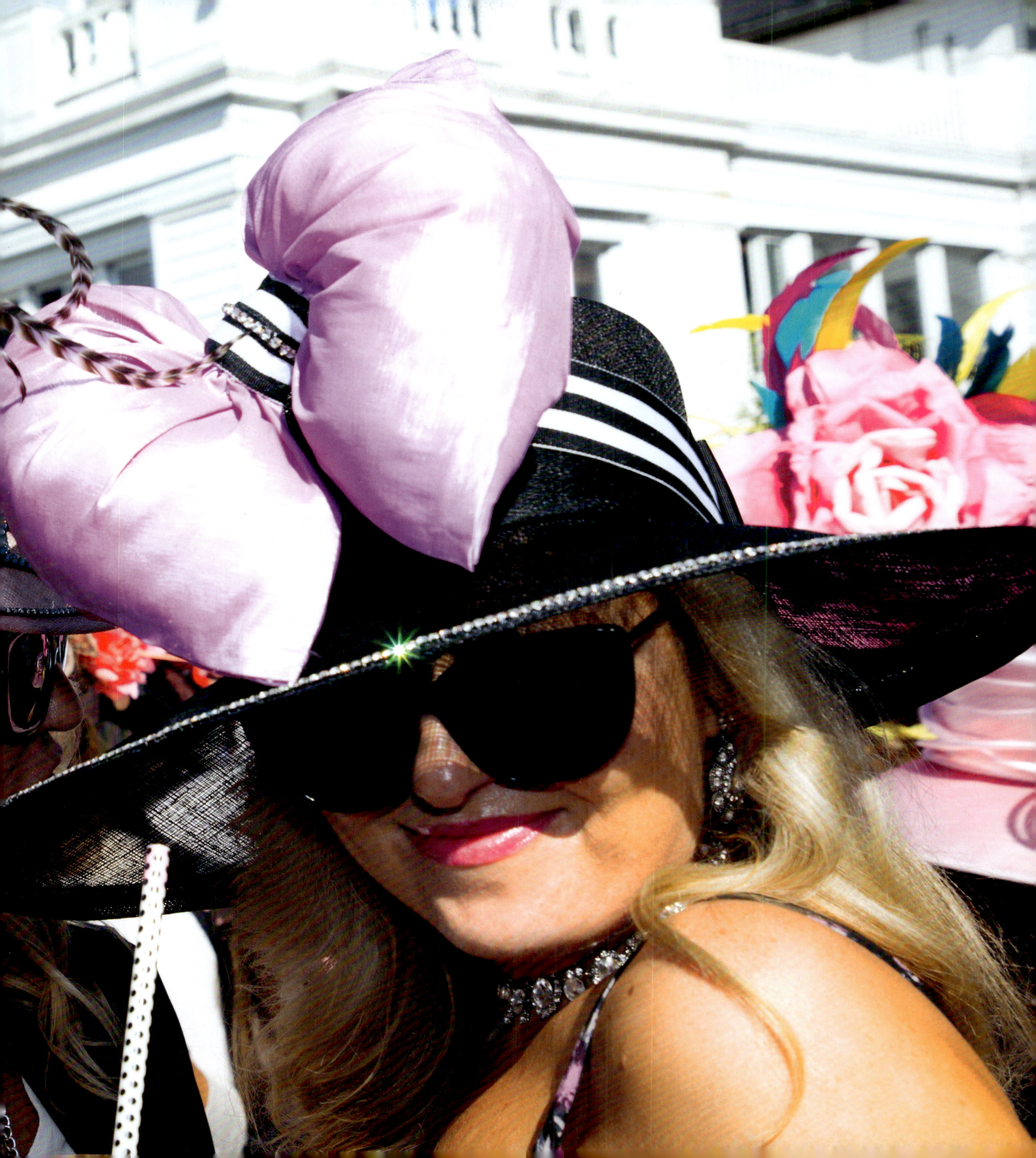

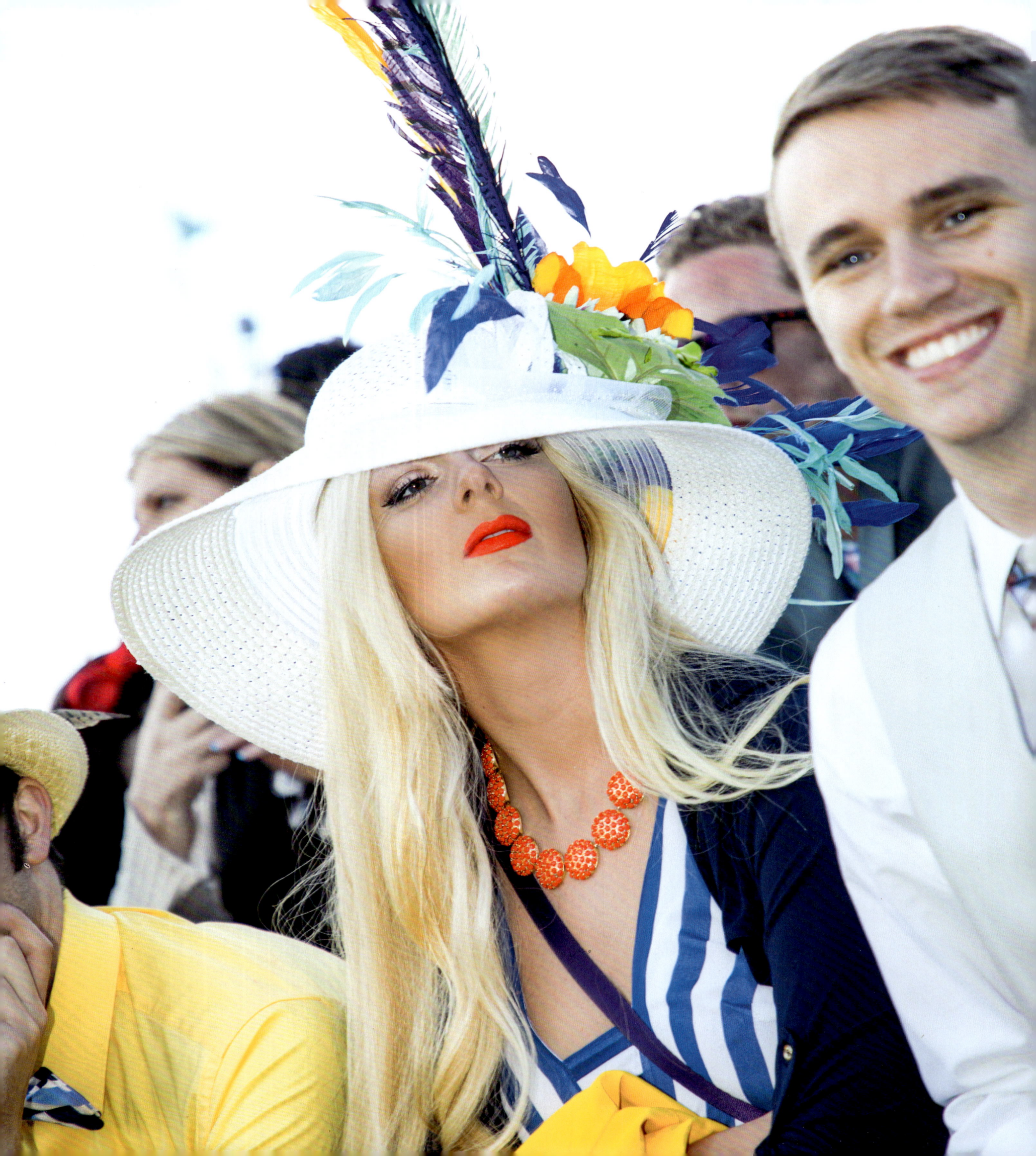

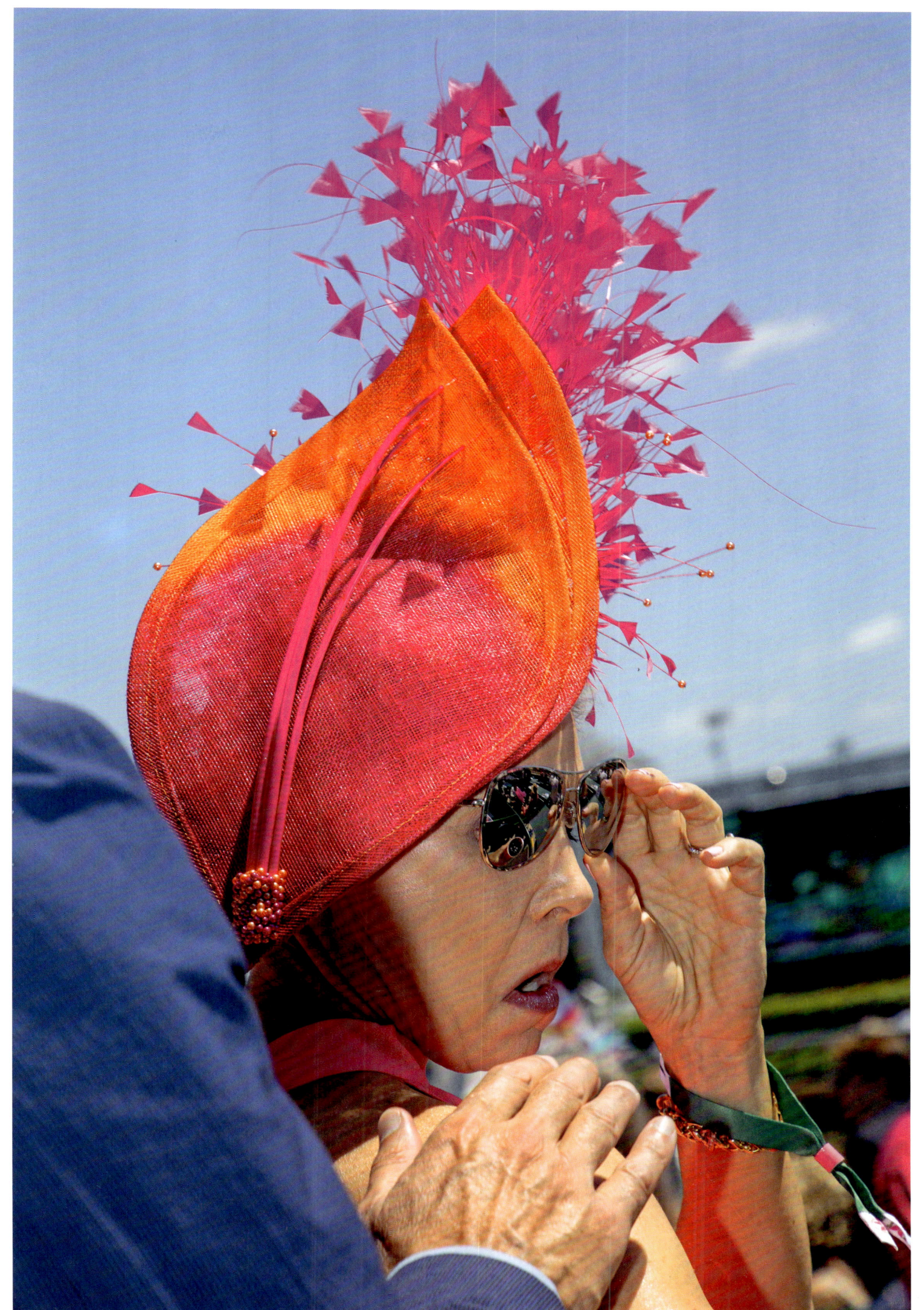

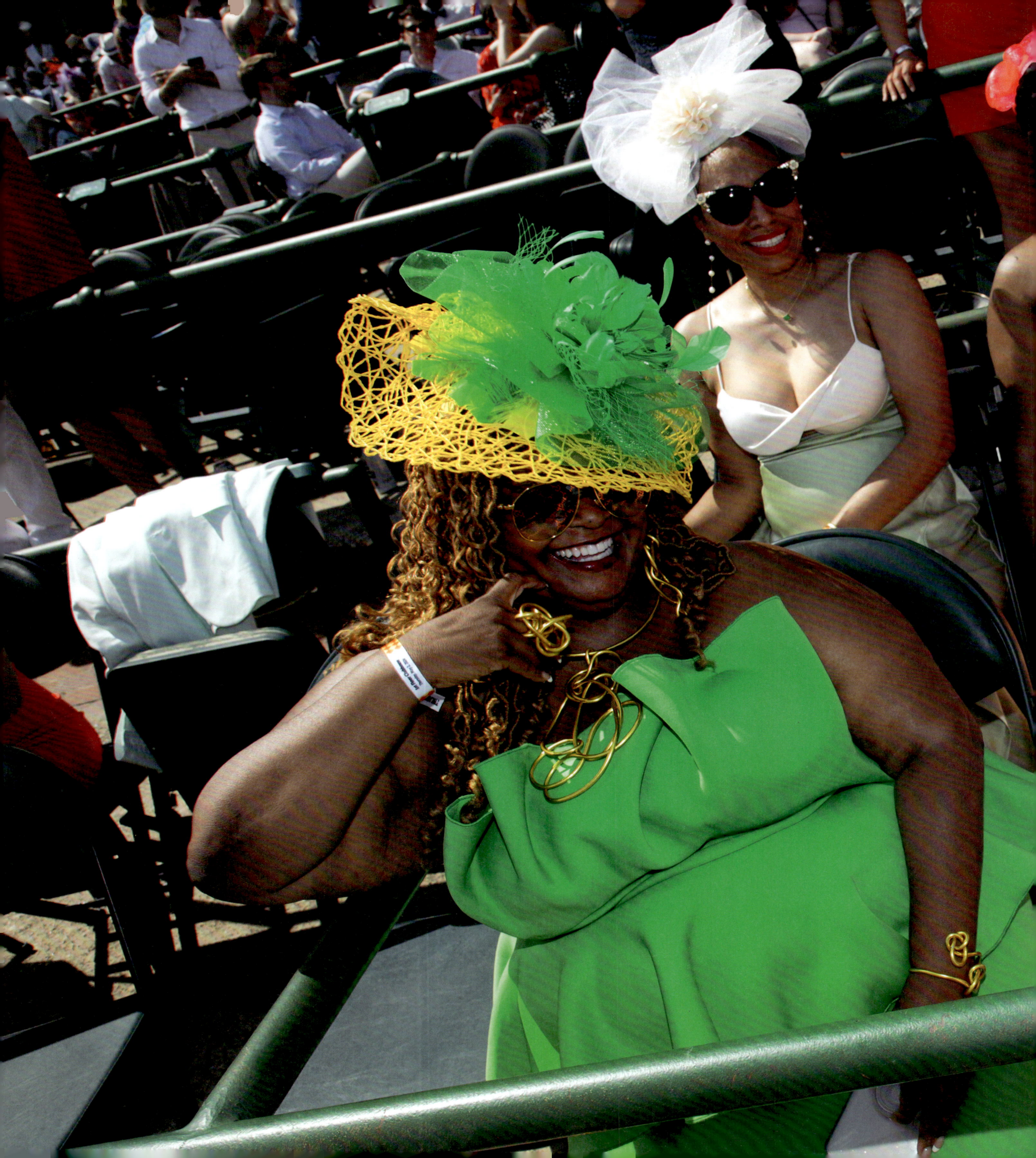

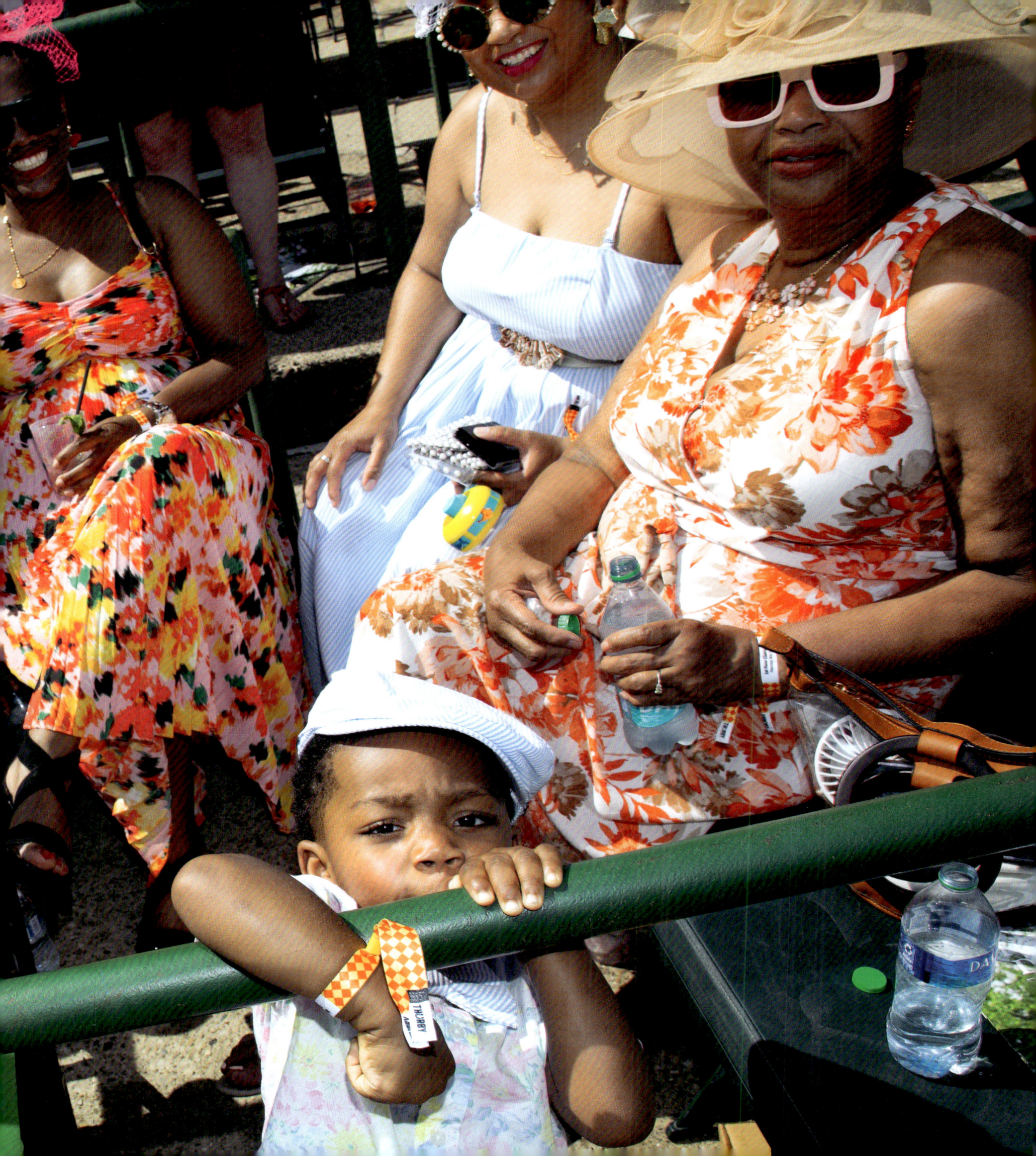

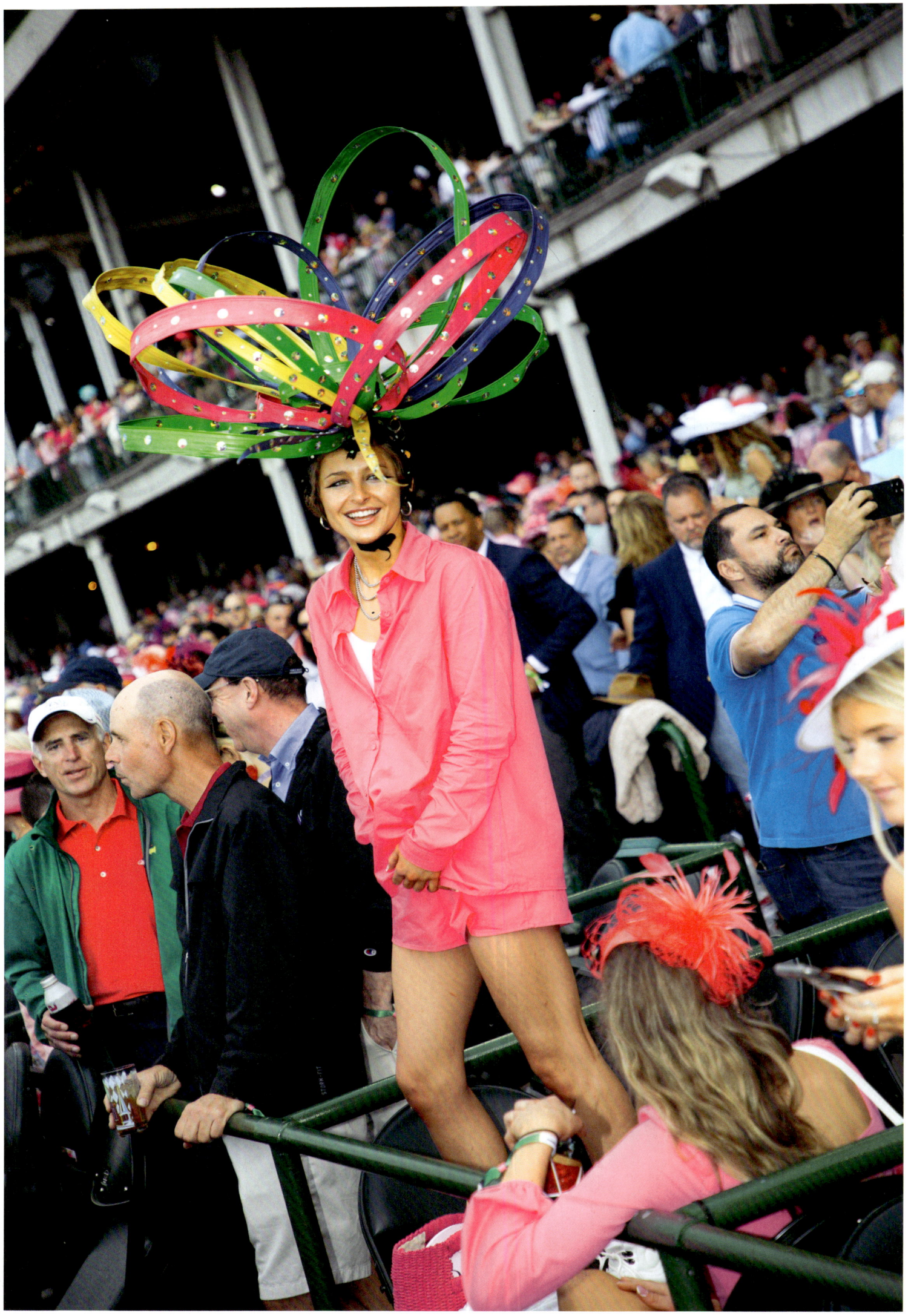

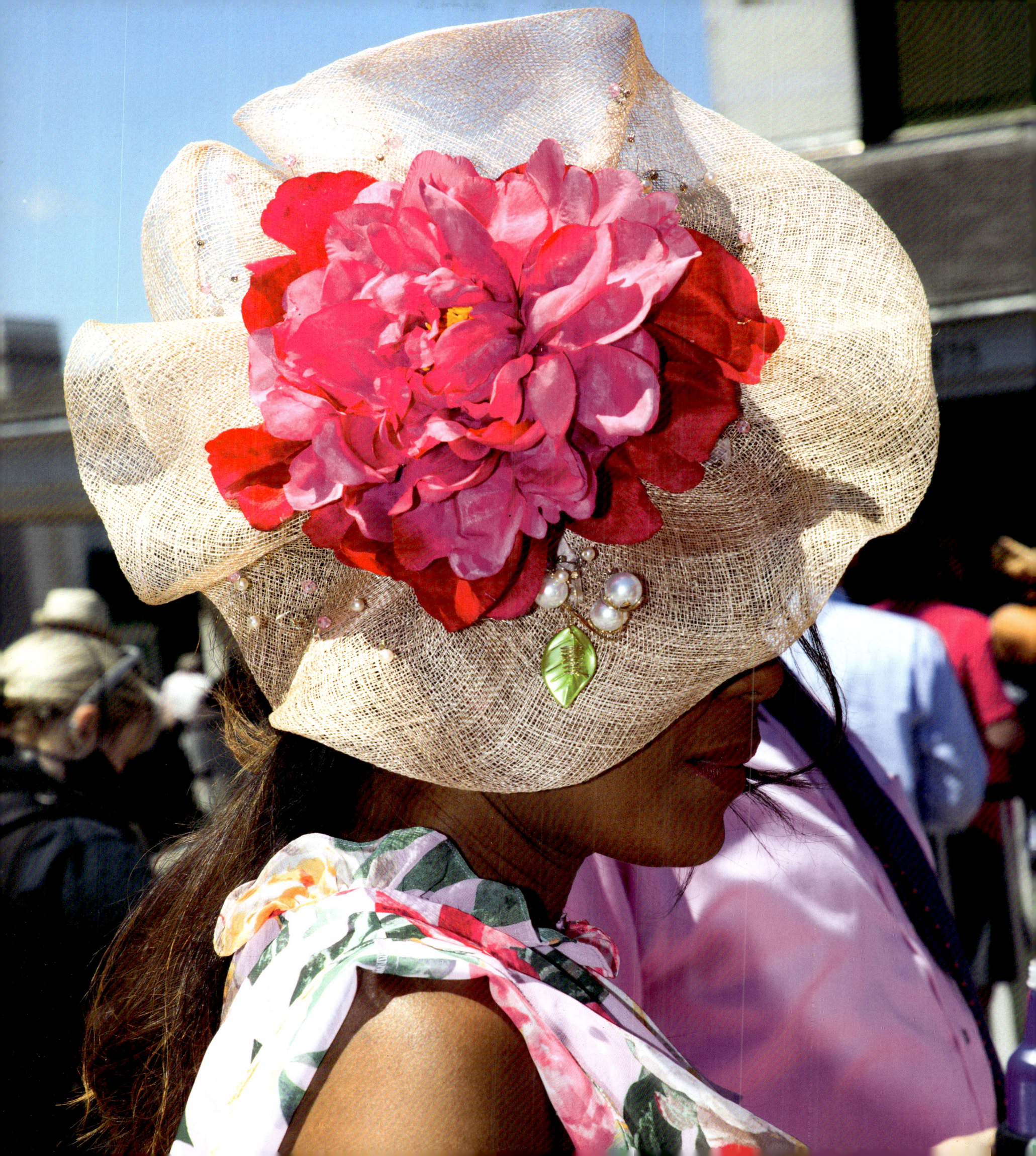

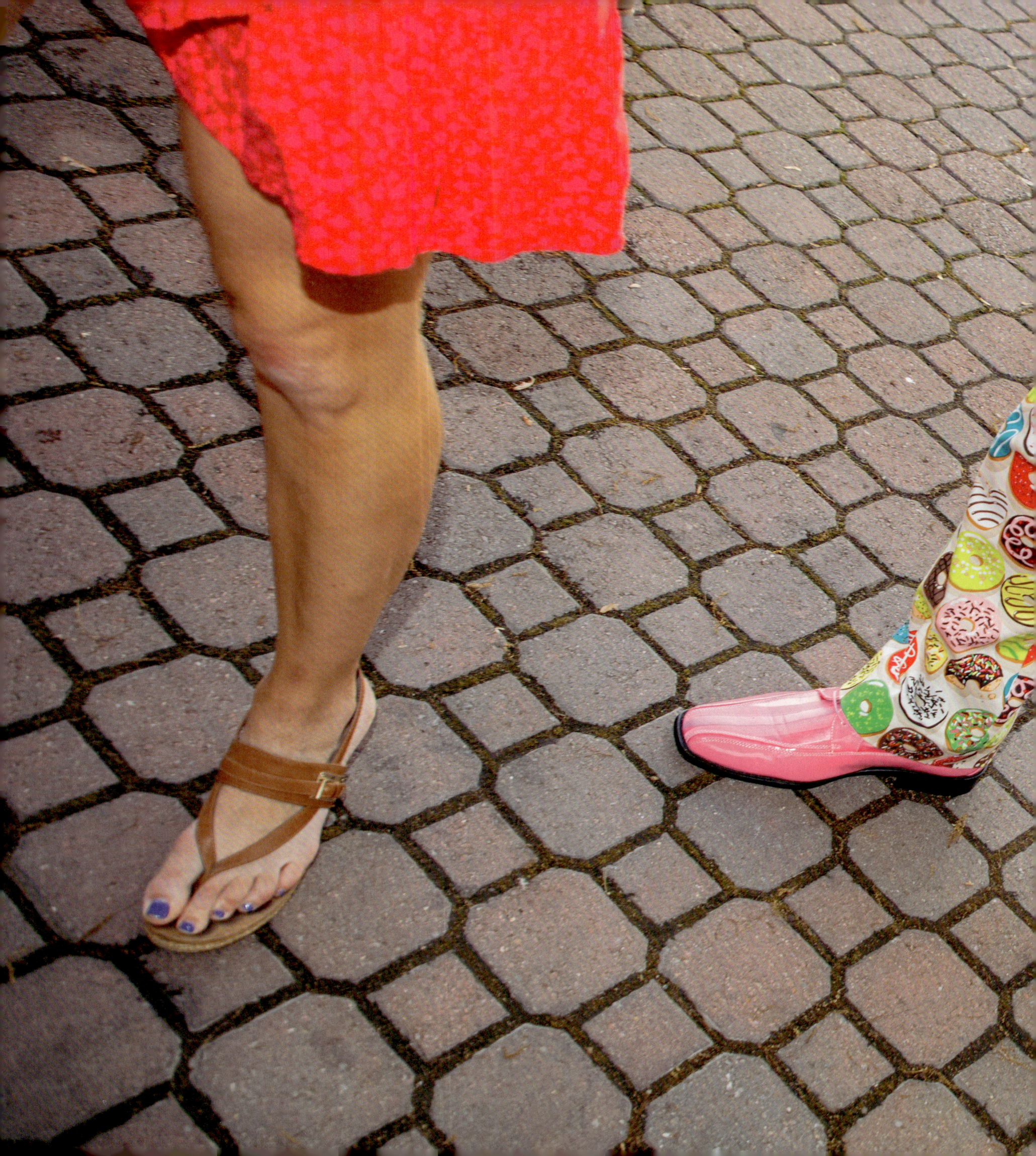

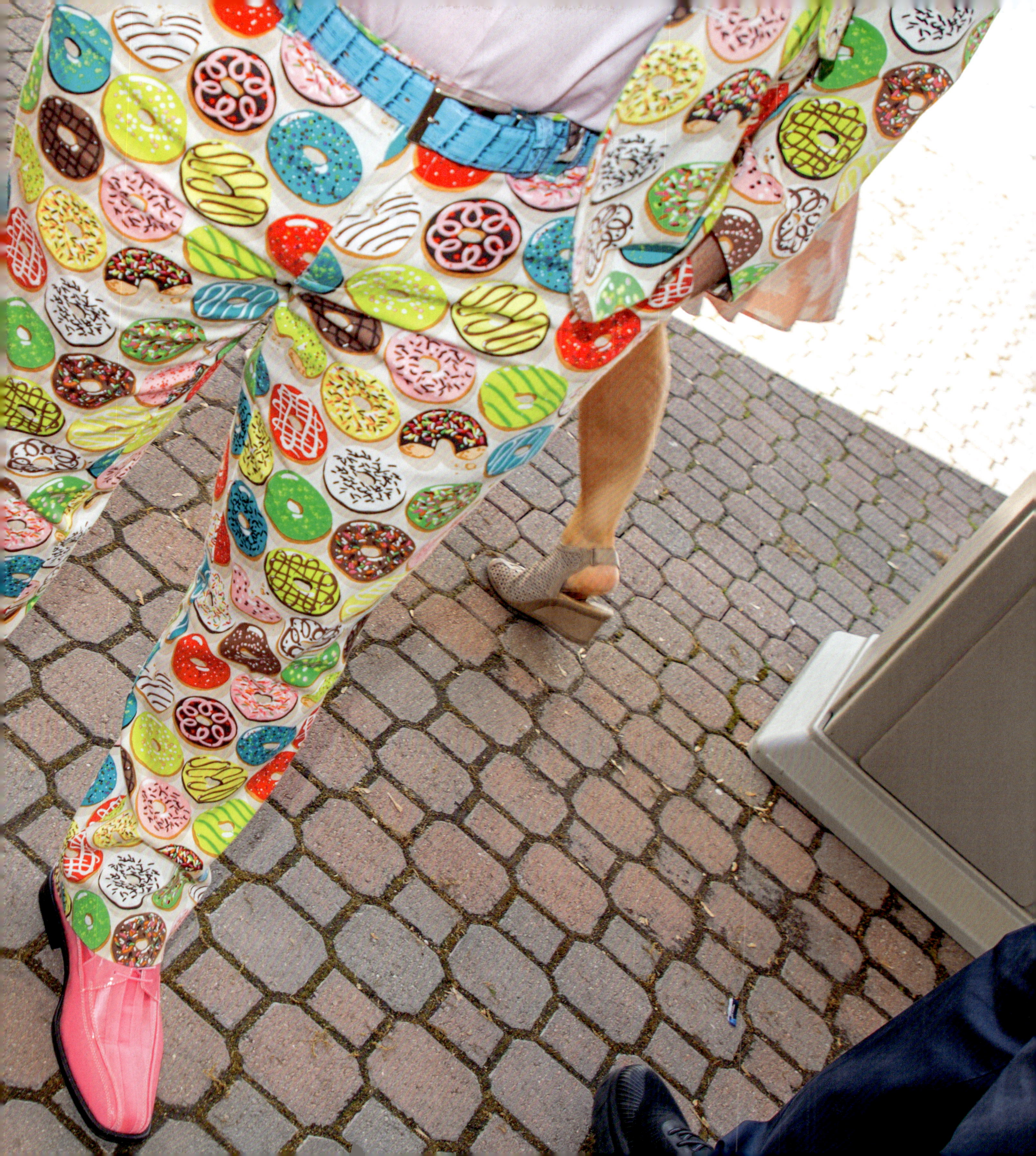

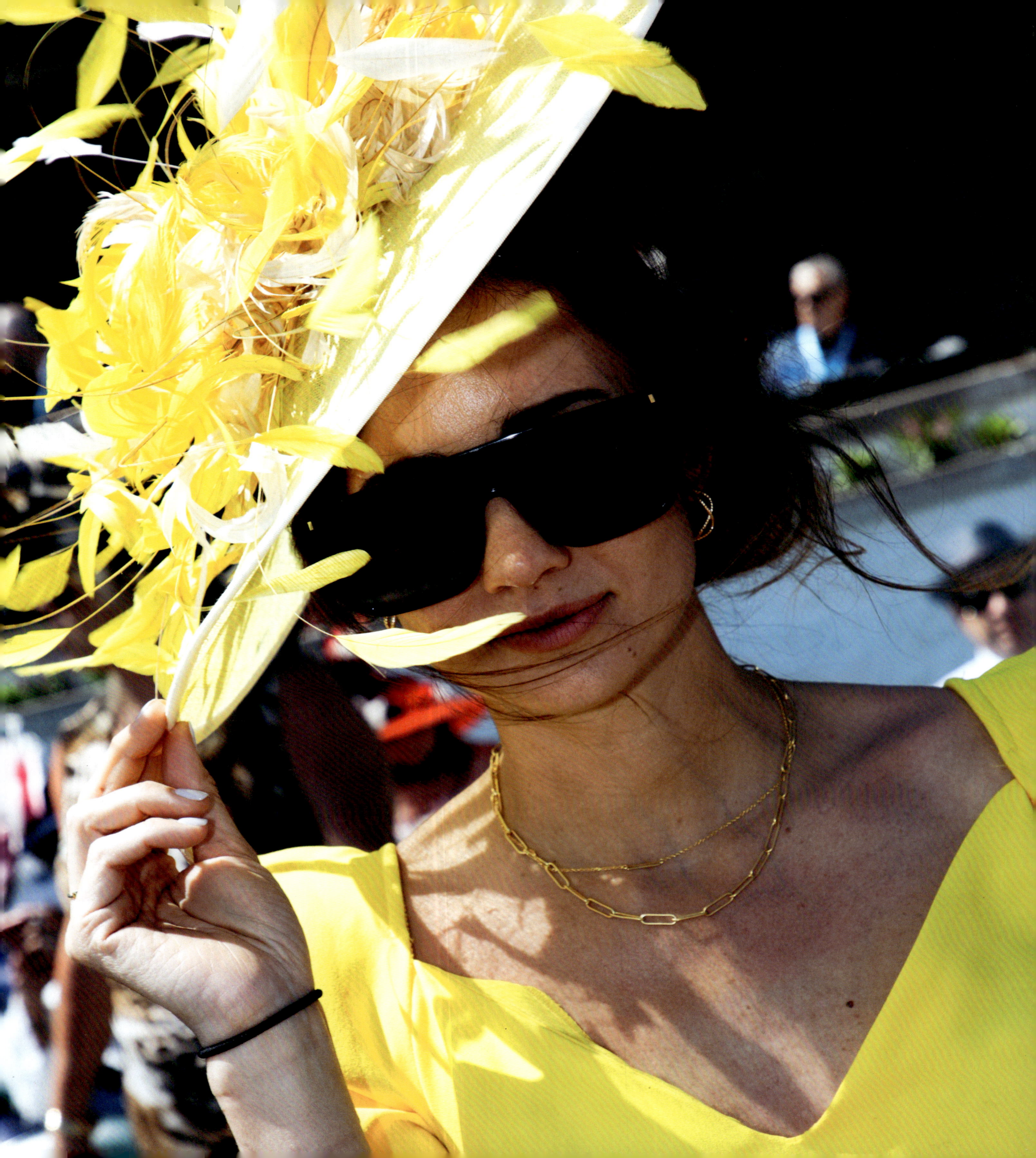

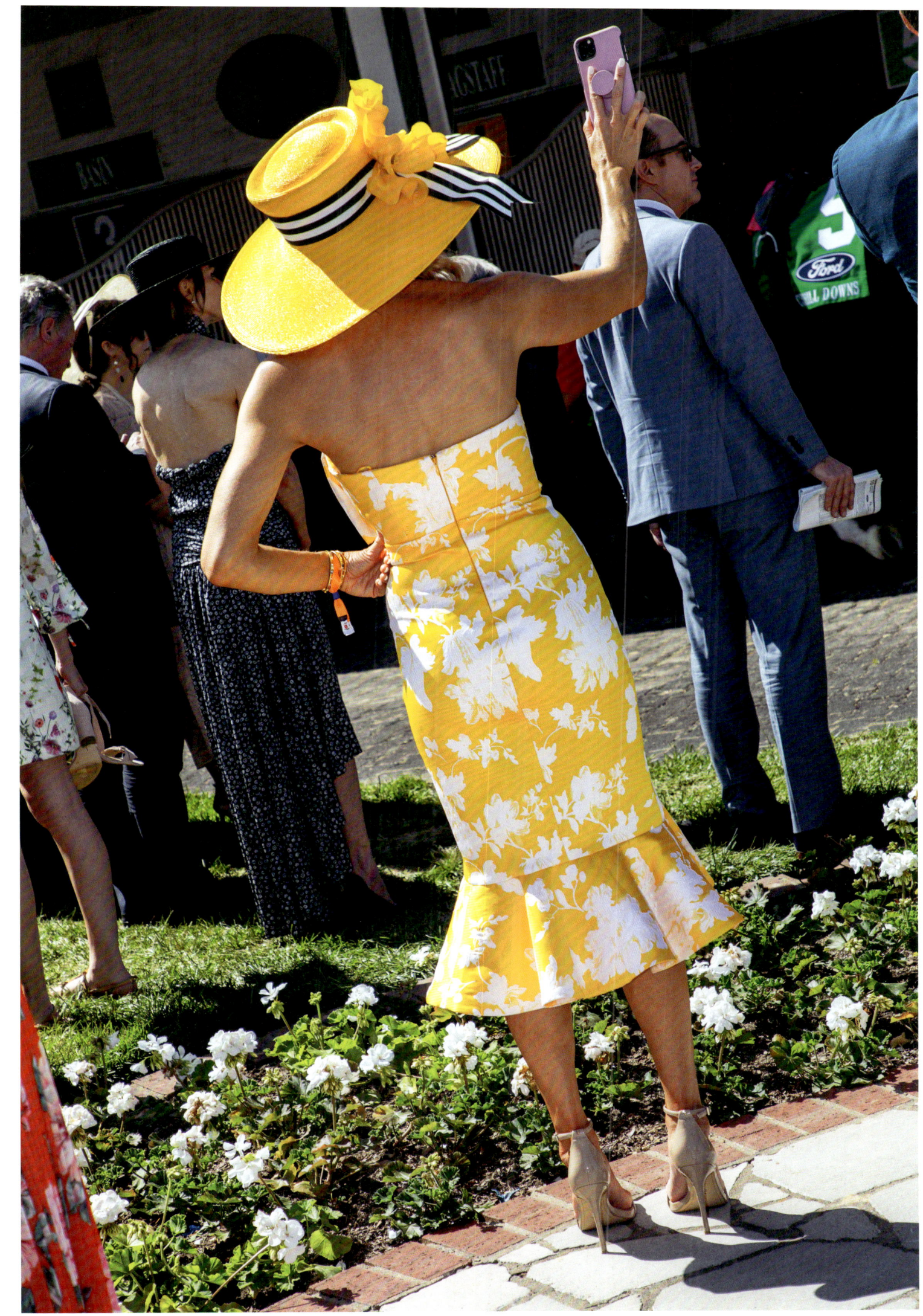

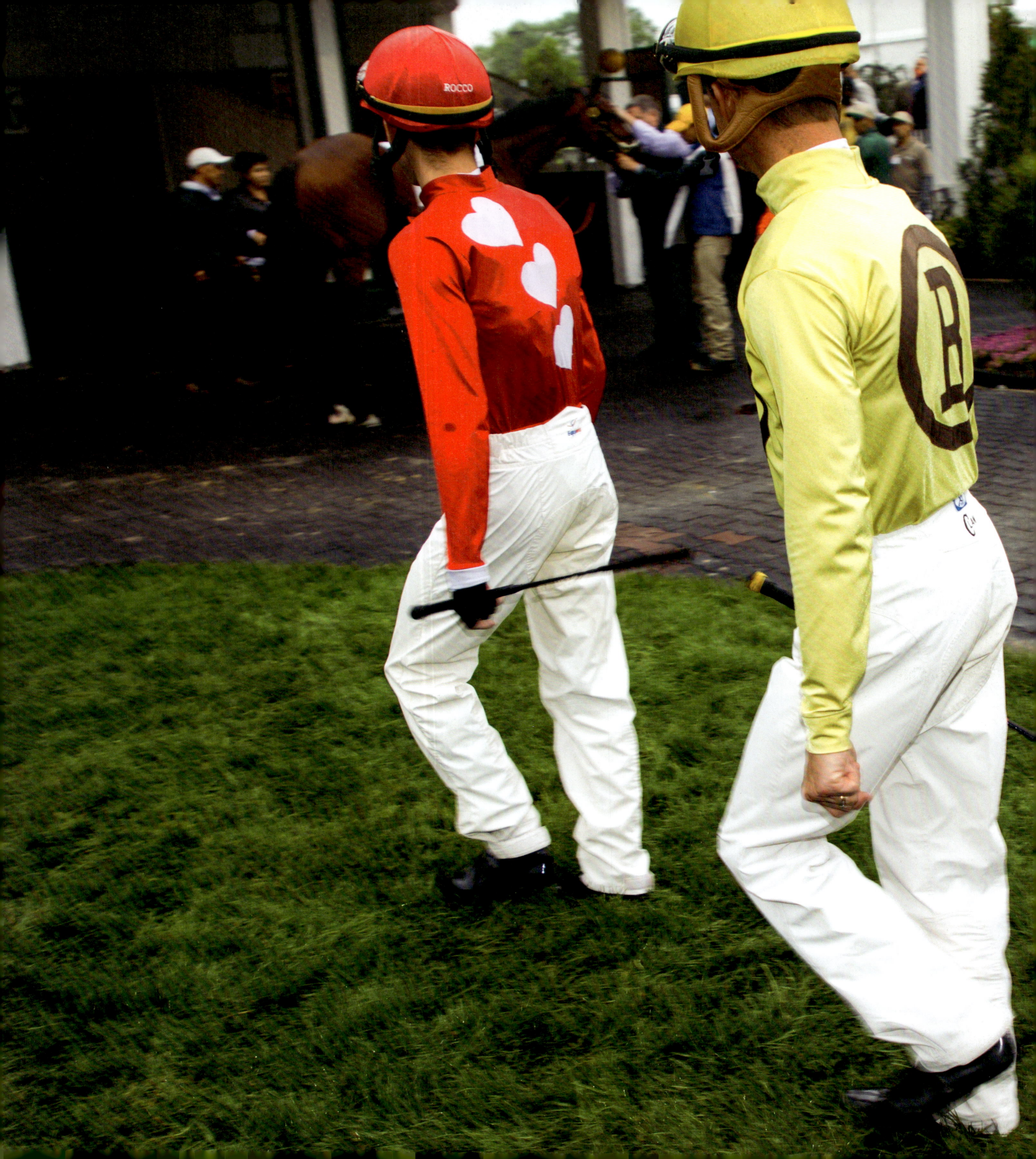

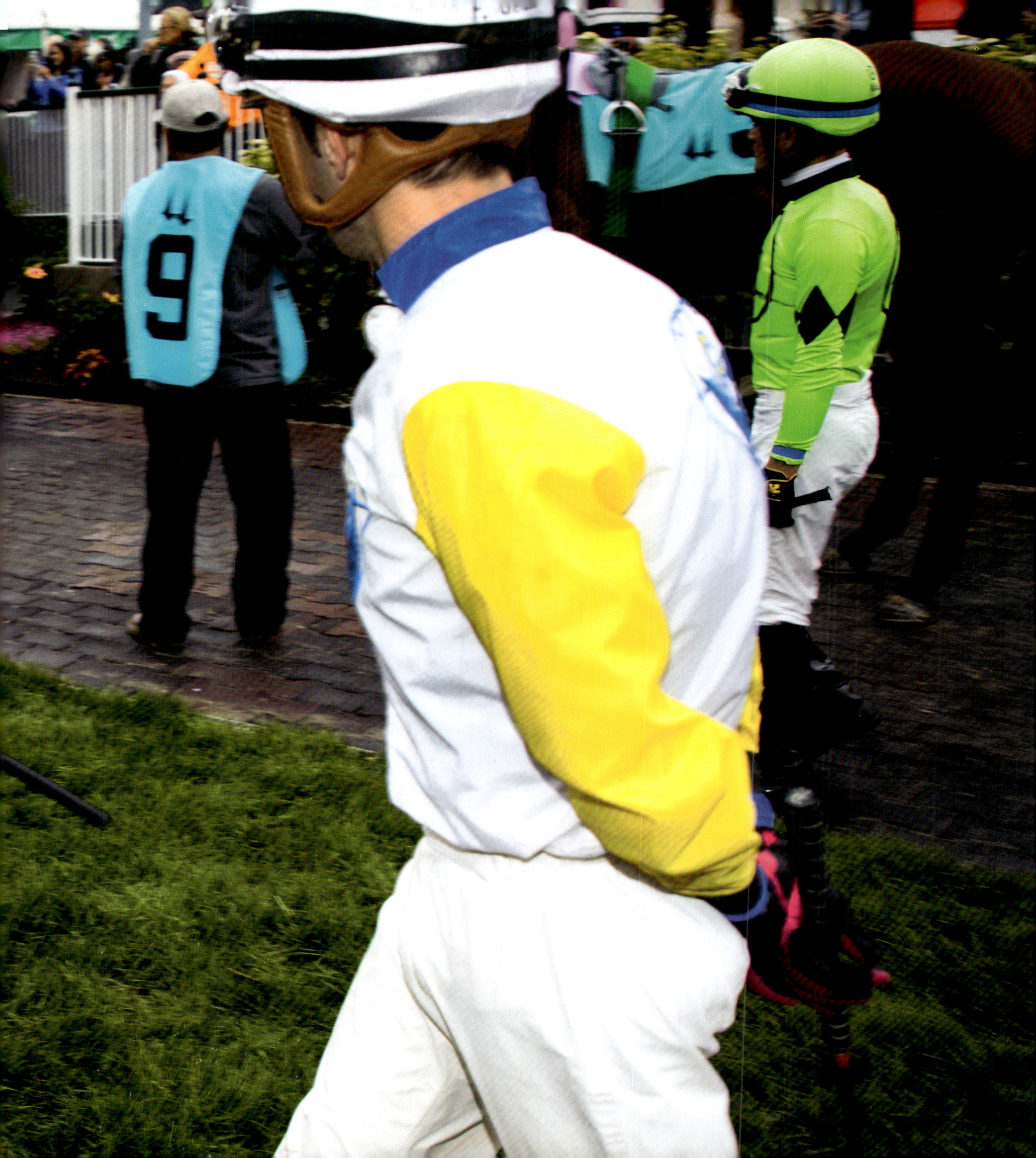

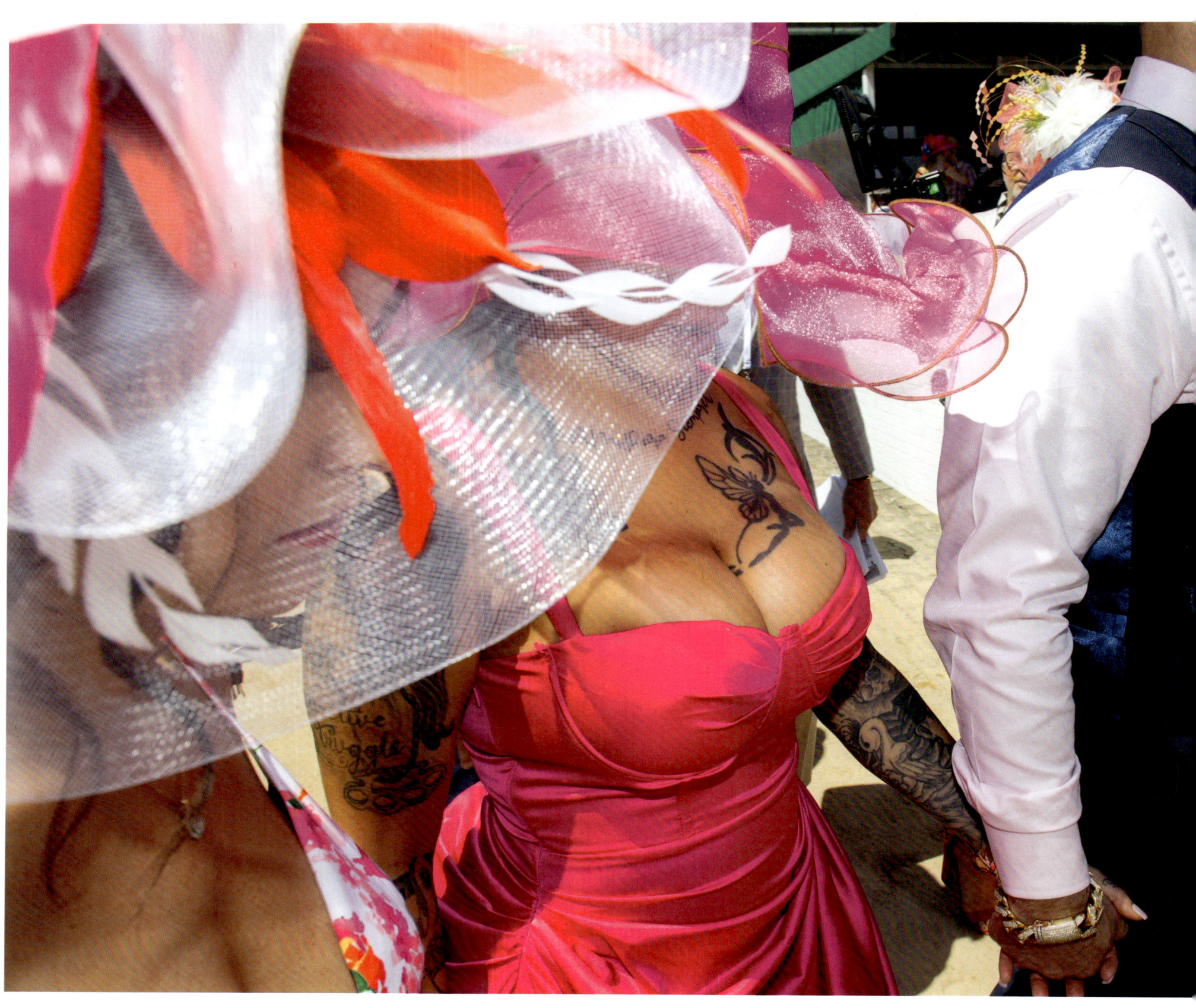

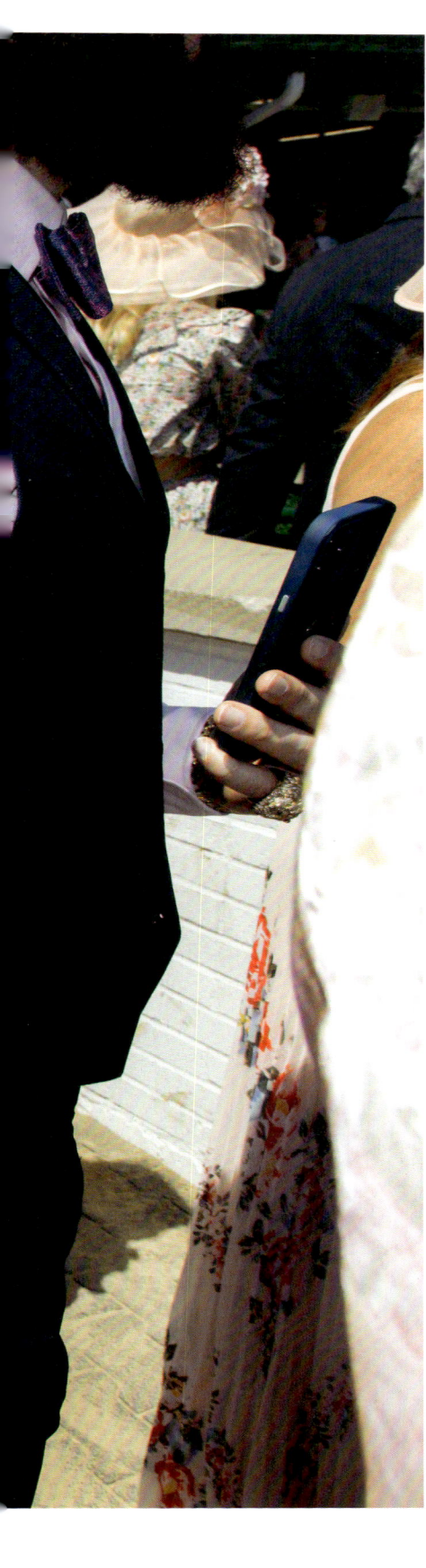

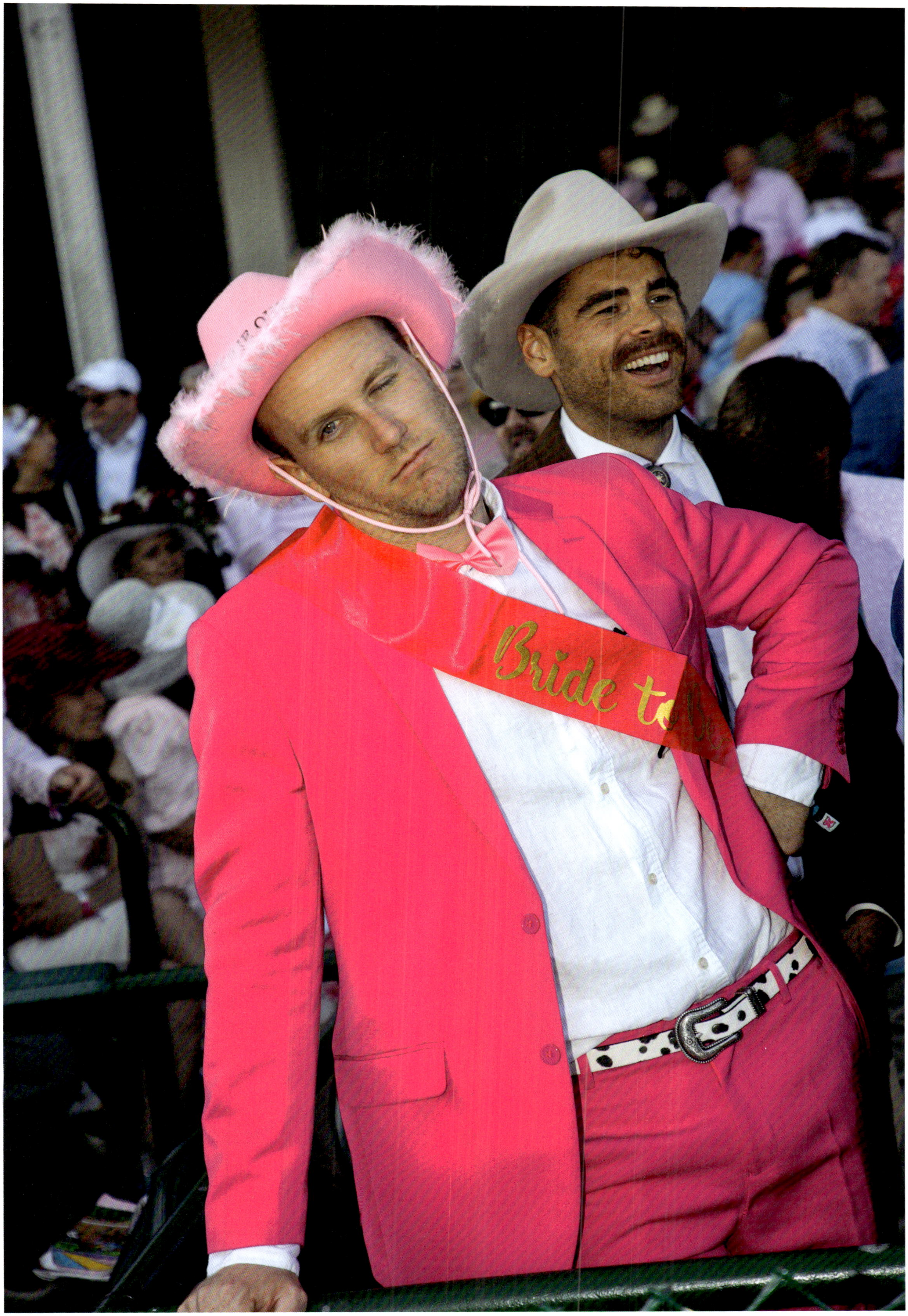

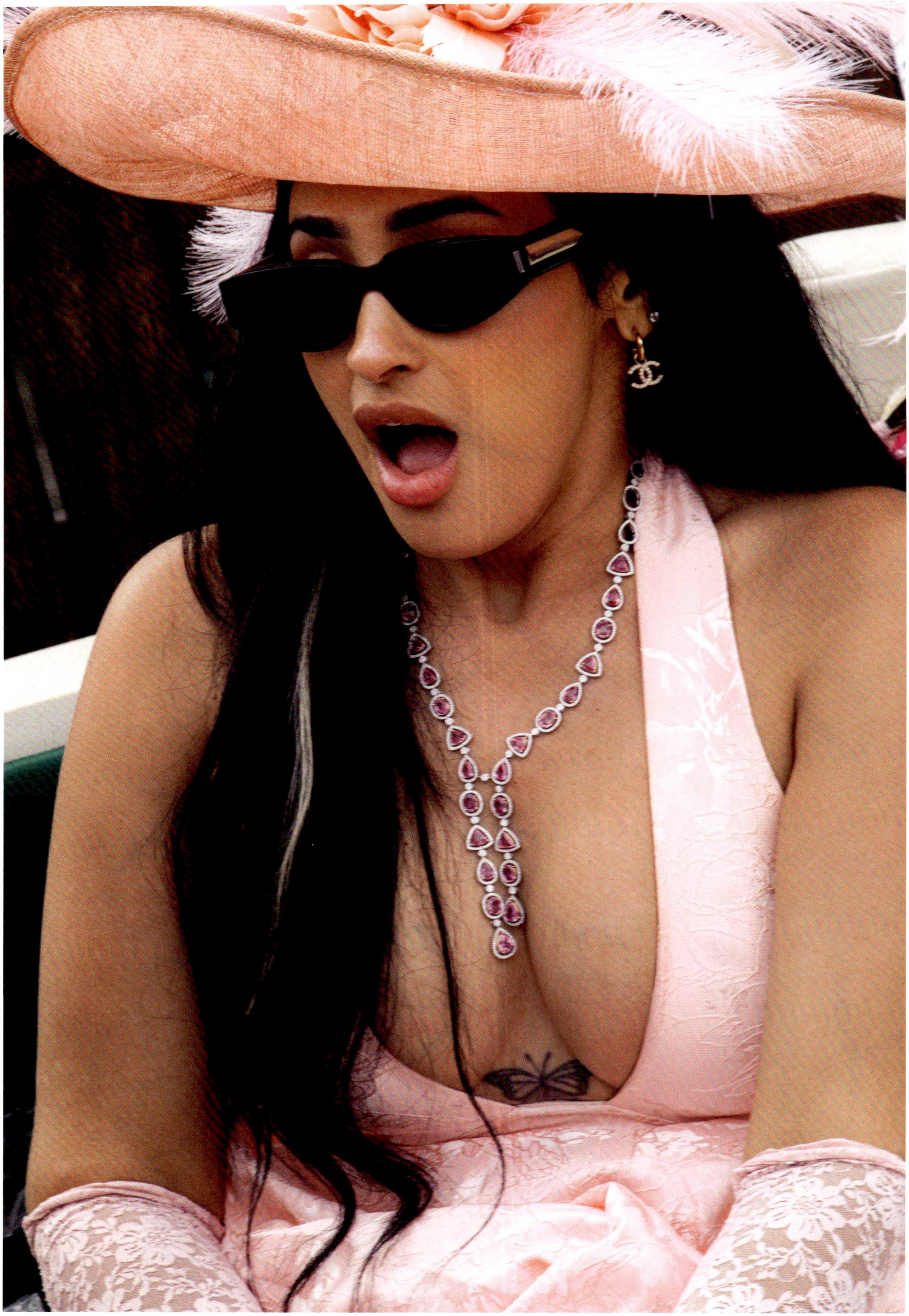

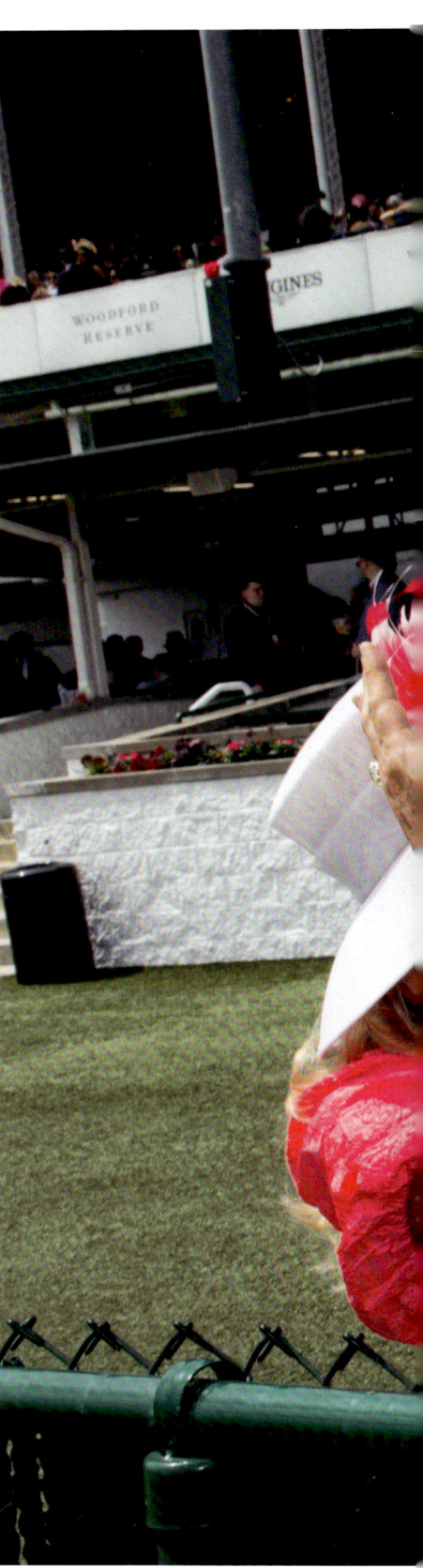

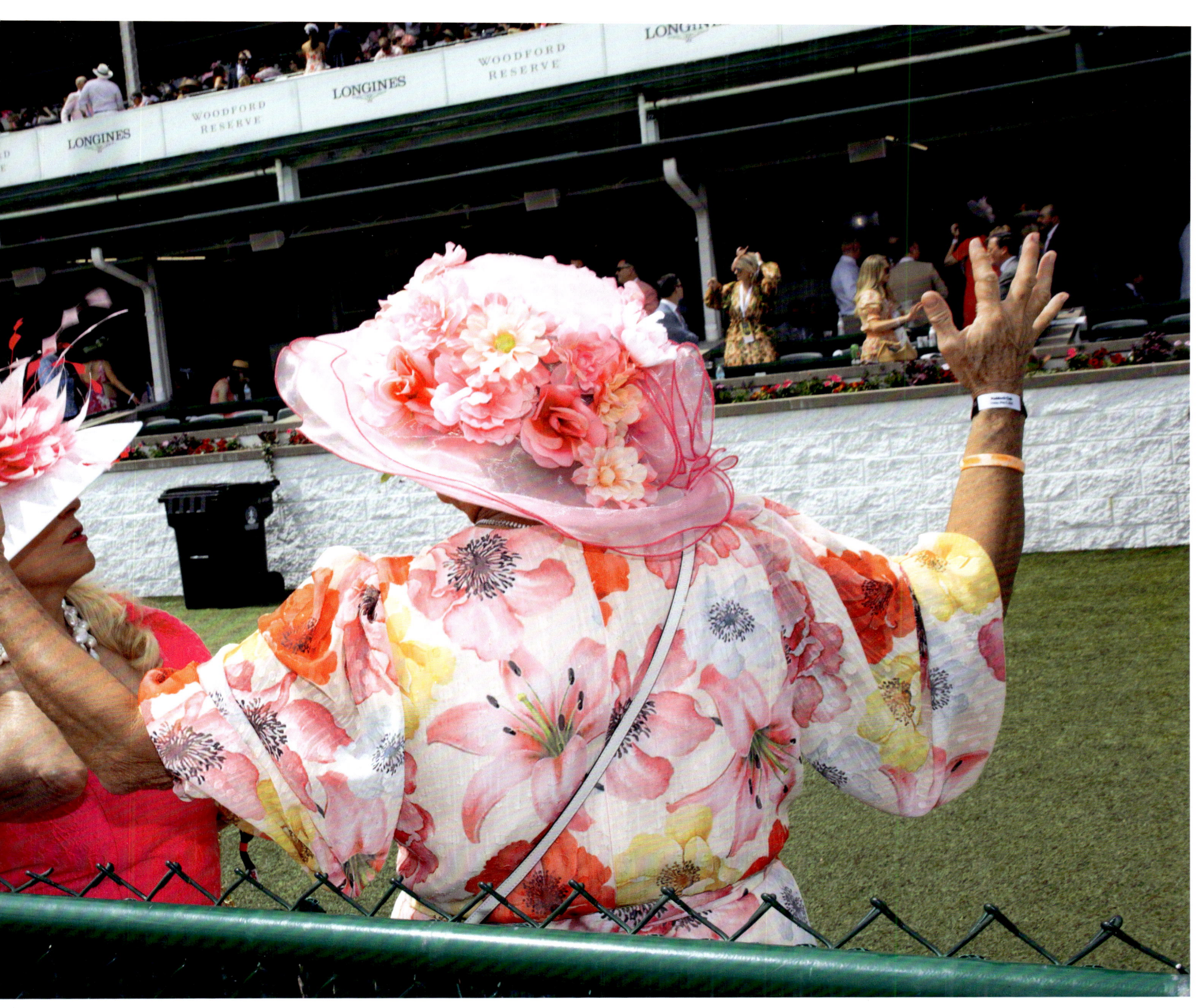

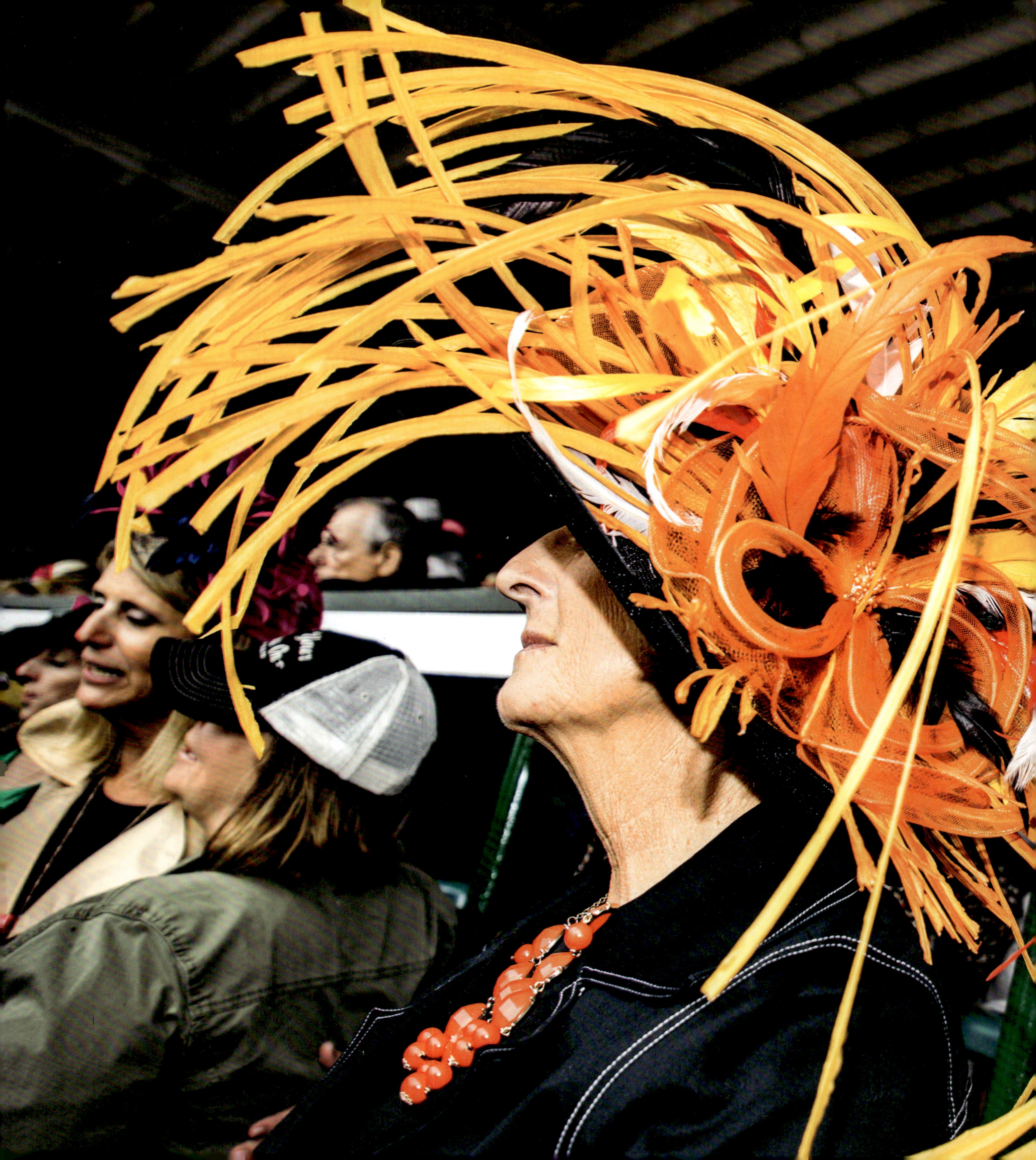

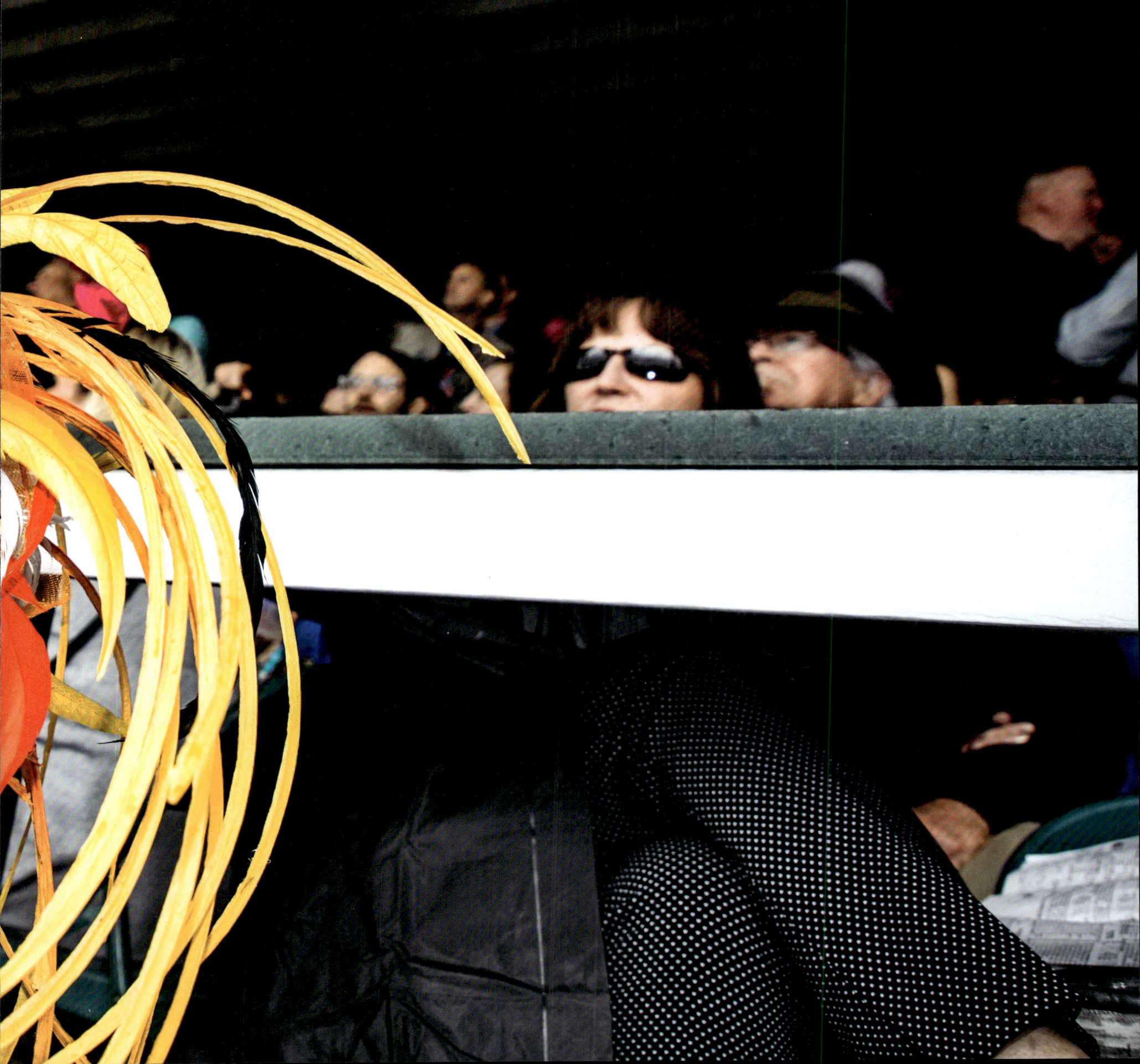

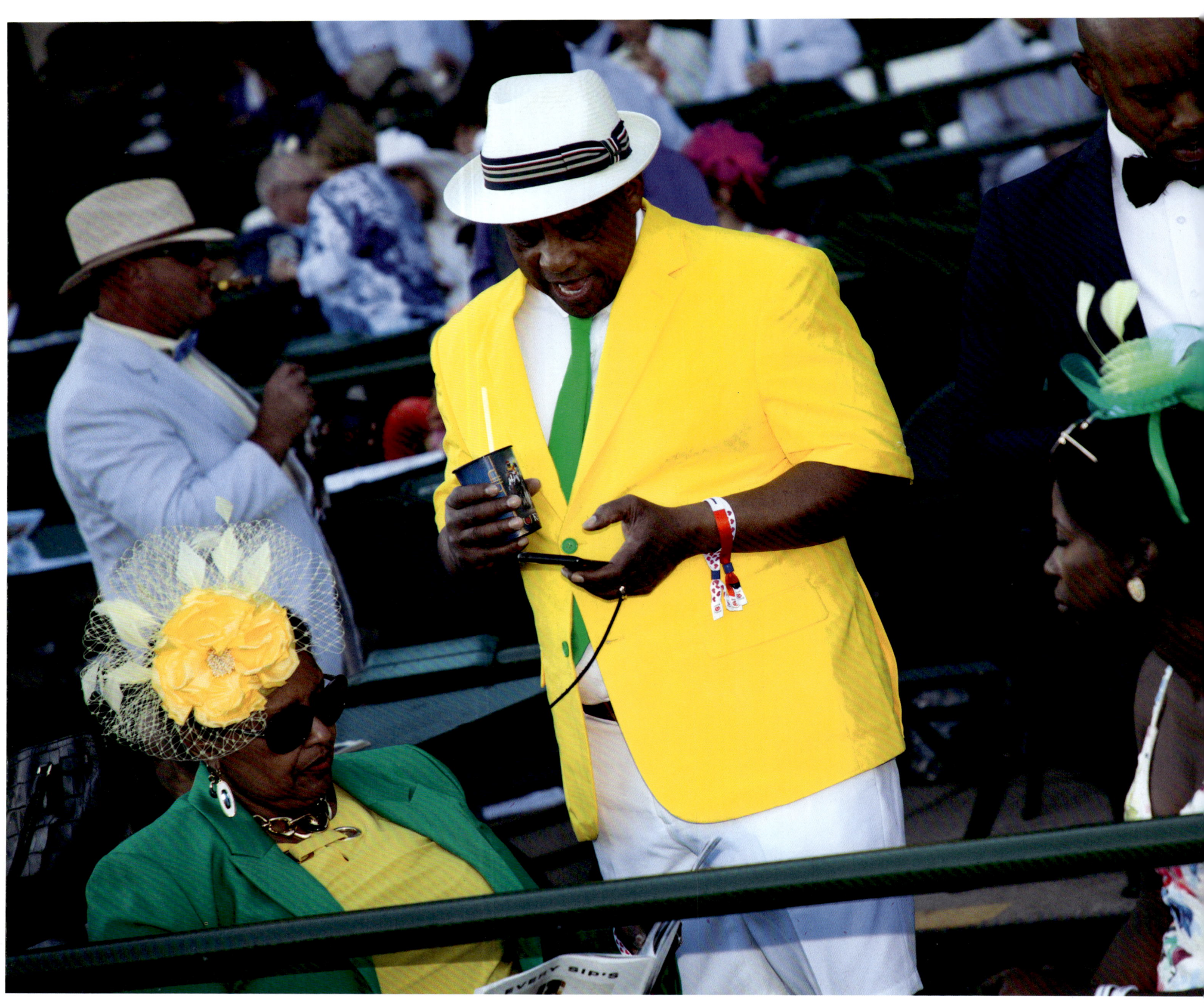

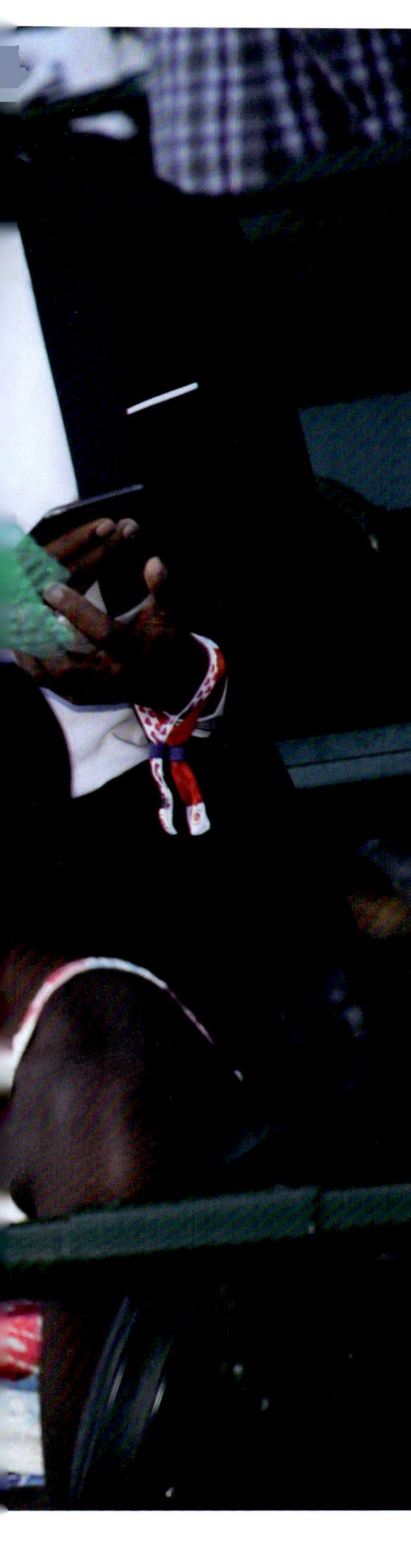

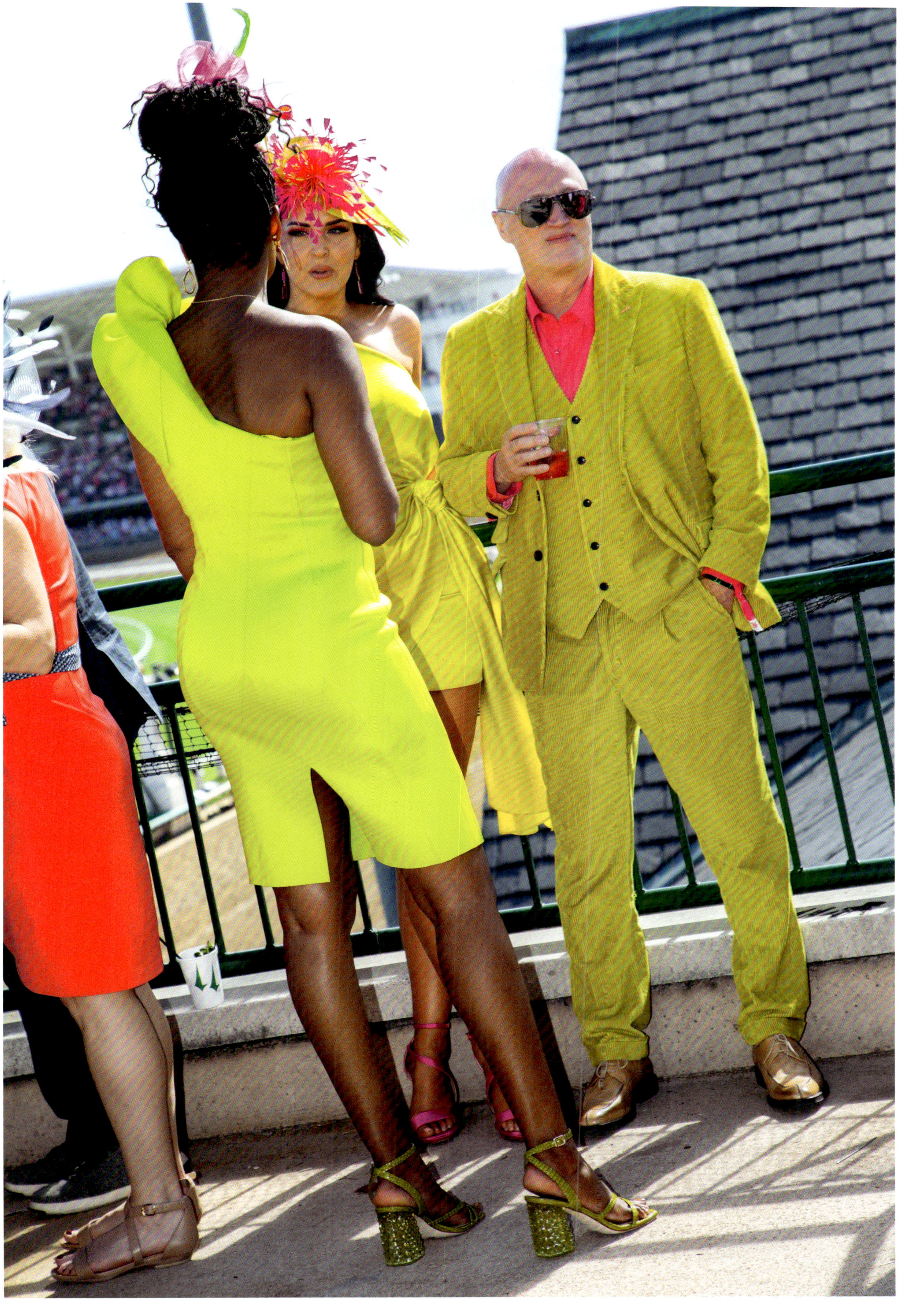

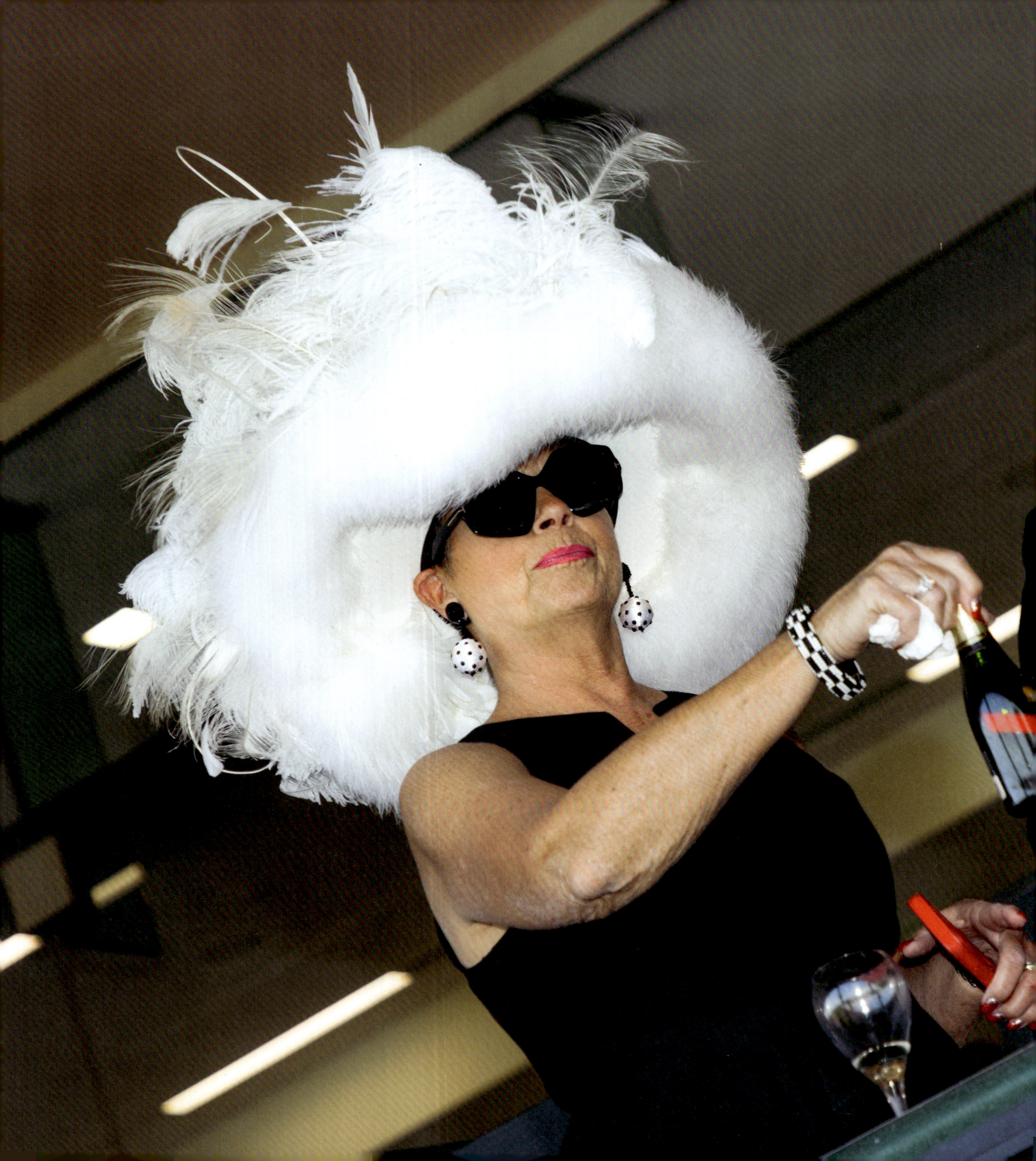

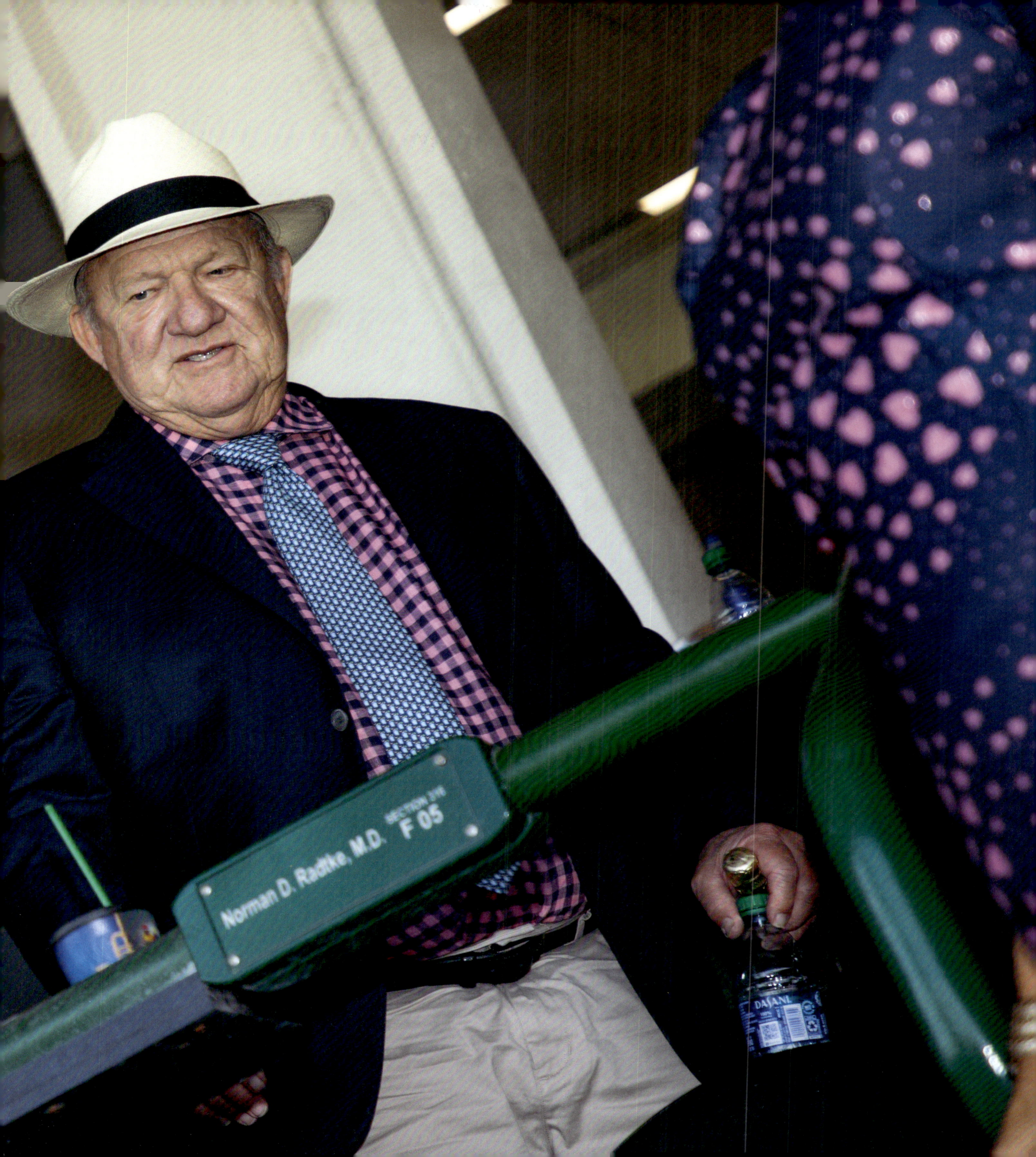

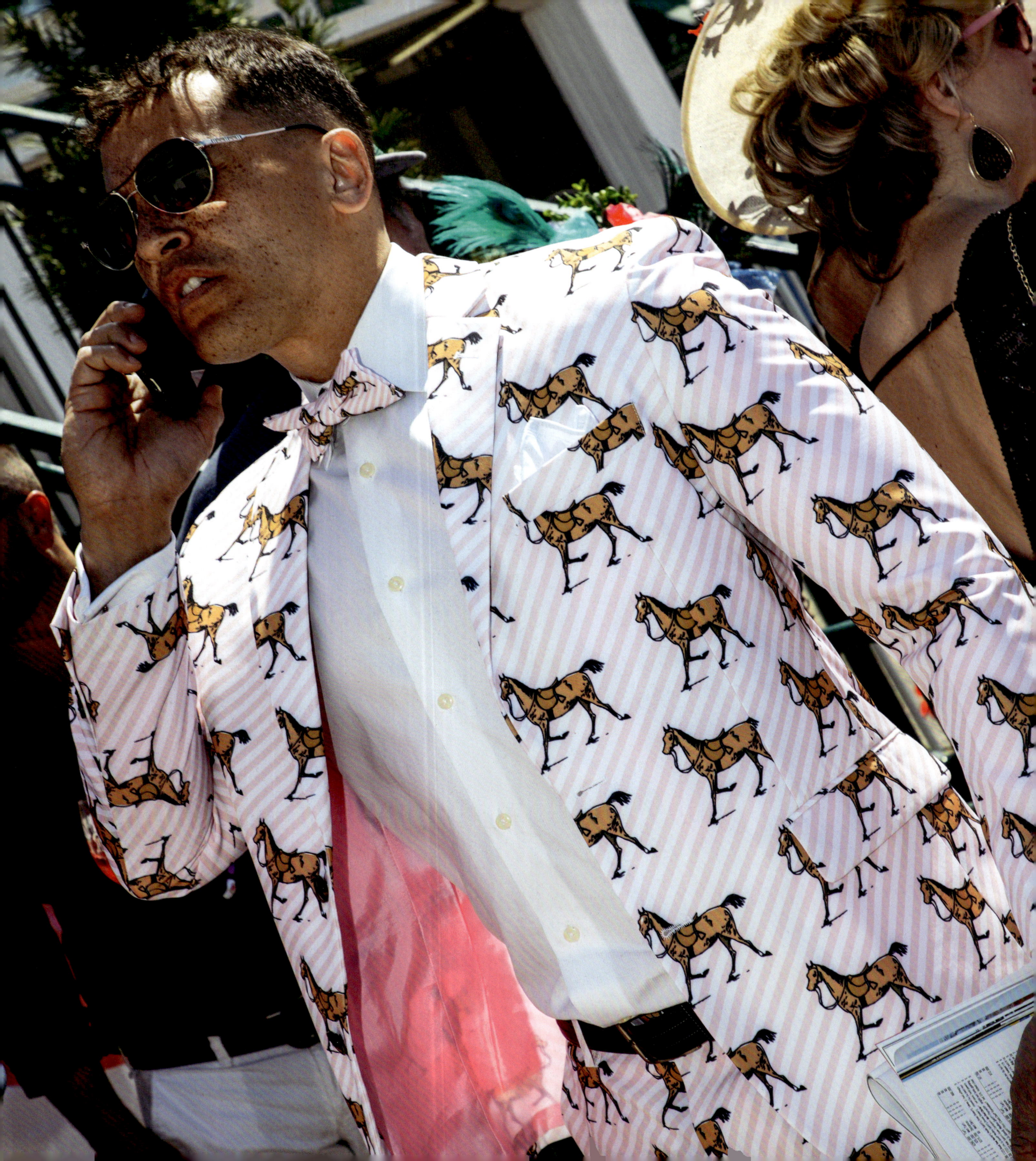

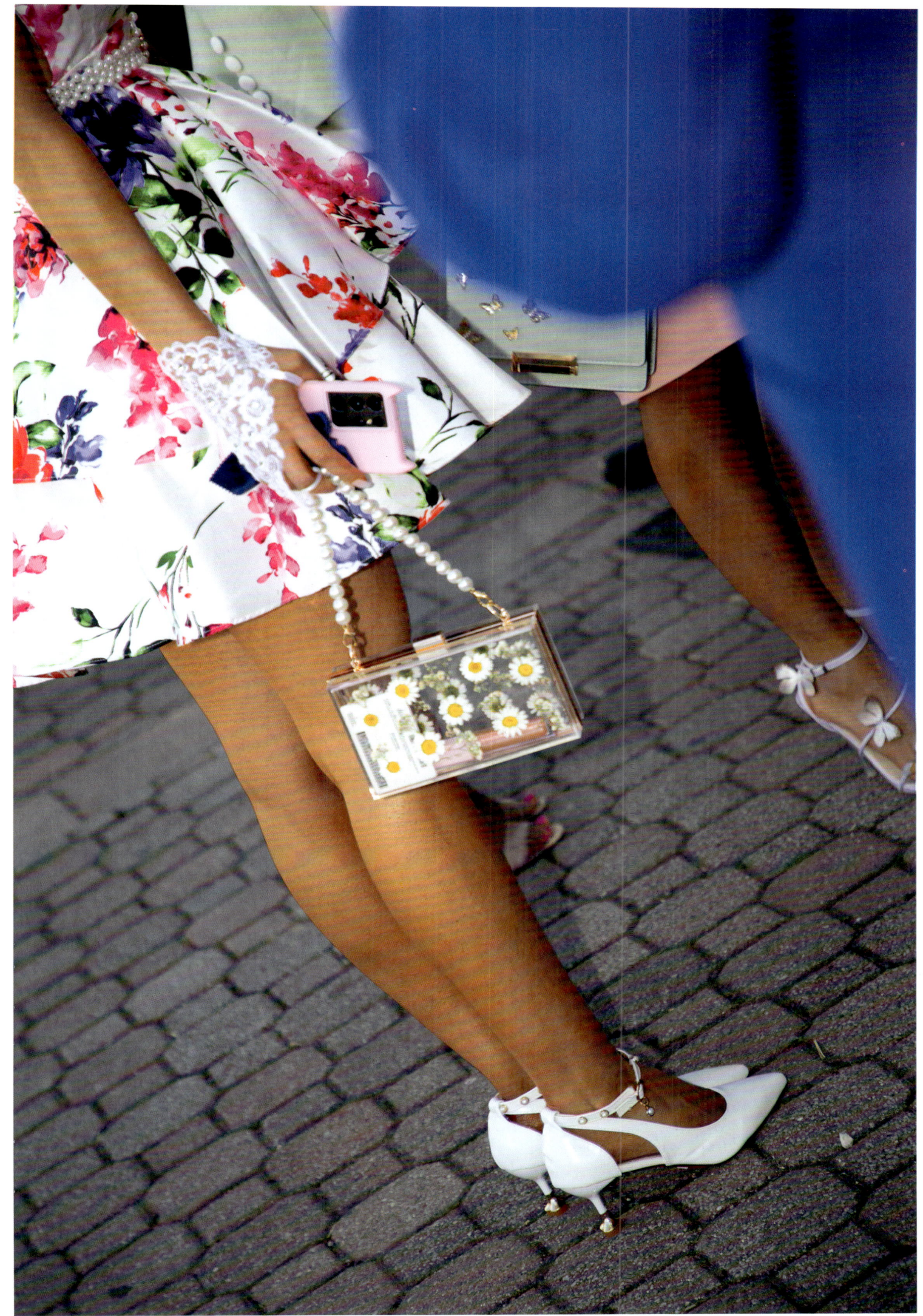

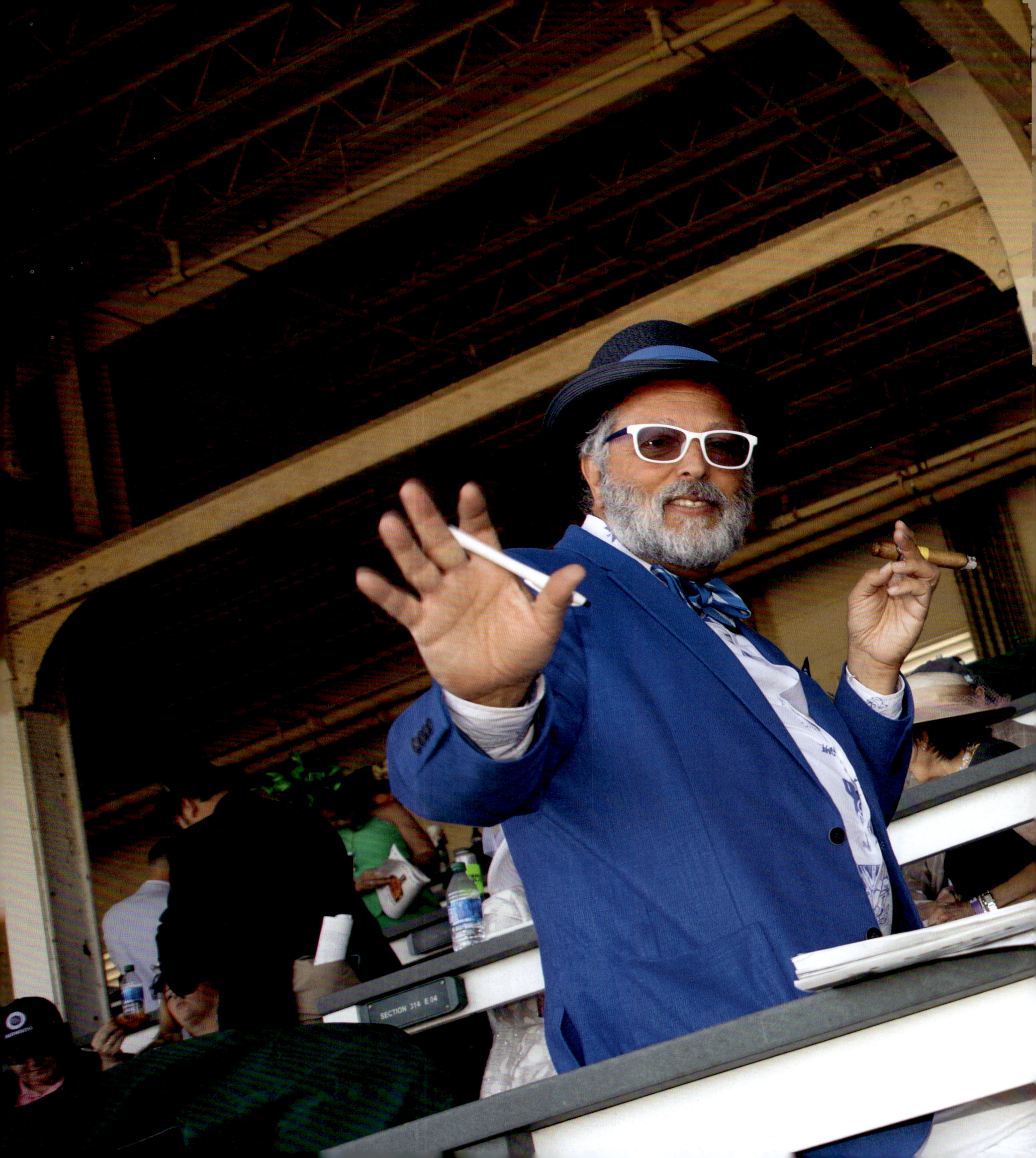

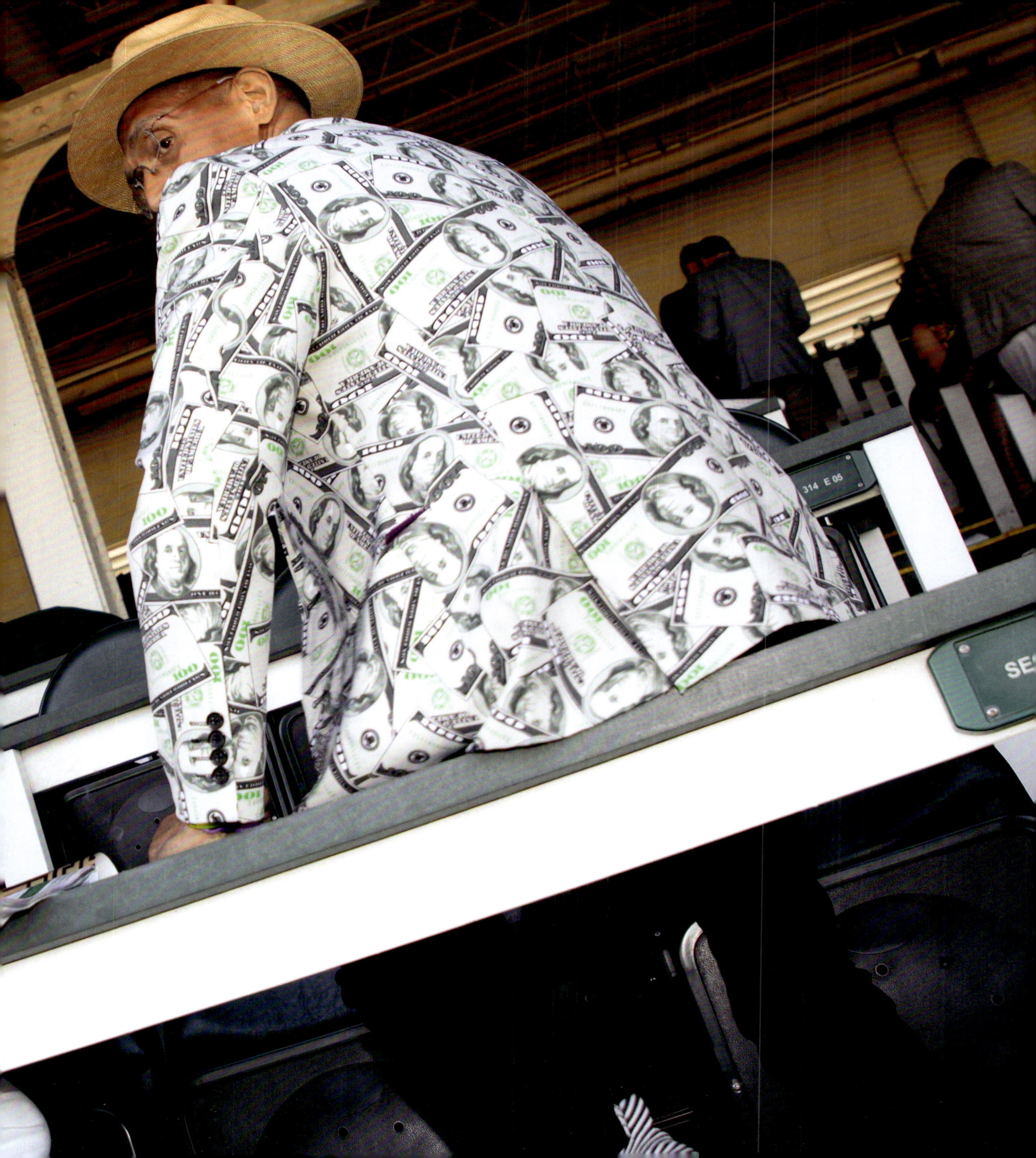

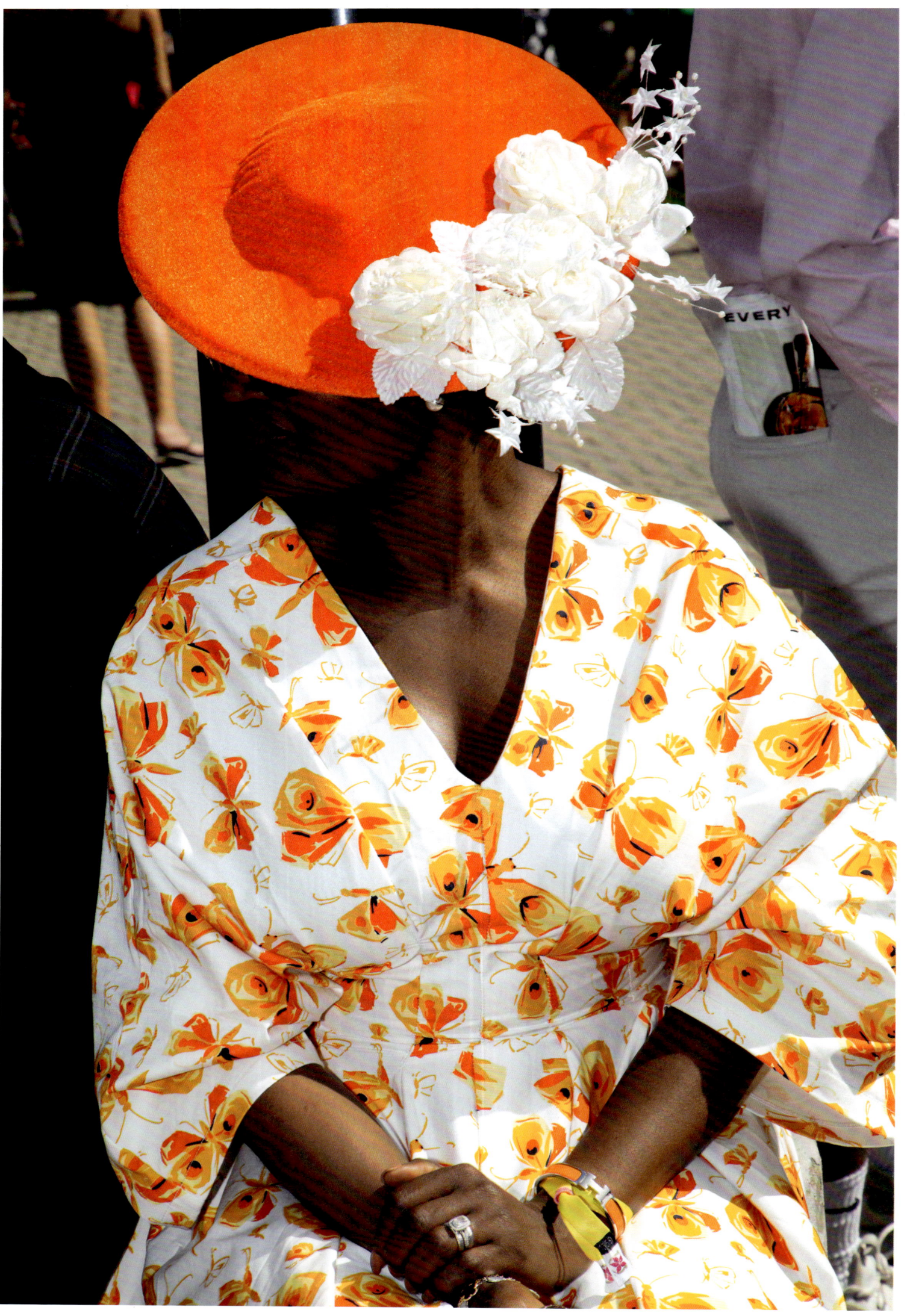

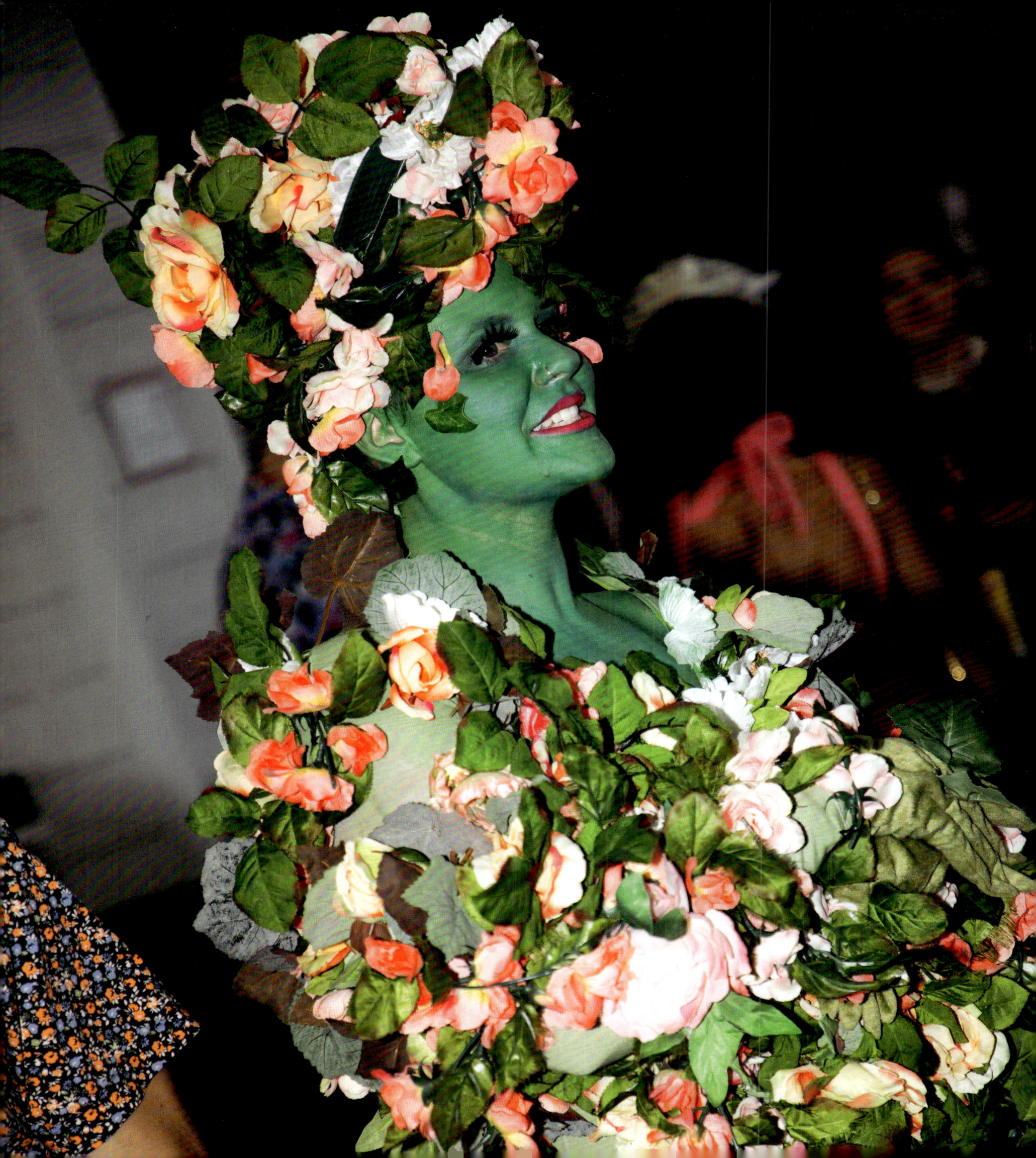

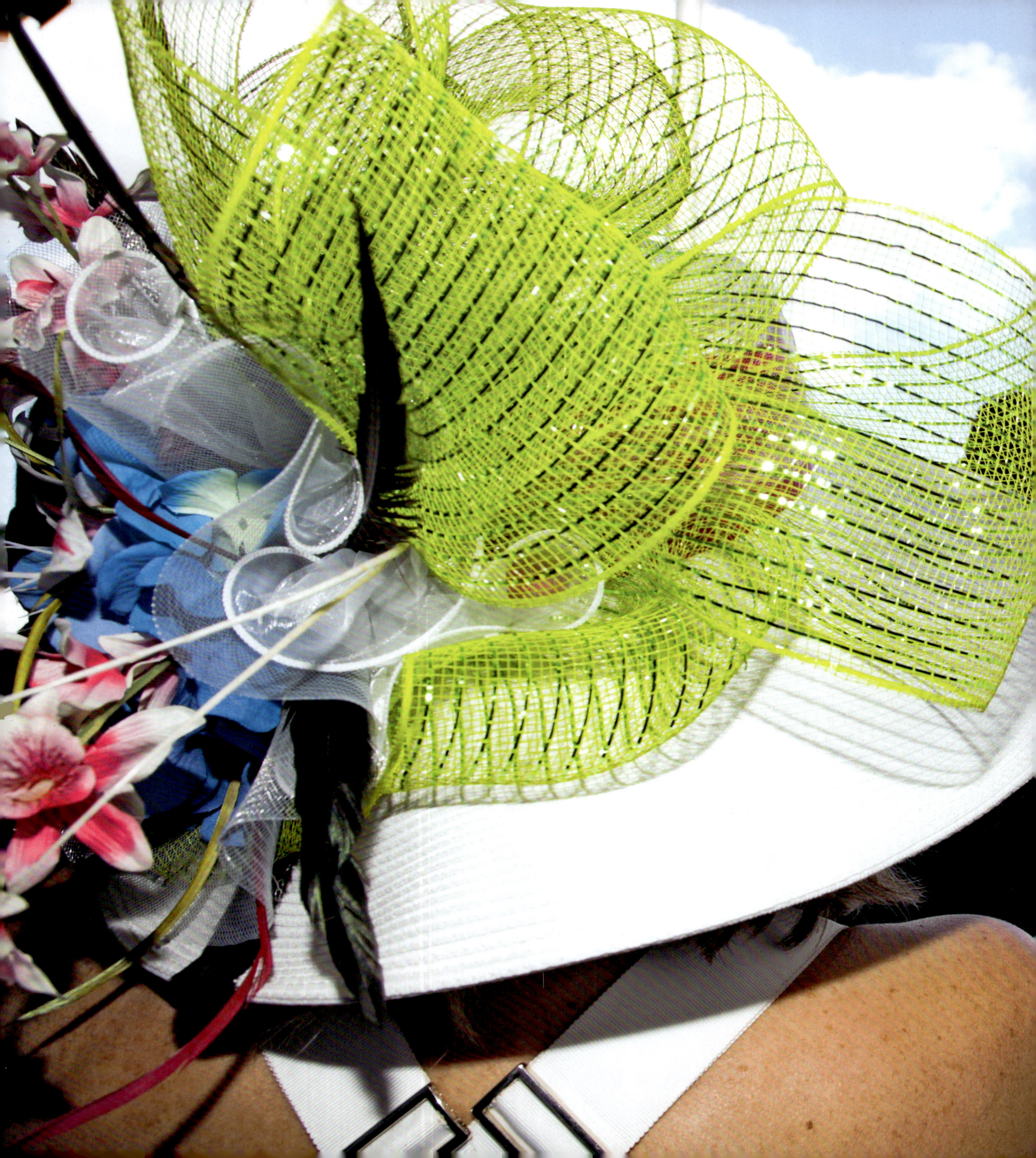

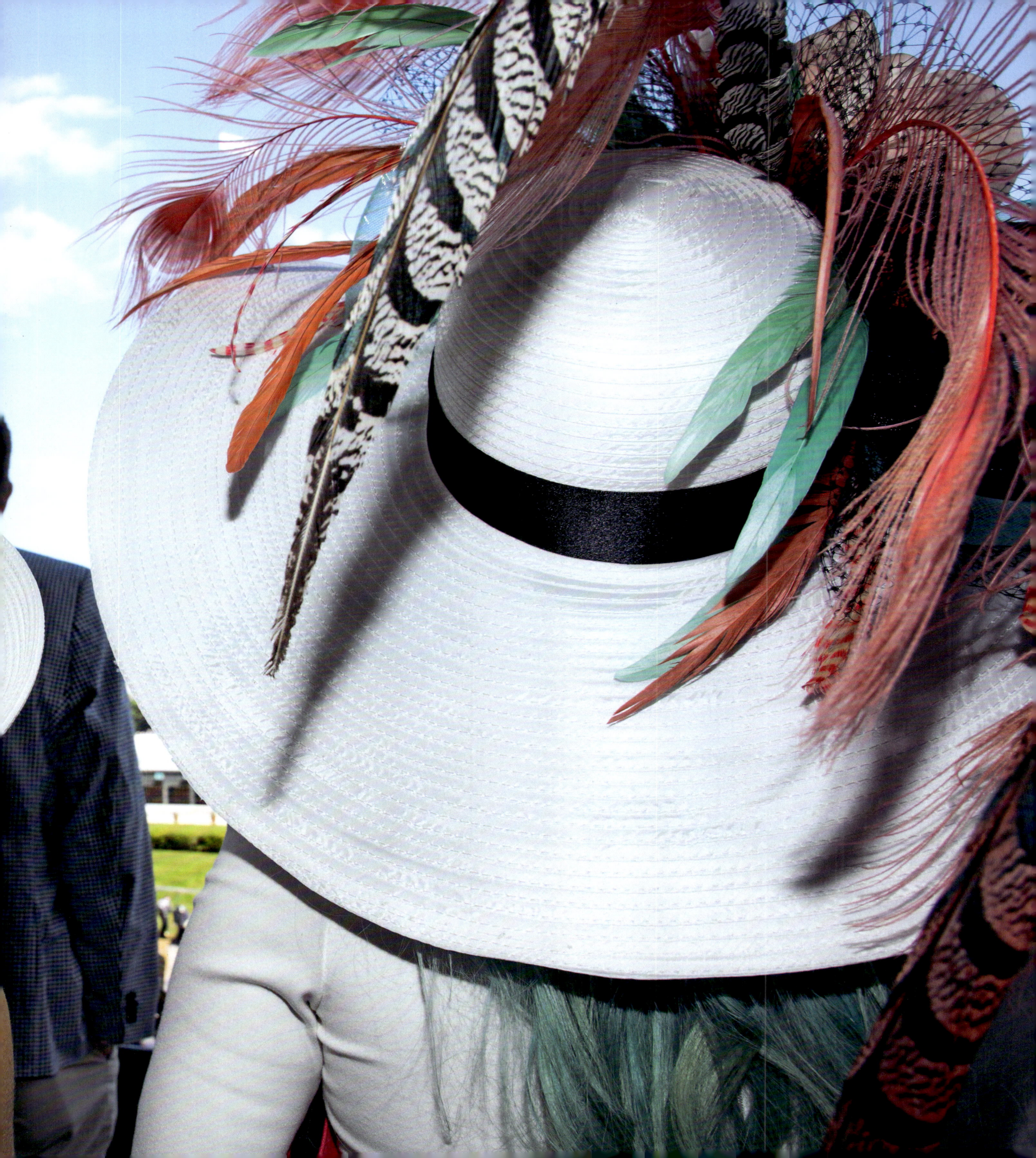

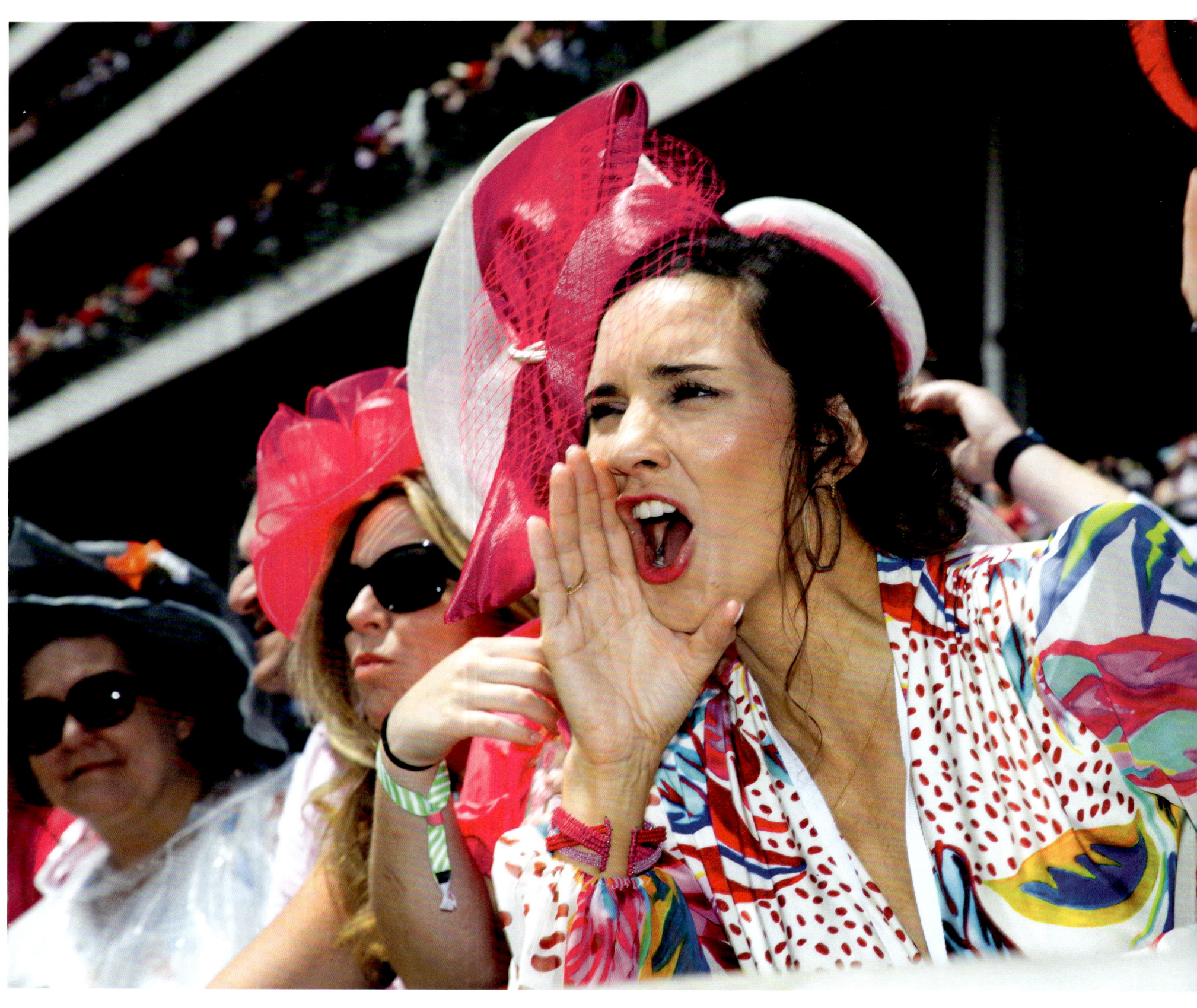

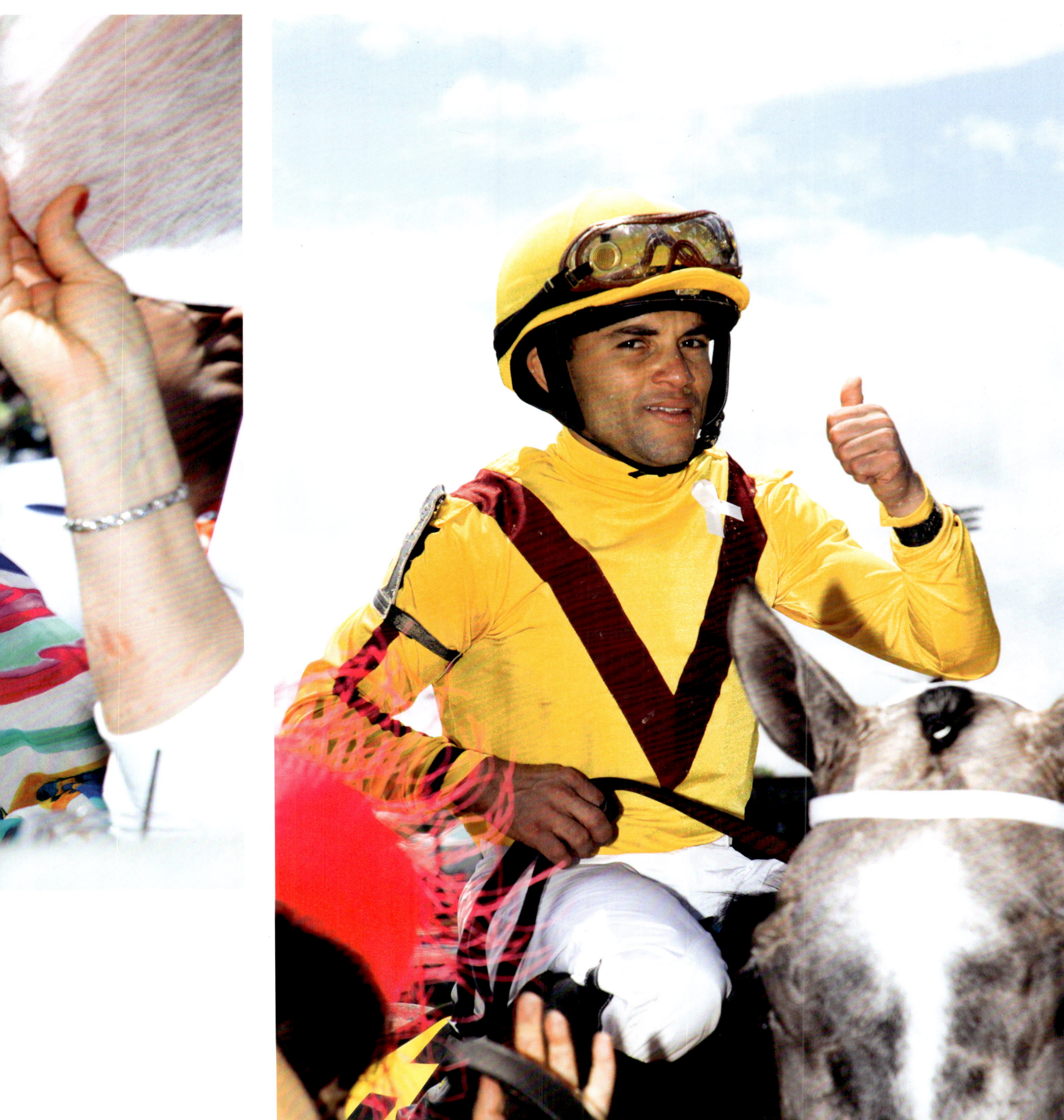

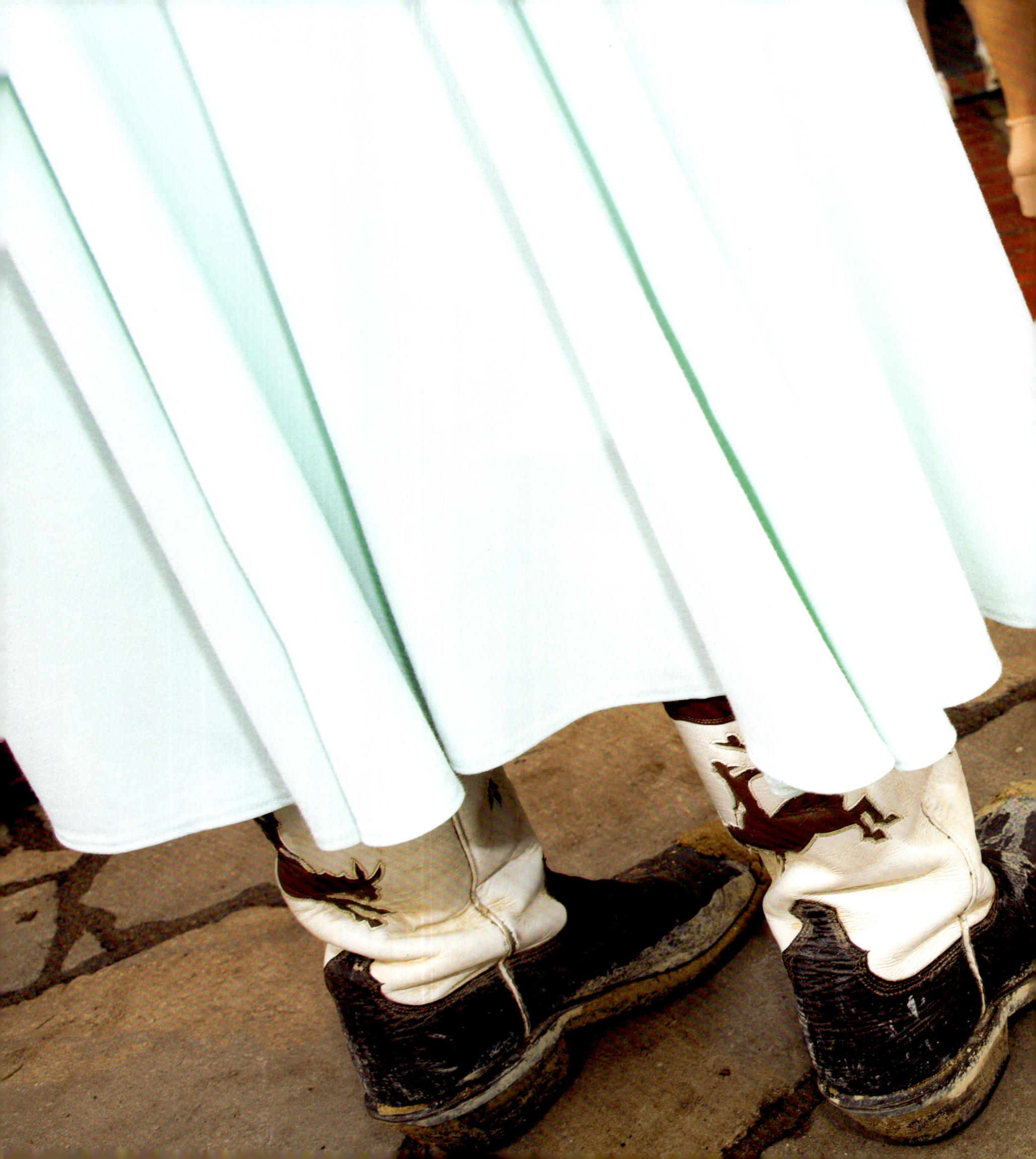

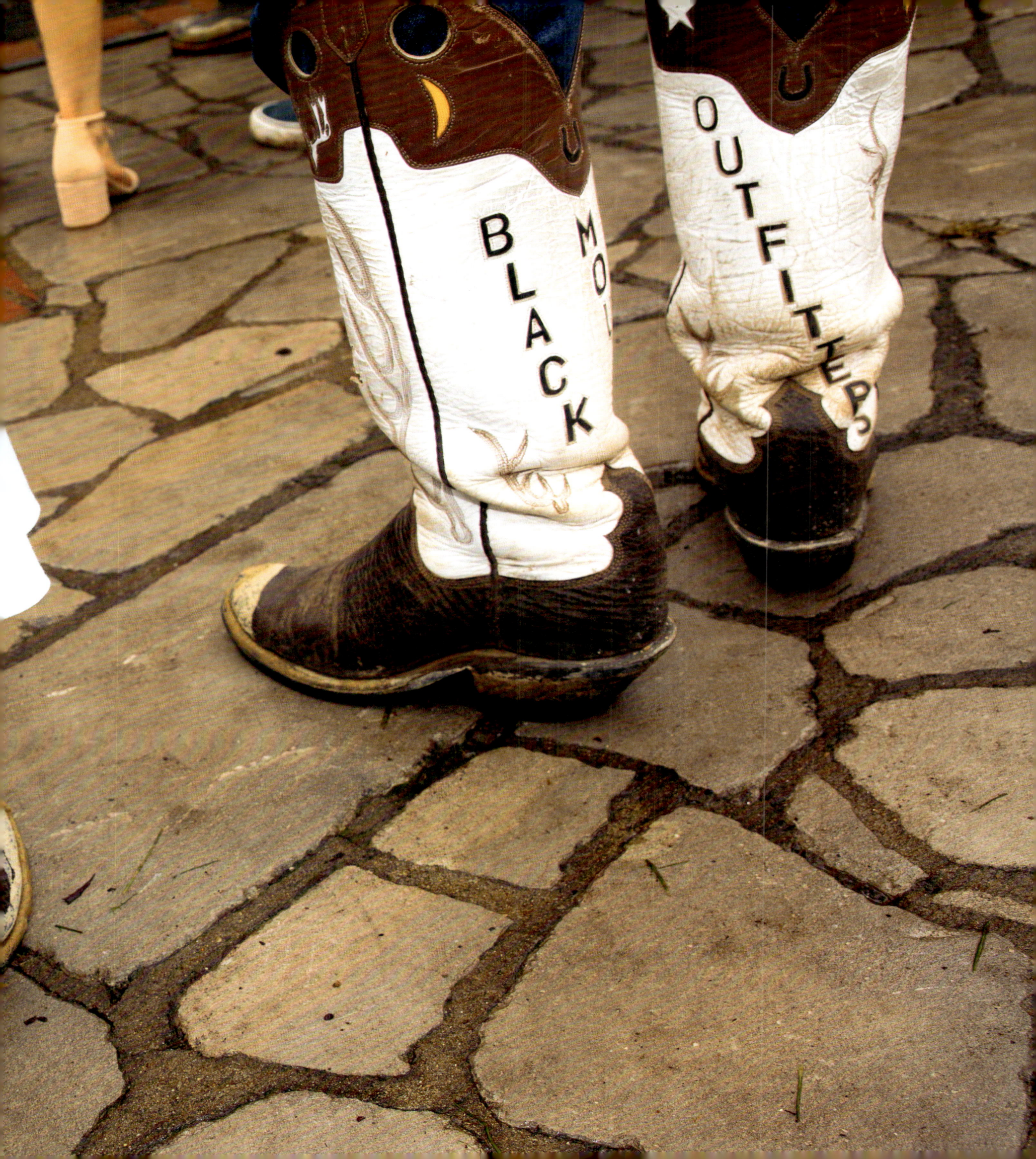

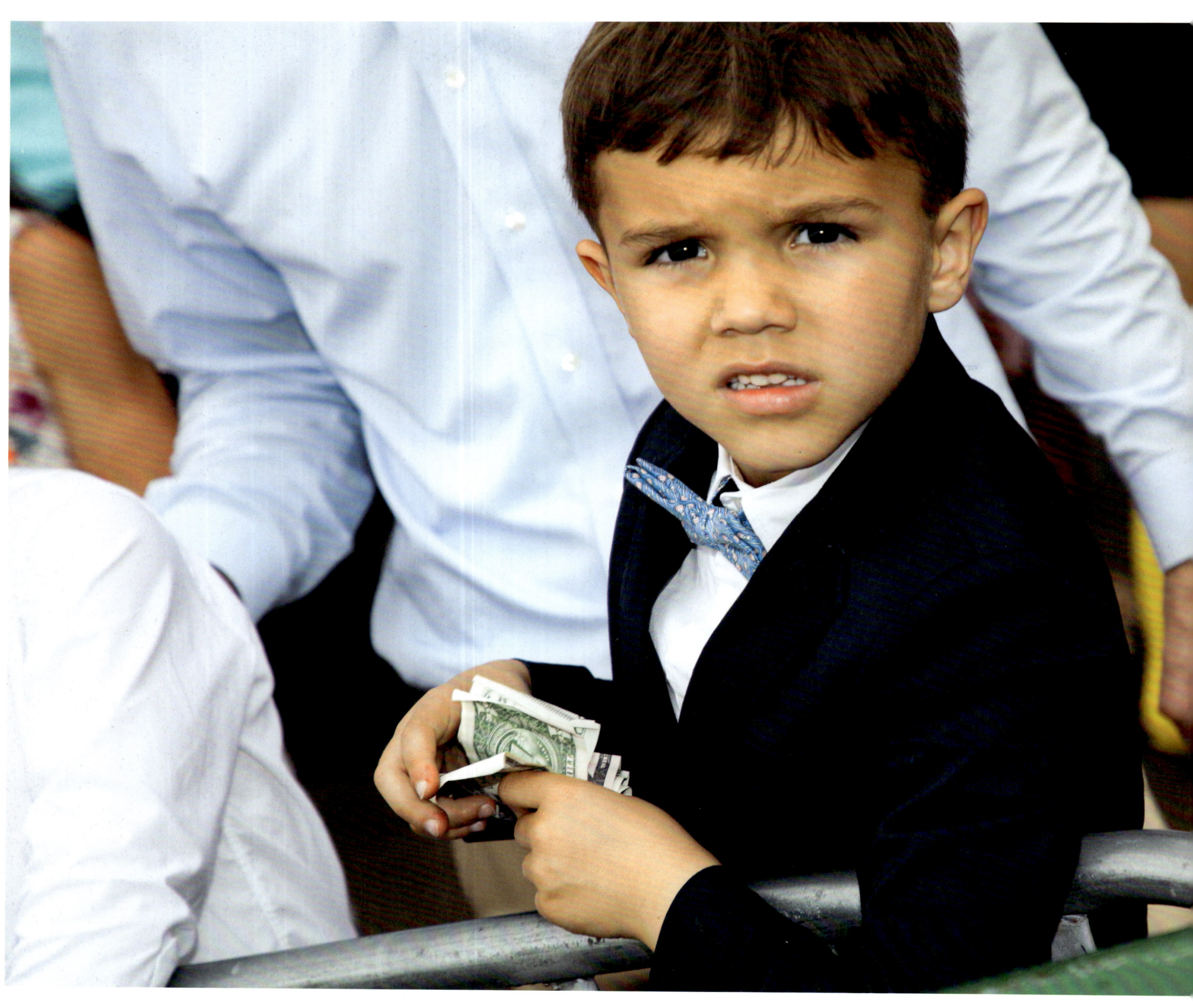

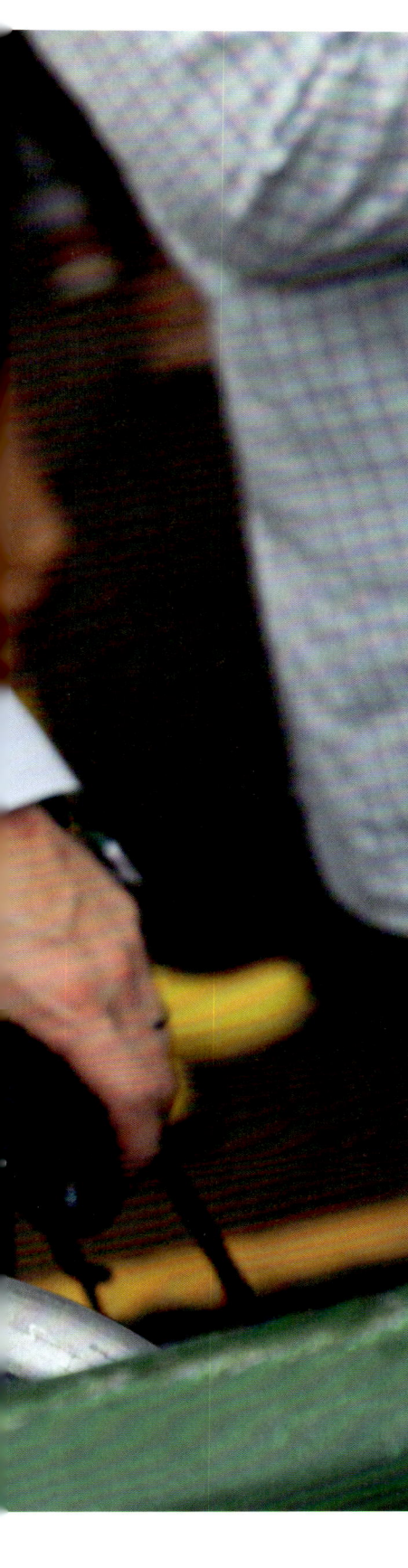

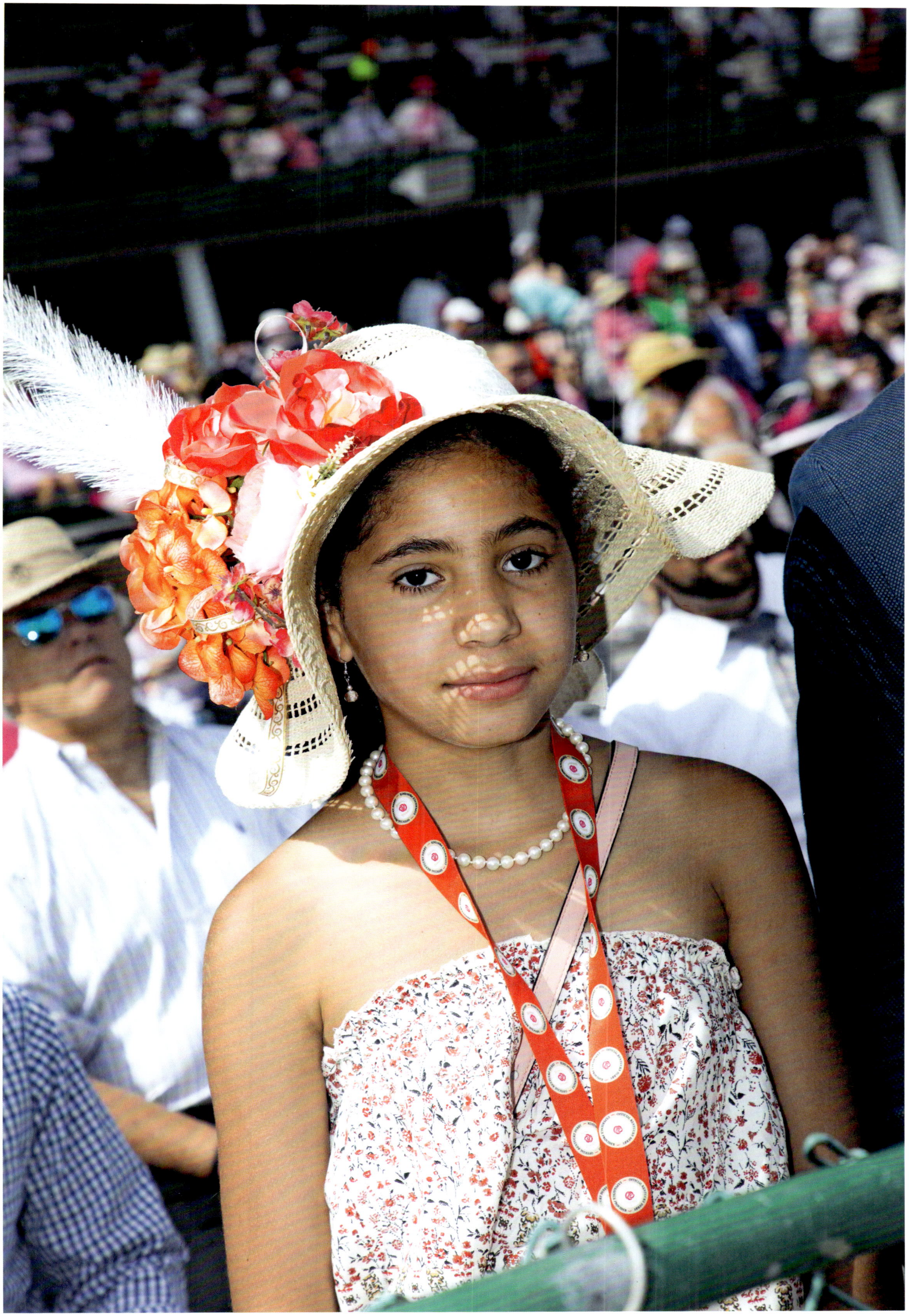

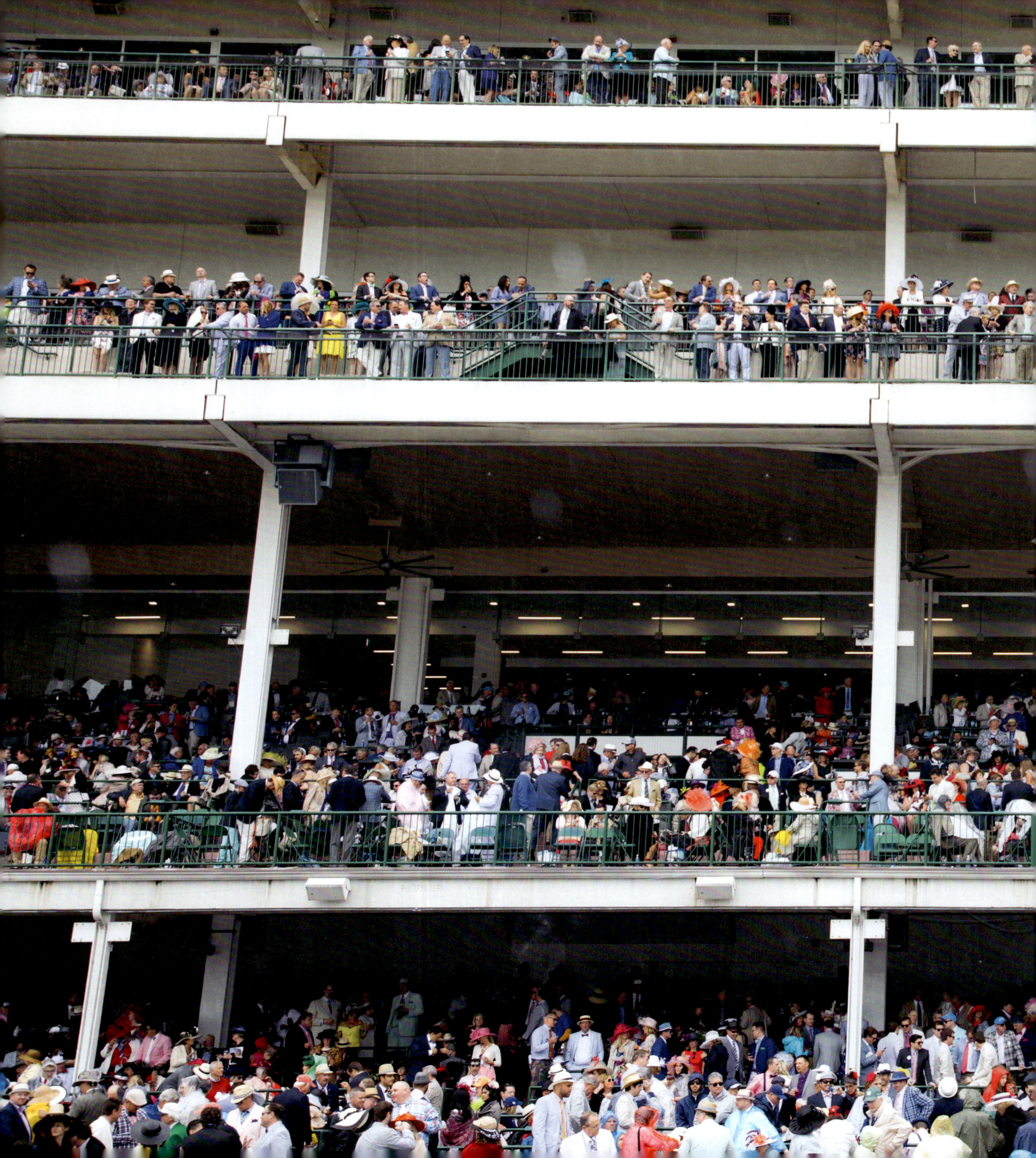

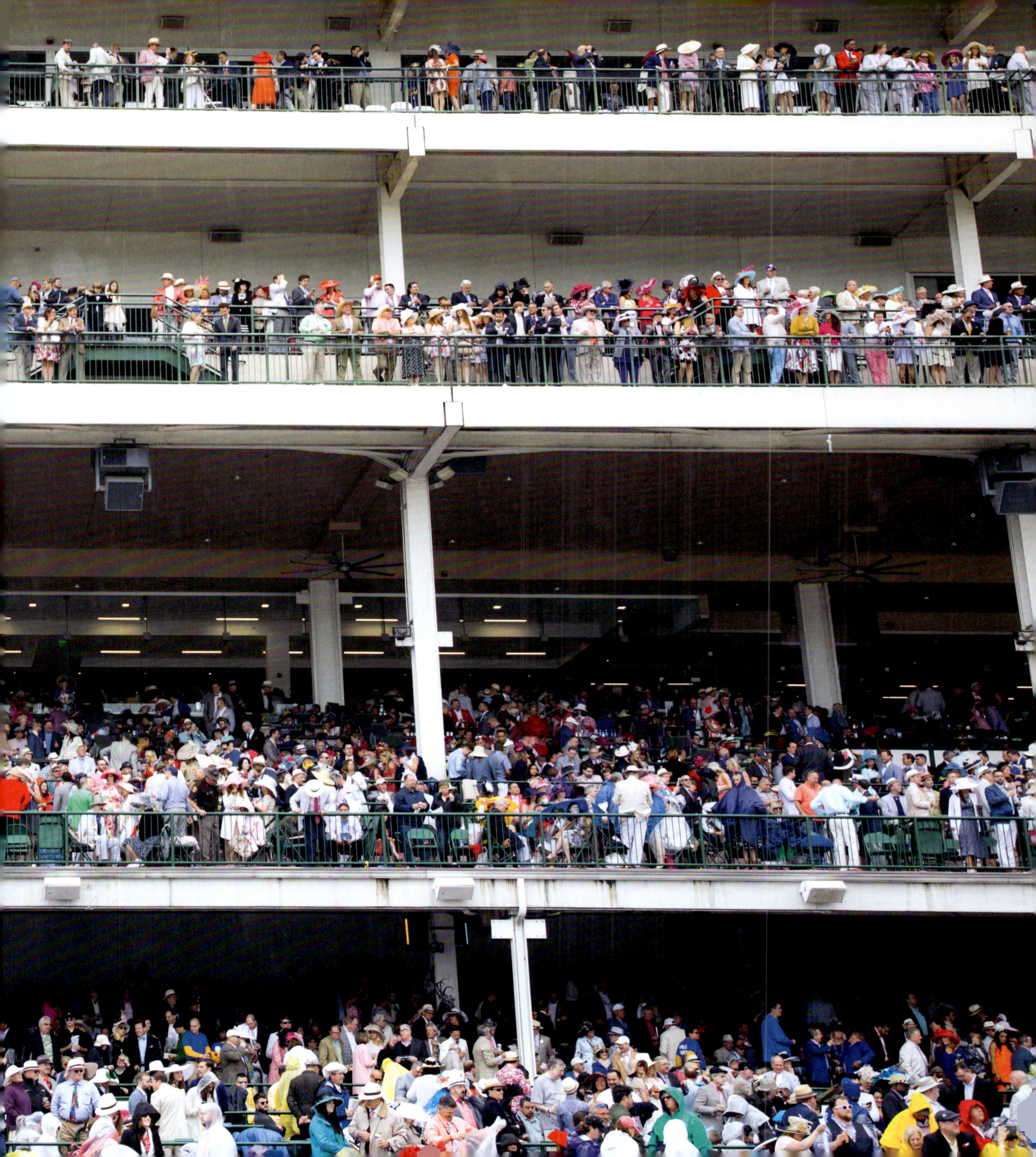

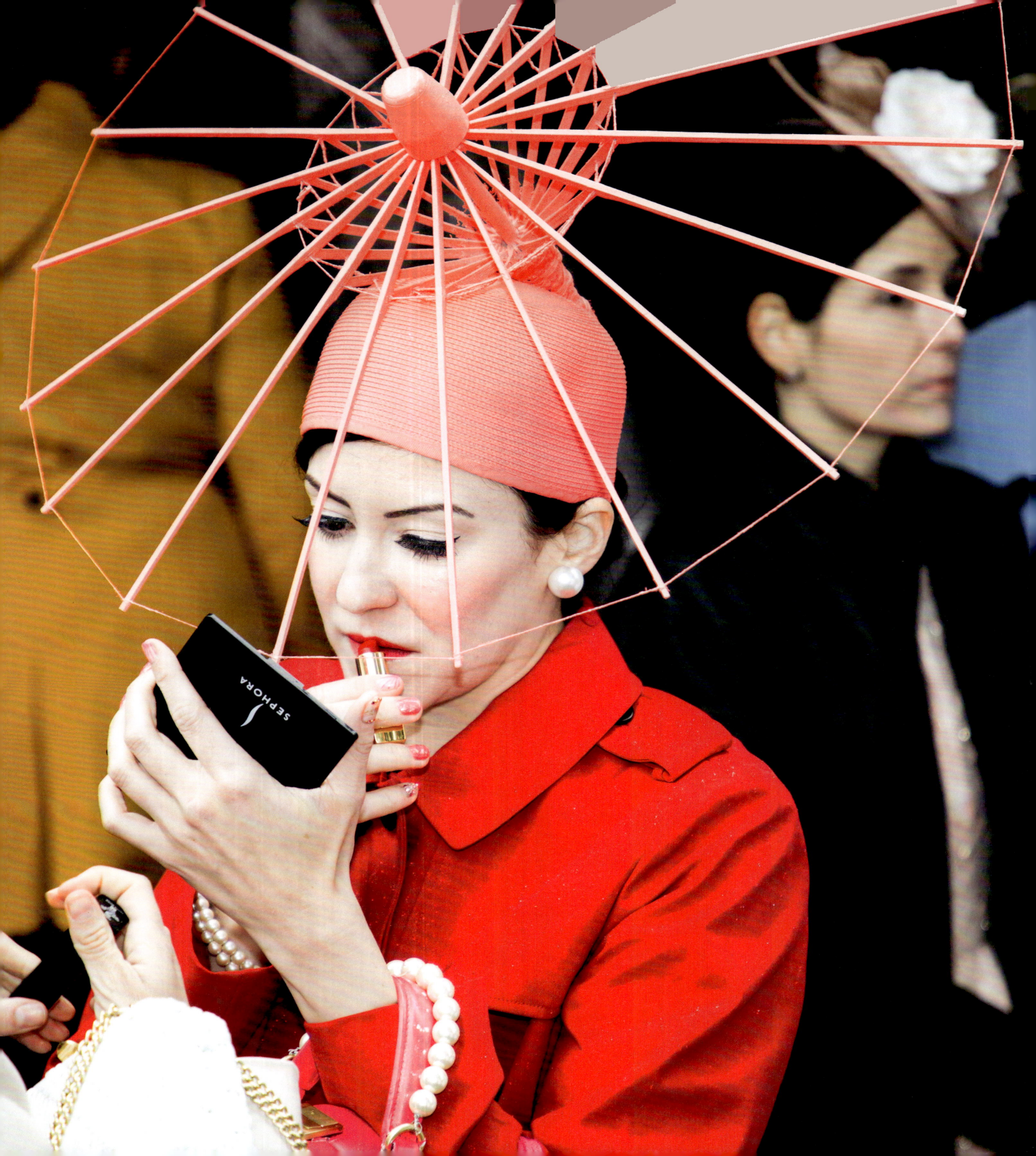

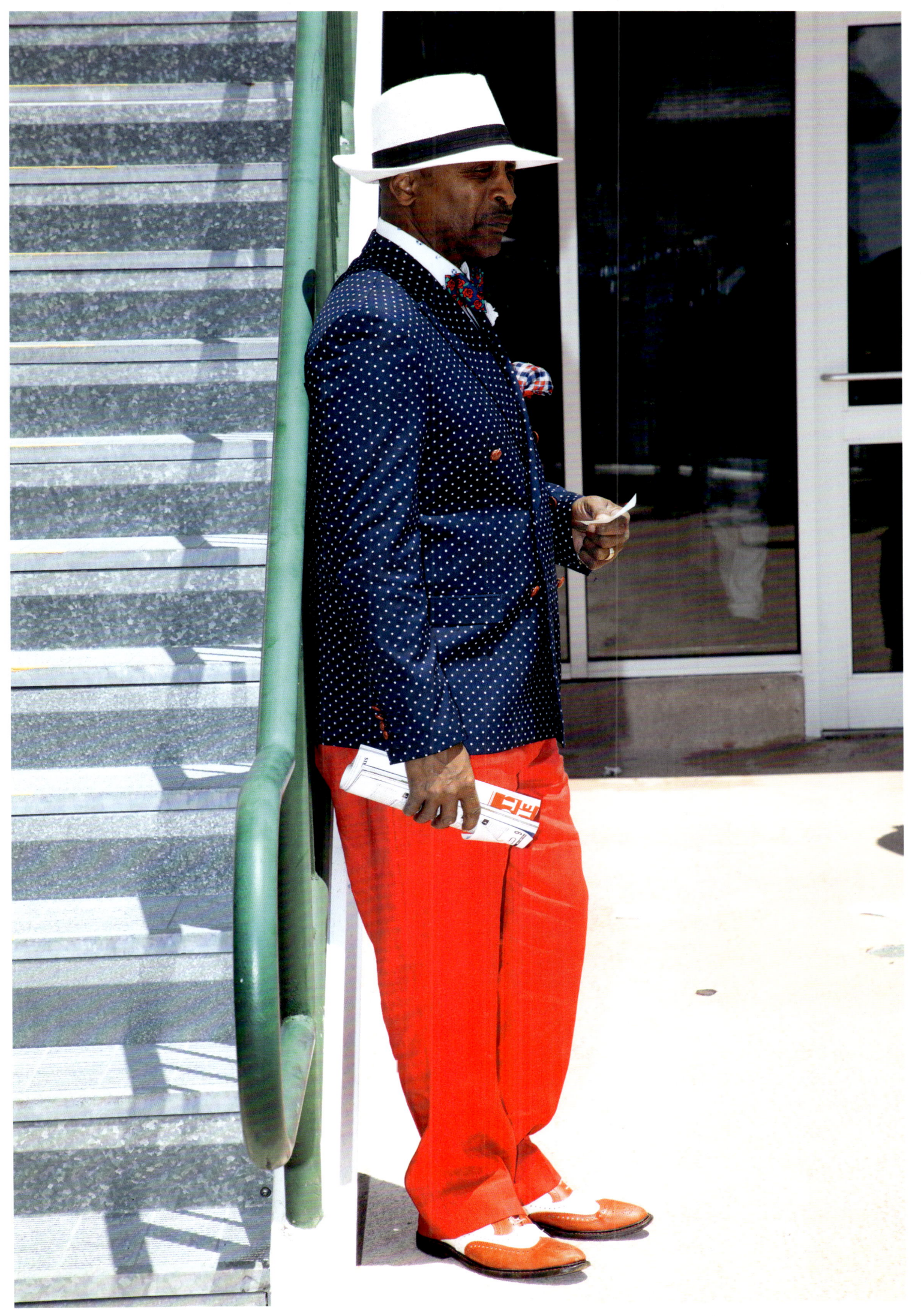

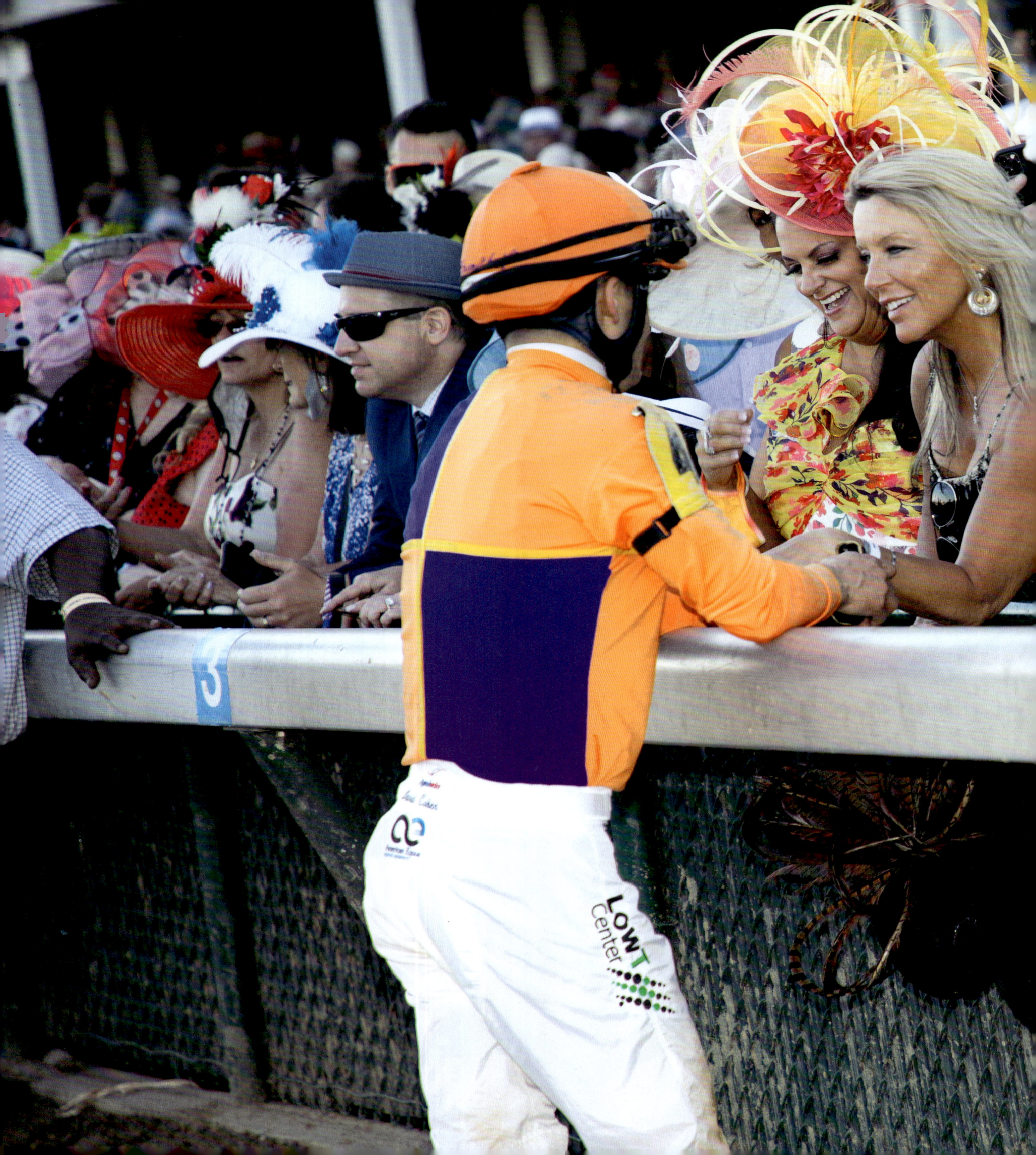

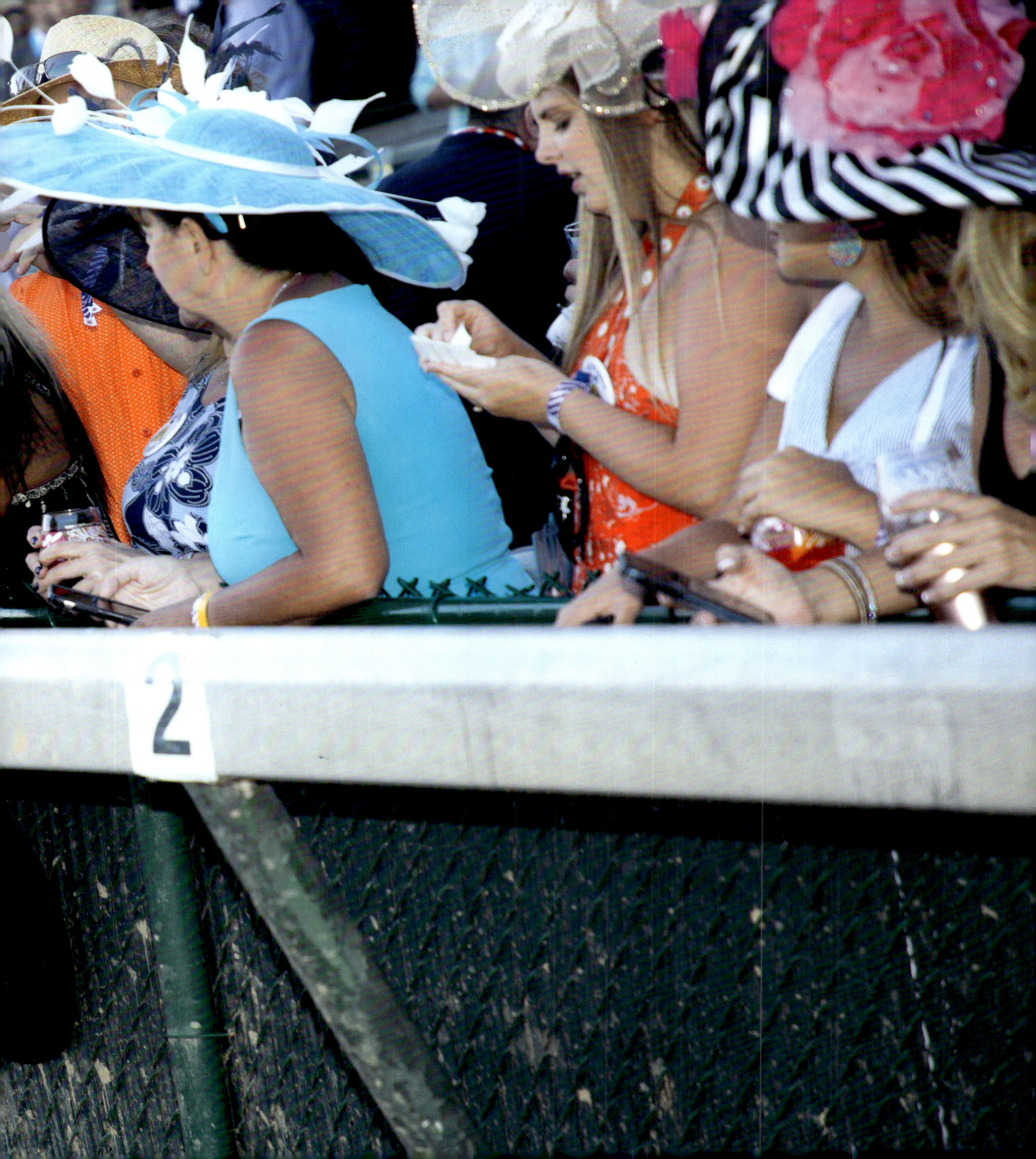

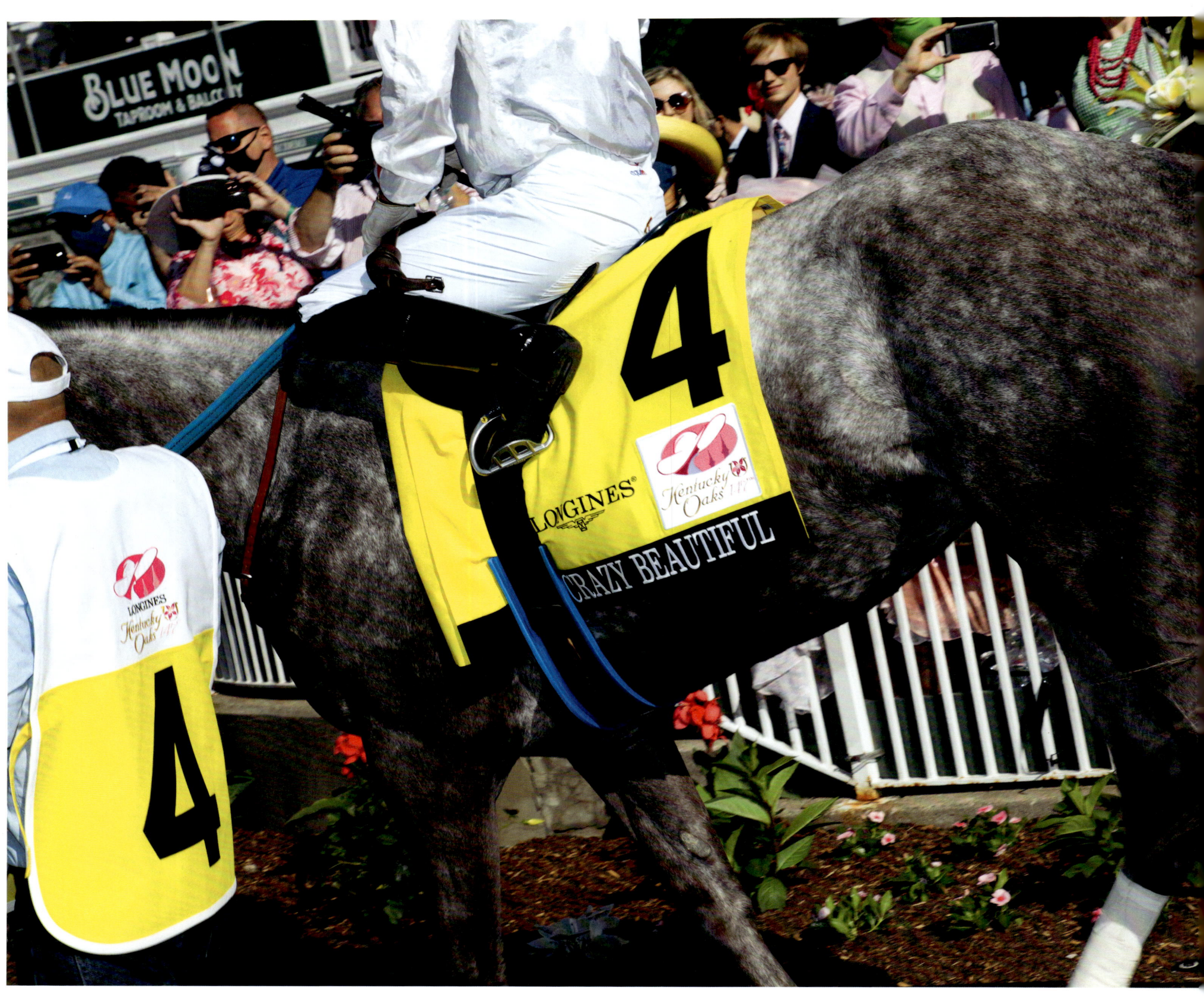

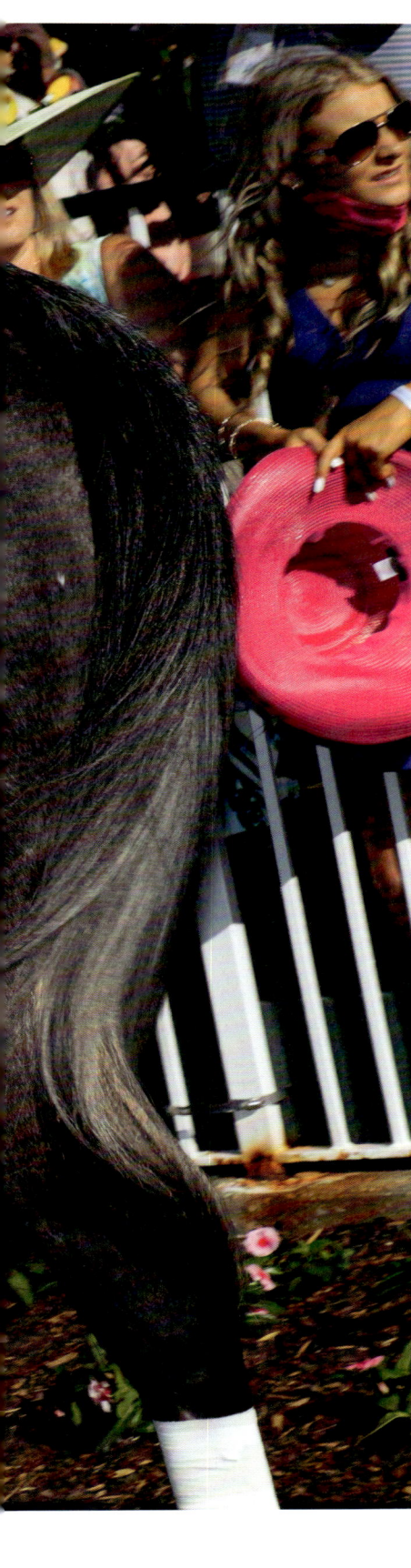

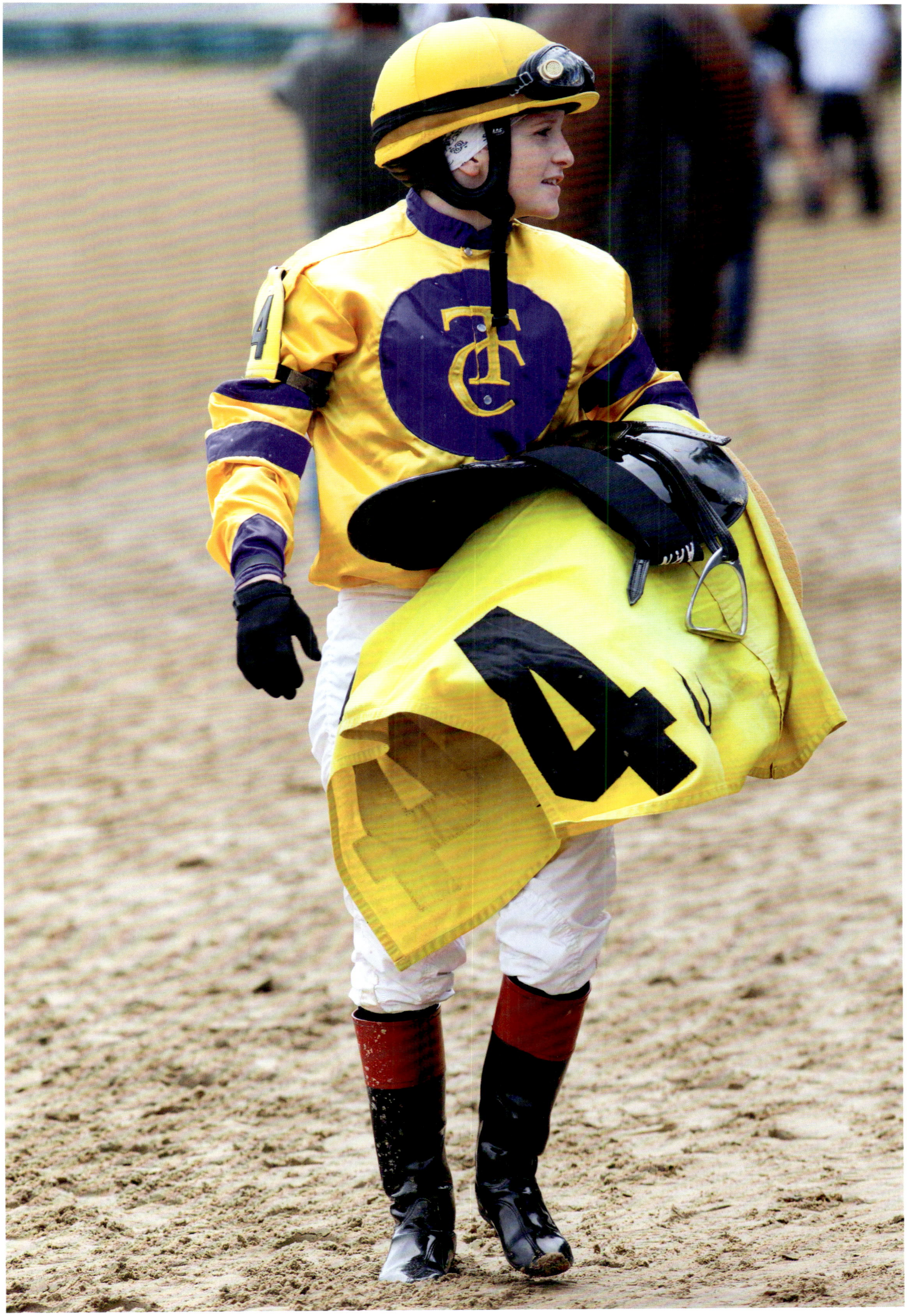

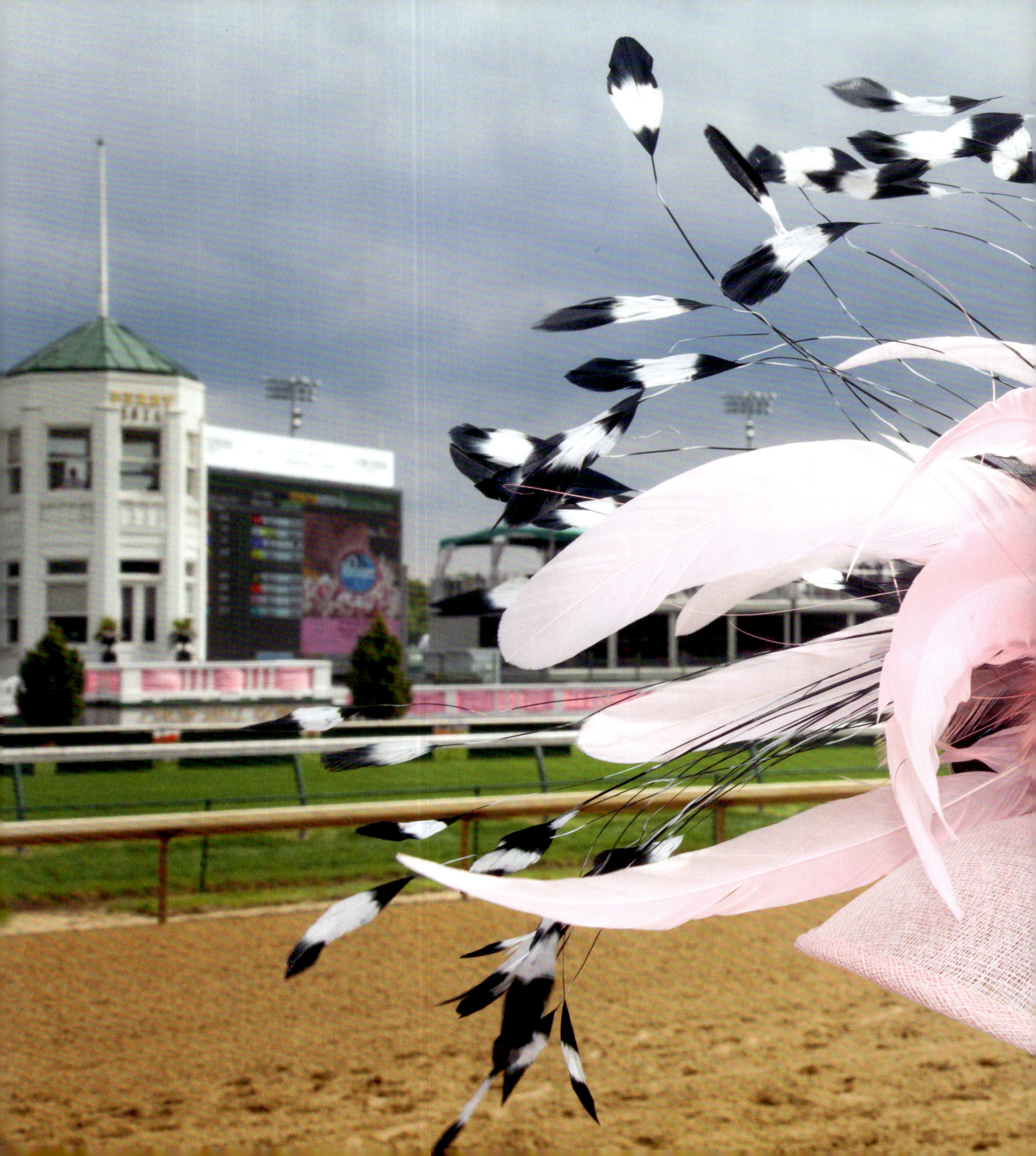

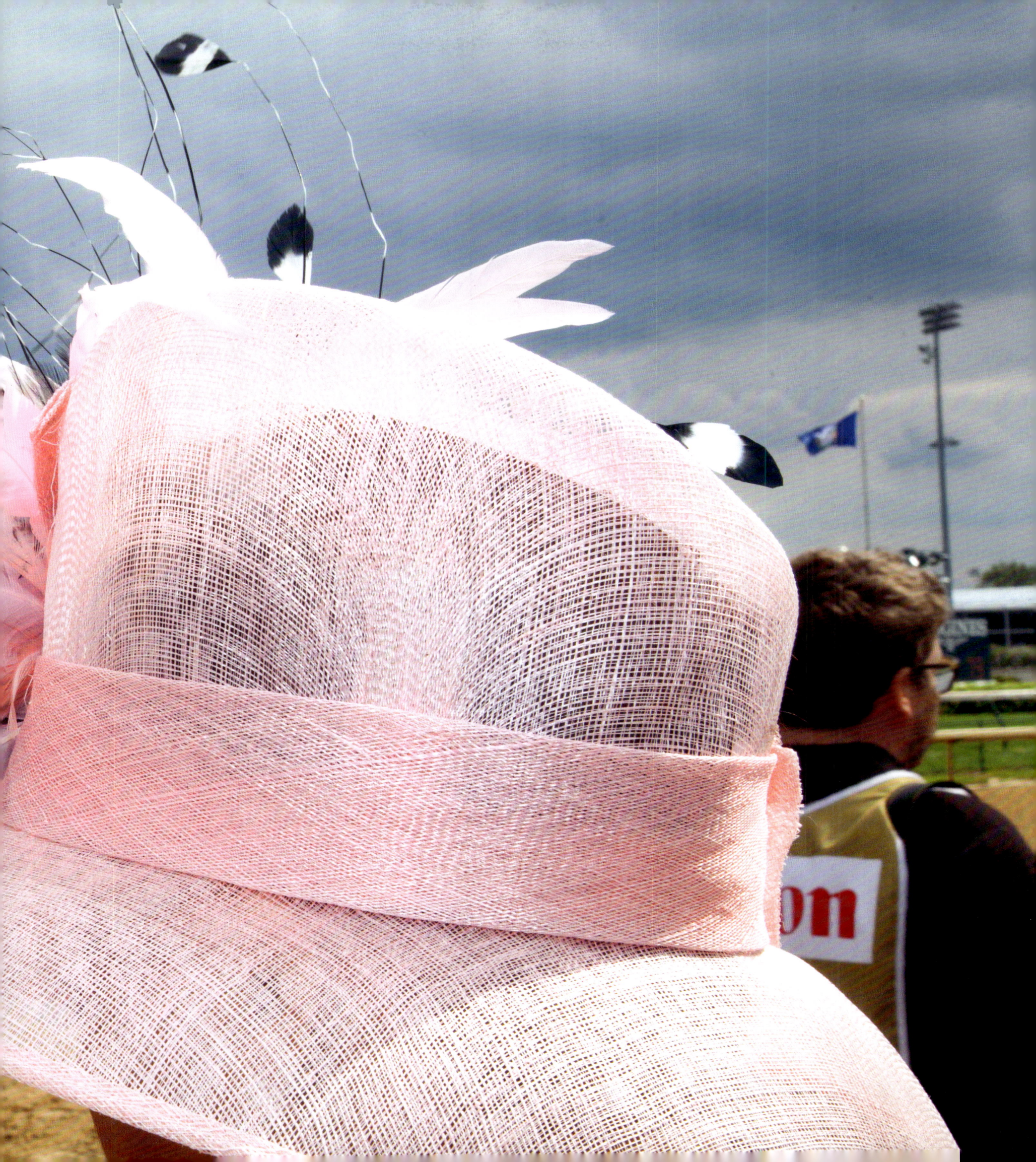

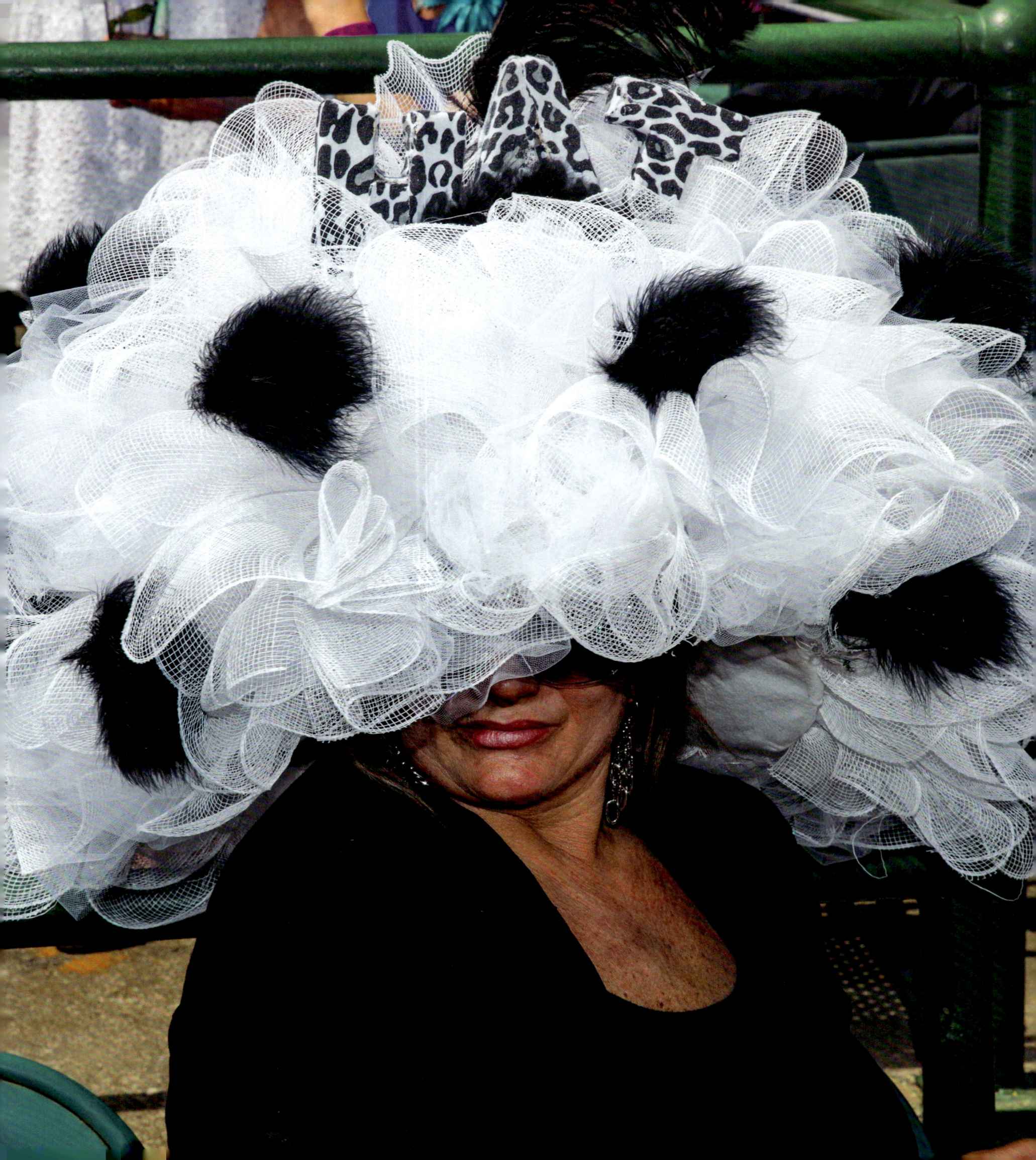

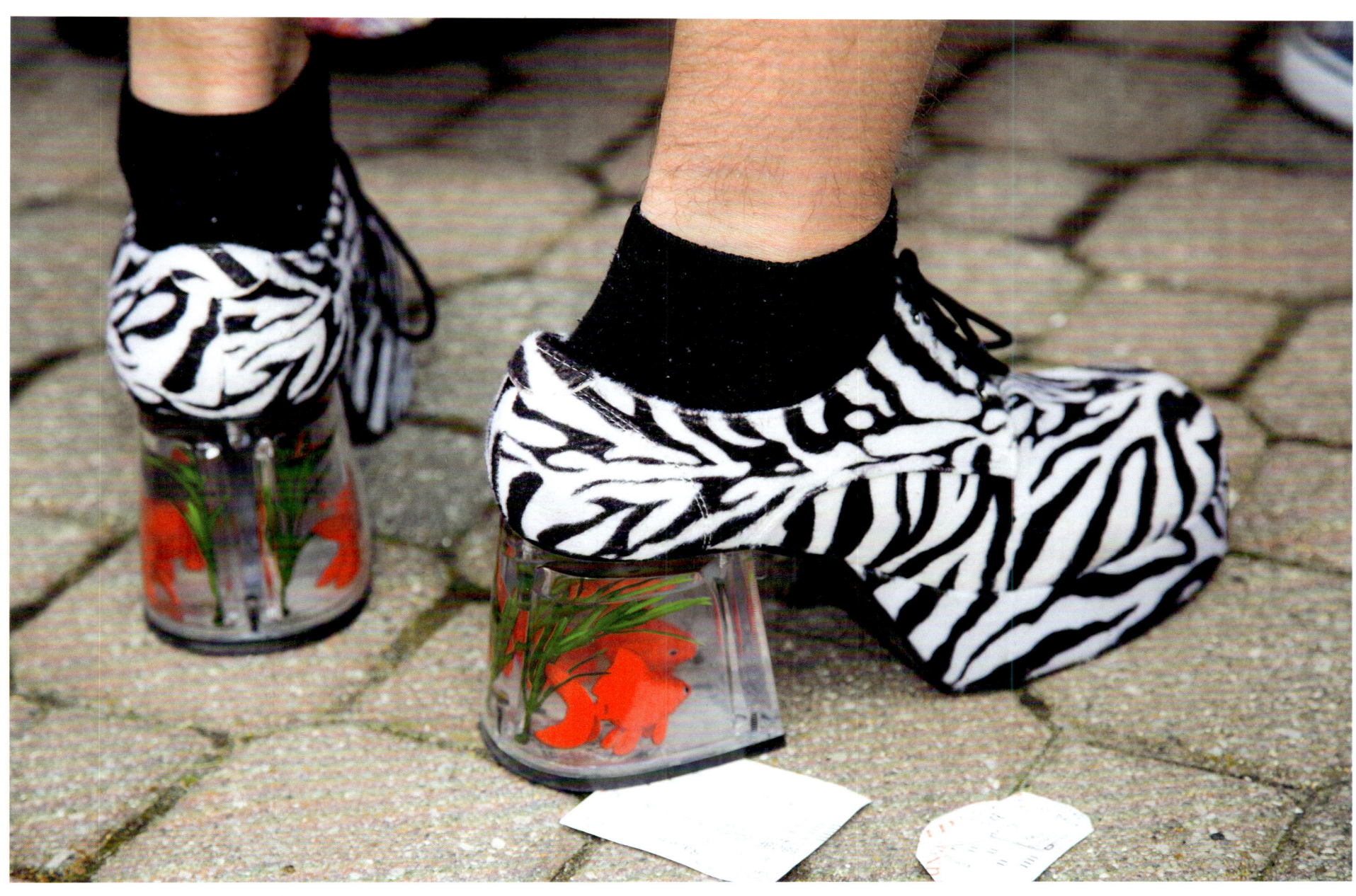

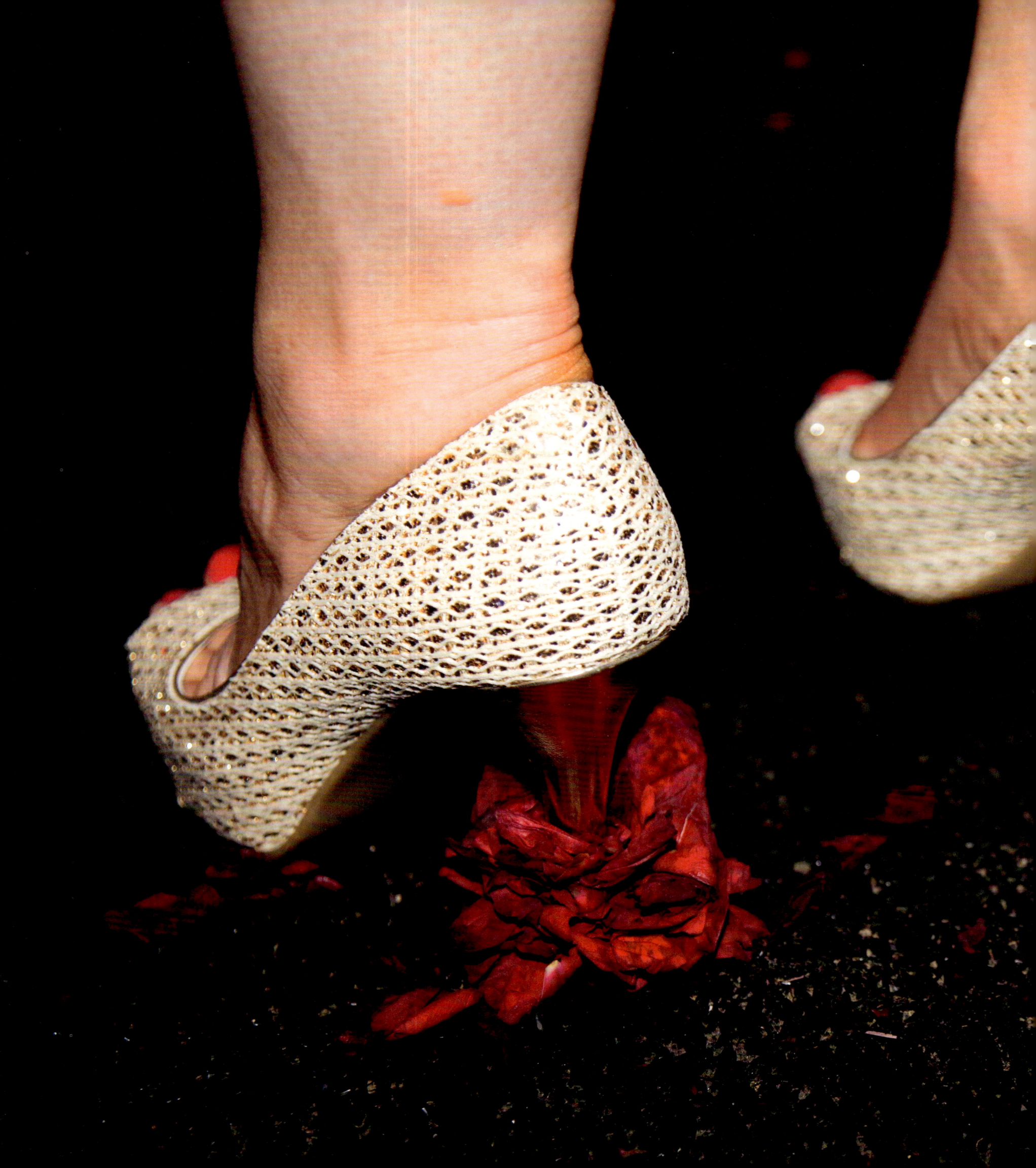

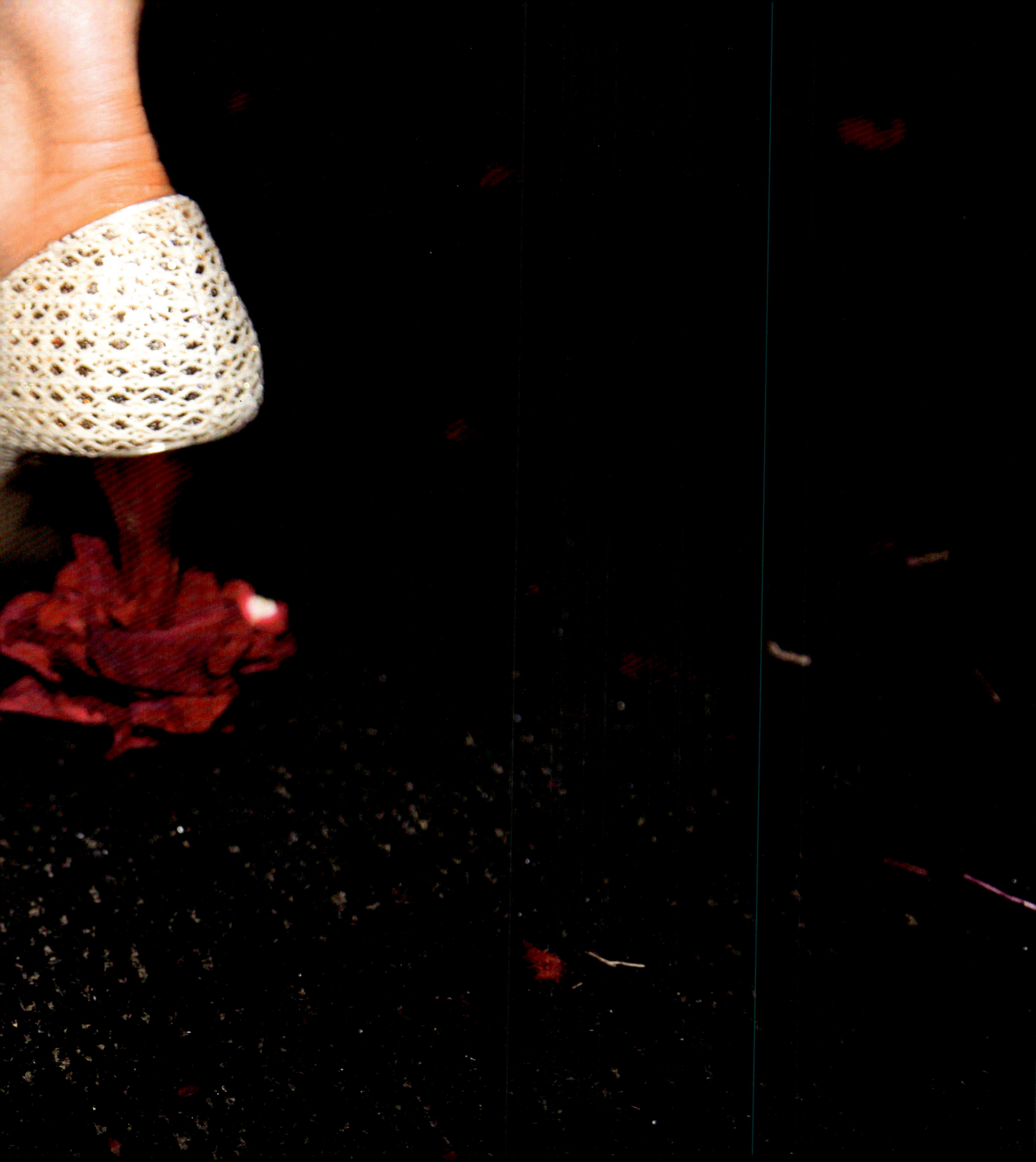

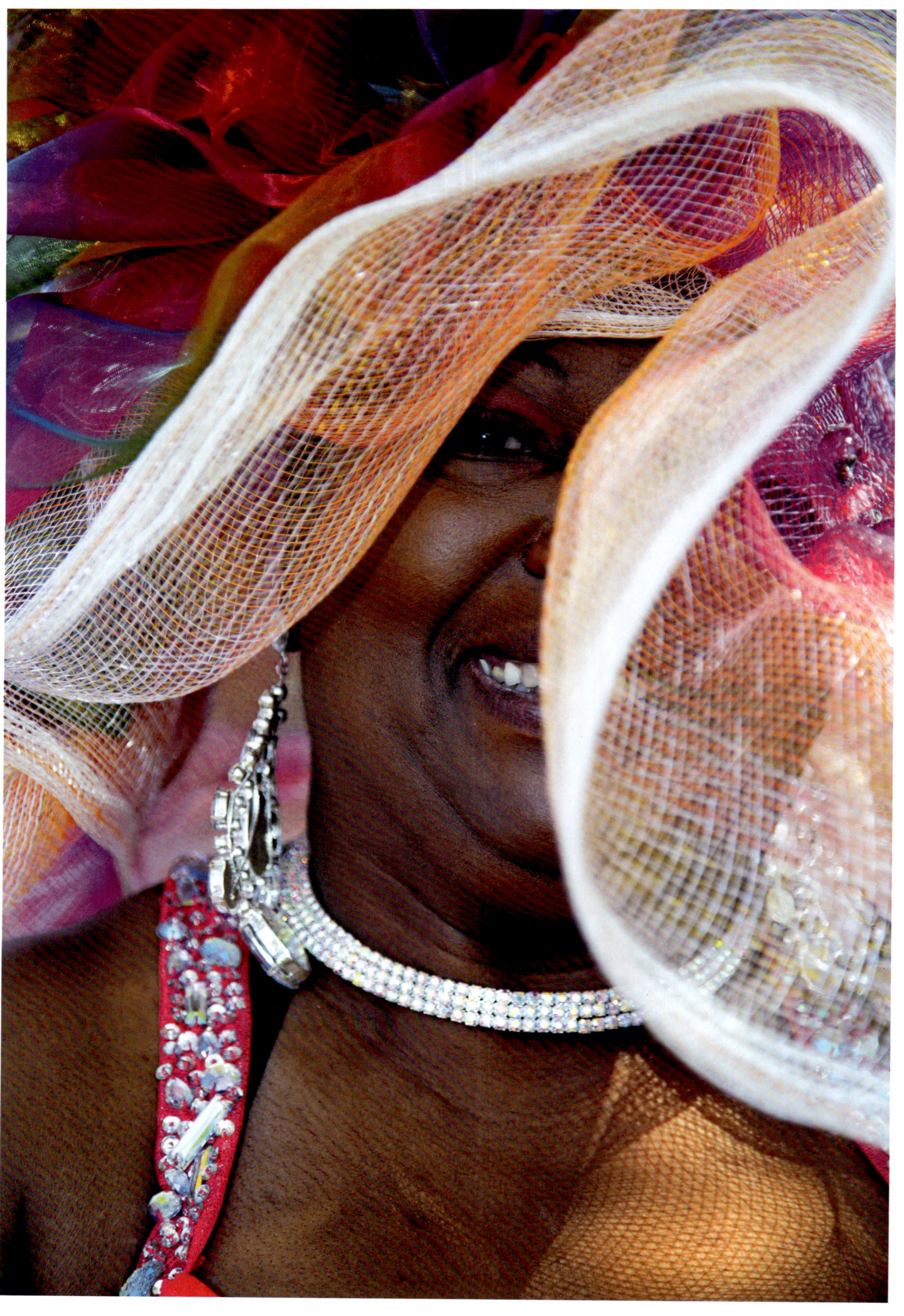

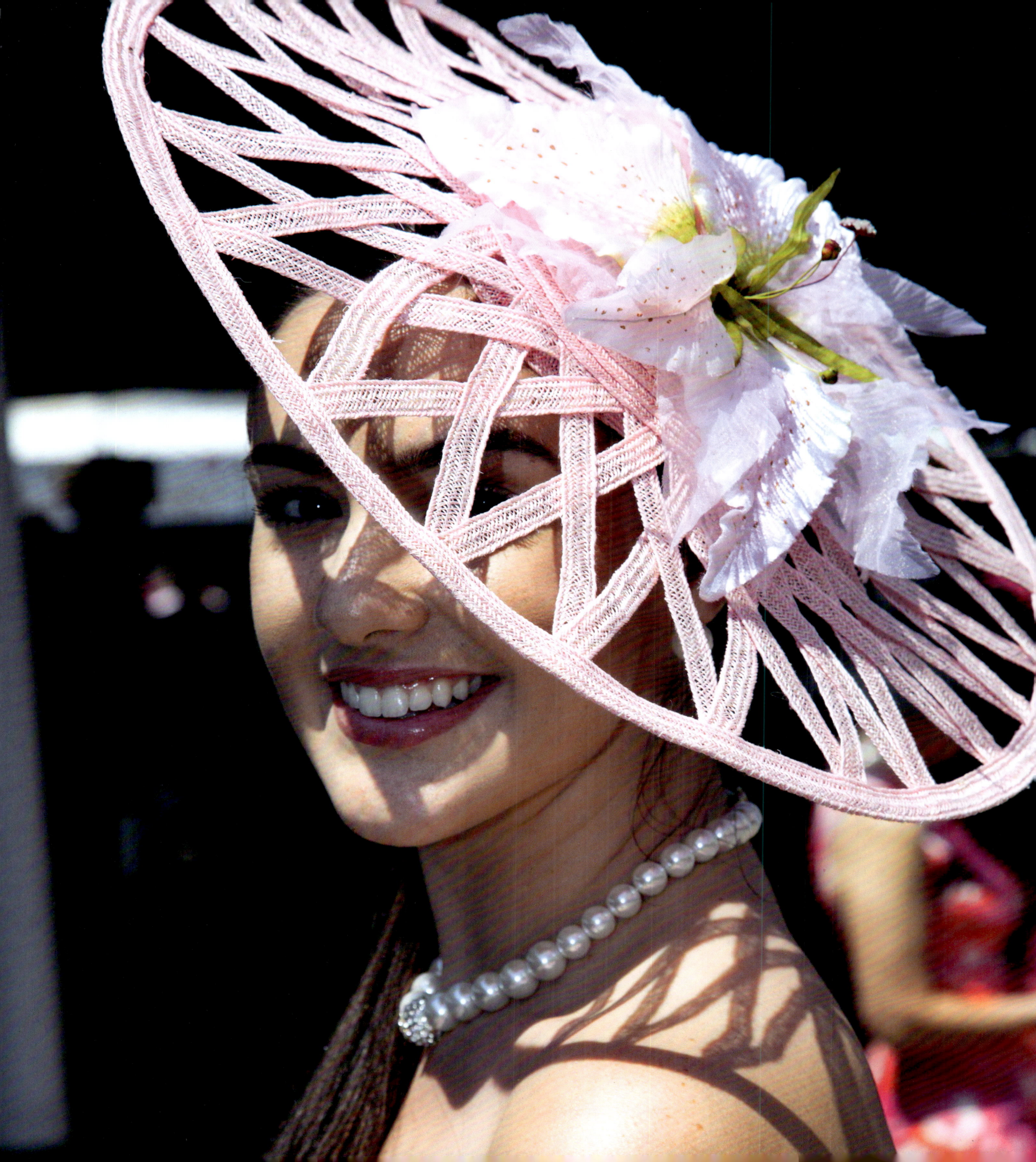

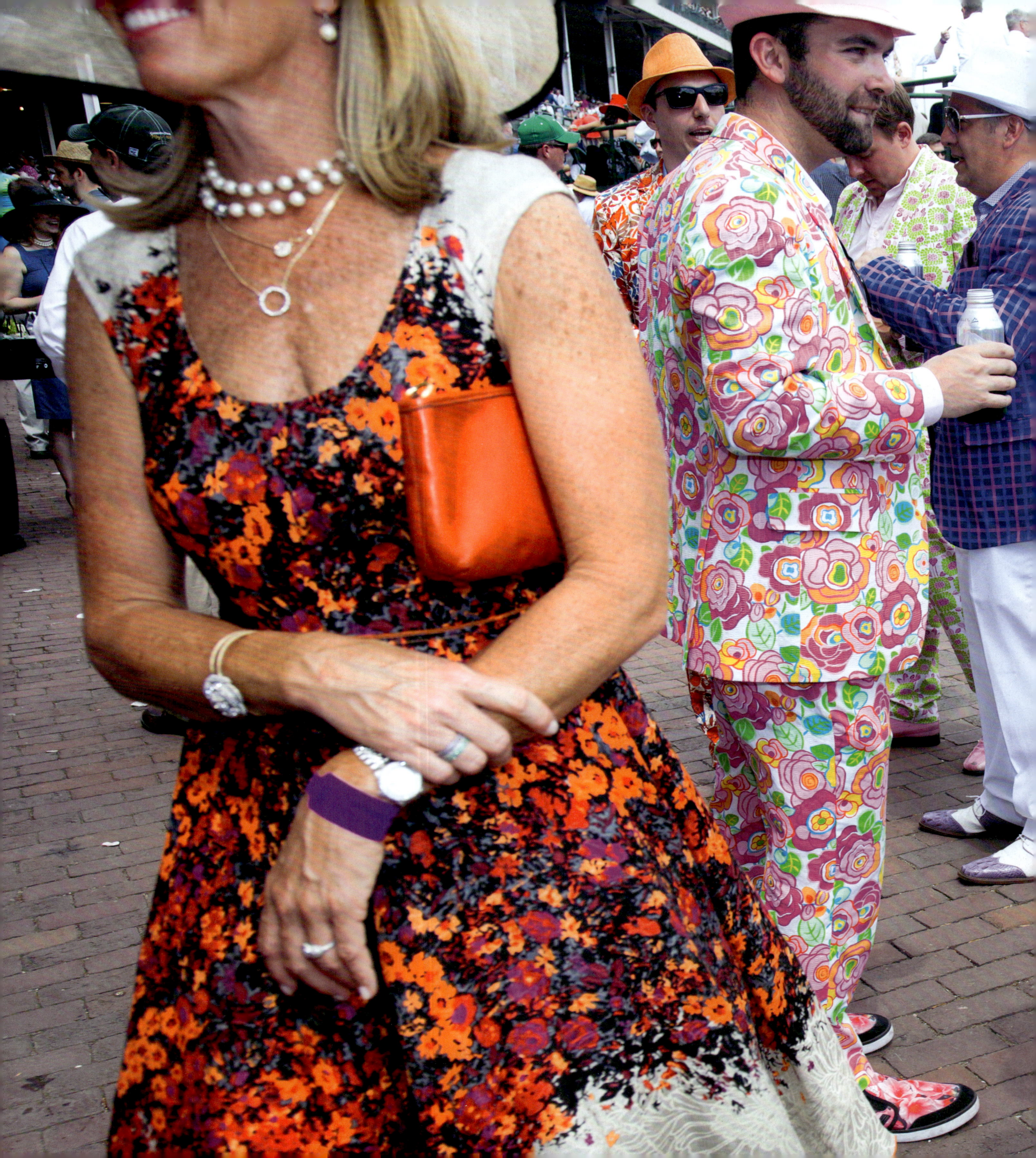

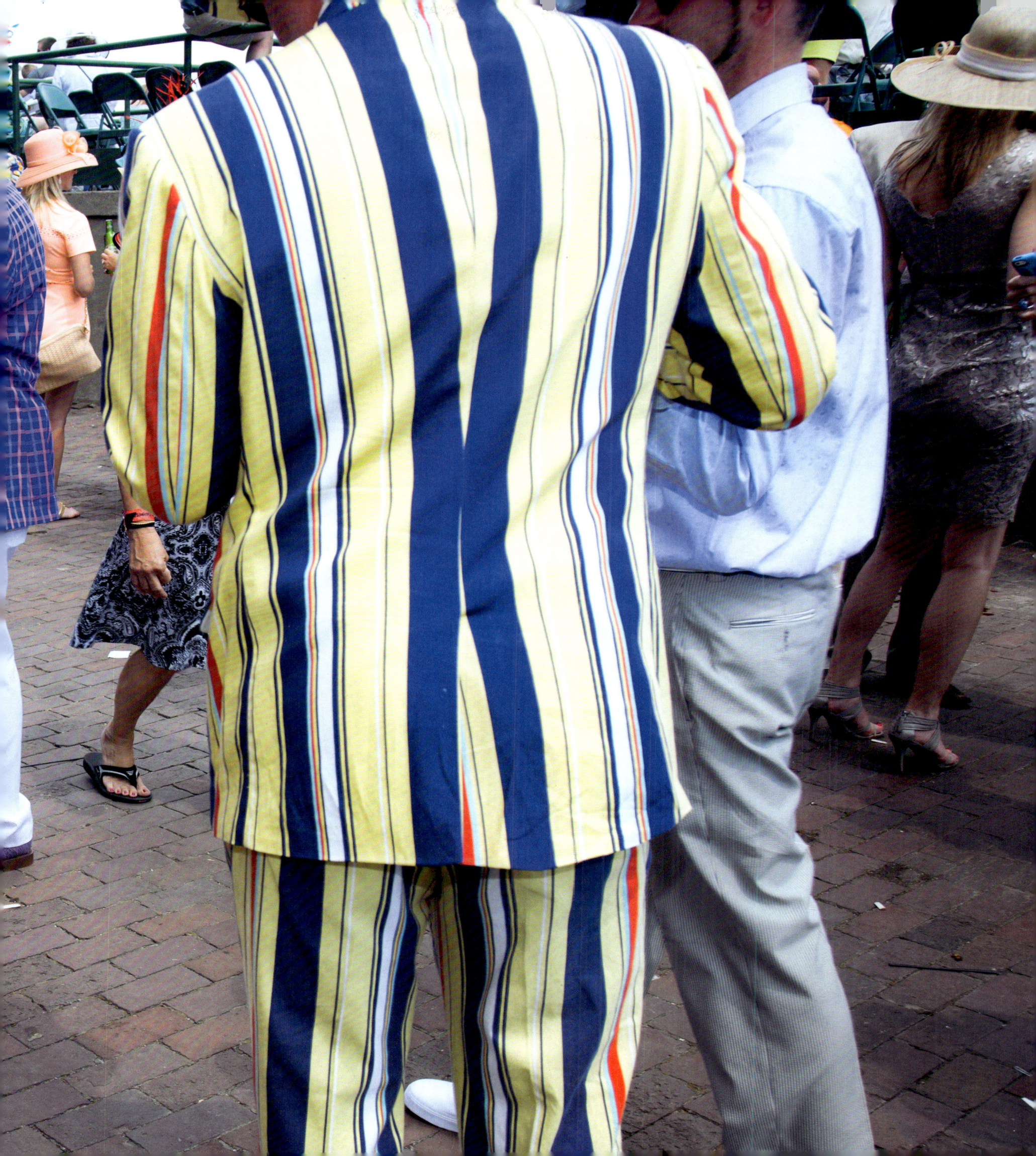

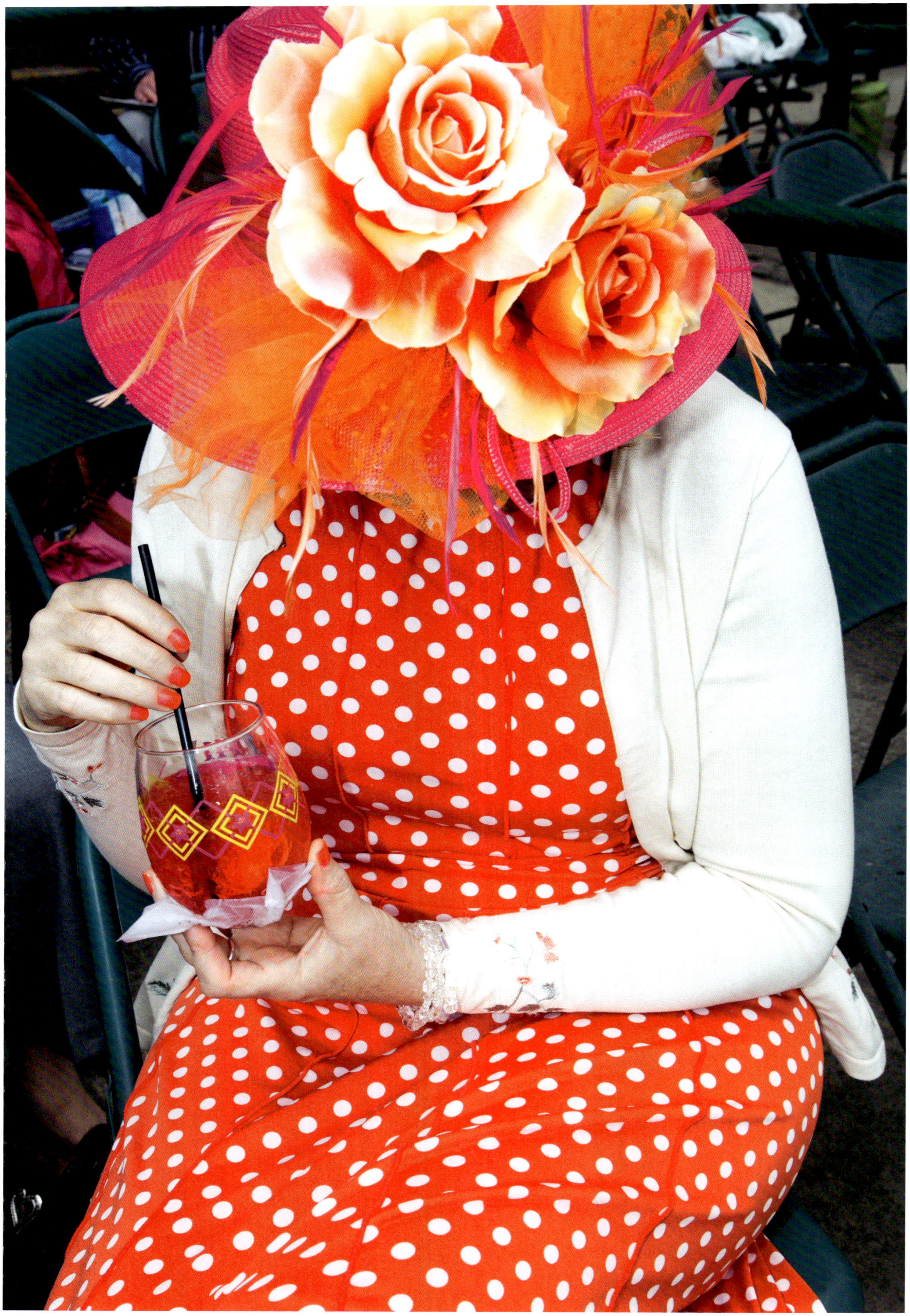

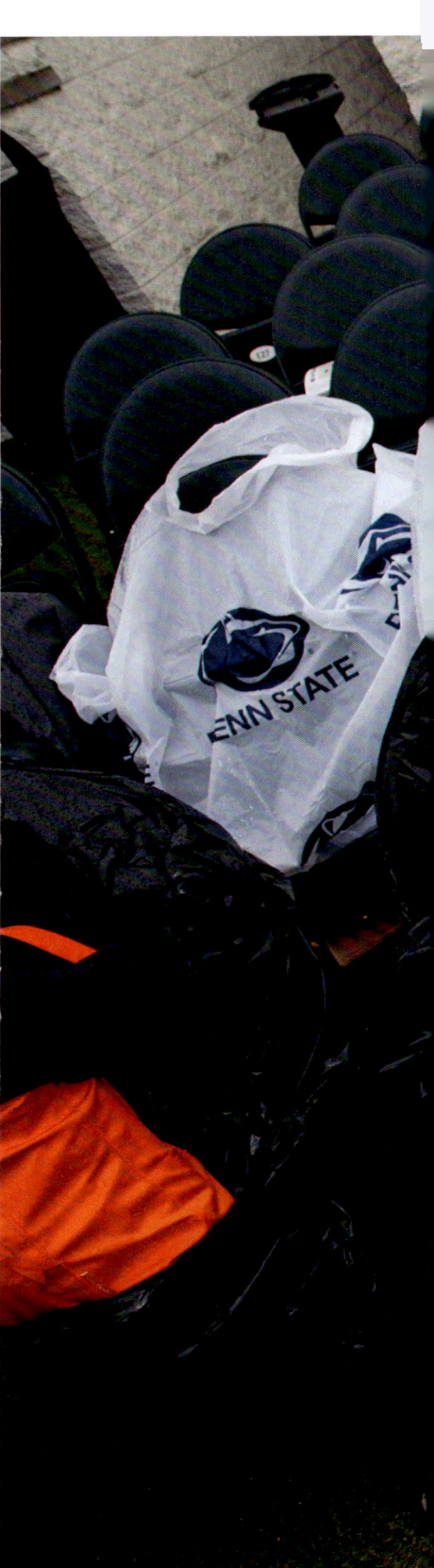

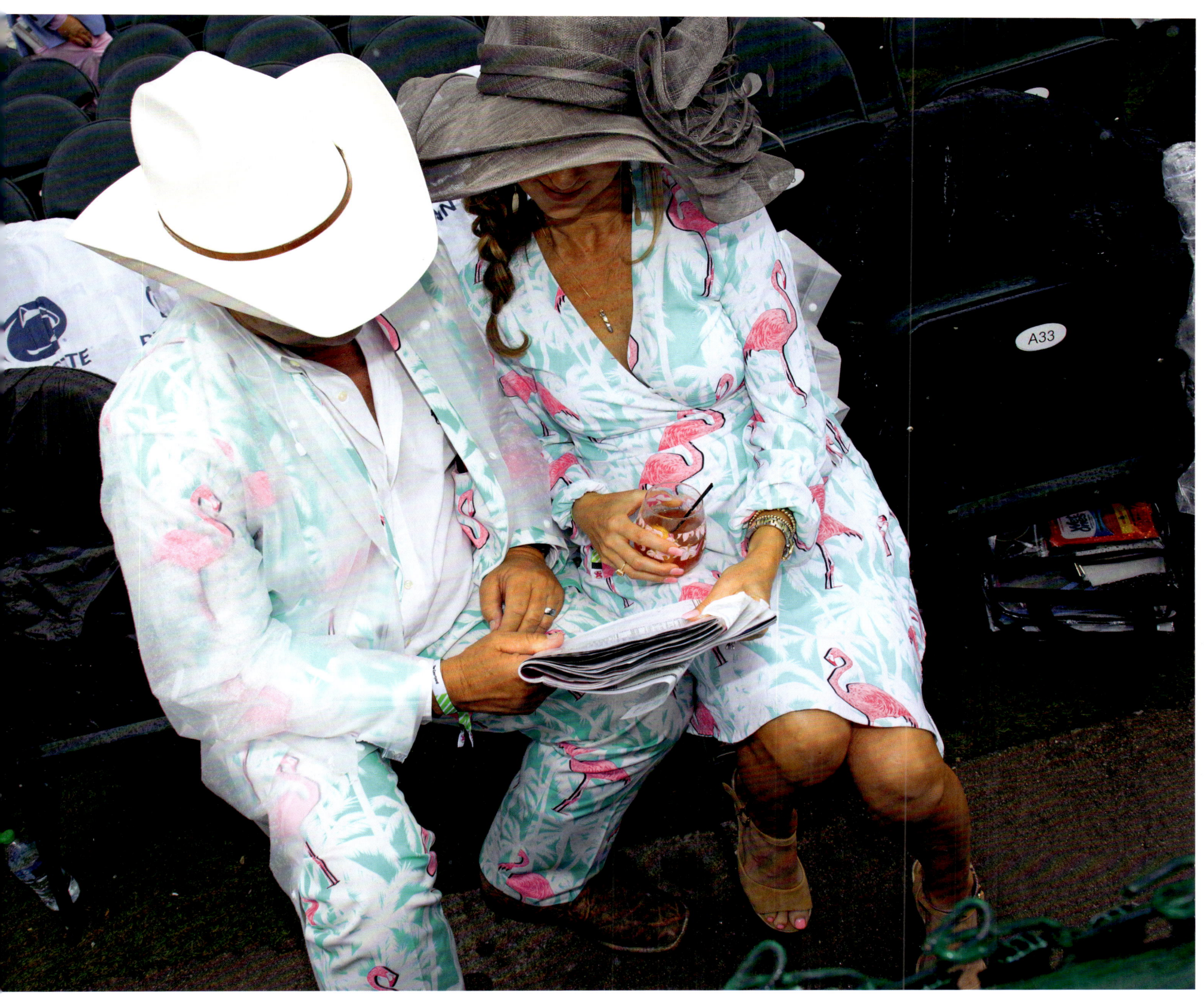

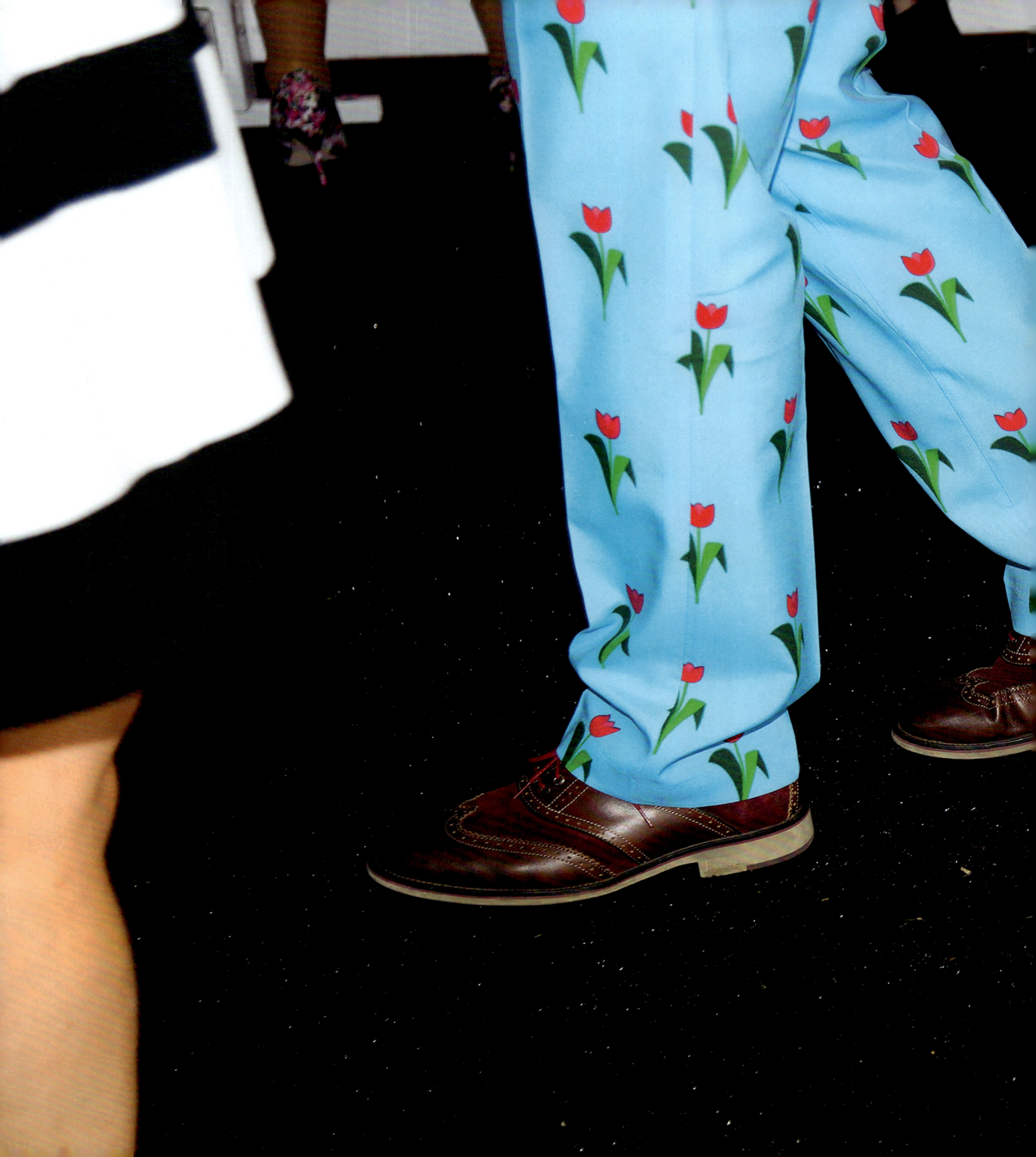

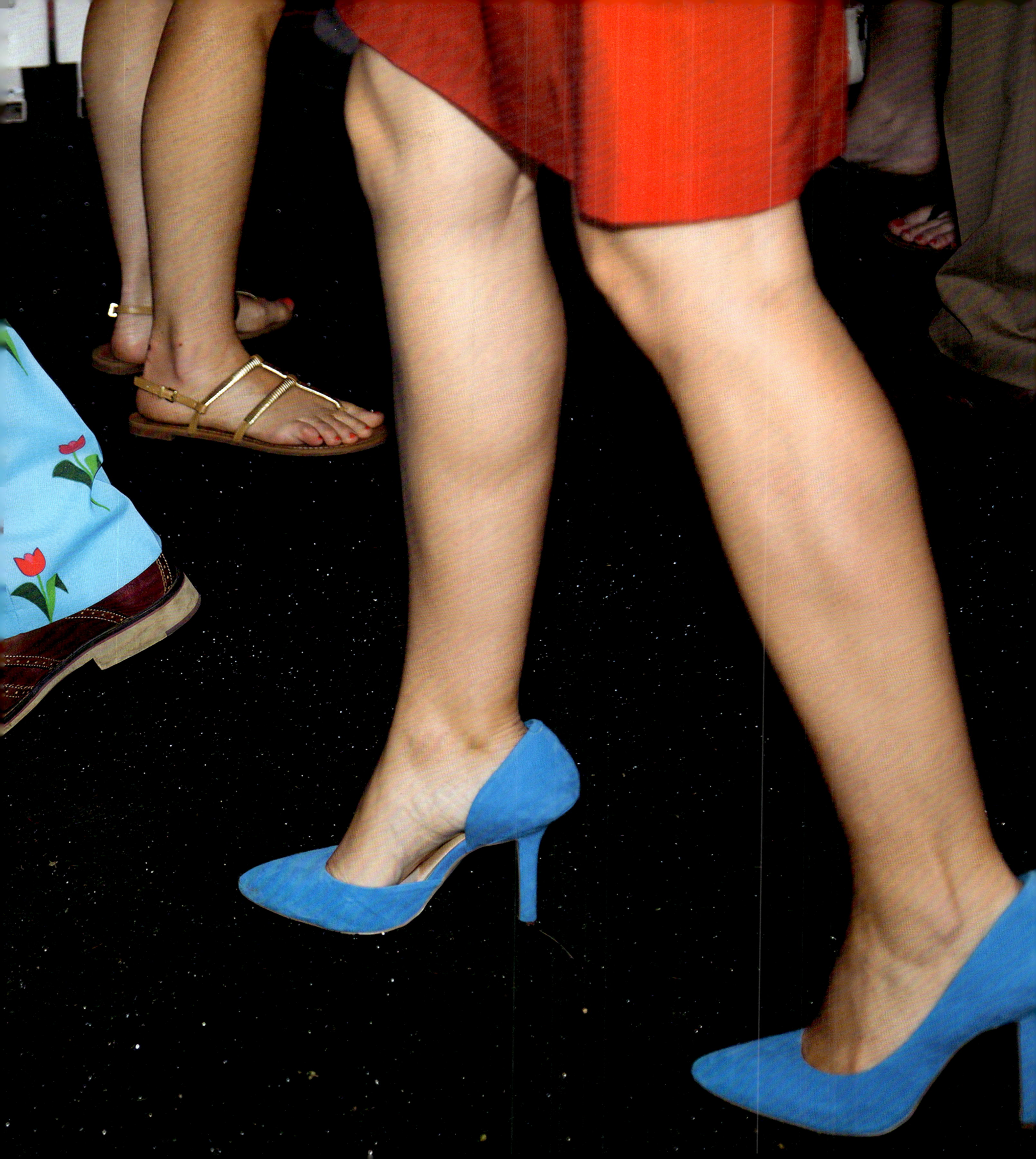

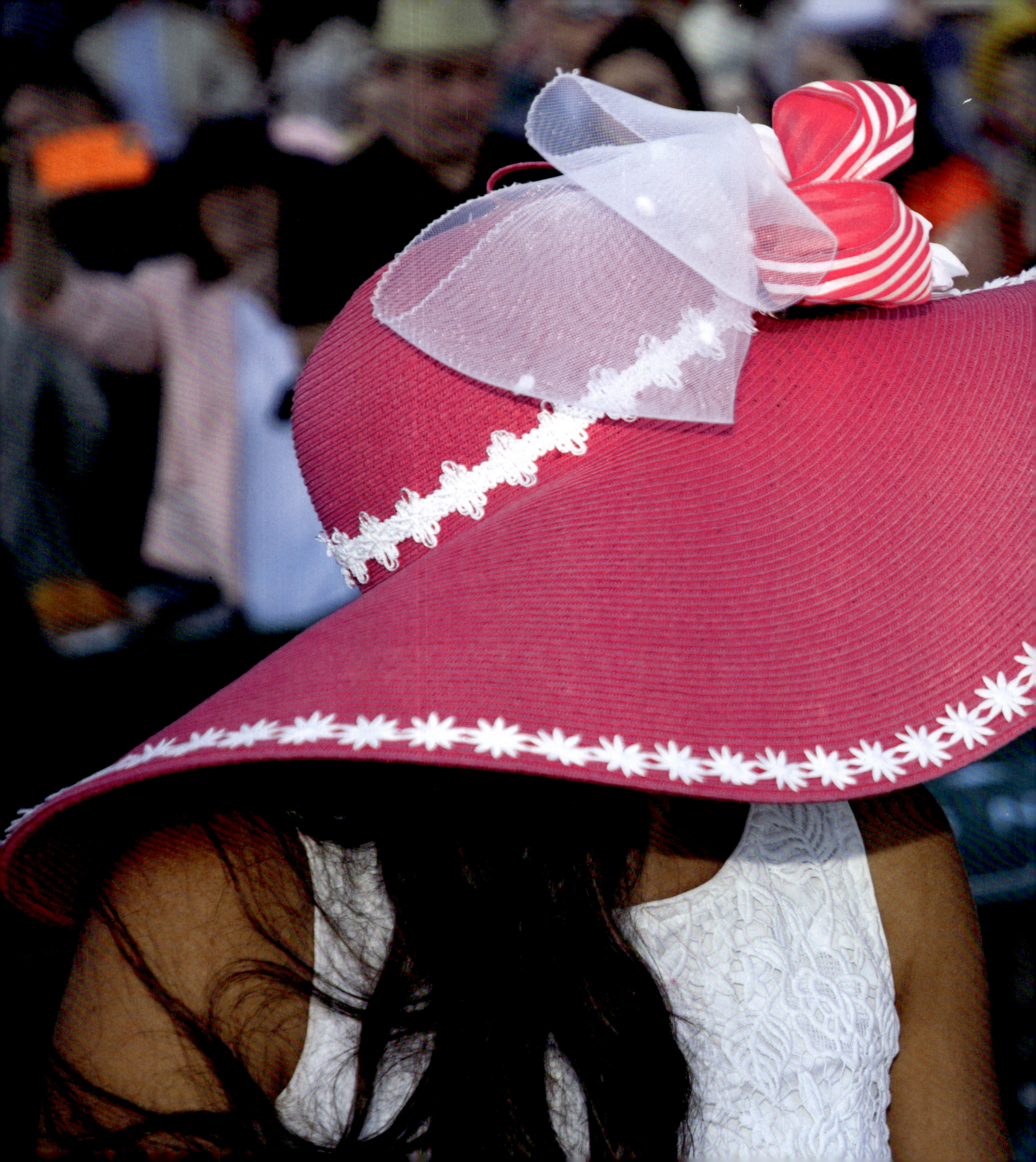

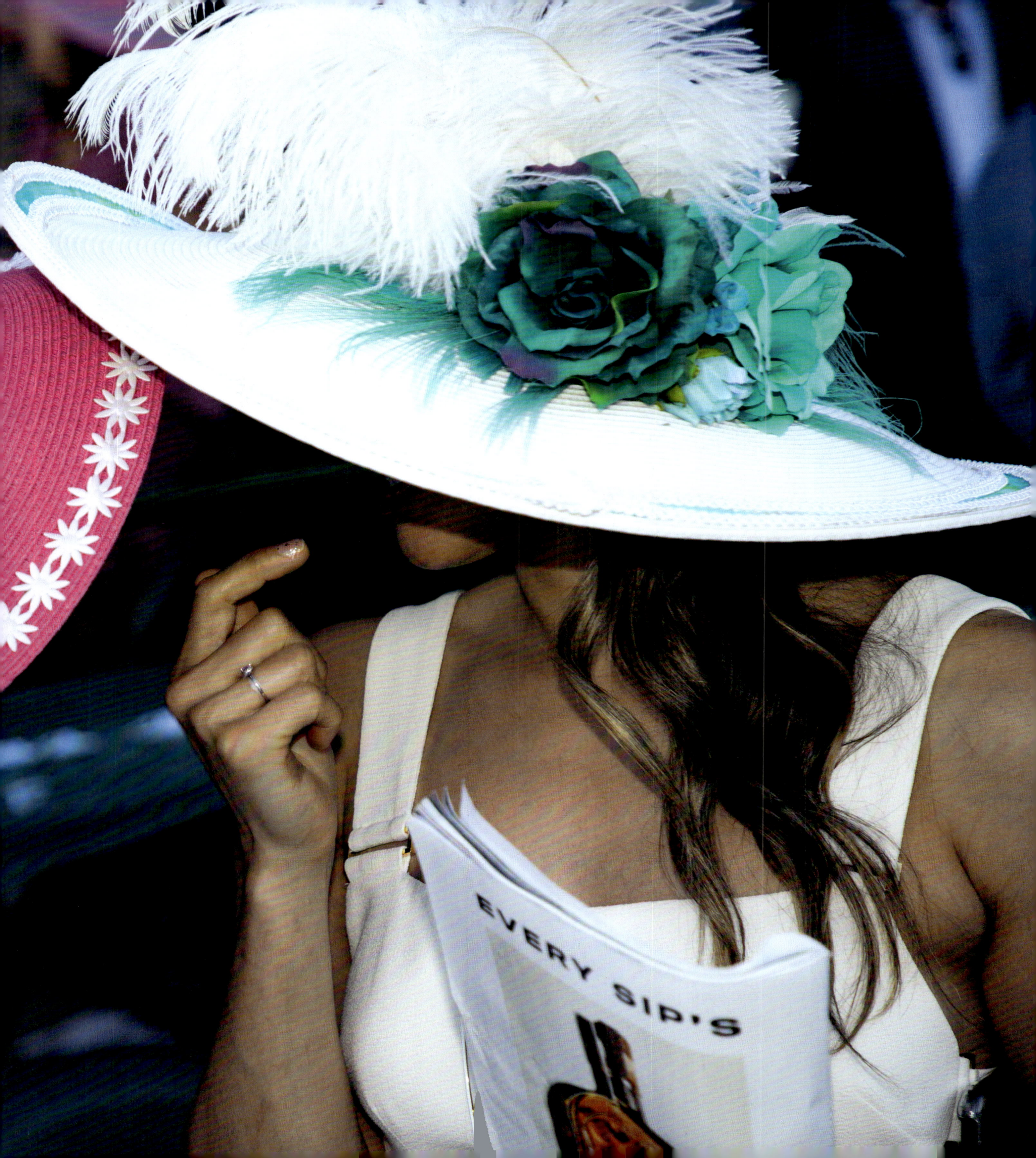

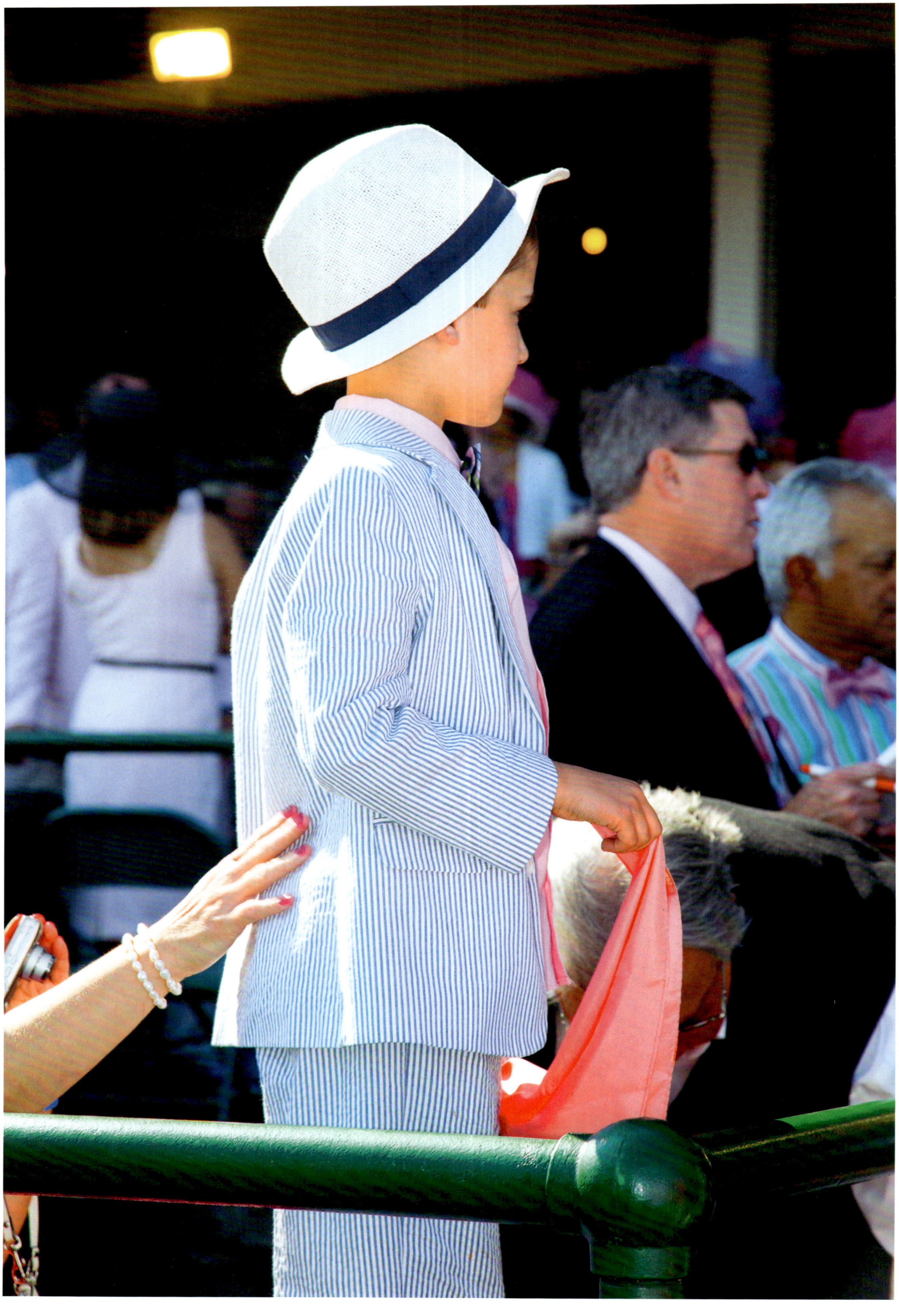

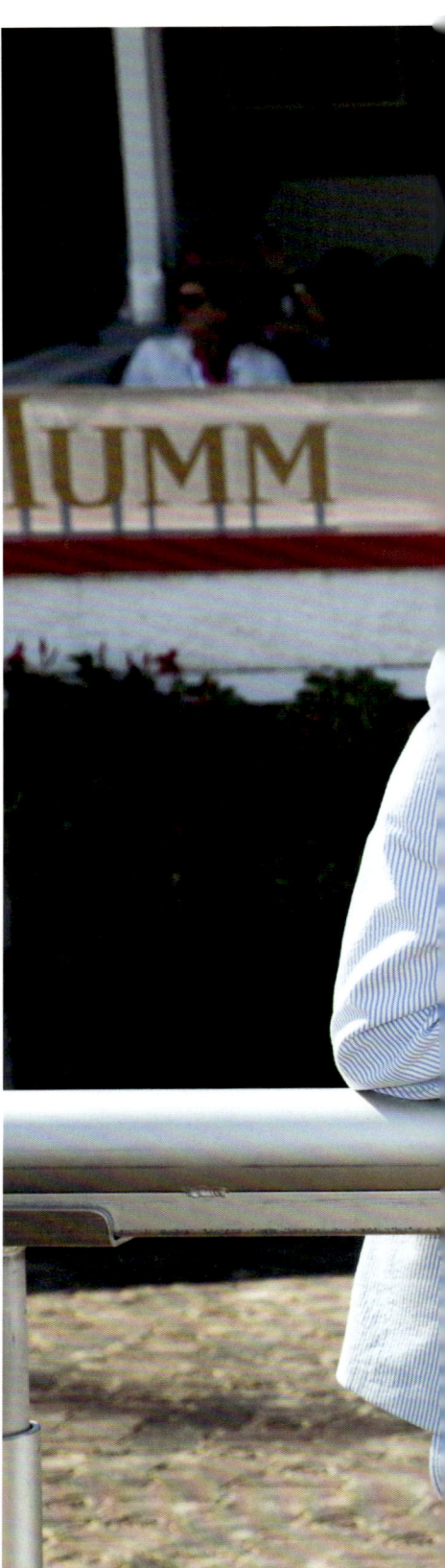

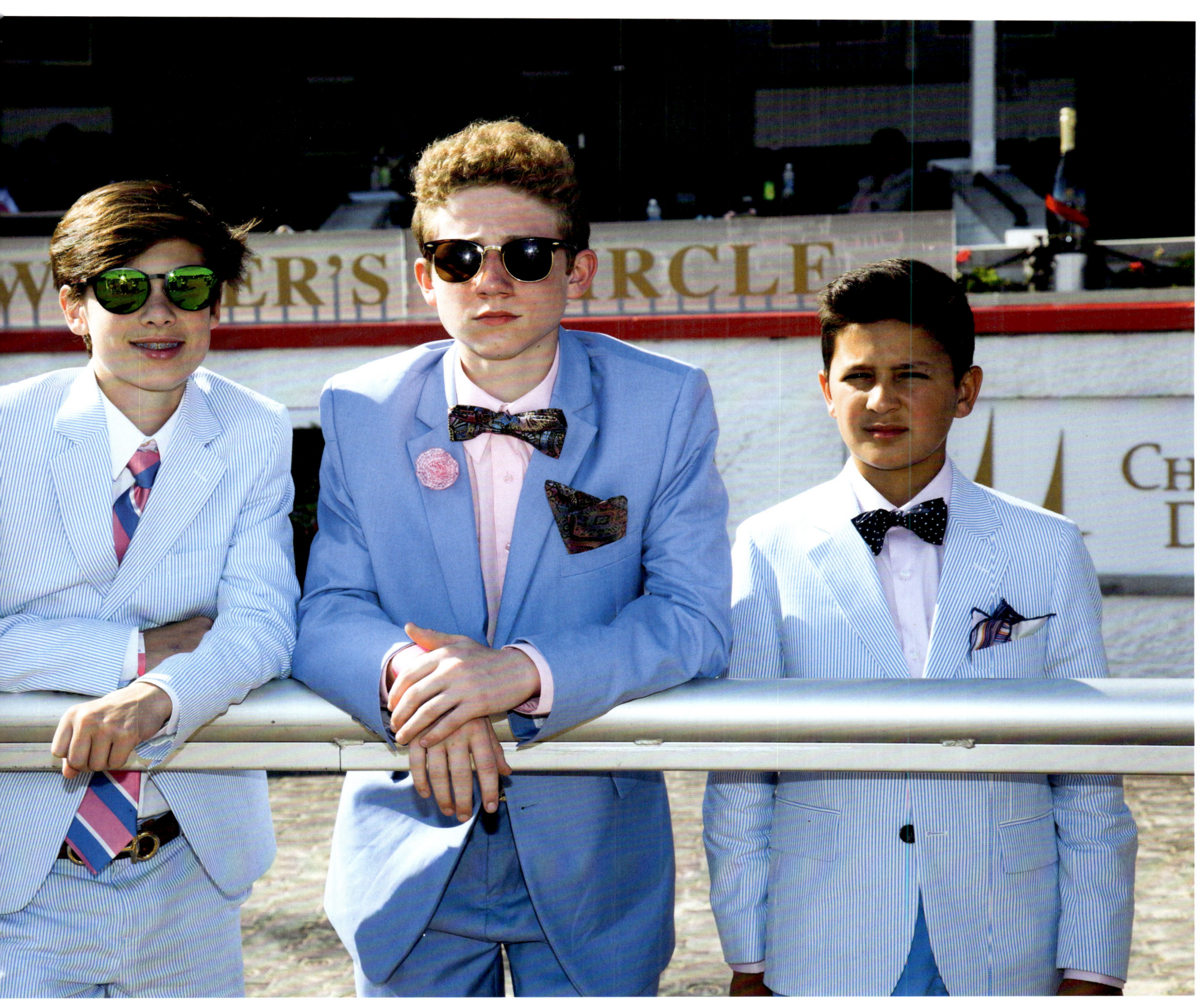

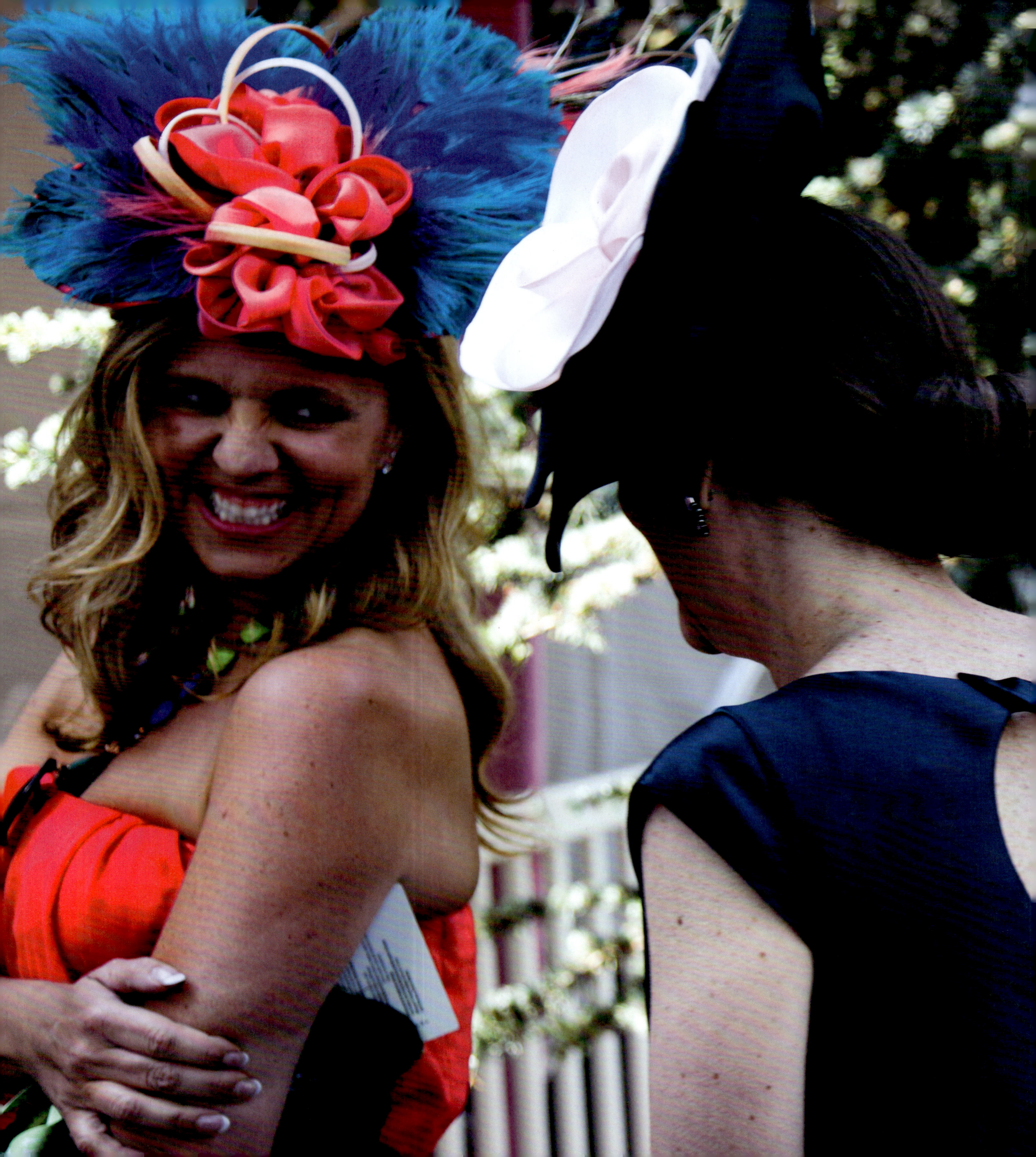

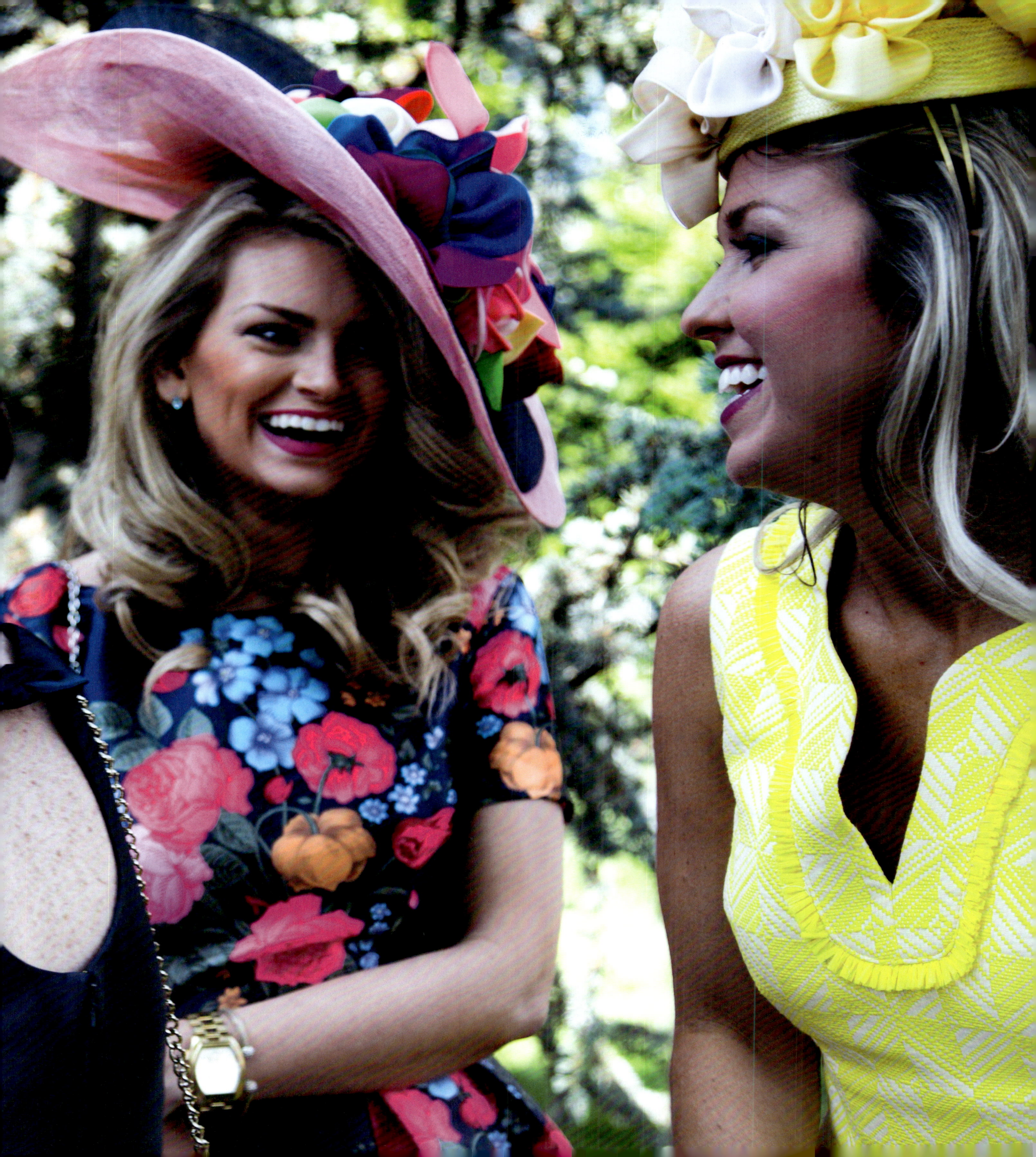

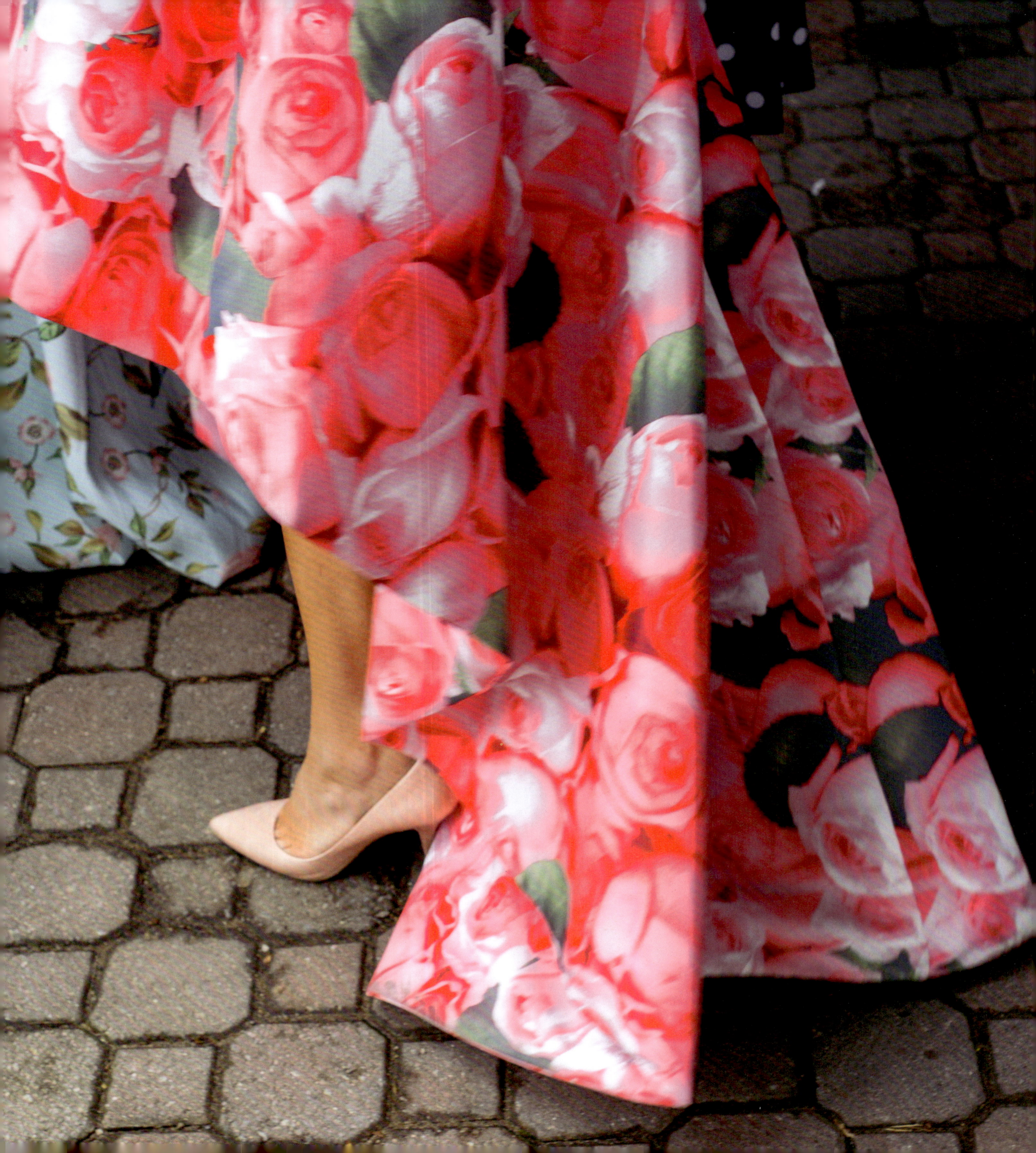

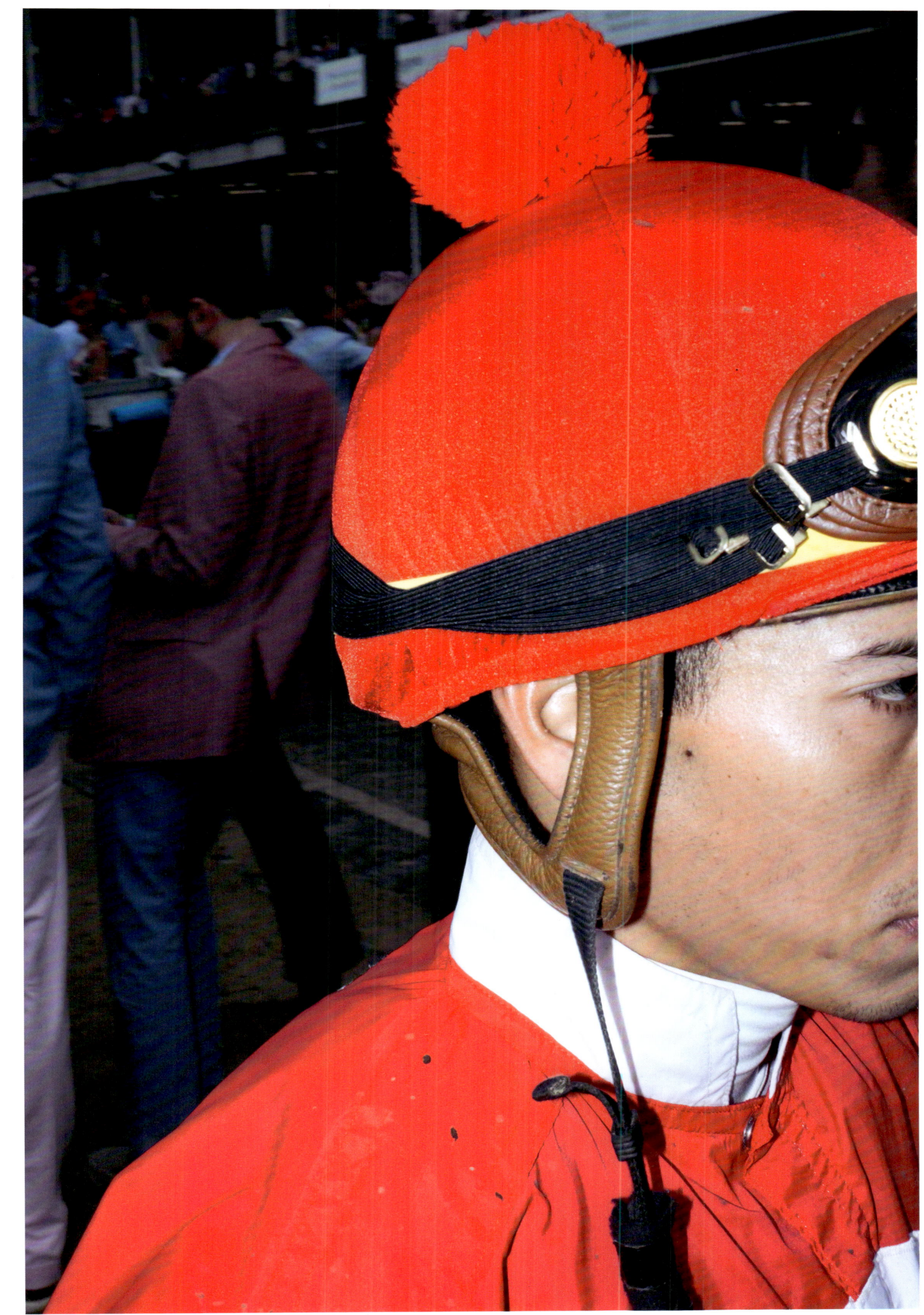

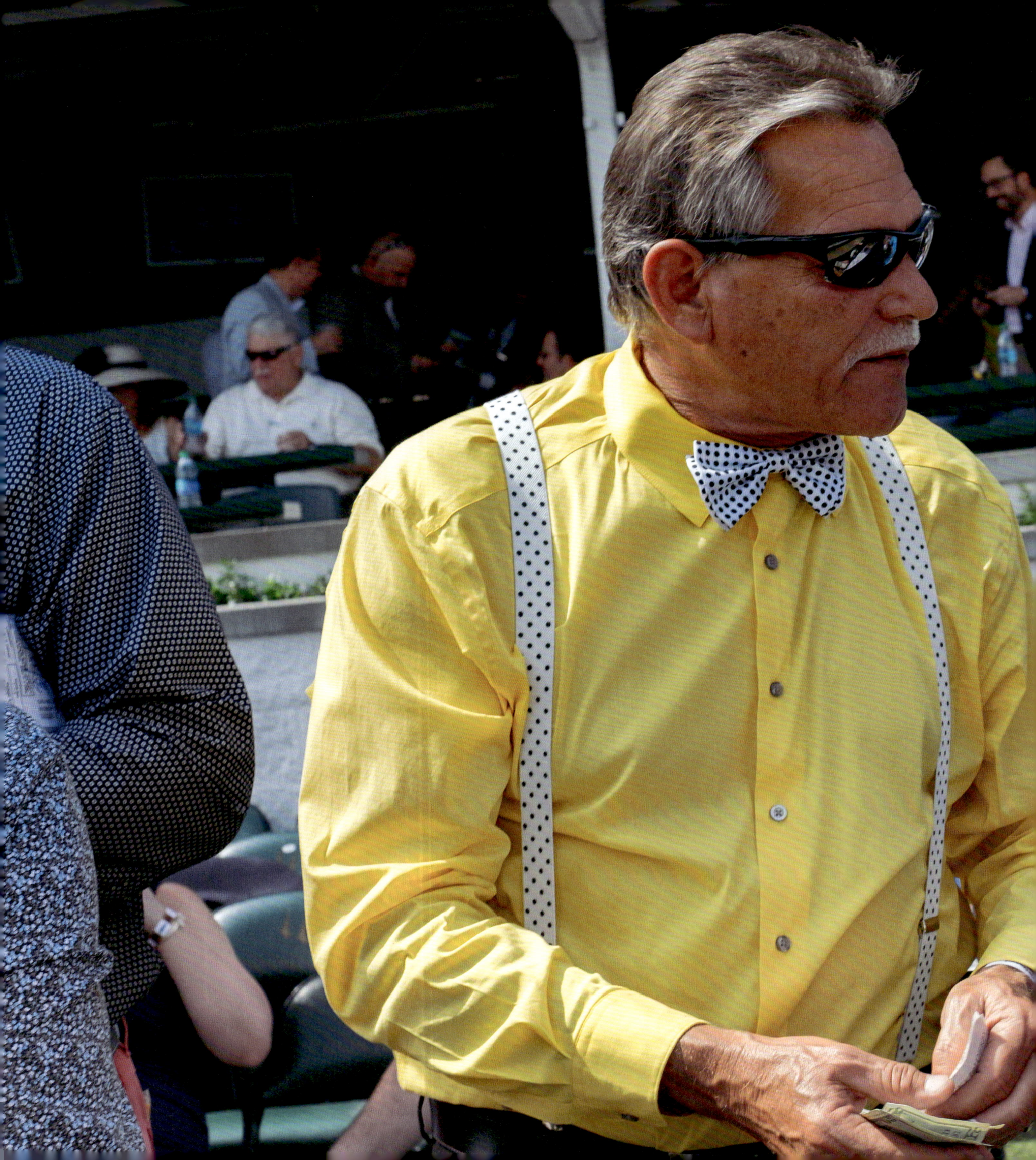

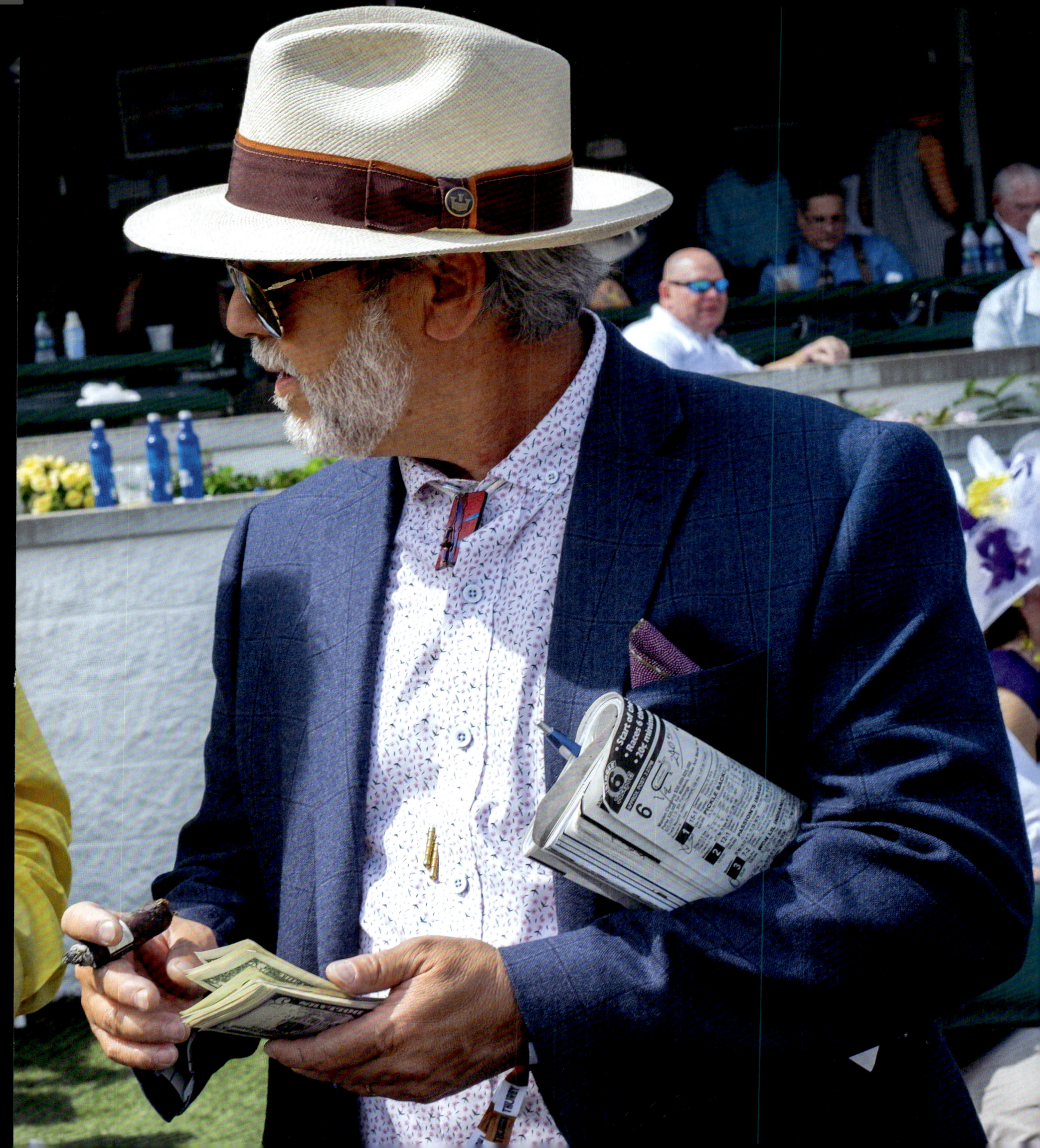

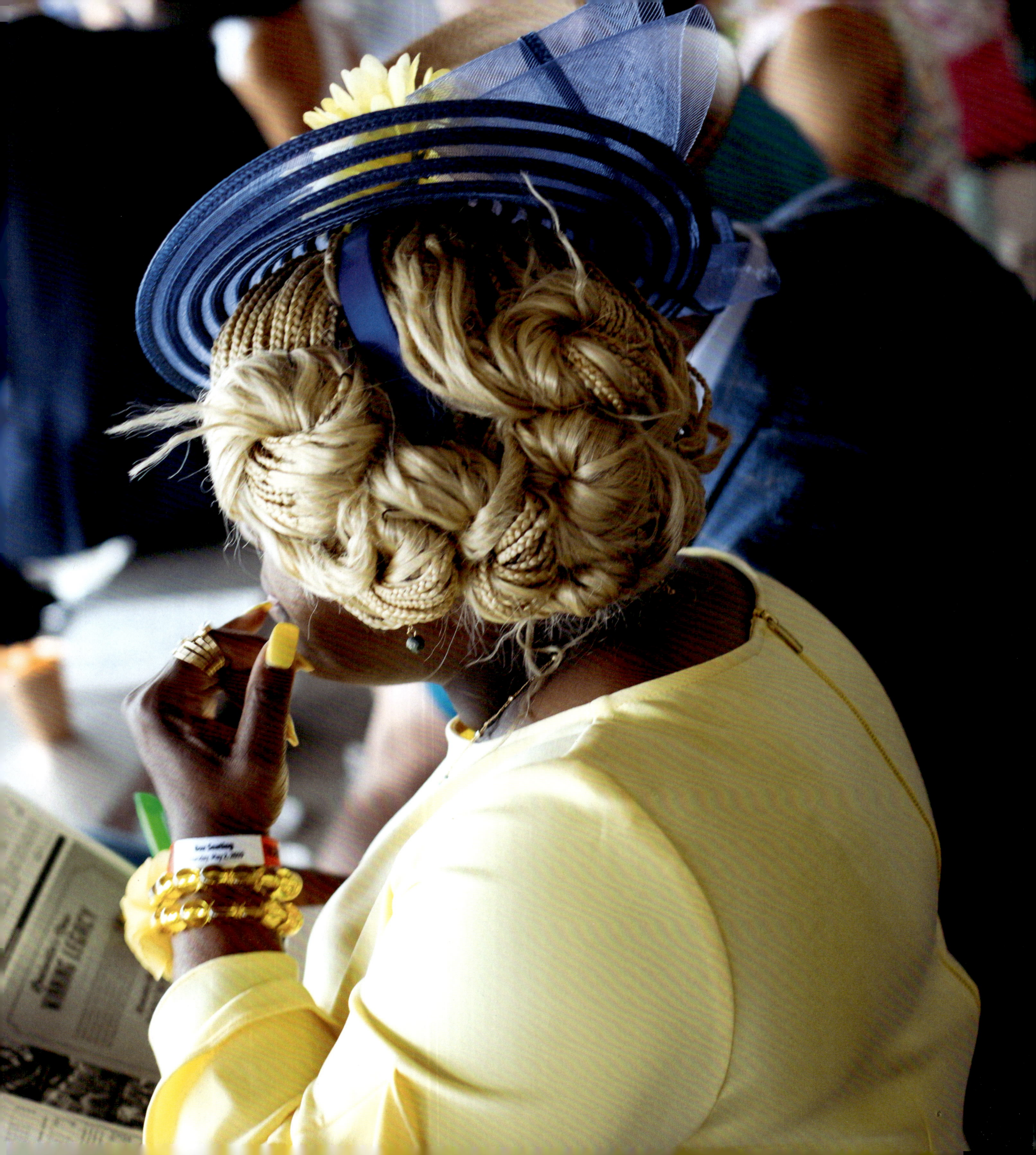

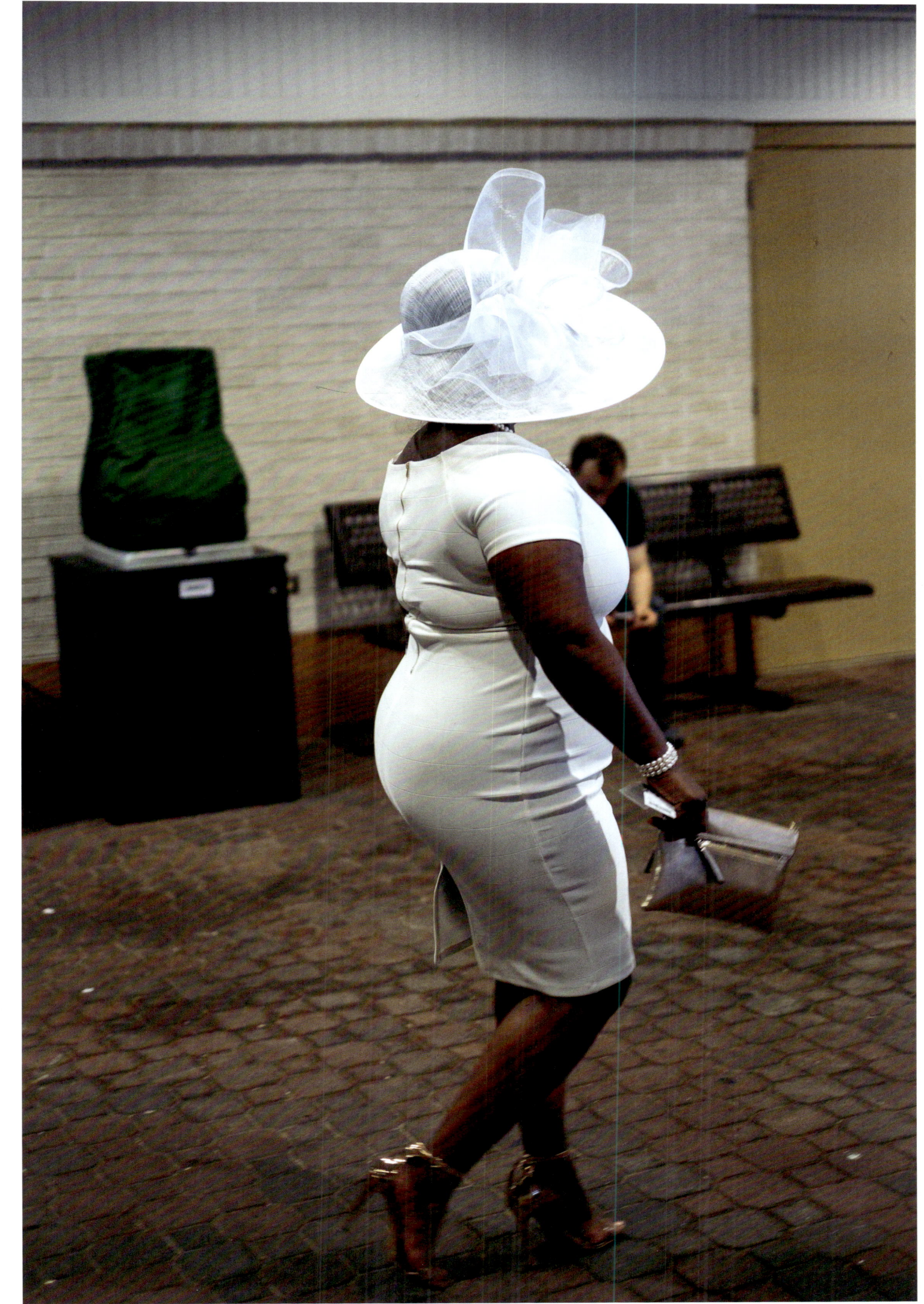

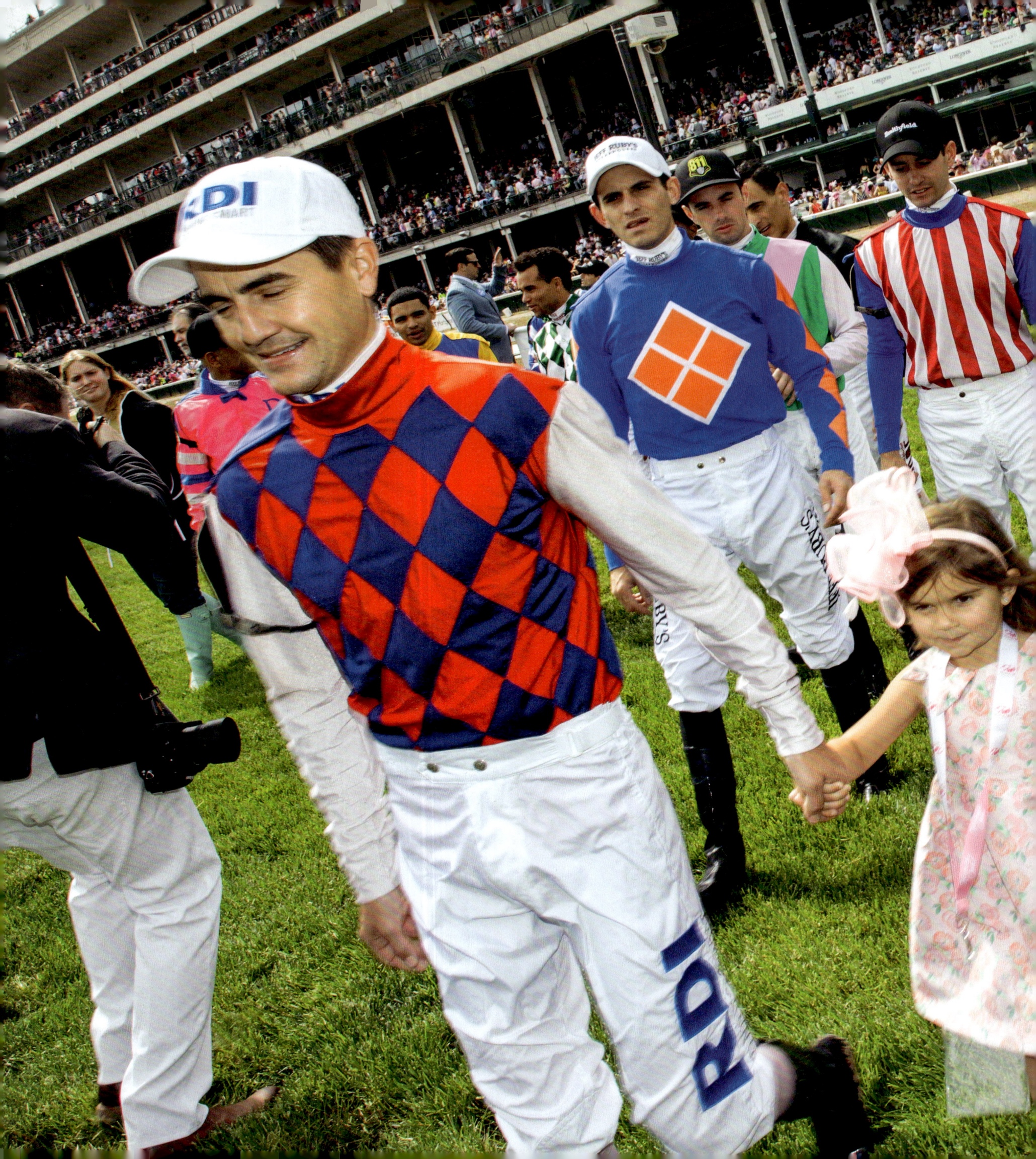

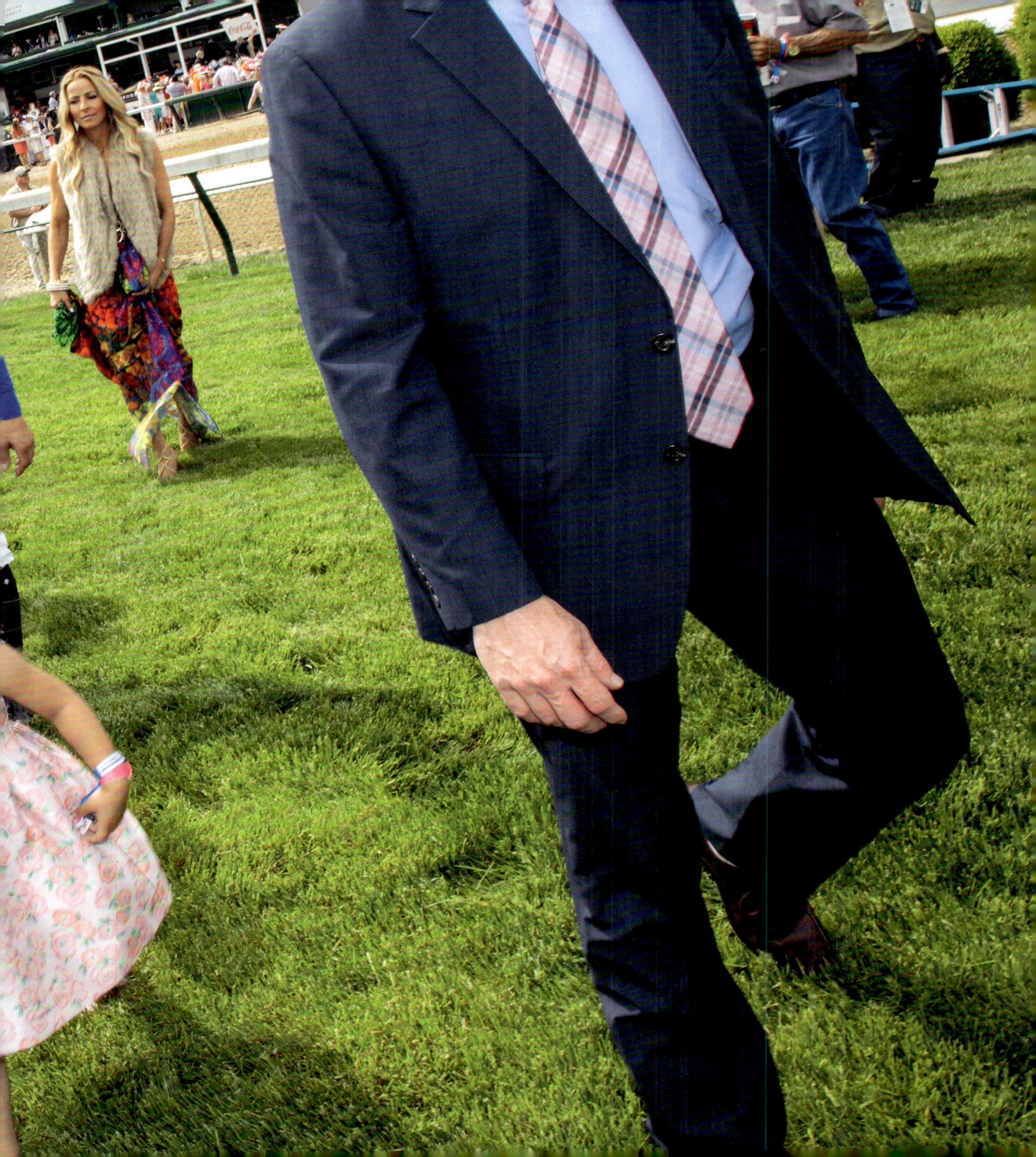

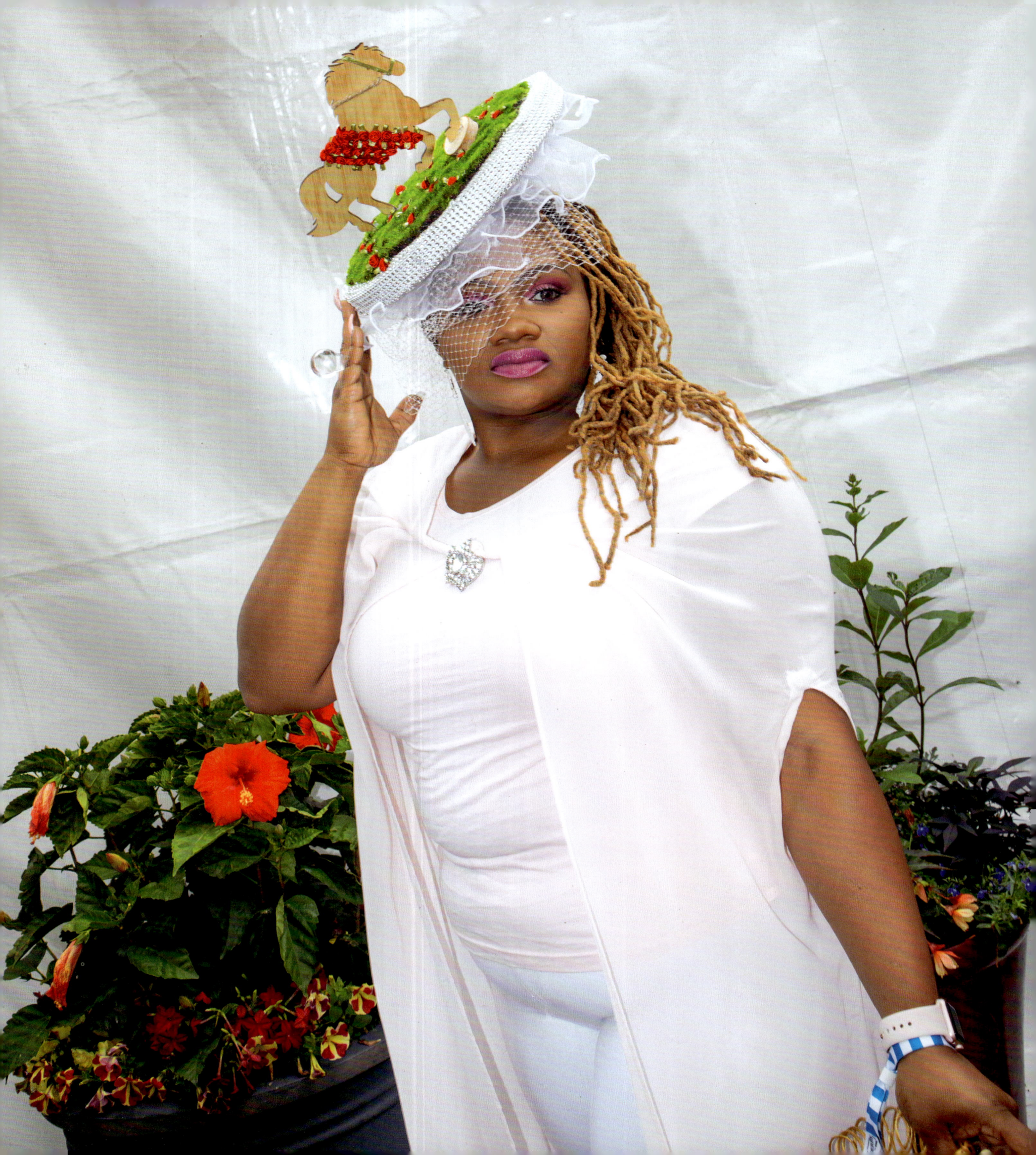

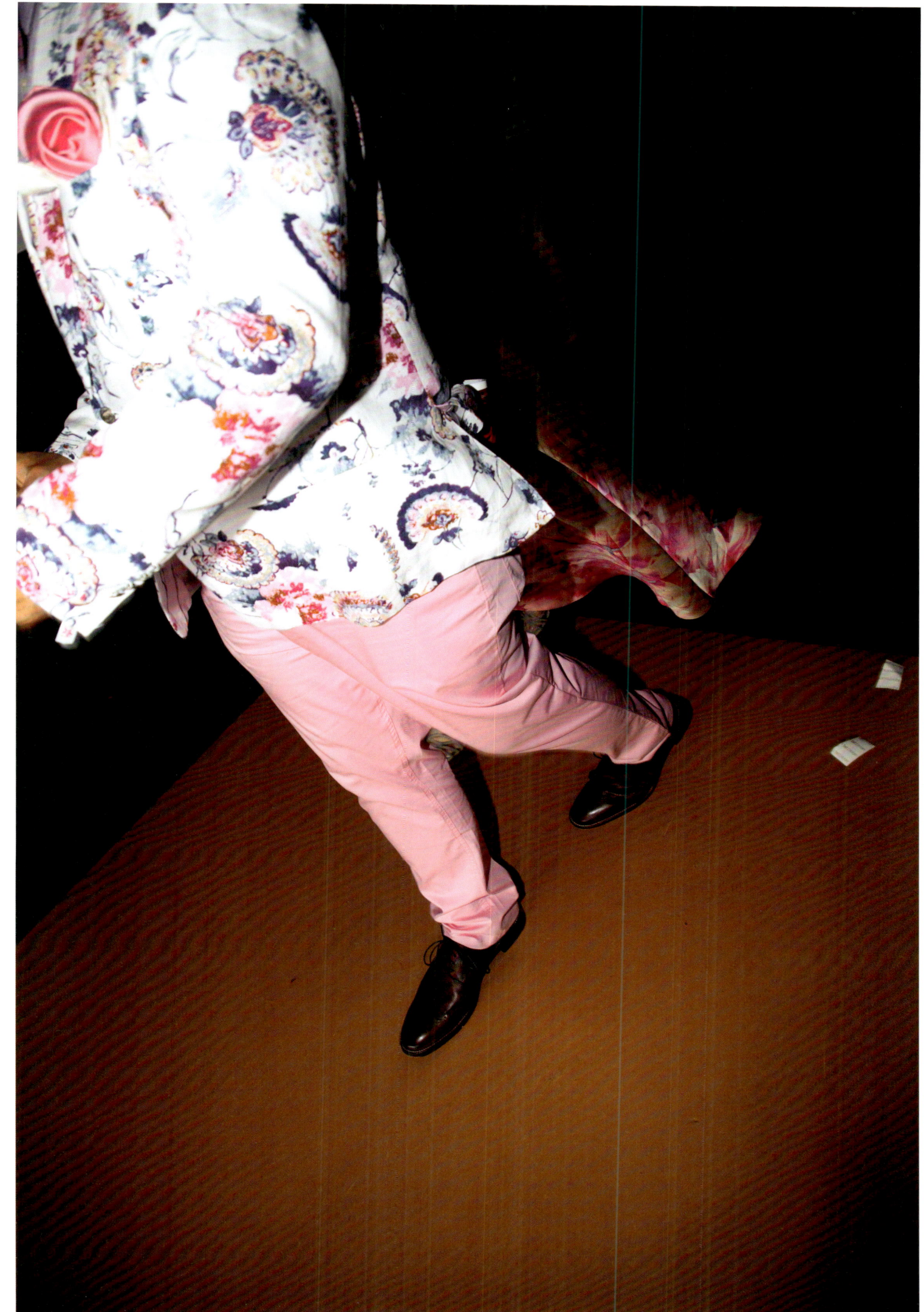

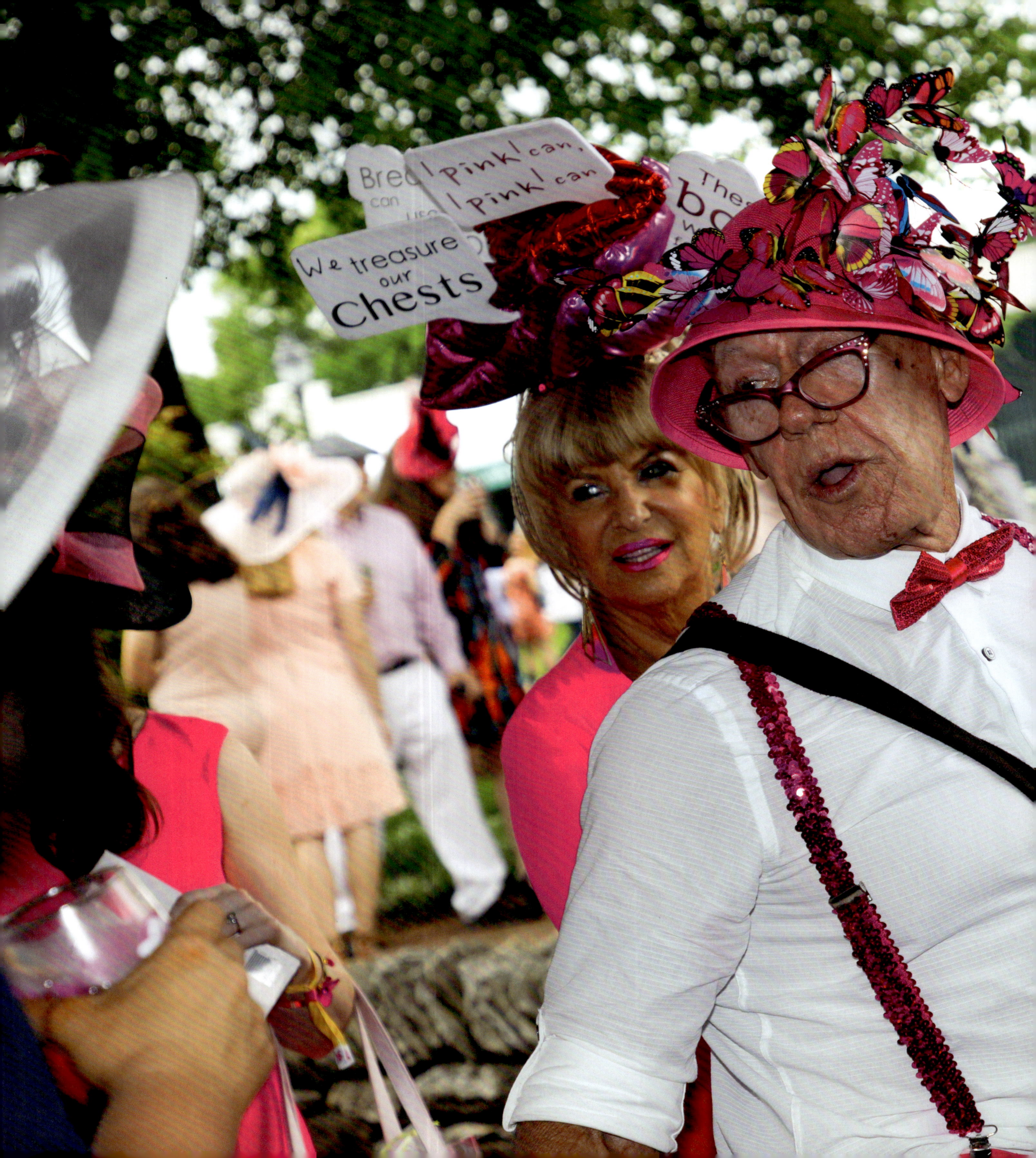

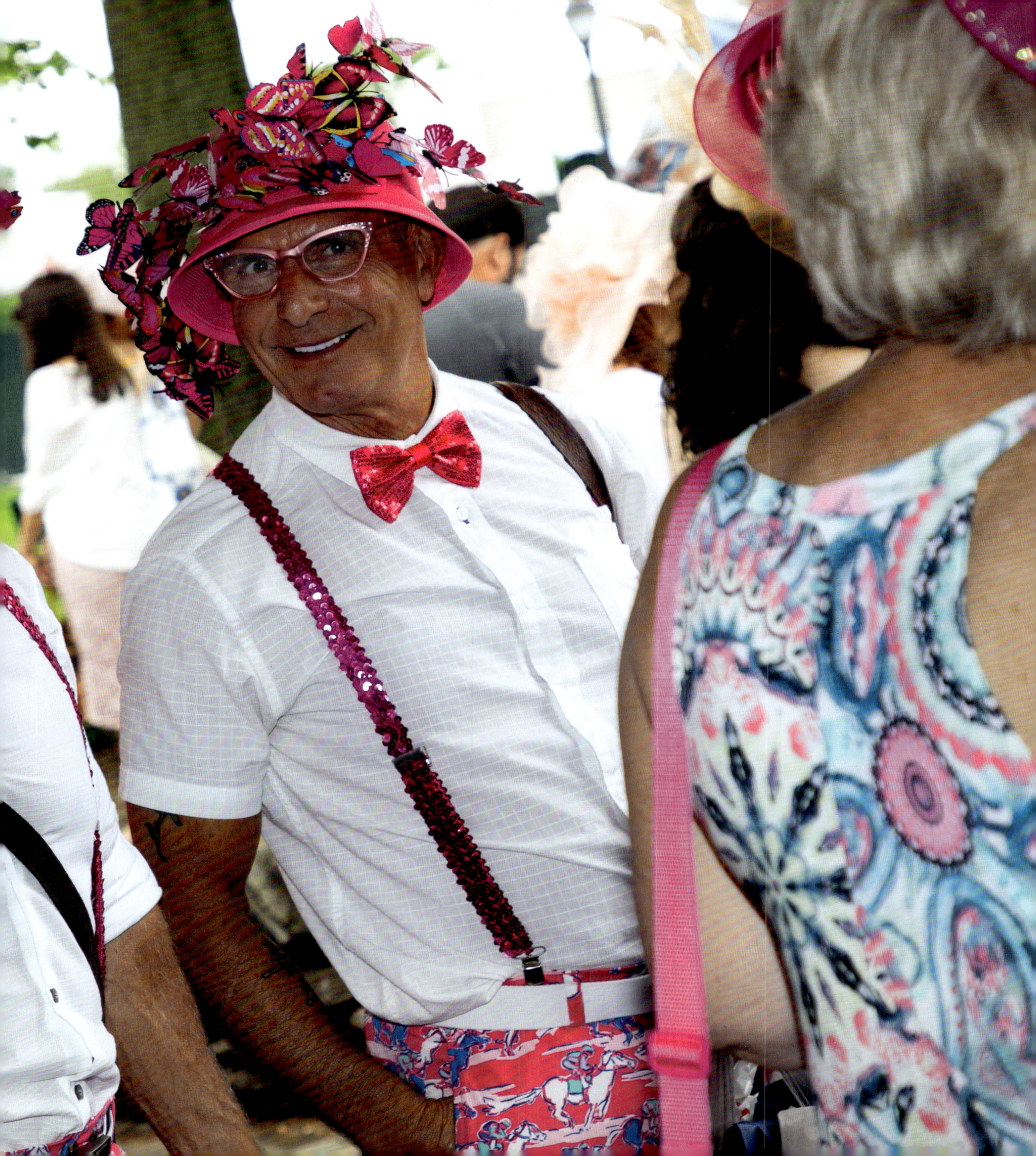

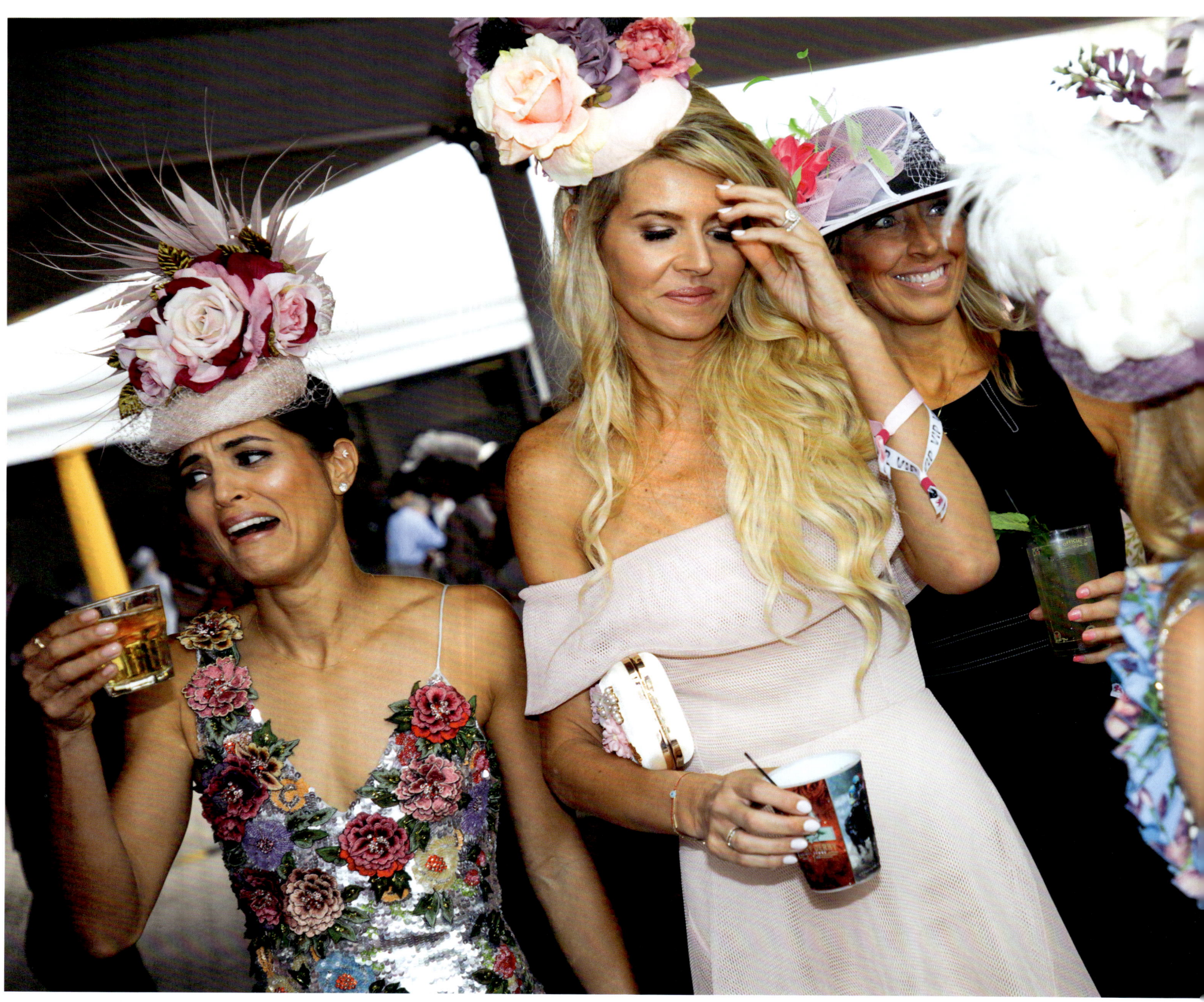

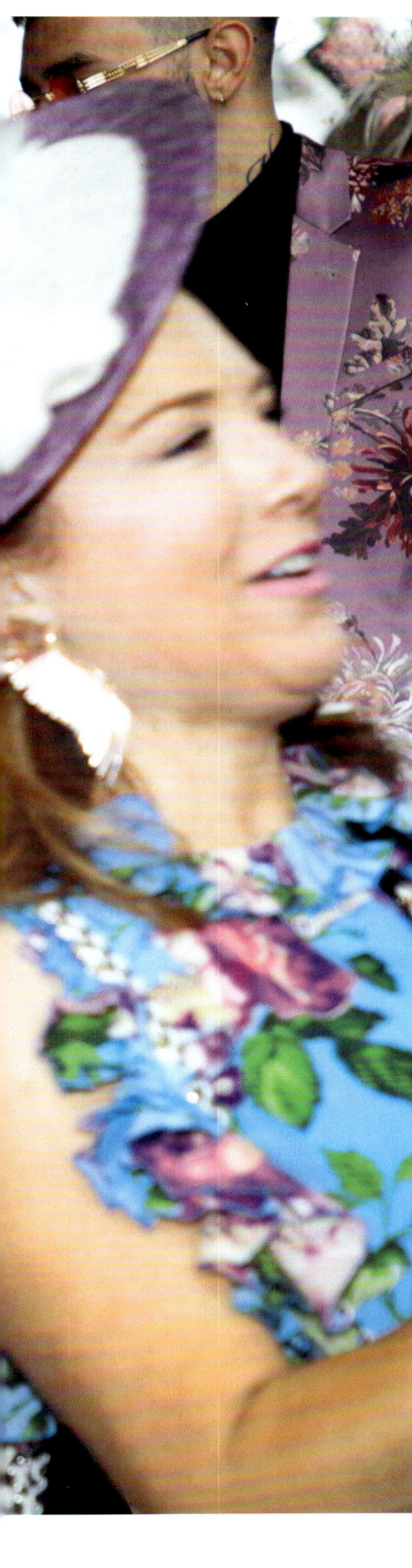

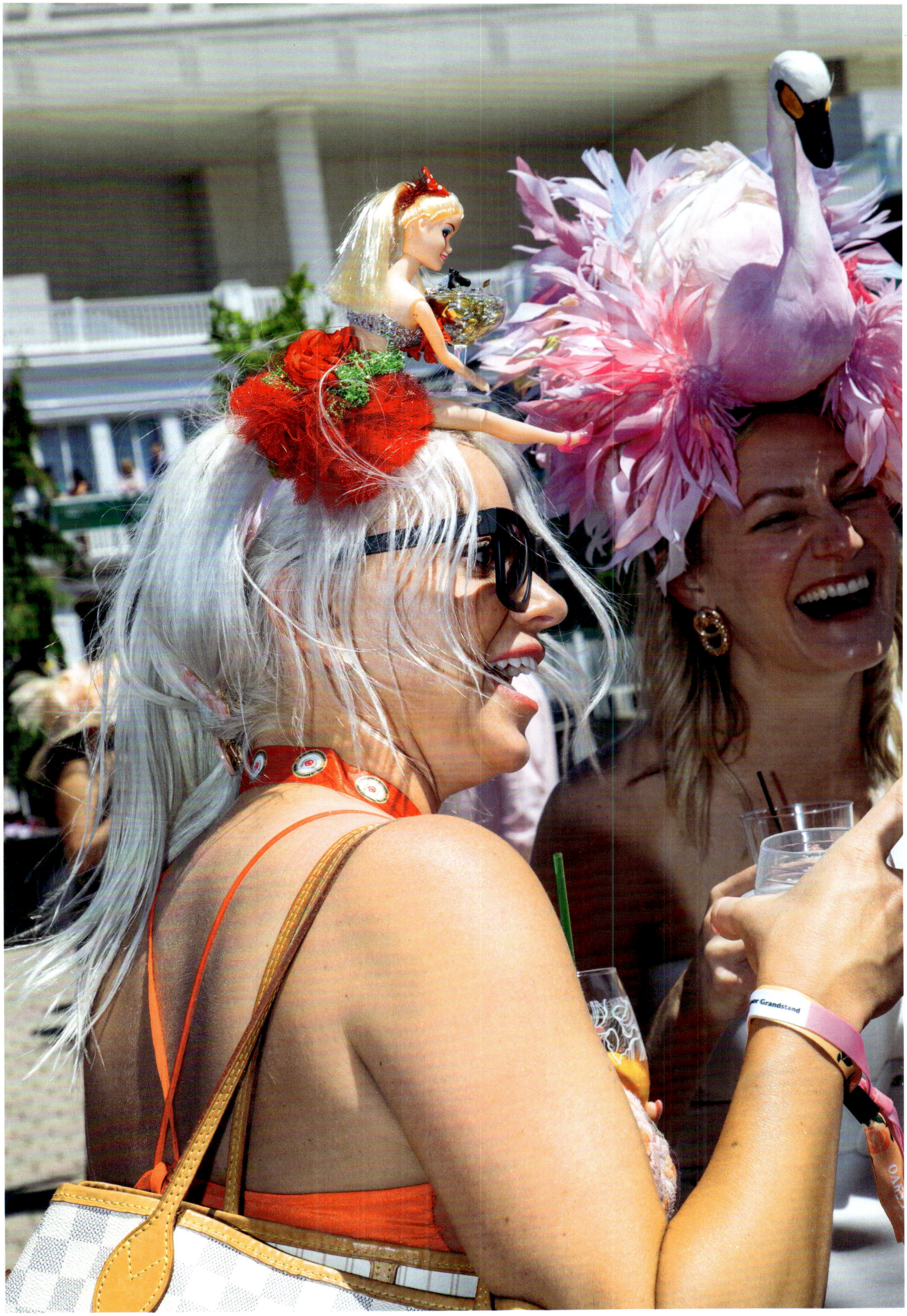

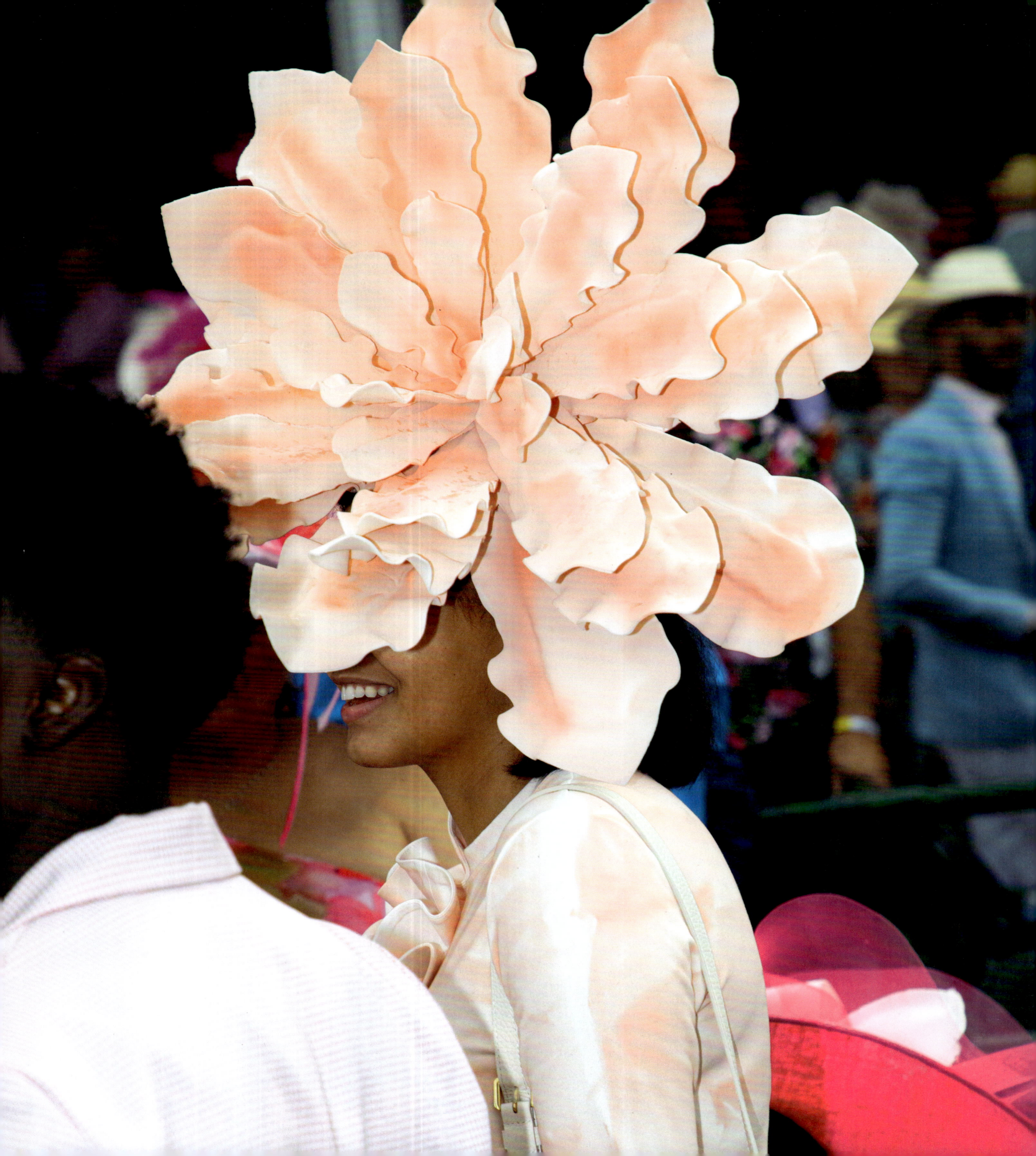

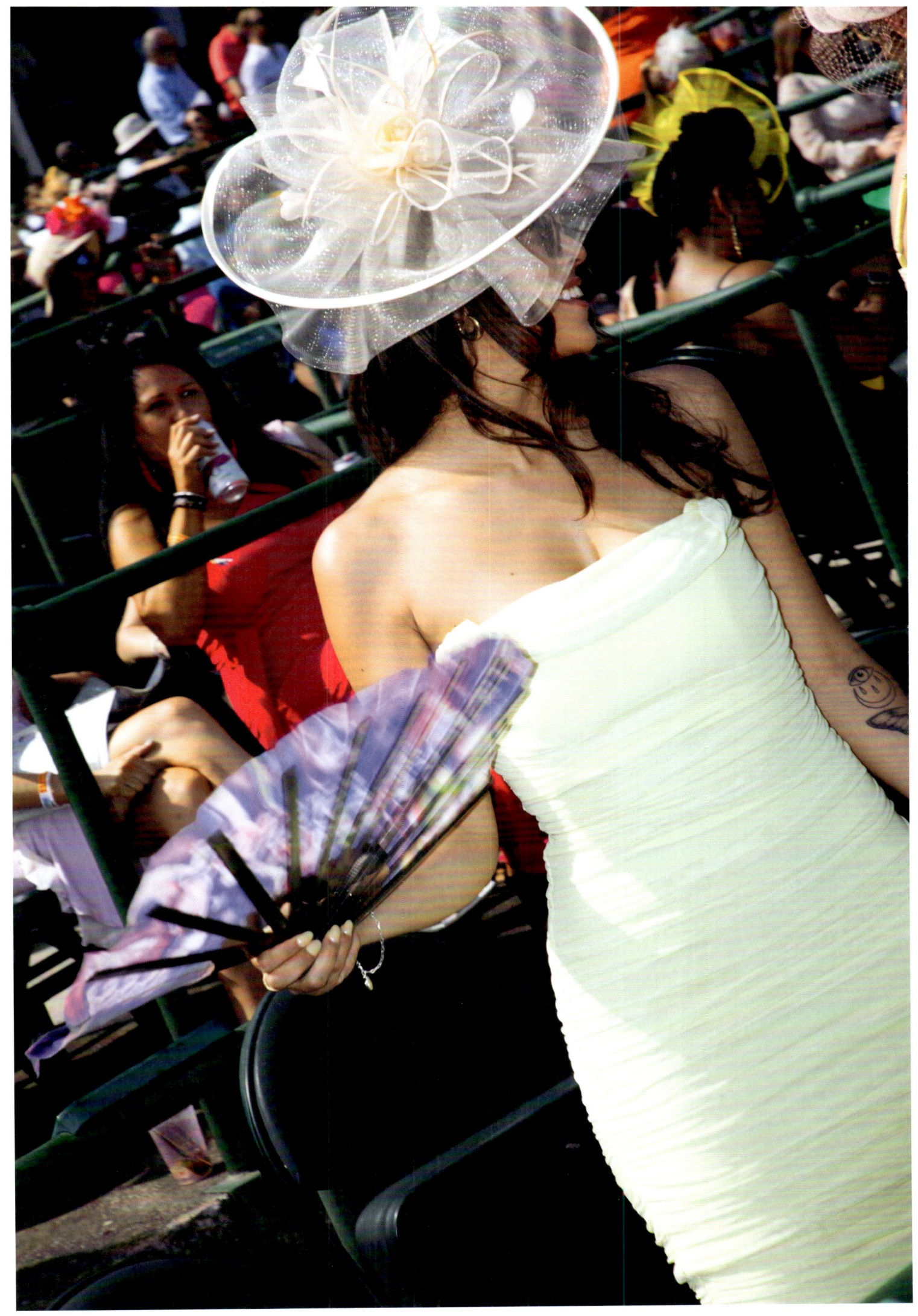

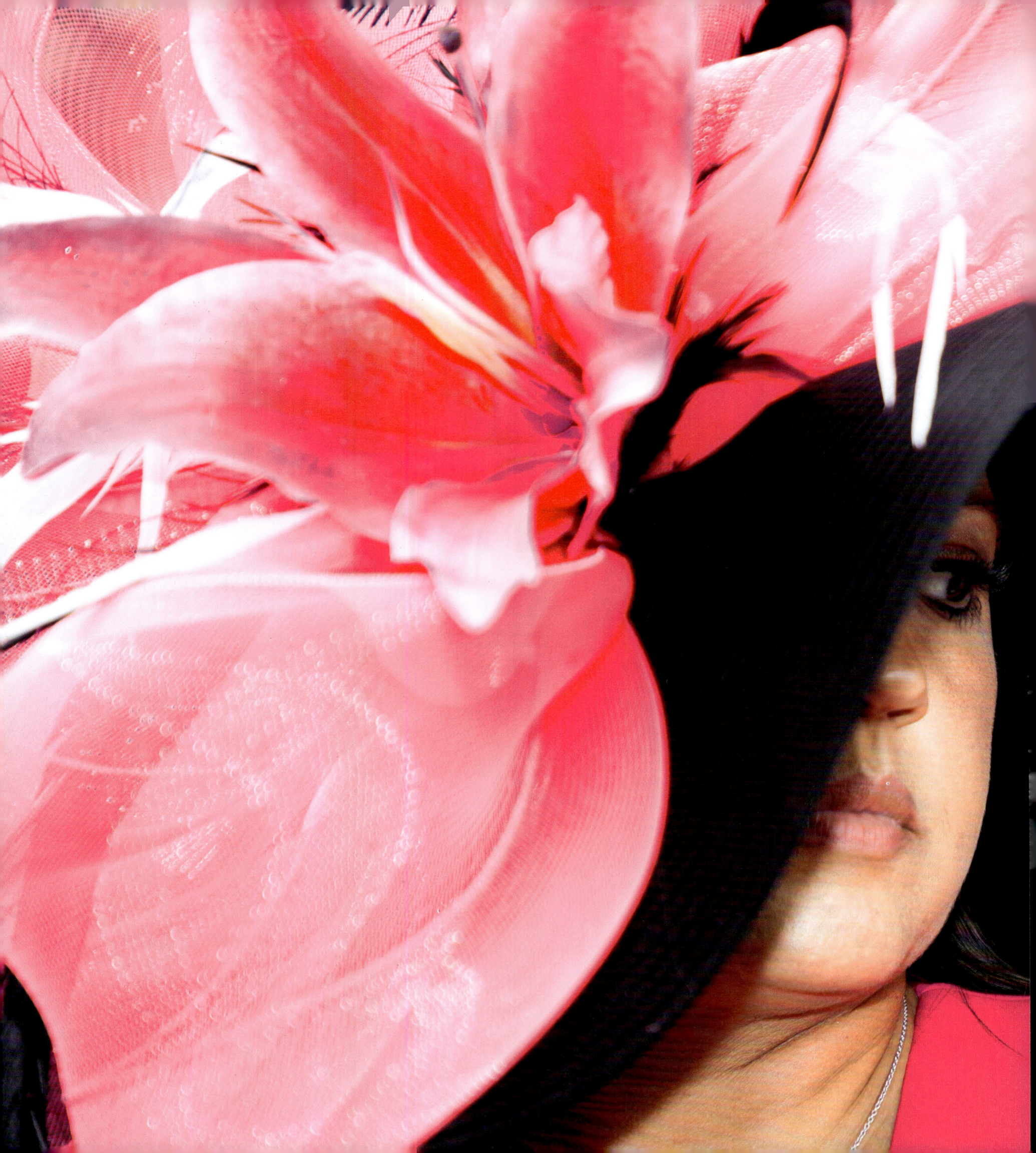

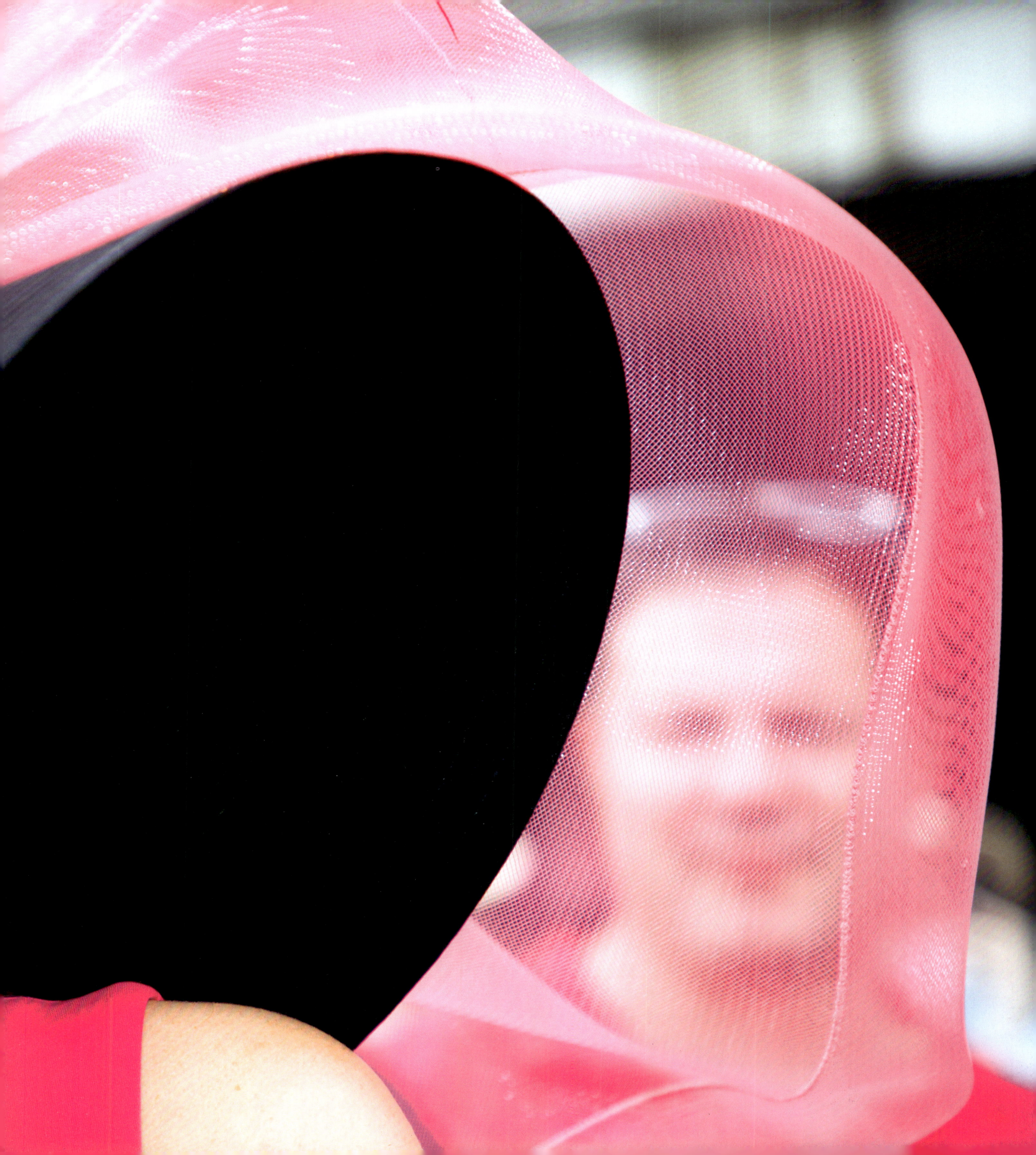

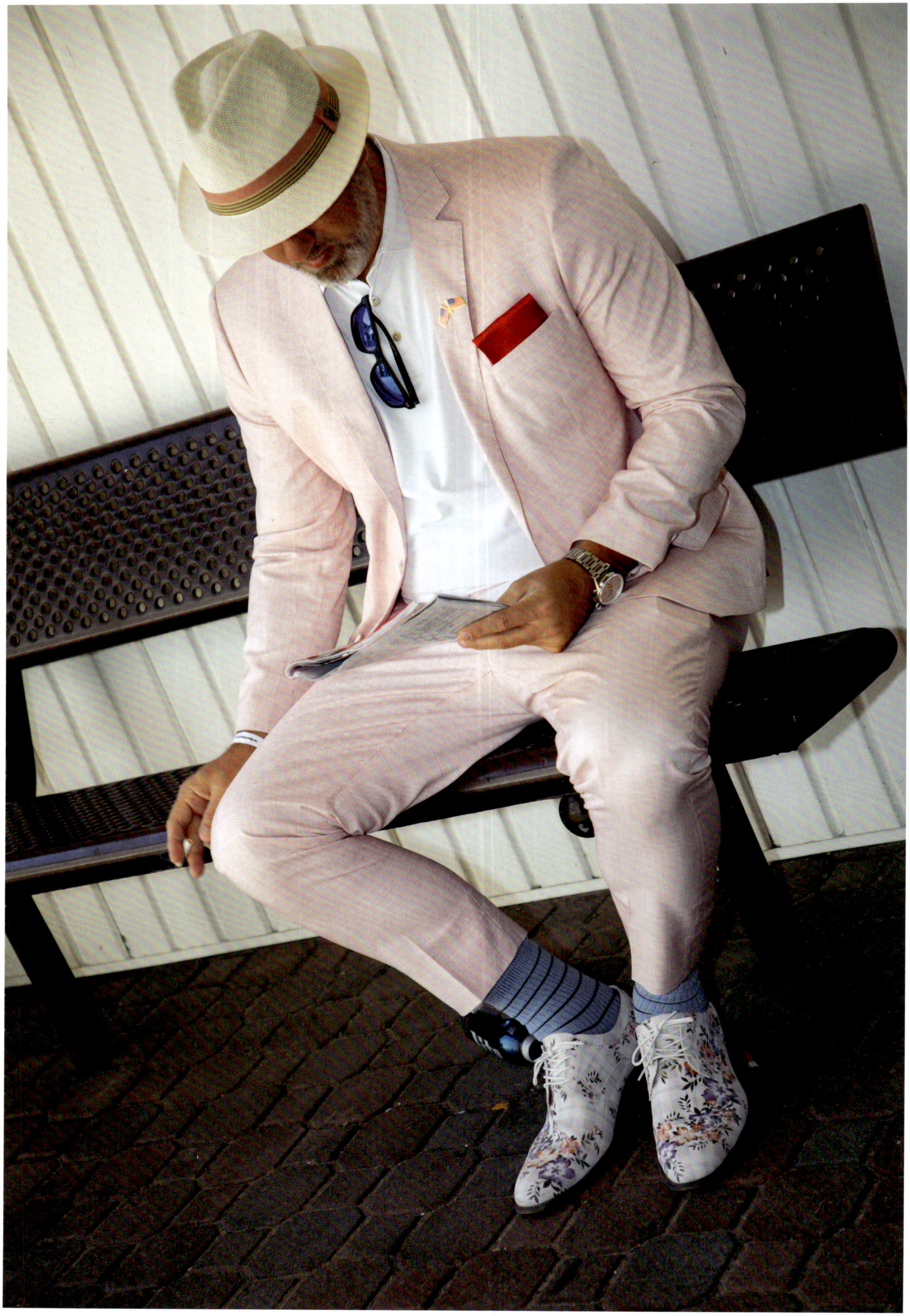

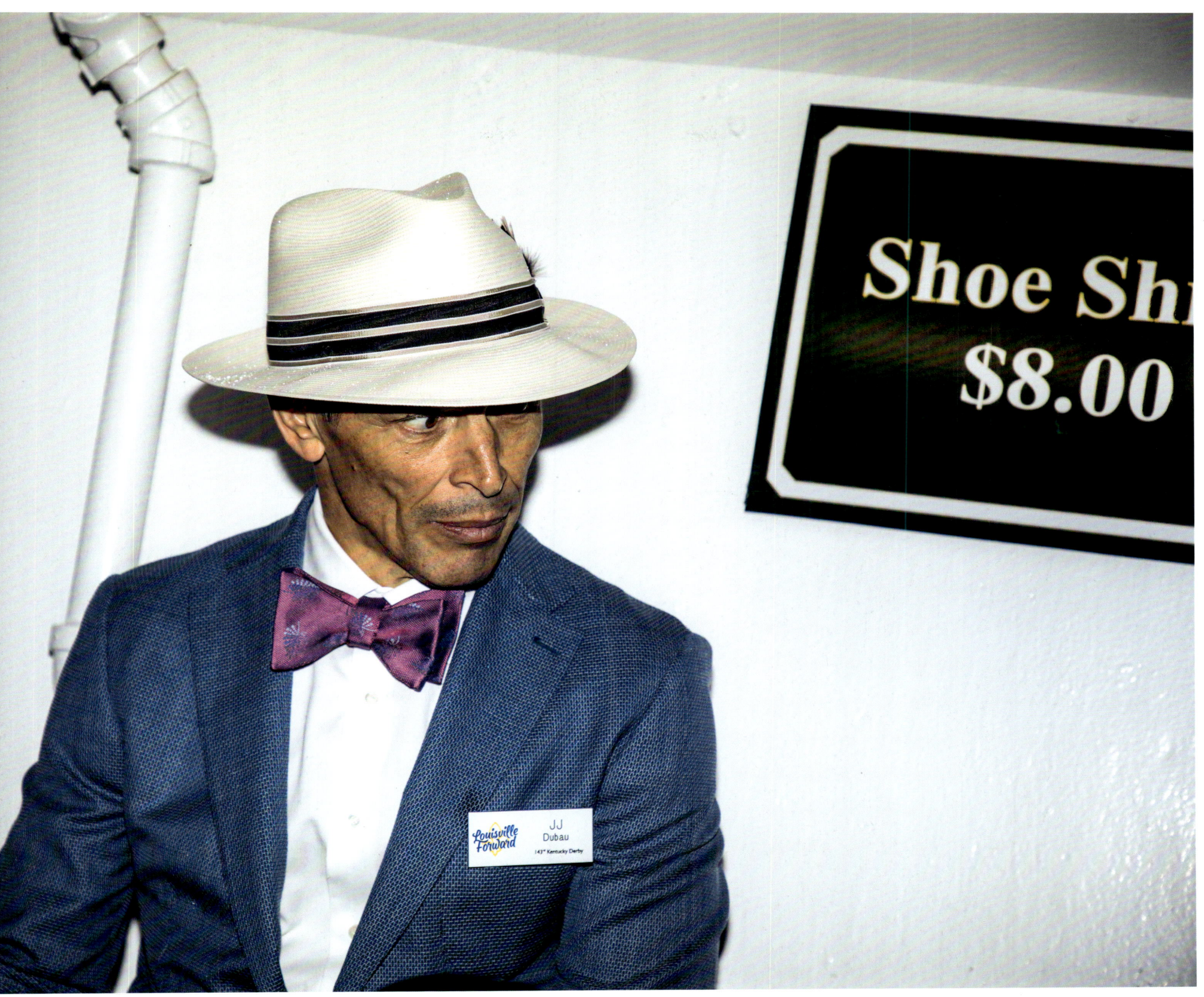

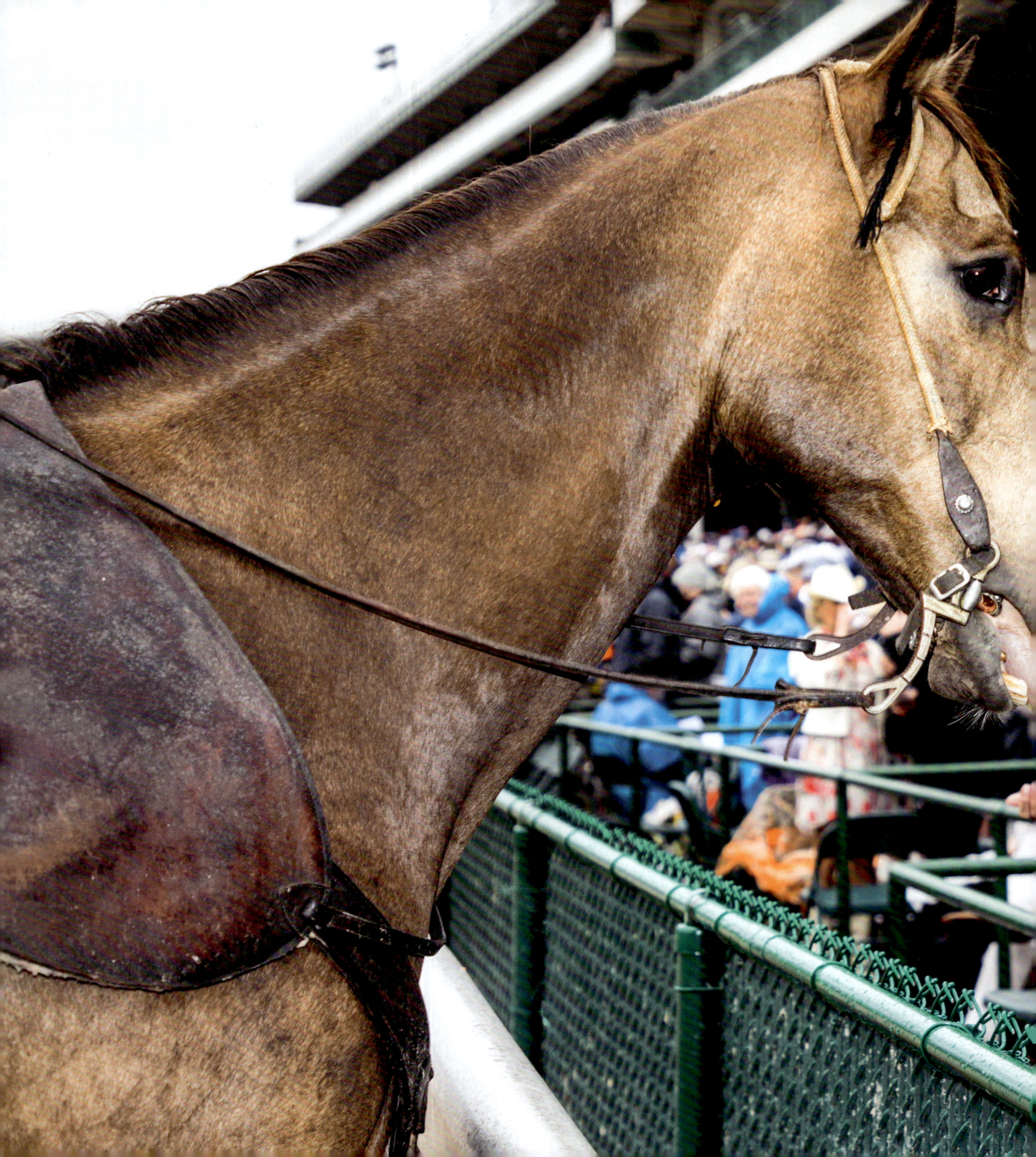

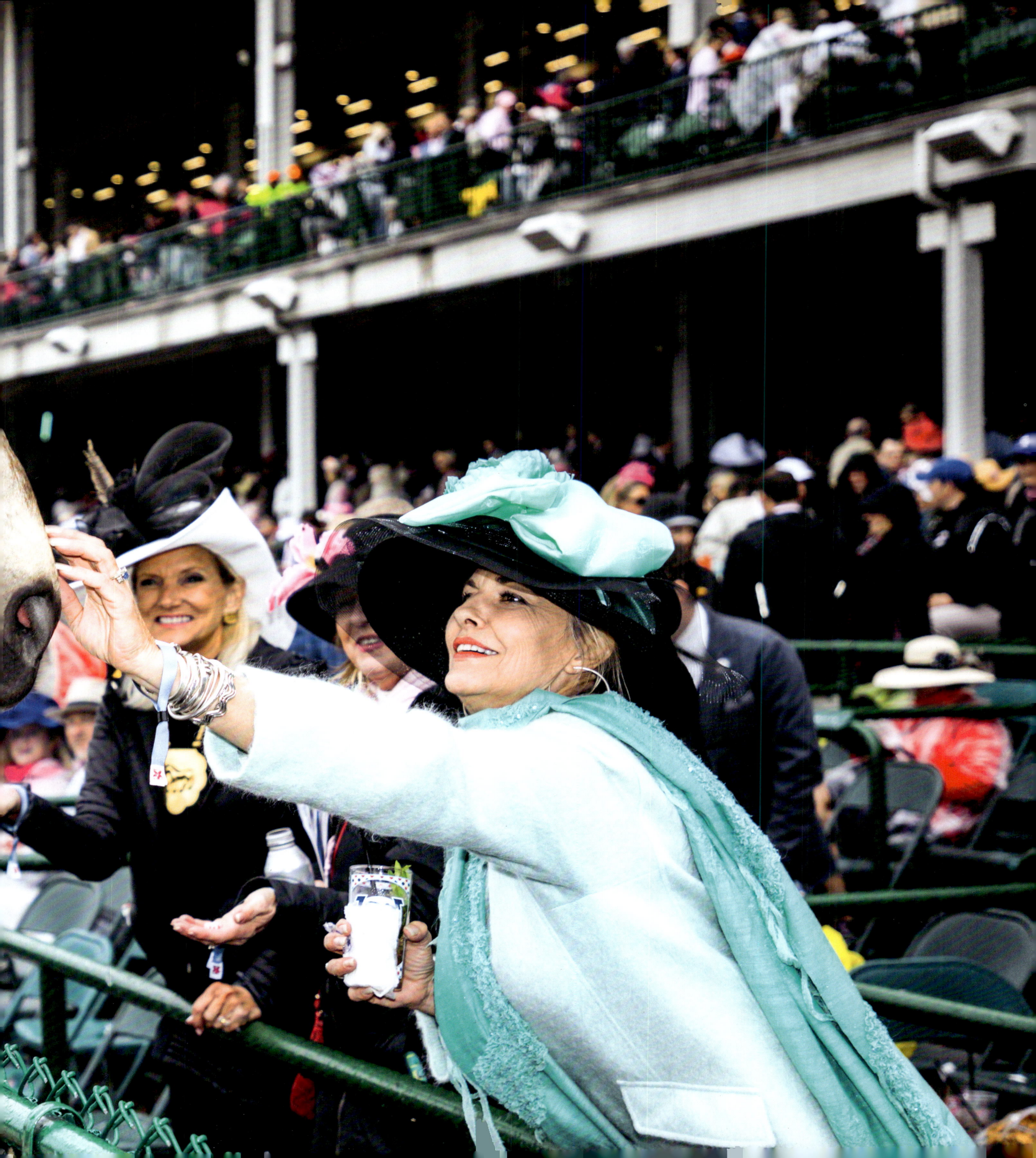

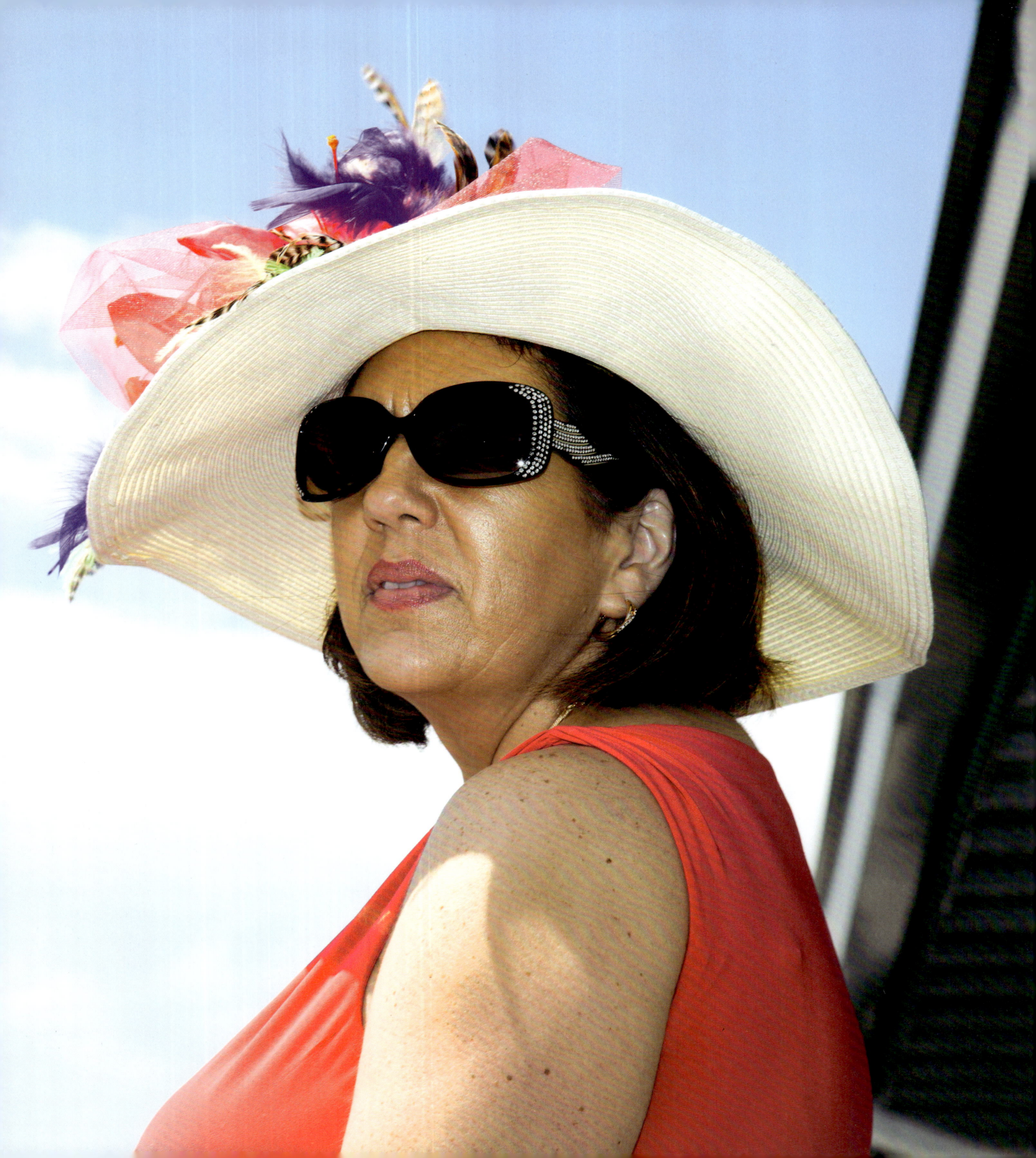

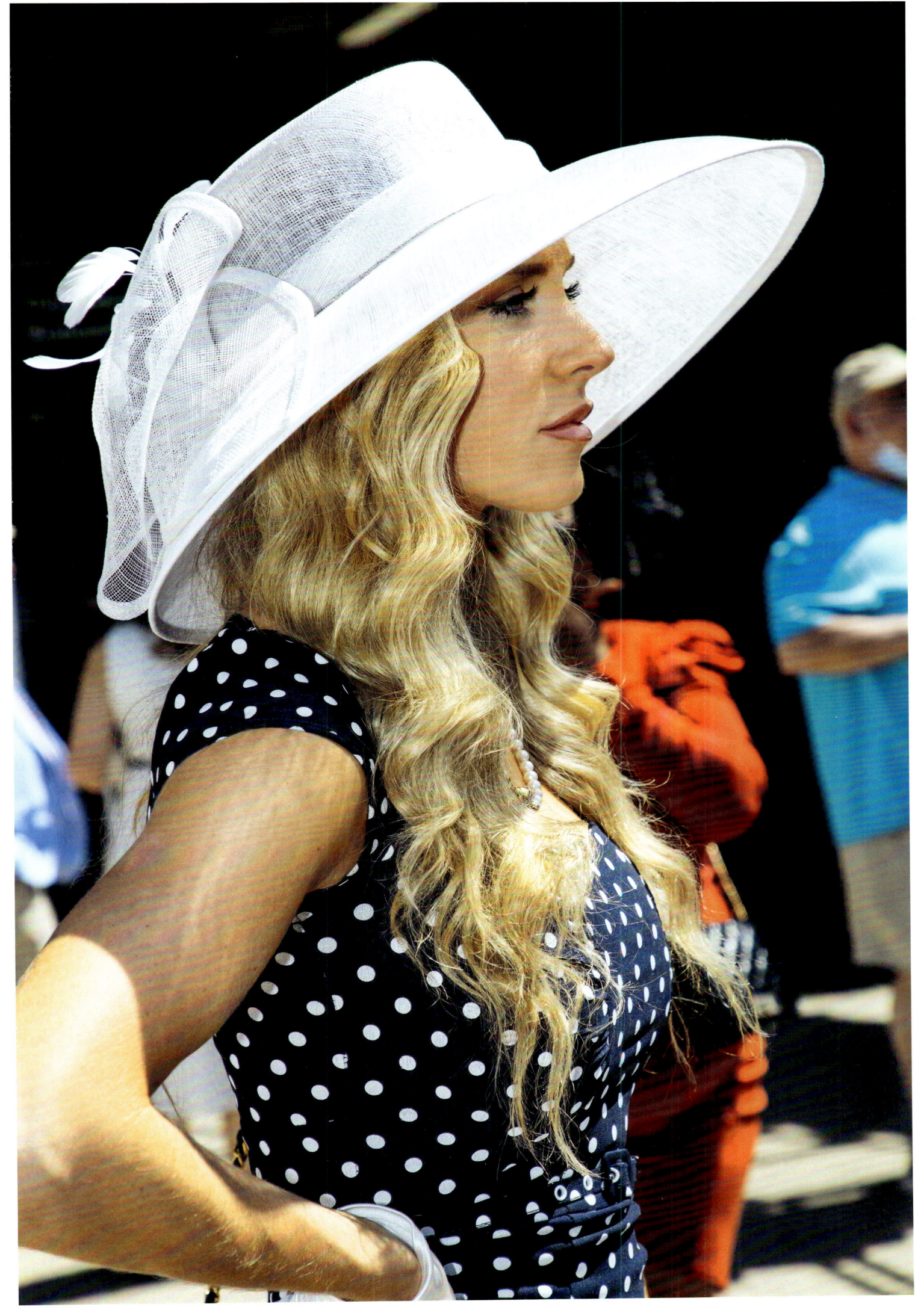

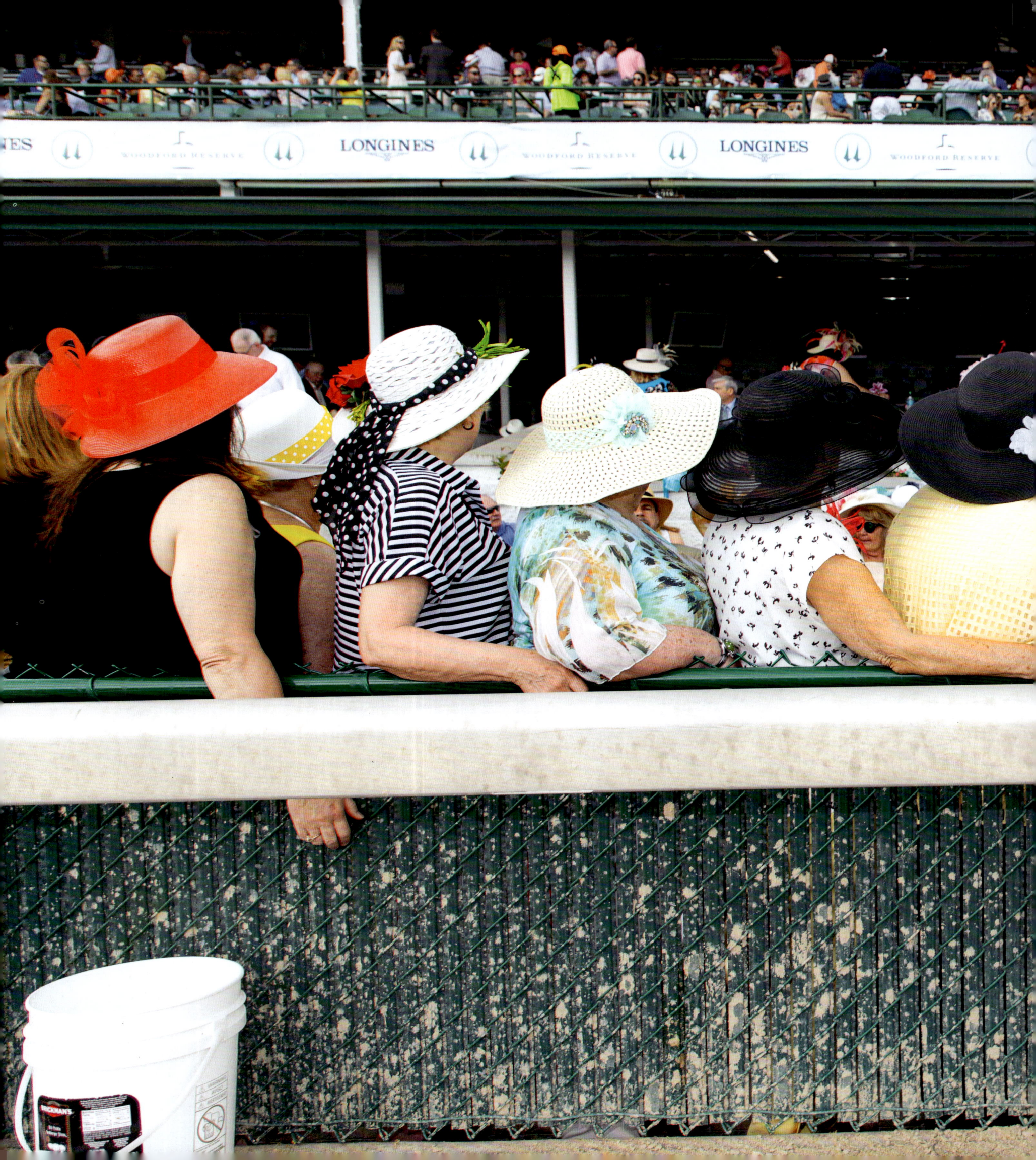

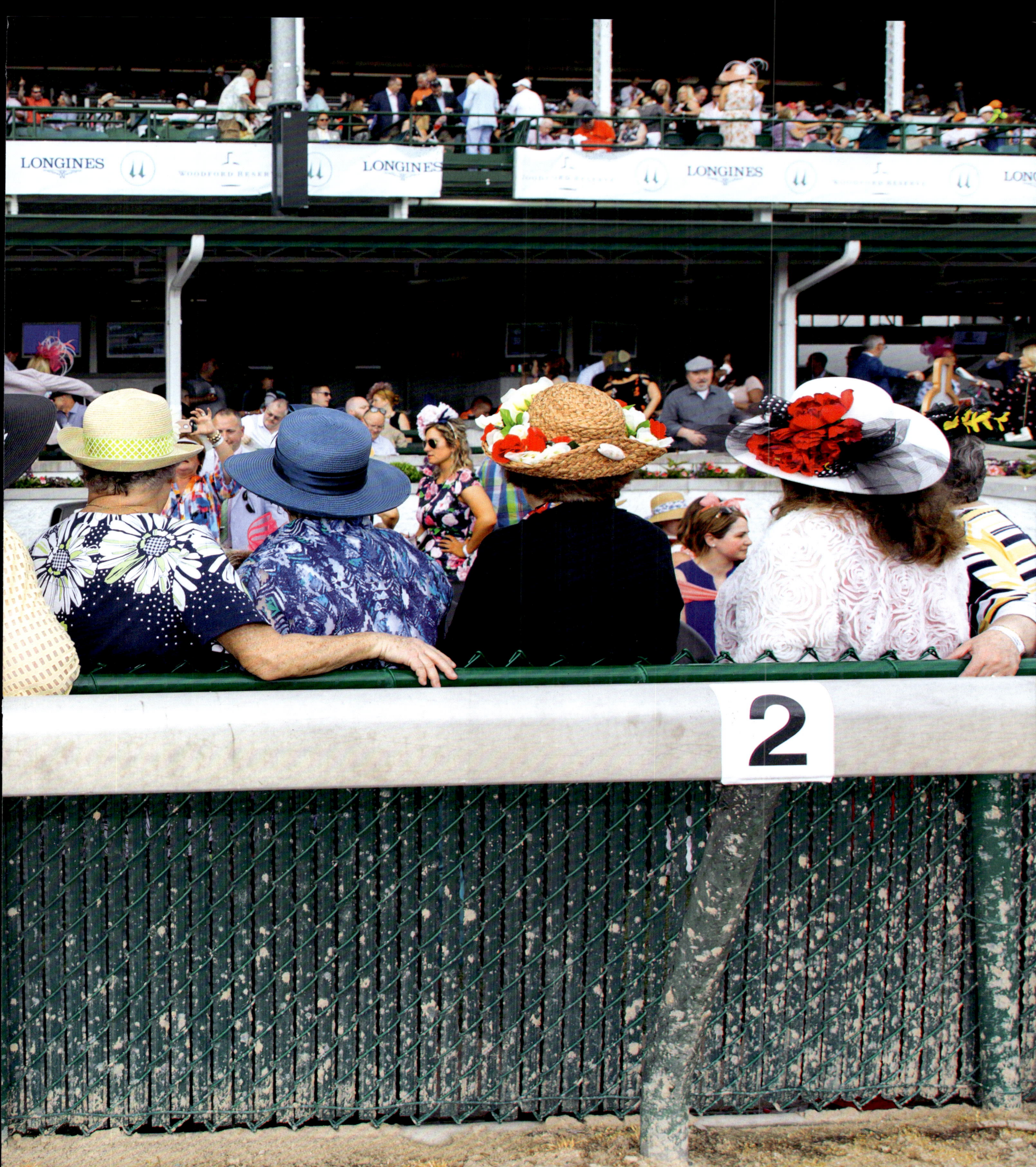

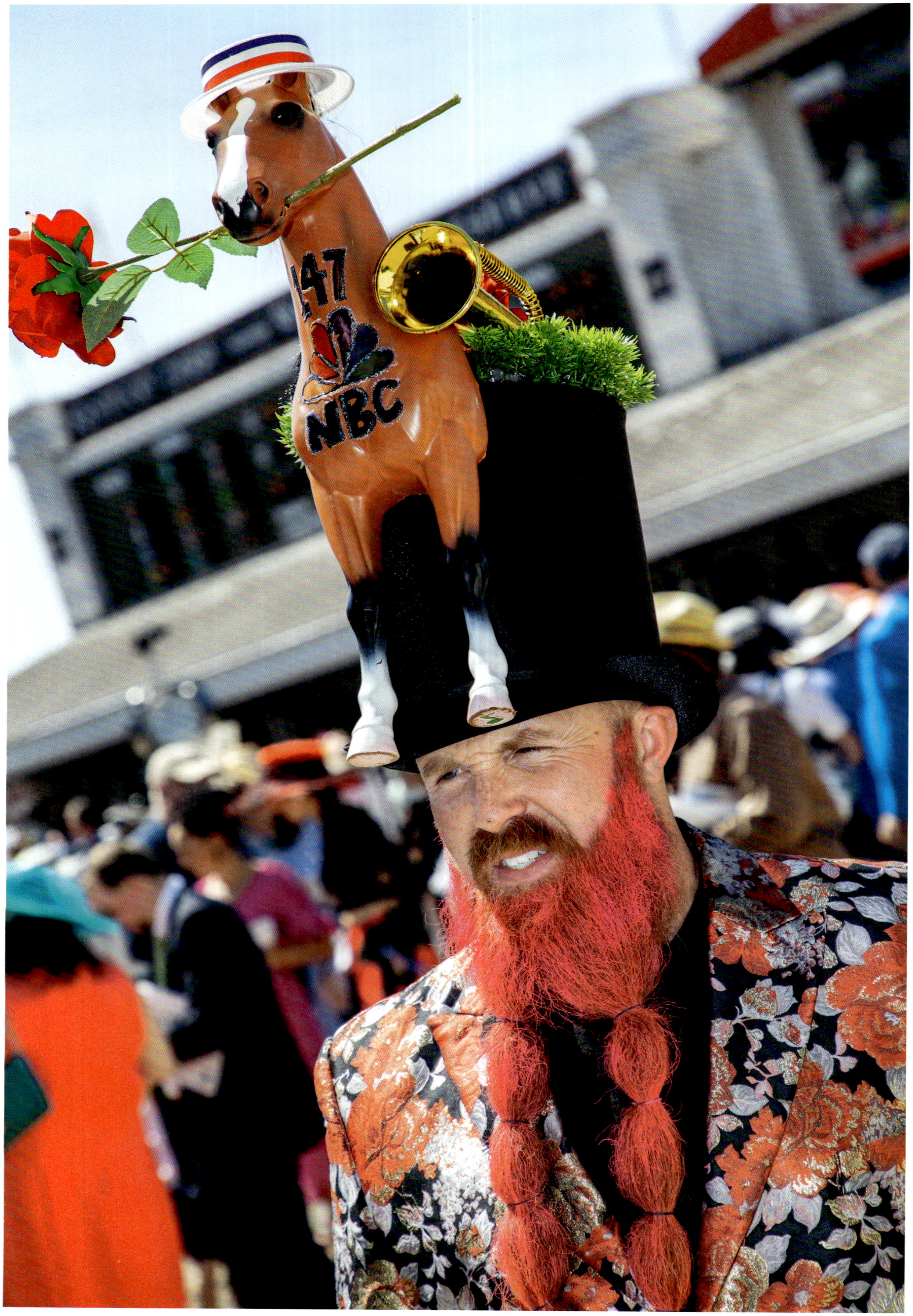

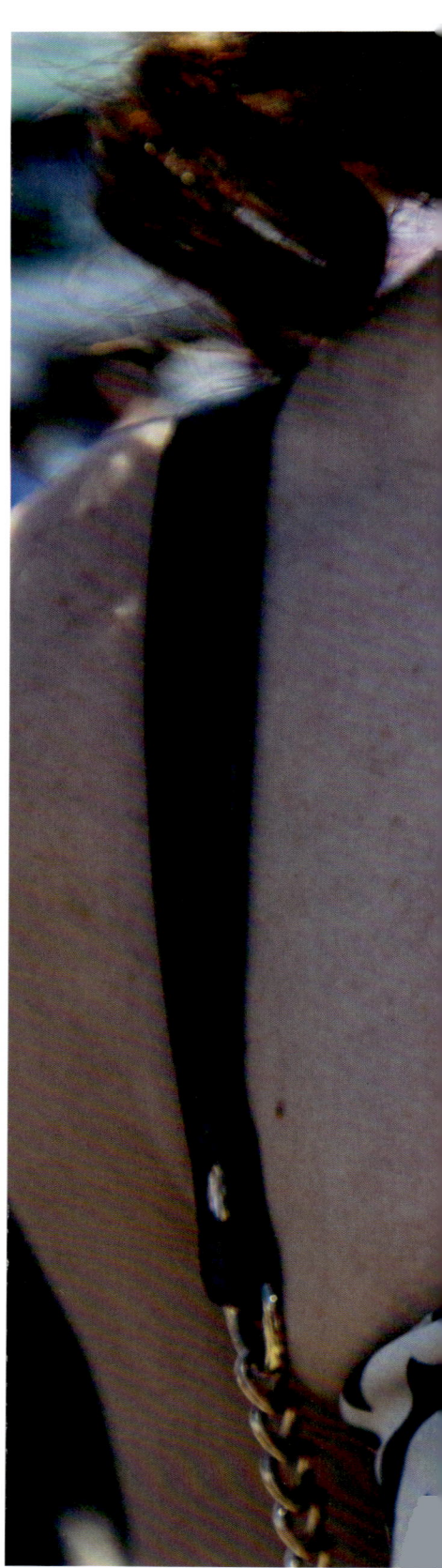

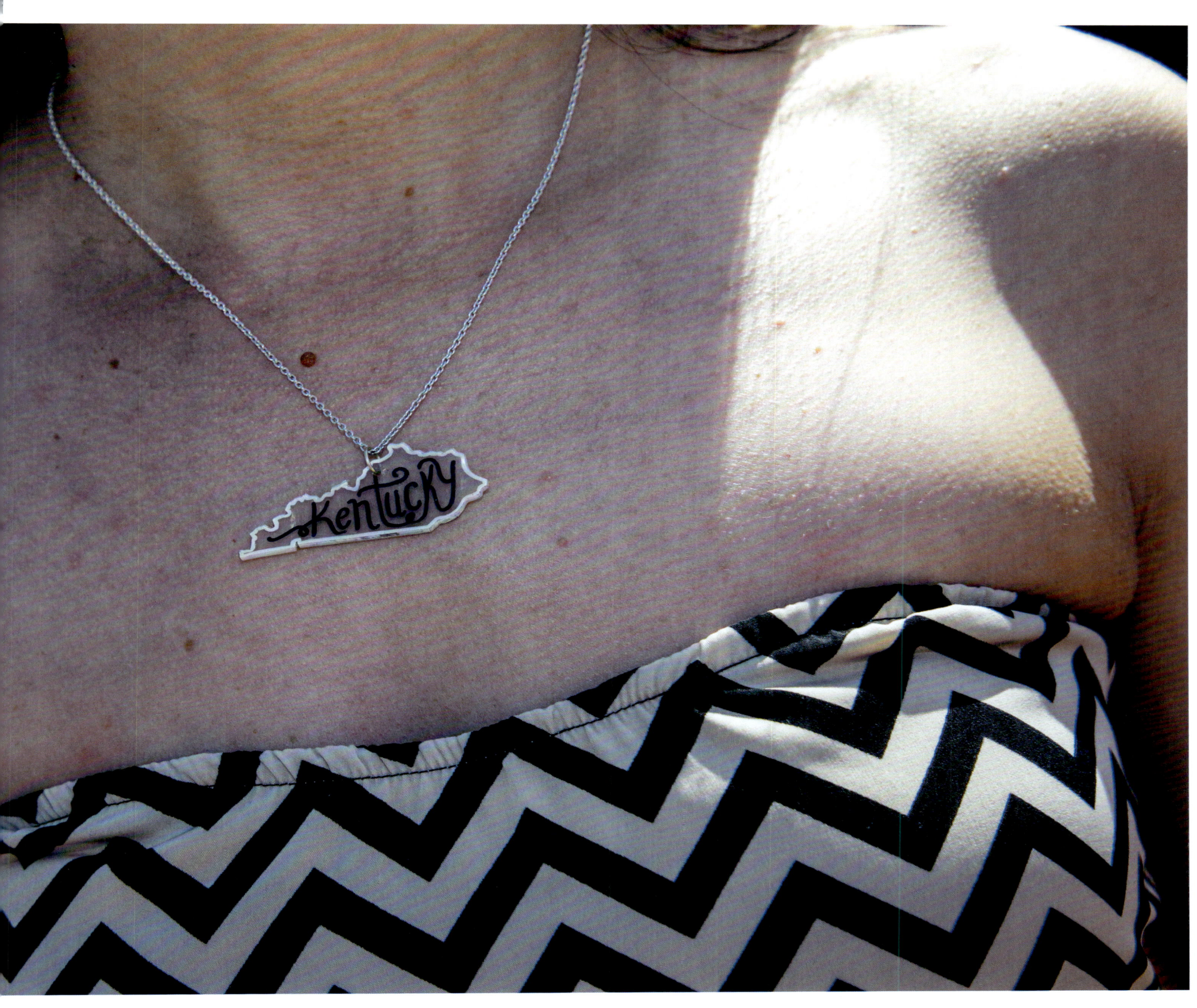

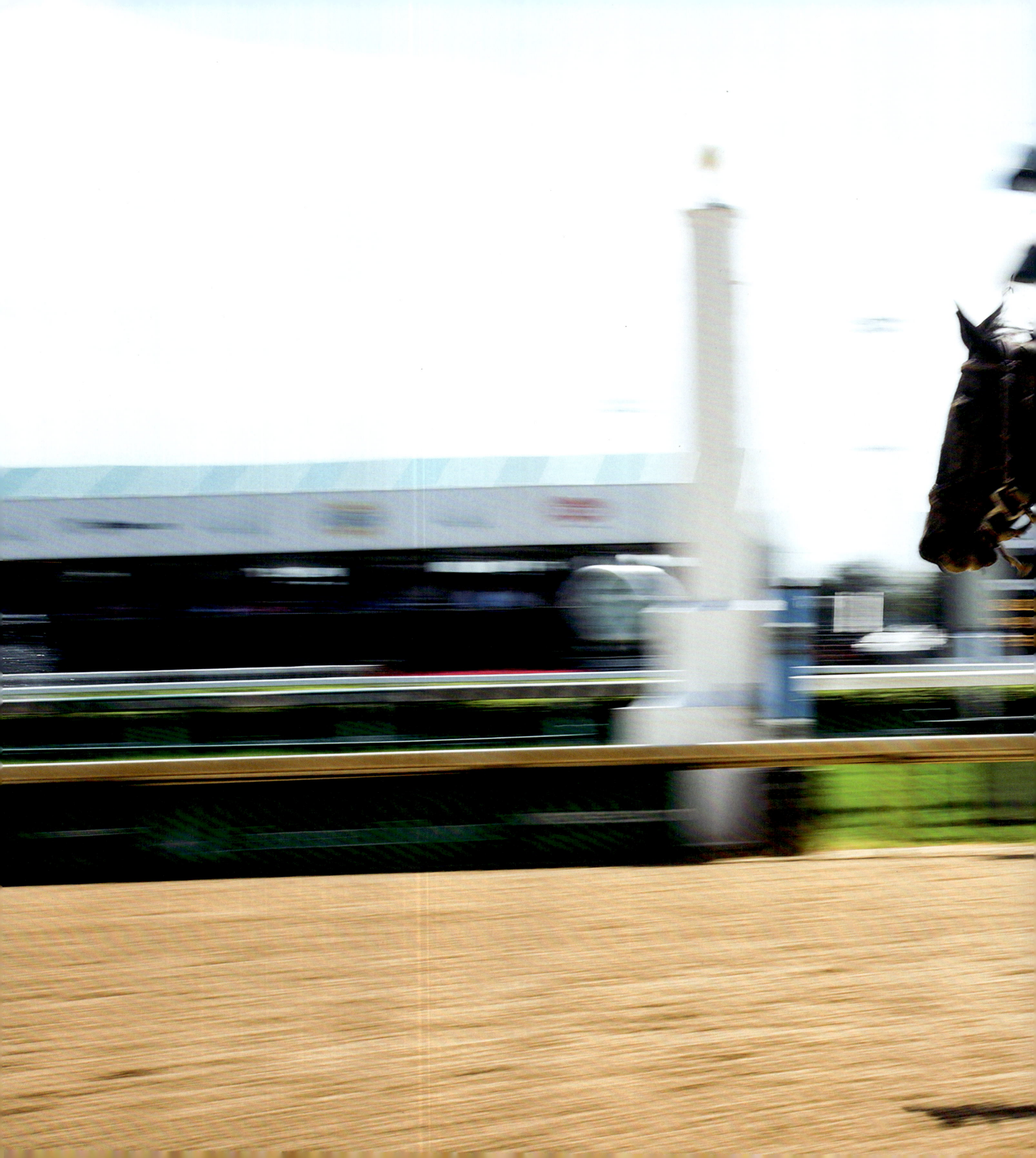

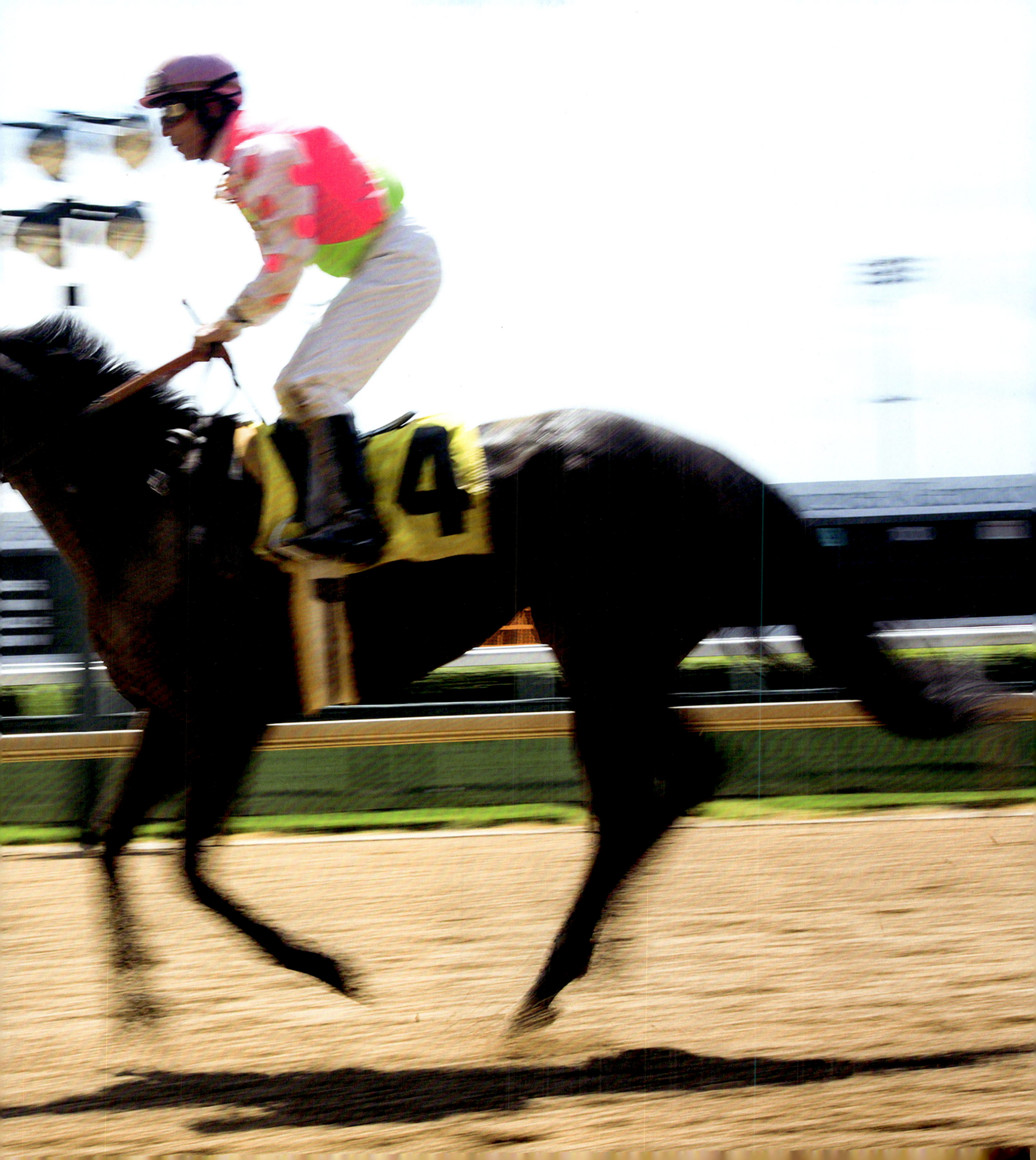

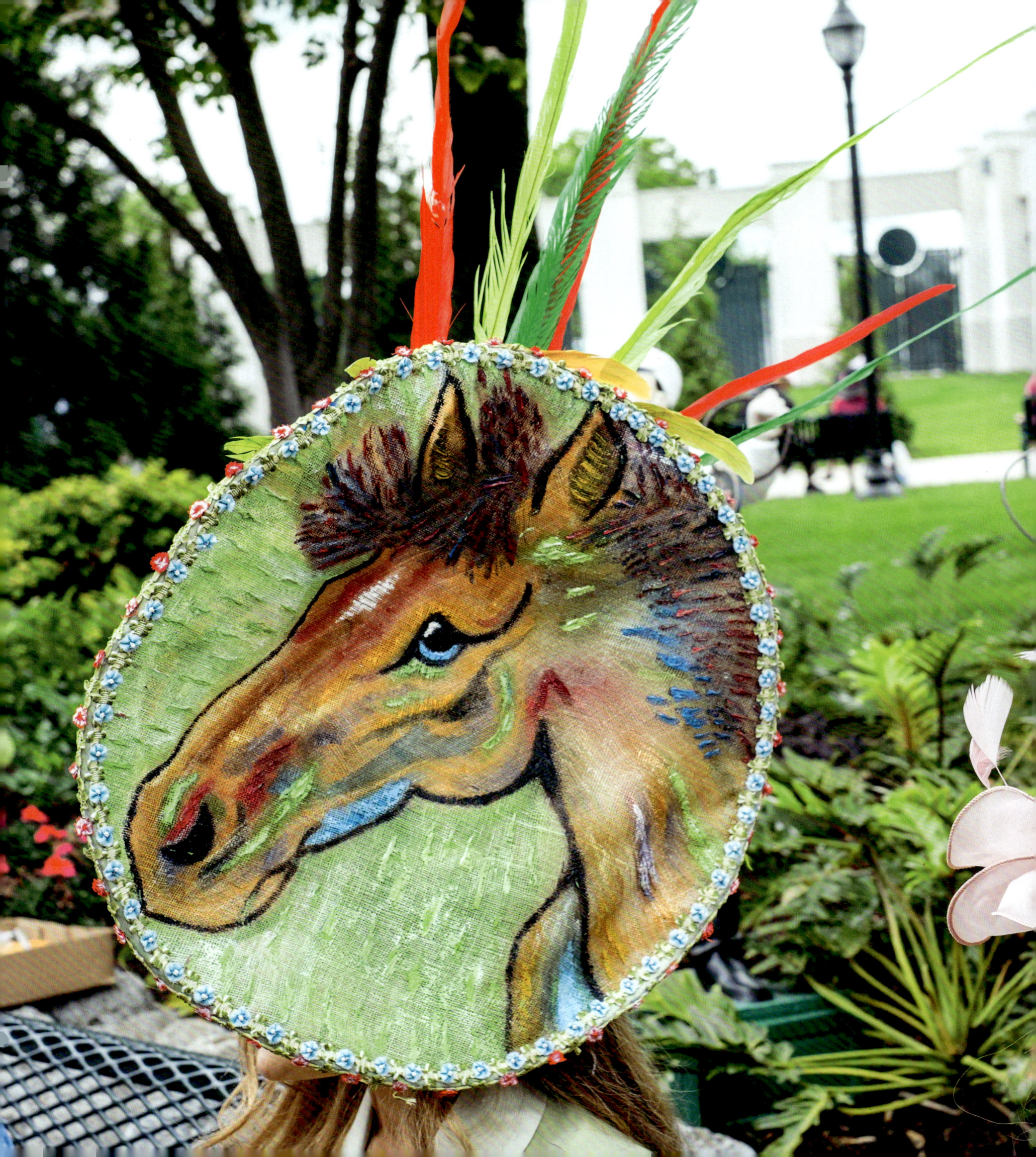

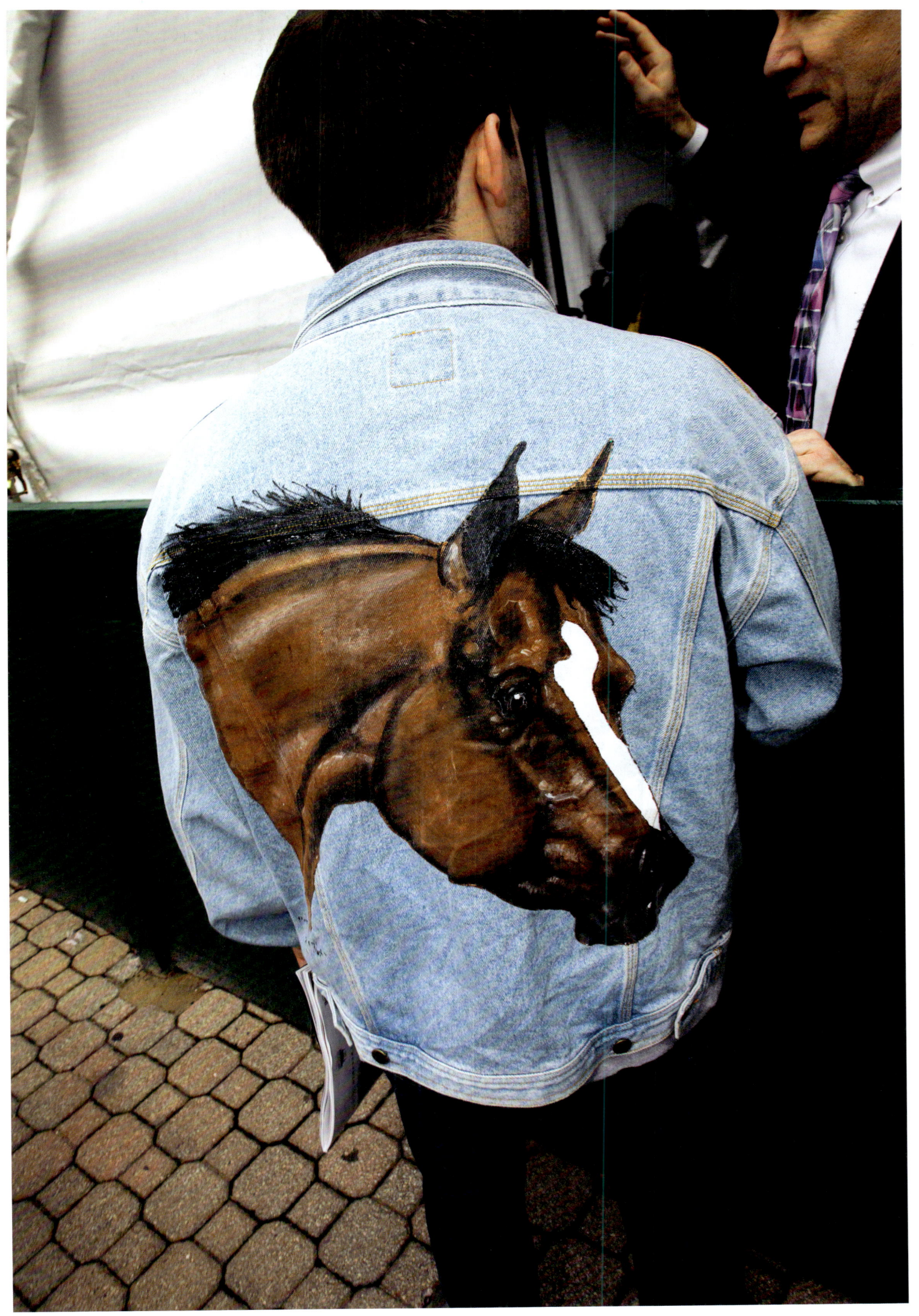

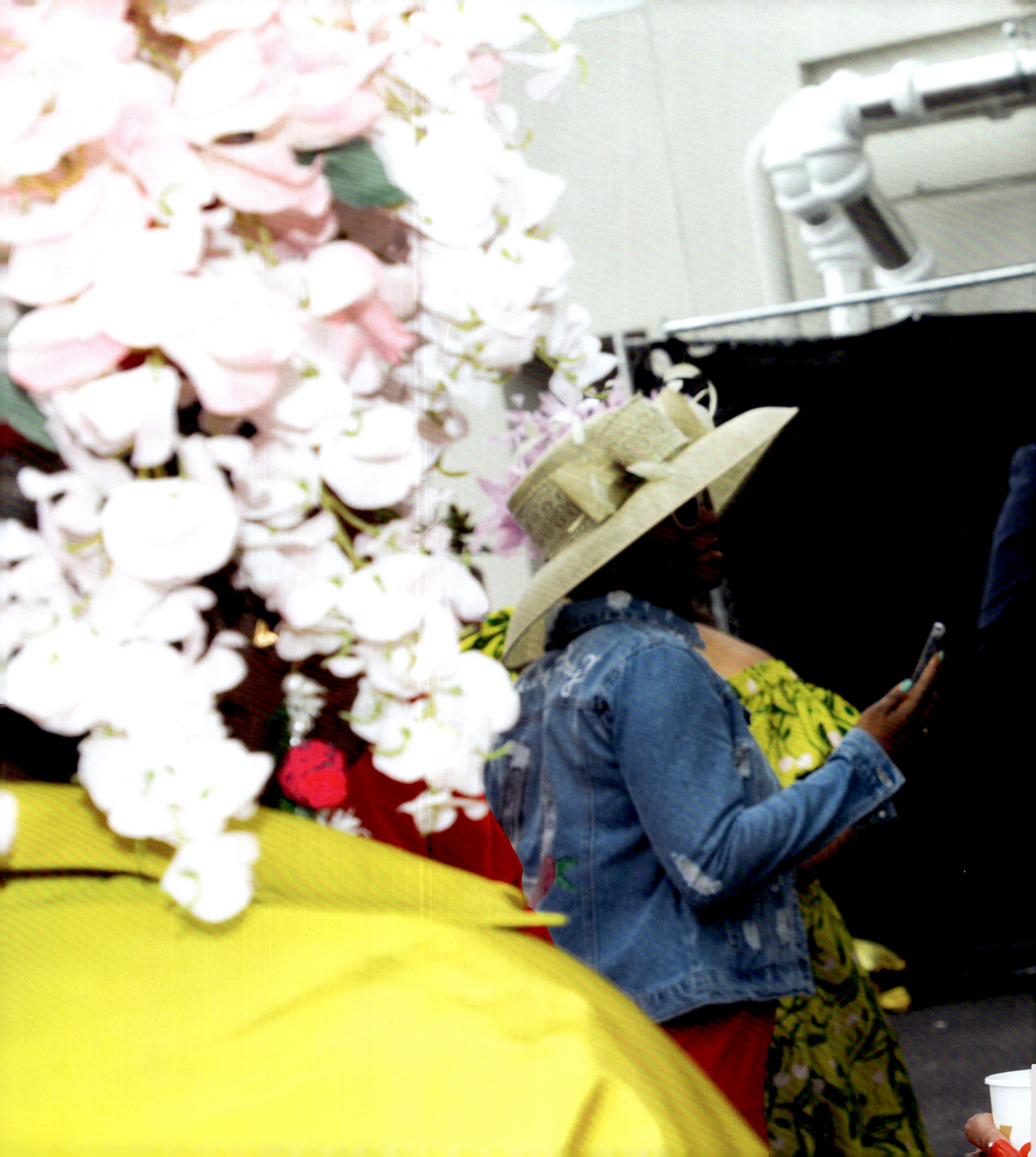

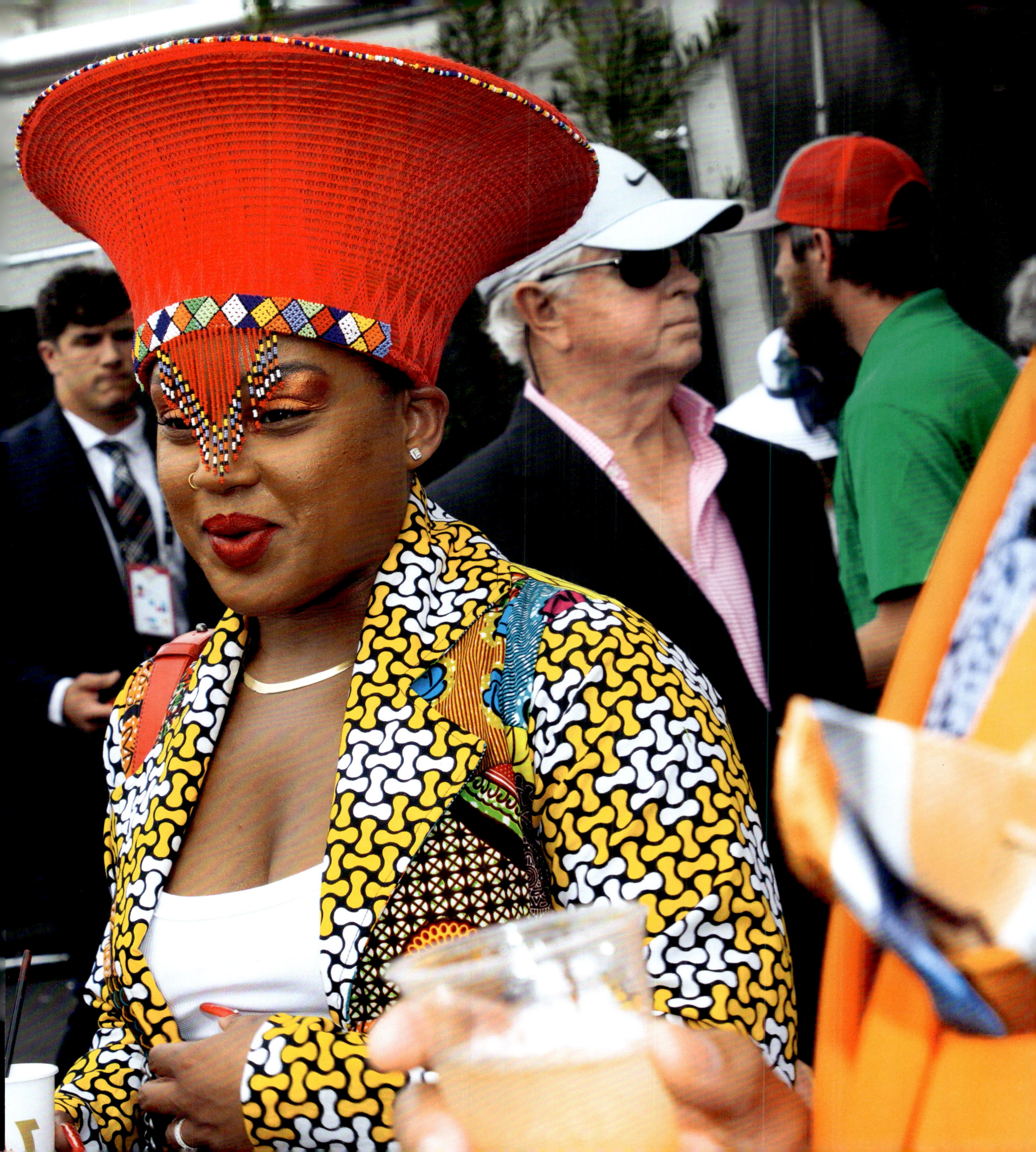

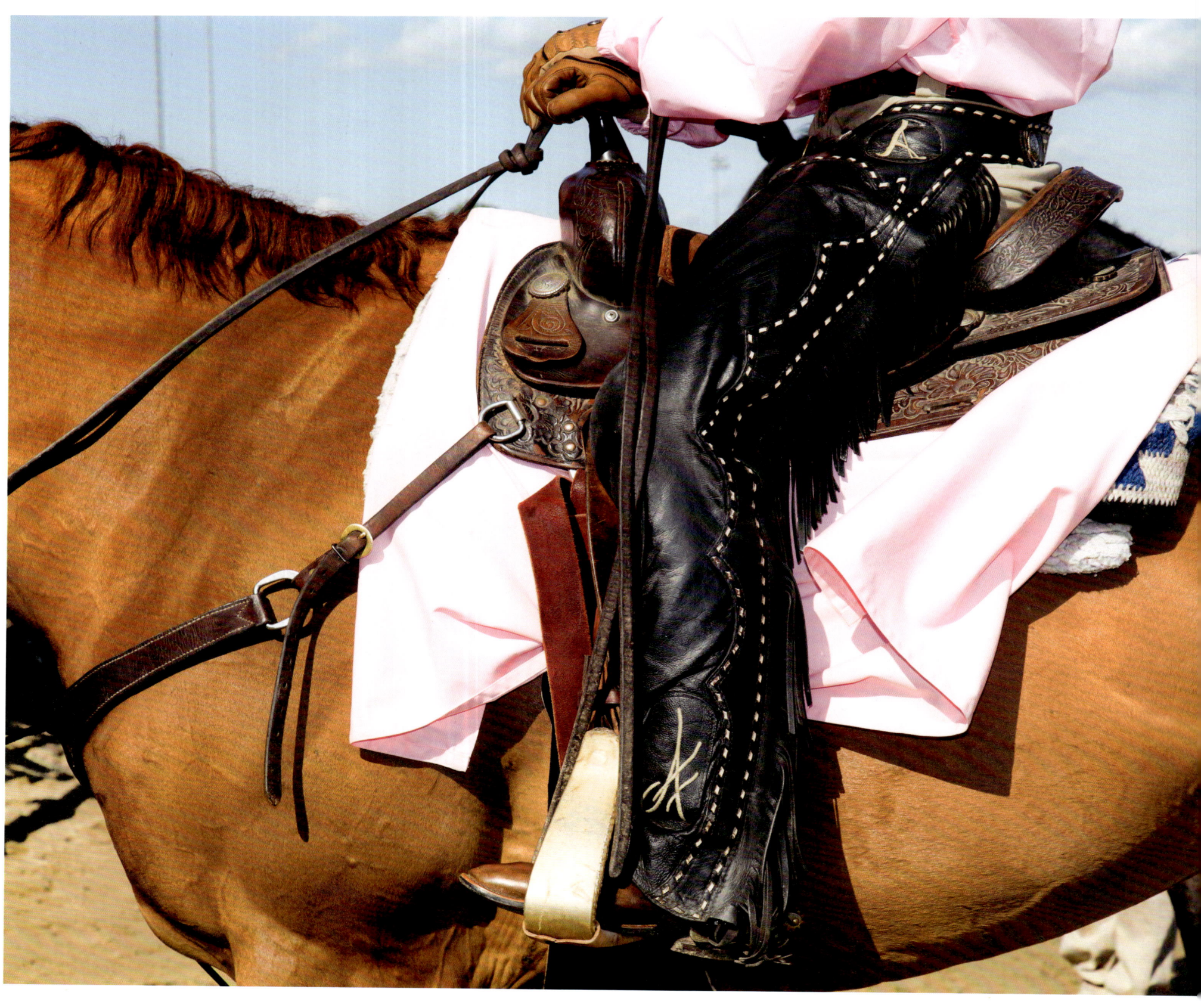

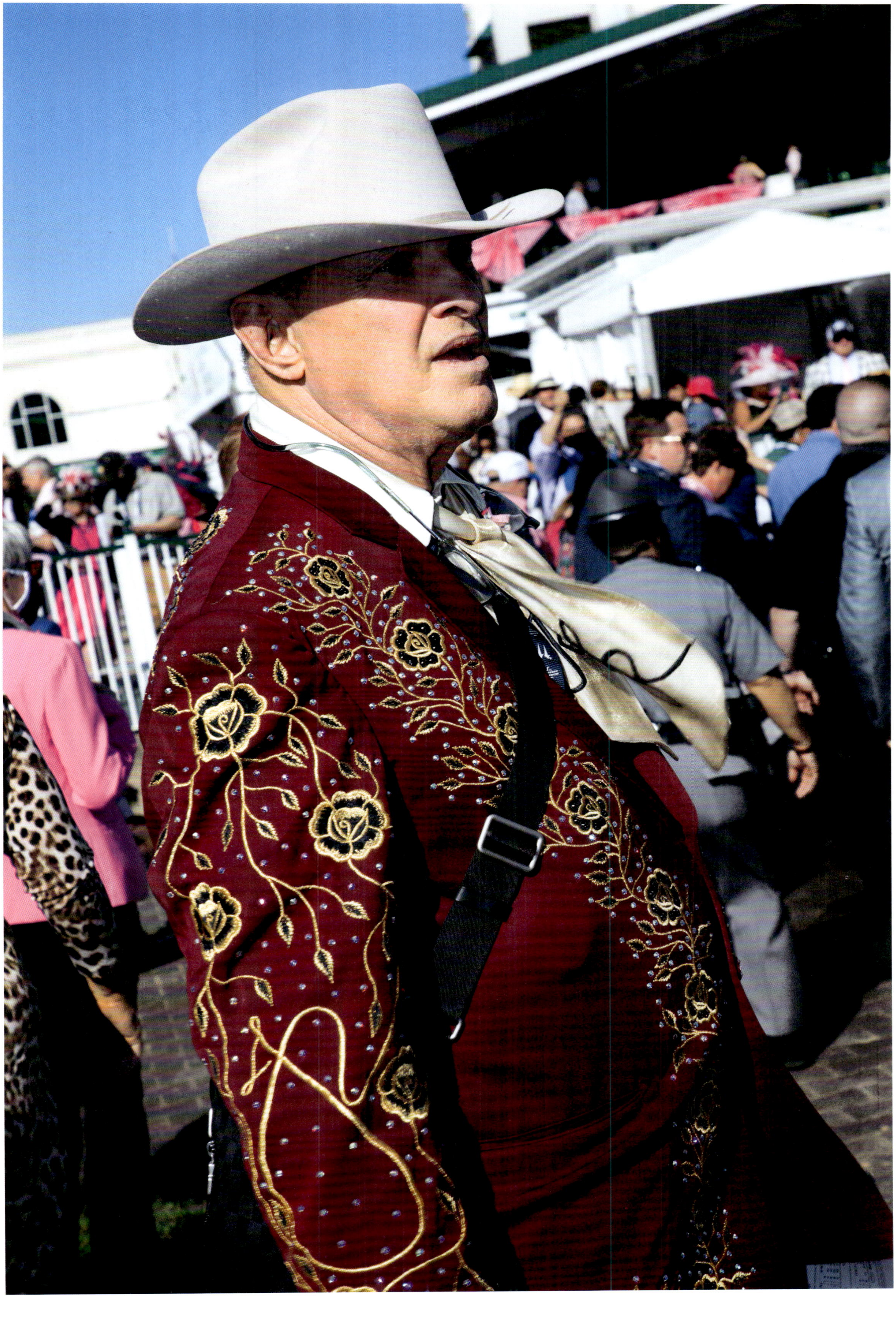

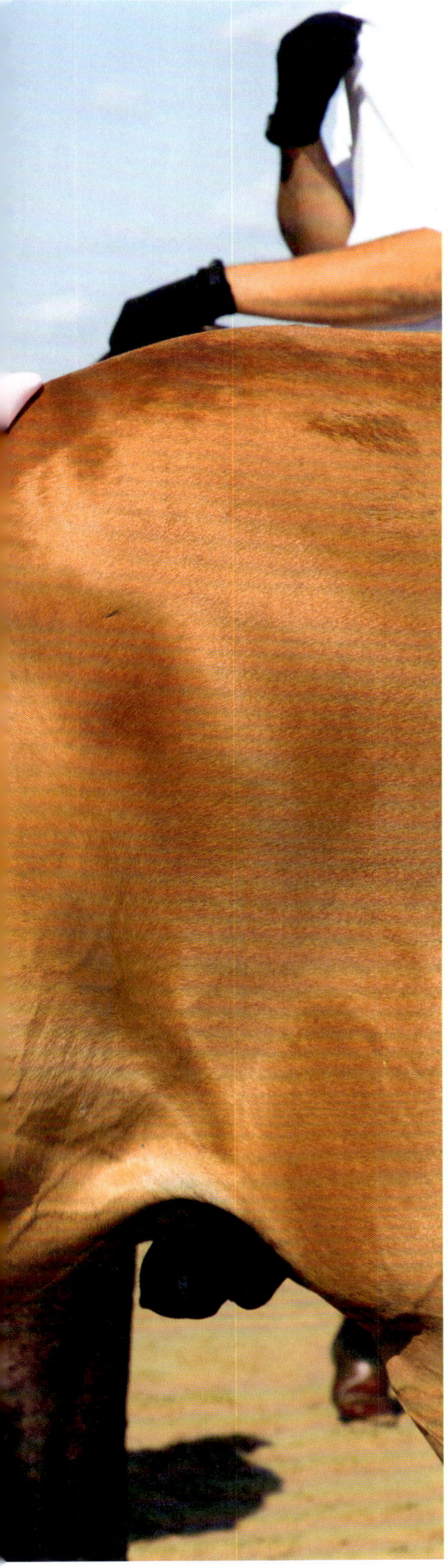

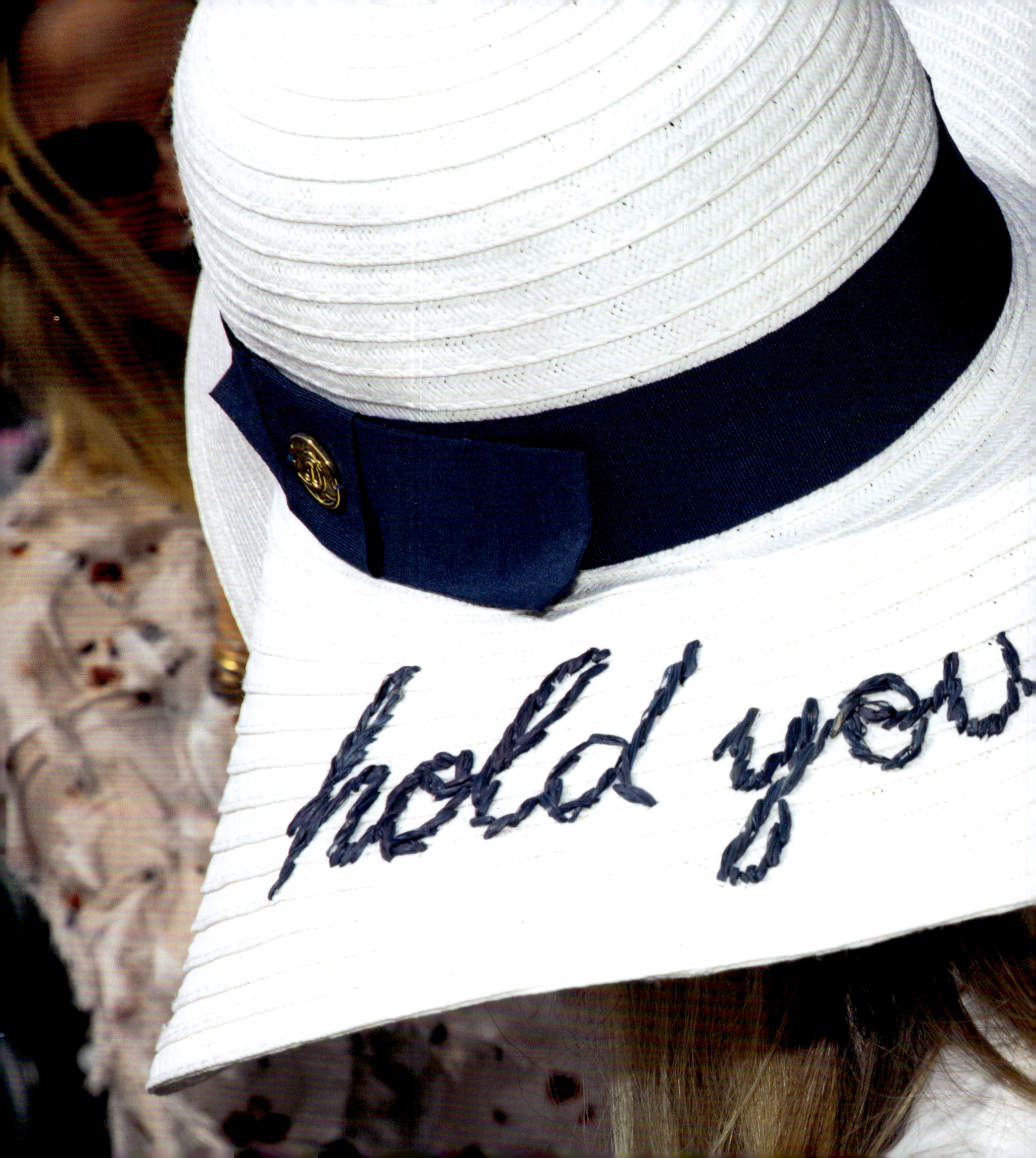

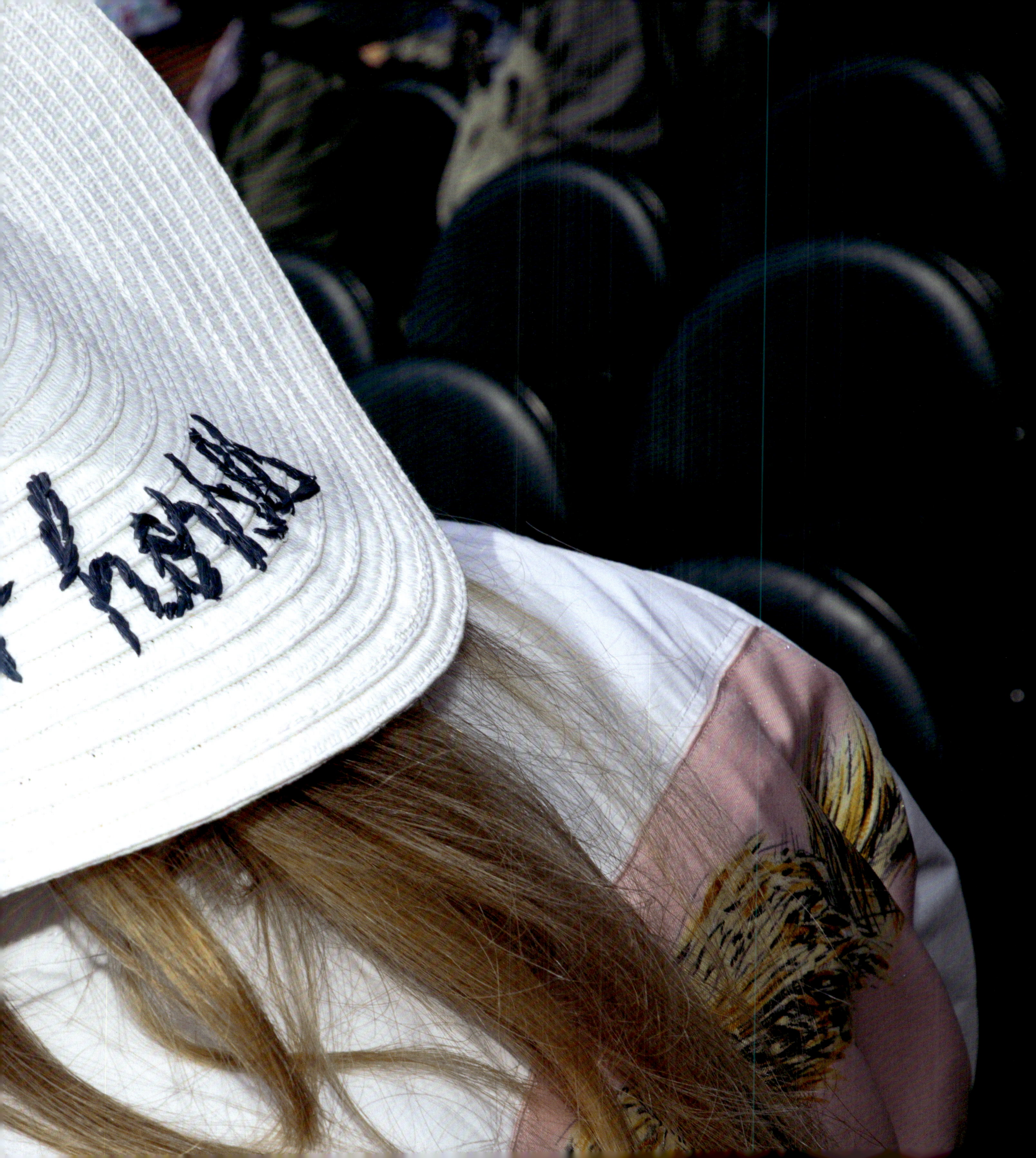

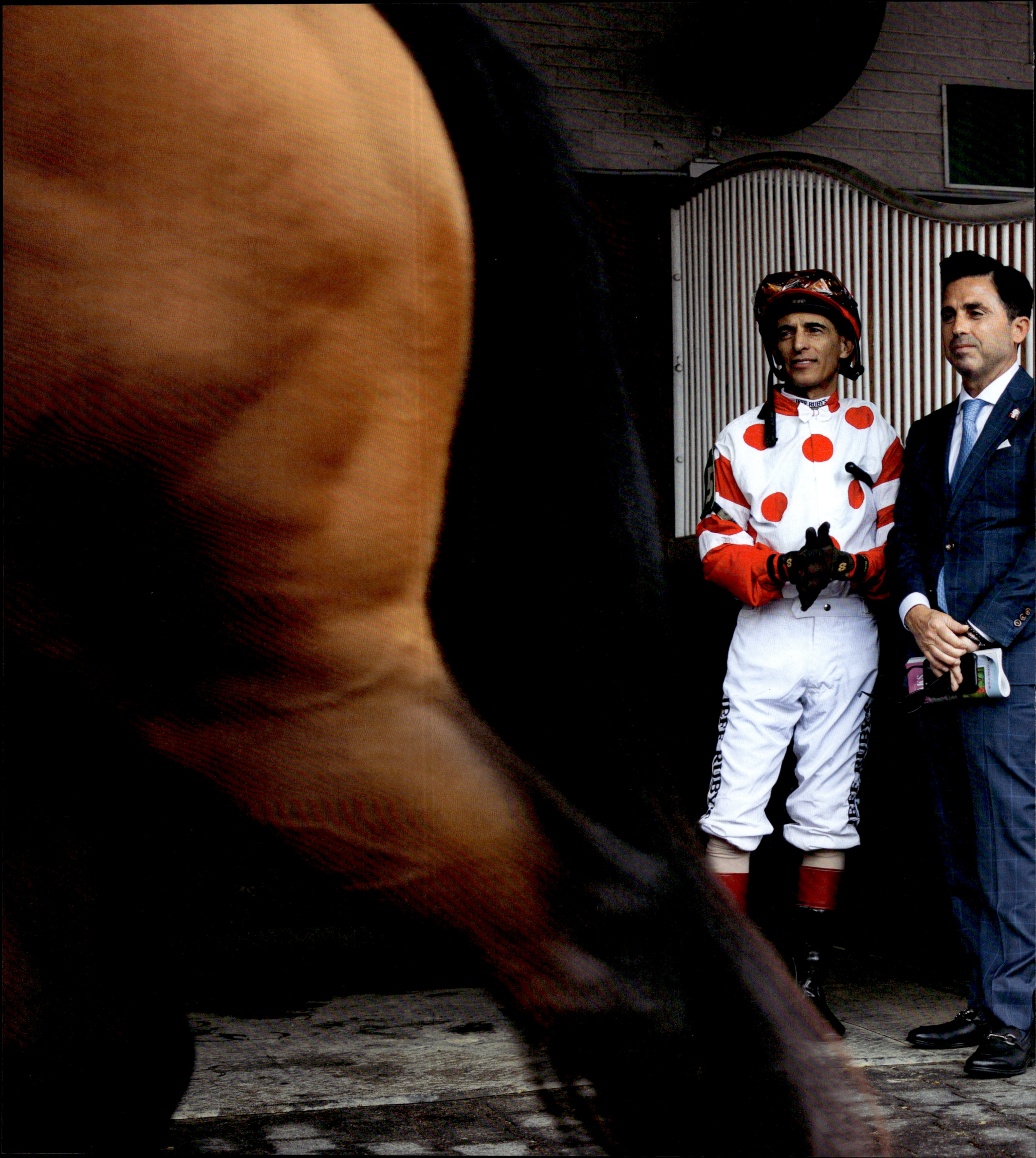

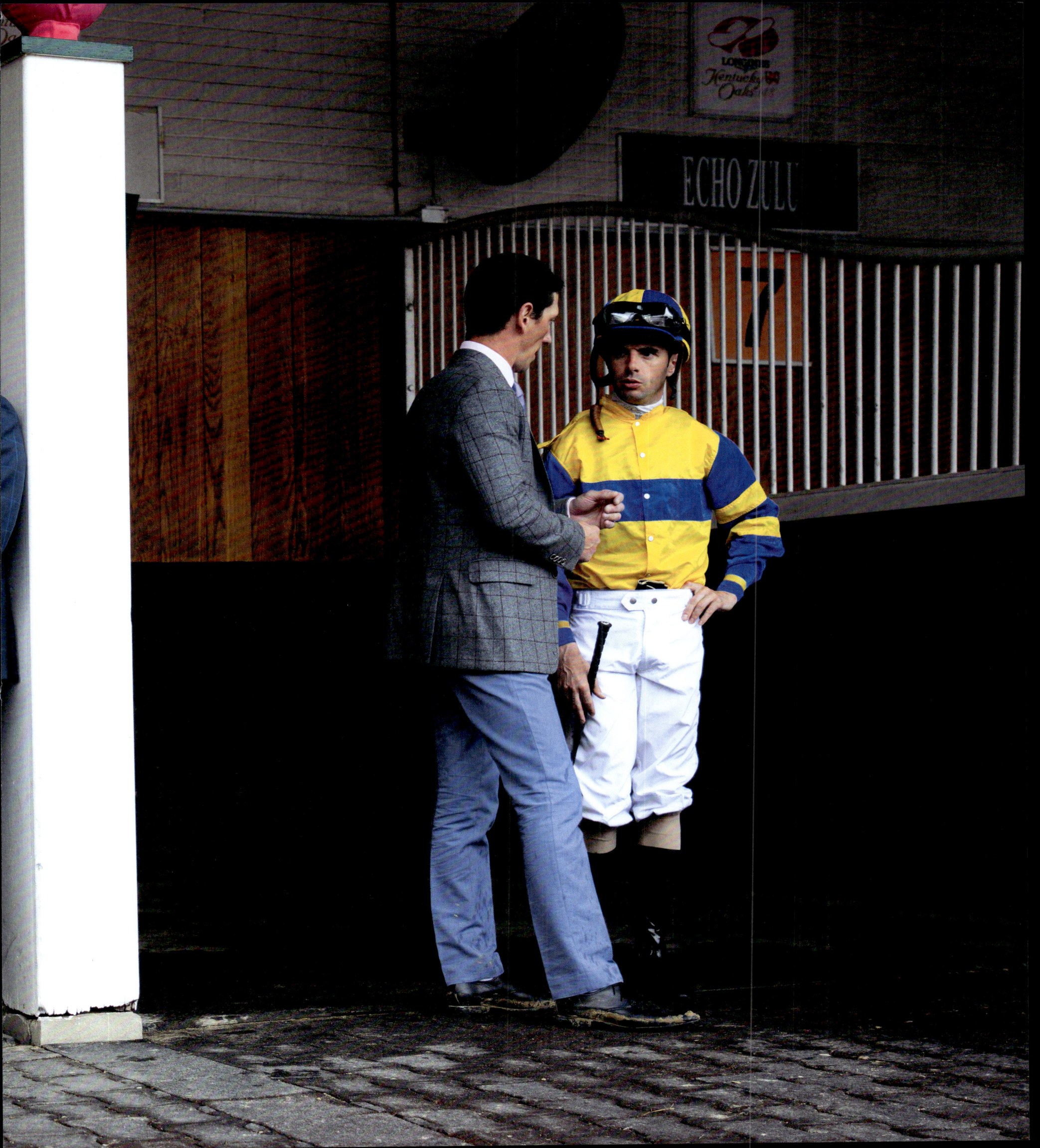

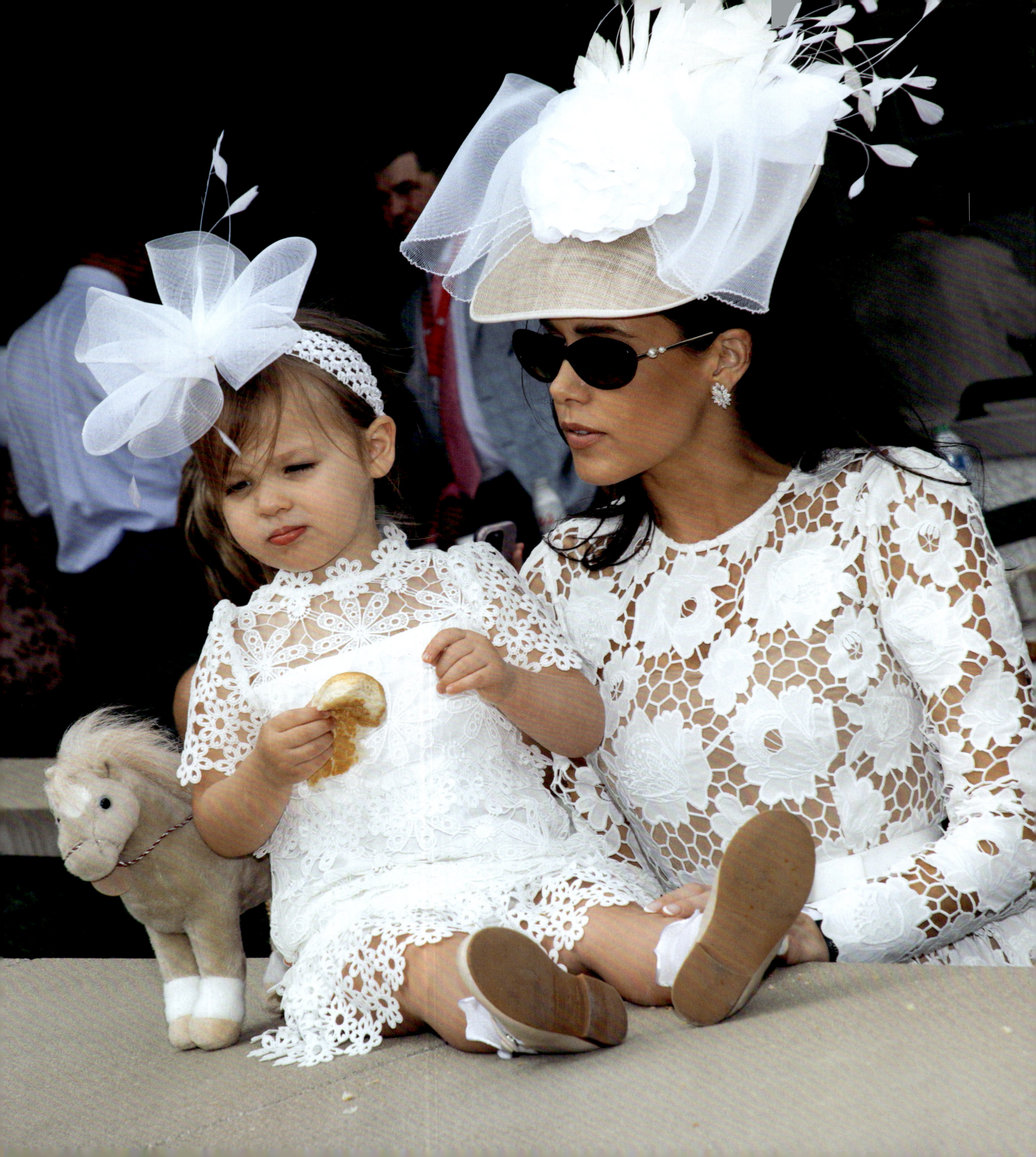

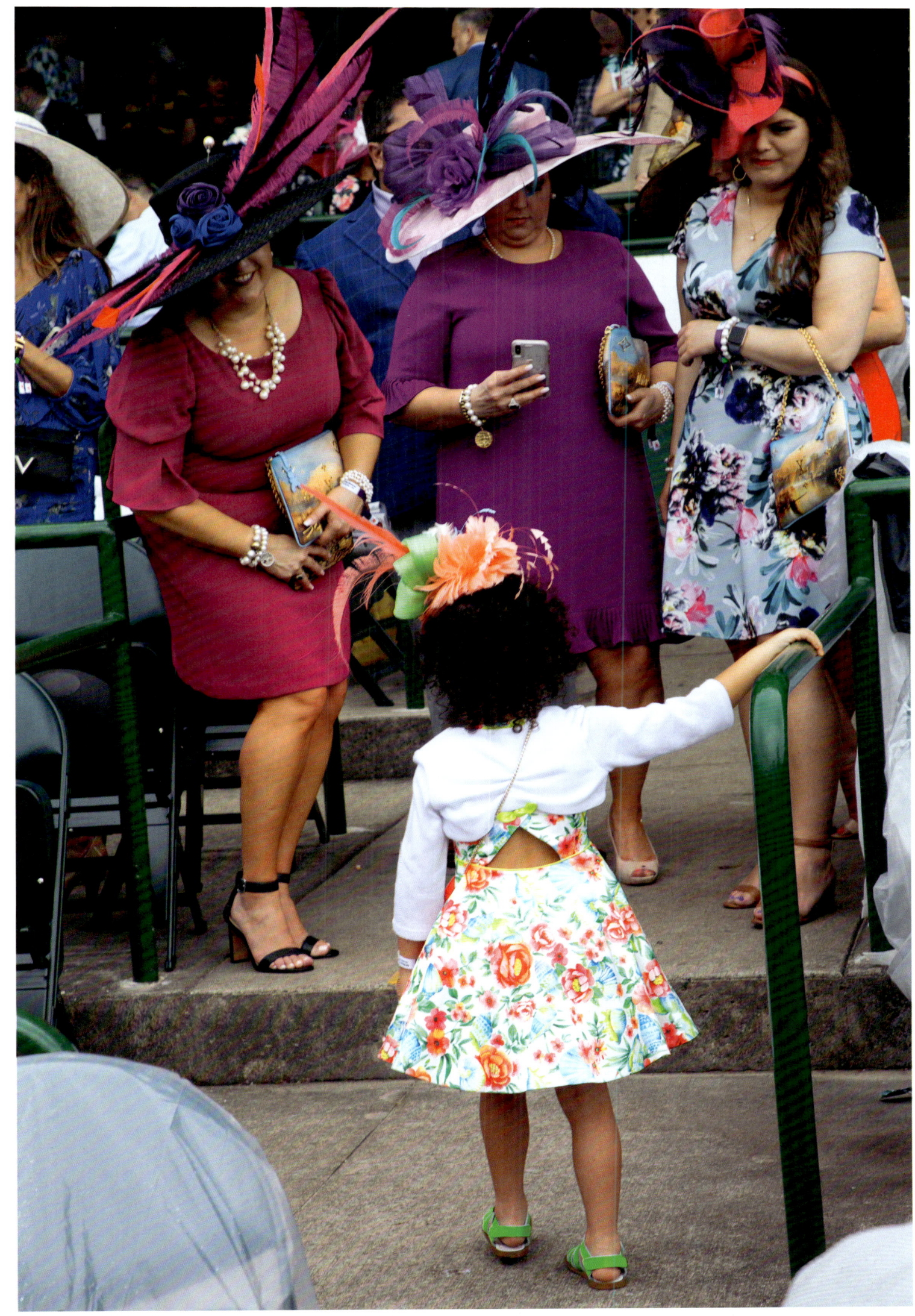

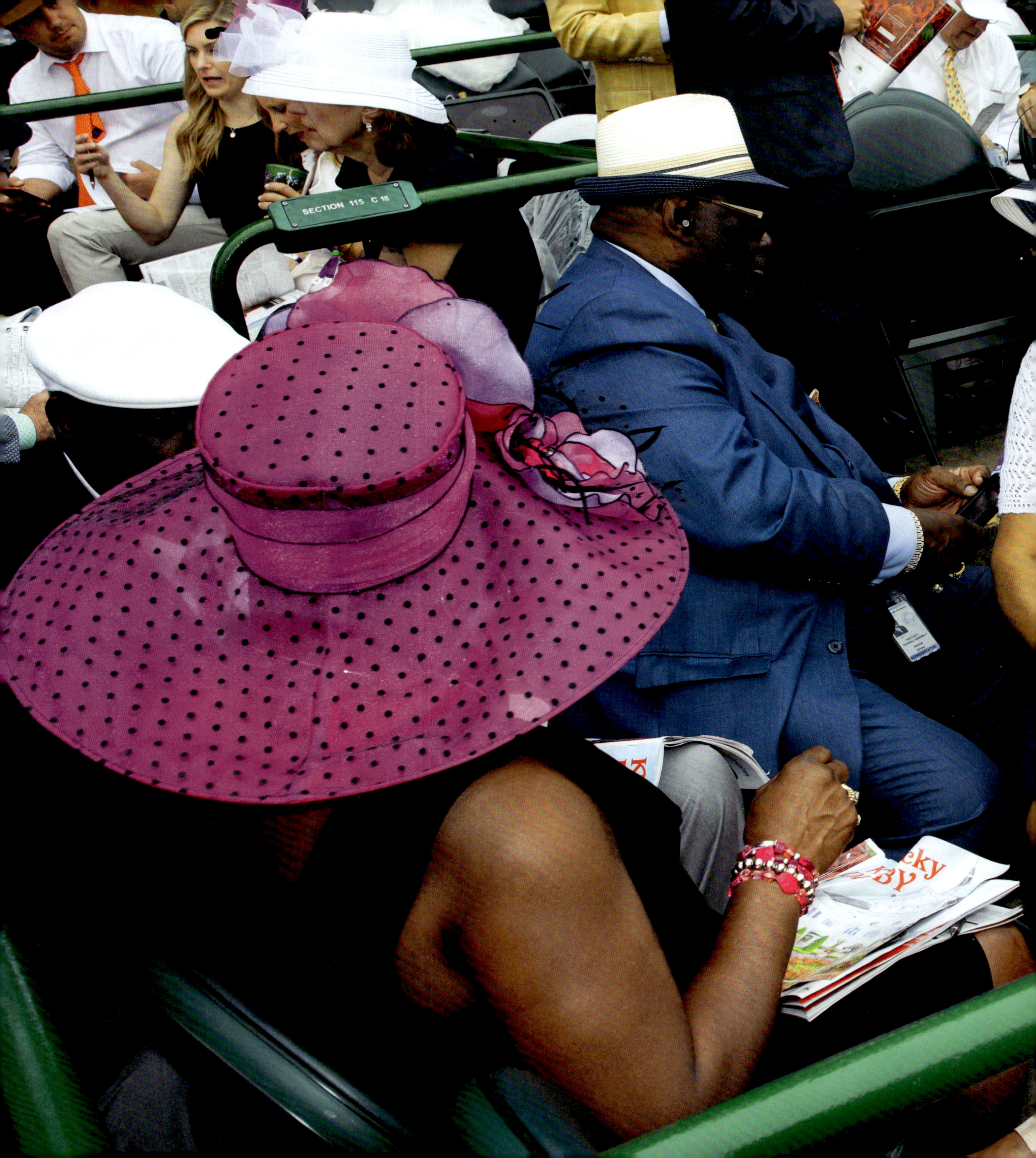

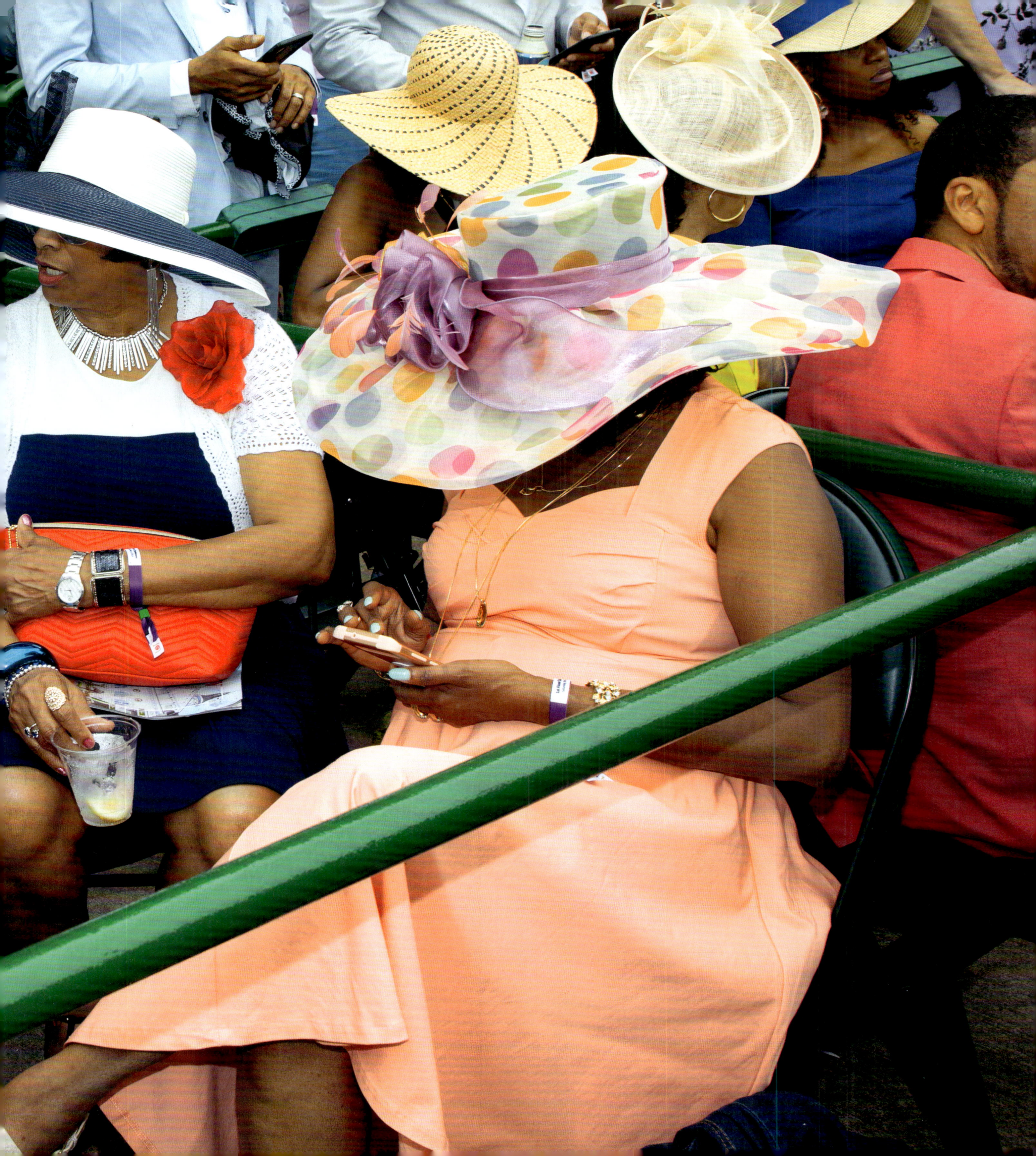

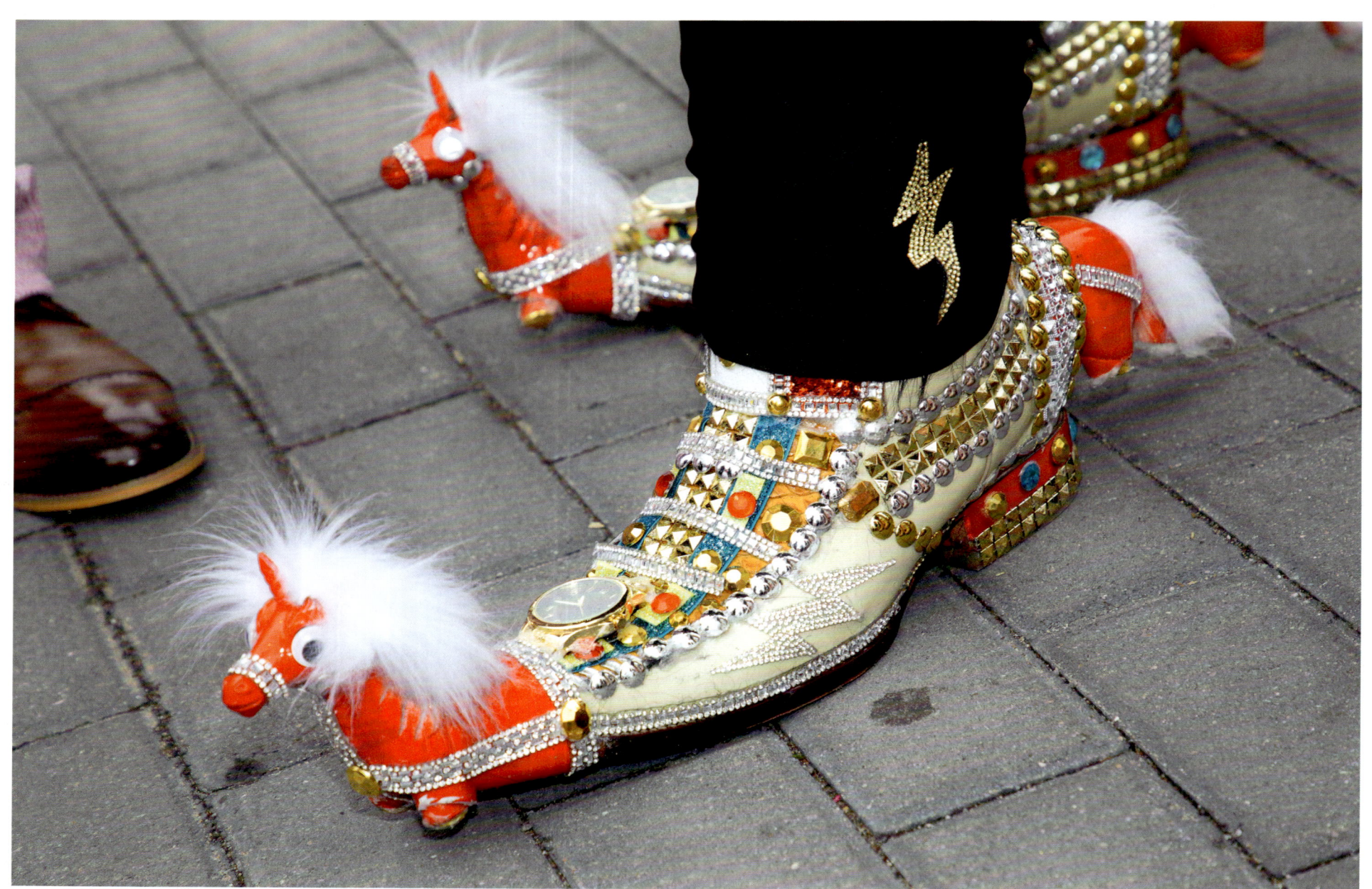

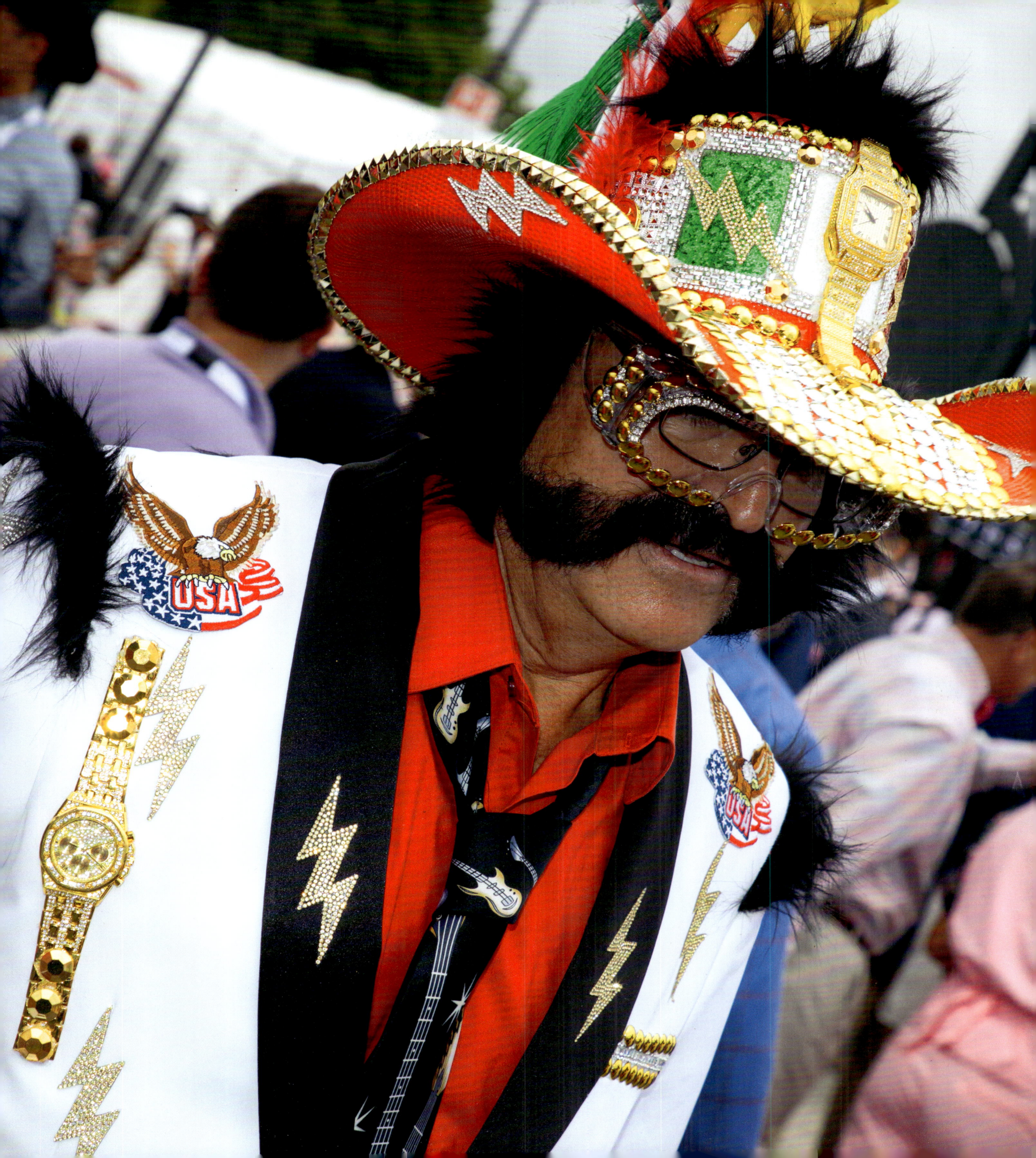

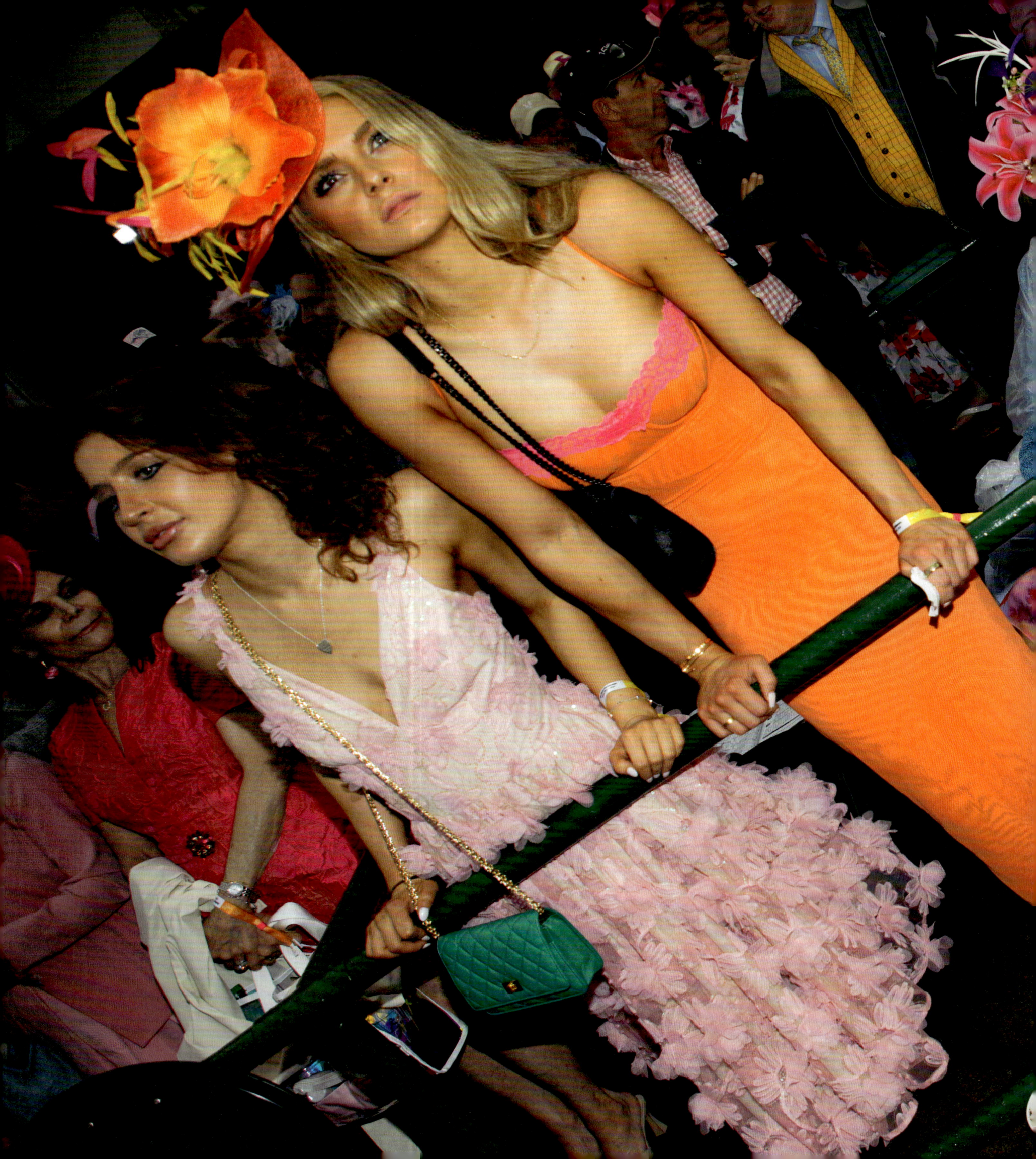

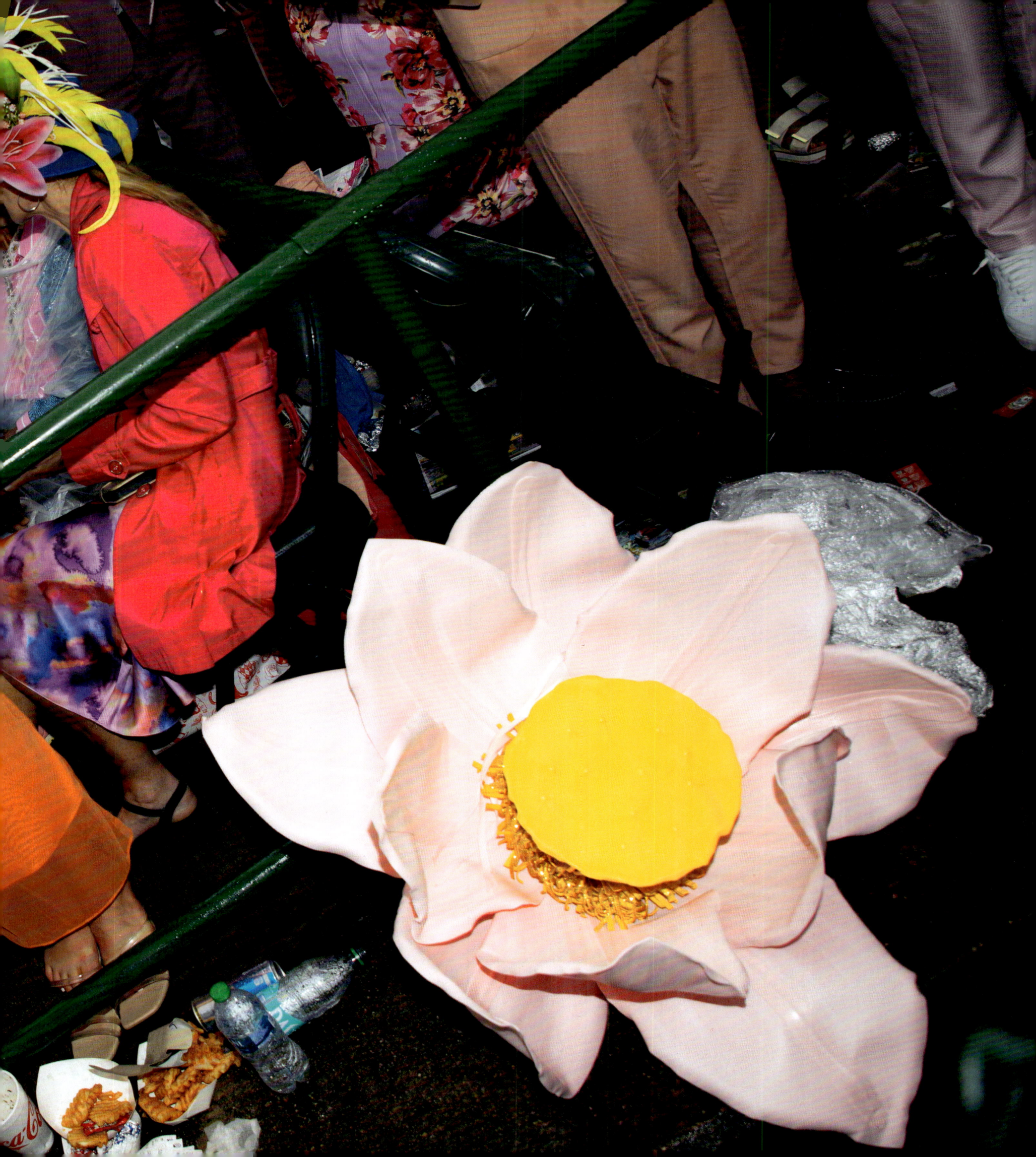

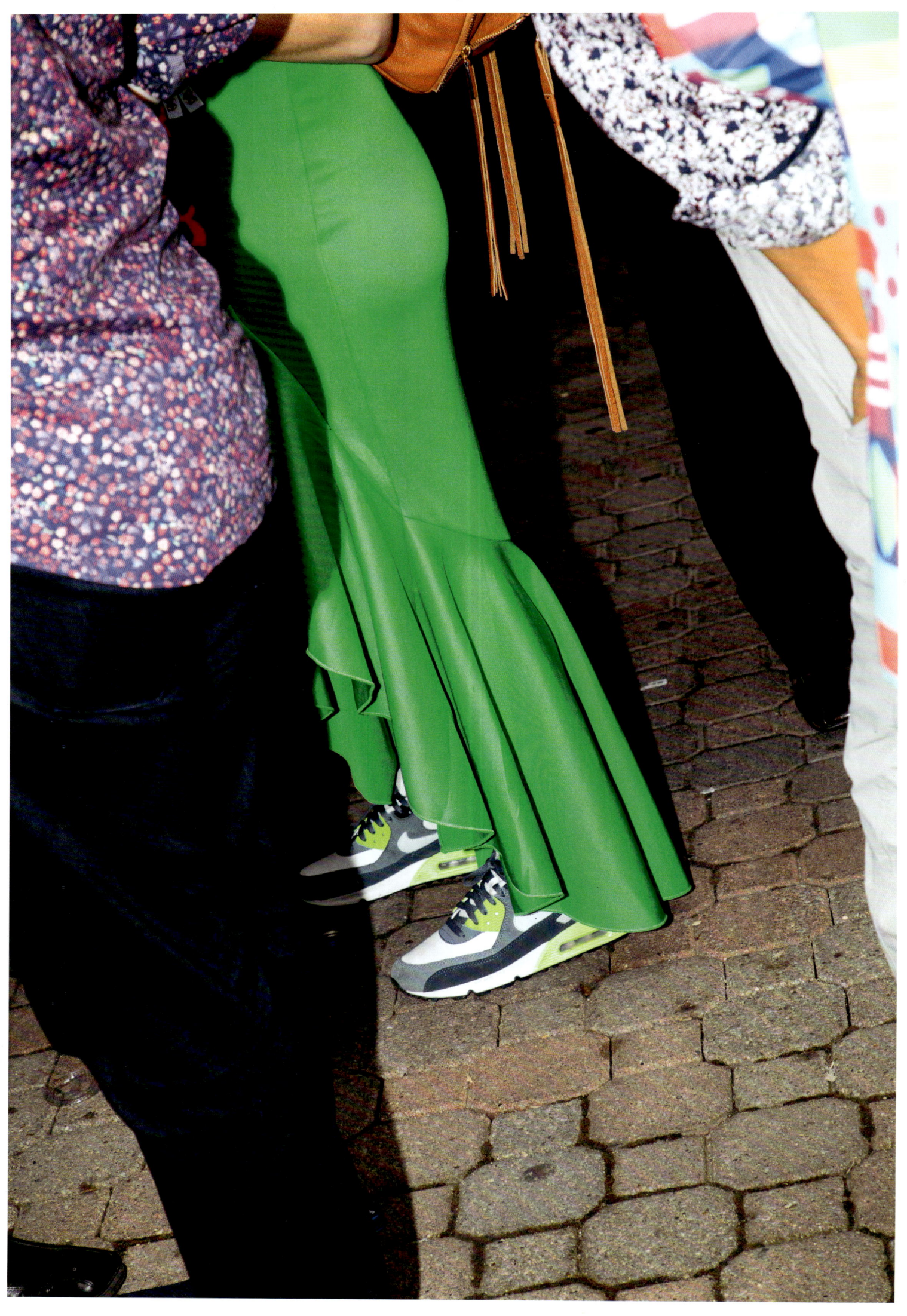

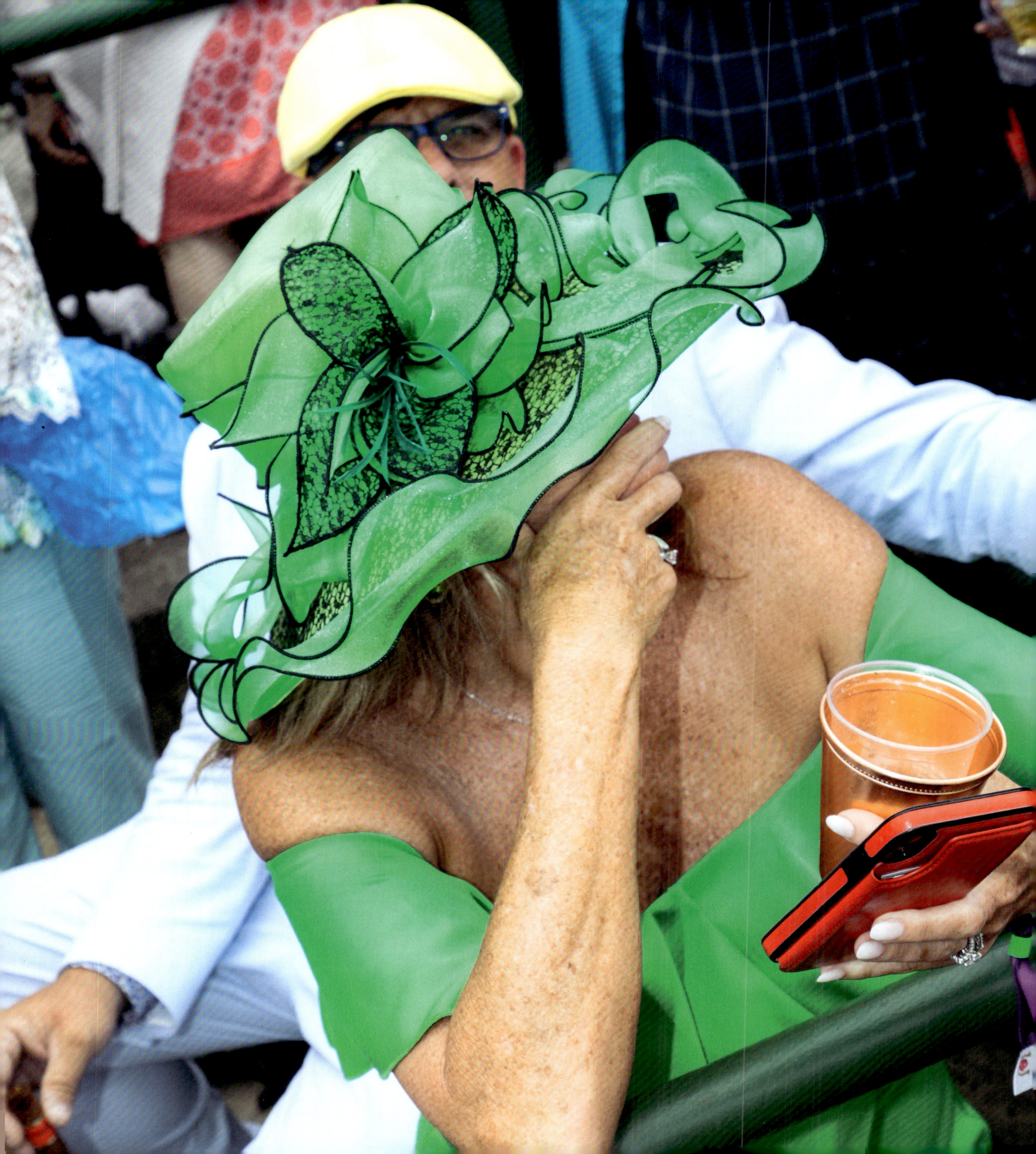

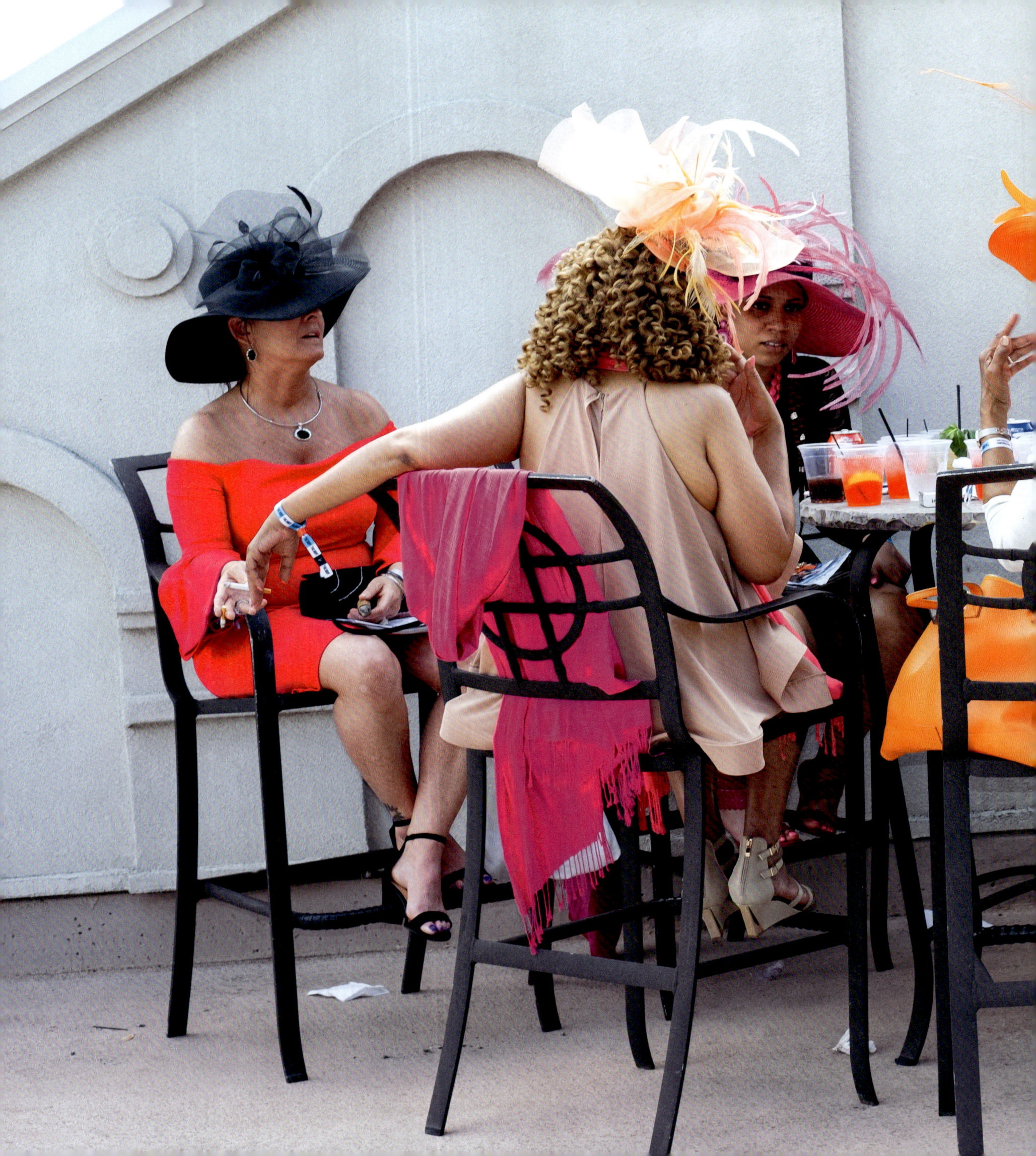

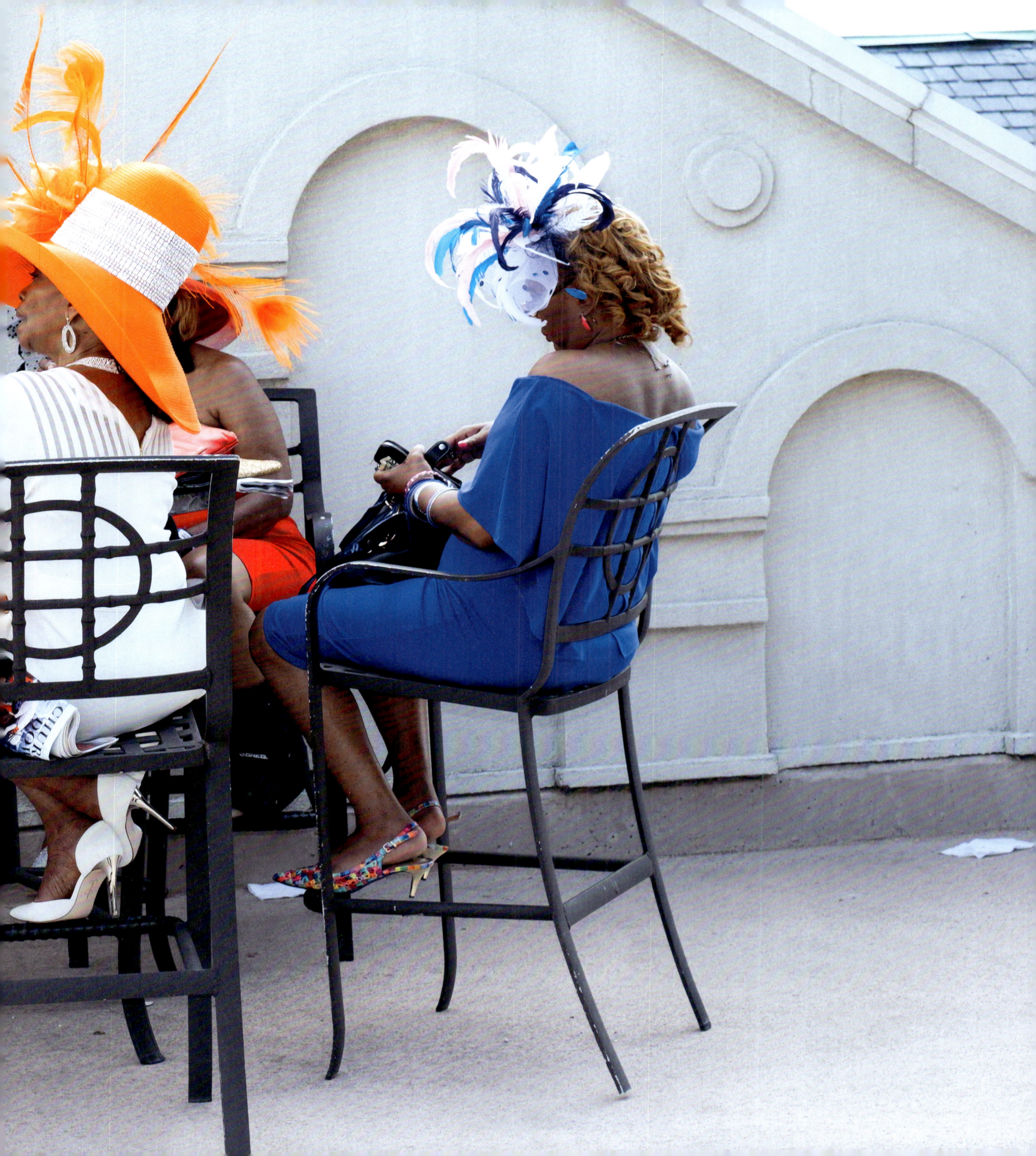

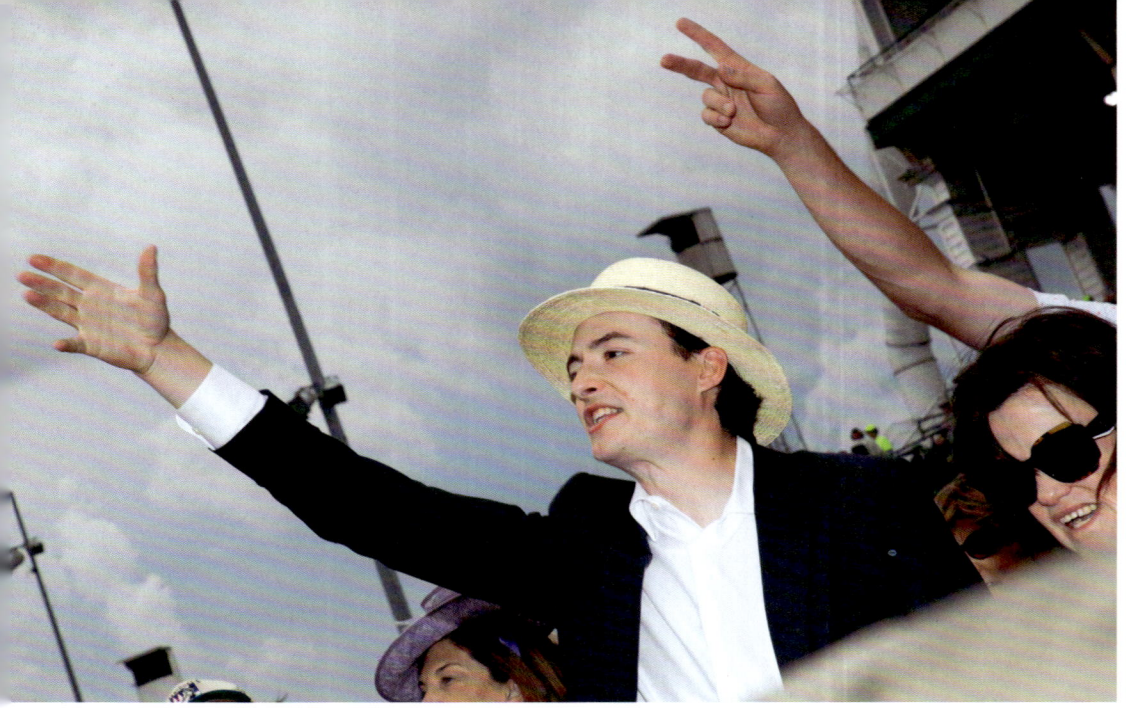

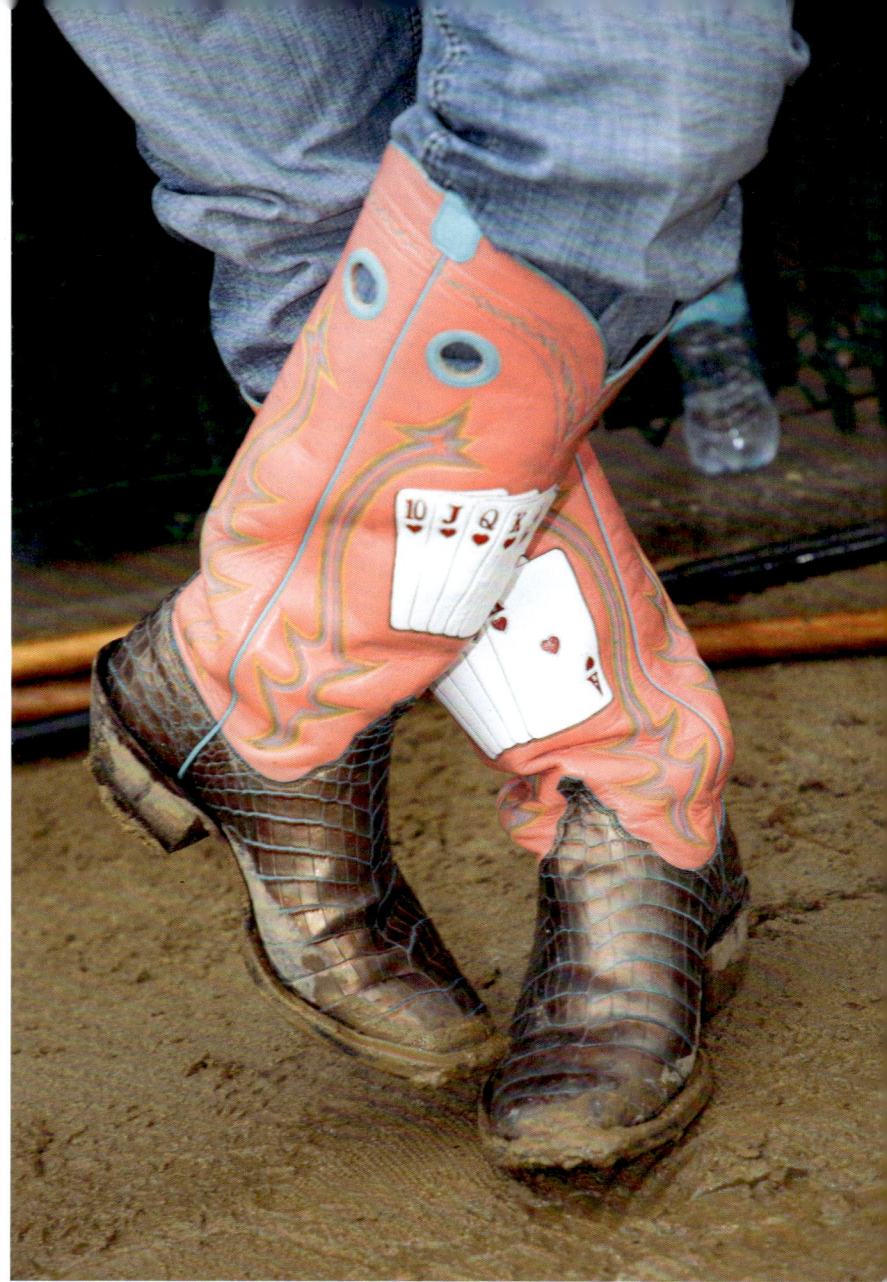

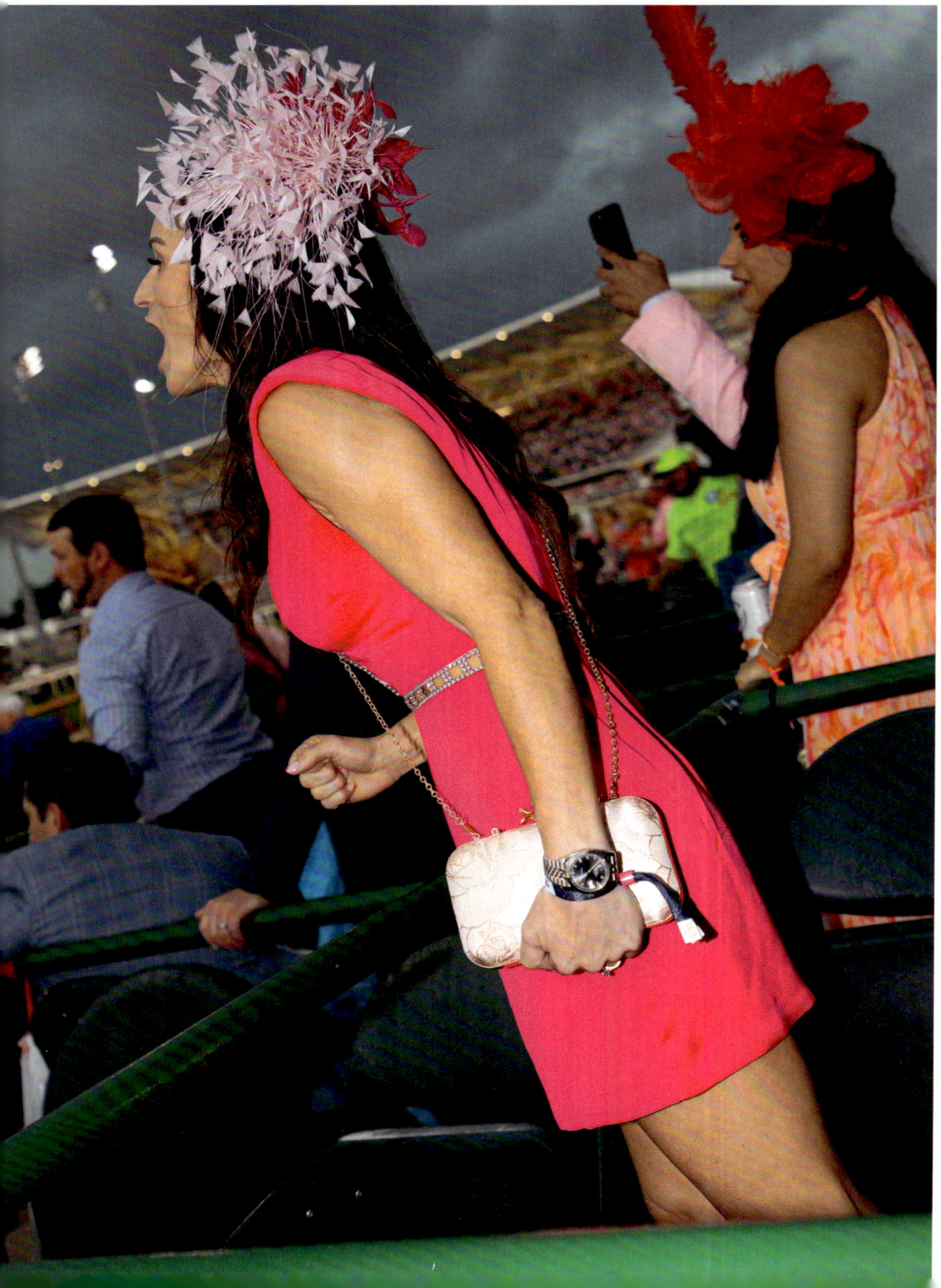

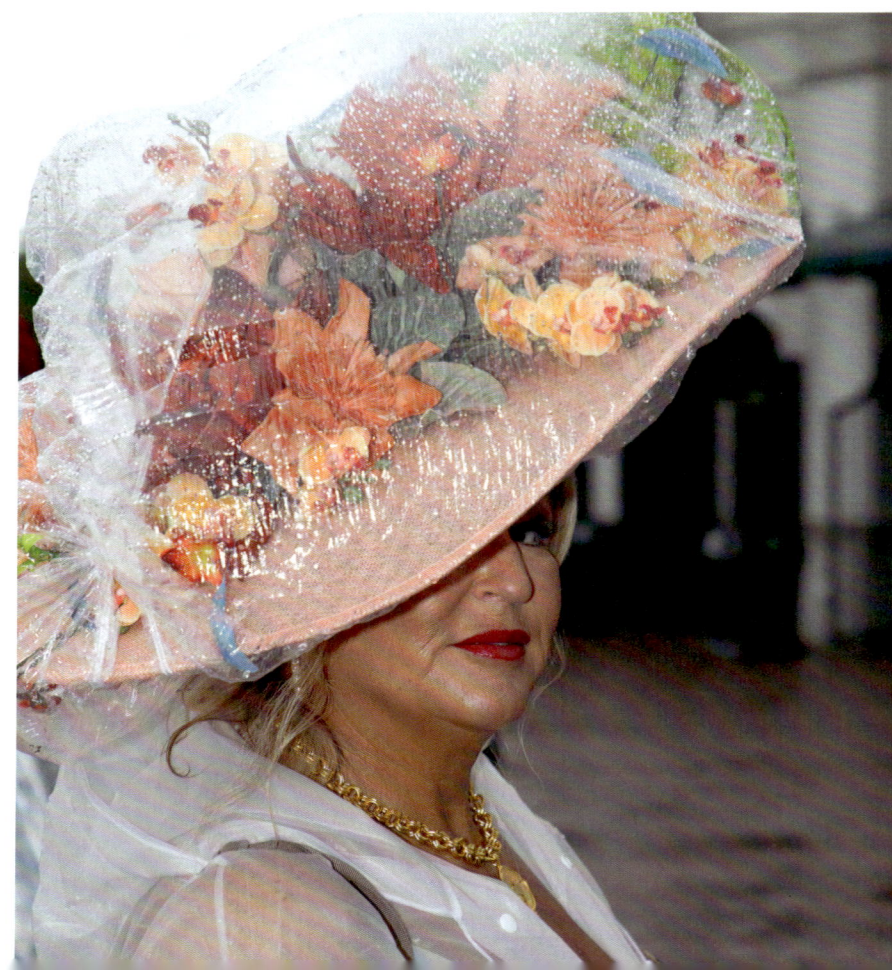

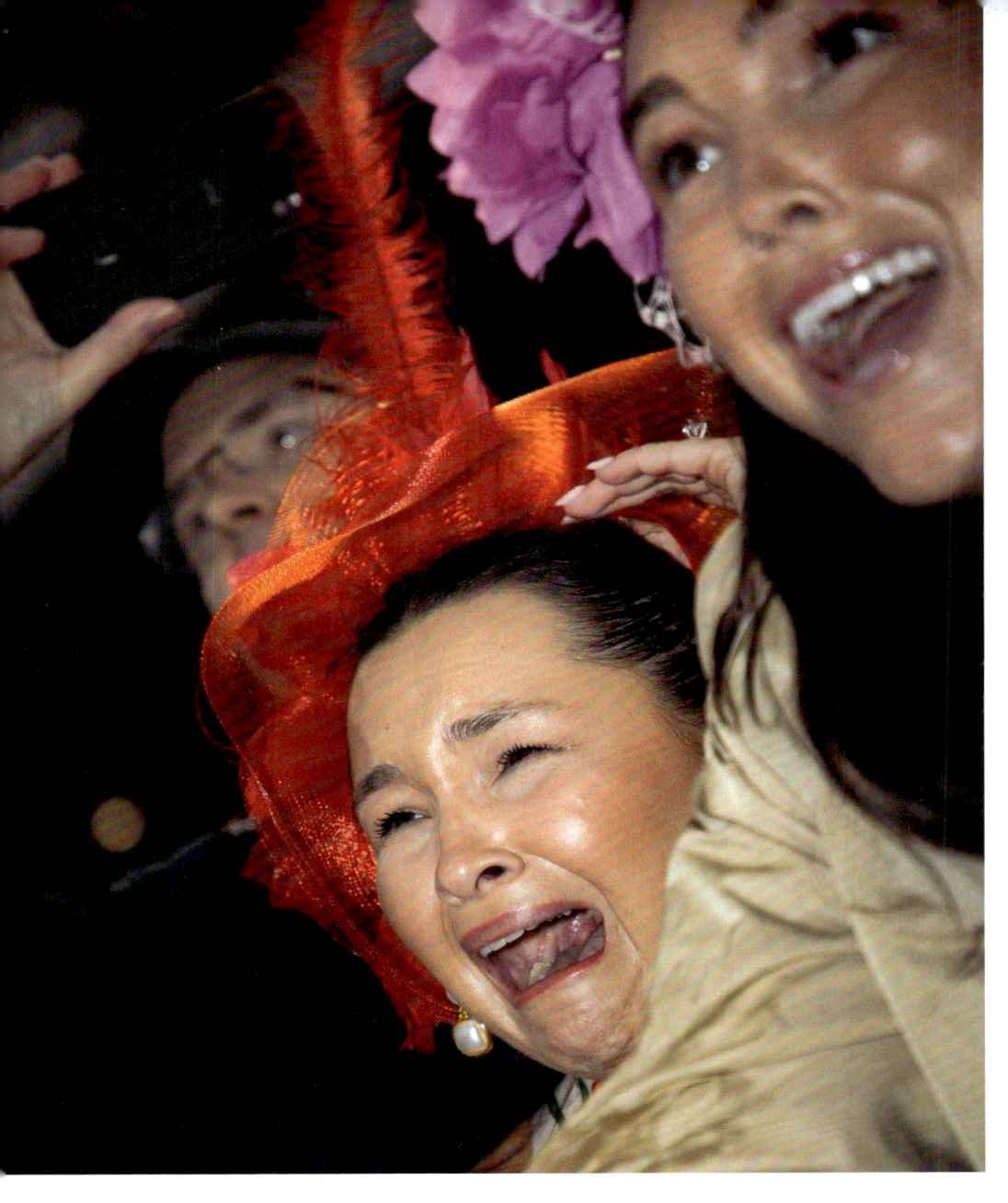
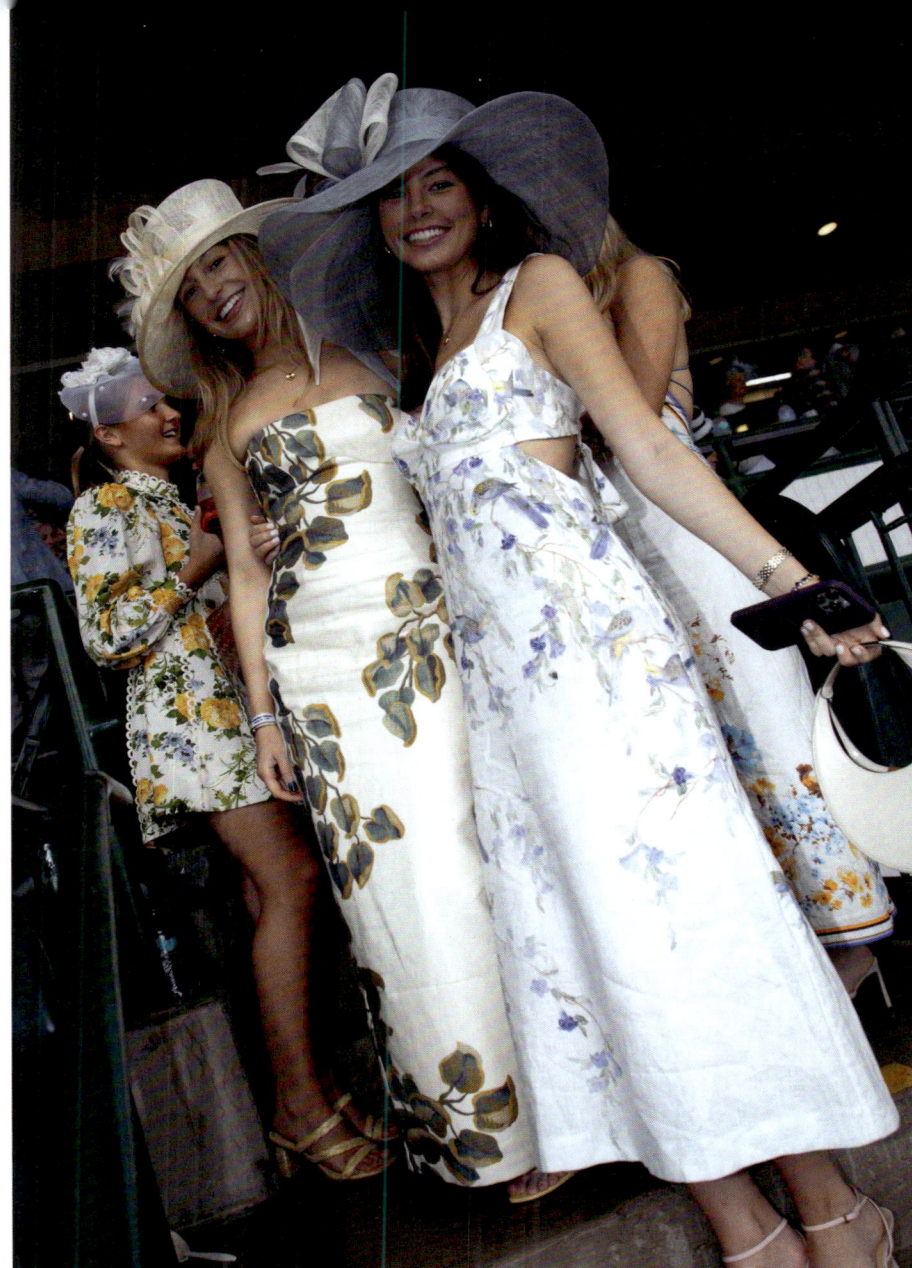
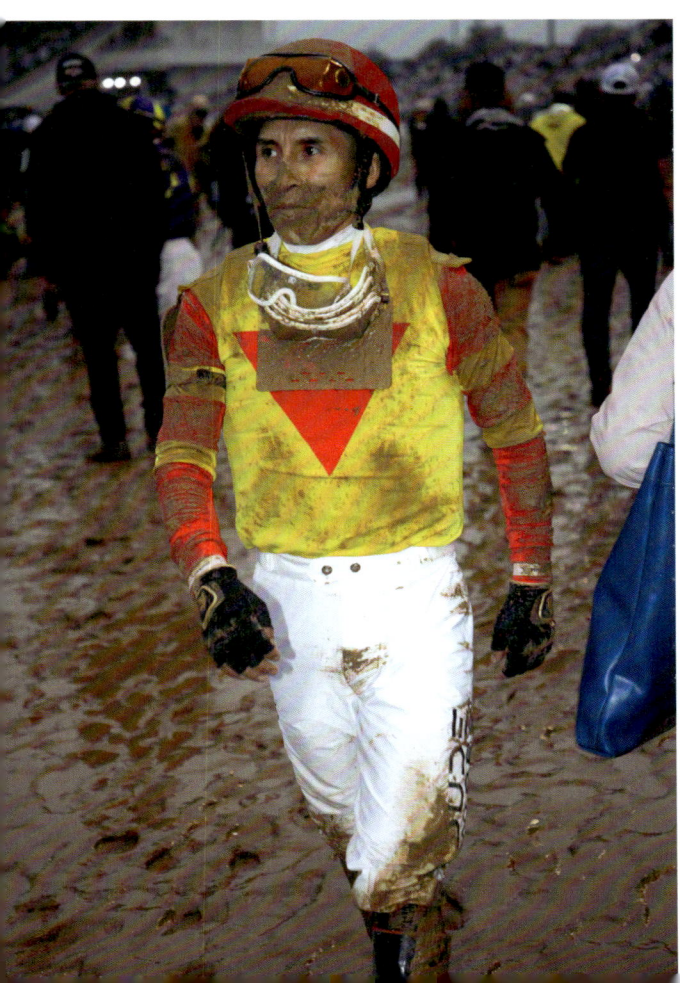
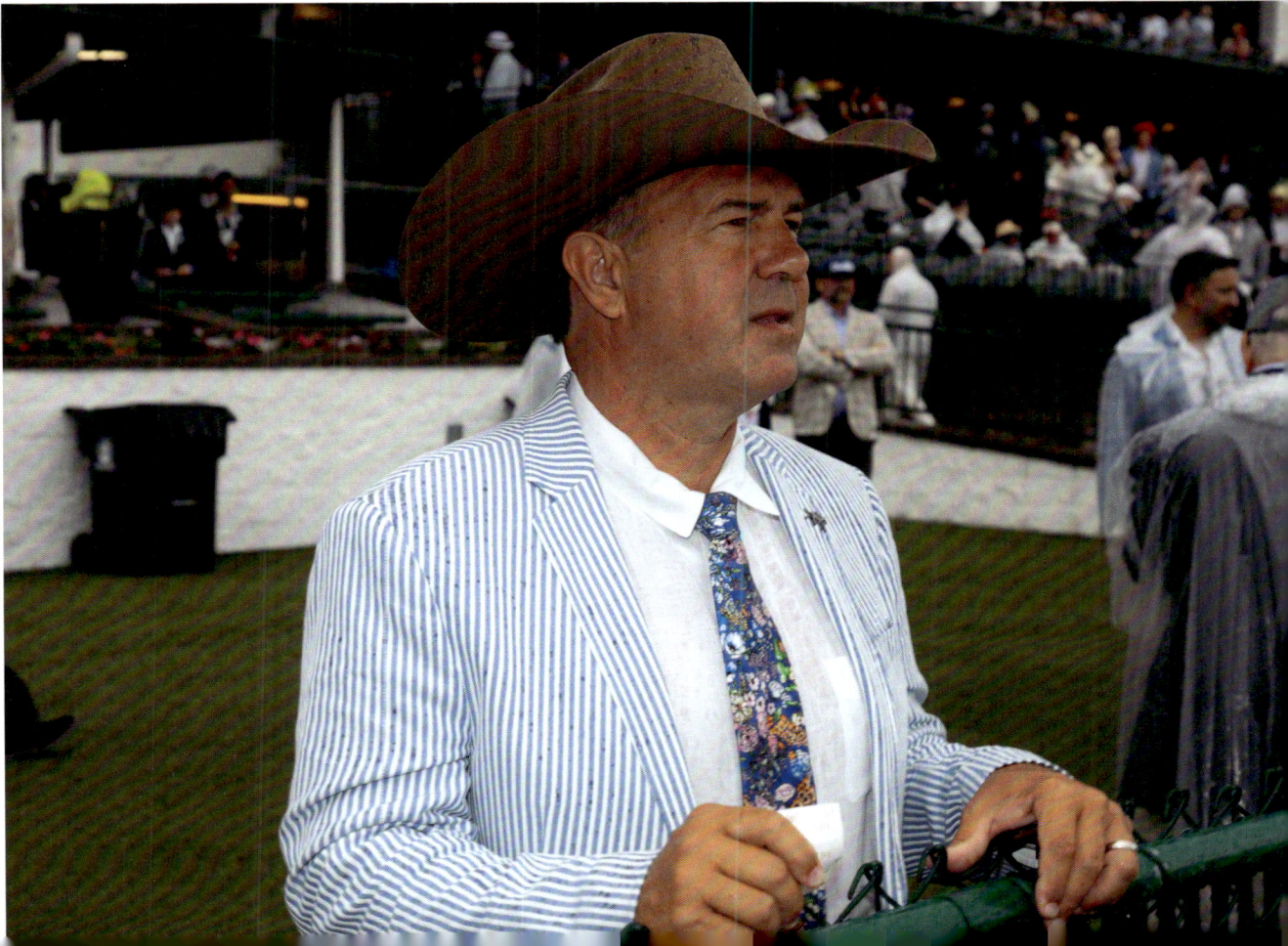

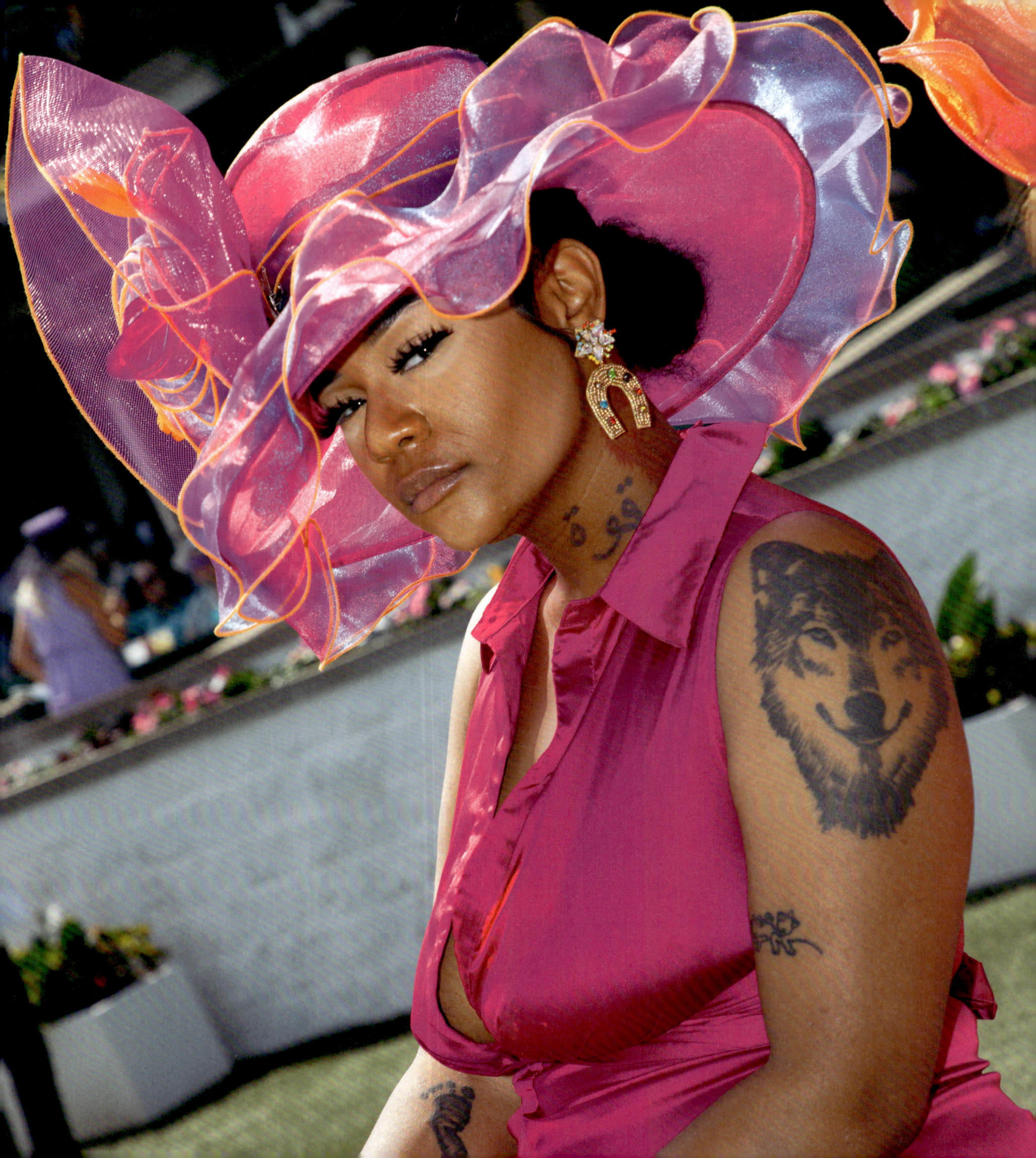

A Visual Celebration of Style and Narrative by Suzanne Shaheen

When I first began envisioning the types of work I wanted to publish as the photo director of *Vogue.com*, Lili Kobielski was one of the first photographers I knew we needed to work with. Her deep narrative quality, love for horses, and keen sense of style made her the perfect candidate to capture the essence of the Kentucky Derby. I knew that Lili's unique perspective would bring a fresh and dynamic energy to our coverage of this iconic event.

Her photographs go beyond mere visuals—they weave narratives that draw viewers into the scenes she captures. This narrative quality is particularly compelling when combined with her love for horses, a passion that resonates deeply with the spirit of the Kentucky Derby. The Derby is not just a horse race; it's a celebration of tradition, fashion, and the unpredictable excitement that defines the sport. Lili's ability to encapsulate these elements in her images made her an ideal choice for this assignment. She was able to capture the action on the track, the behind-the-scenes energy, and the outlandish style of the audience in the stands, all with the same narrative prowess.

The Kentucky Derby is renowned for its fashion as much as its racing. It's an event where the boundaries of style are pushed and individuality is celebrated. From the extravagant hats to the vibrant dresses, the Derby is a spectacle of sartorial expression. Lili's keen sense of style allows her to capture this celebration of fashion in a broad sense. She doesn't just focus on the expected; she seeks out the unique and the unconventional, highlighting the wackier and more celebratory side of fashion for which the Derby is famous.

Lili's work at the Kentucky Derby is a visual feast that encapsulates the whimsical and elegant spirit of the event. Her photographs are a blend of vibrant colors, dynamic compositions, and intimate moments that tell the story of the Derby from multiple perspectives. She captures the grandeur of the event, the excitement of the race, and the personal stories of the attendees. Each image is a testament to her ability to find beauty and meaning in the chaos and glamour of the Derby.

One of the most striking aspects of Lili's Derby photography is her attention to detail. Whether it's the intricate design of a hat, the spontaneous joy of a winning bet, or the quiet moments of reflection of the jockeys between races, Lili's images are rich with details that convey the full experience of the Derby. This attention to detail is what makes her work stand out; it's what makes viewers feel like they are a part of the event, experiencing the thrill and elegance firsthand.

Having worked on three Kentucky Derbies together, I have seen Lili's work evolve and grow with each year. A sense of discovery marked her first year at the Derby—she captured the grandeur of the event with a fresh perspective, bringing new angles and insights to our coverage. Her second year showed a deeper understanding of the Derby's unique culture; she began to explore the stories behind the fashion, delving into the motivations and inspirations of the attendees.

By the third year, Lili had truly found her stride. Her work had become more nuanced, capturing not just the surface glamour but also the underlying emotions and stories that make the Derby so special. She began experimenting with new techniques, playing with light and shadow, and using her camera to explore the contrasts and contradictions that define the Derby. The result was a body of work that is both visually stunning and emotionally resonant.

Lili Kobielski's work at the Kentucky Derby is a testament to her exceptional talent and unique vision. Her deep narrative quality, love for horses, and keen sense of style make her the perfect photographer to capture the spirit, and, over the past decade, she has created a body of work that celebrates its whimsy, elegance, and individuality. Her photographs are more than just images; they are stories that bring the Kentucky Derby to life for viewers, making them feel a part of this extraordinary event. As we look to the future, I am incredibly excited to see where Lili's work will go next.

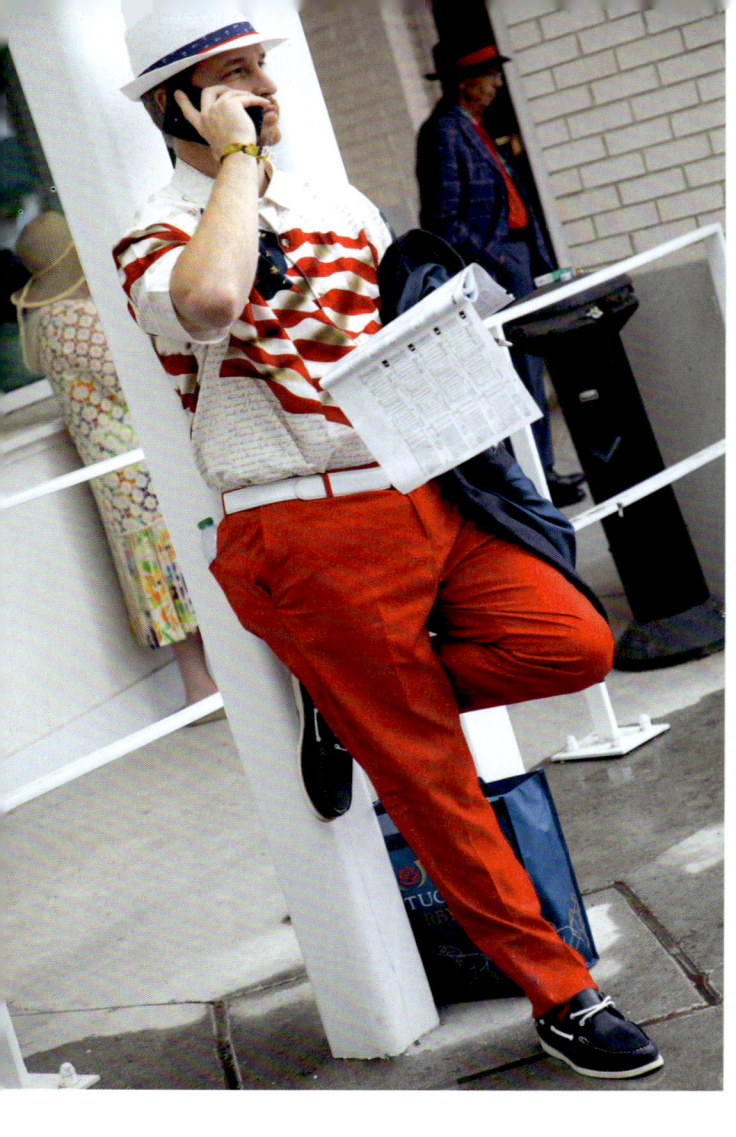
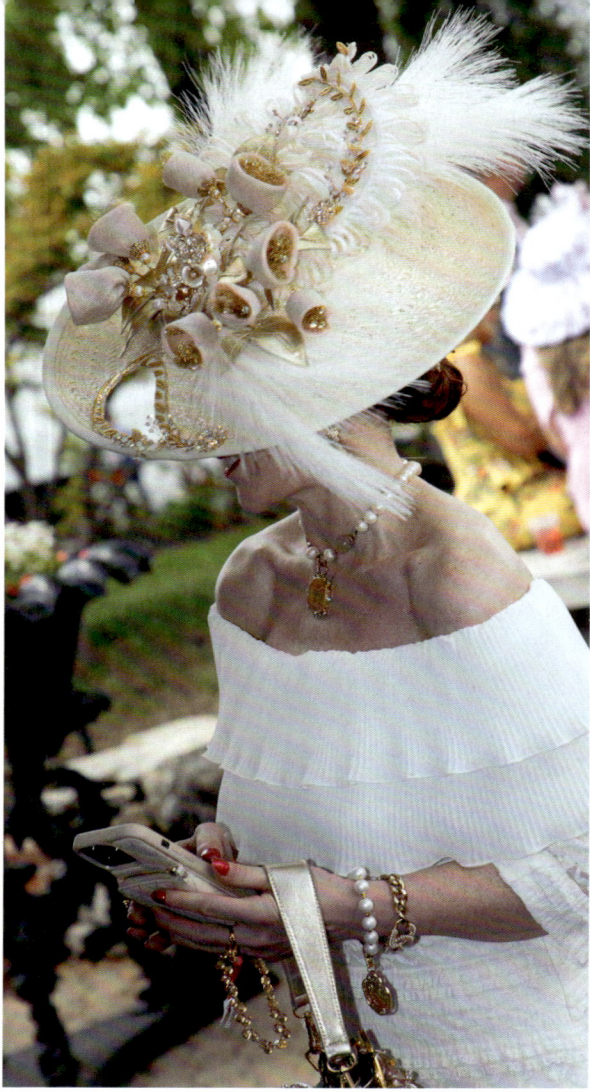
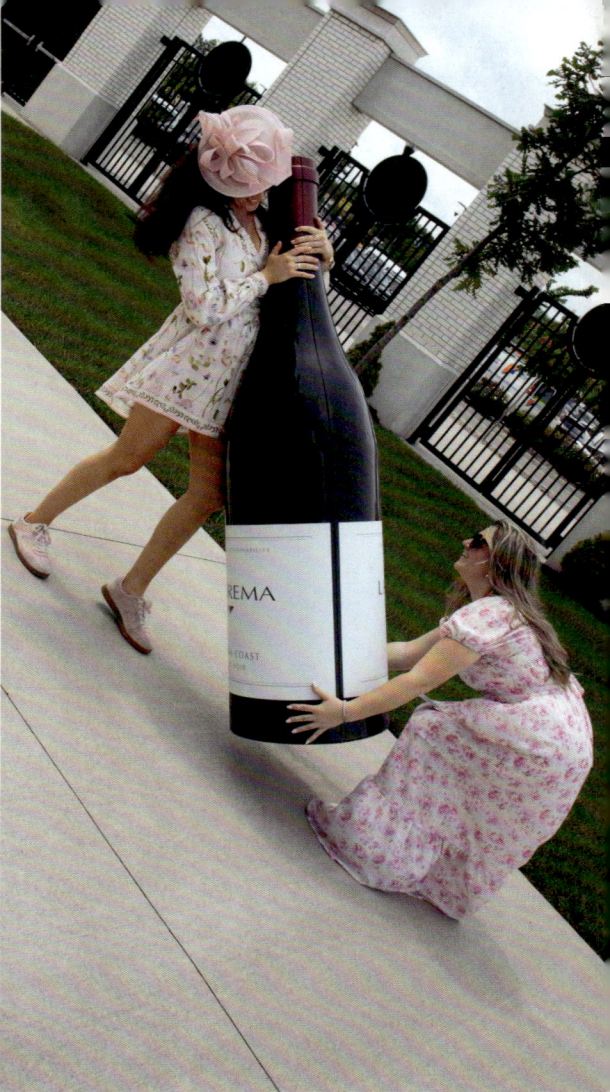

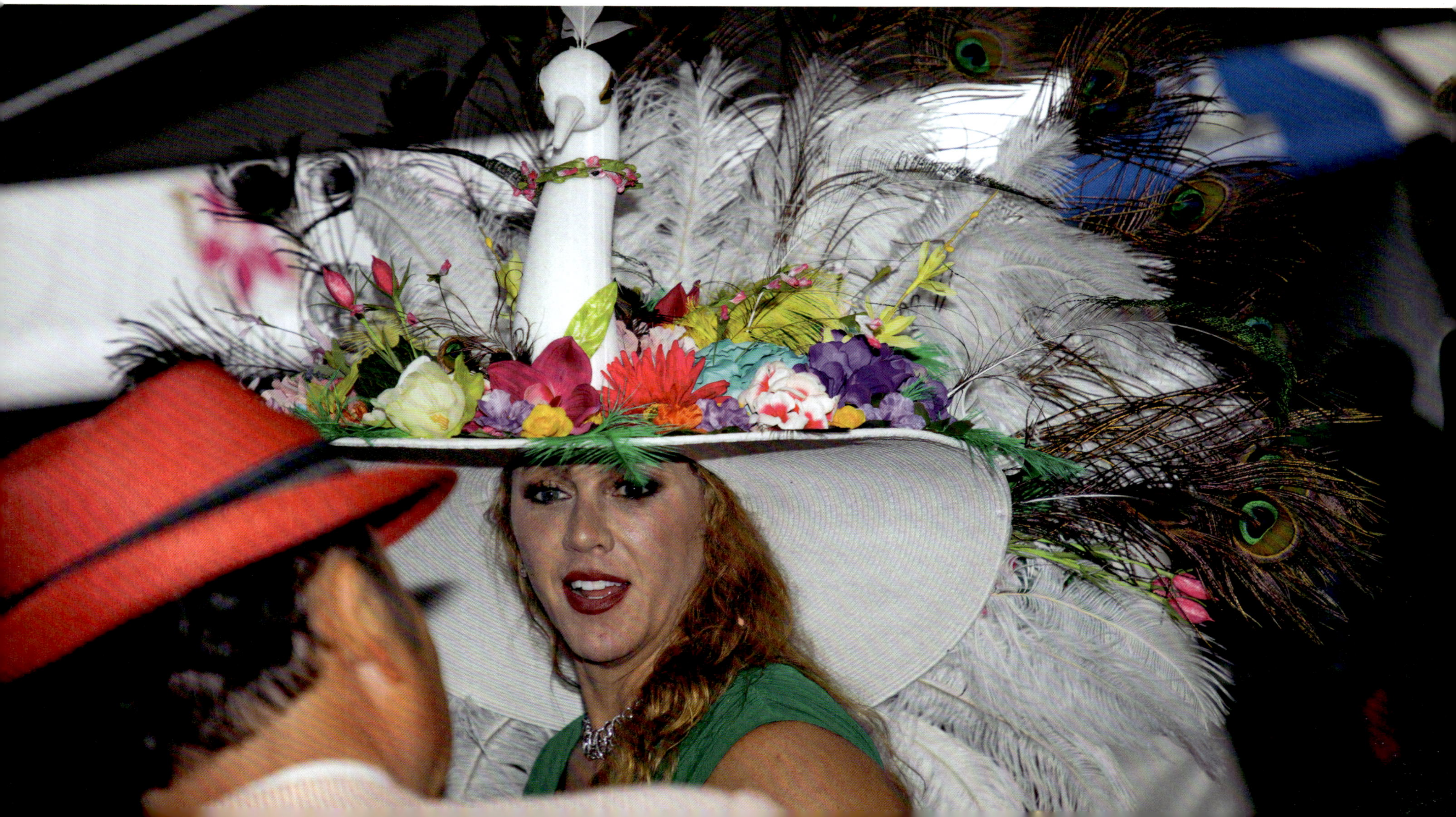

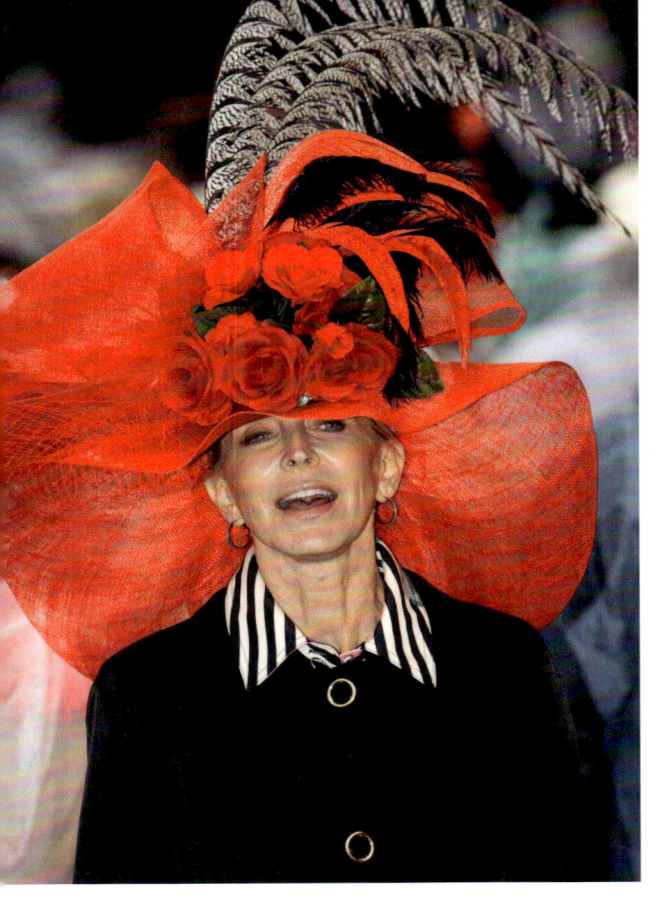

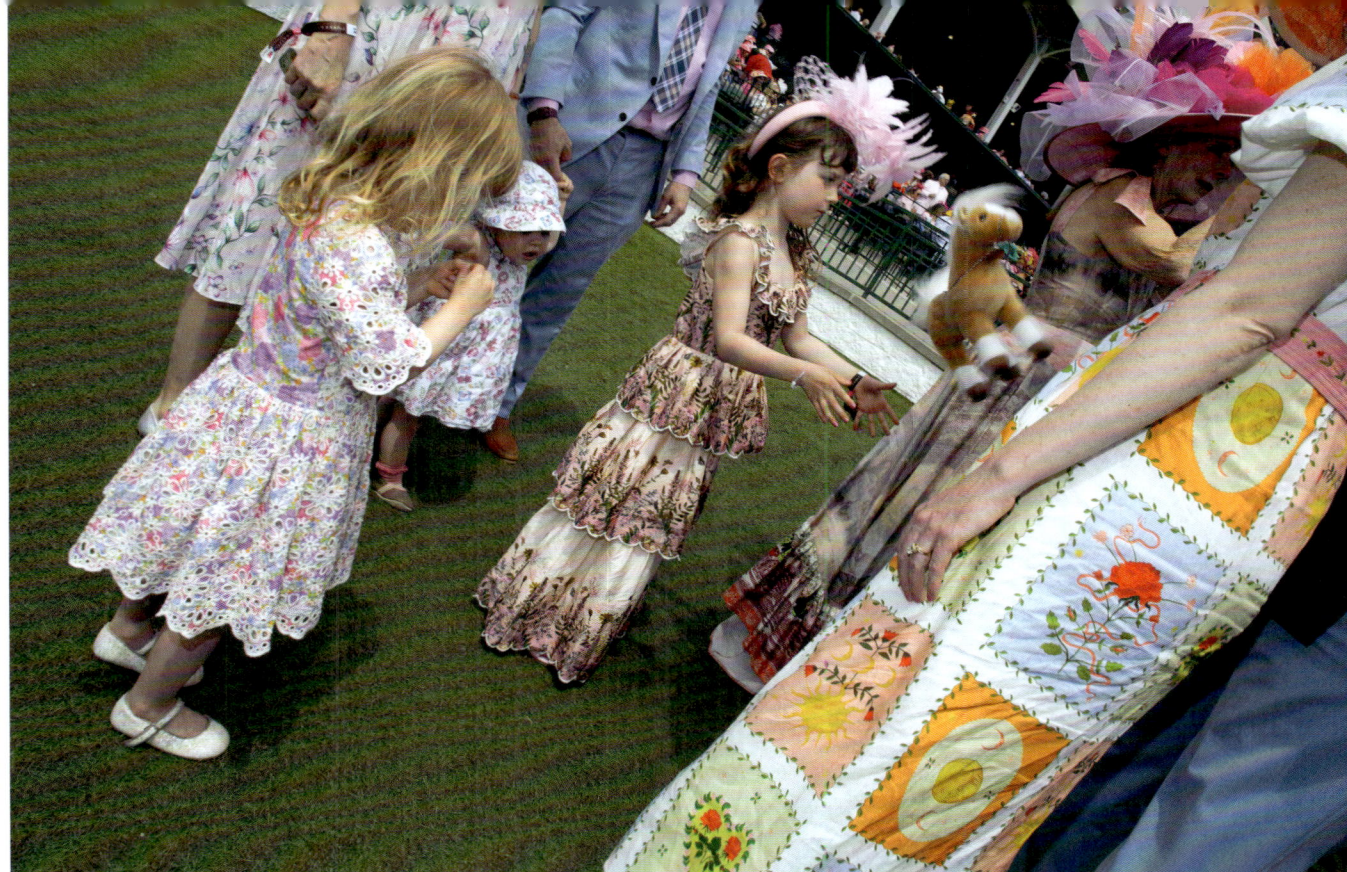

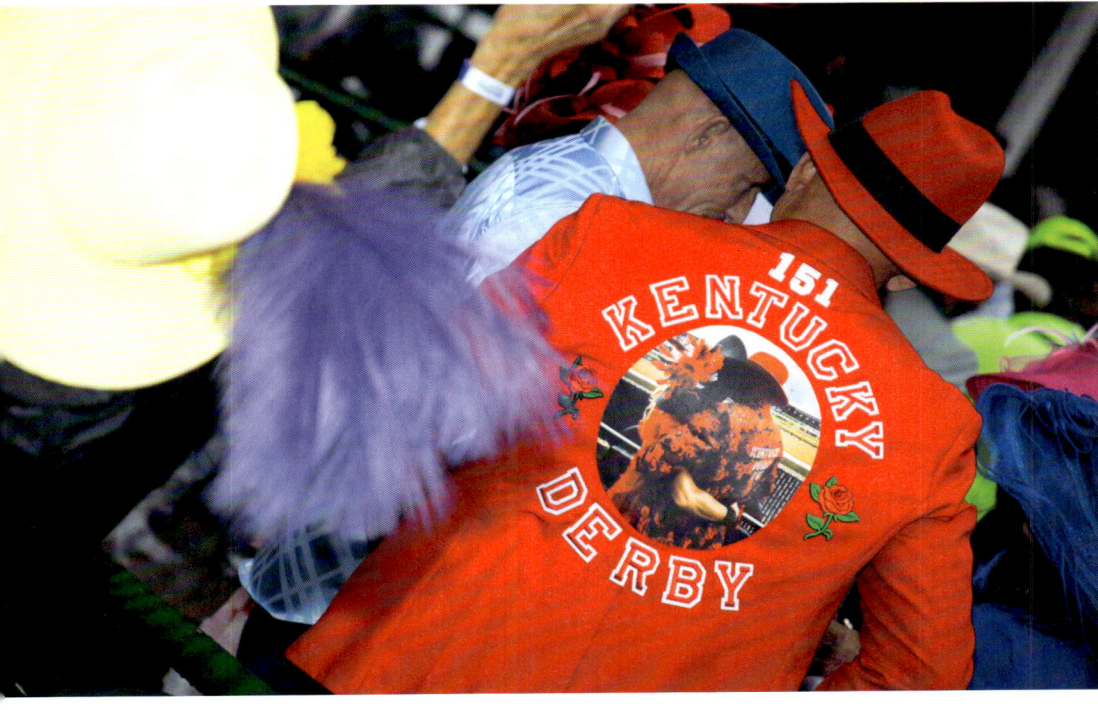

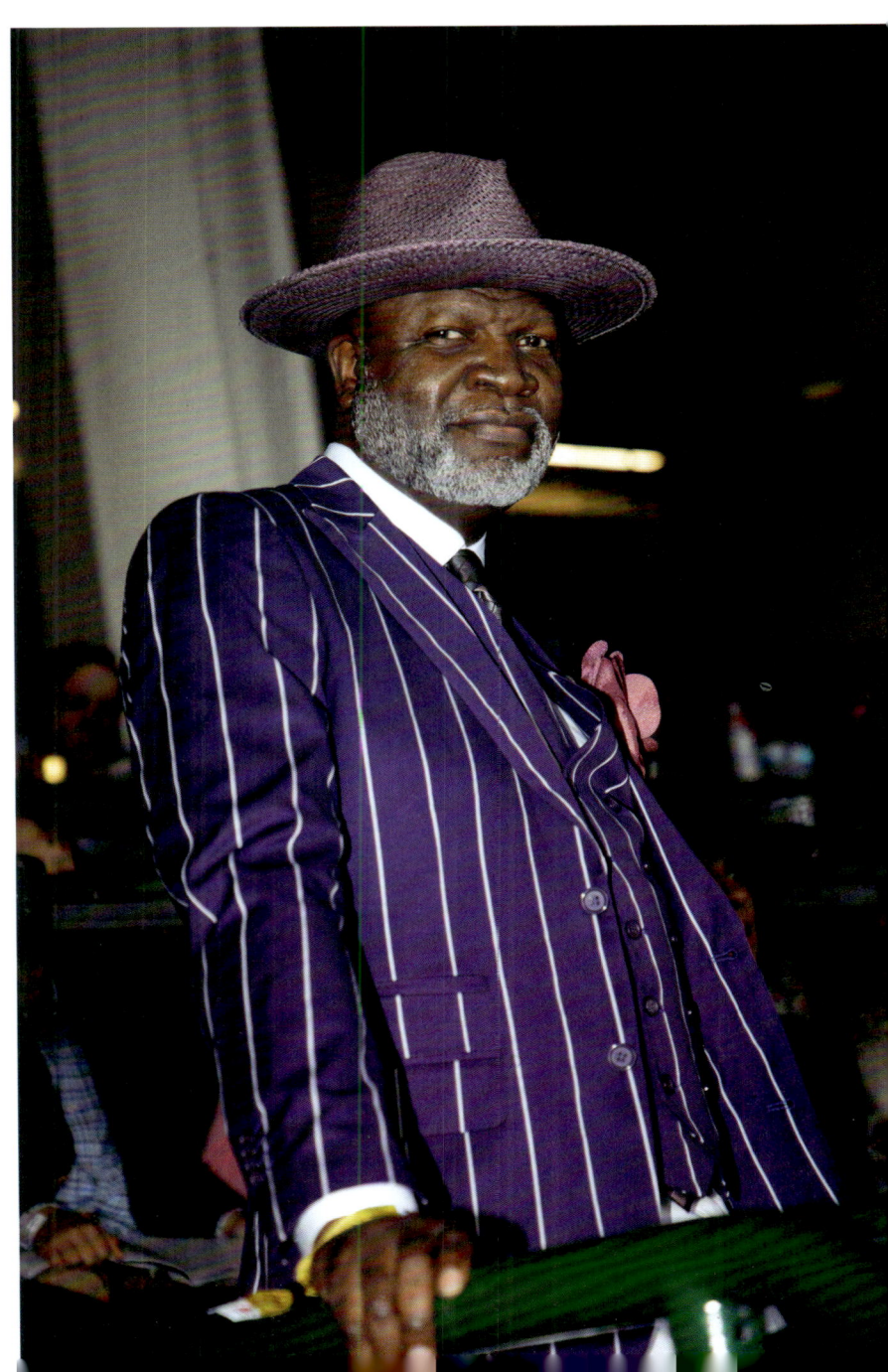

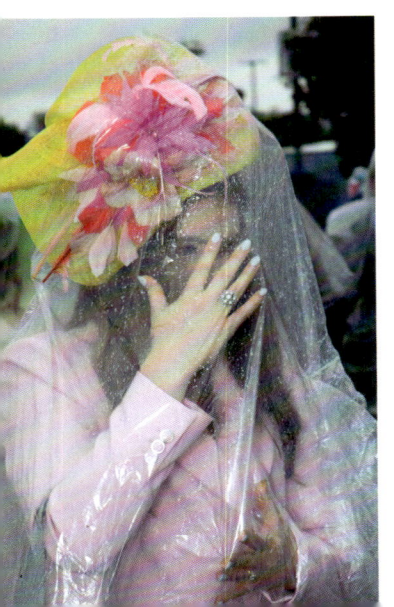

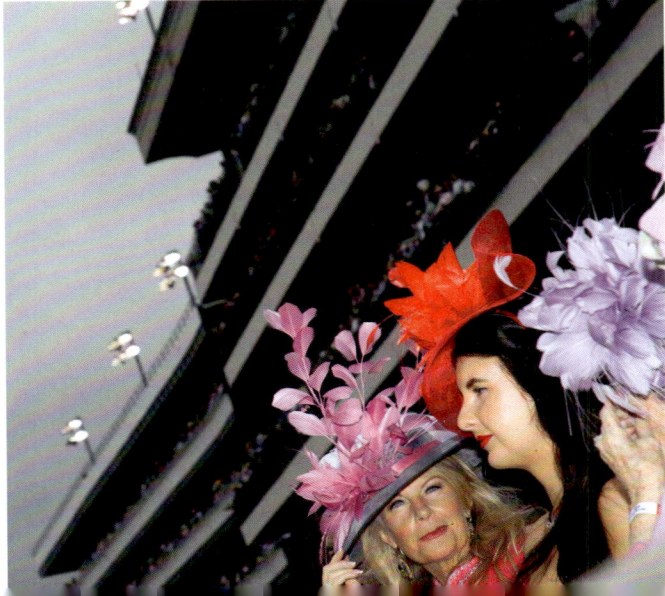

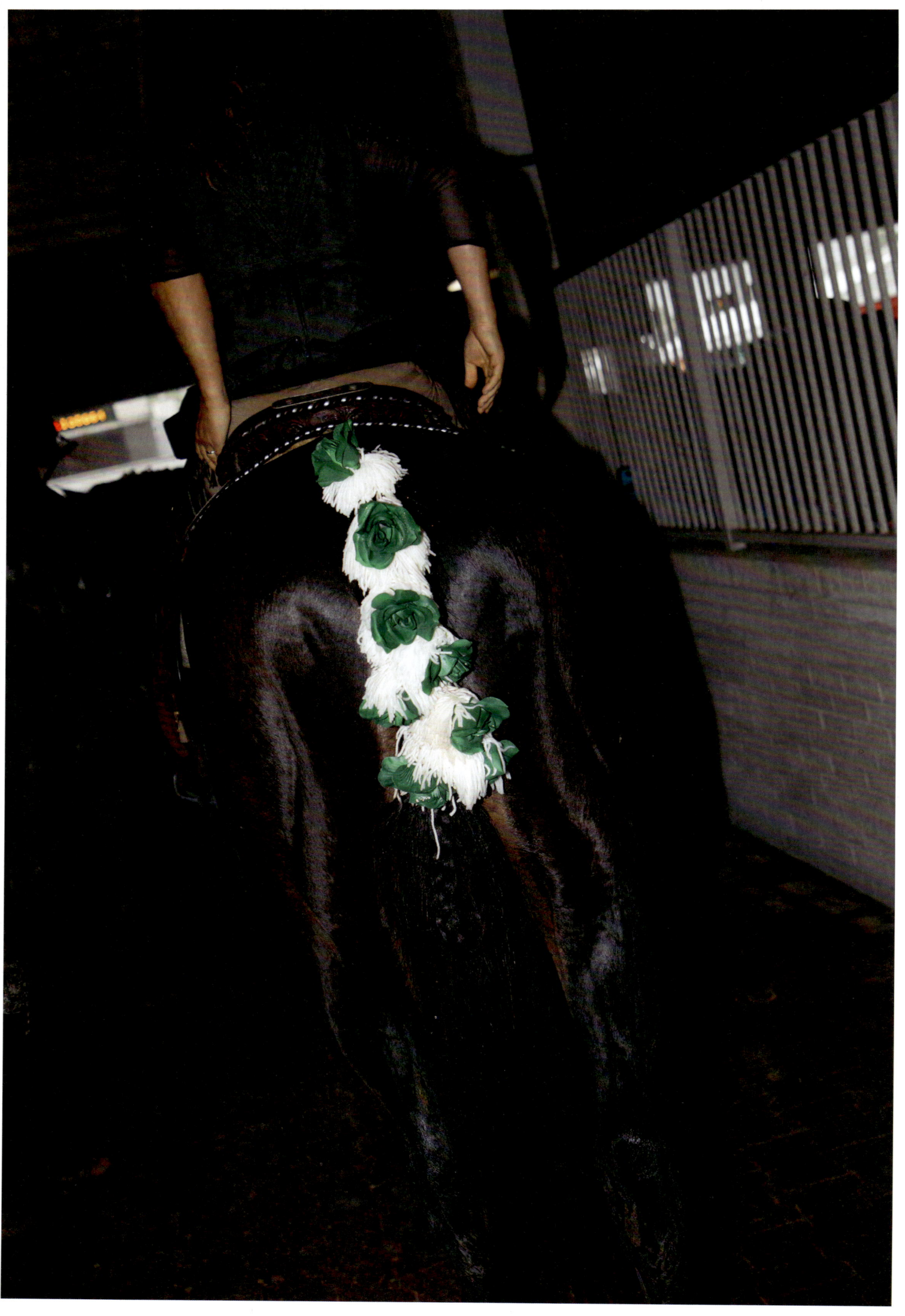

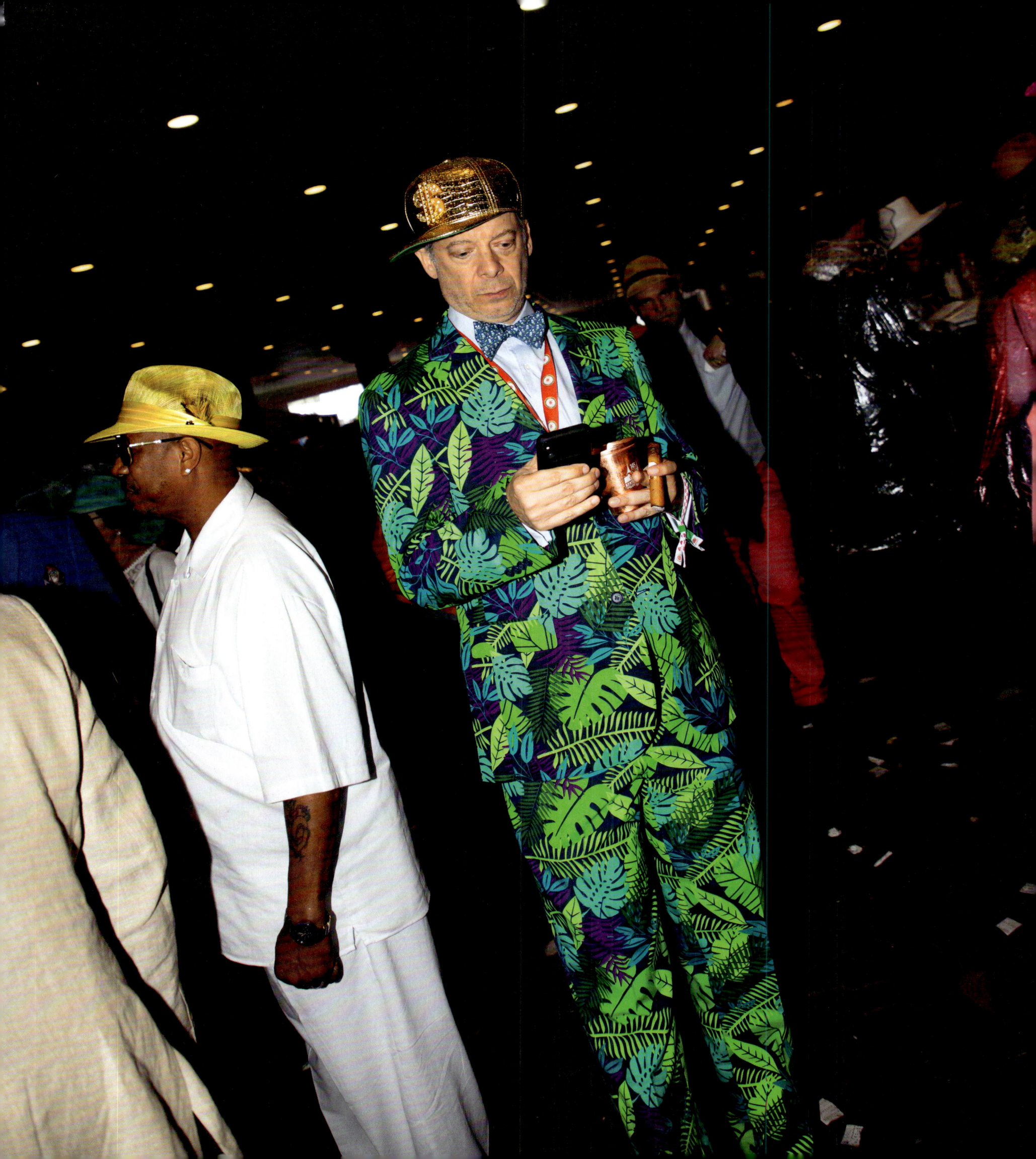

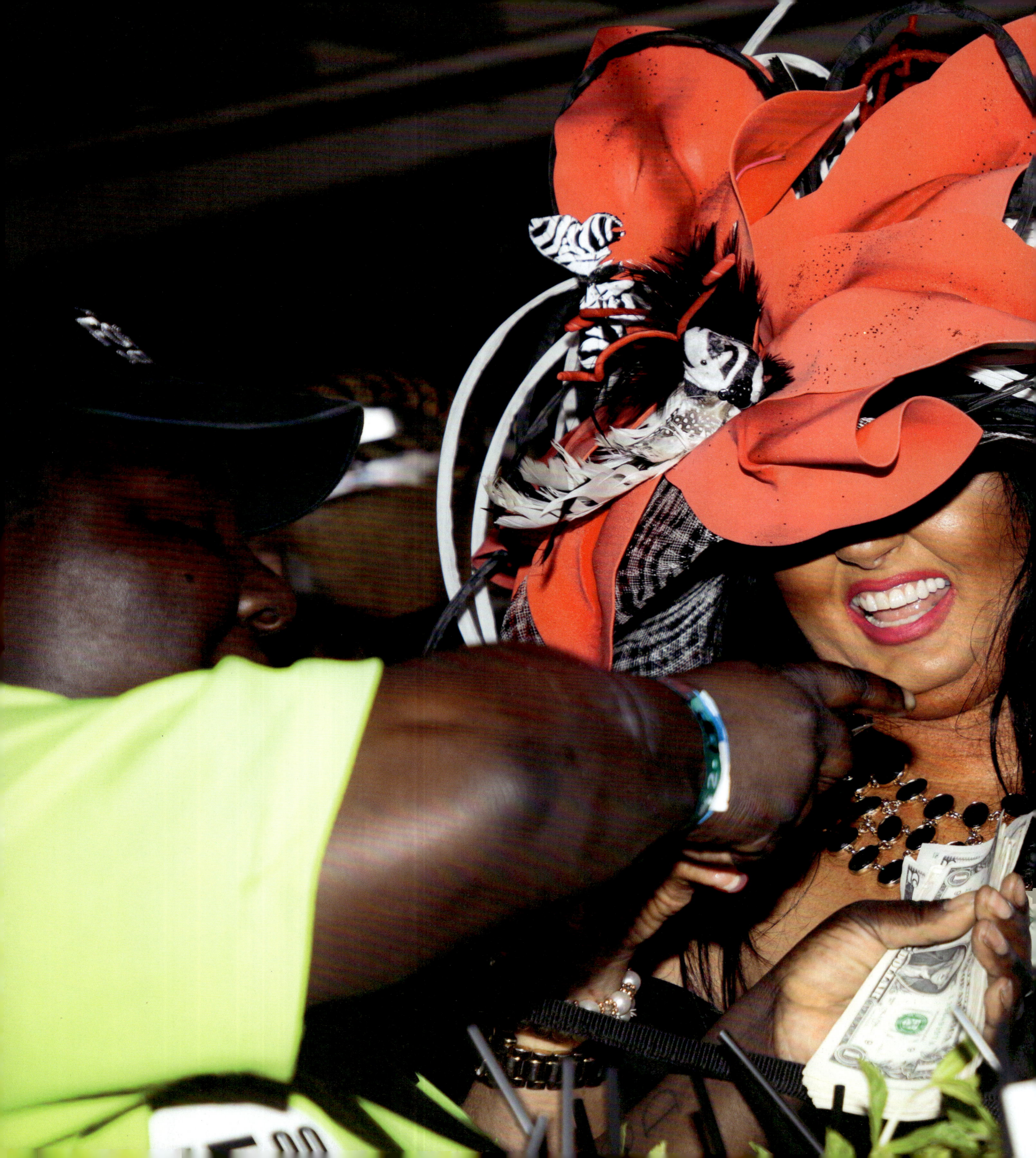

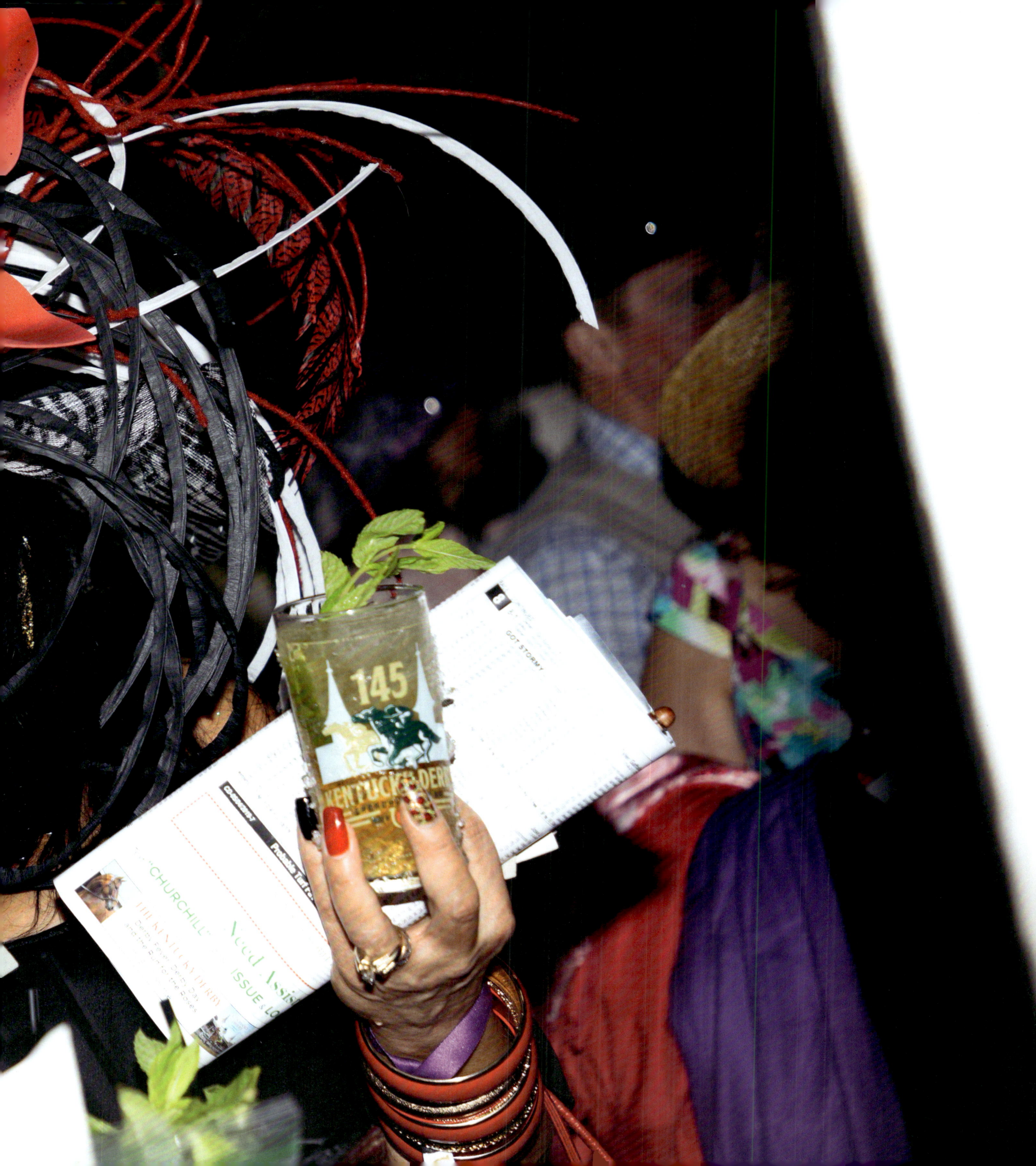

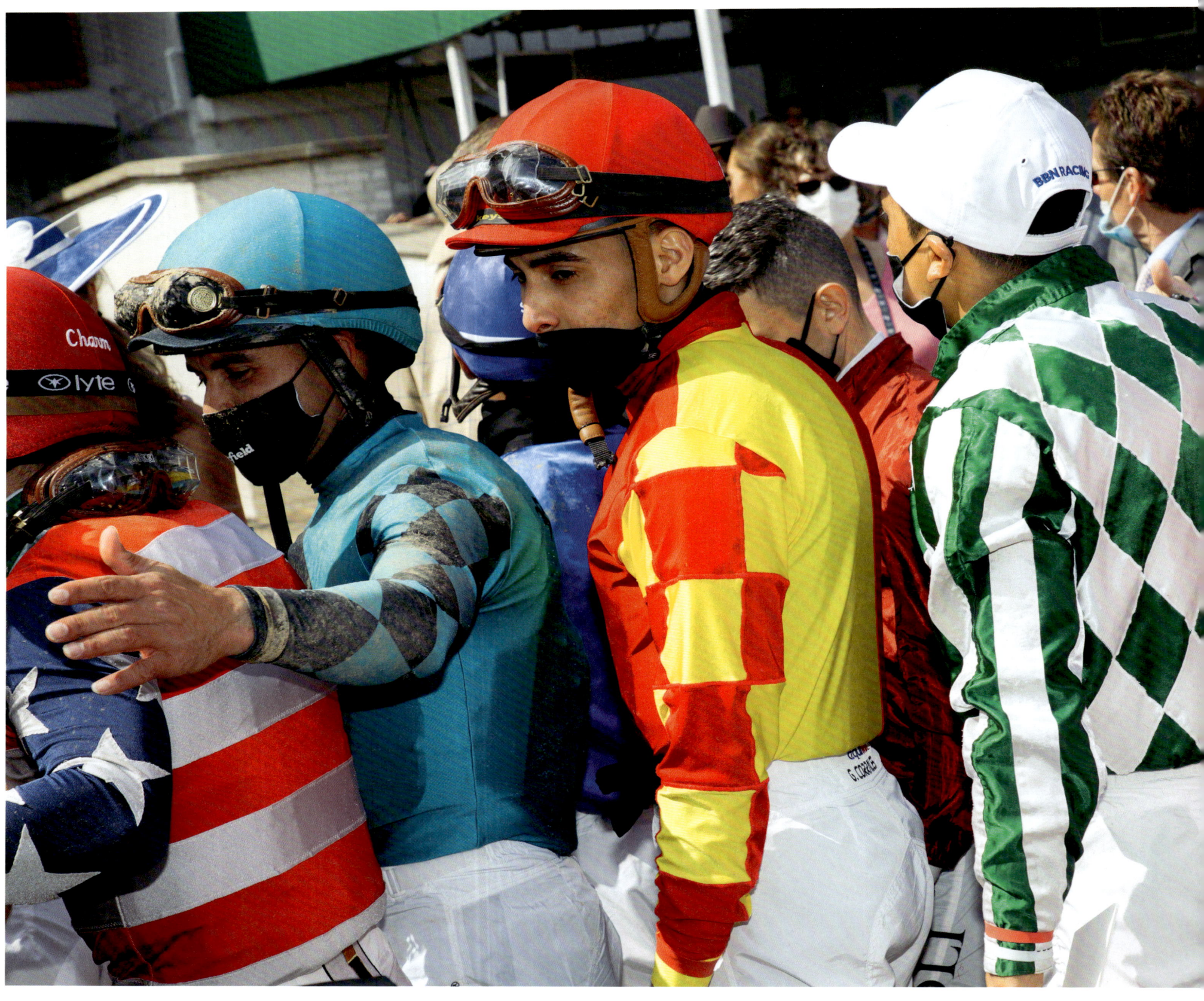

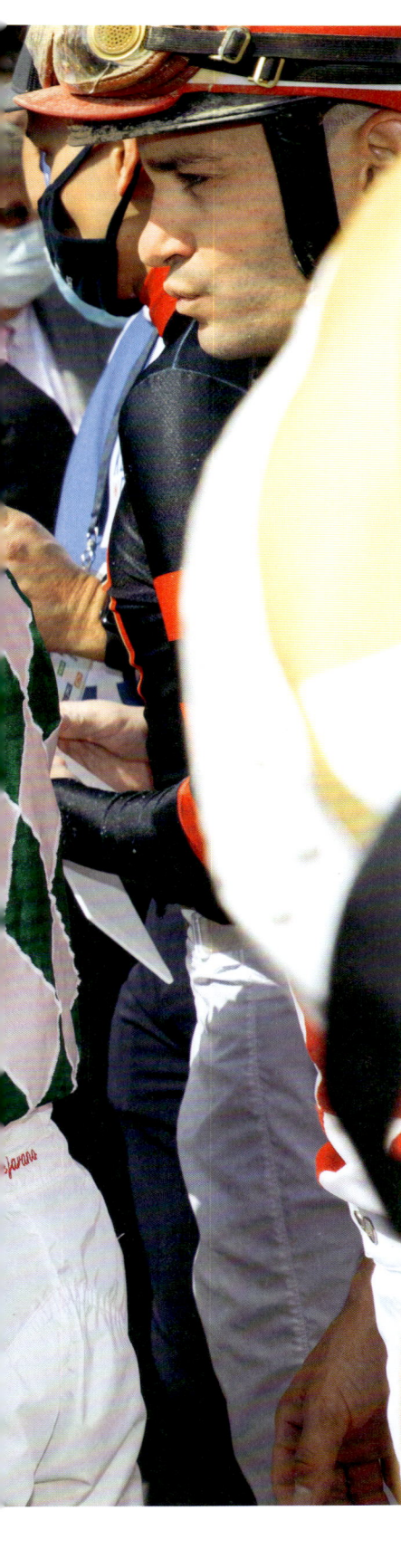

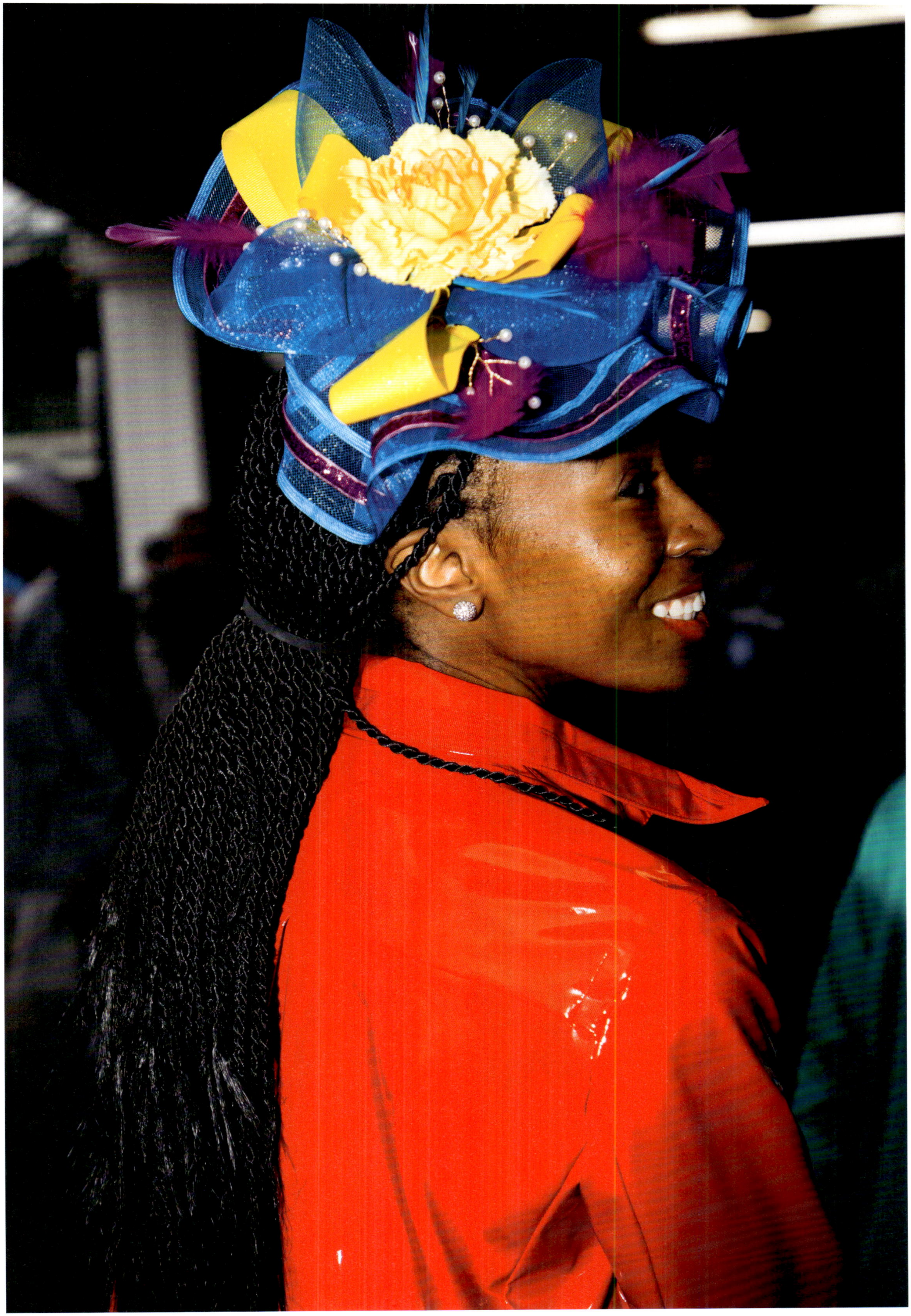

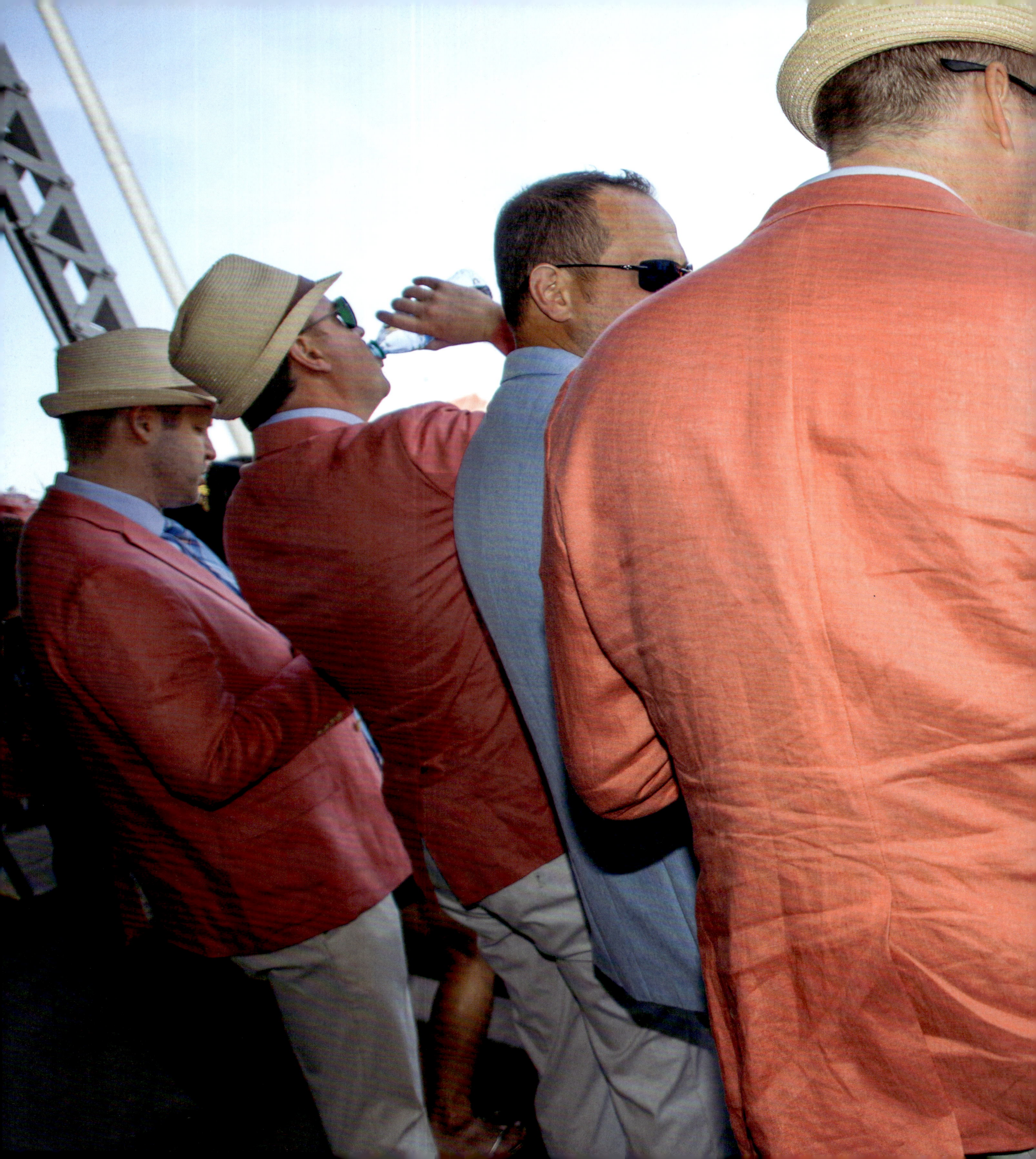

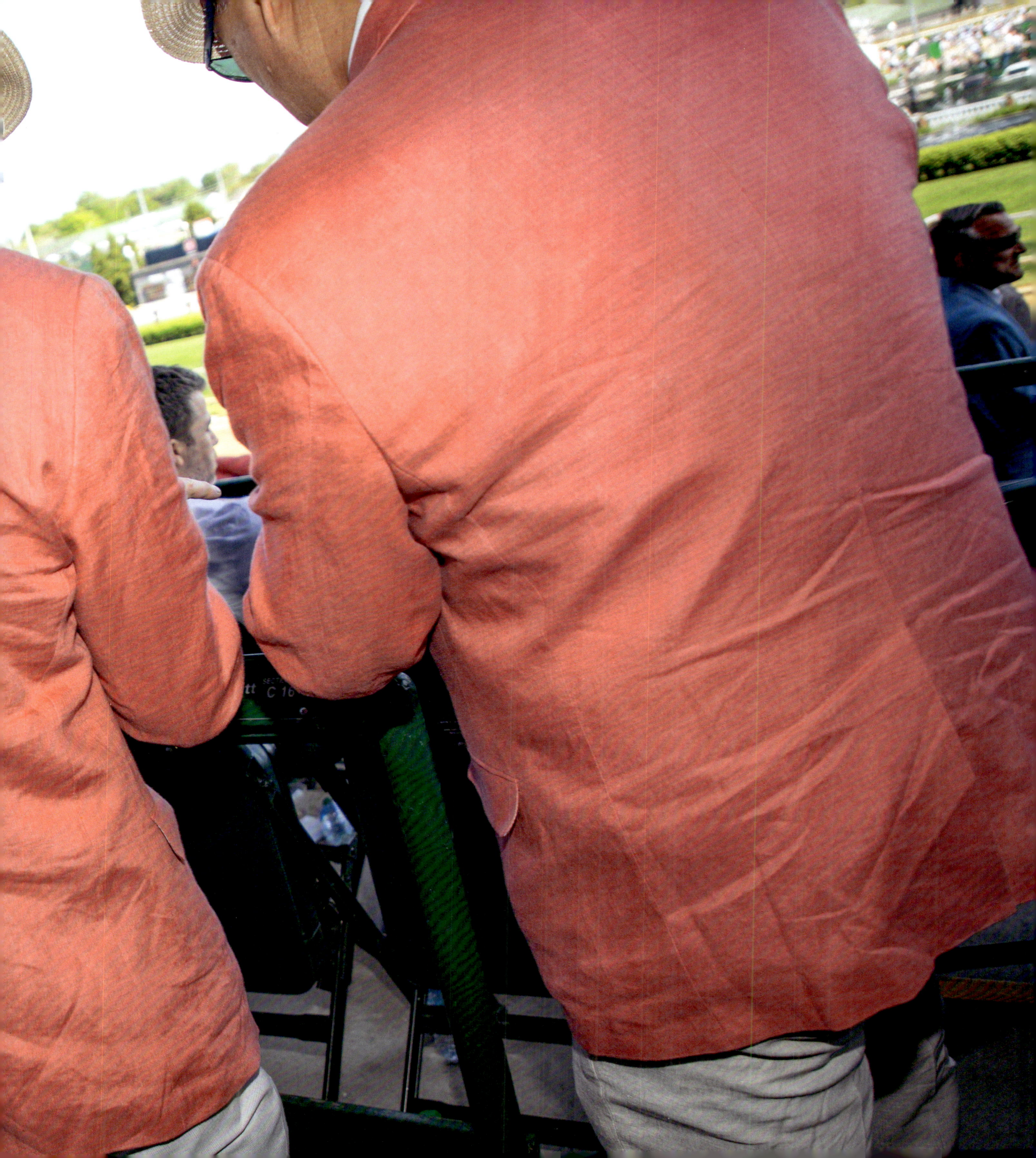

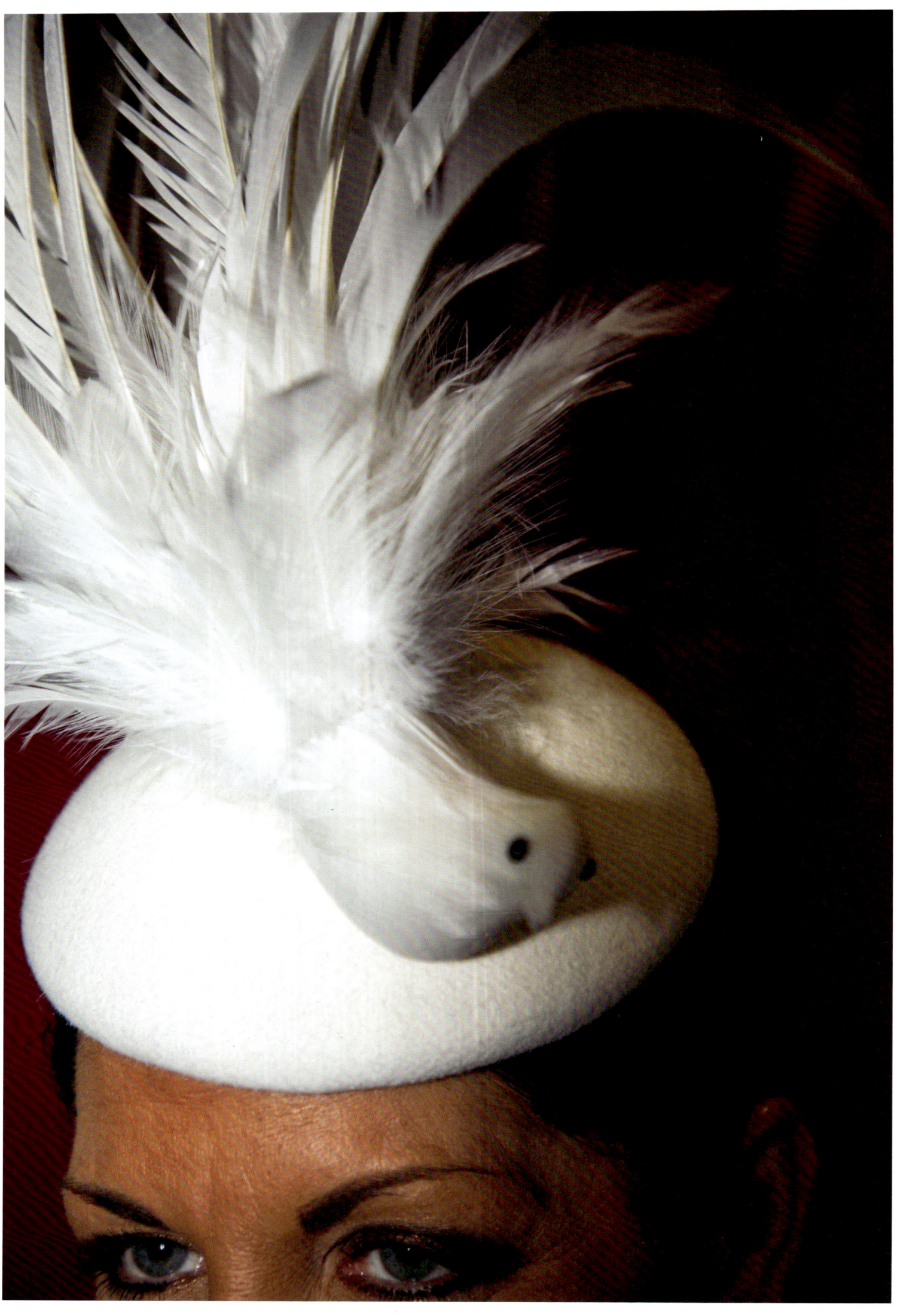

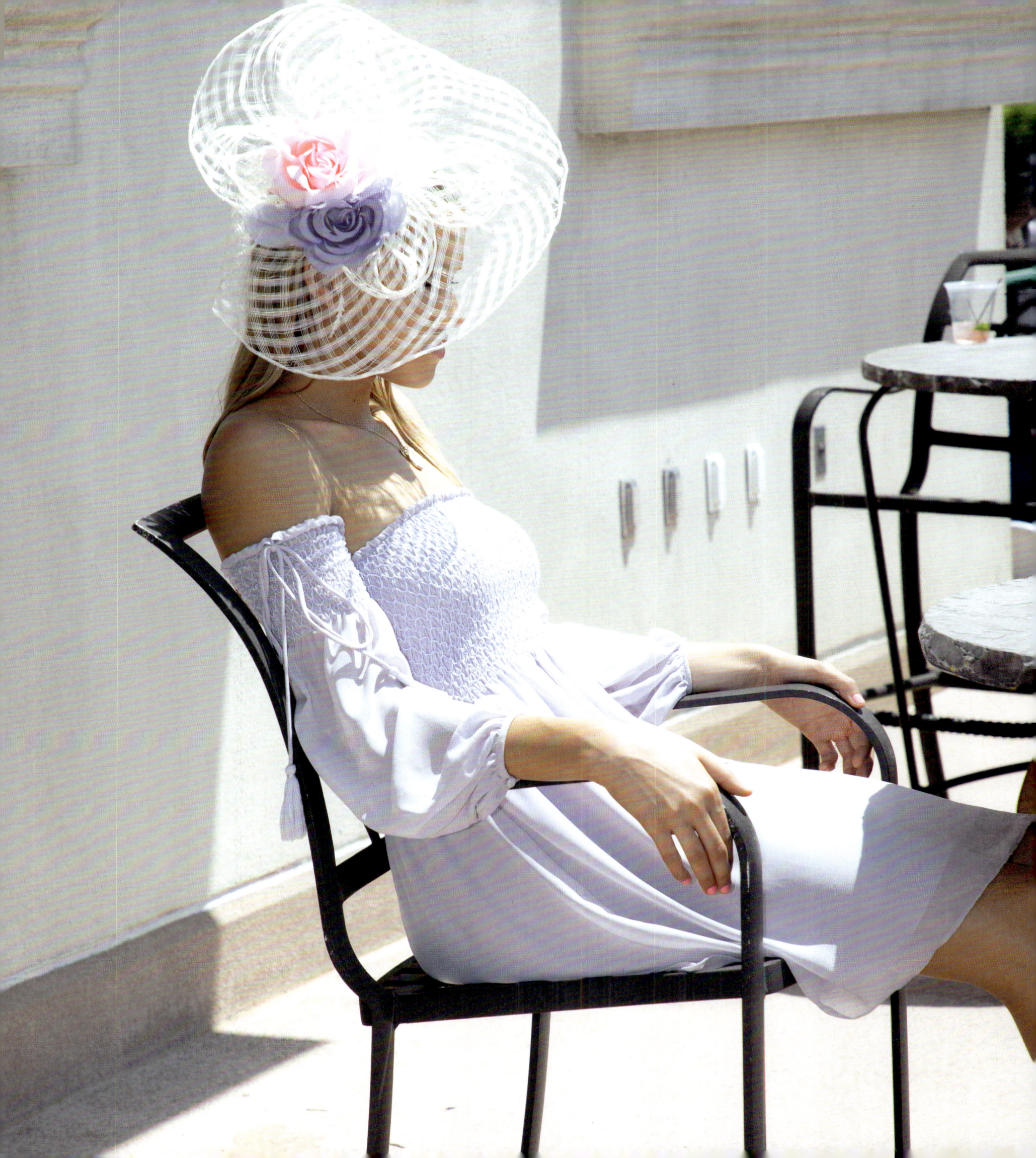

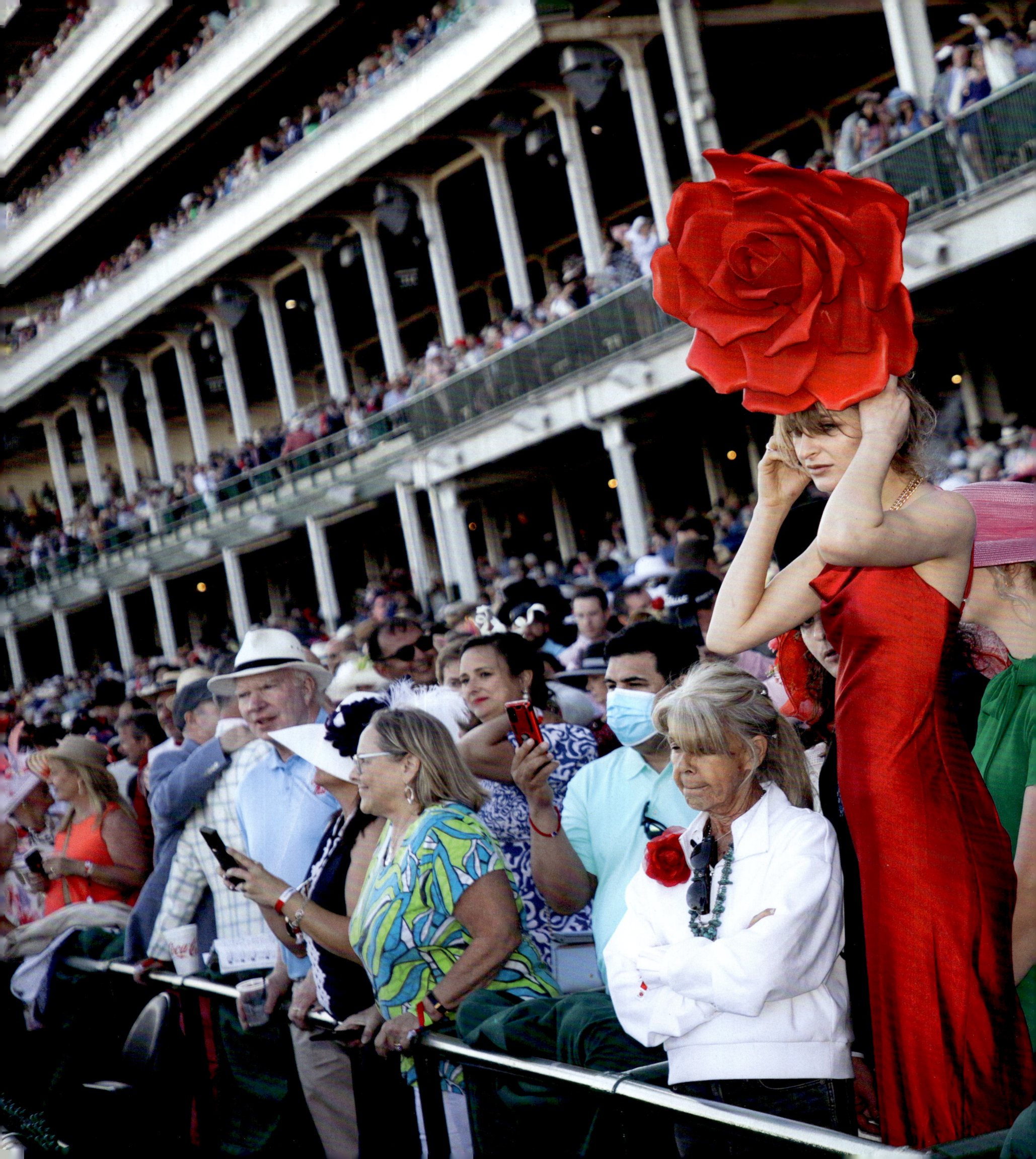

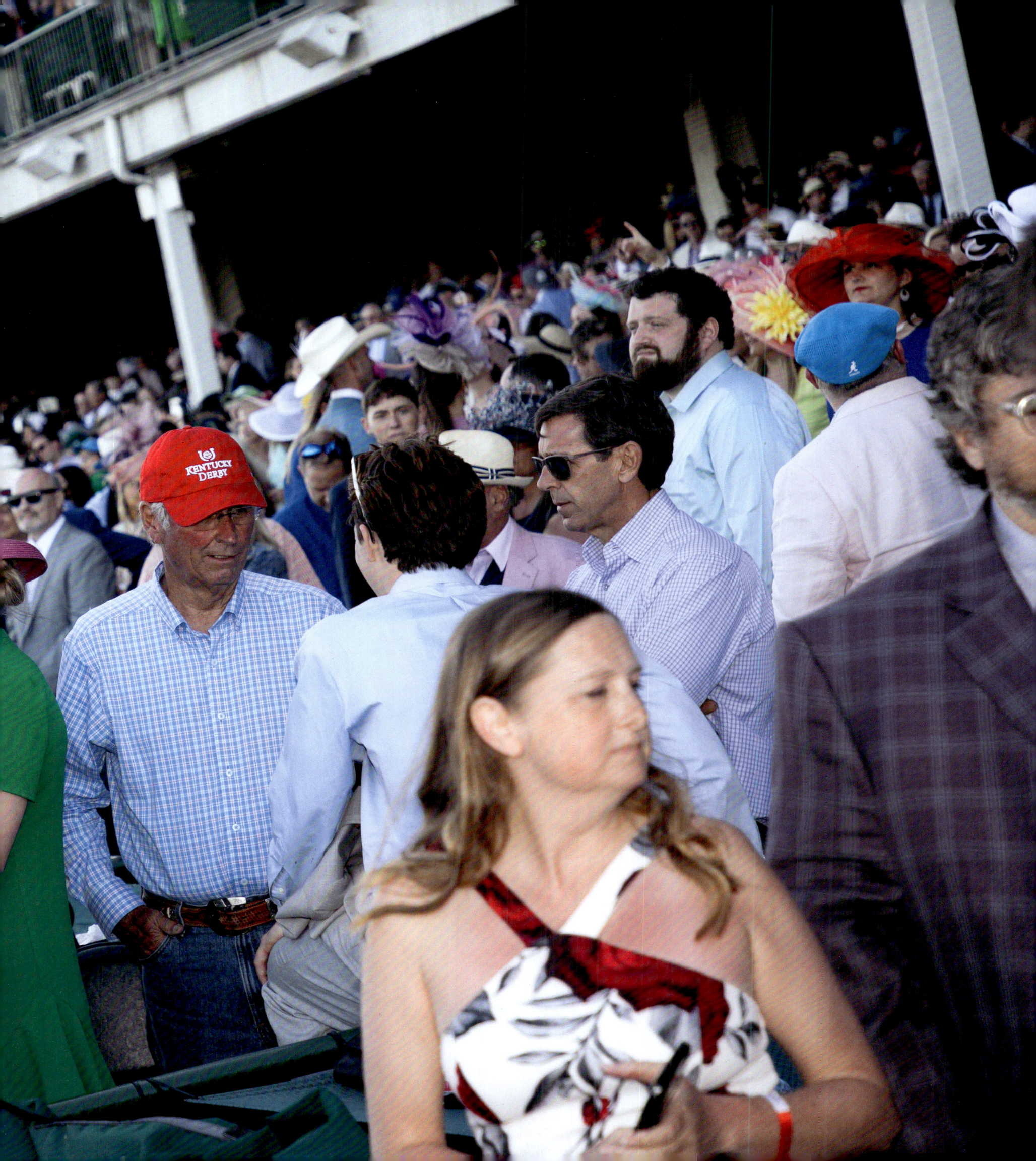

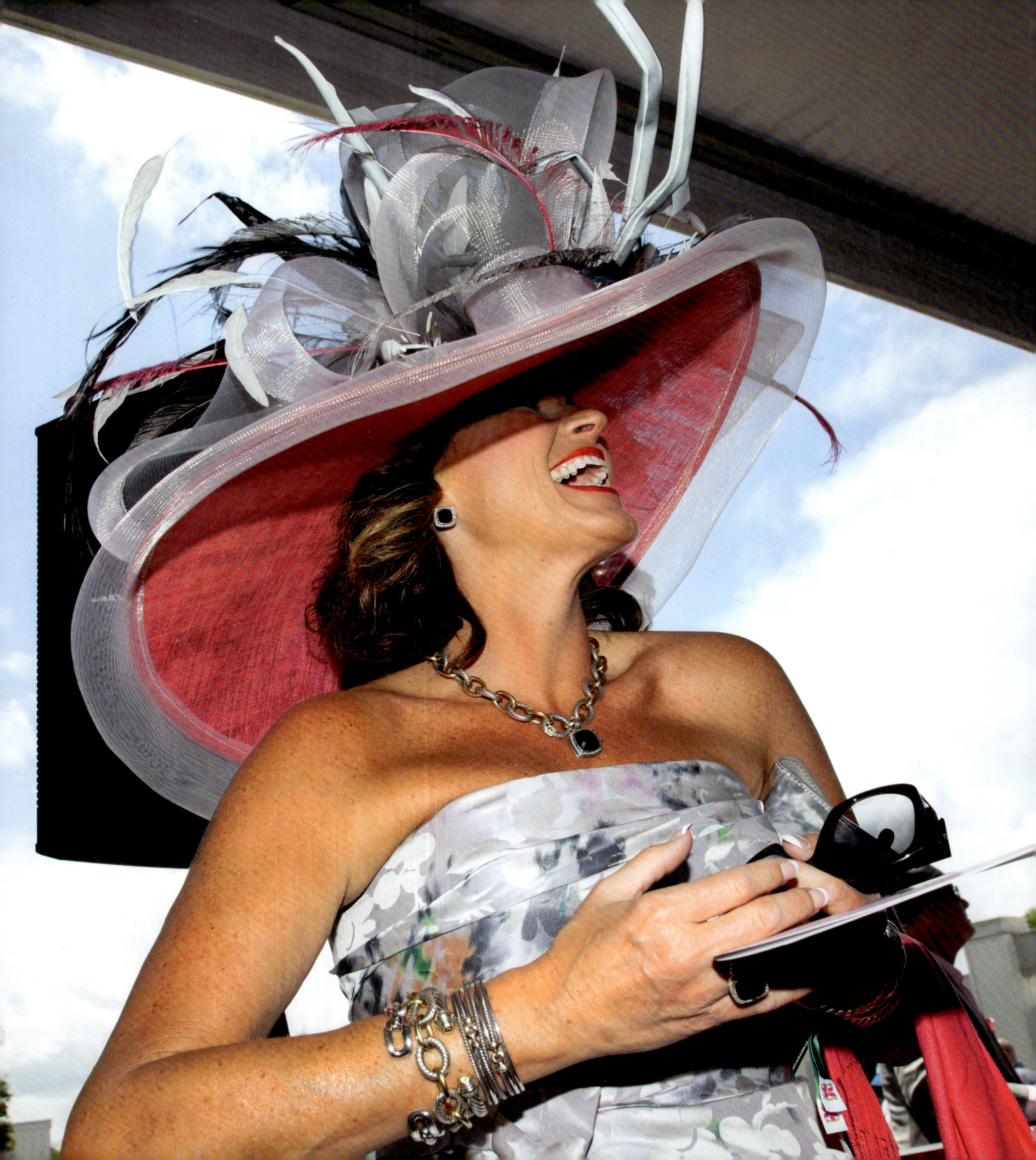

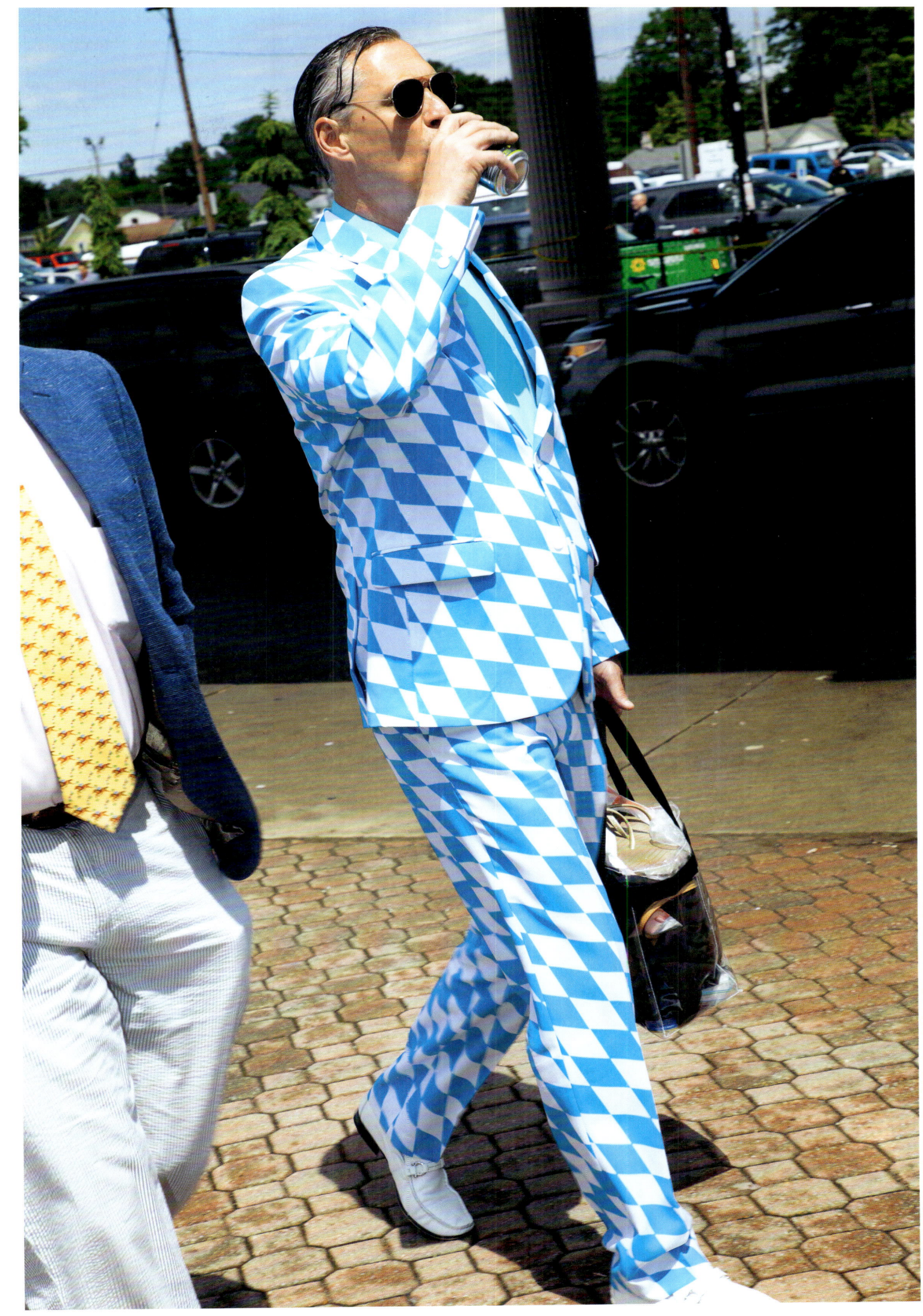

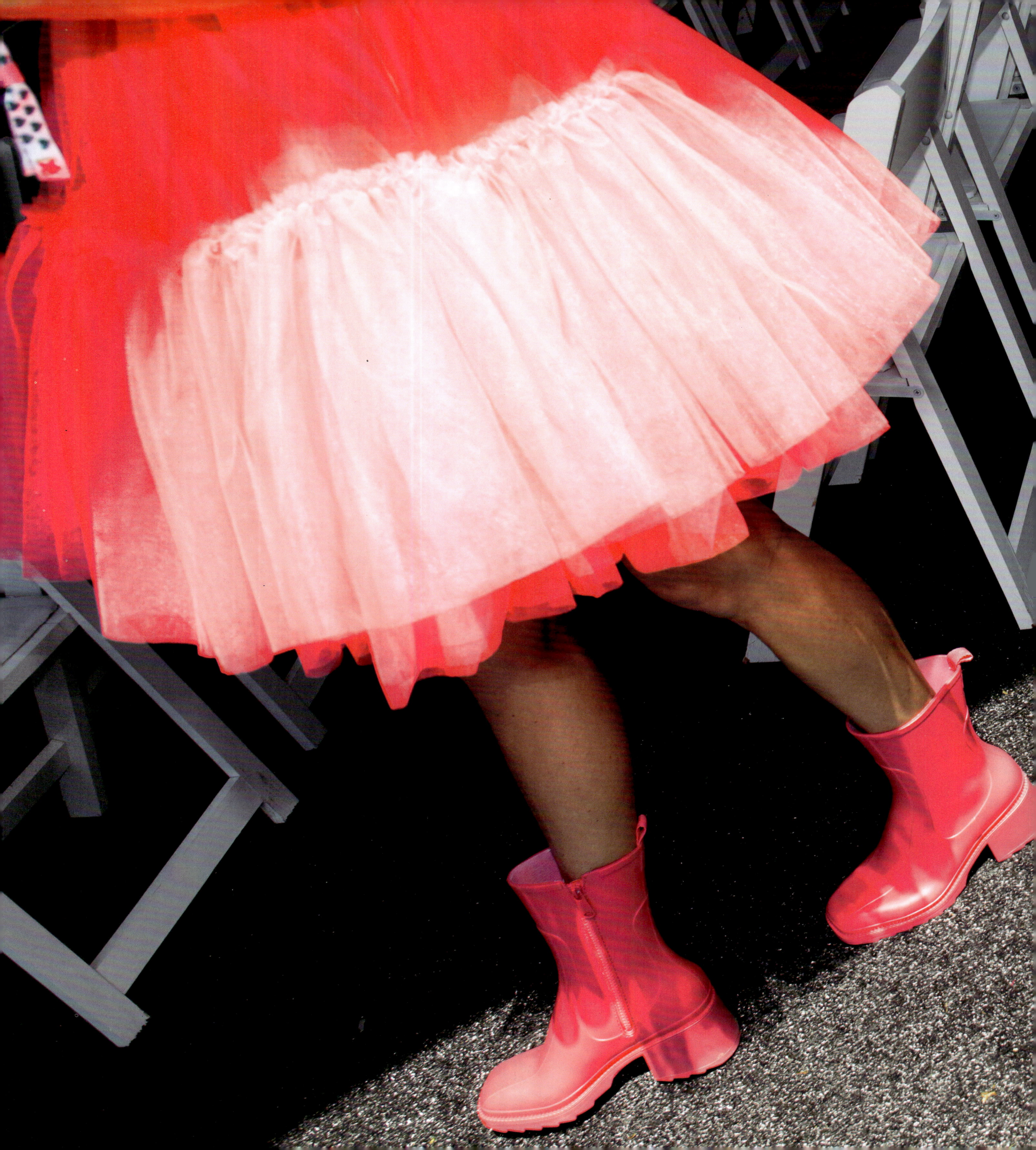

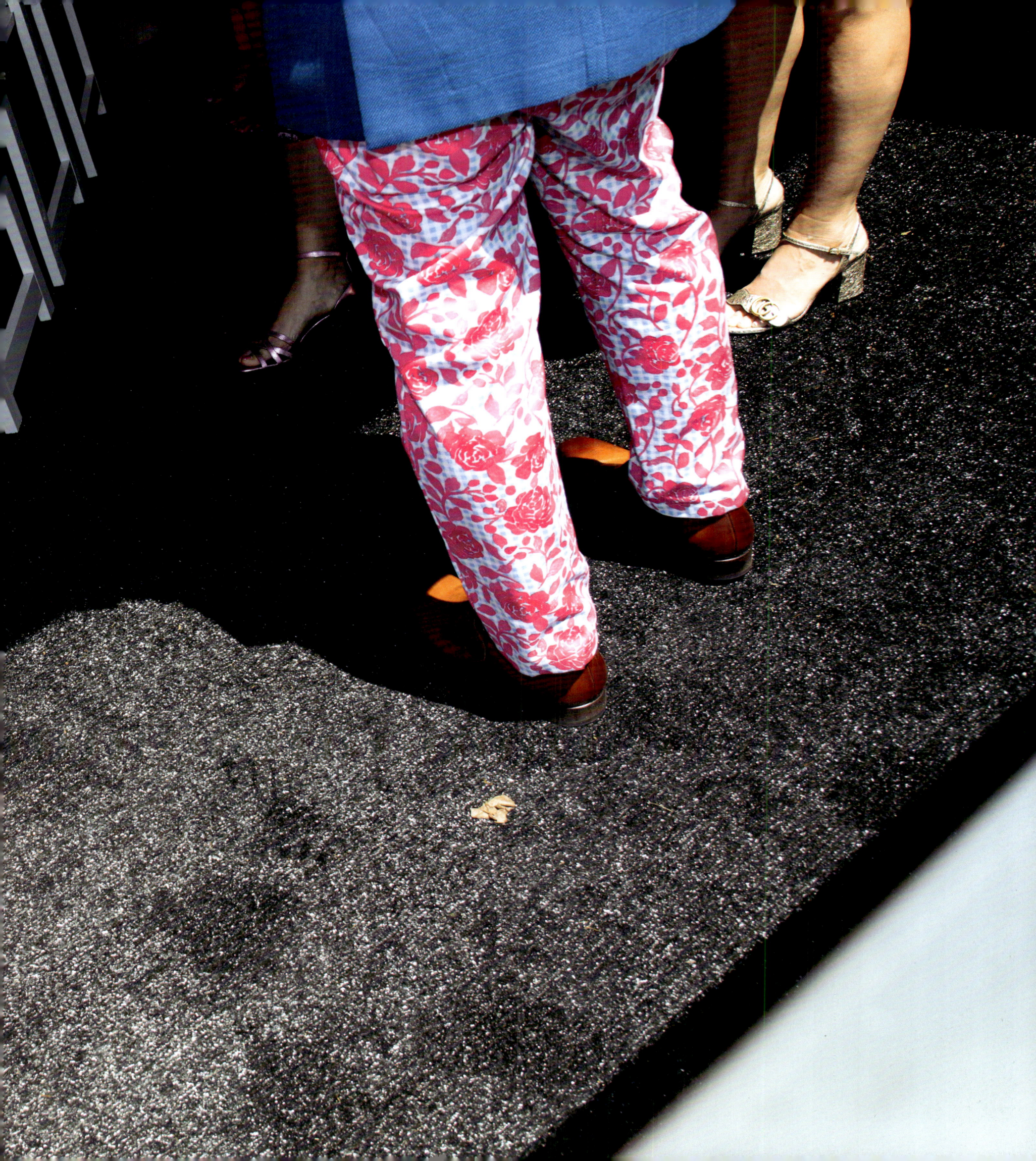

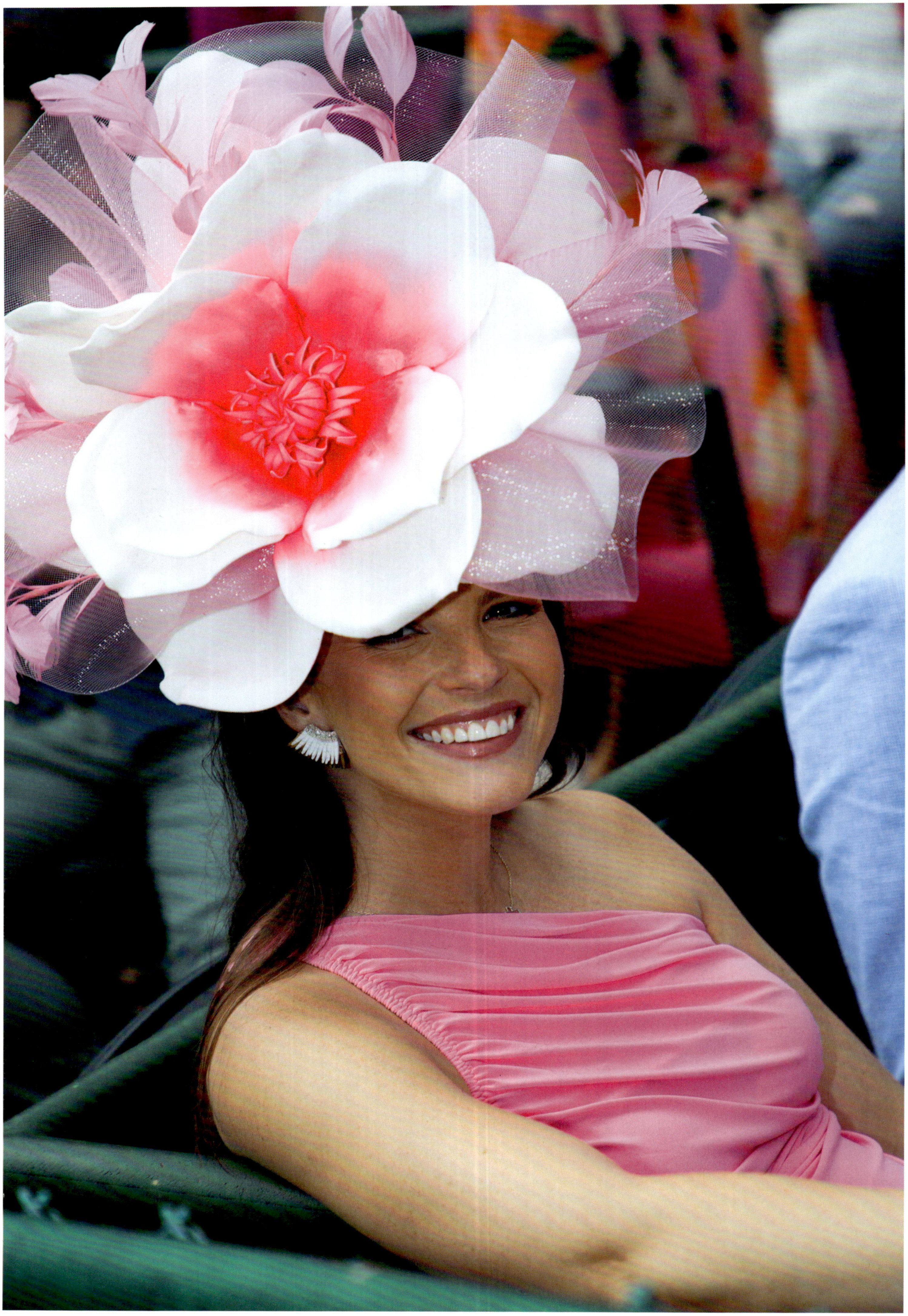

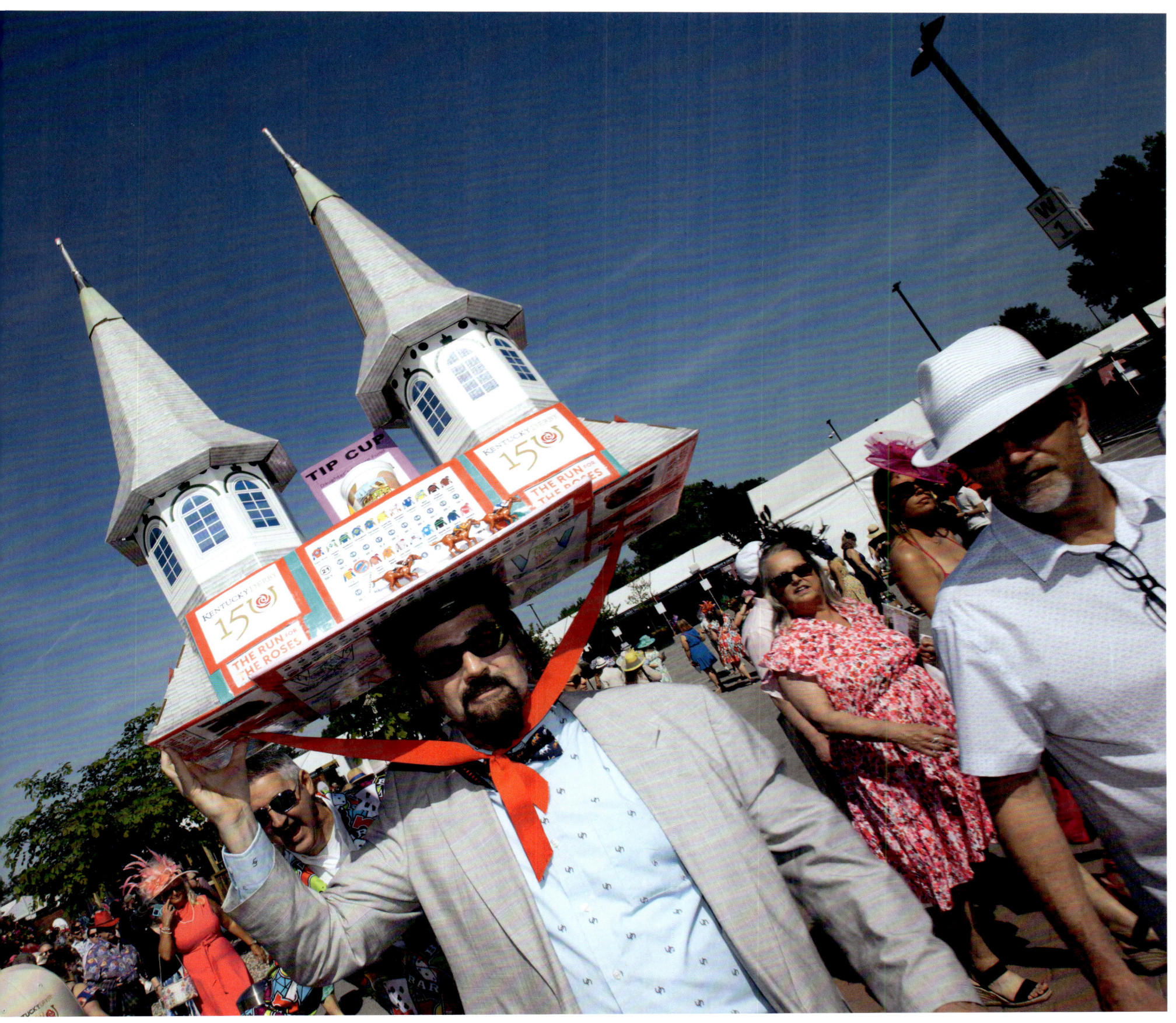

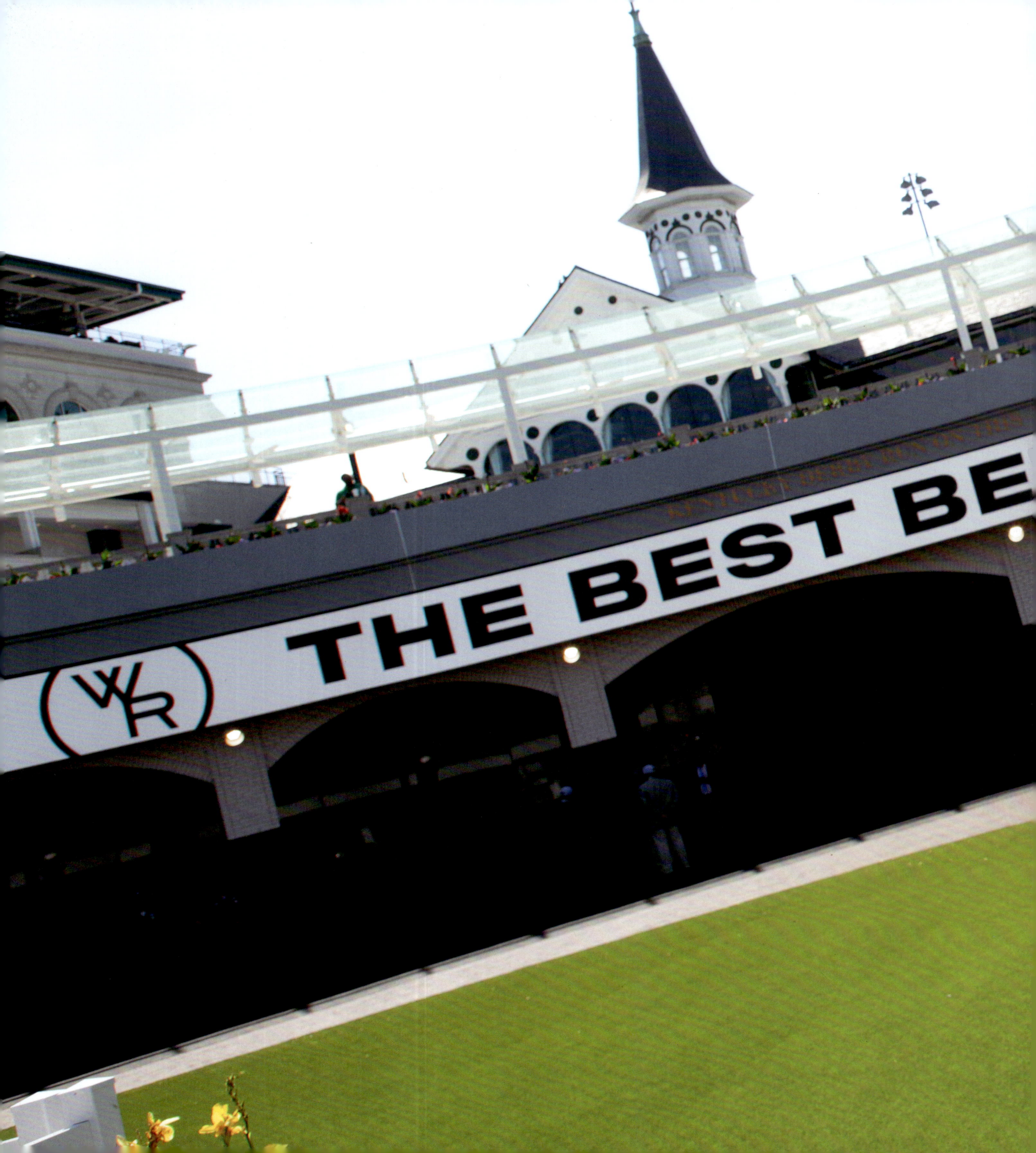

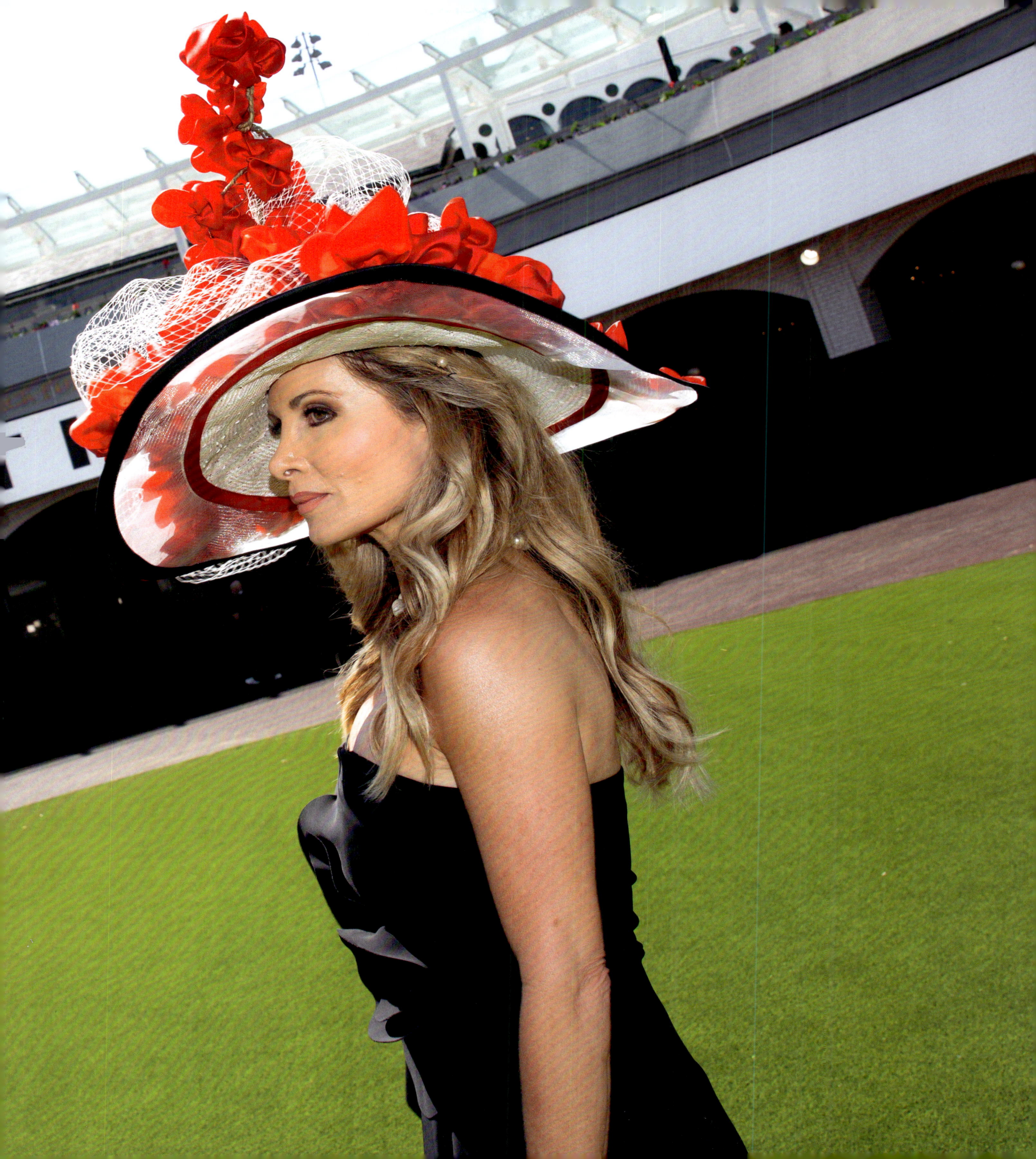

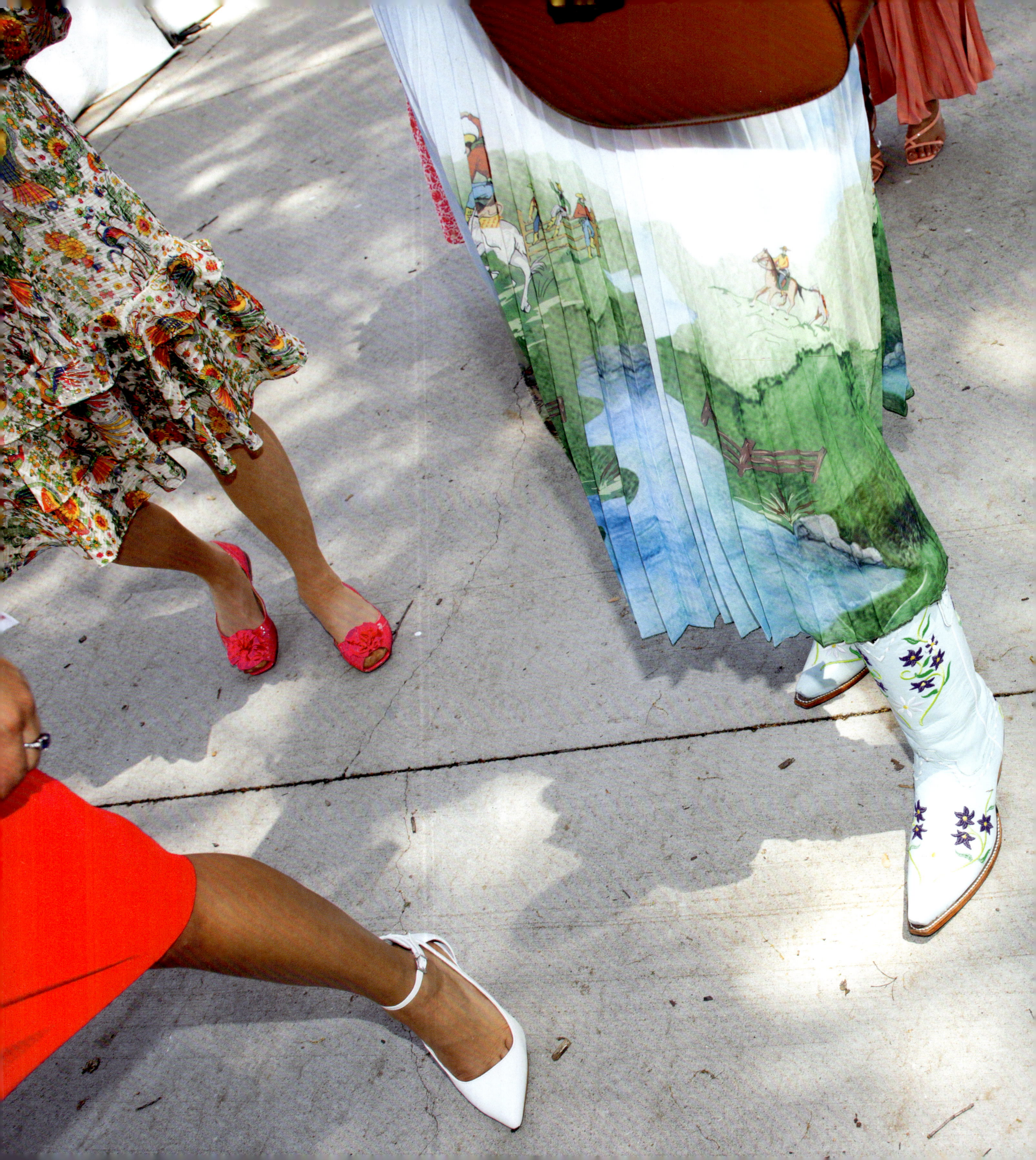

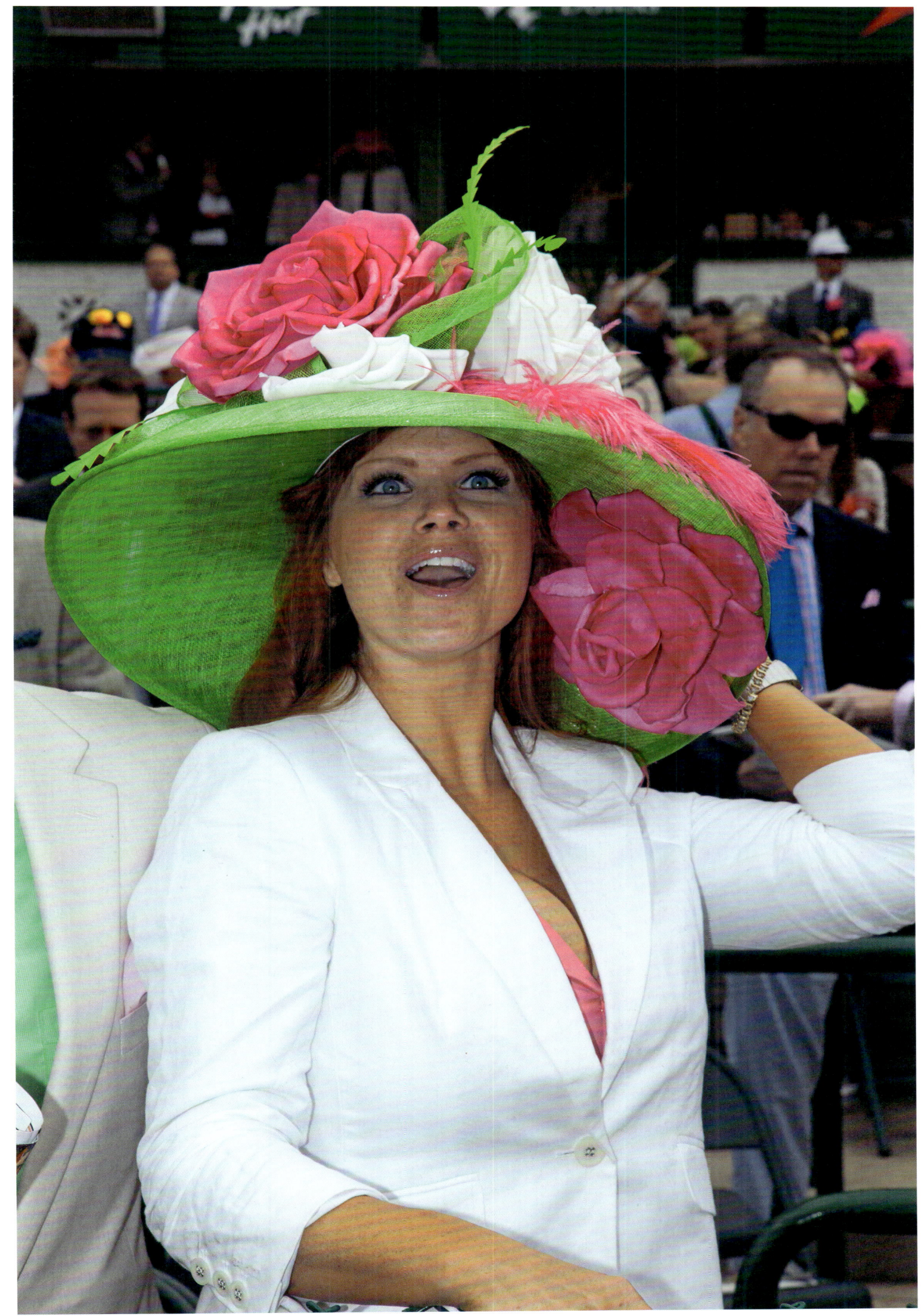

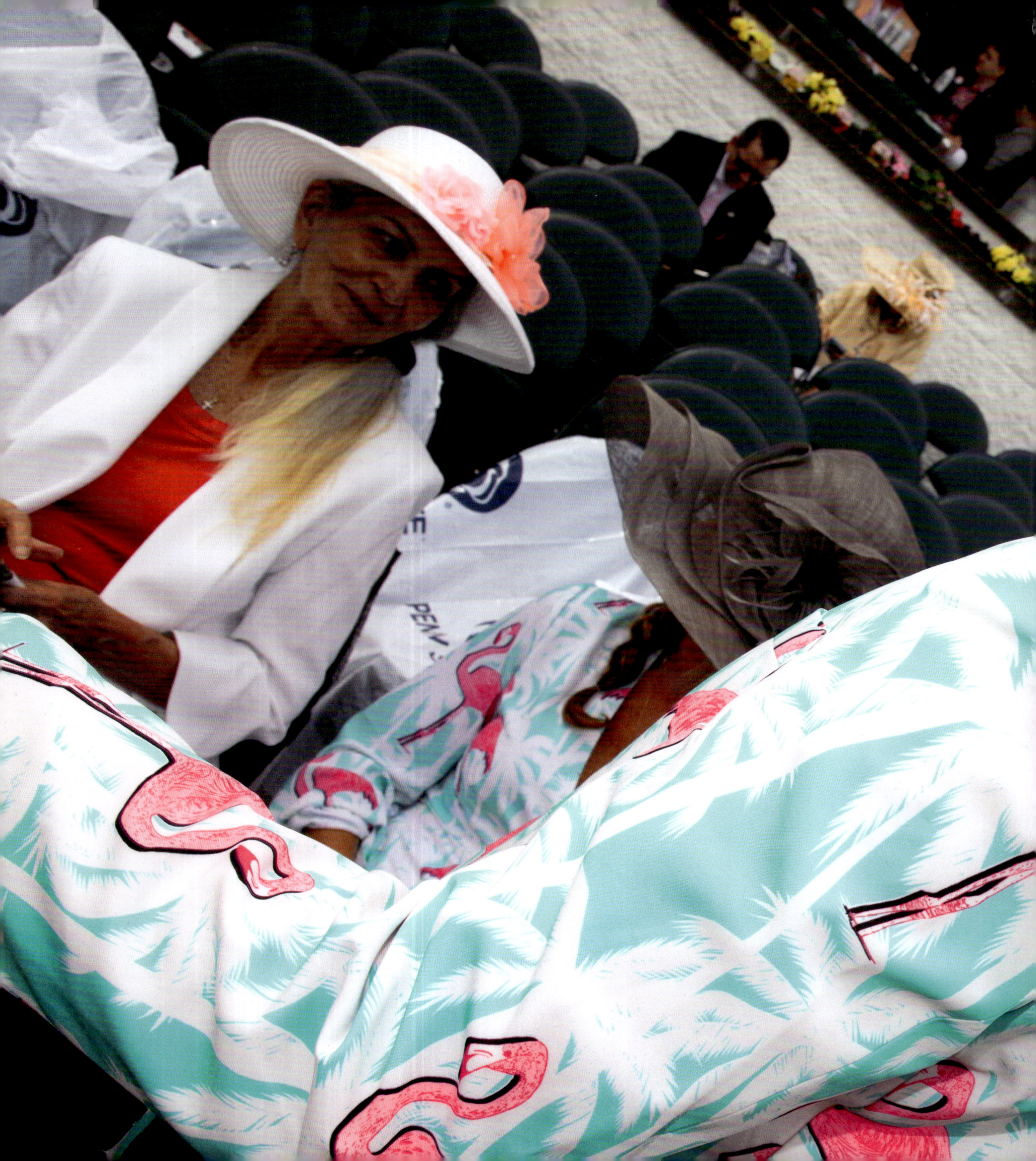

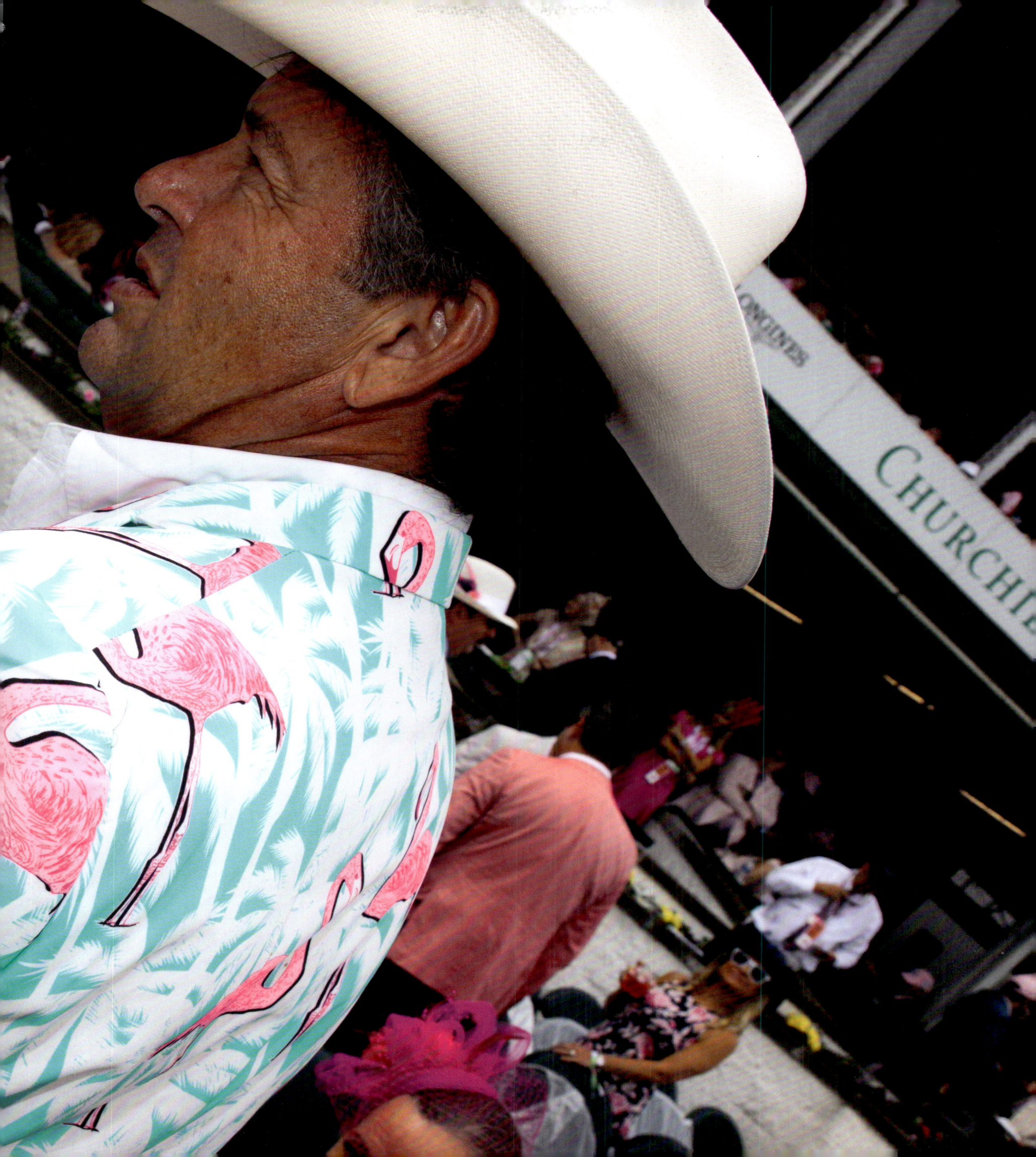

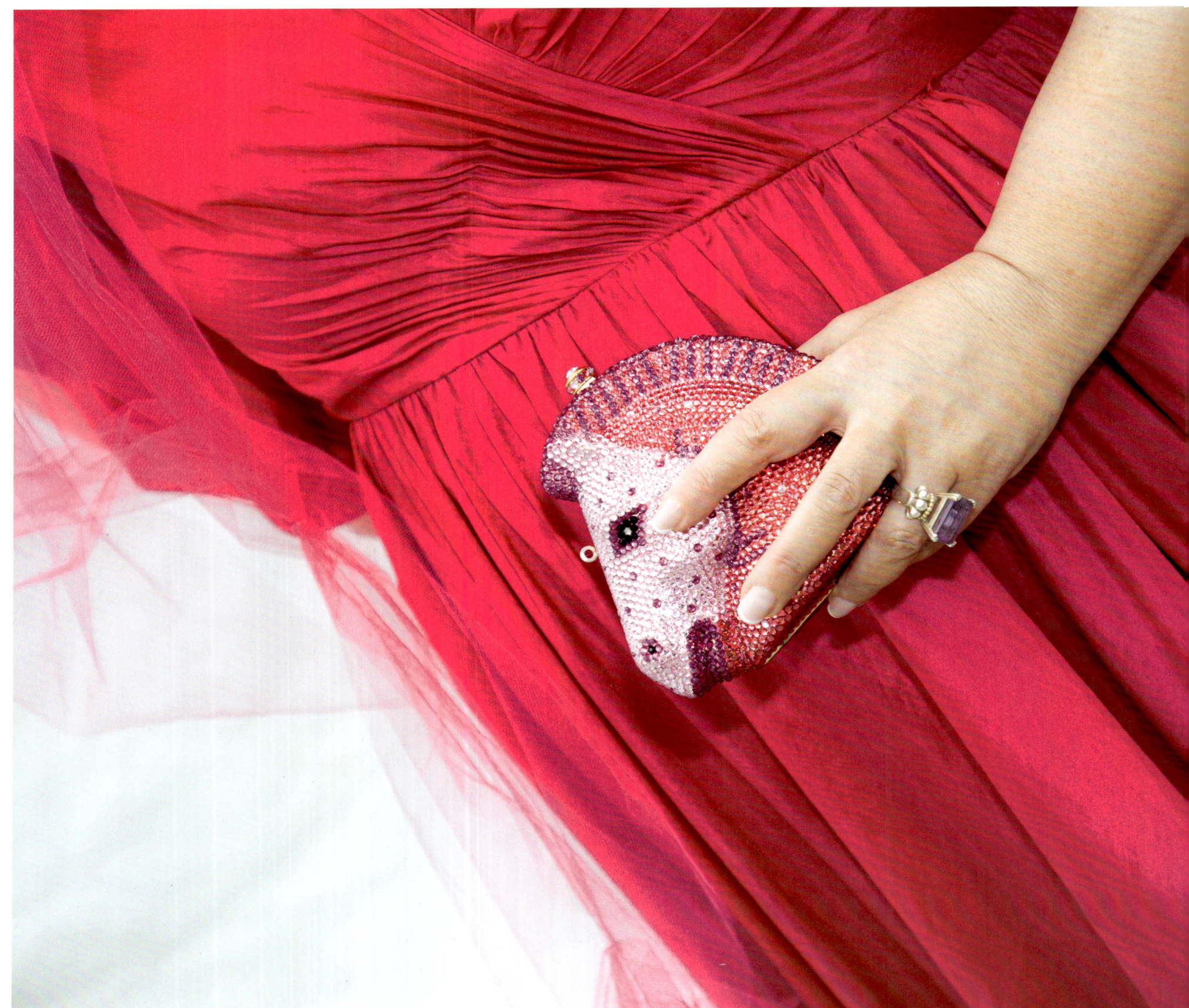

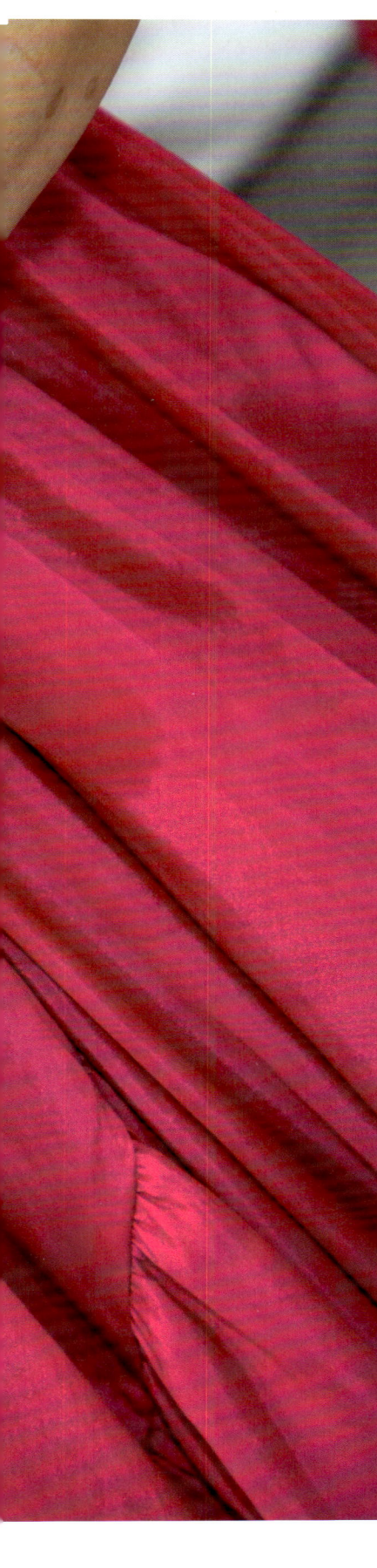

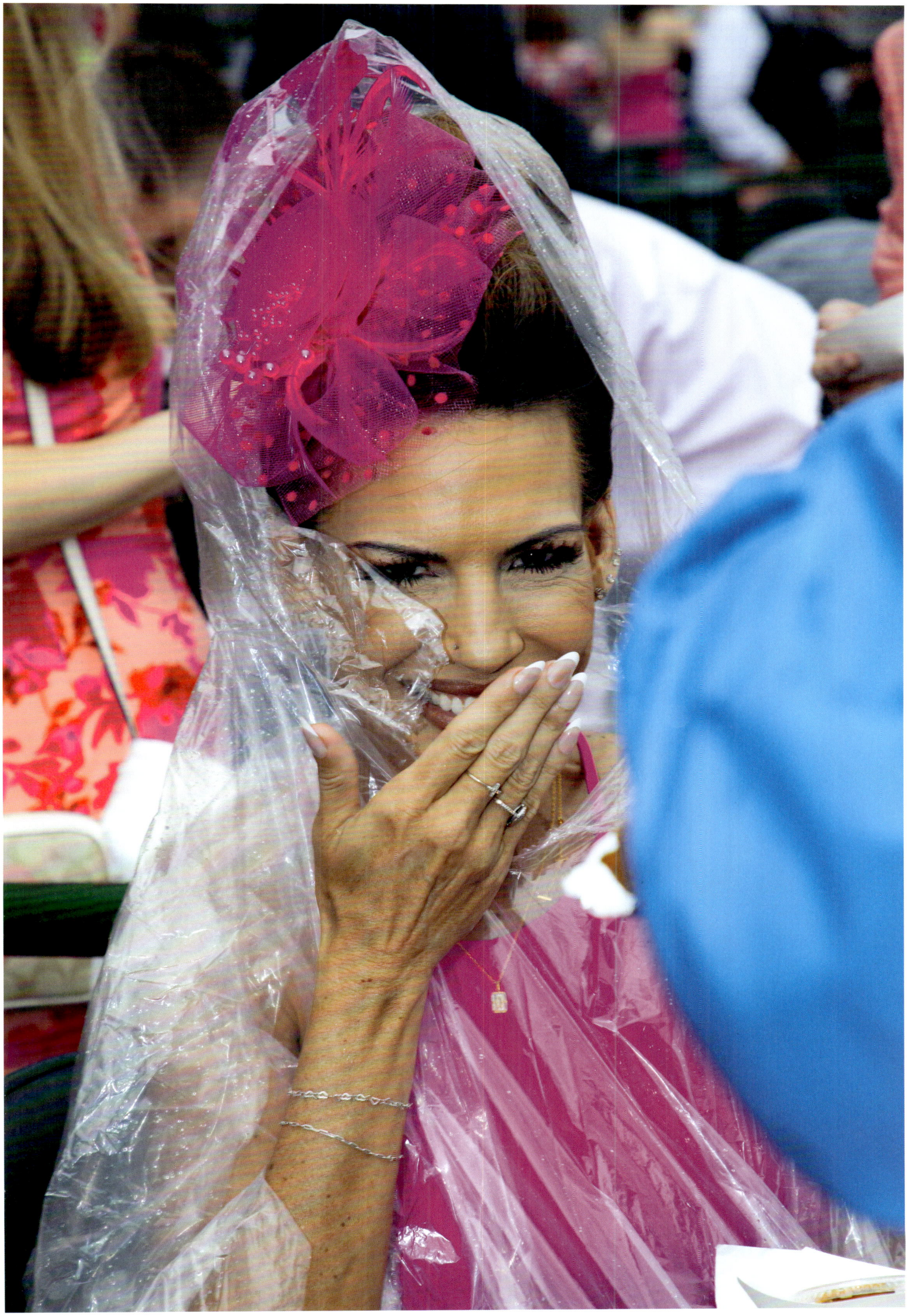

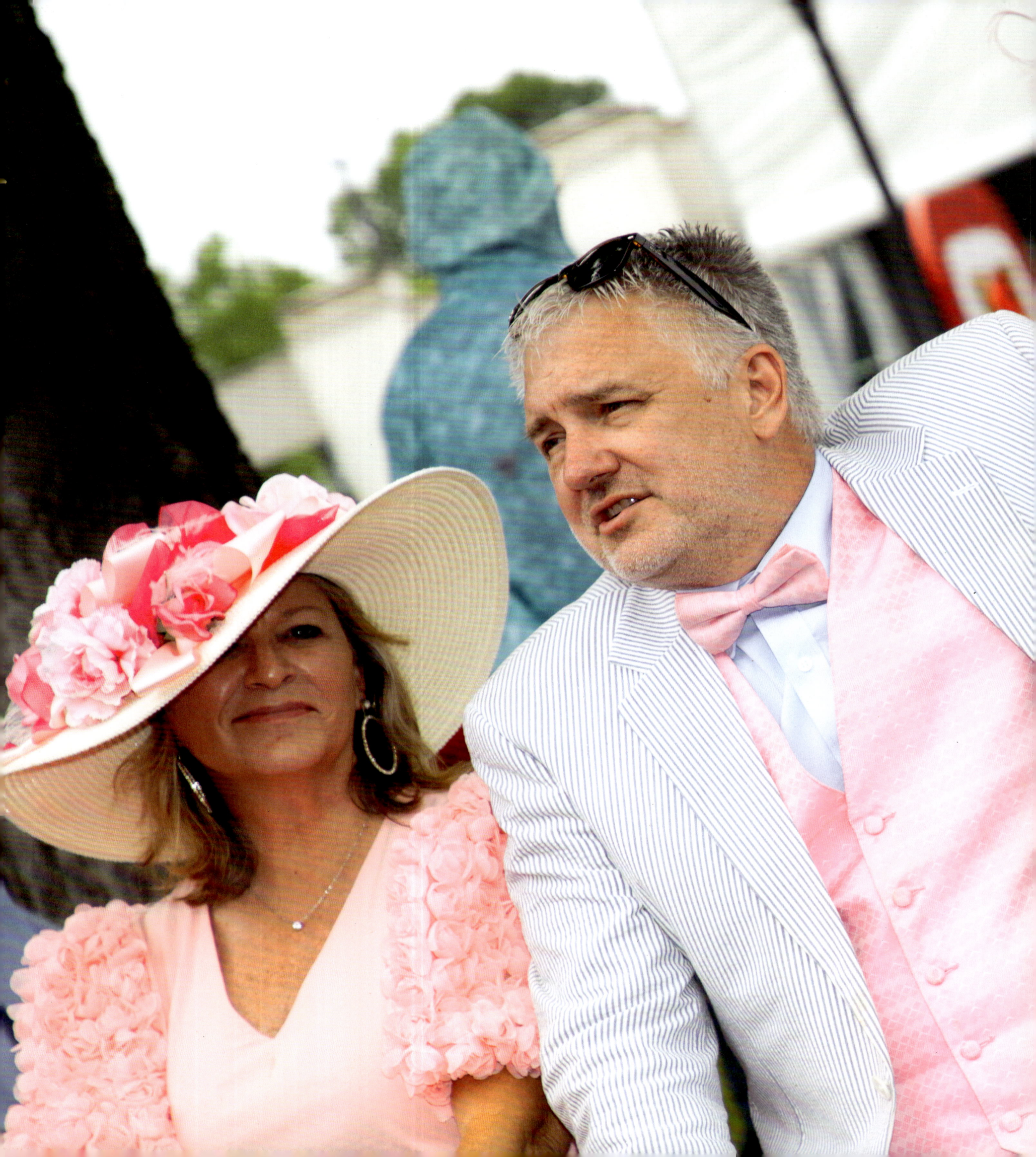

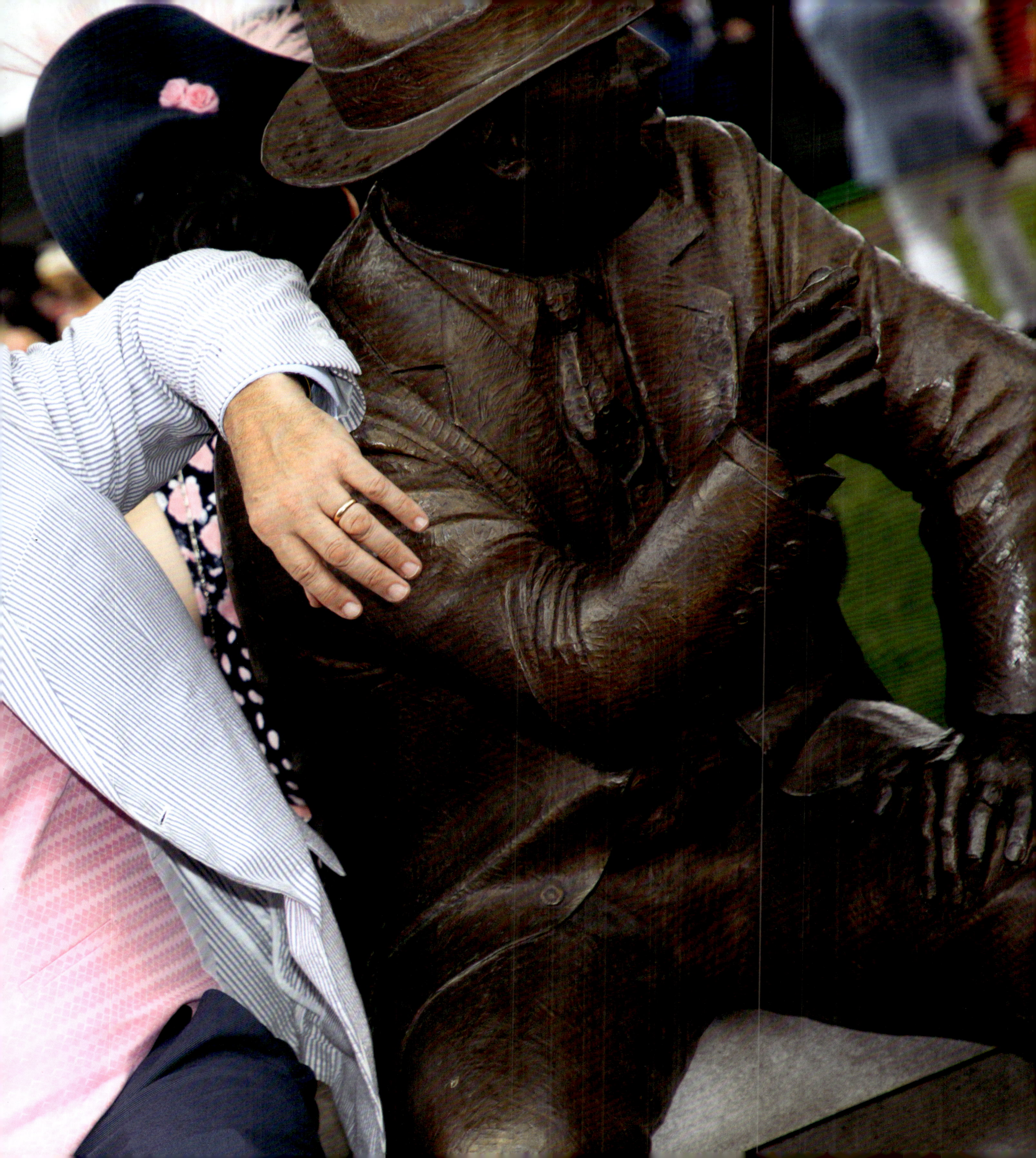

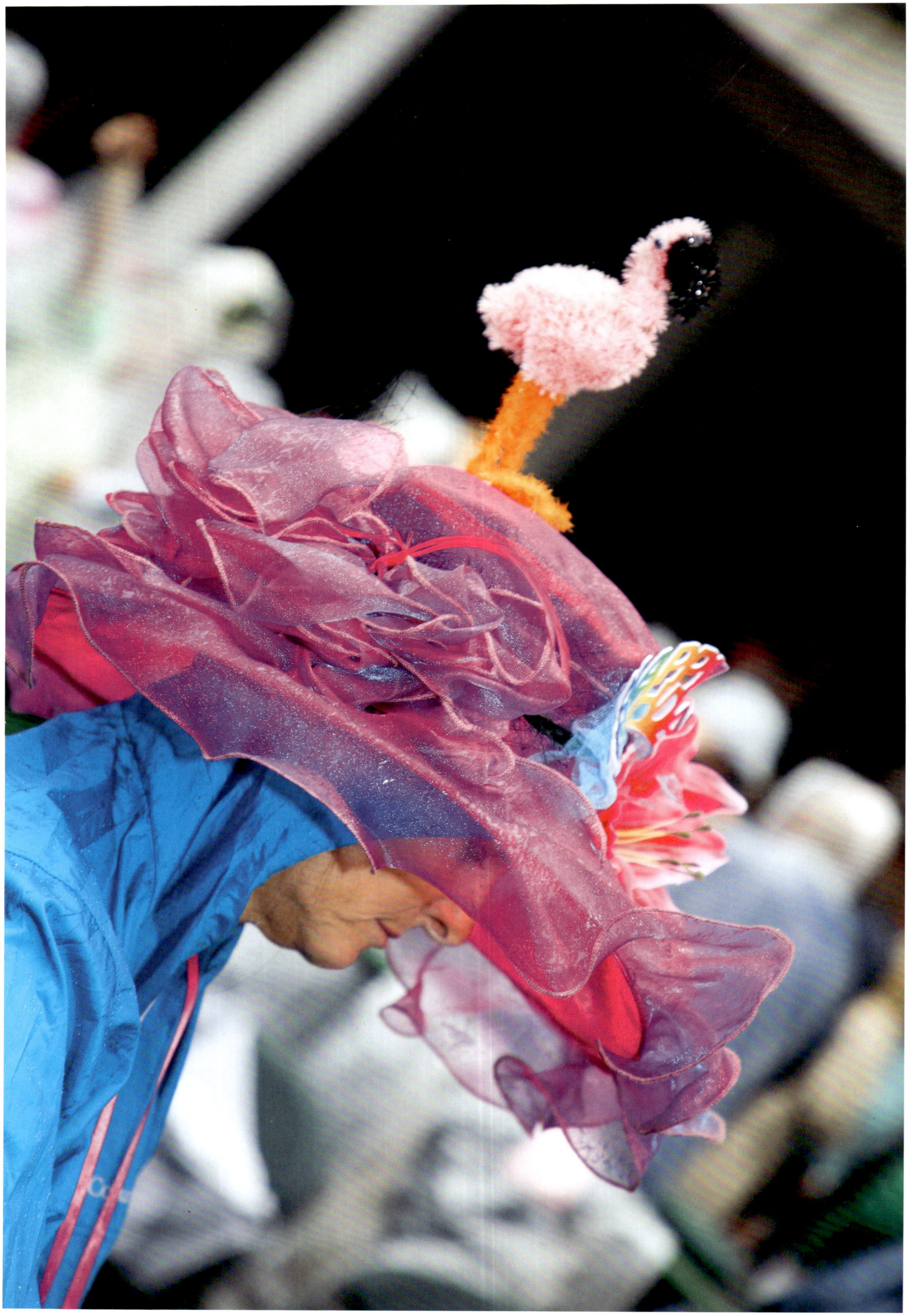

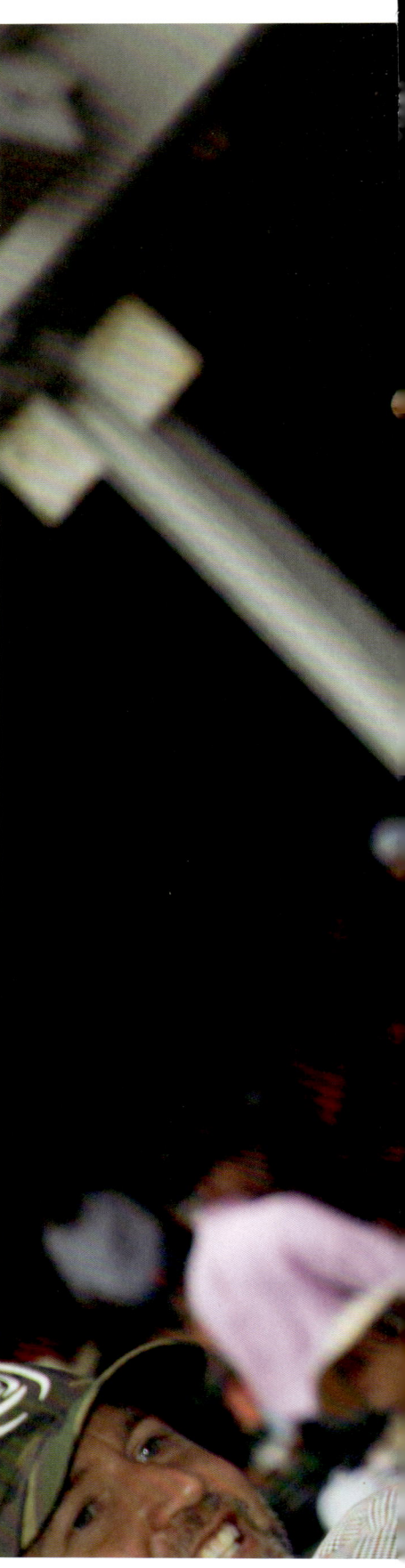

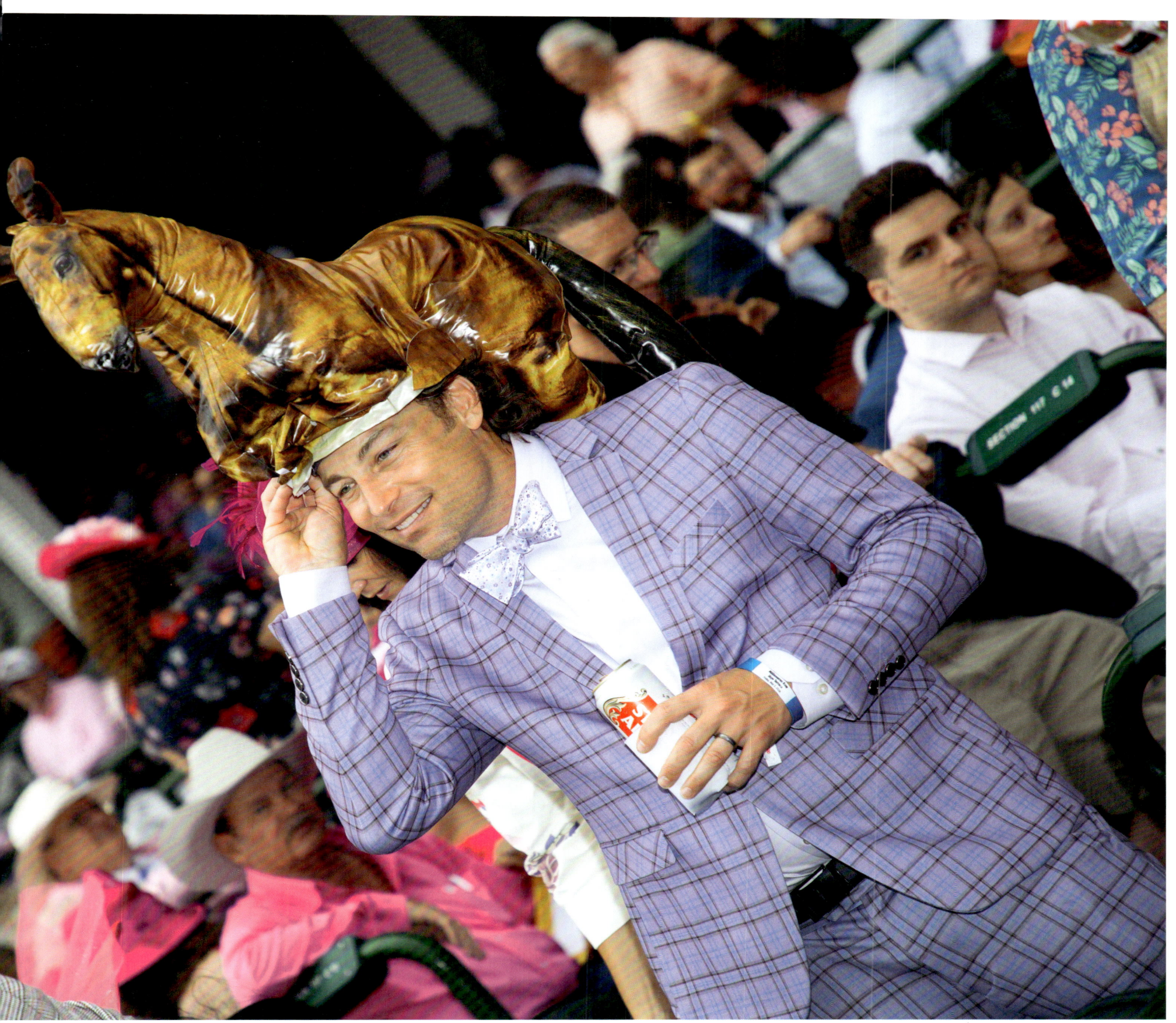

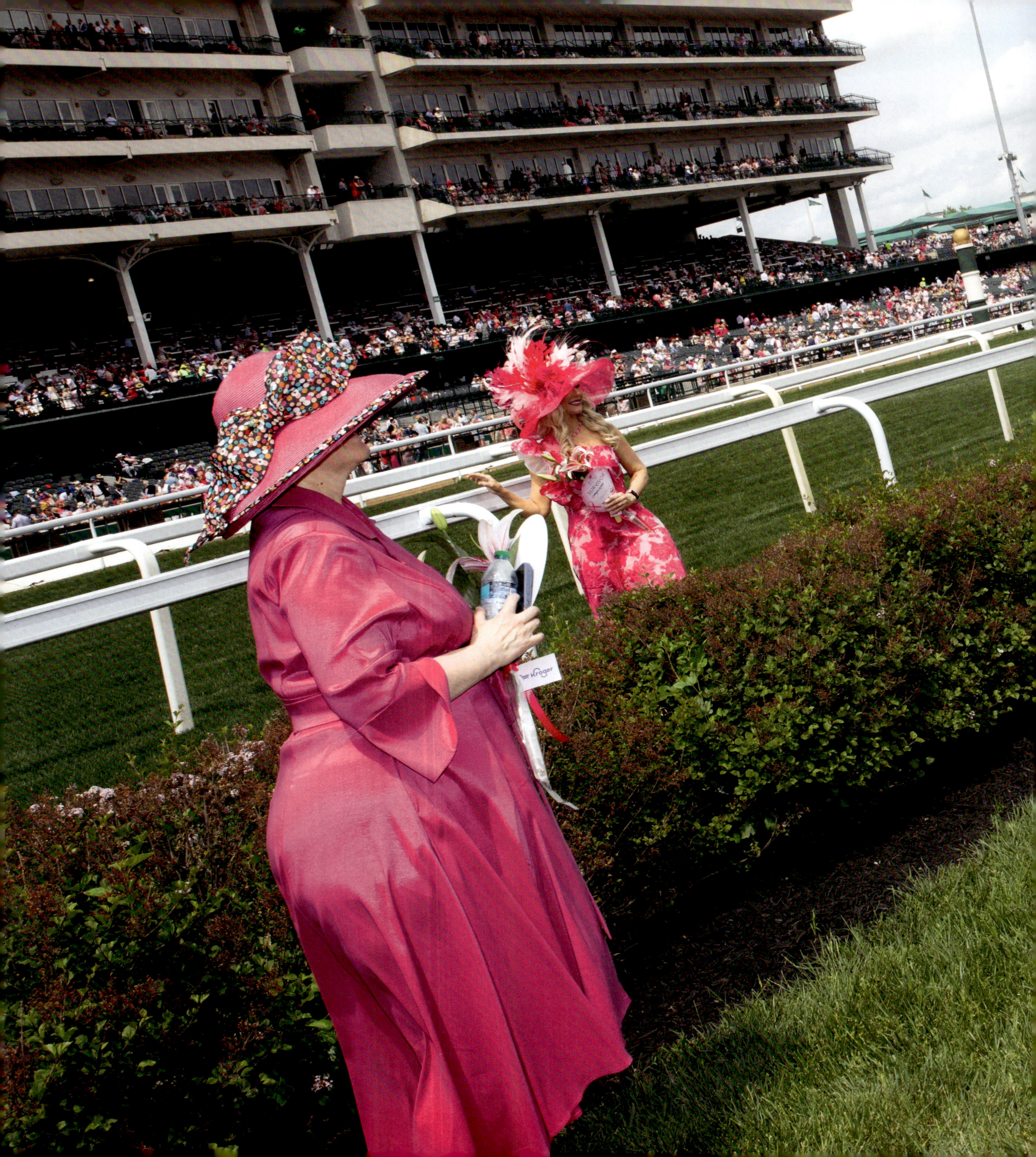

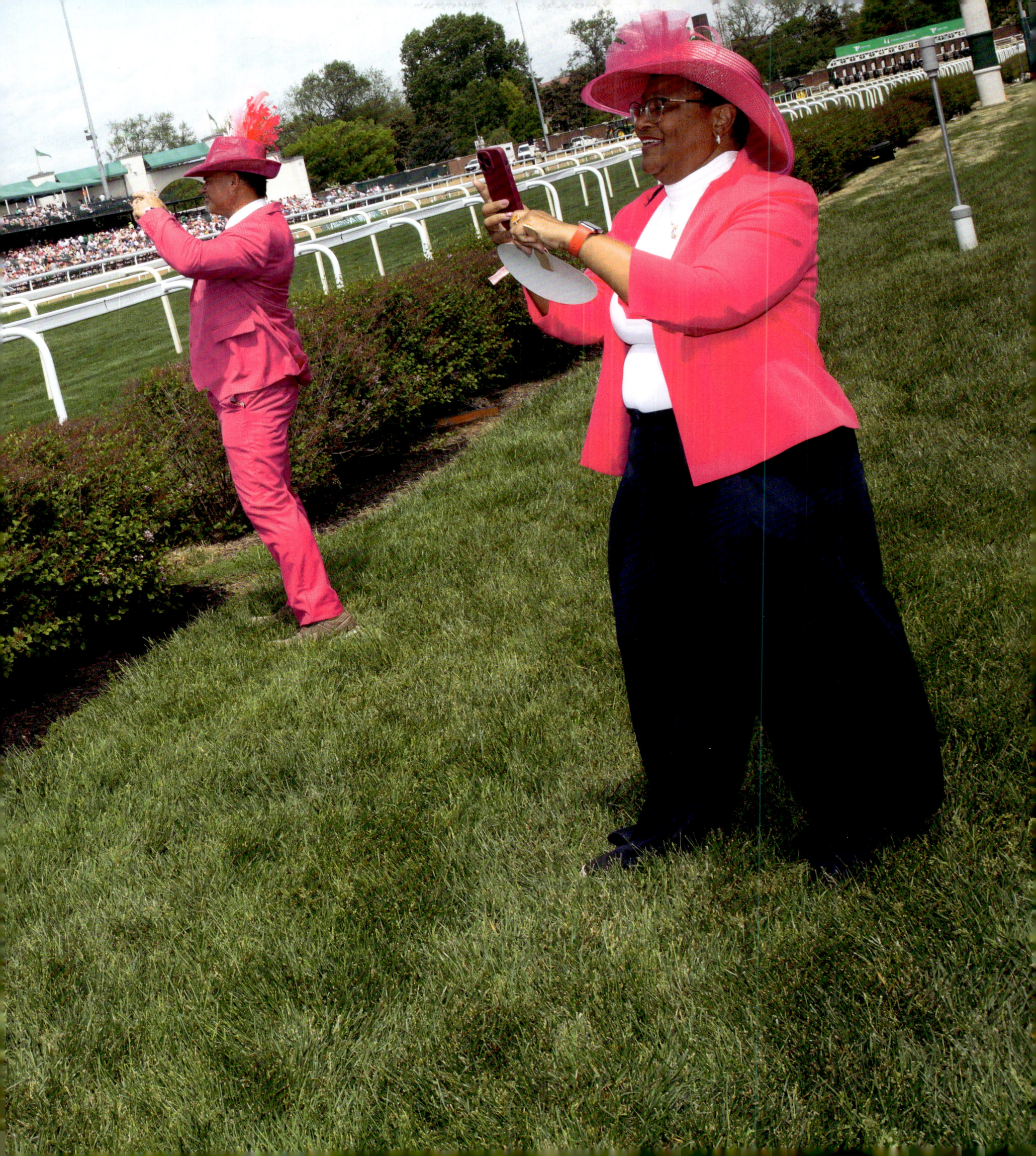

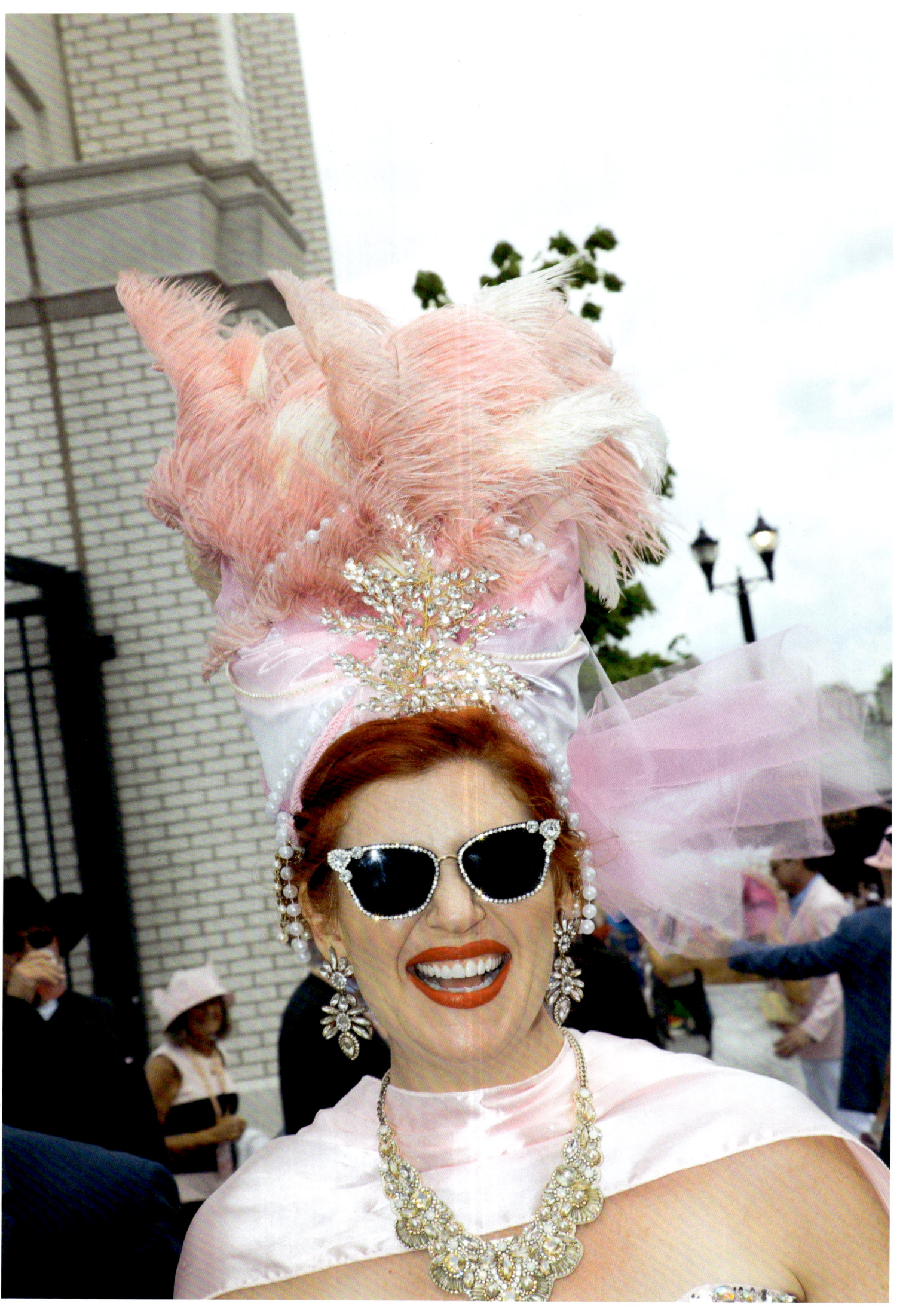

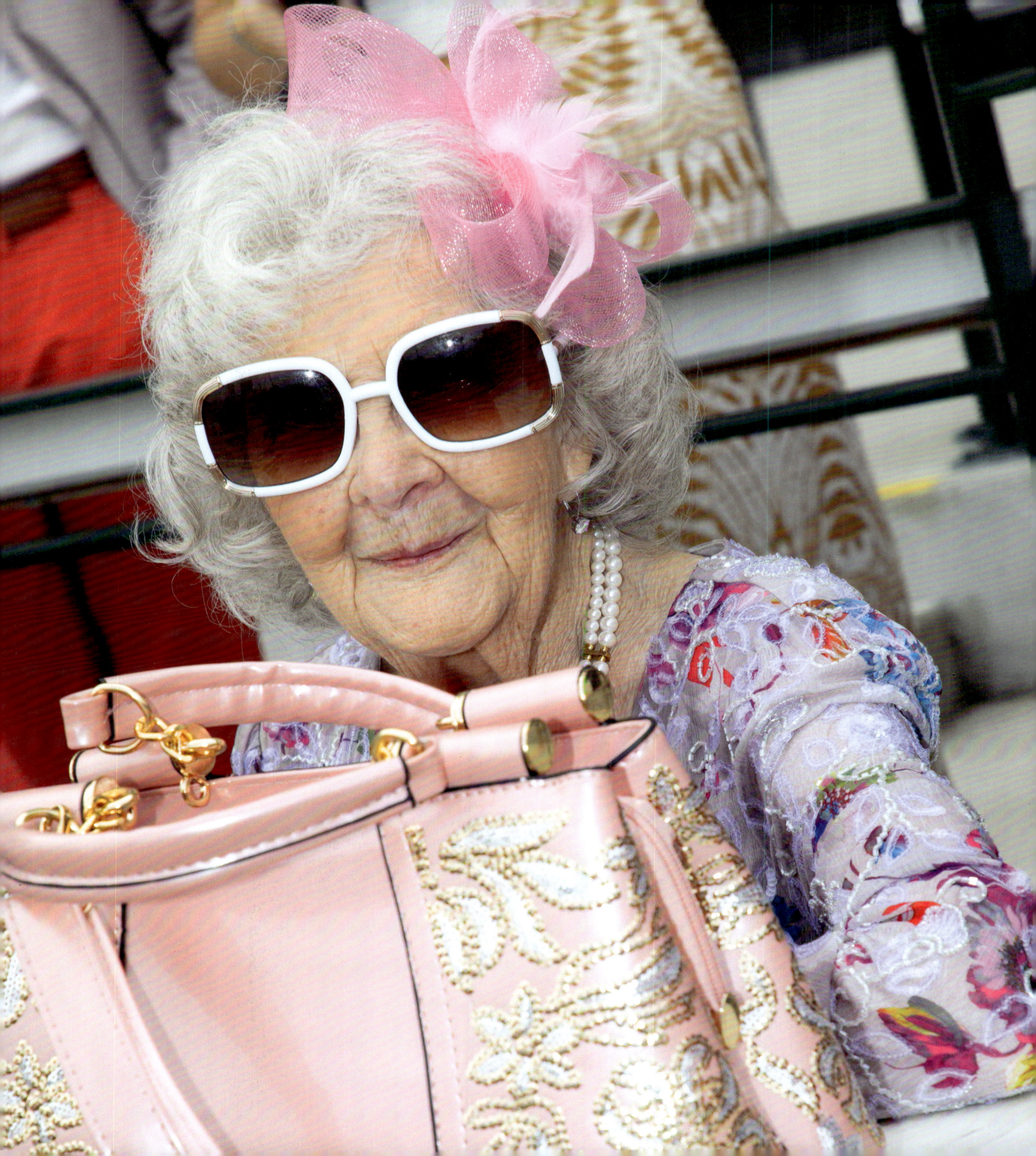

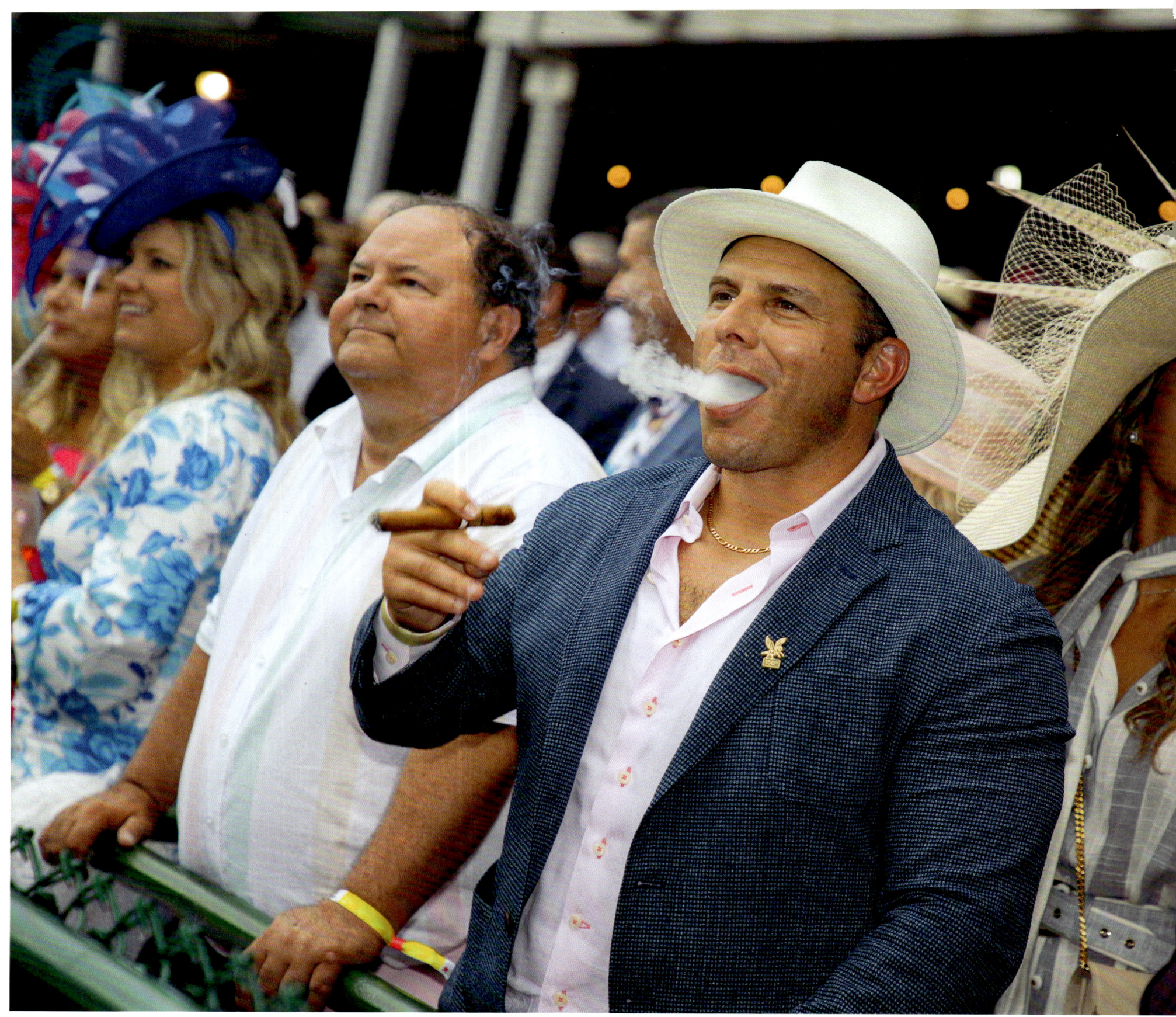

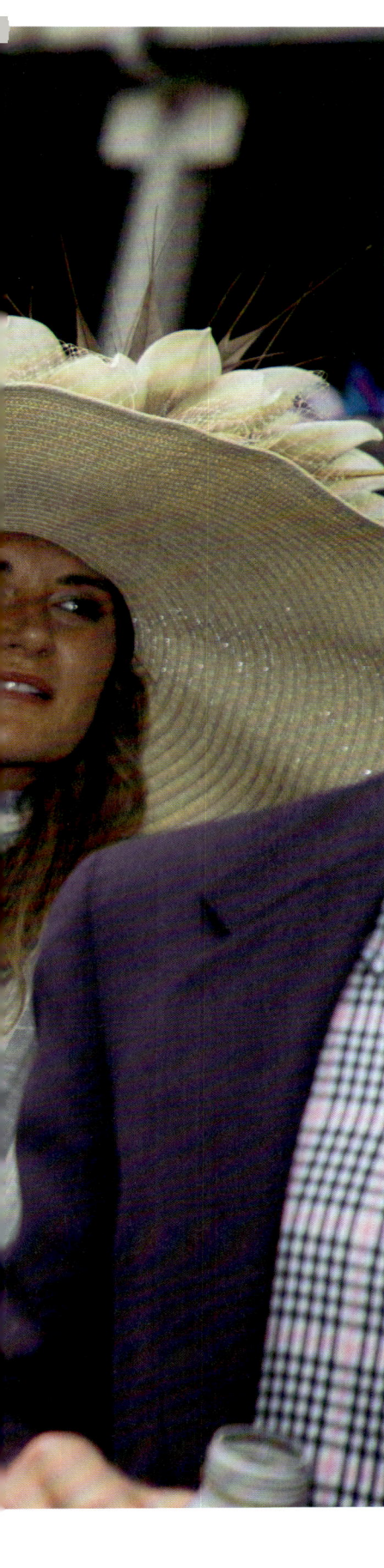

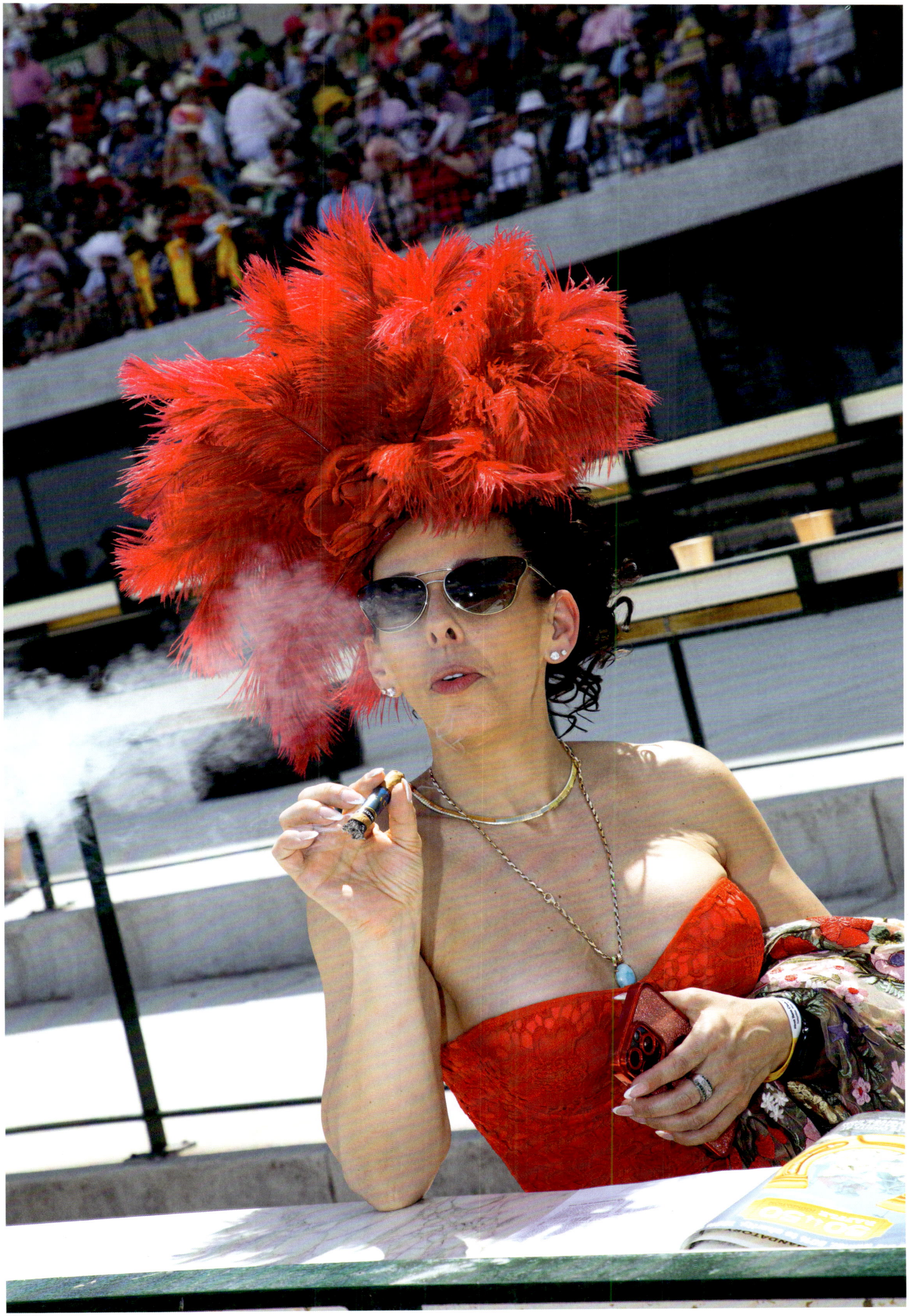

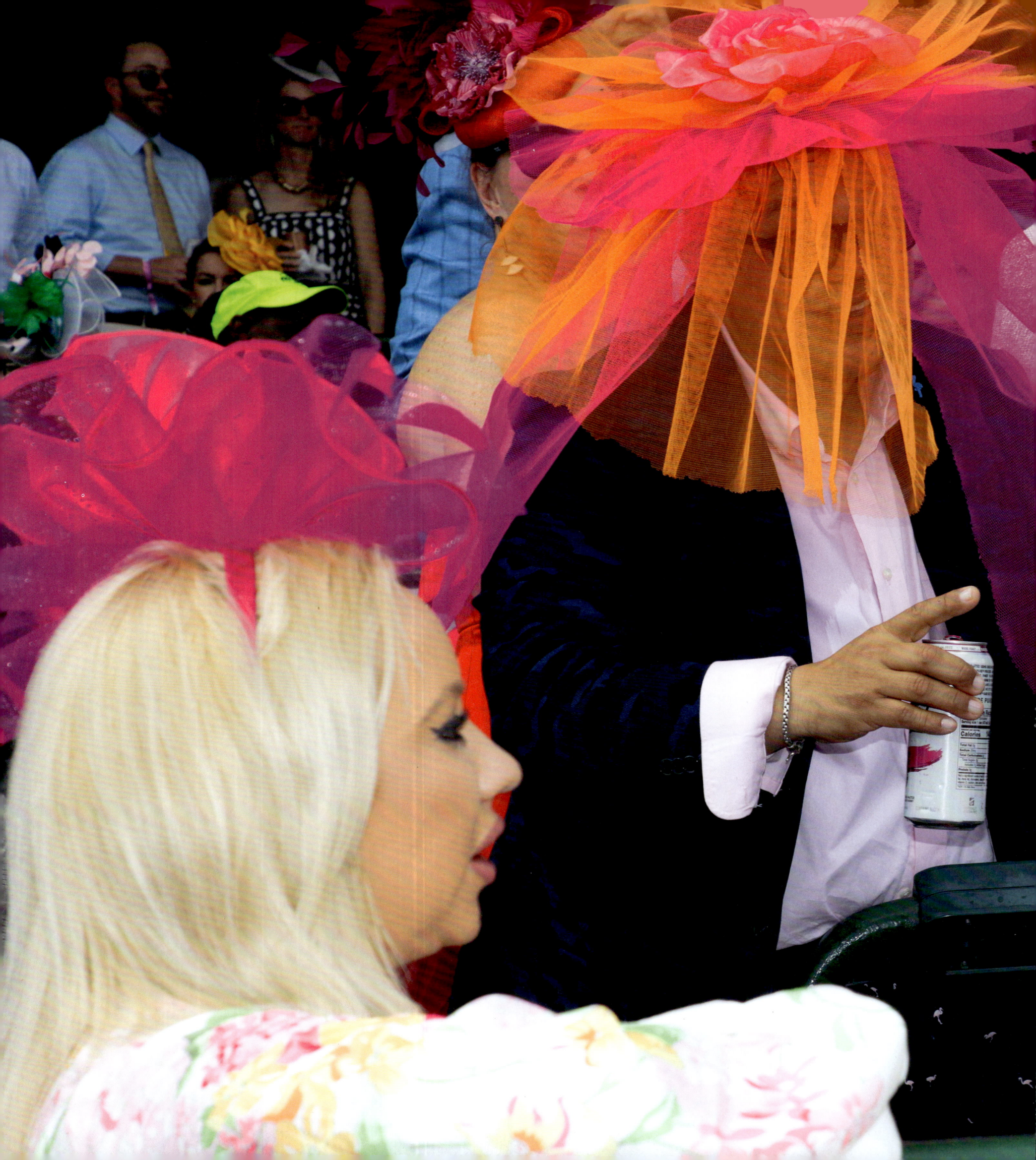

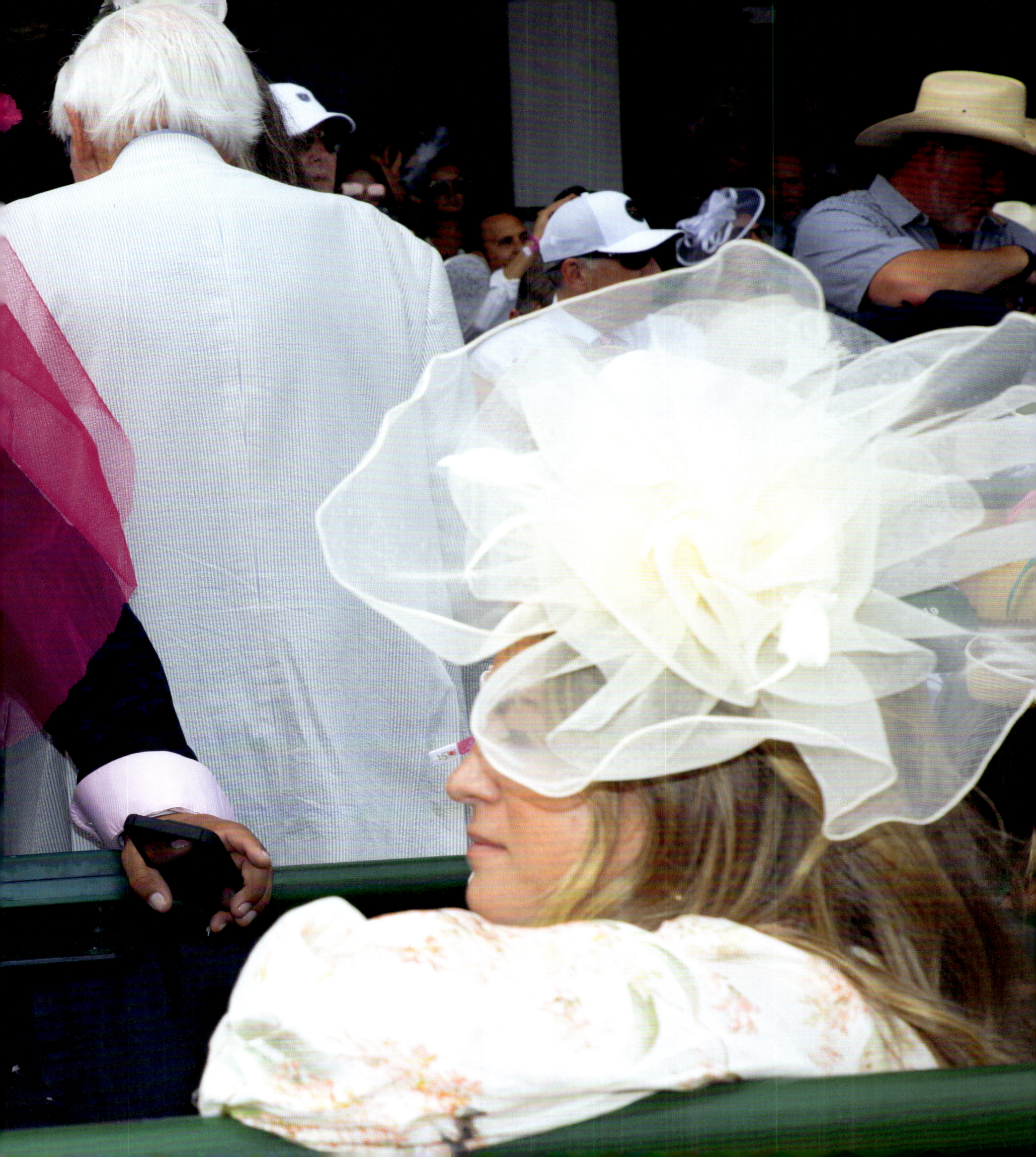

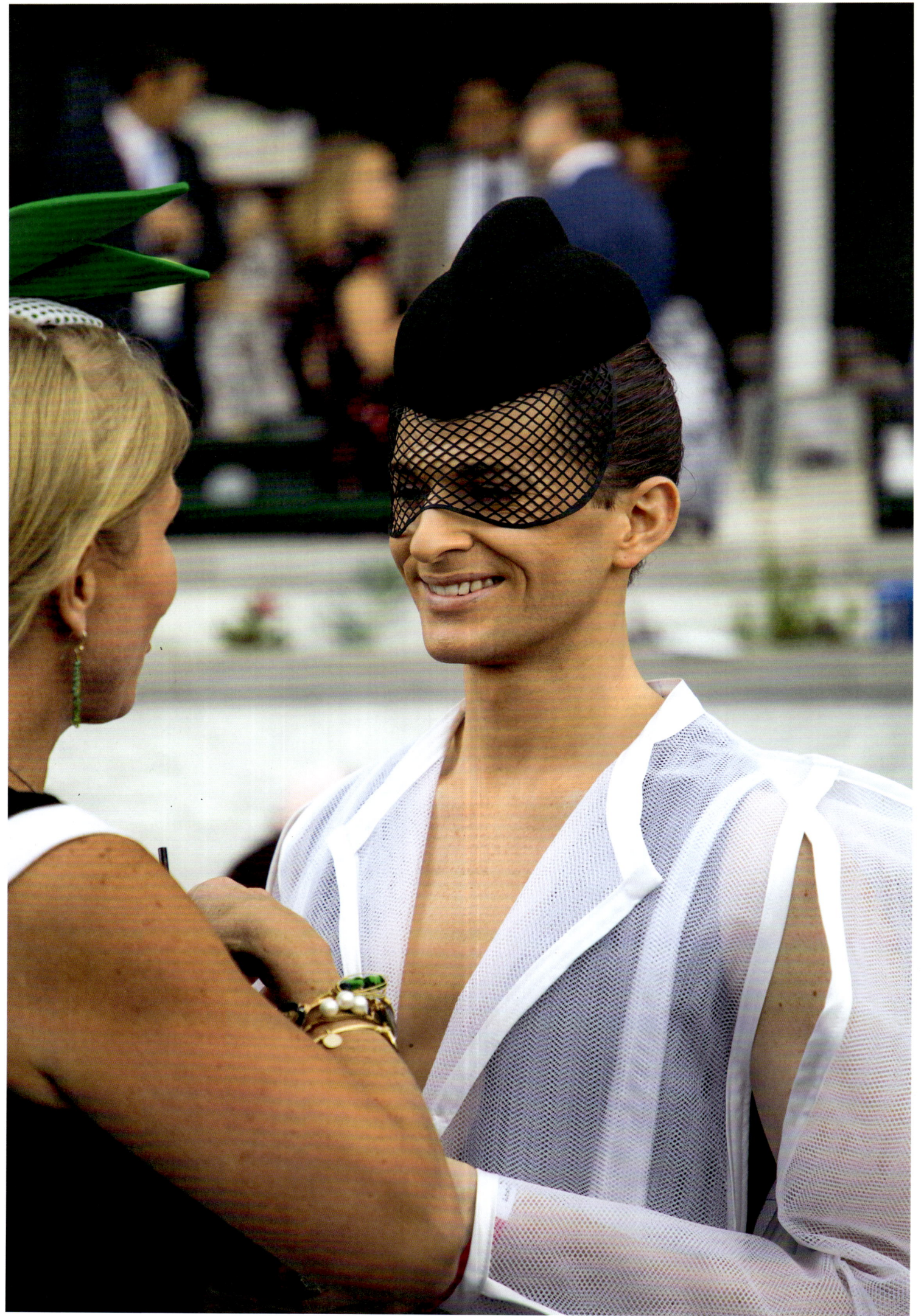

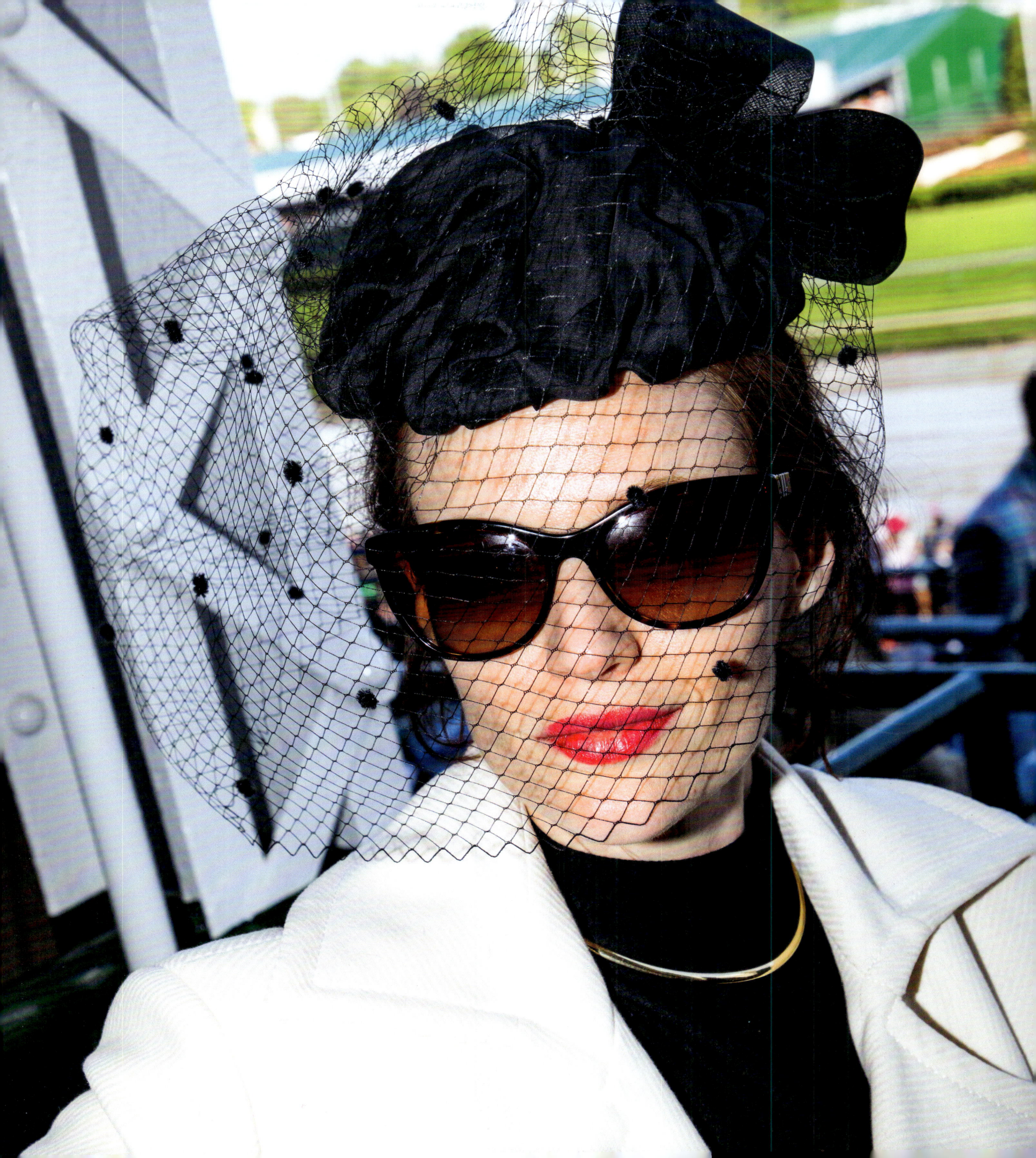

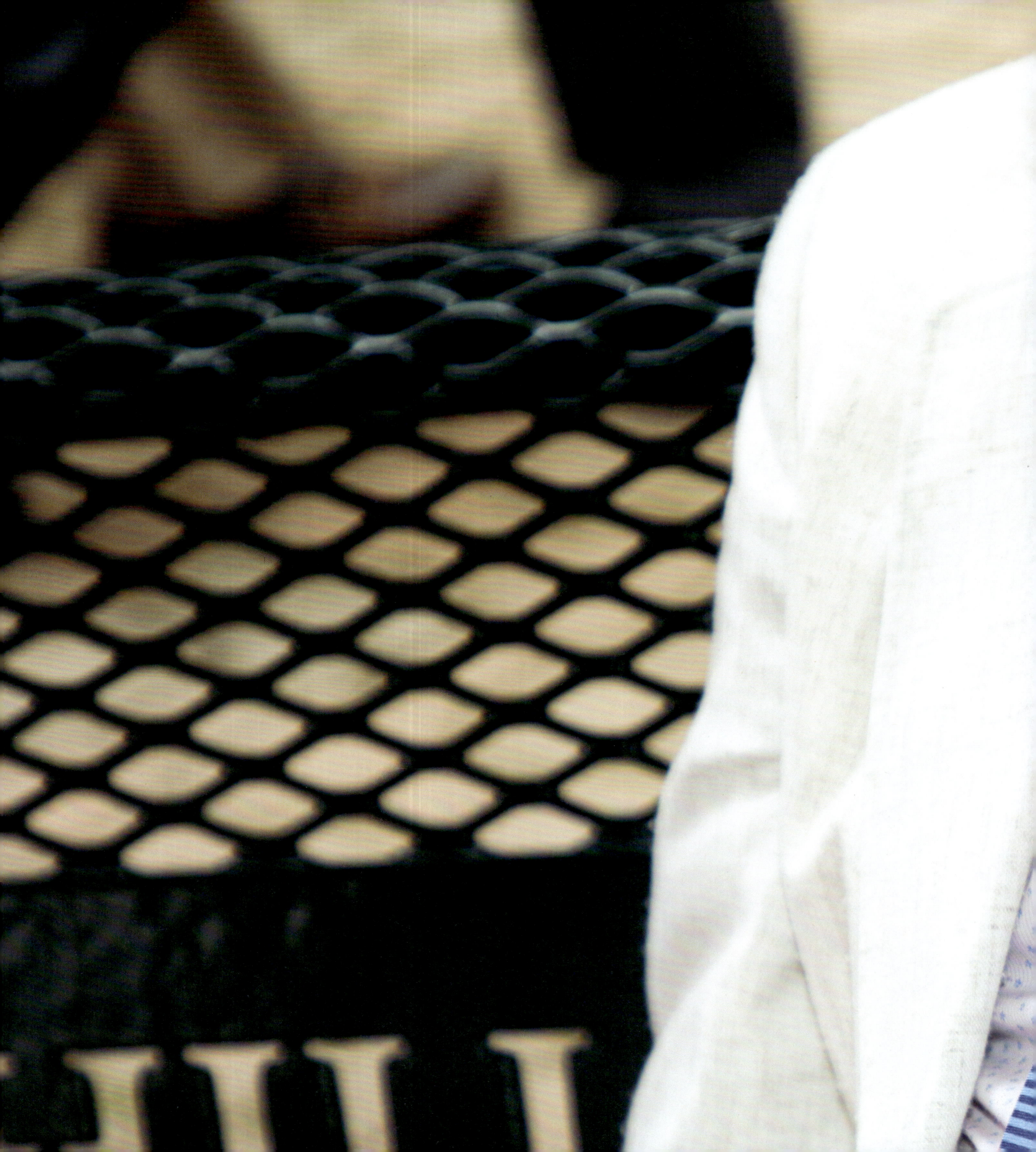

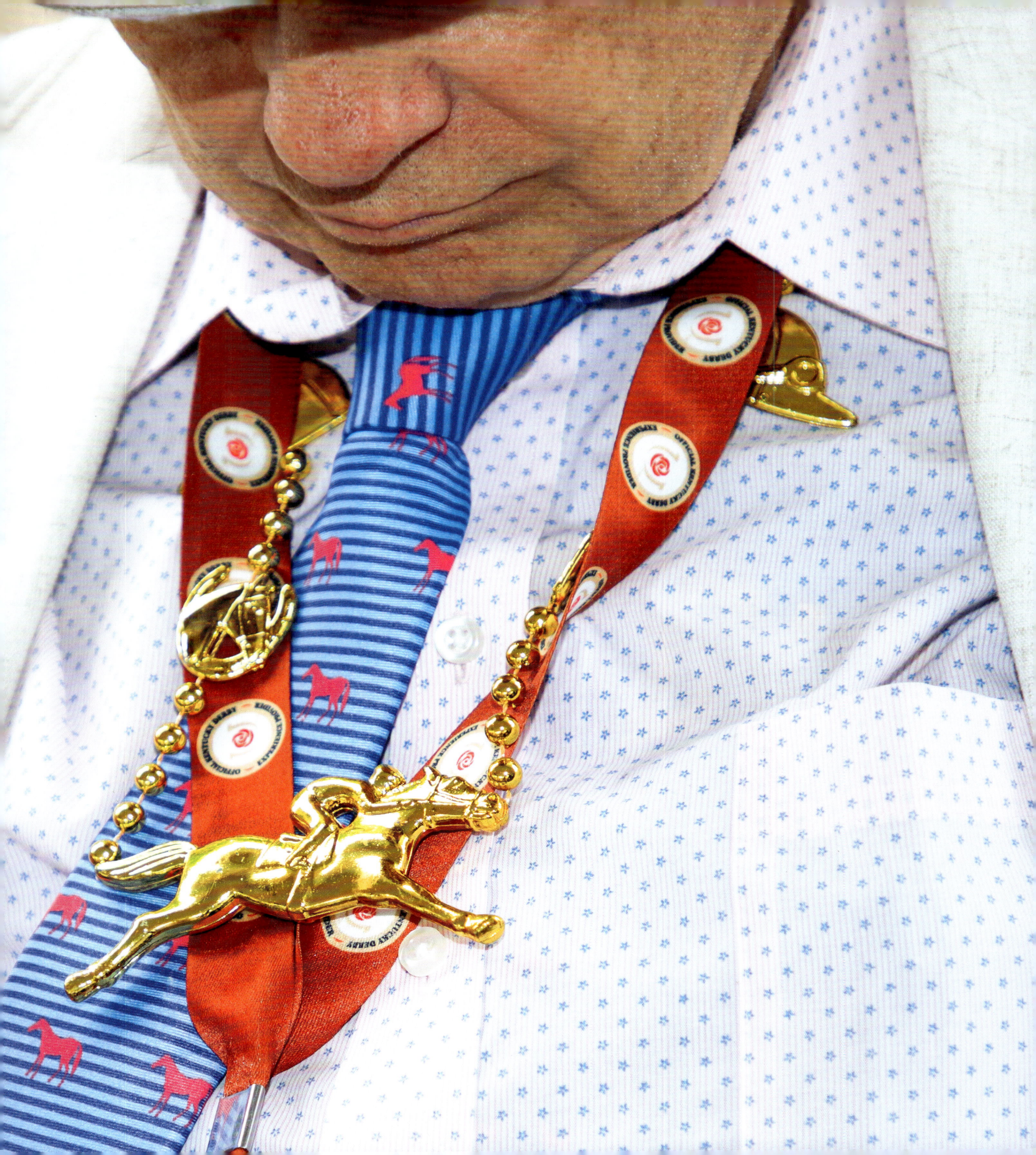

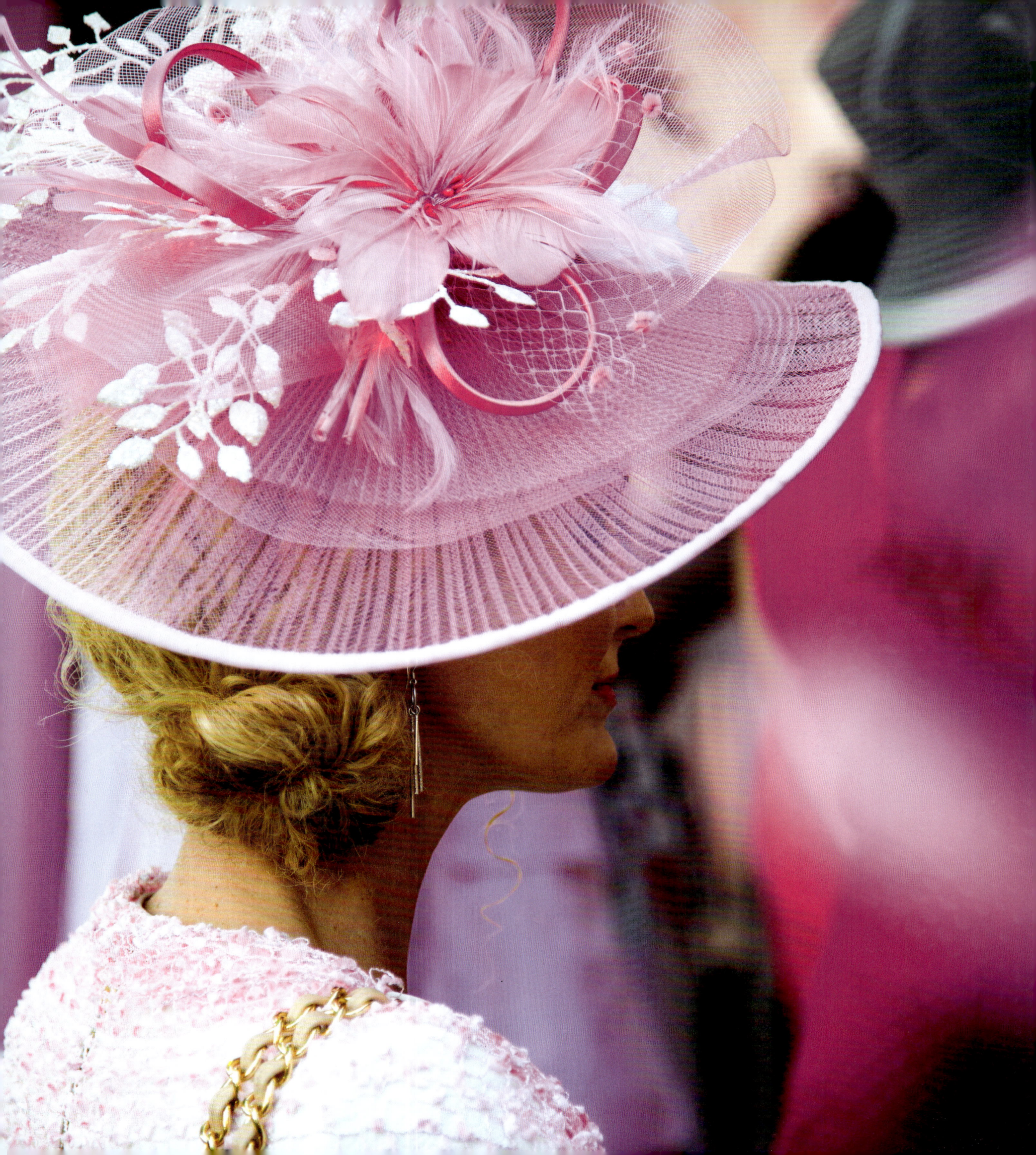

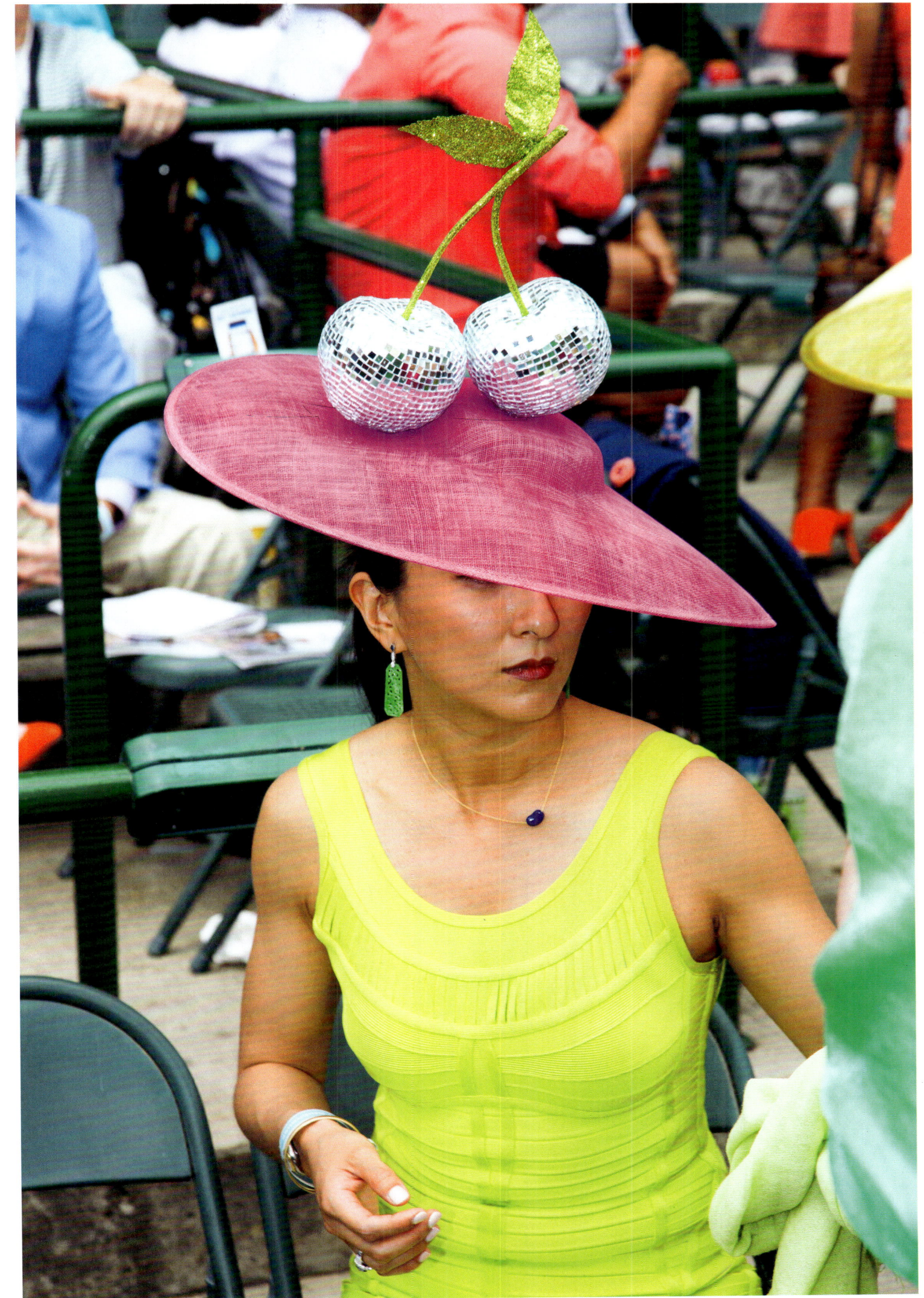

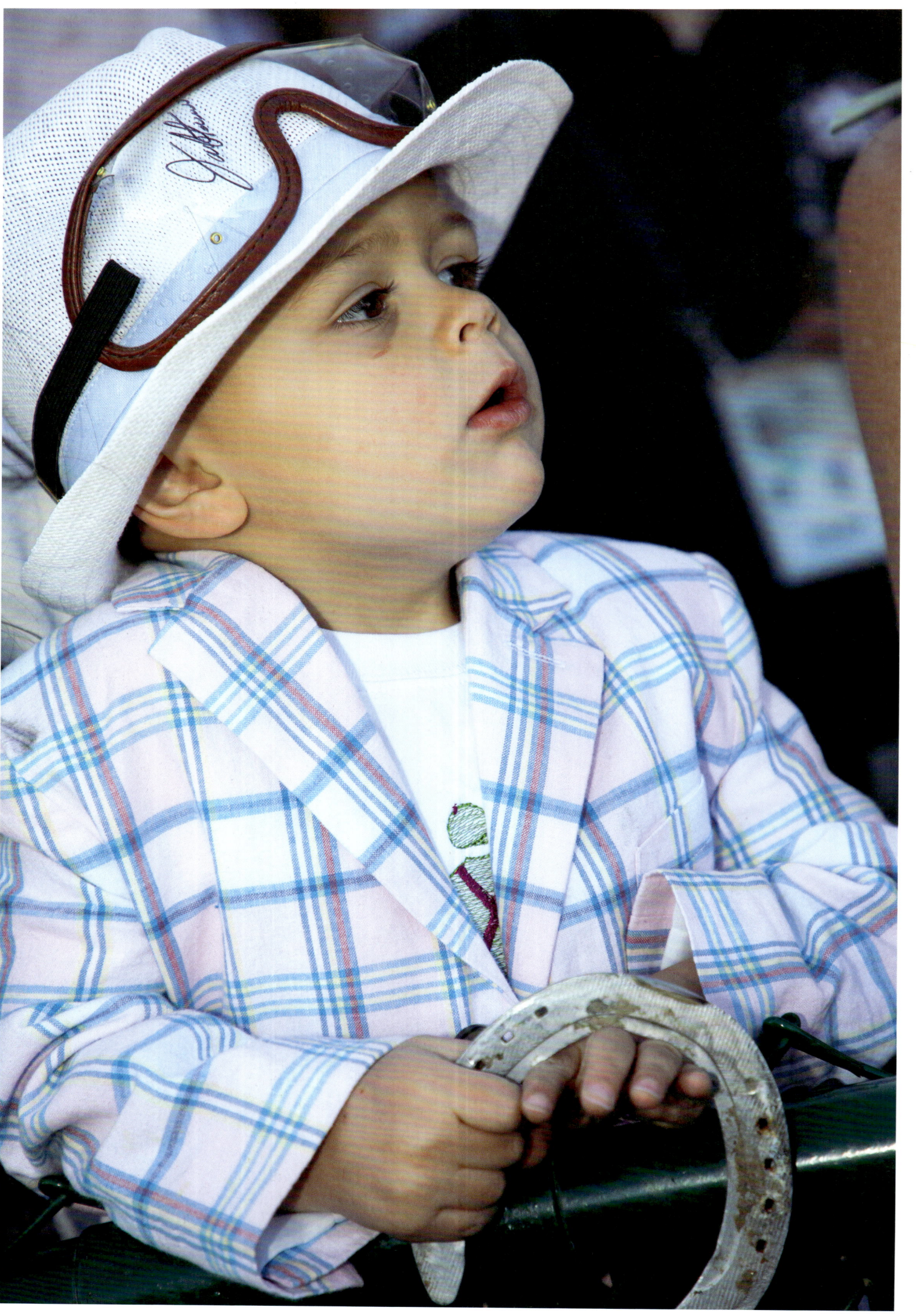

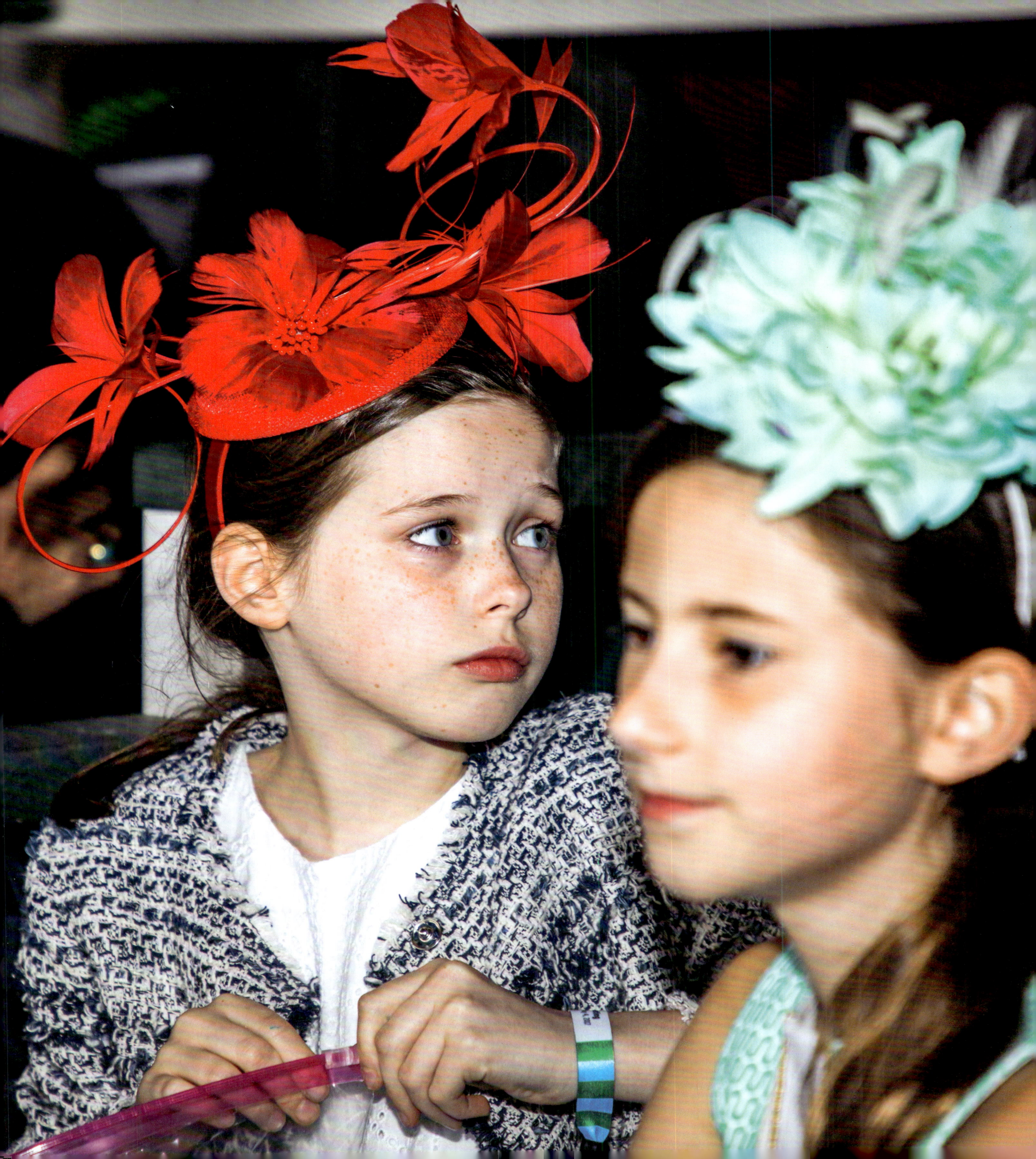

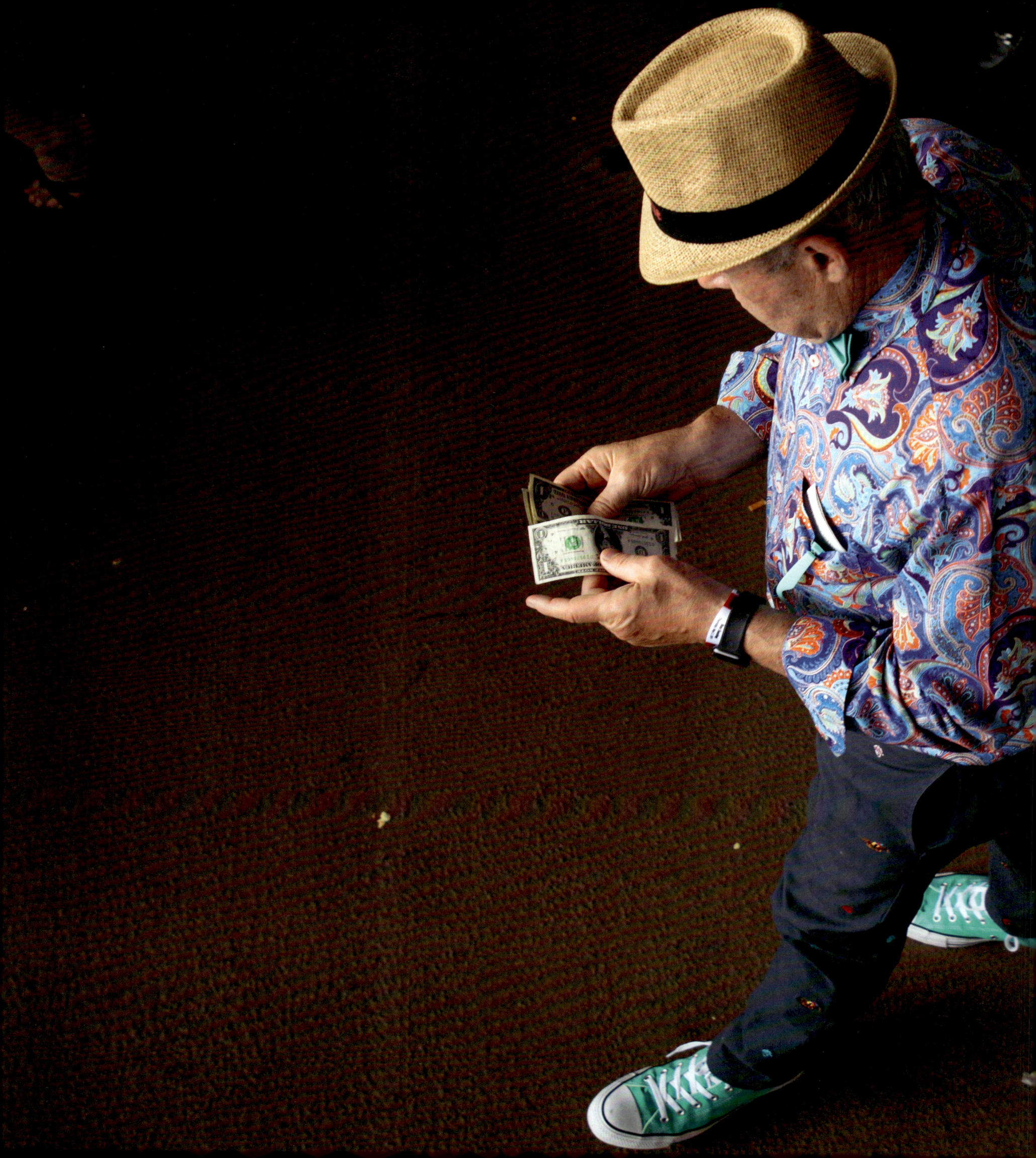

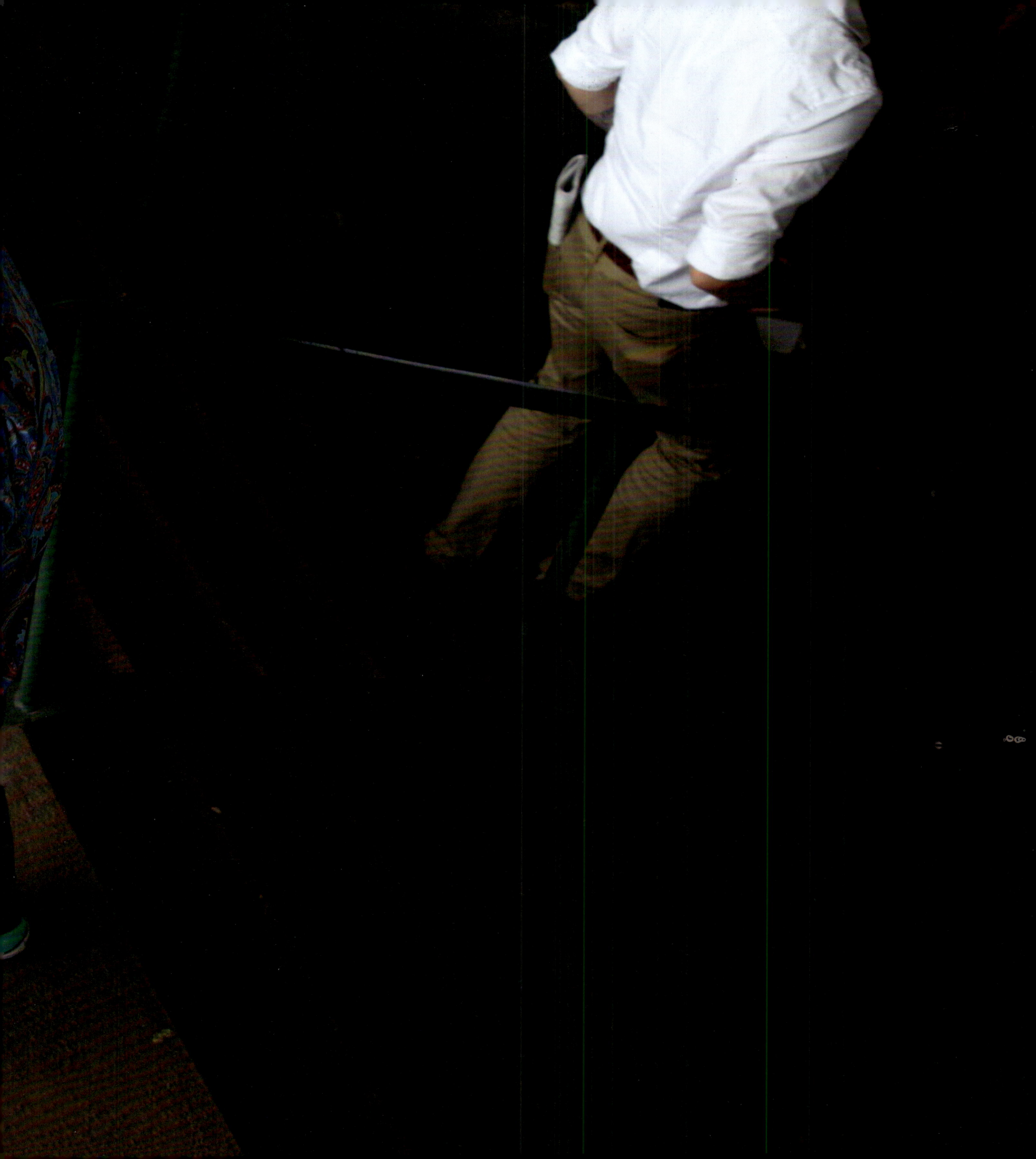

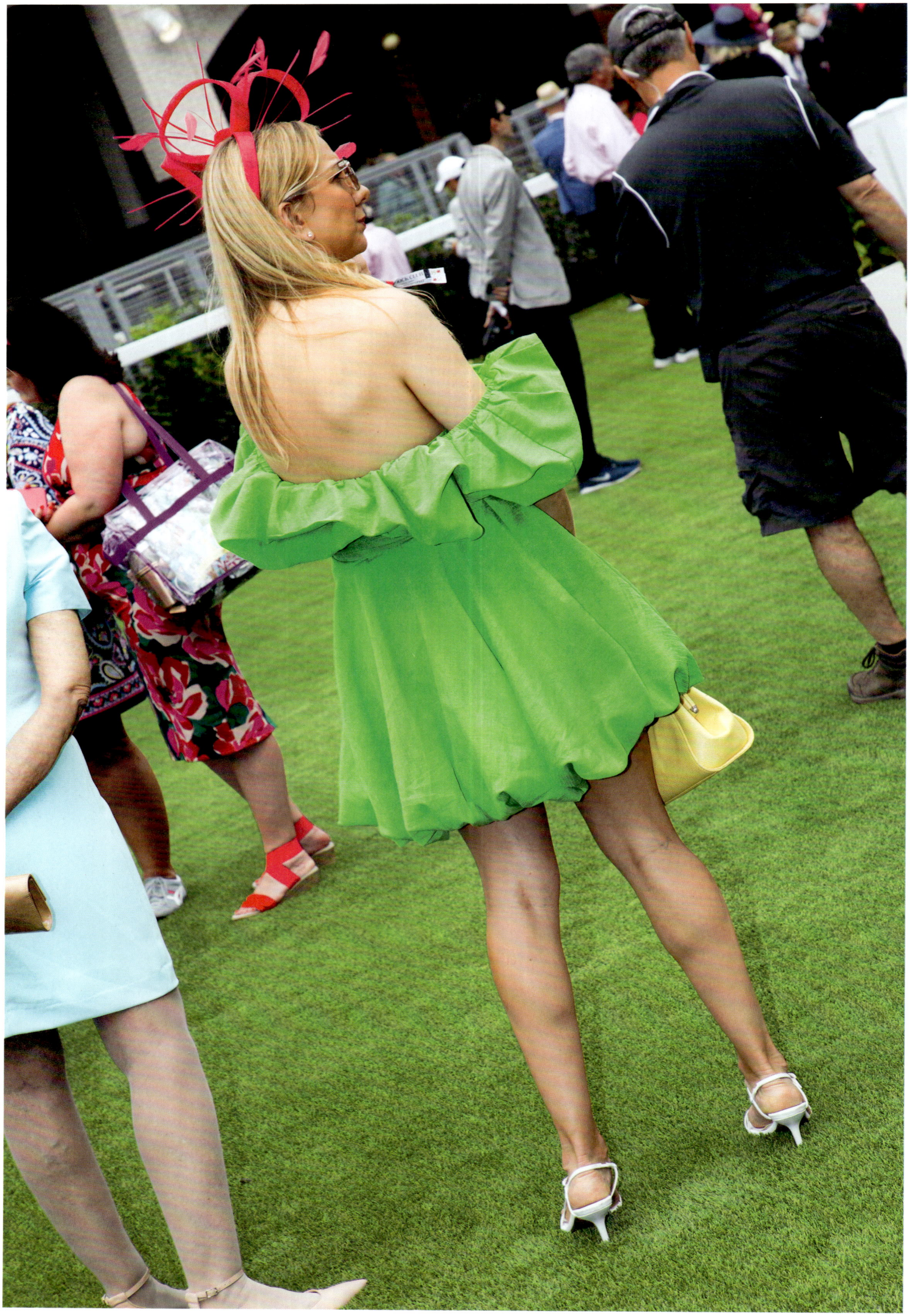

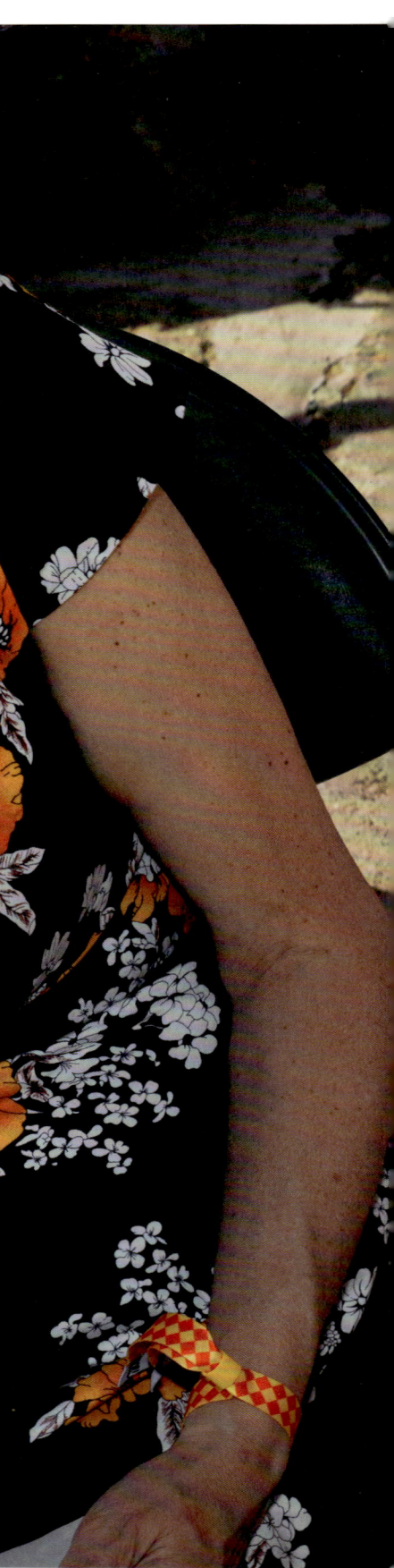

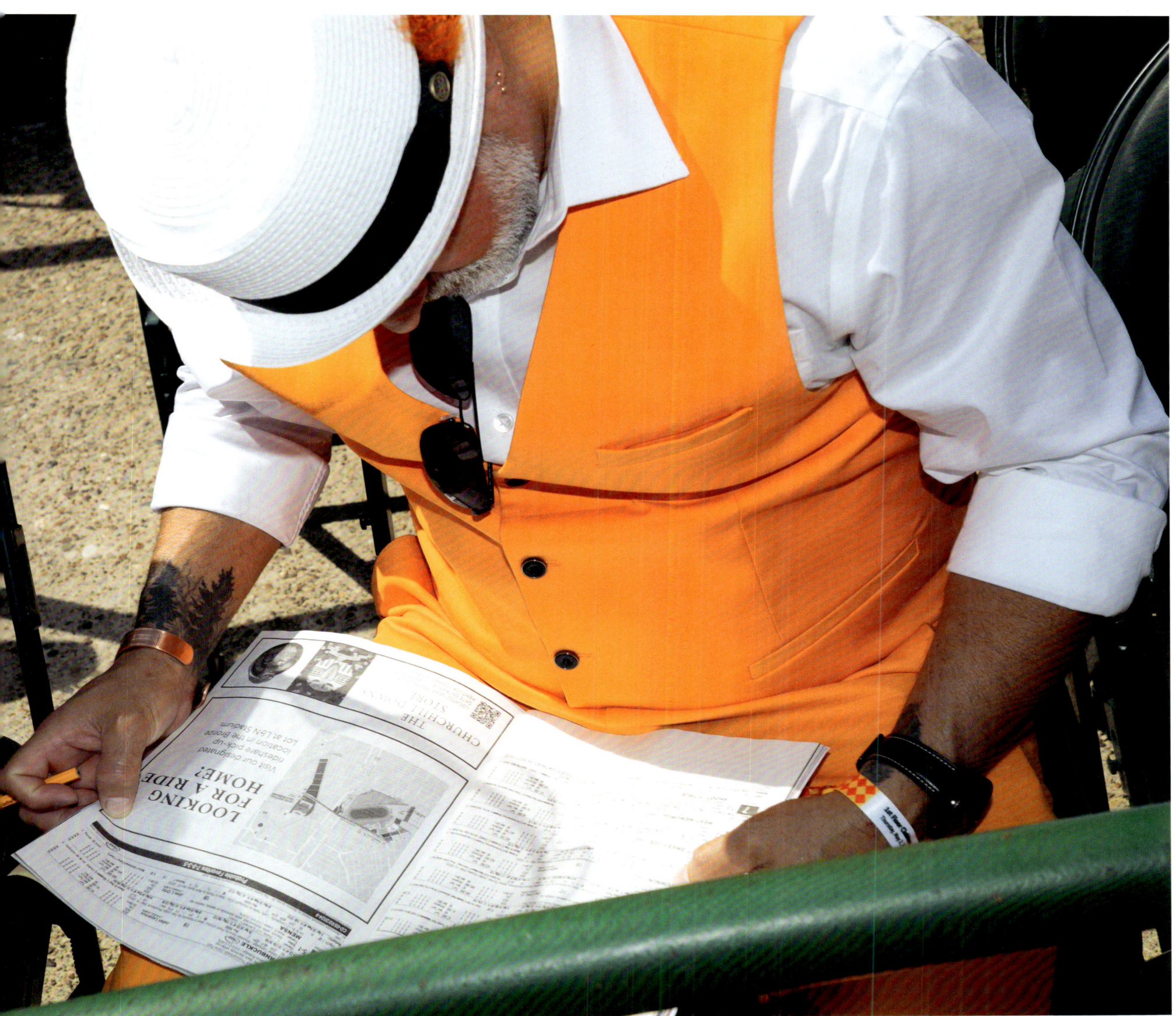

LOOKING
FOR A RIDE
HOME!

Visit our designated
rideshare pick-up
location in the Bronx
Lot at LSN Stadium.

THE CHURCHILL DOWNS
STORE

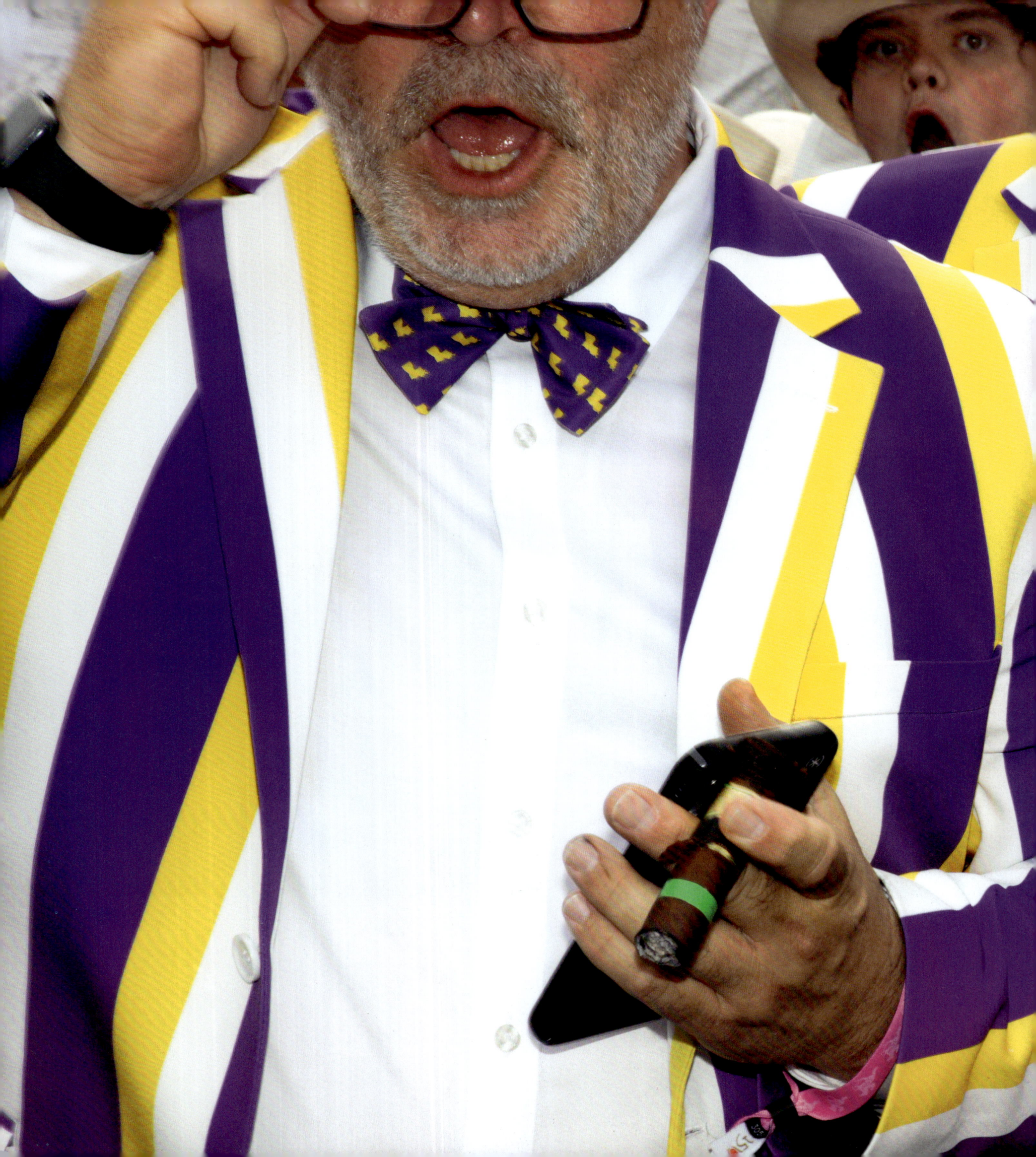

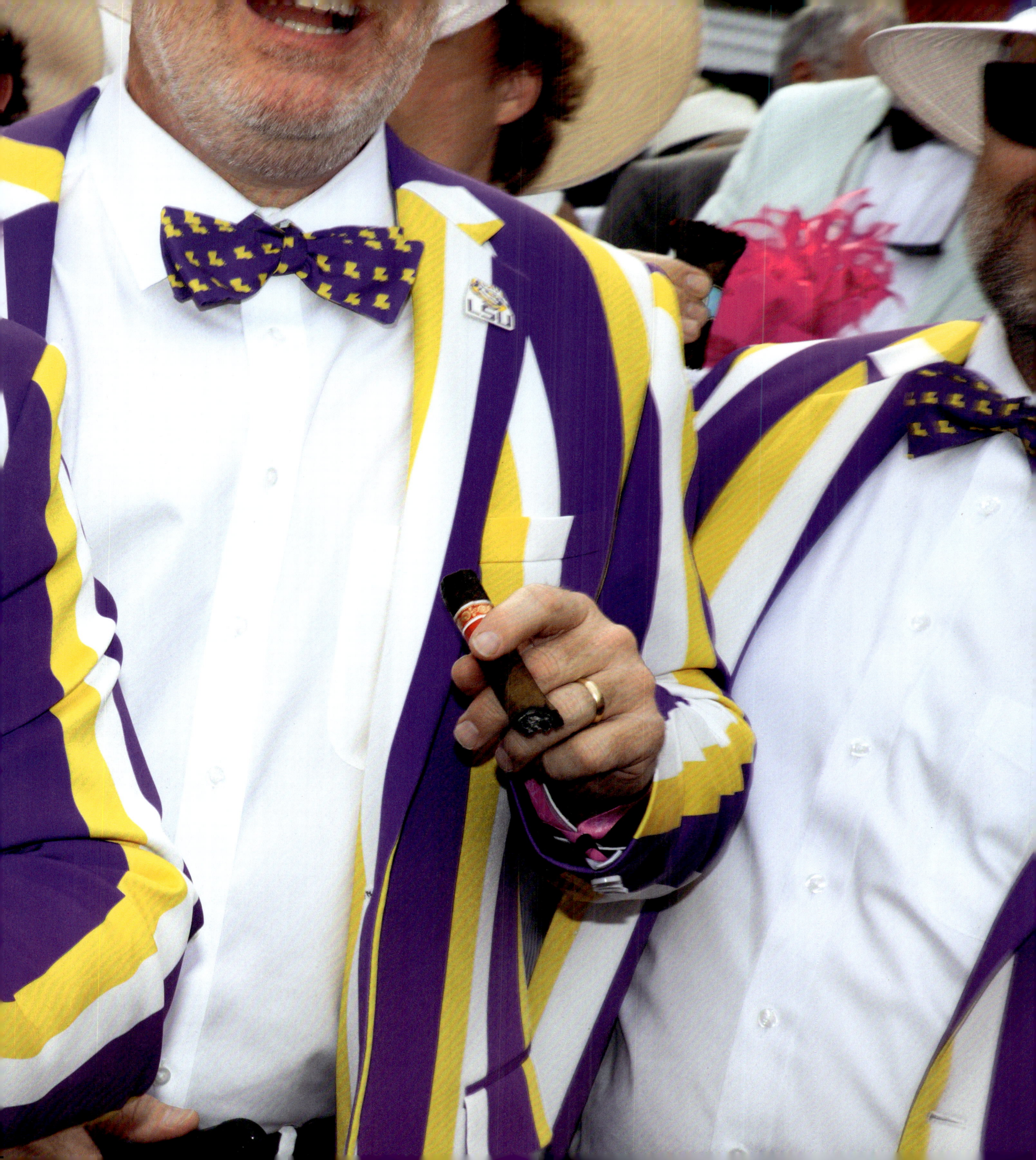

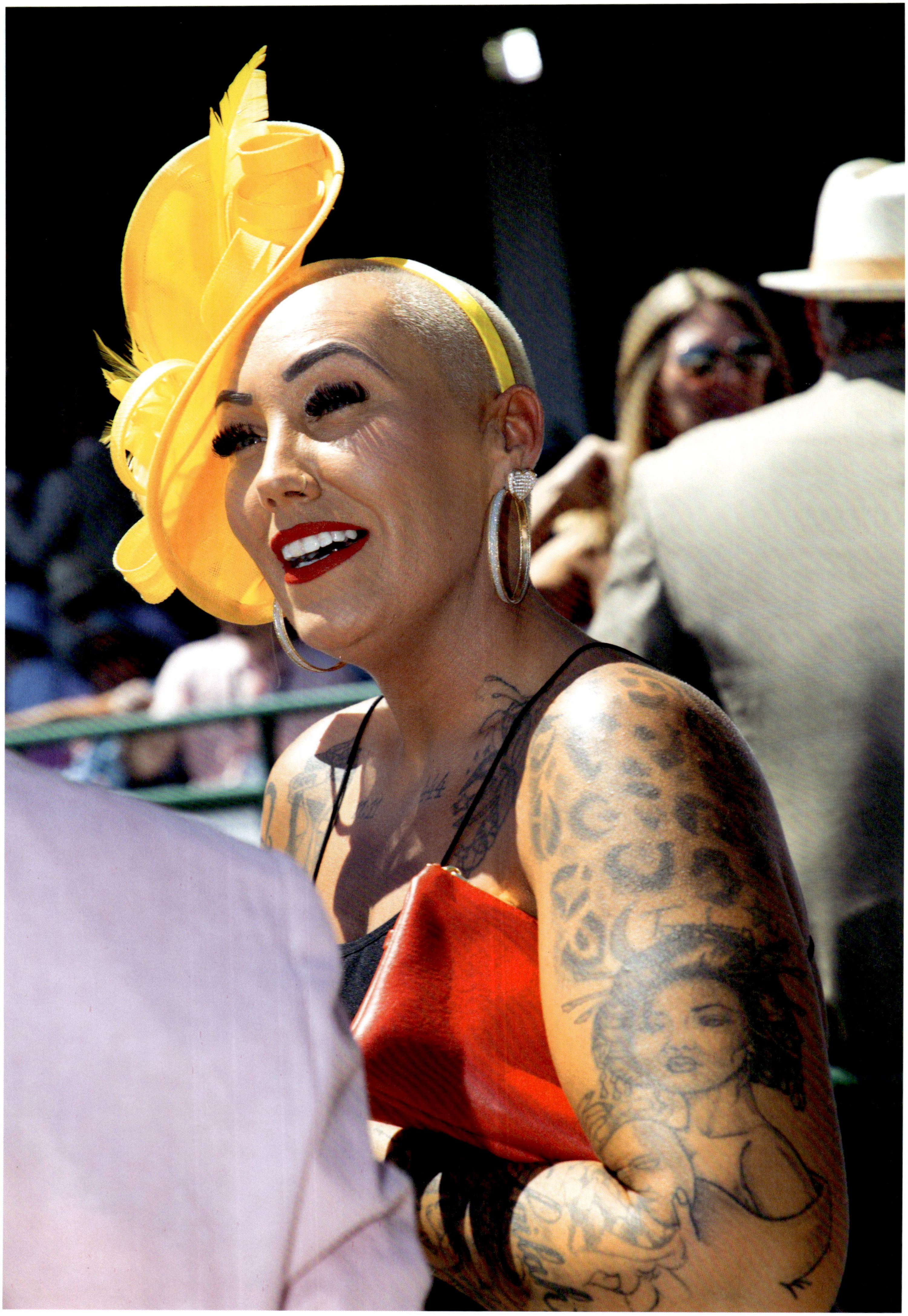

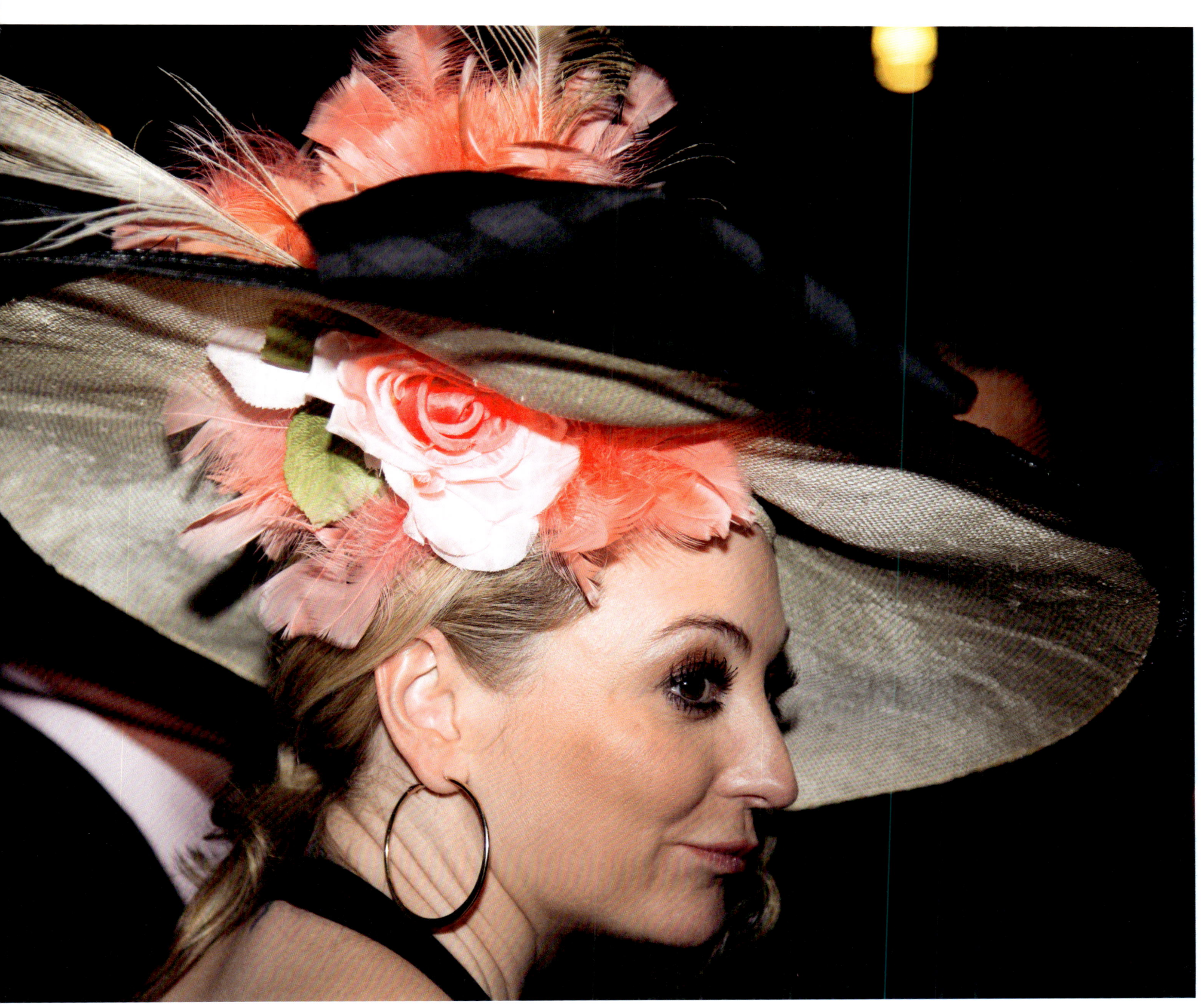

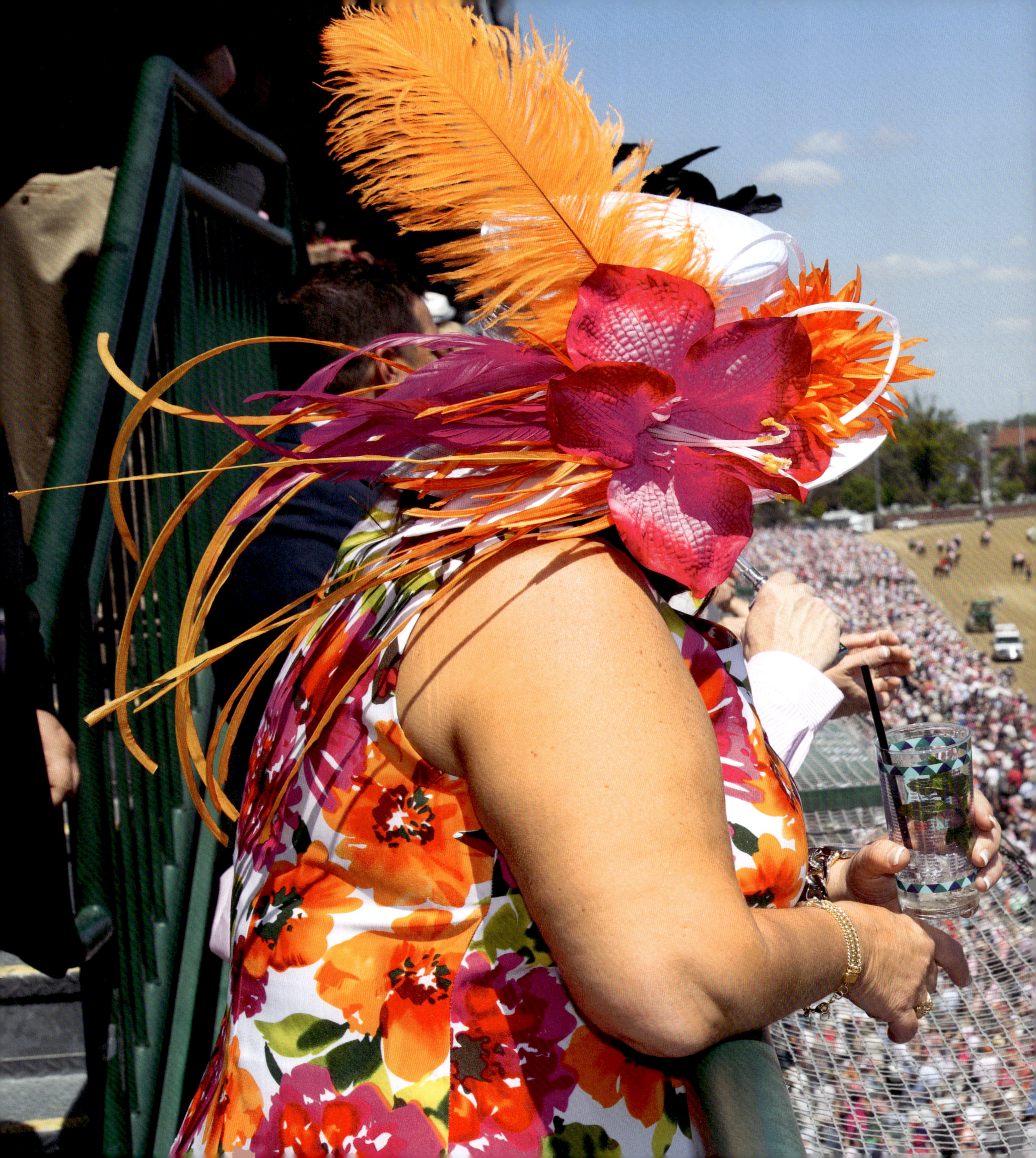

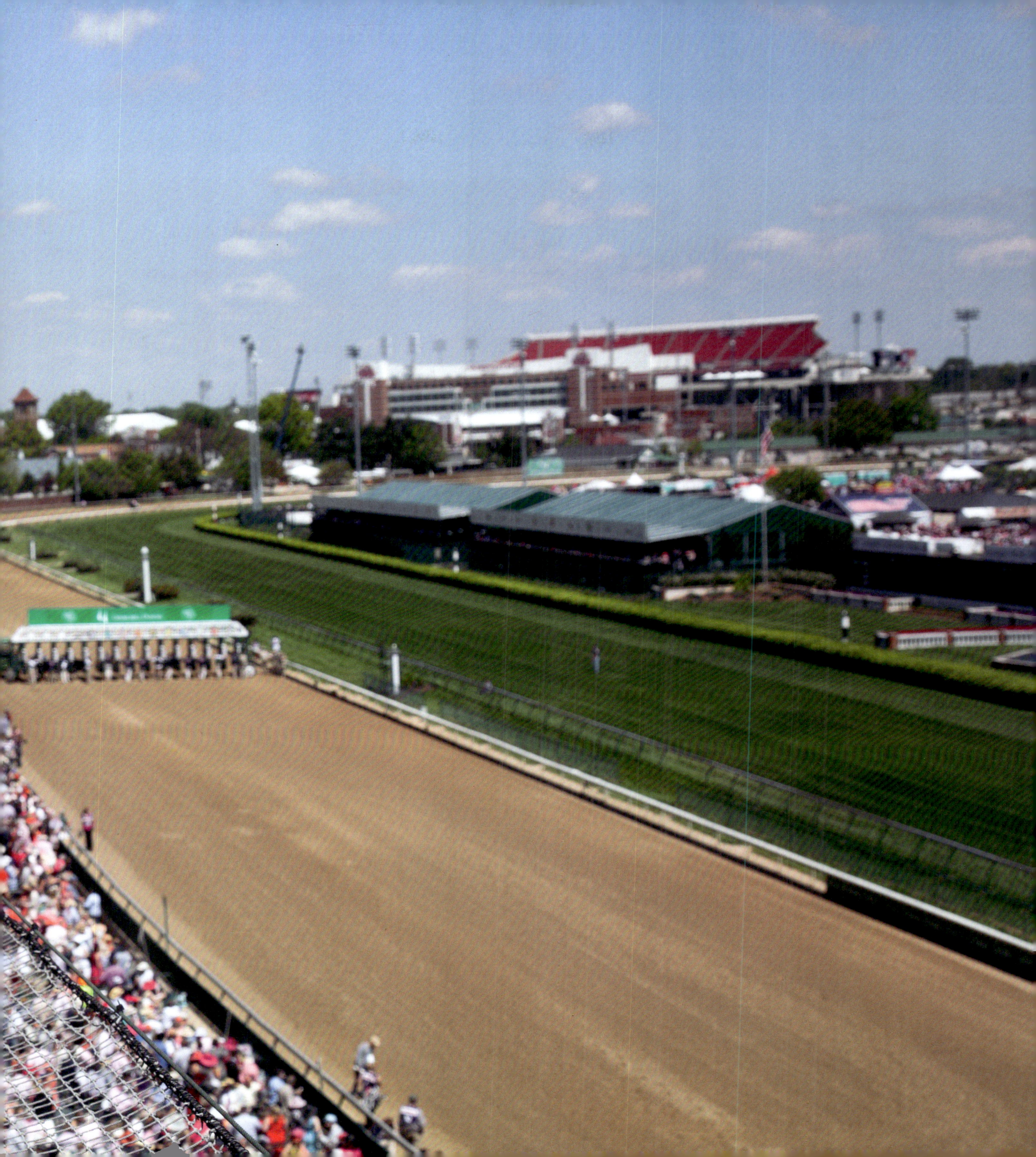

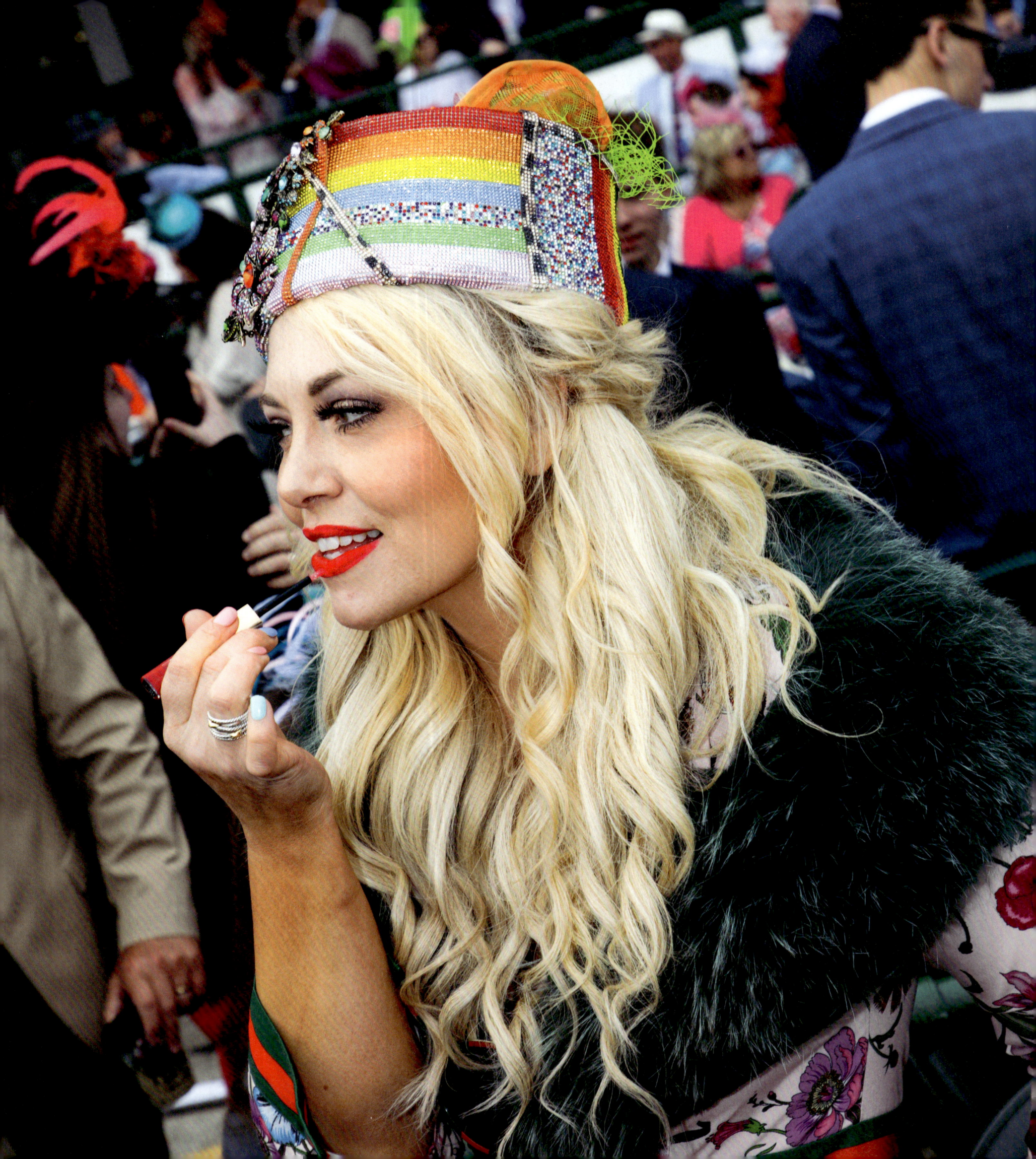

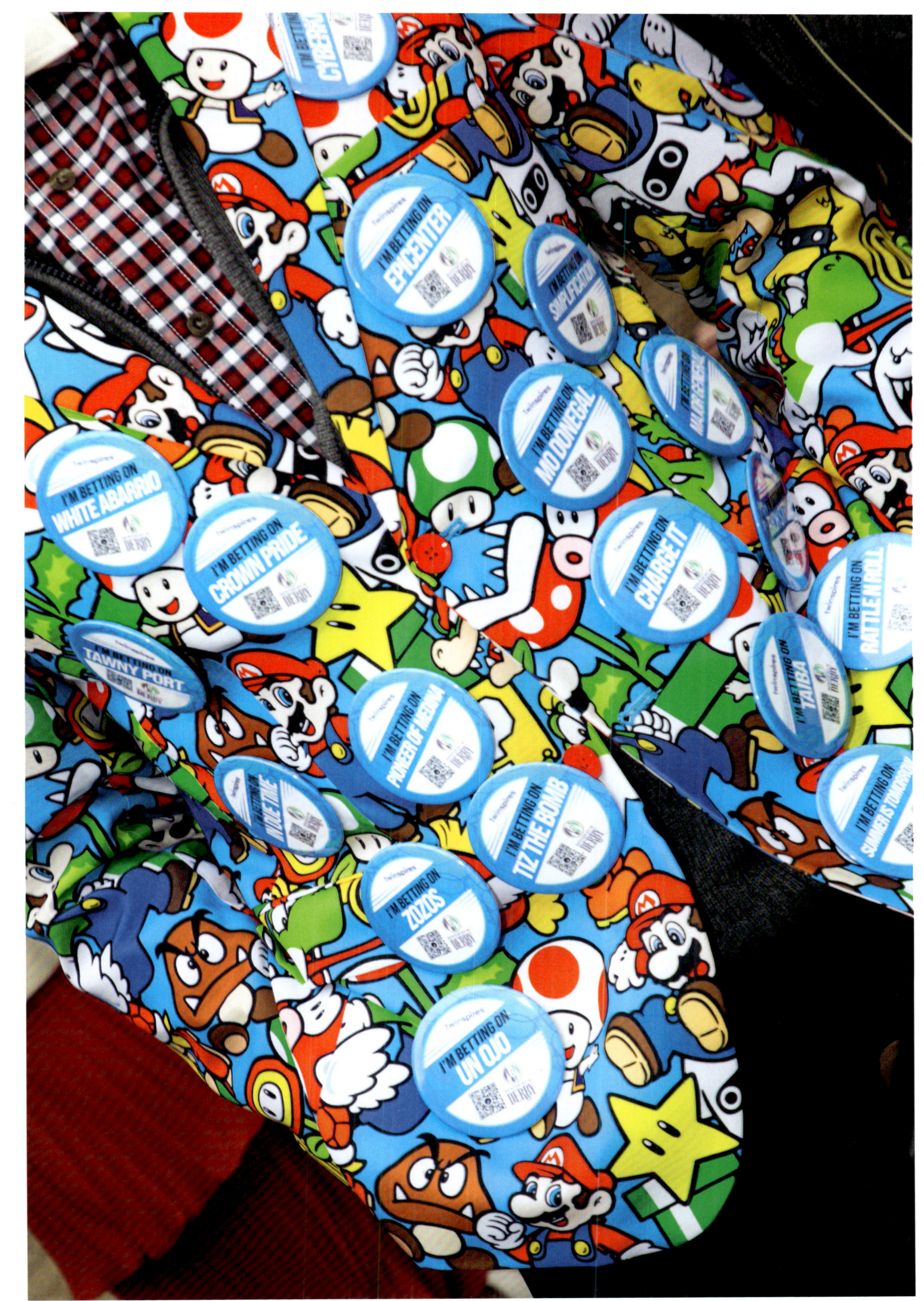

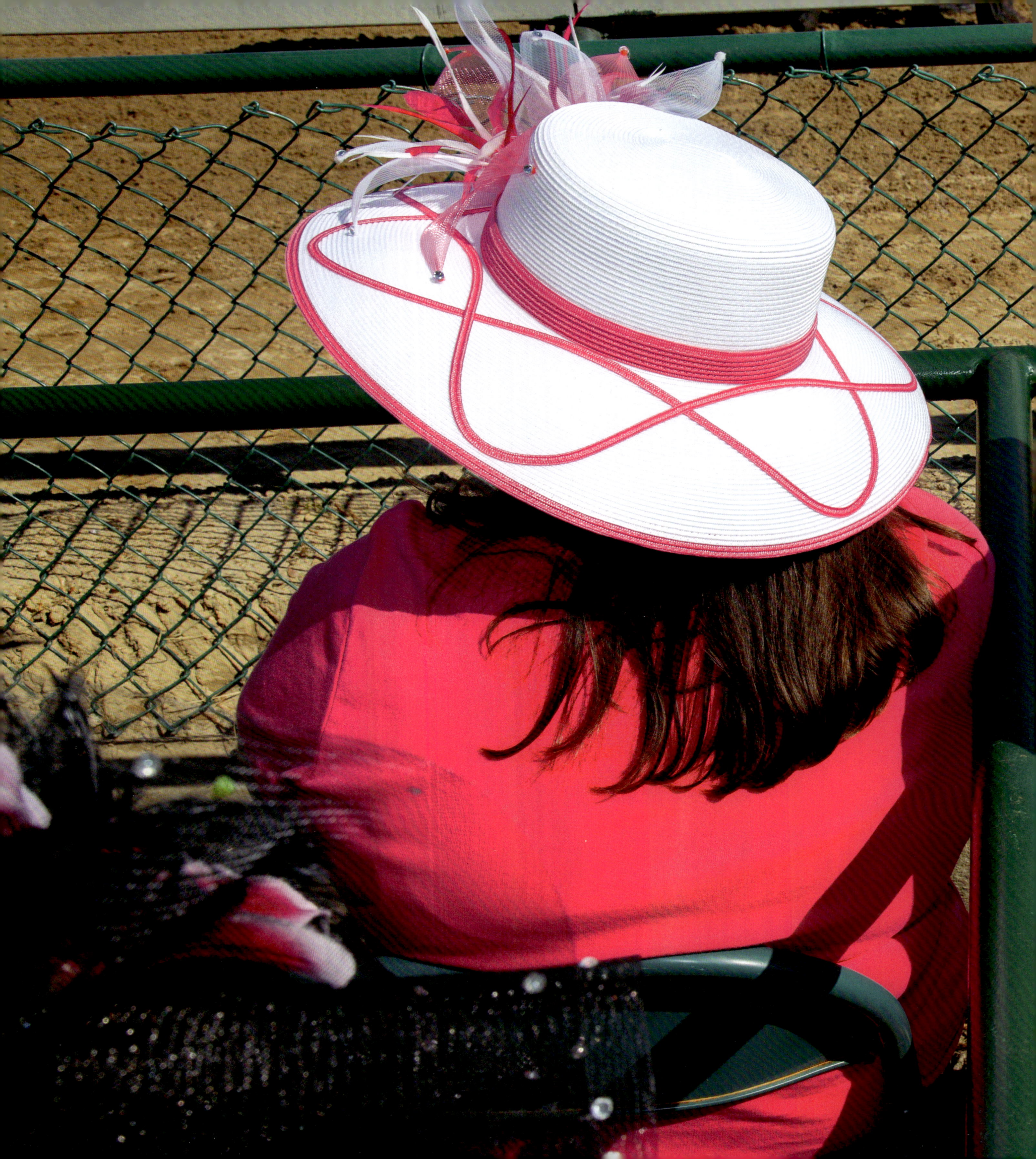

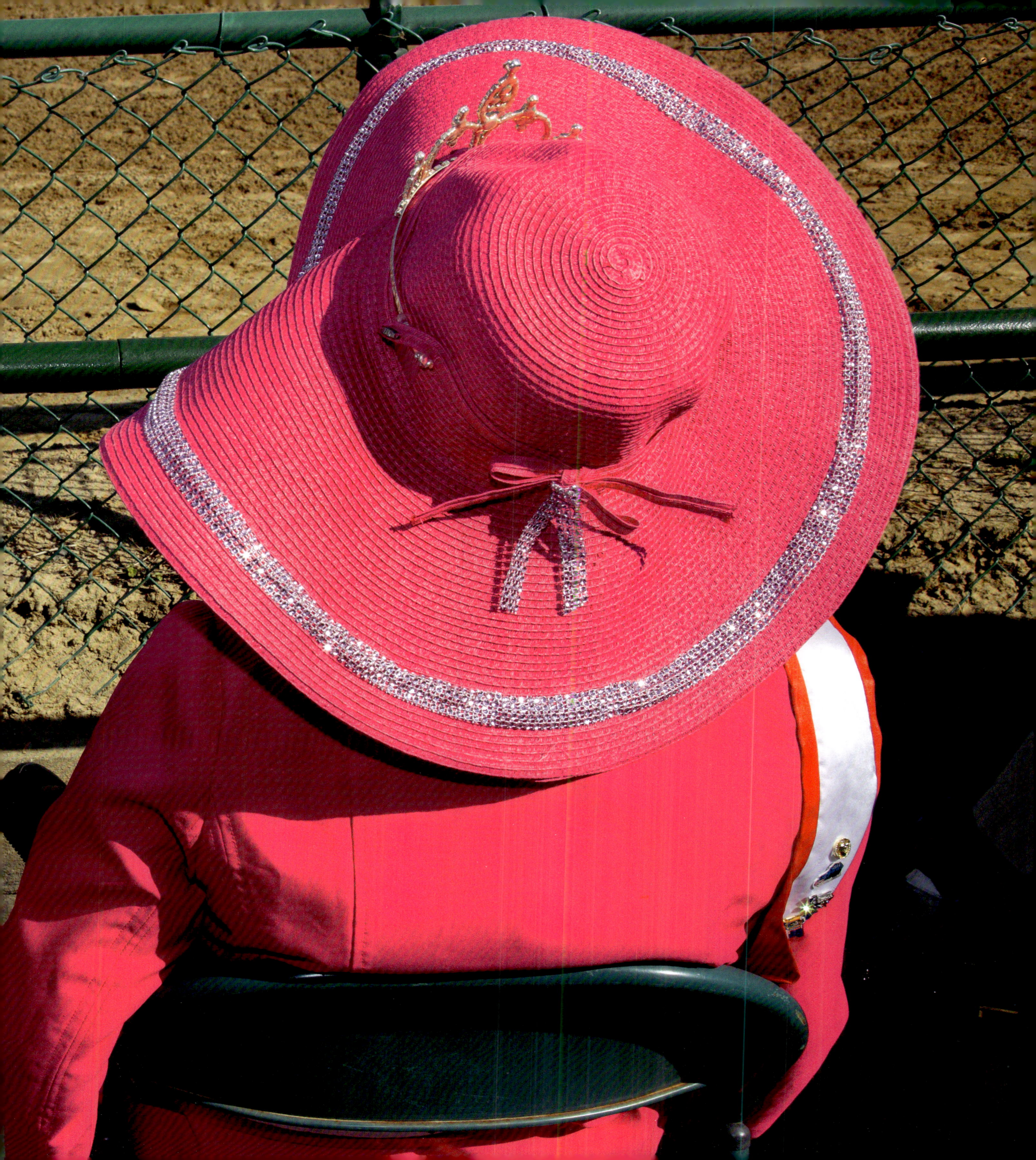

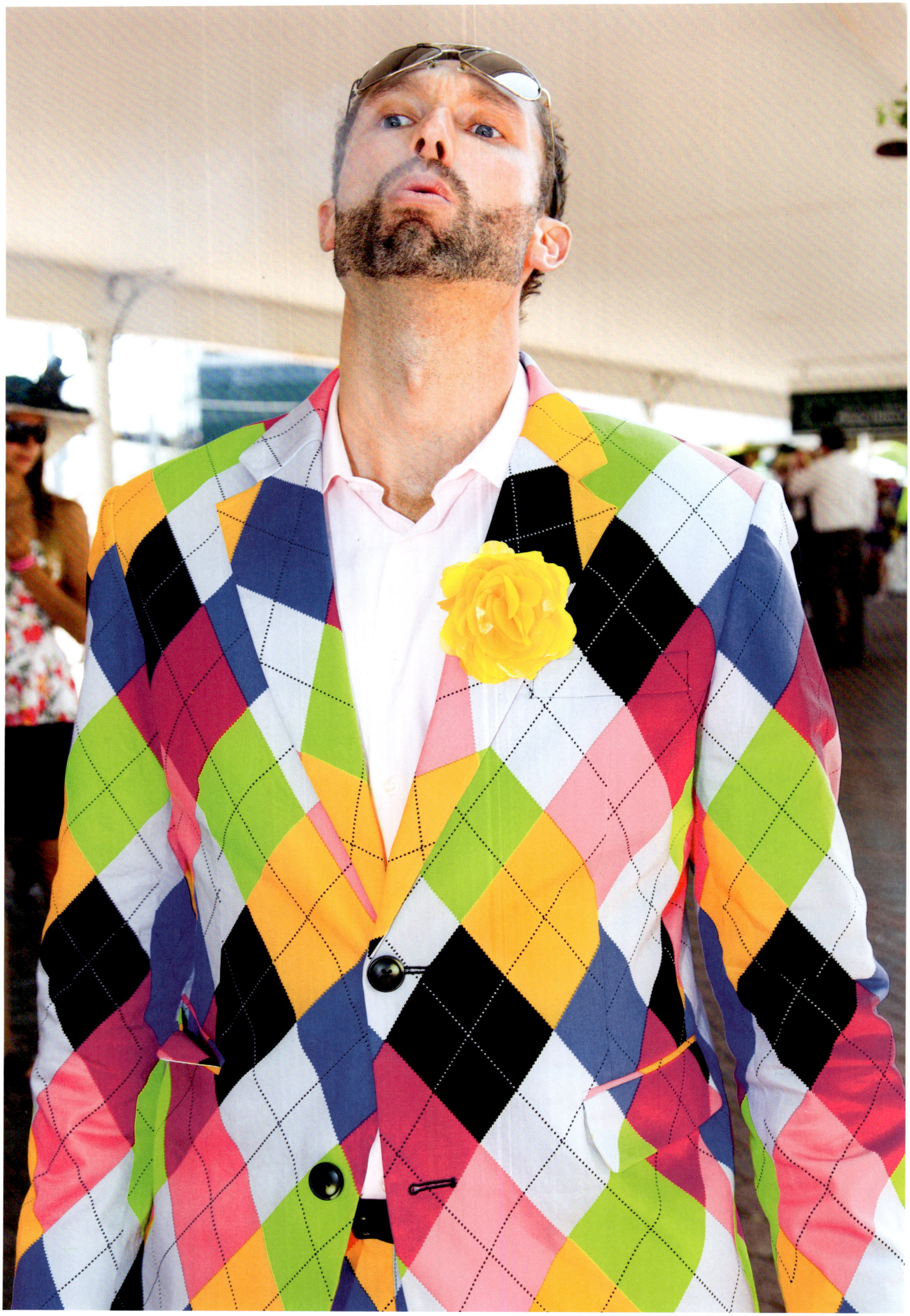

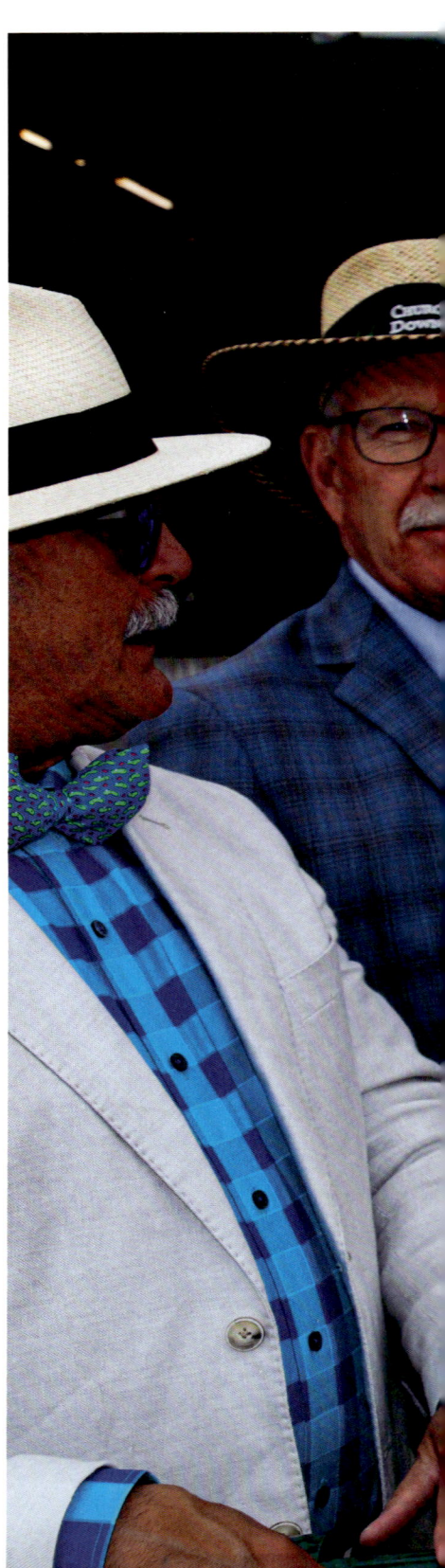

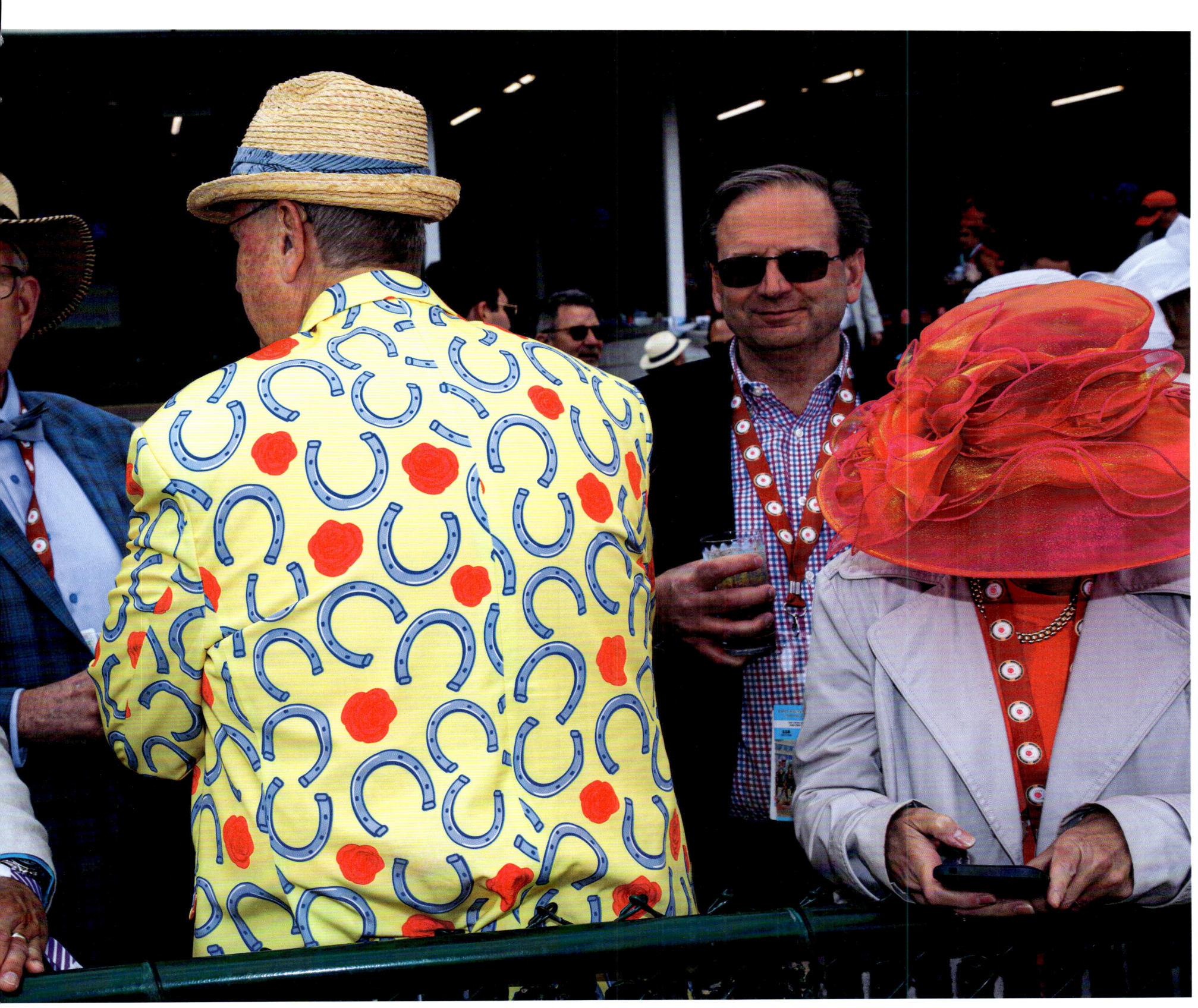

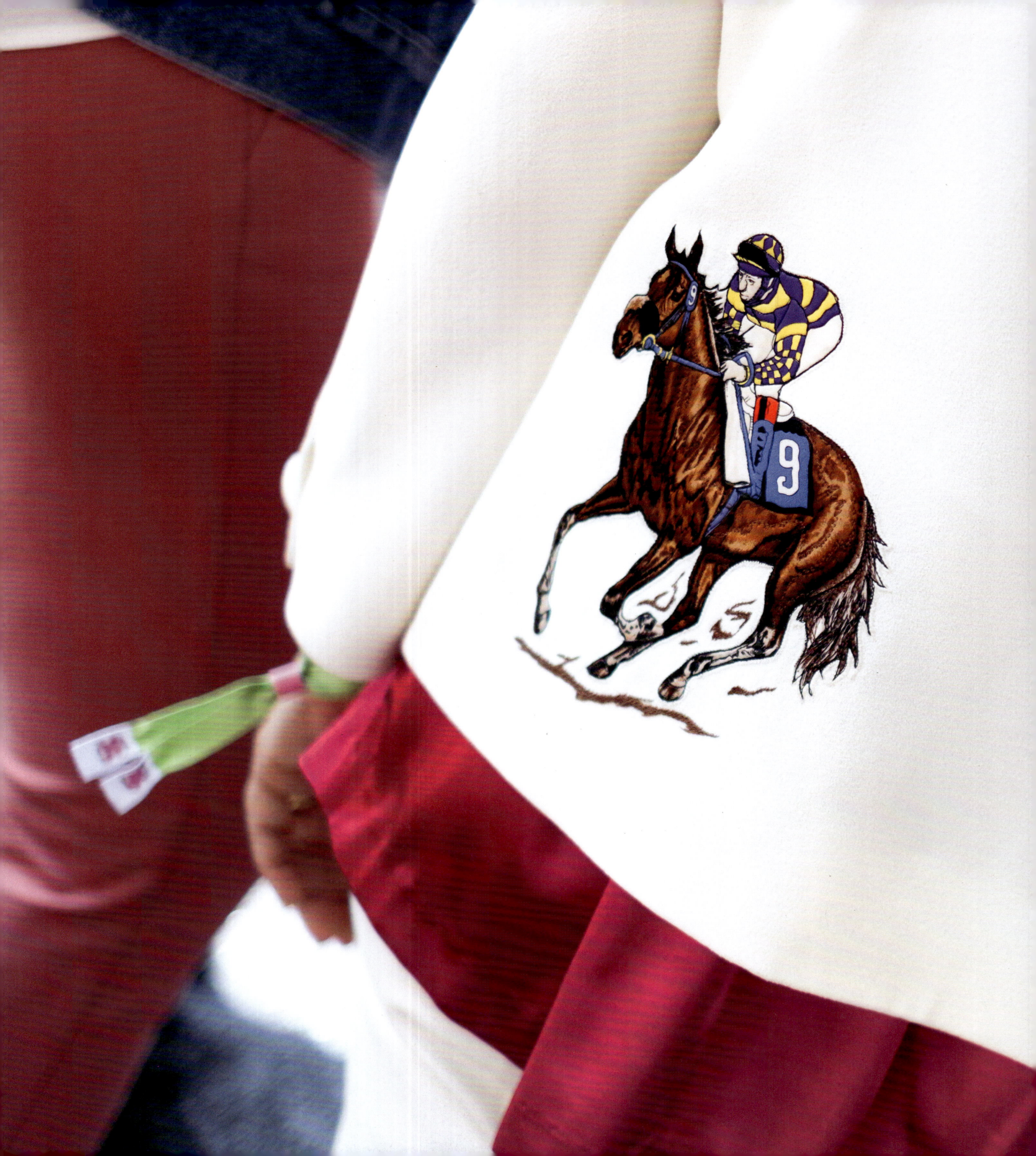

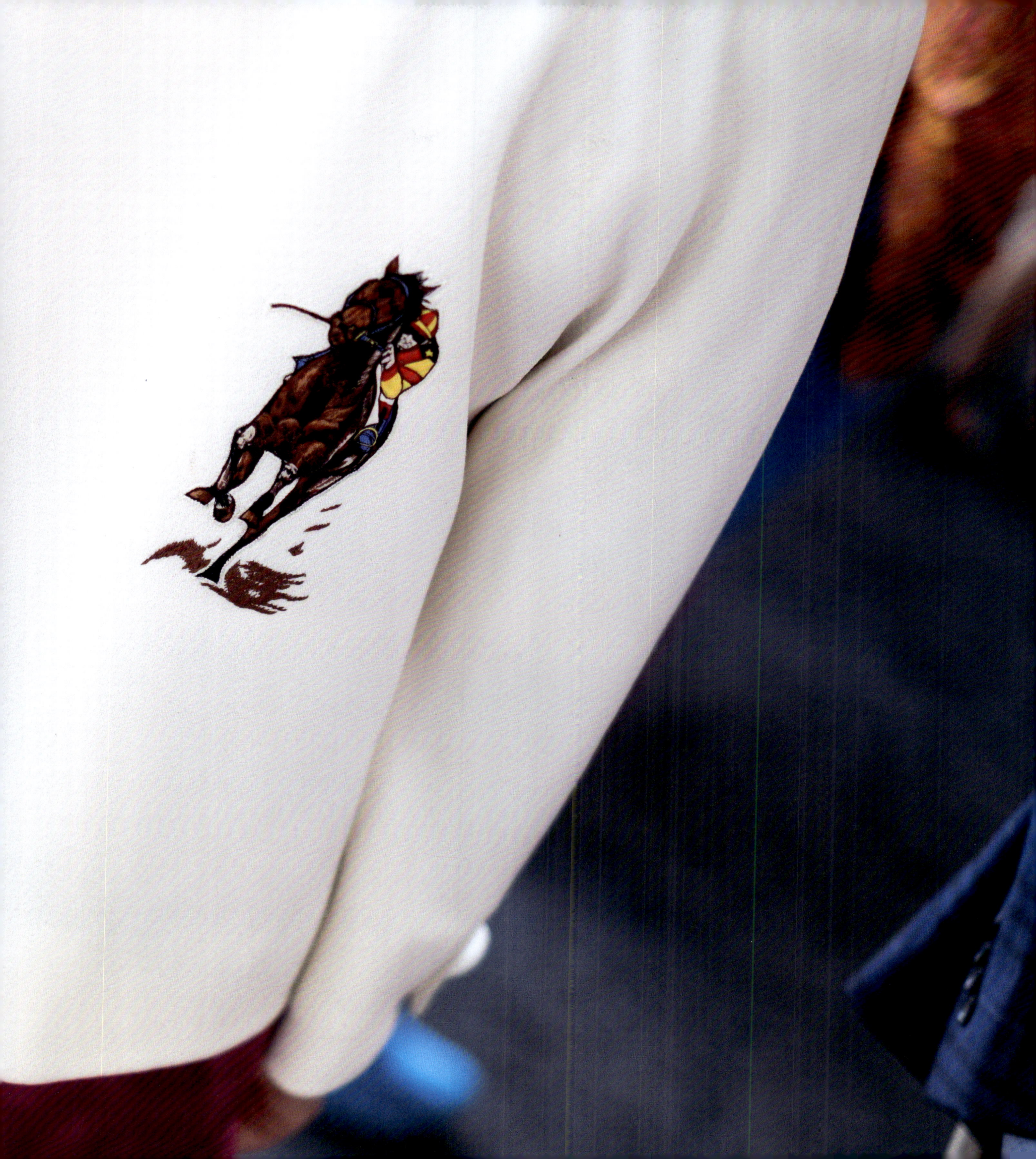

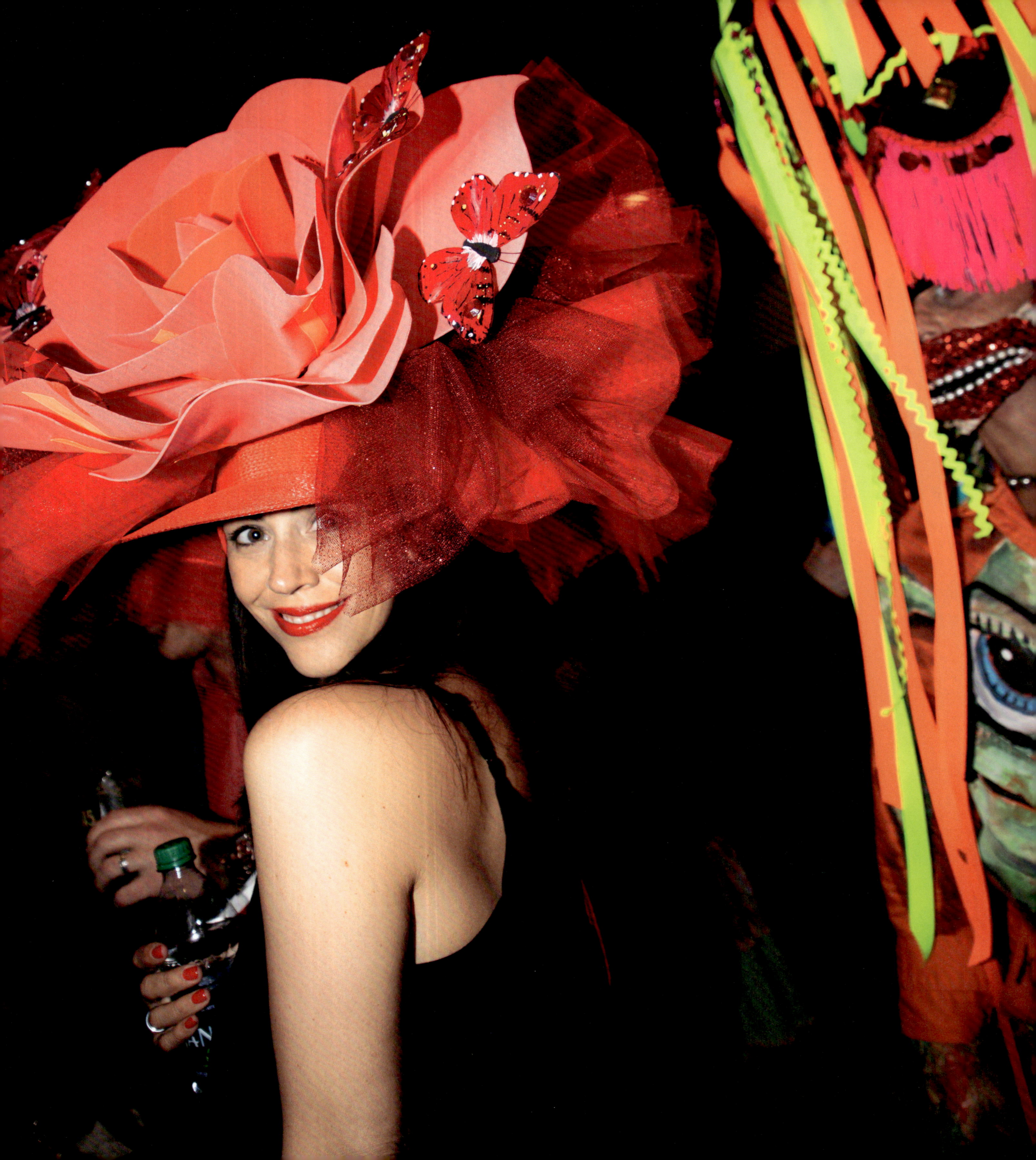

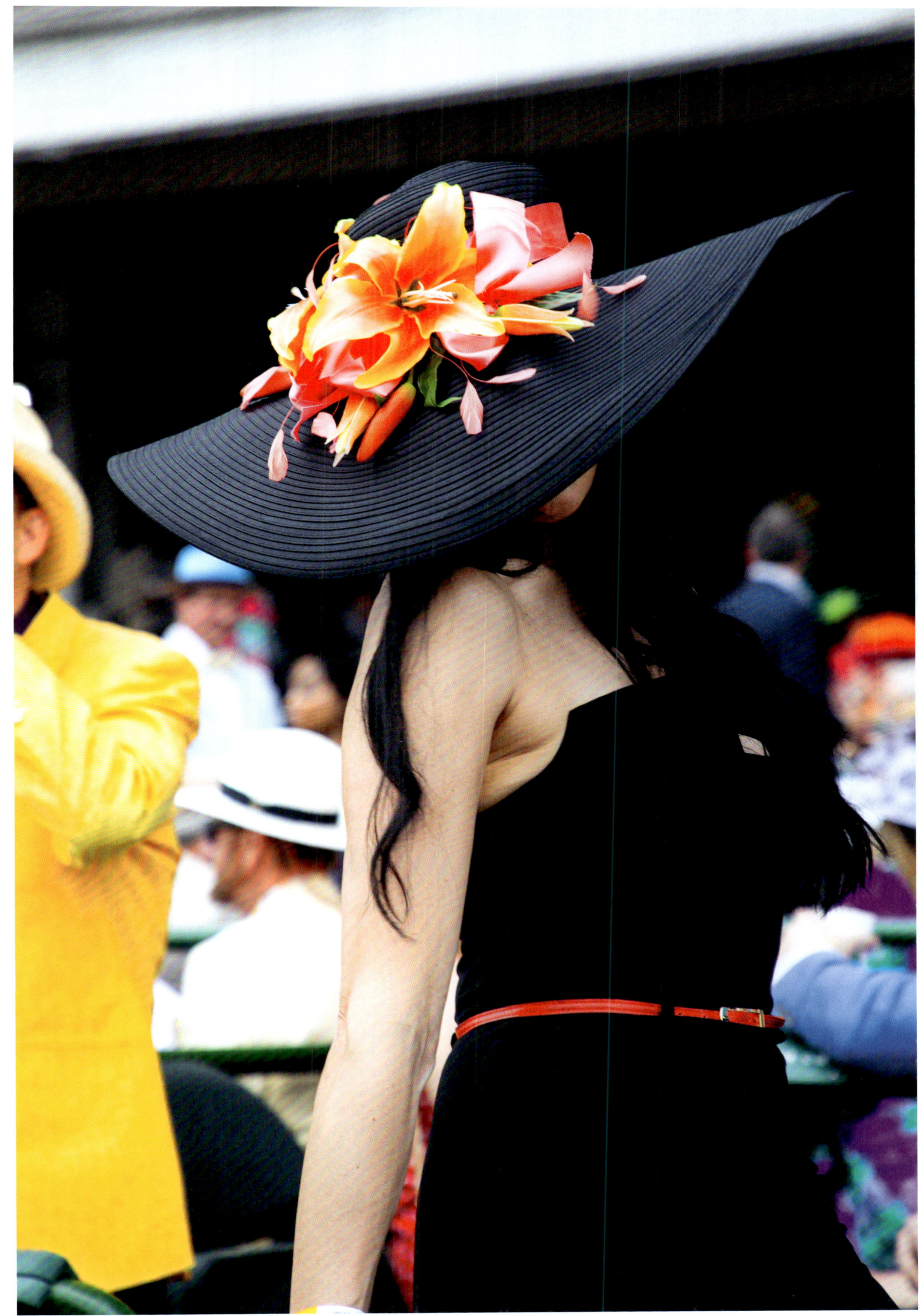

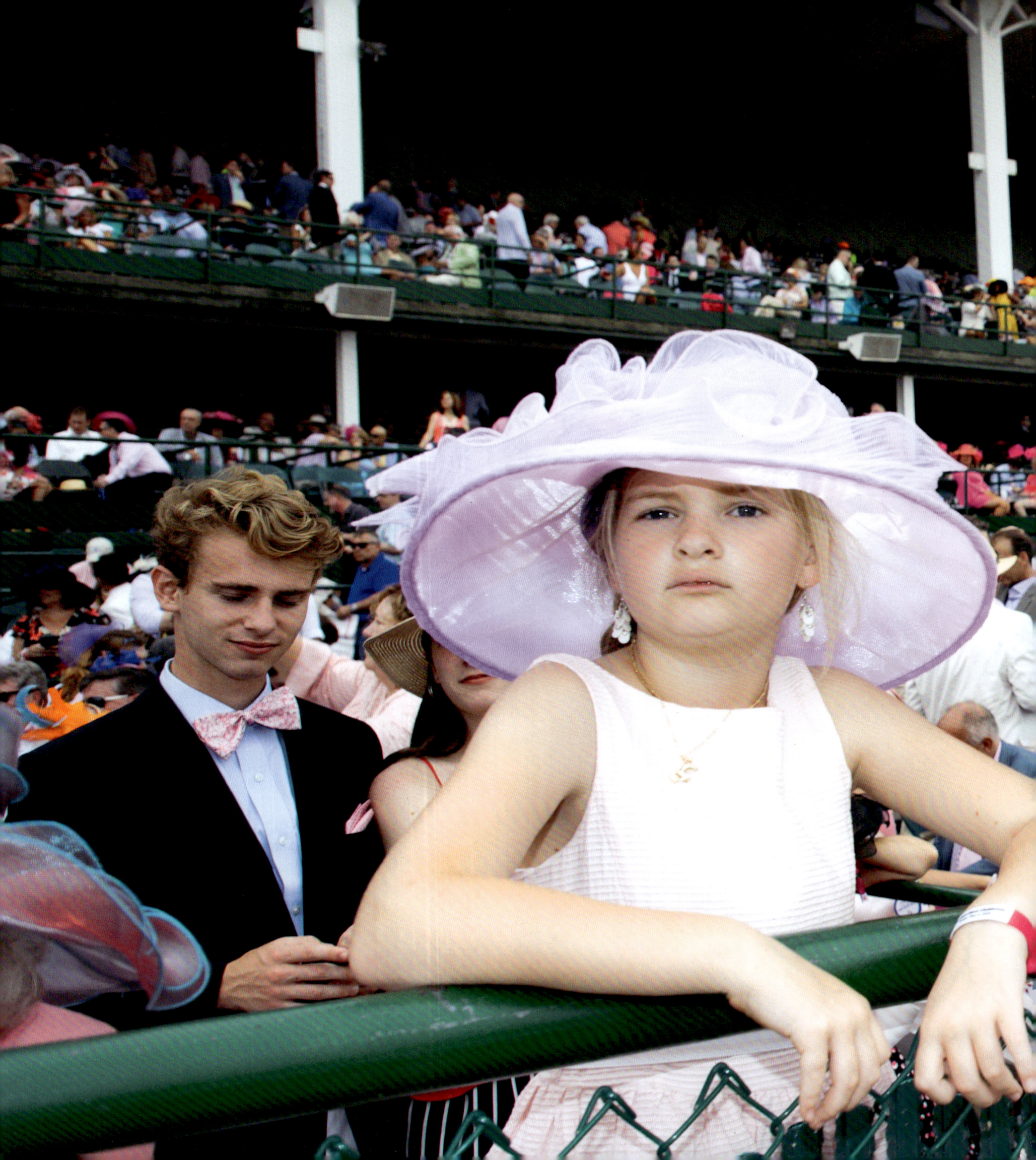

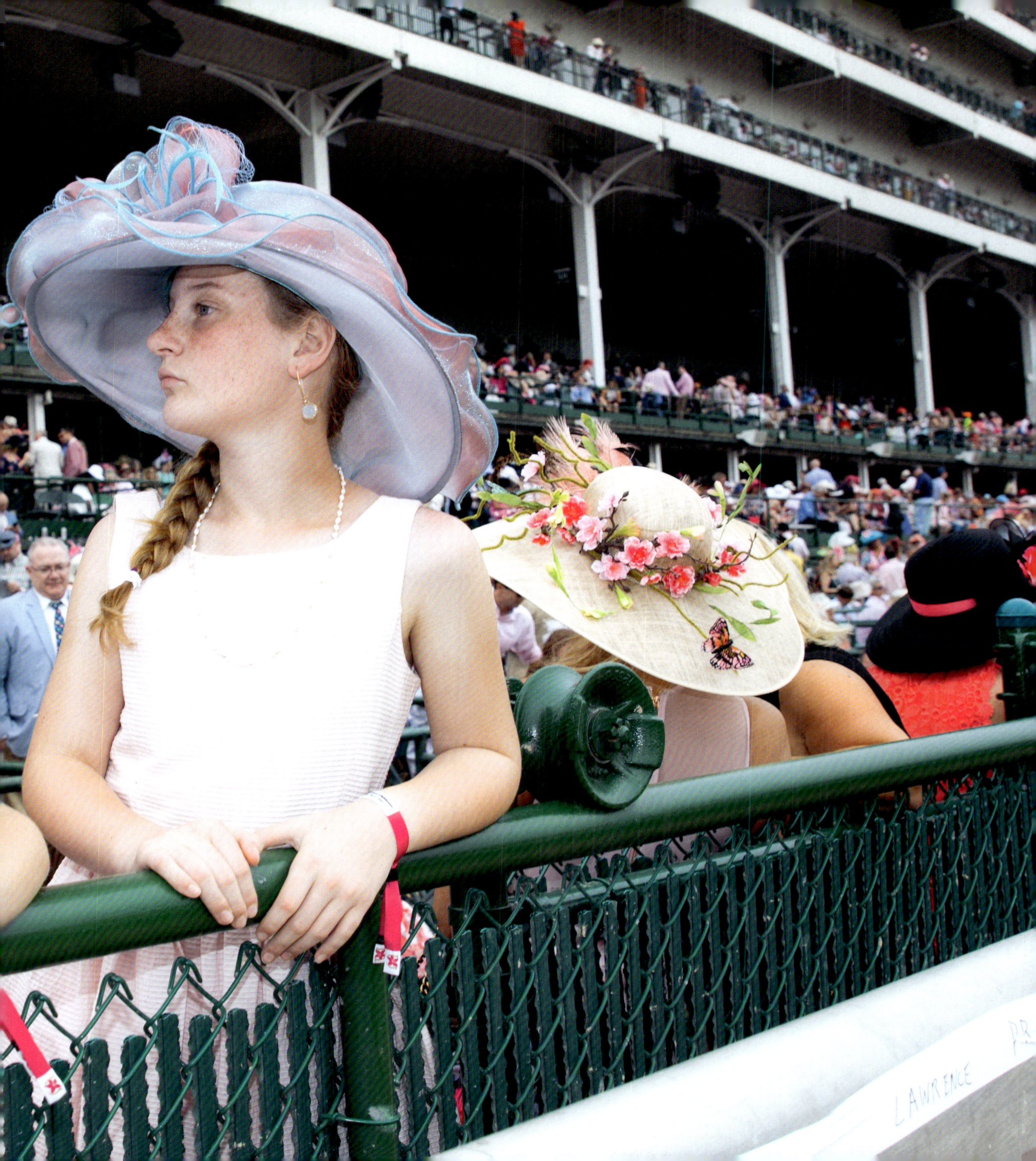

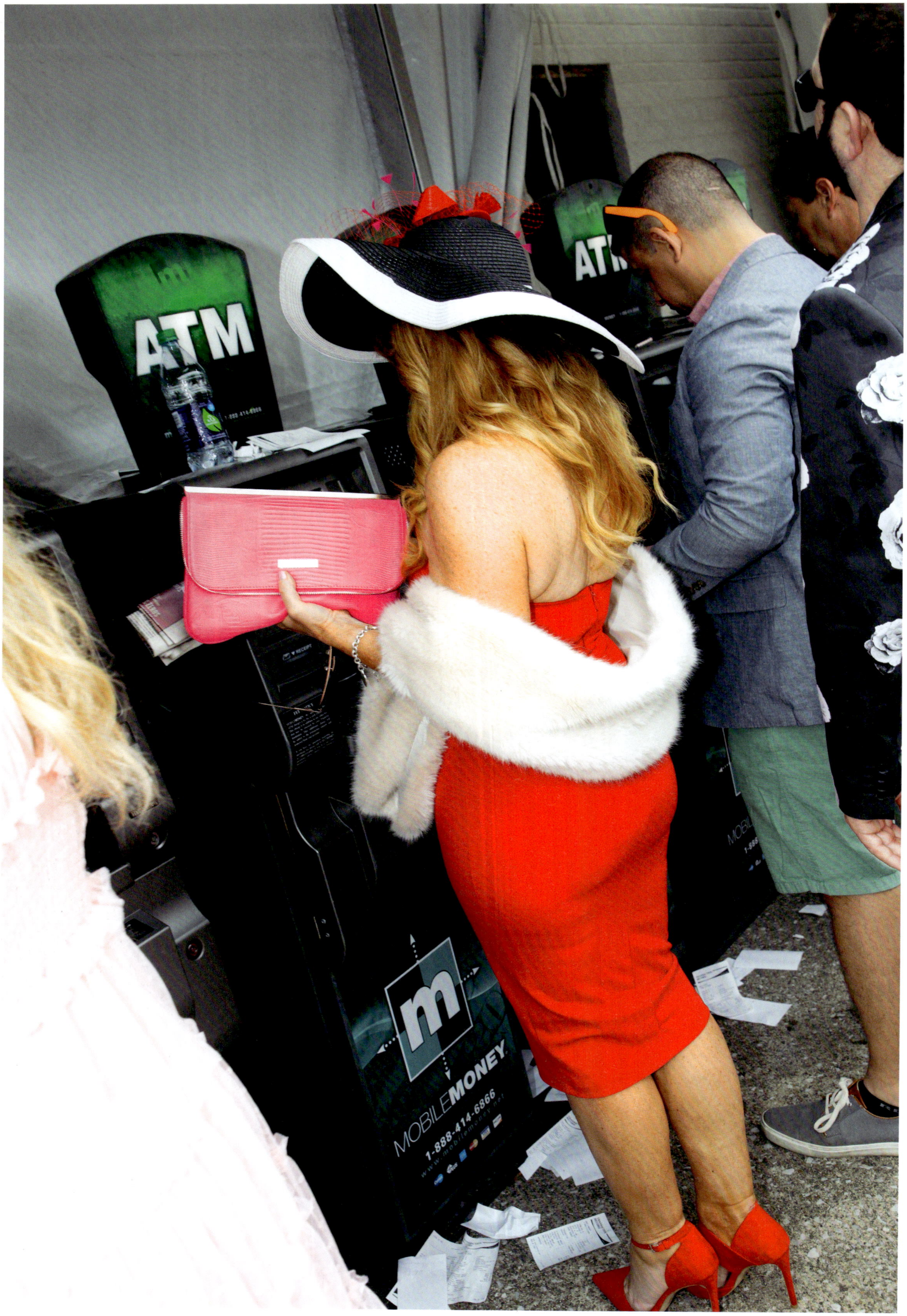

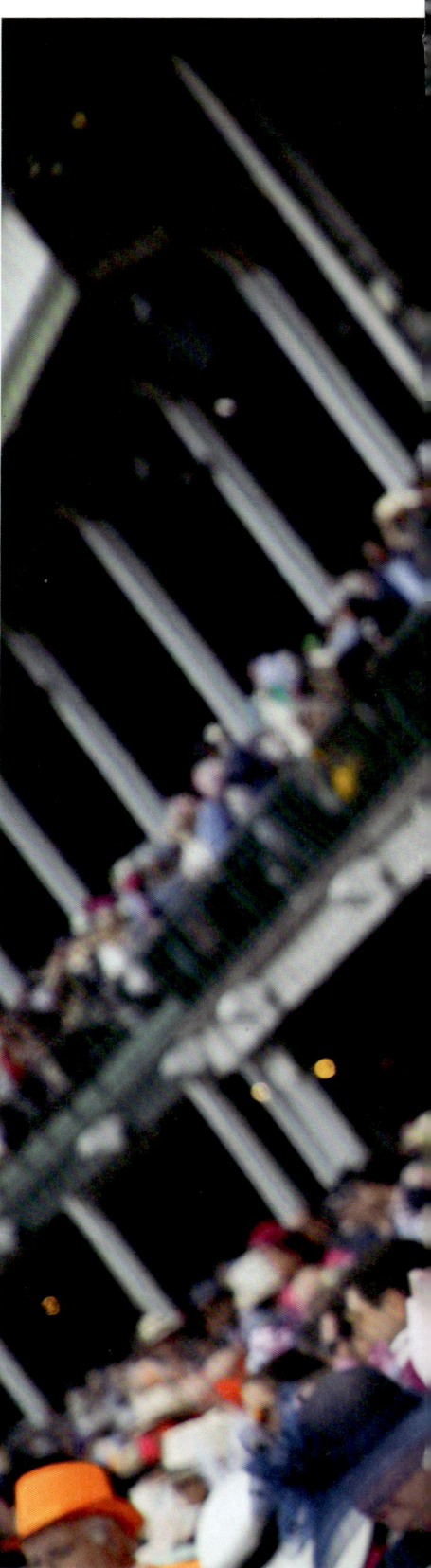

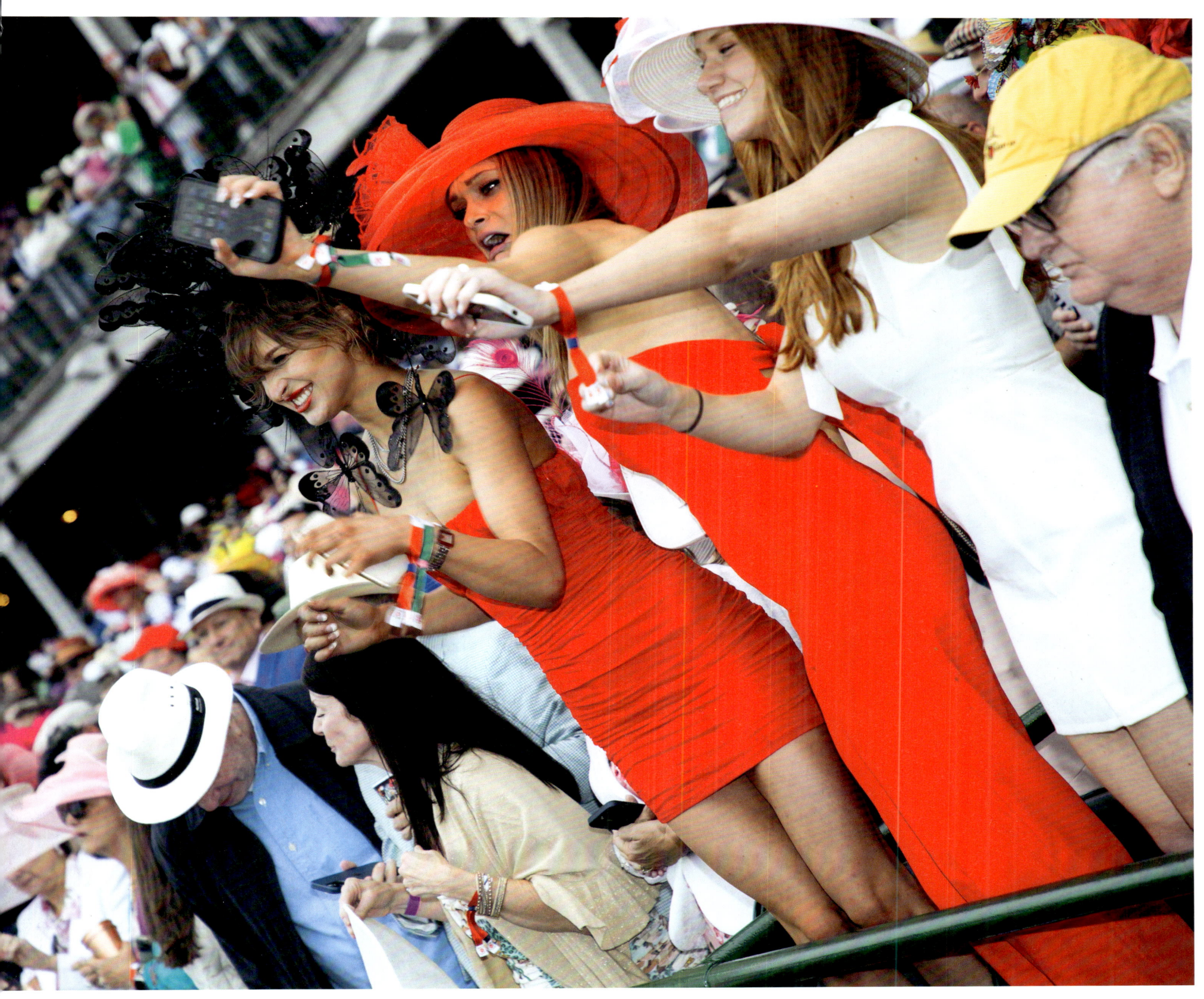

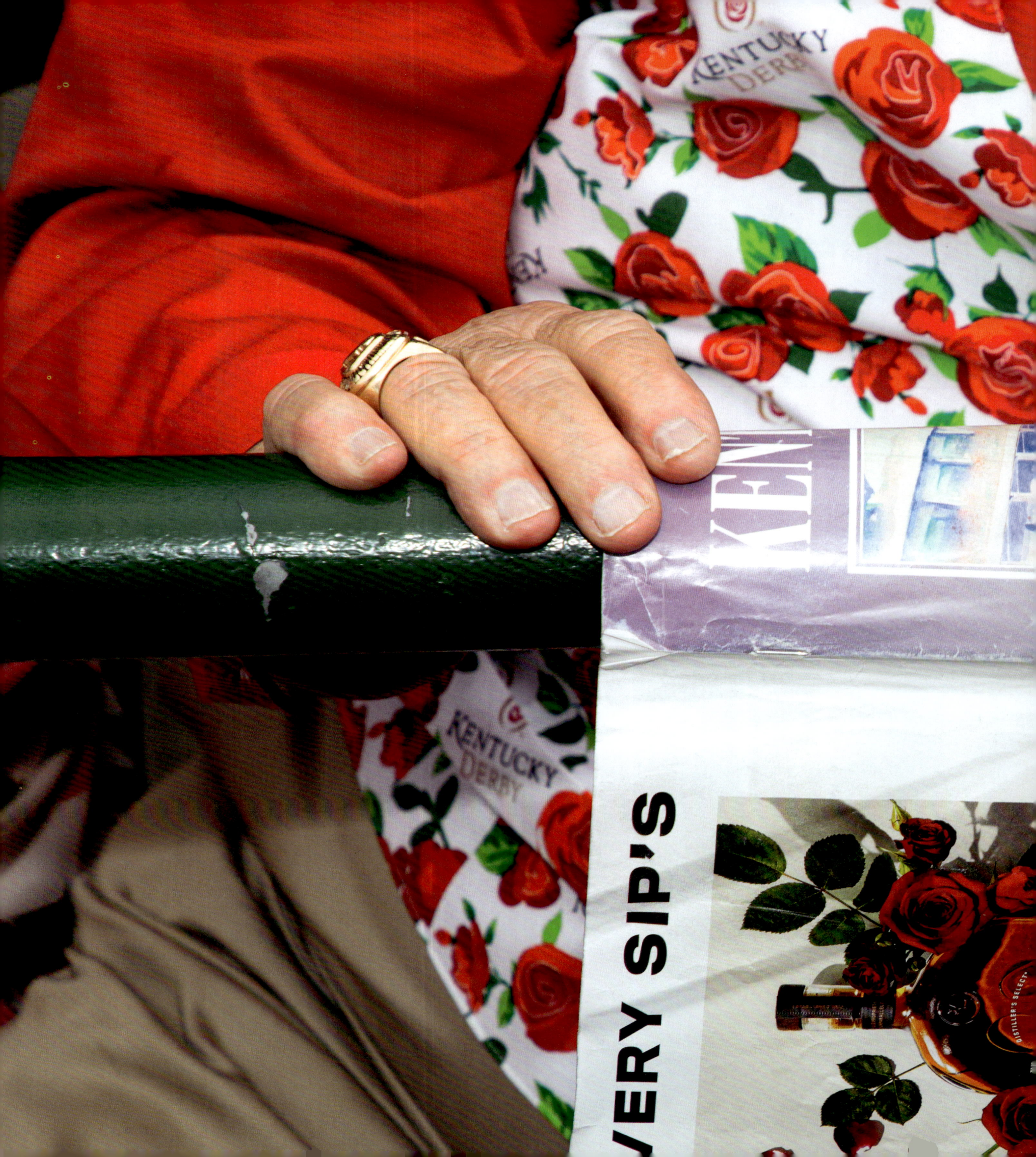

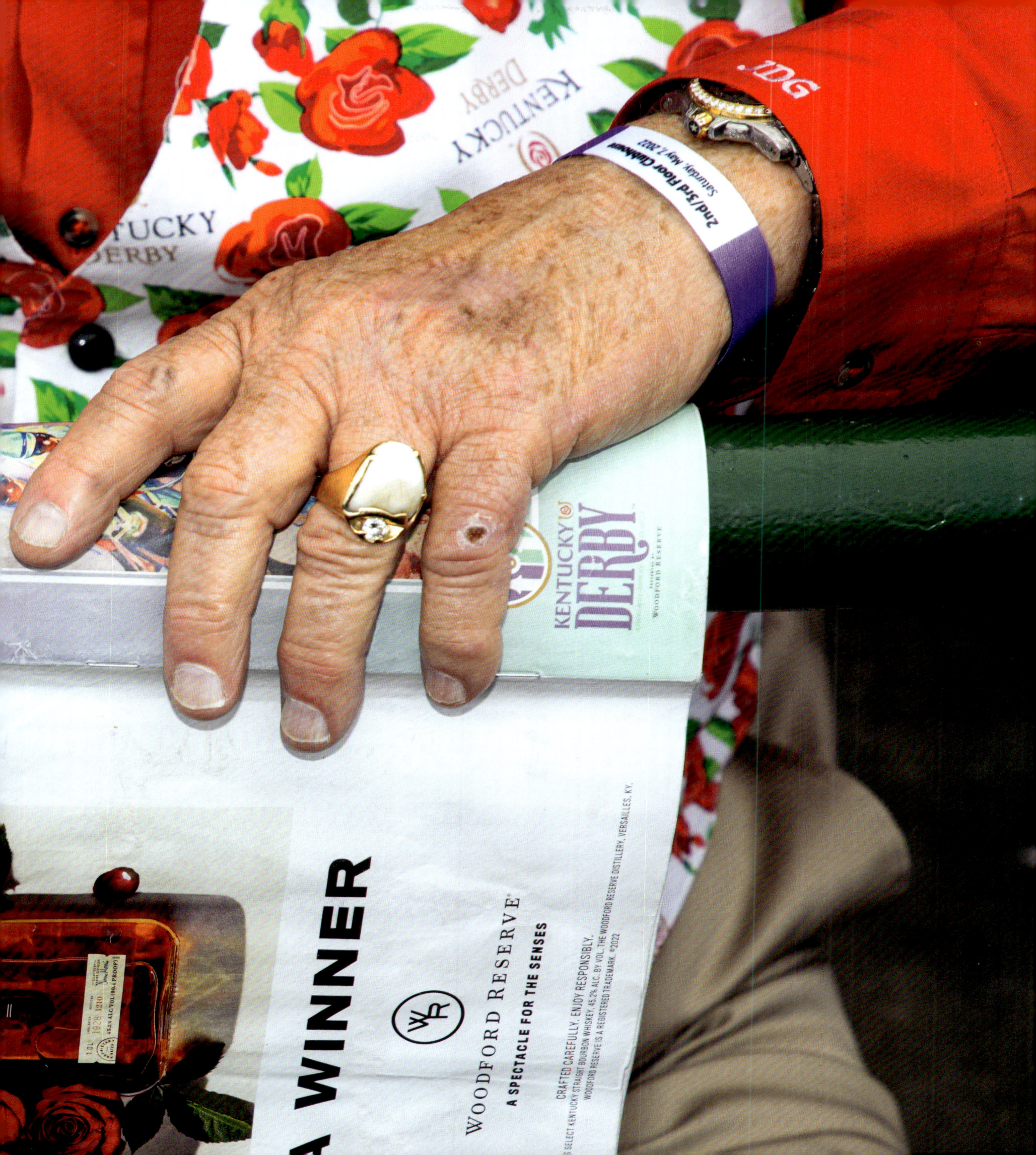

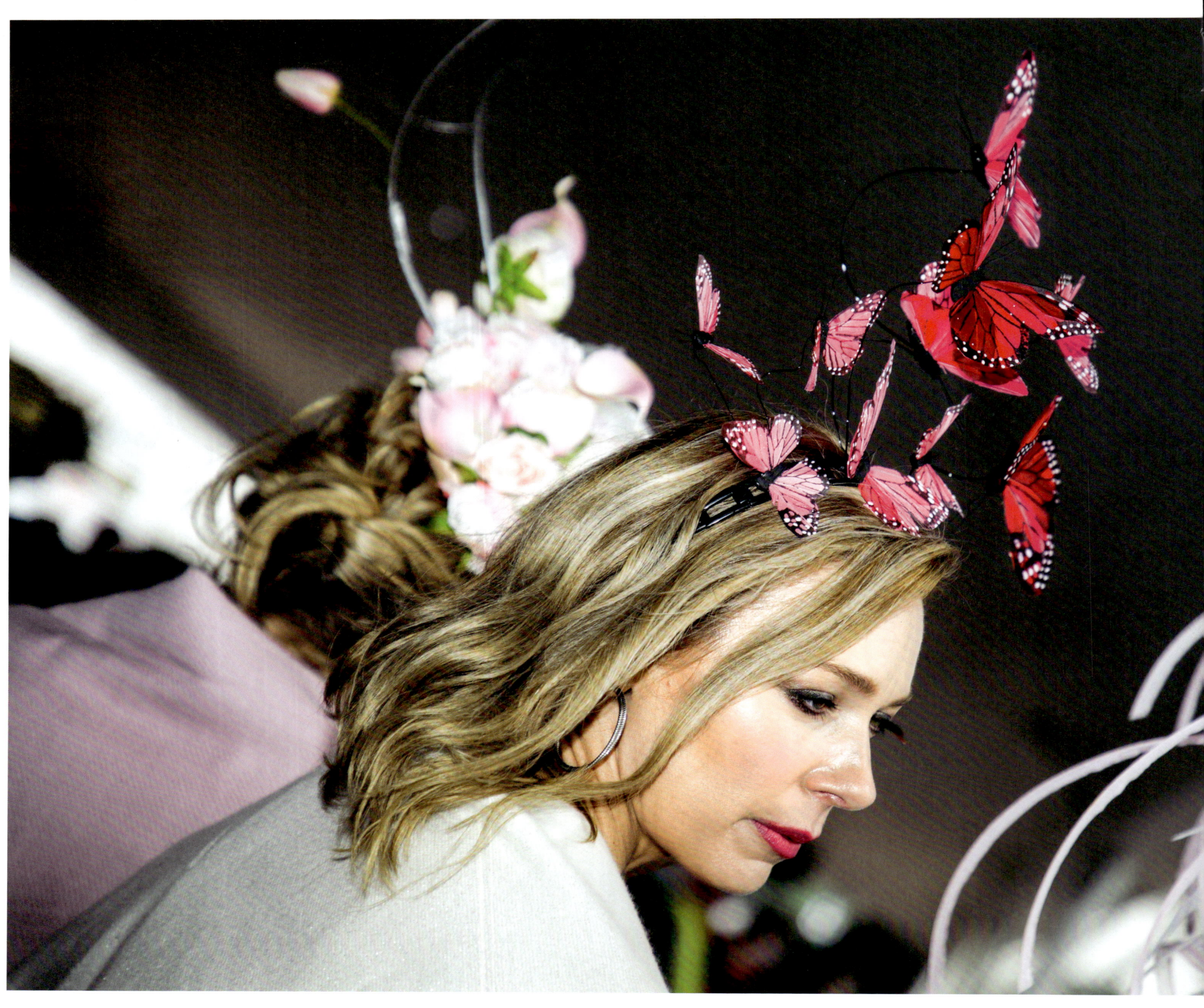

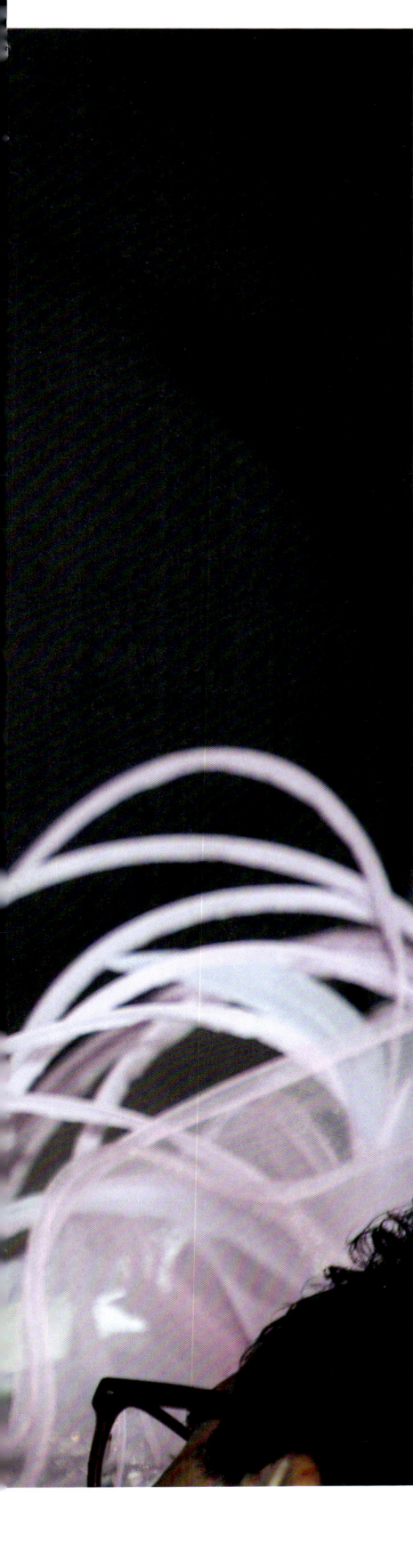

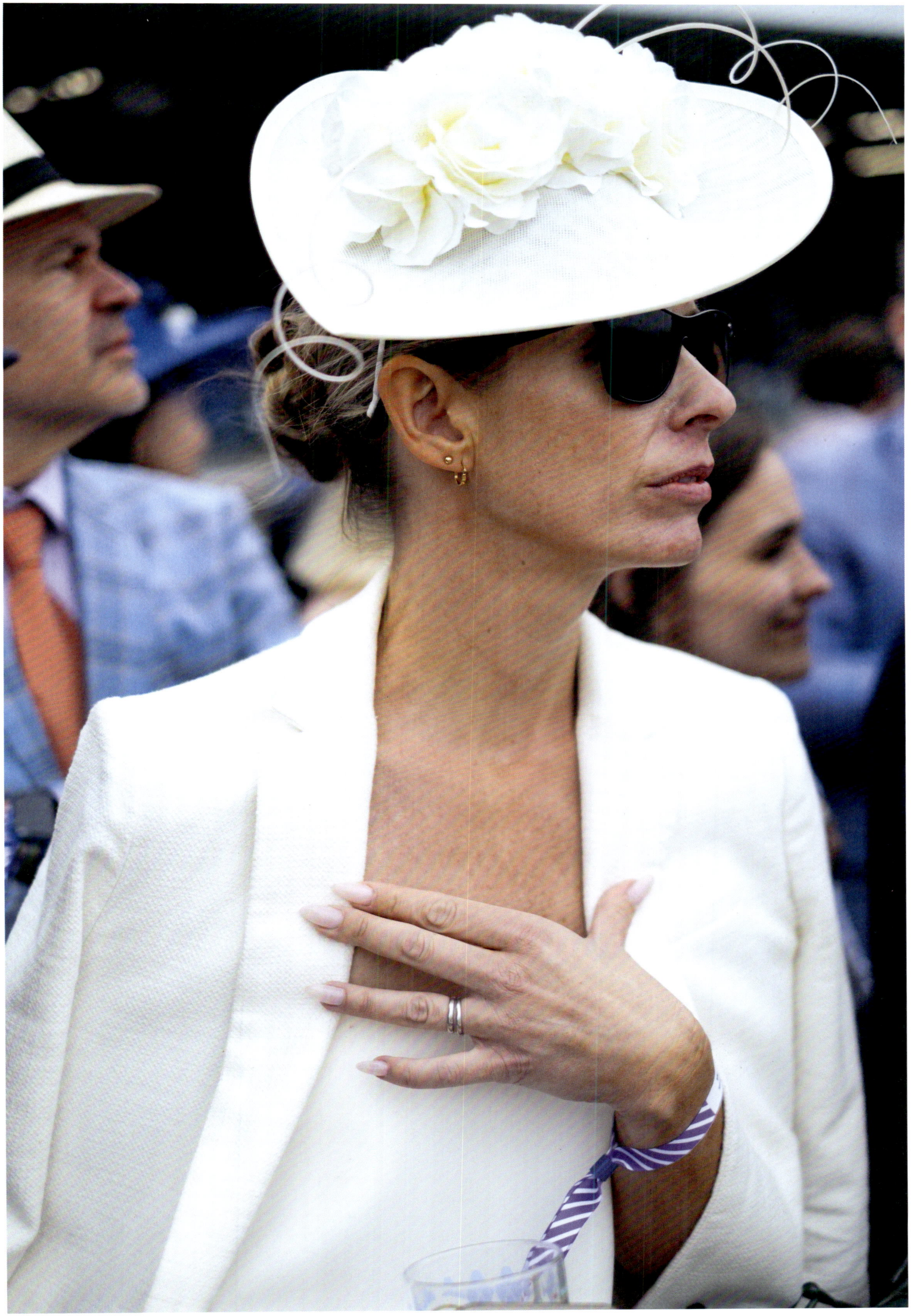

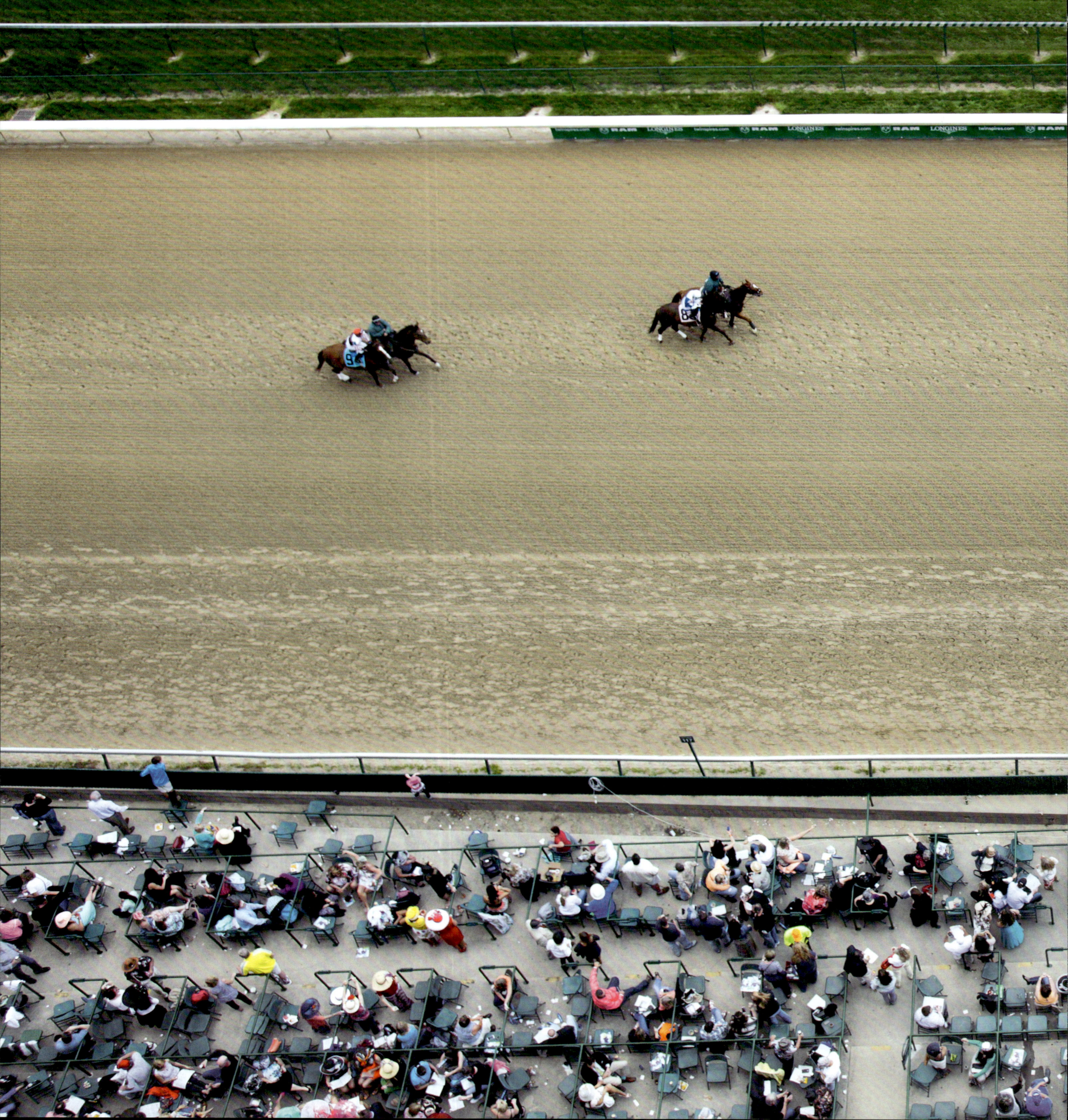

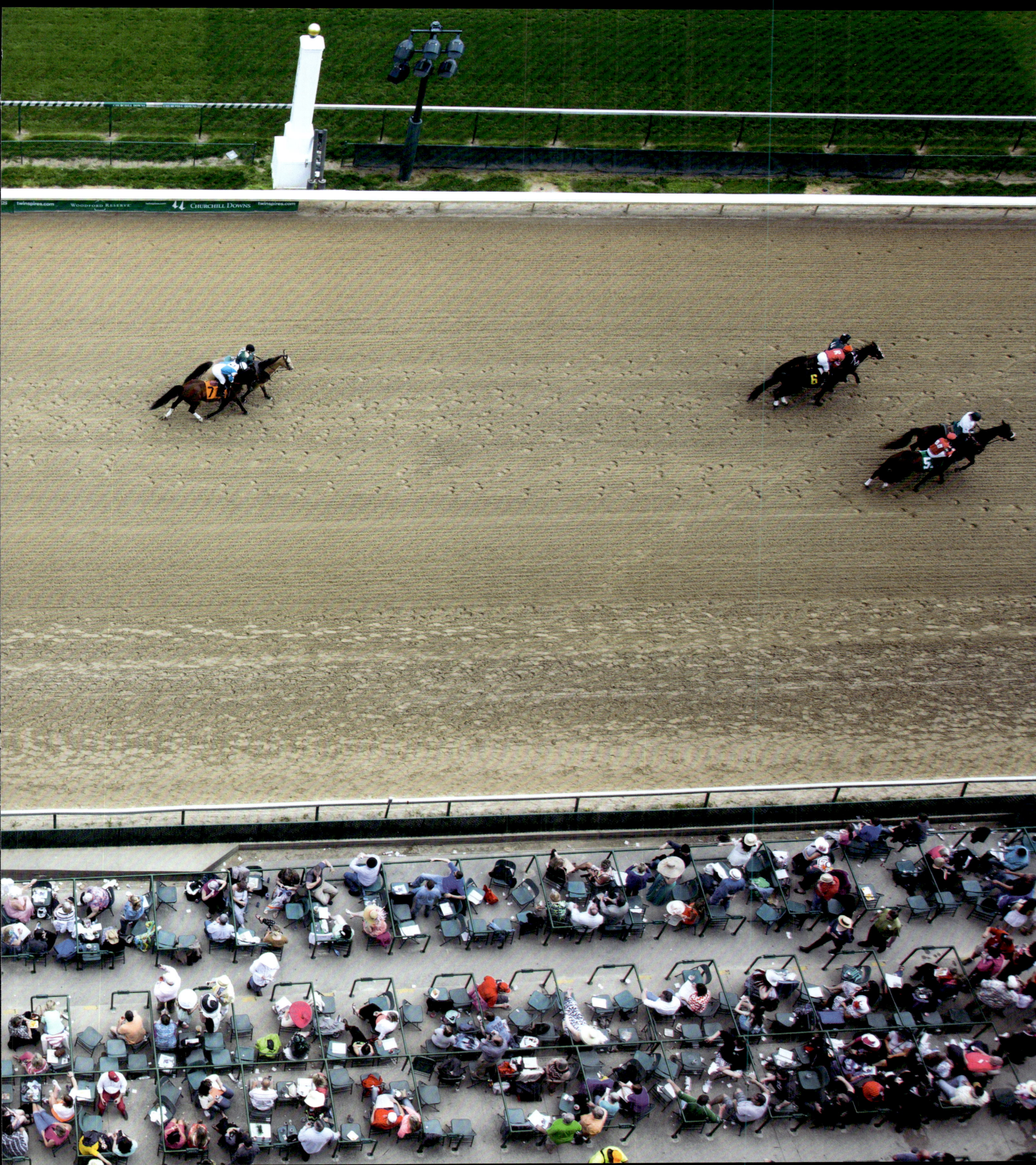

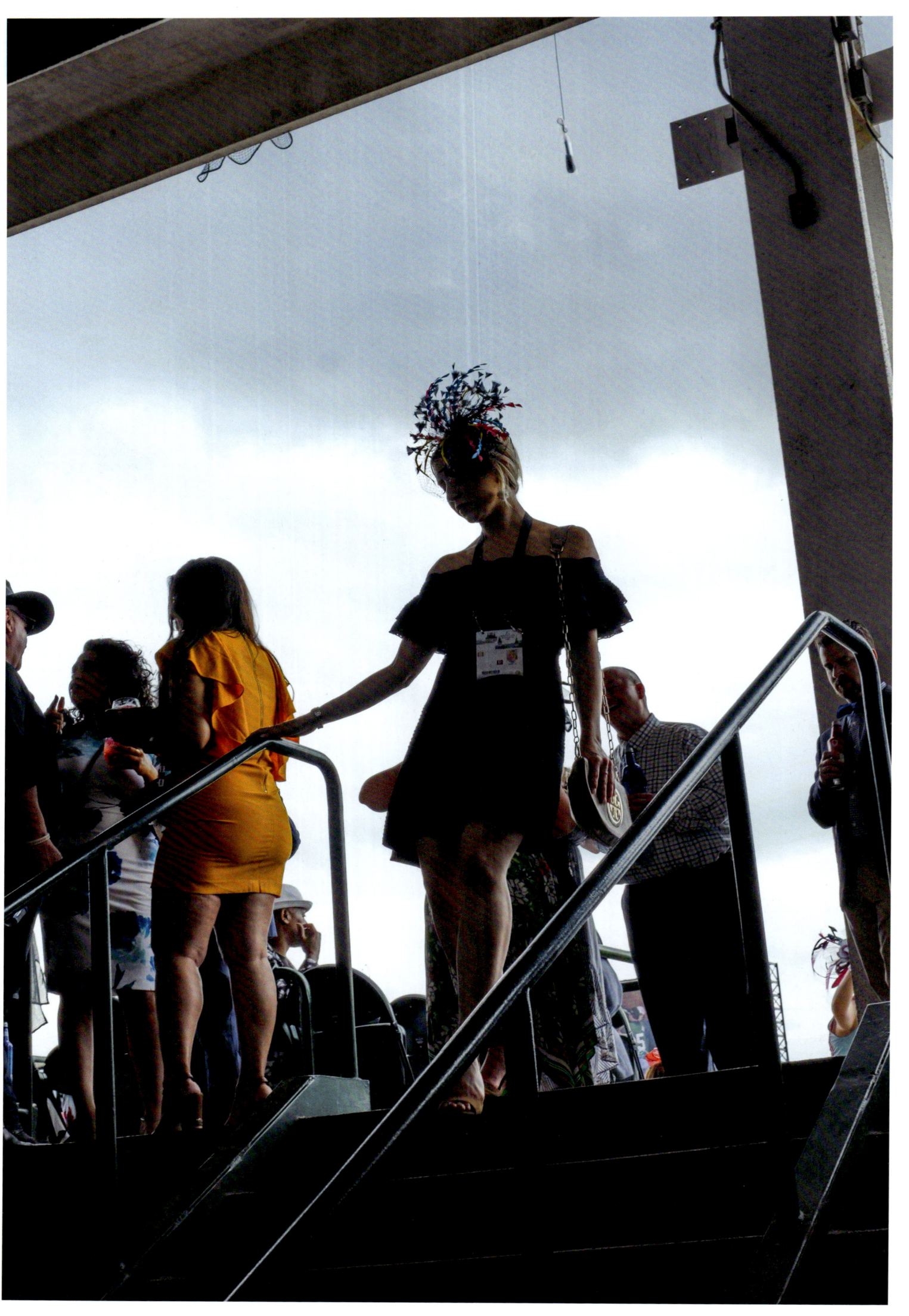

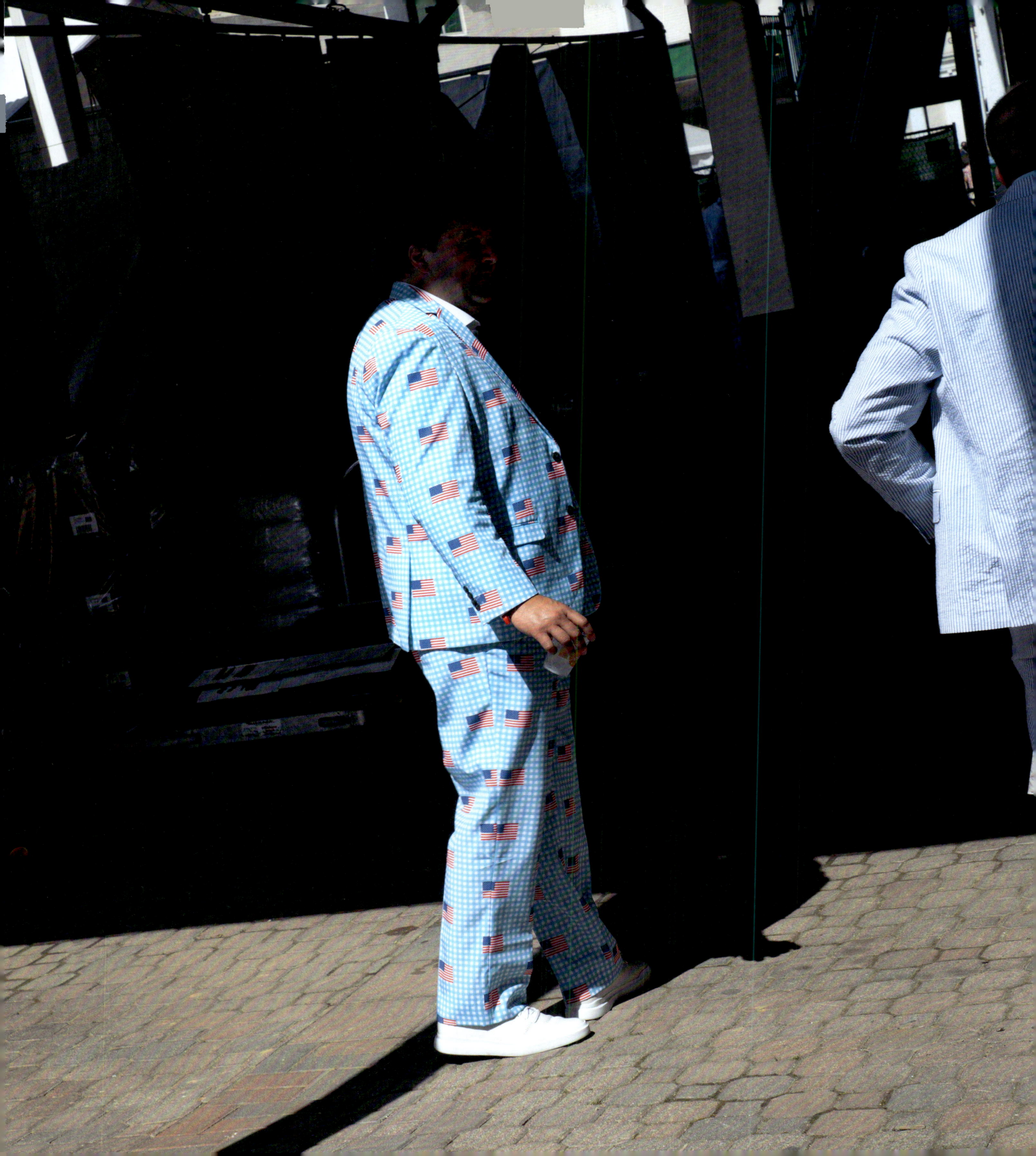

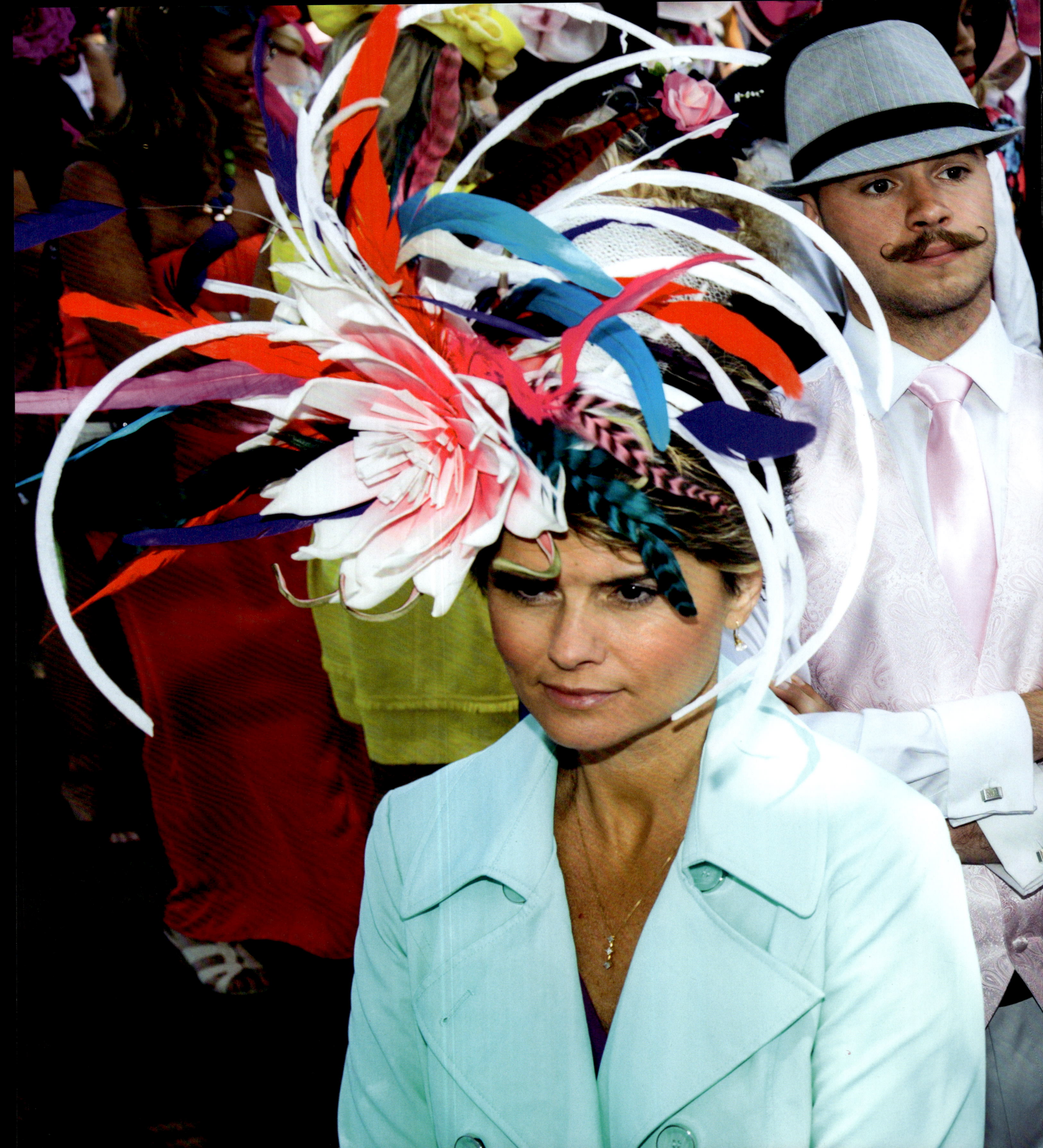

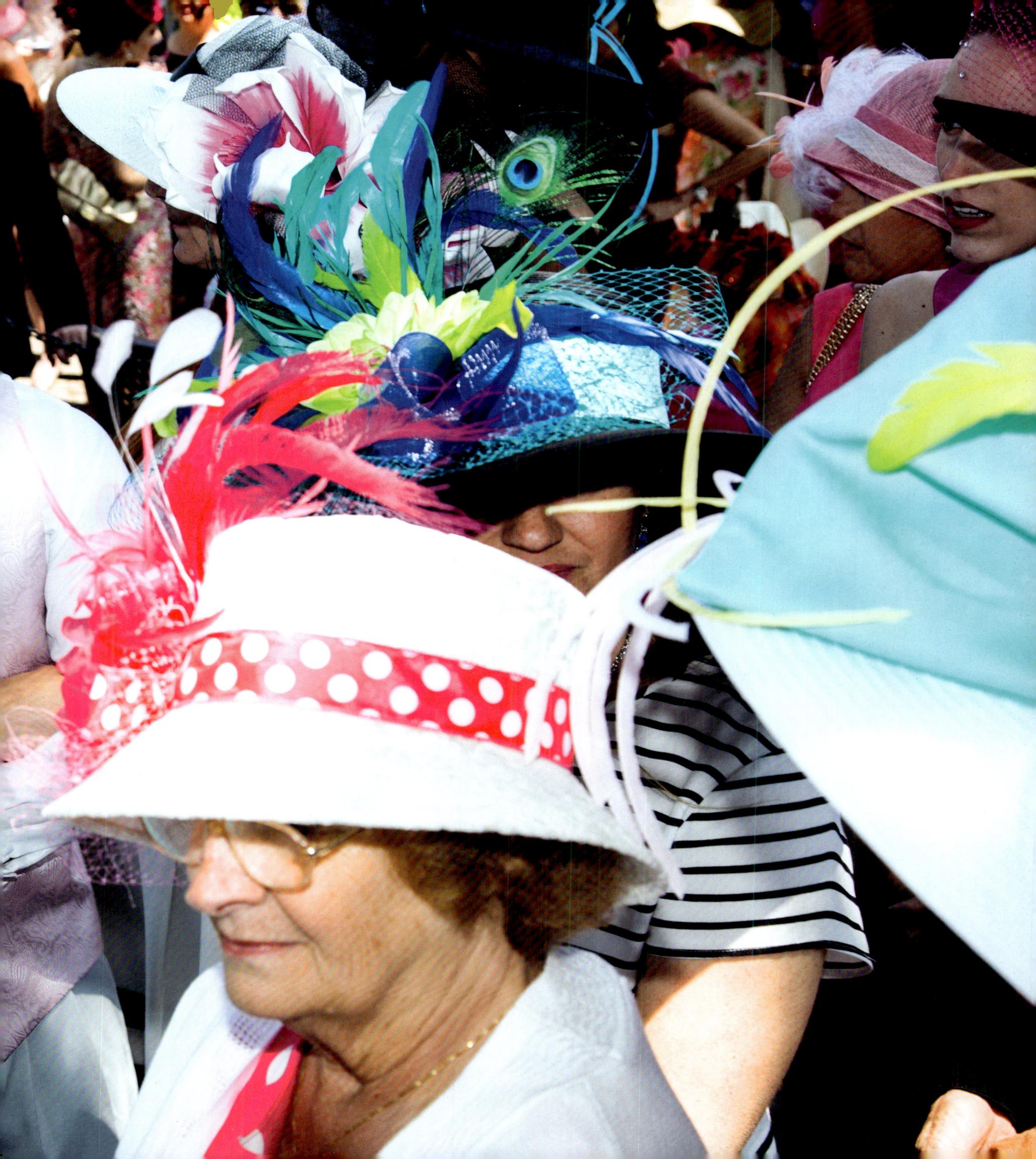

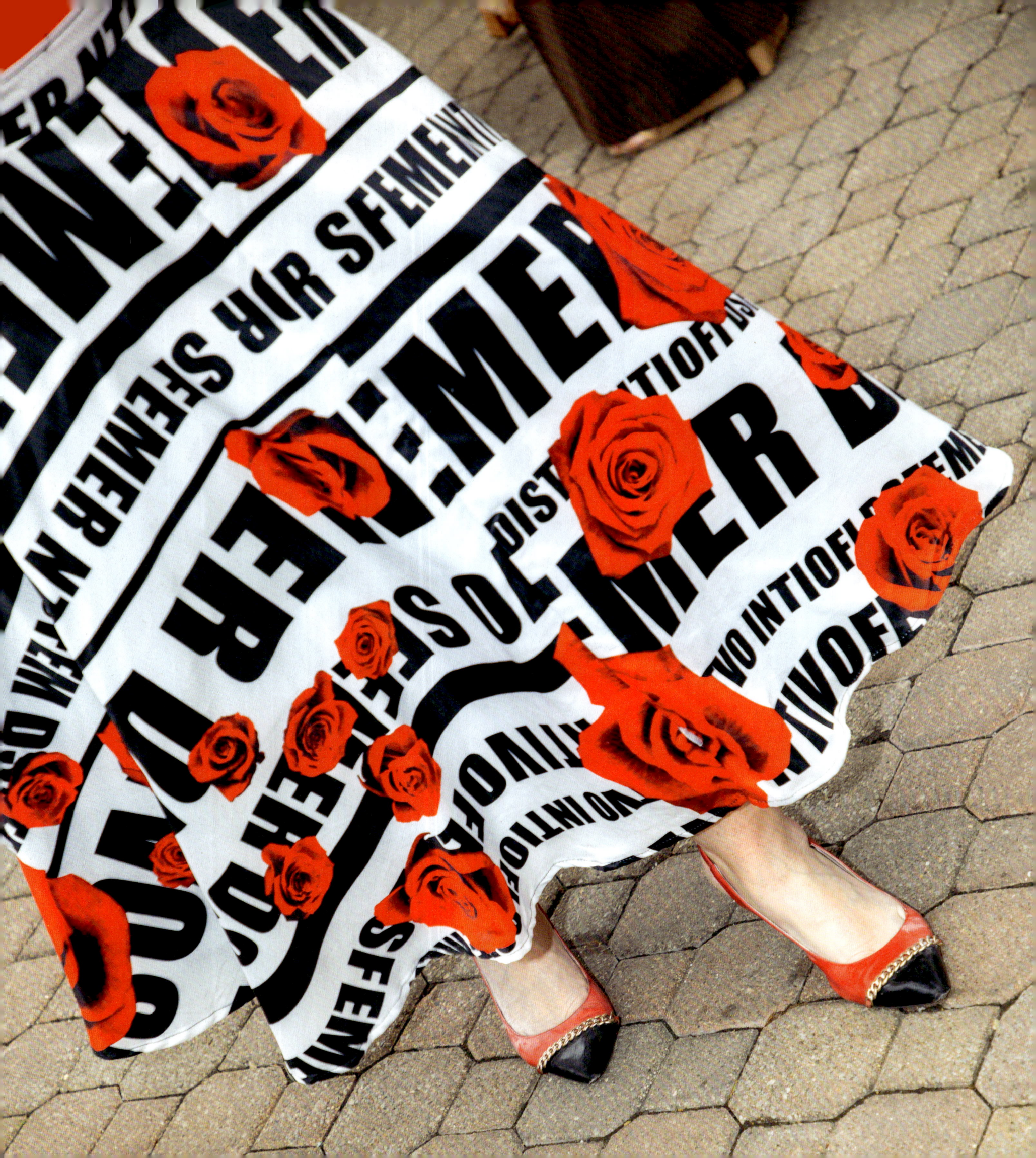

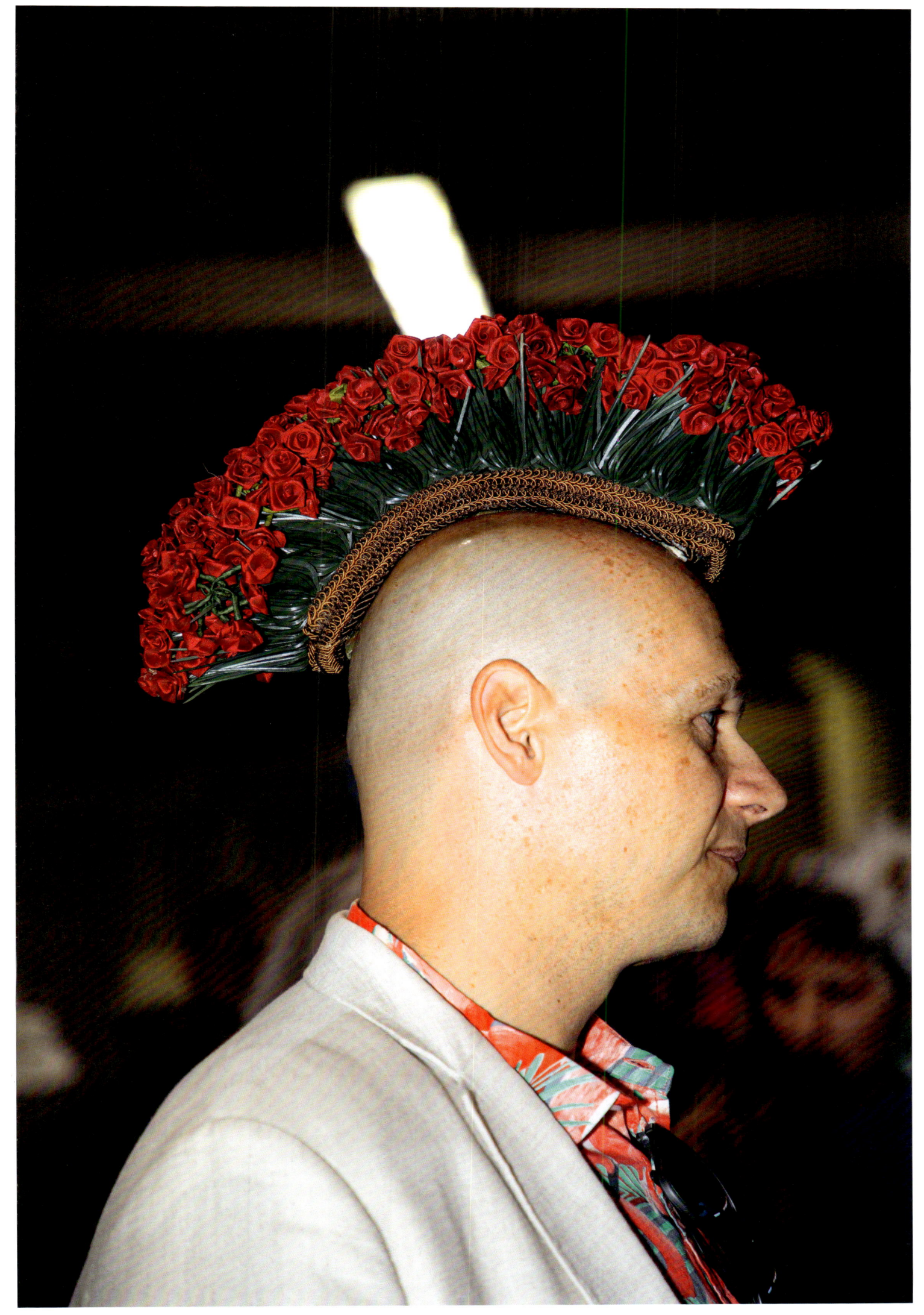

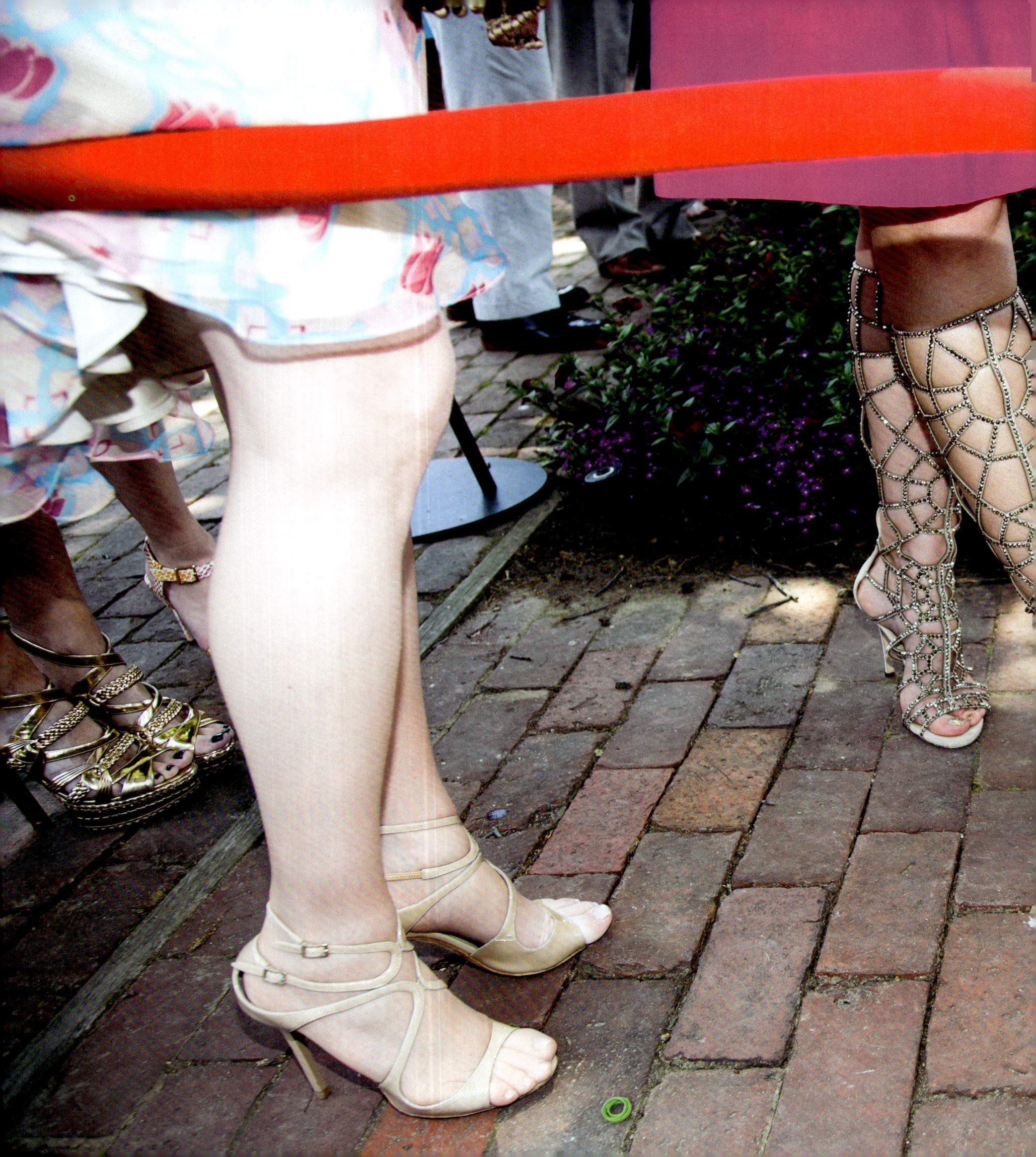

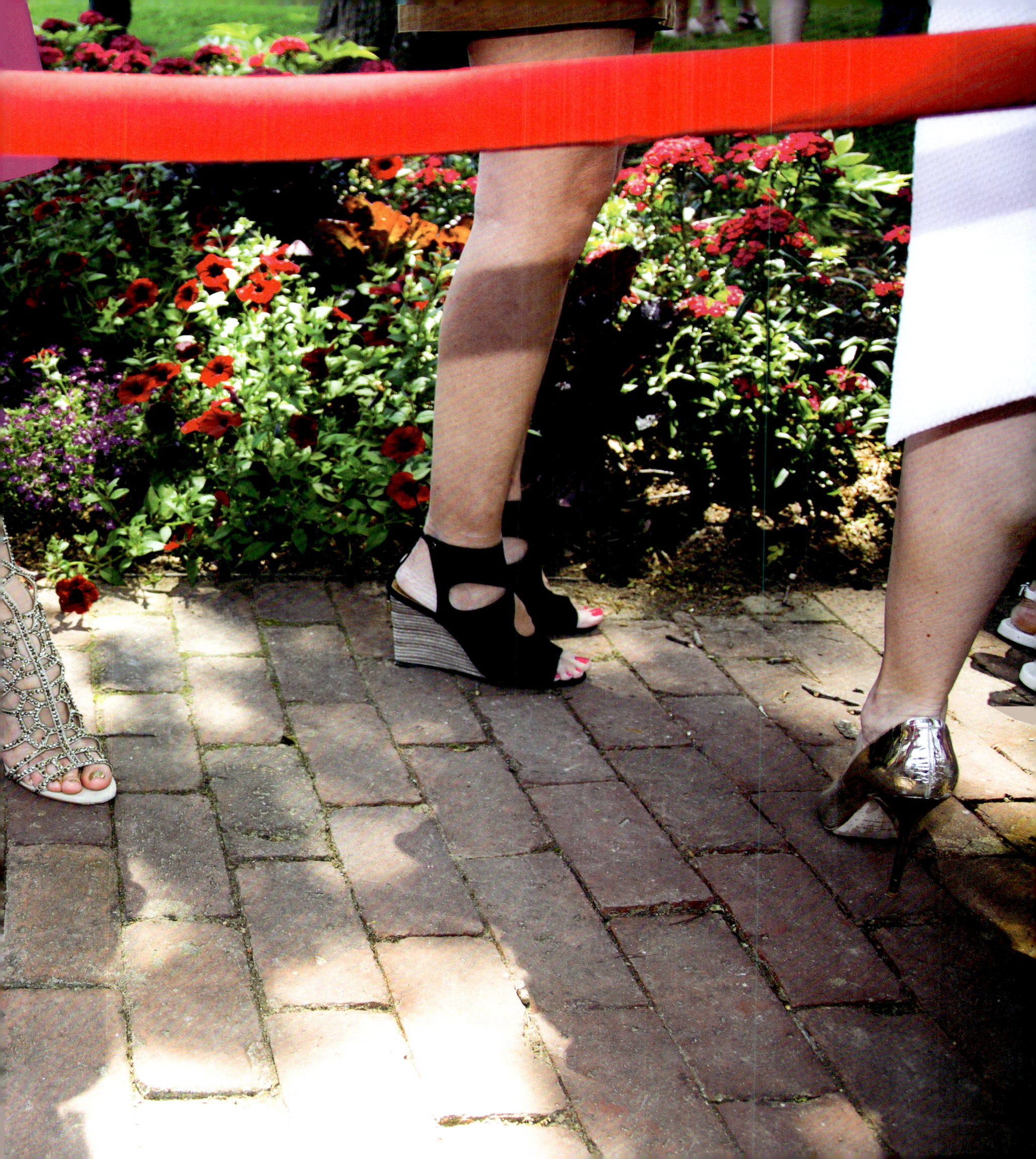

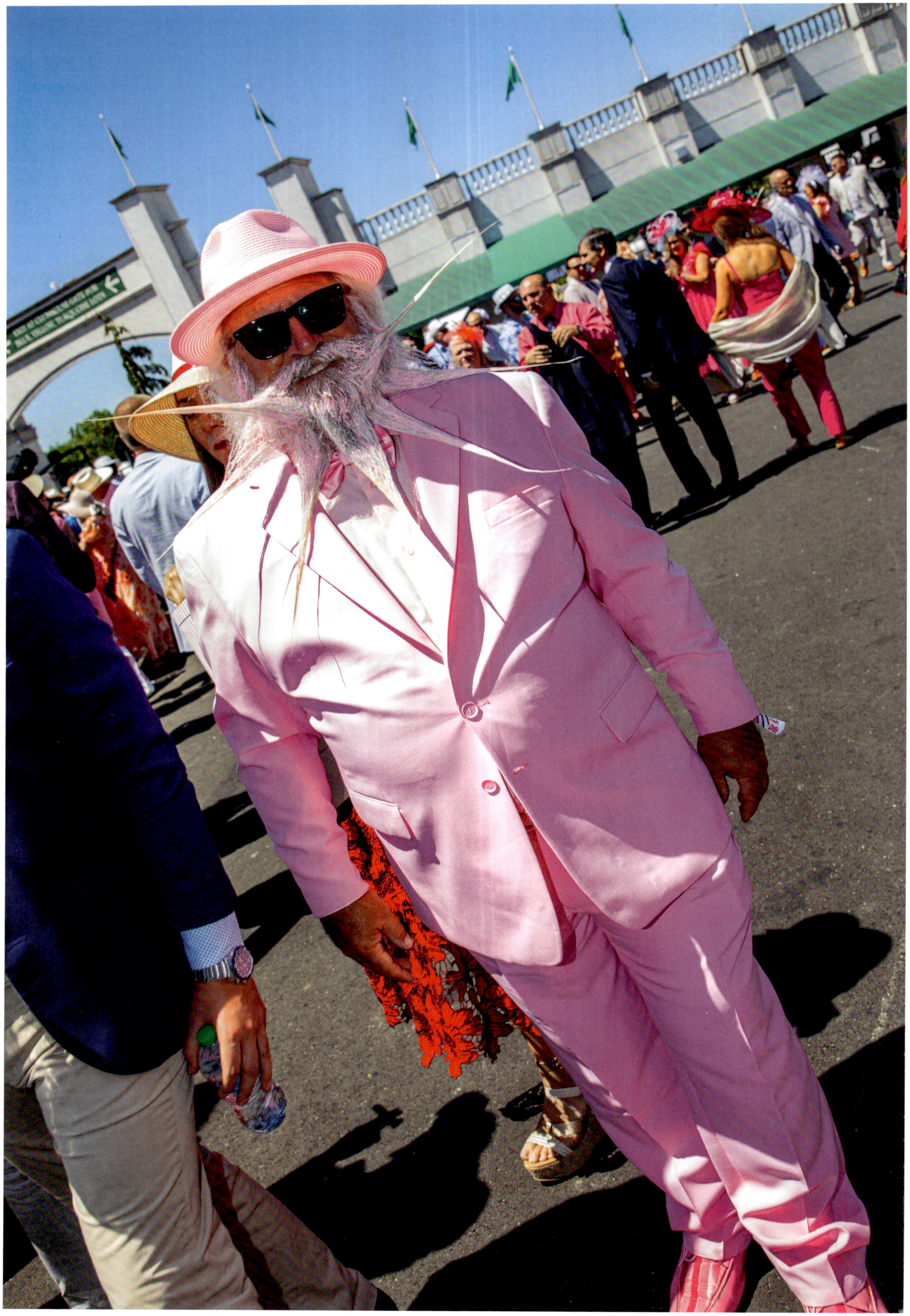

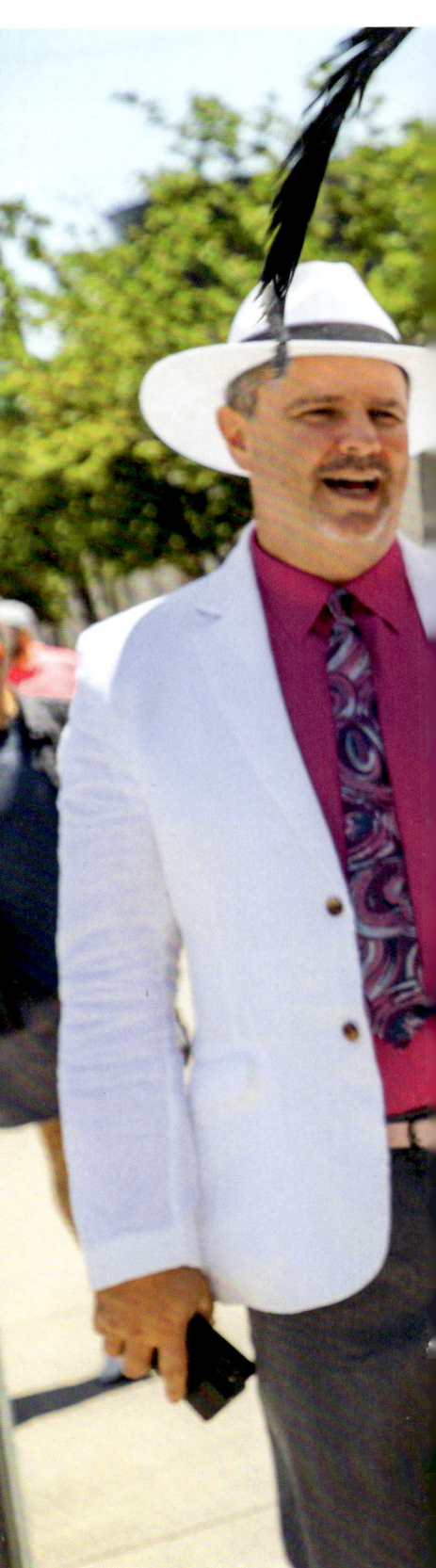

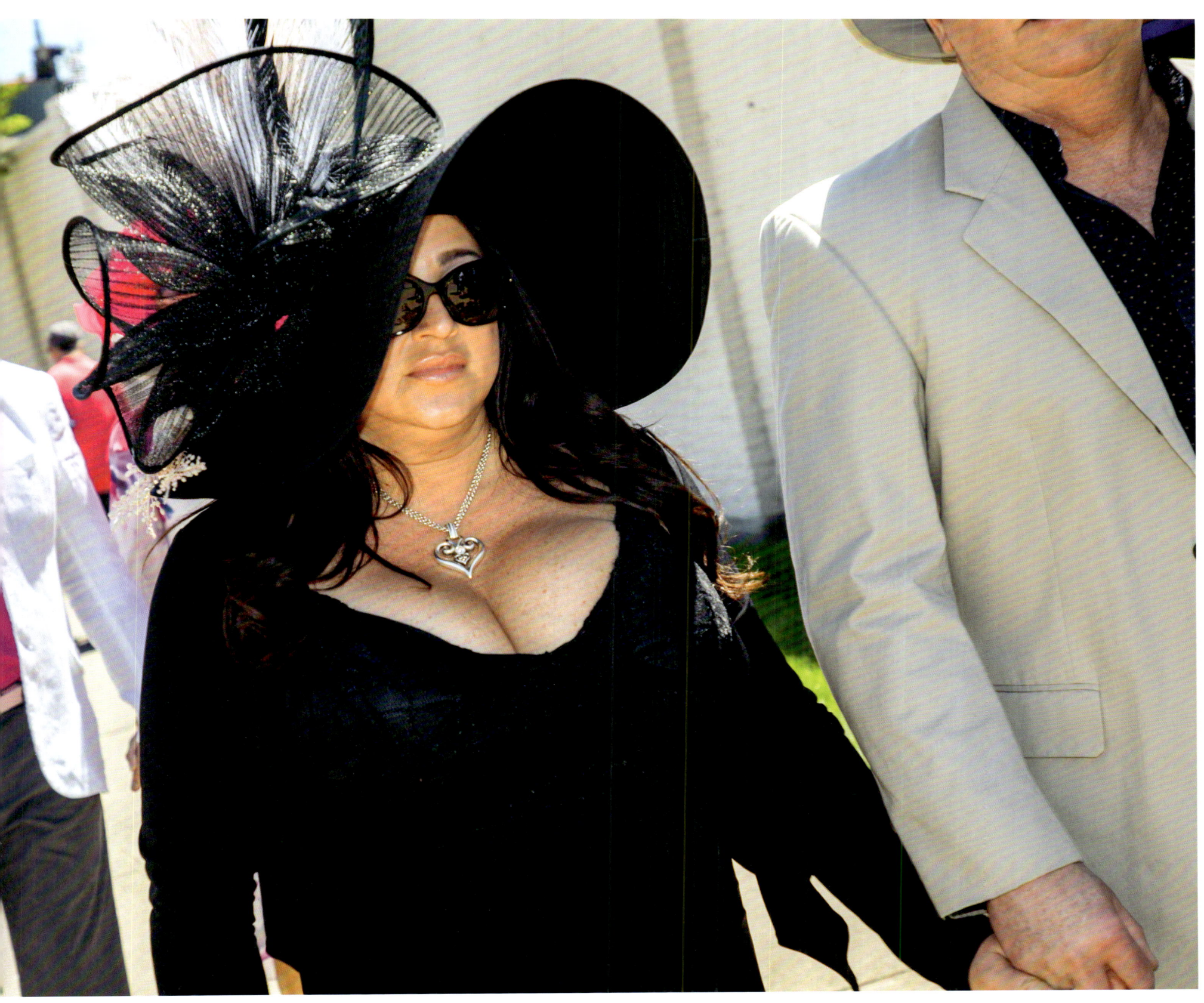

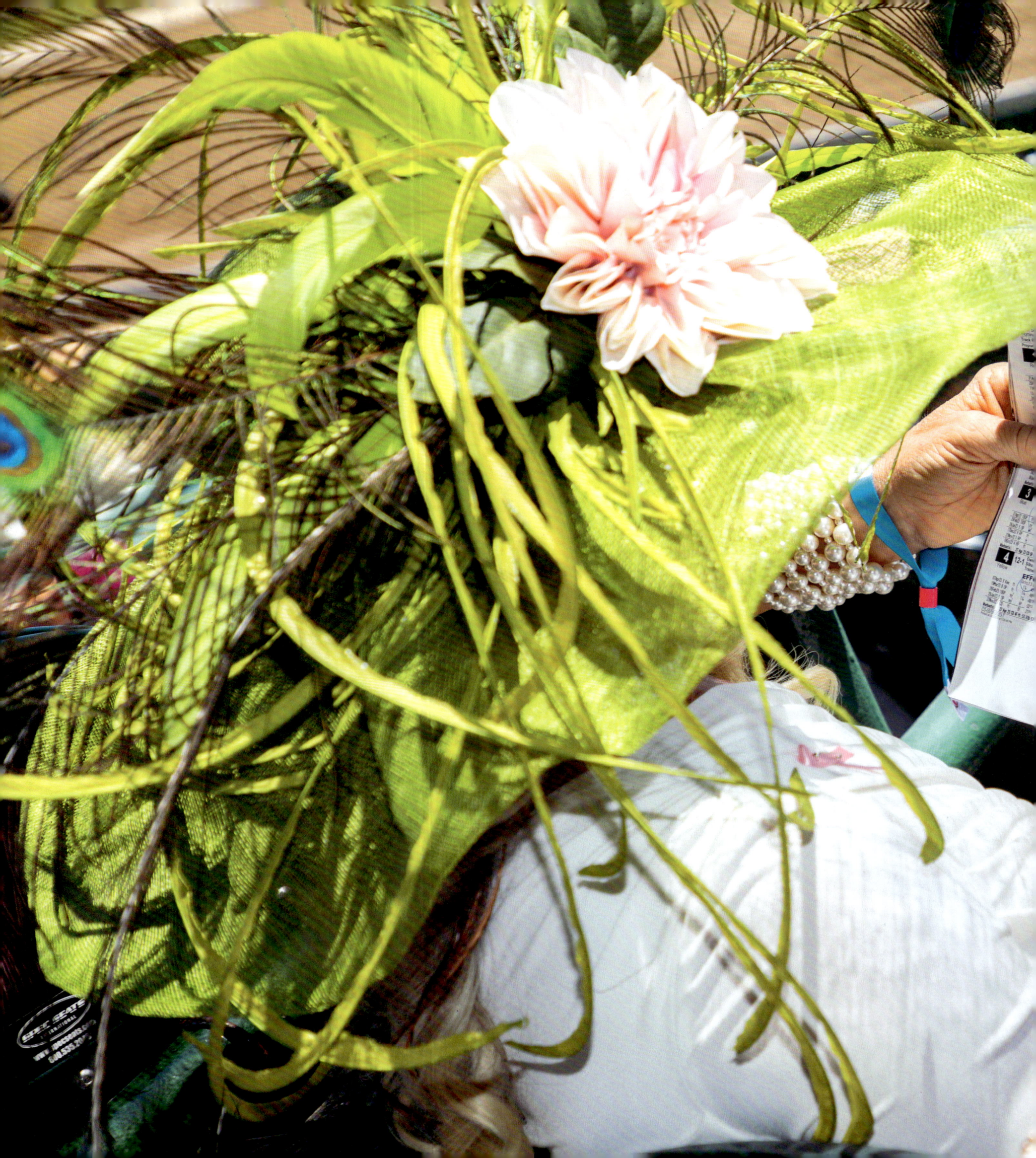

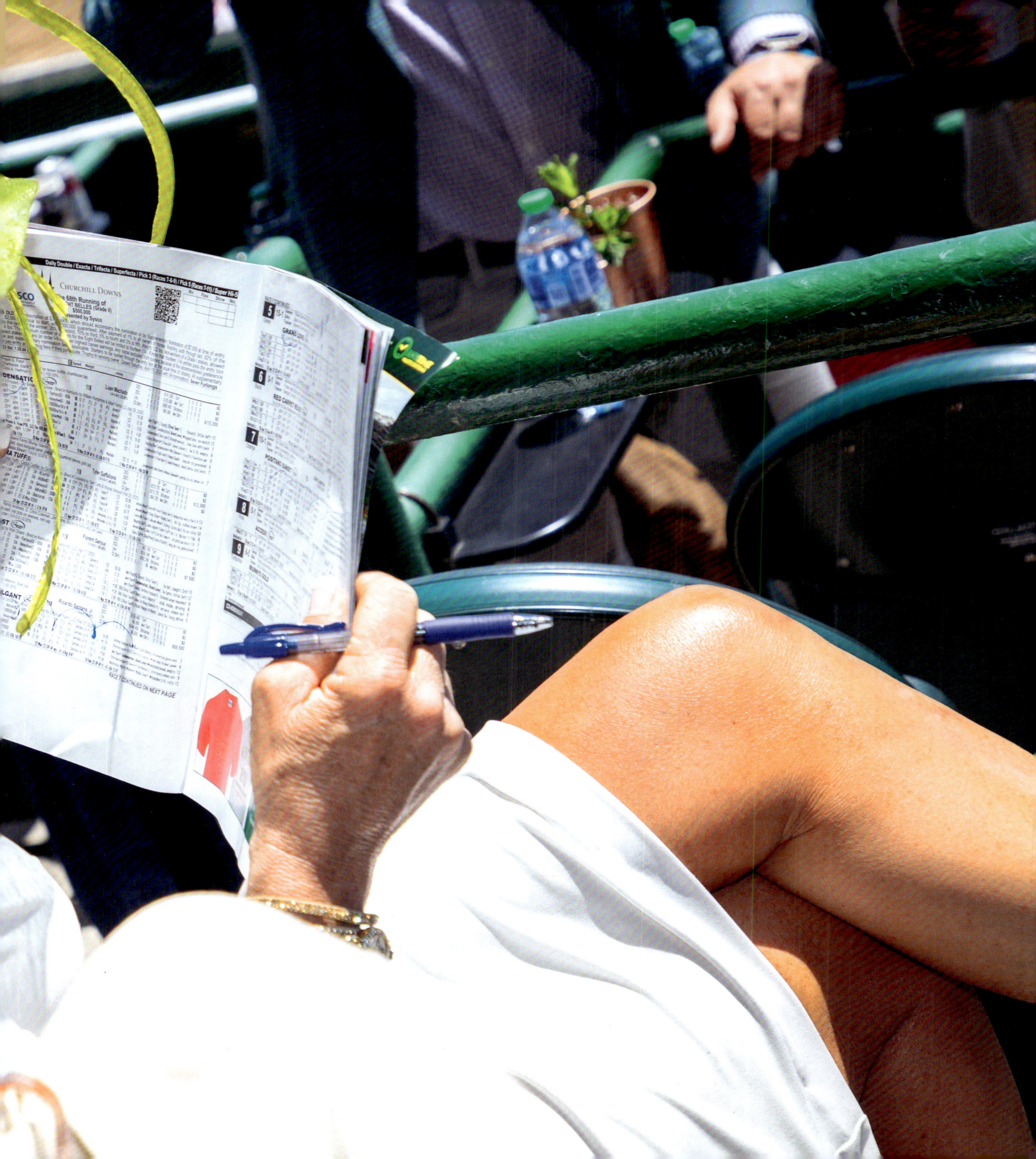

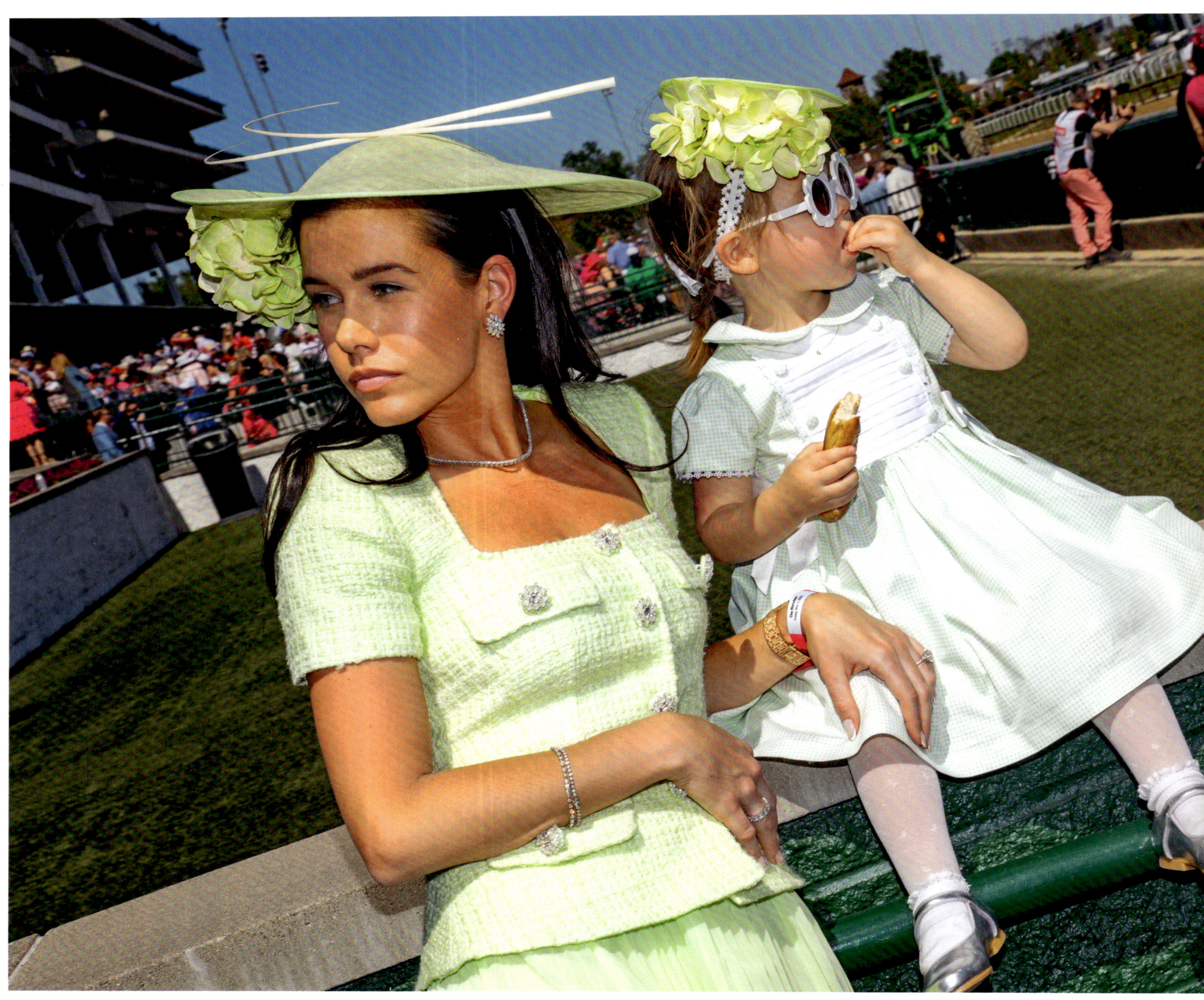

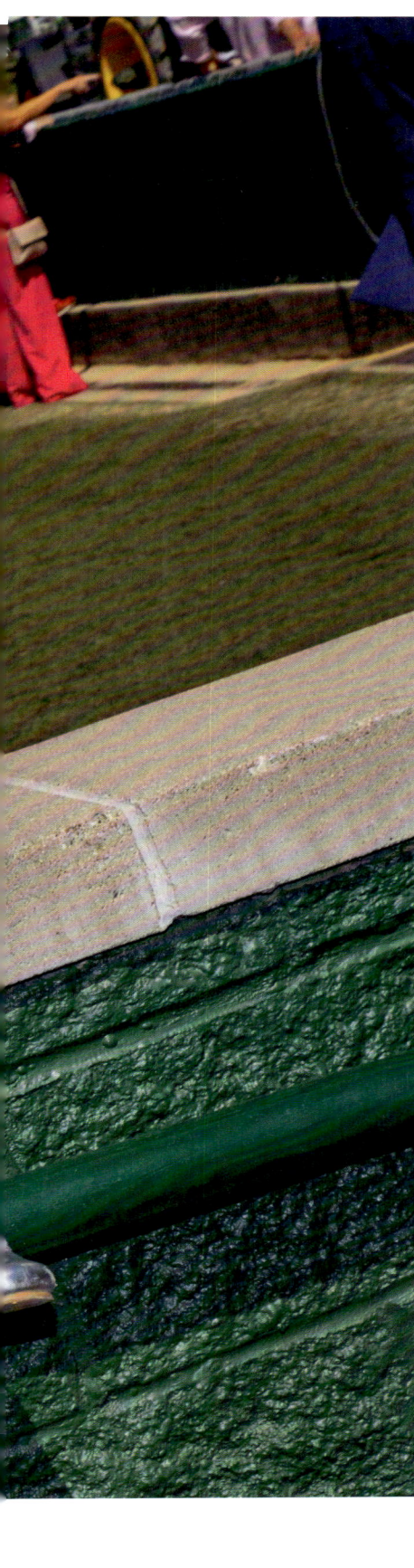

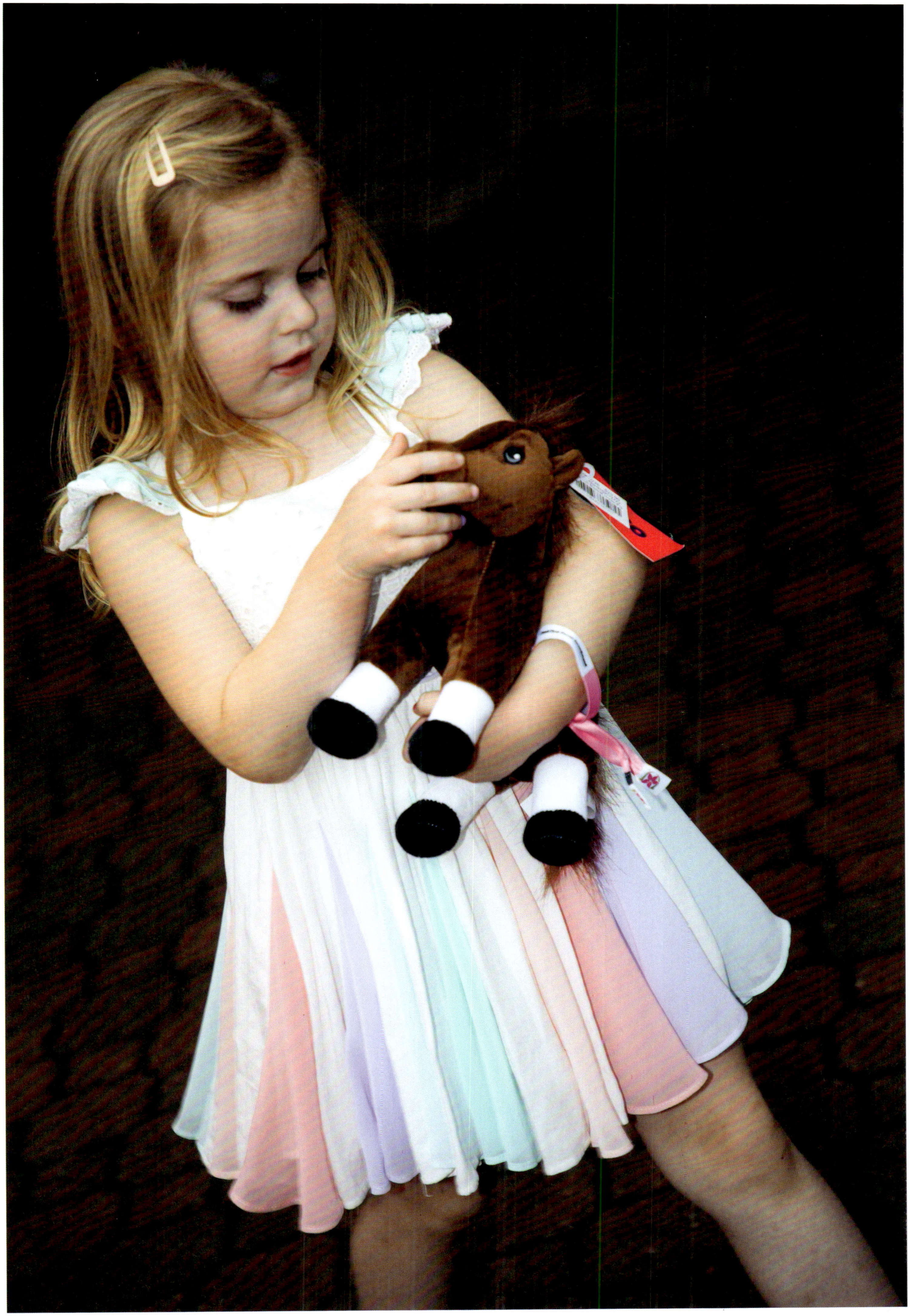

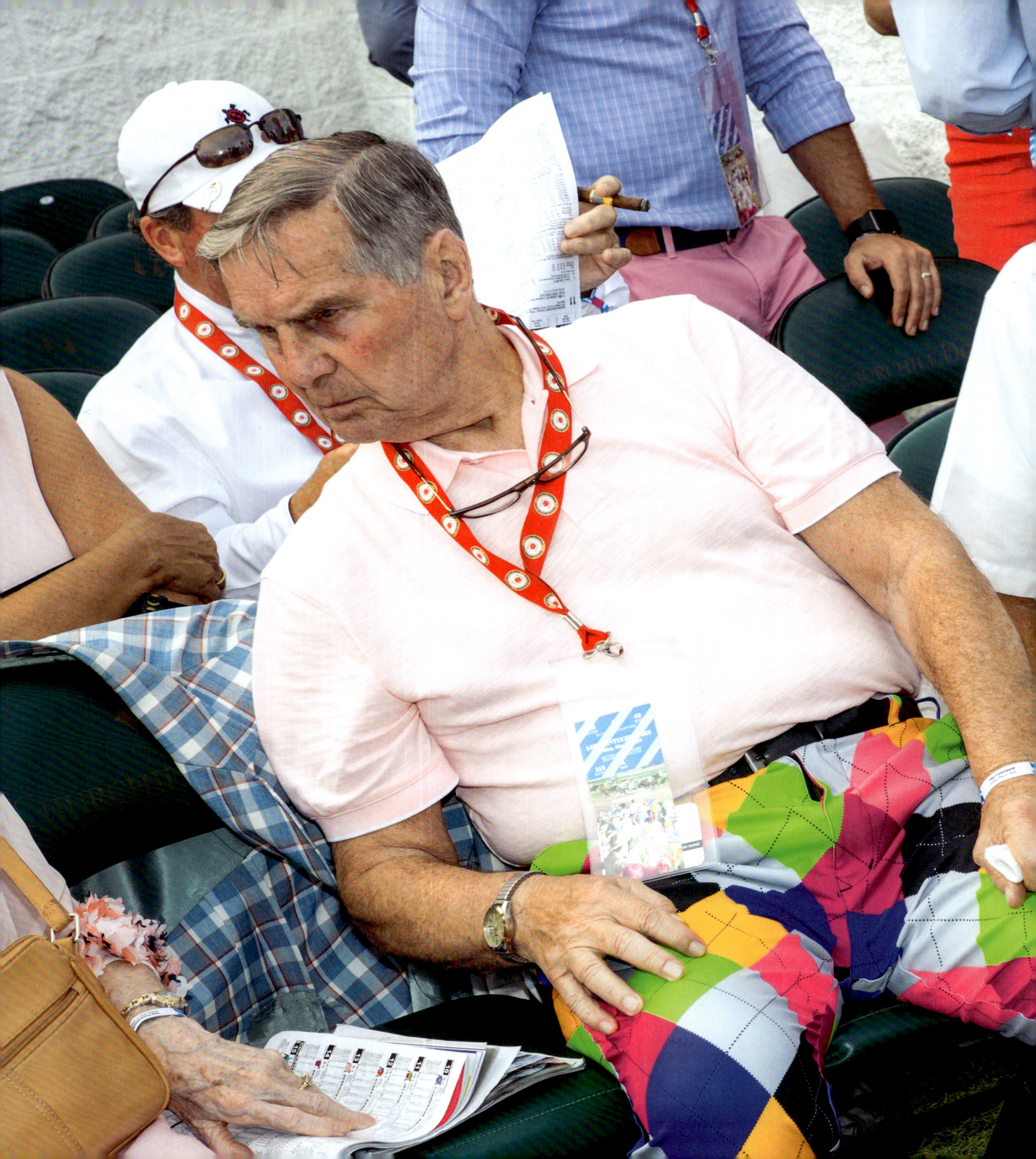

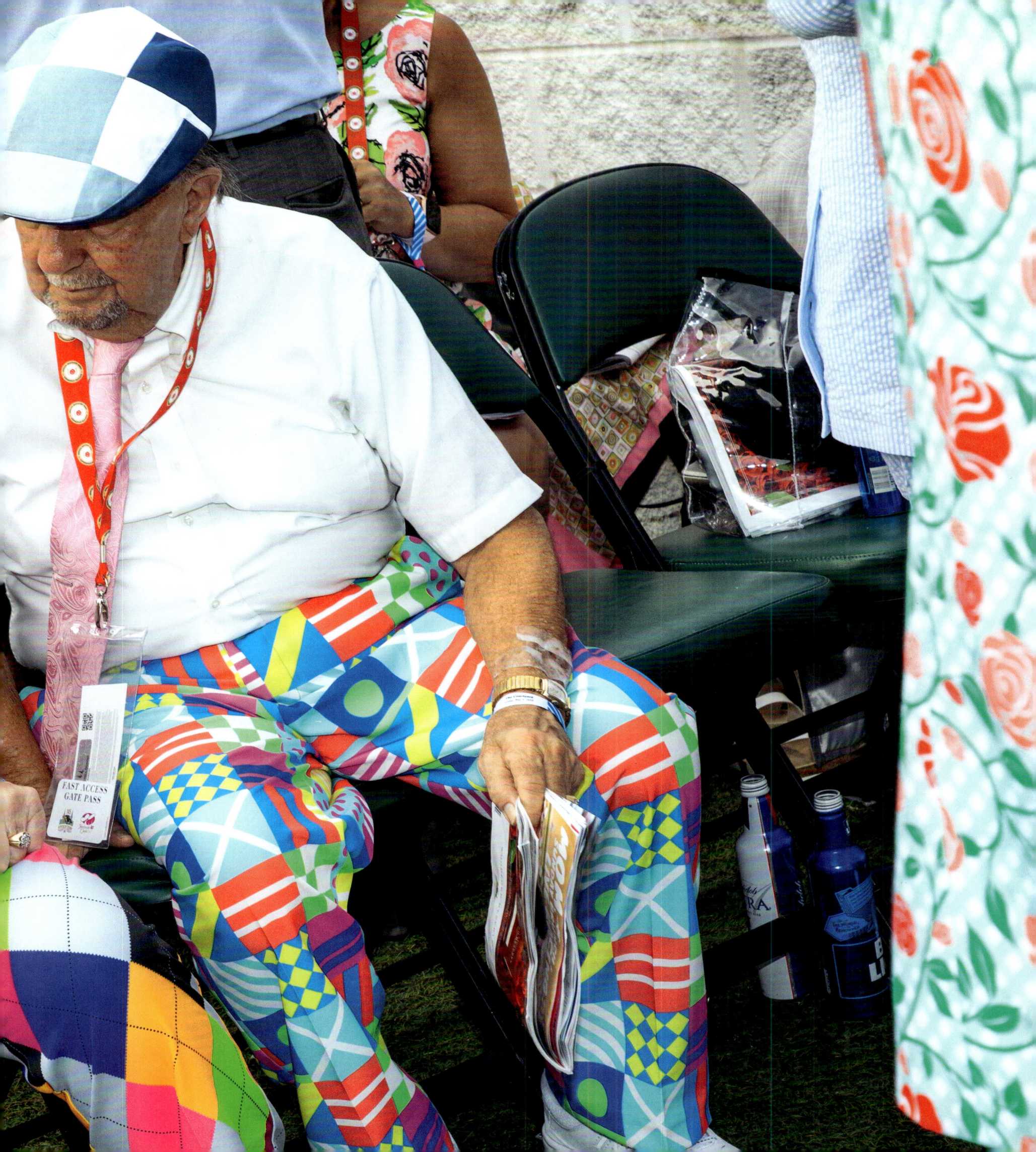

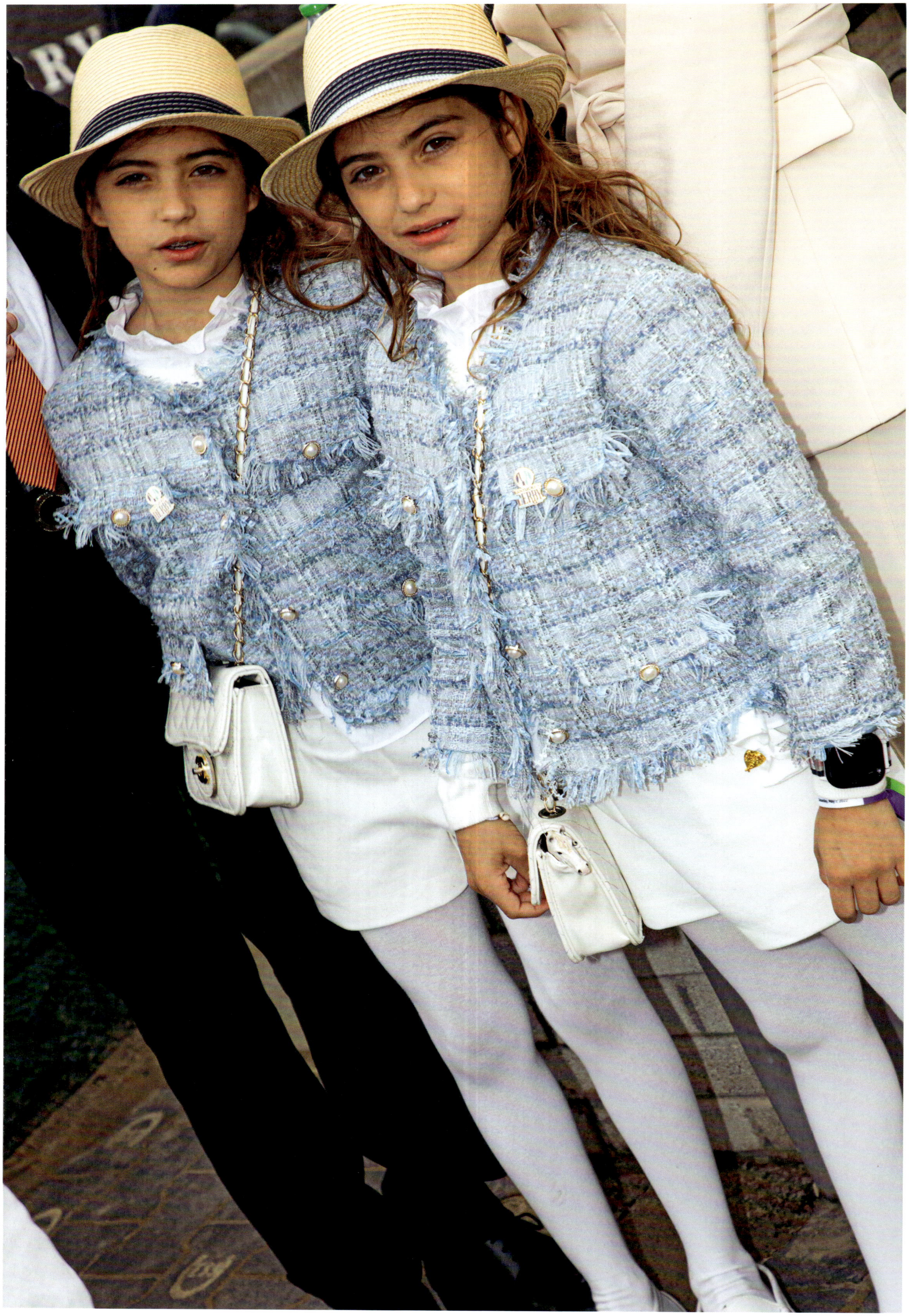

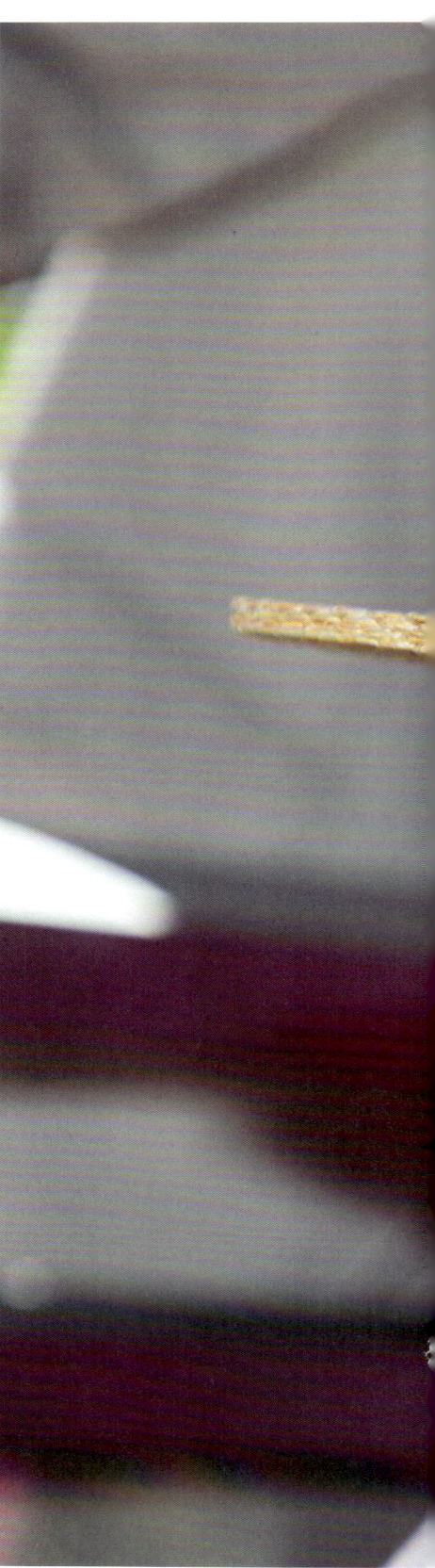

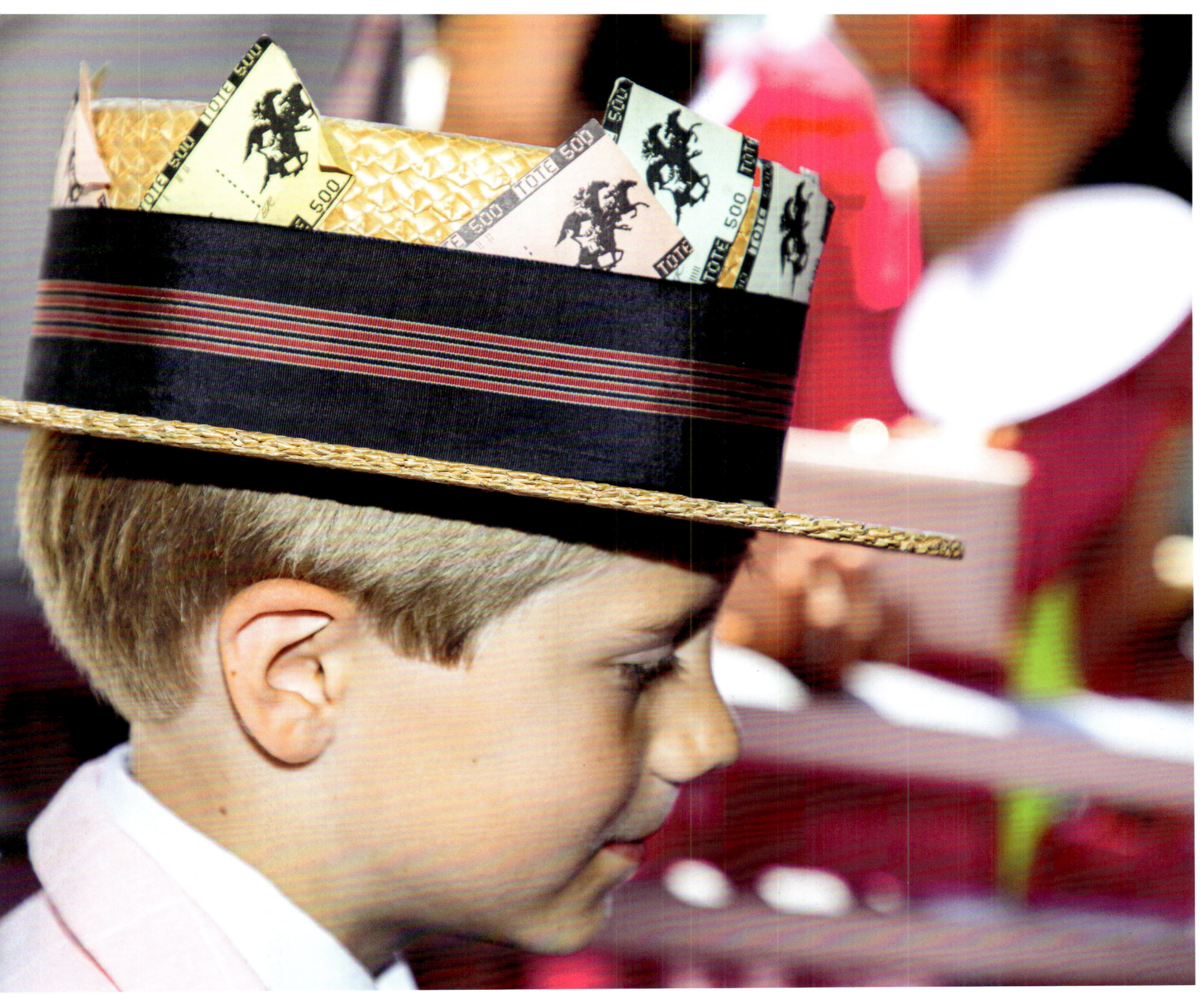

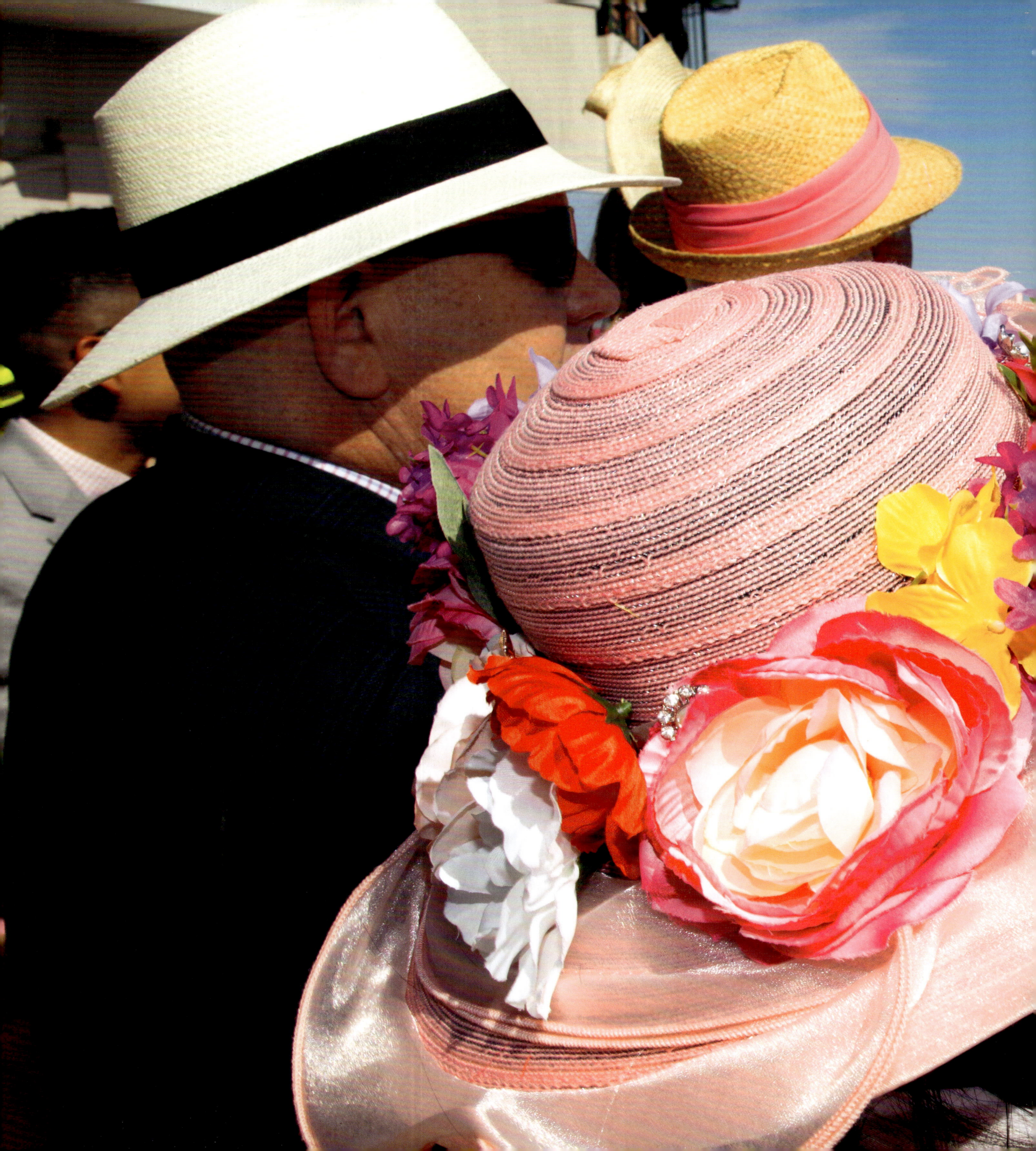

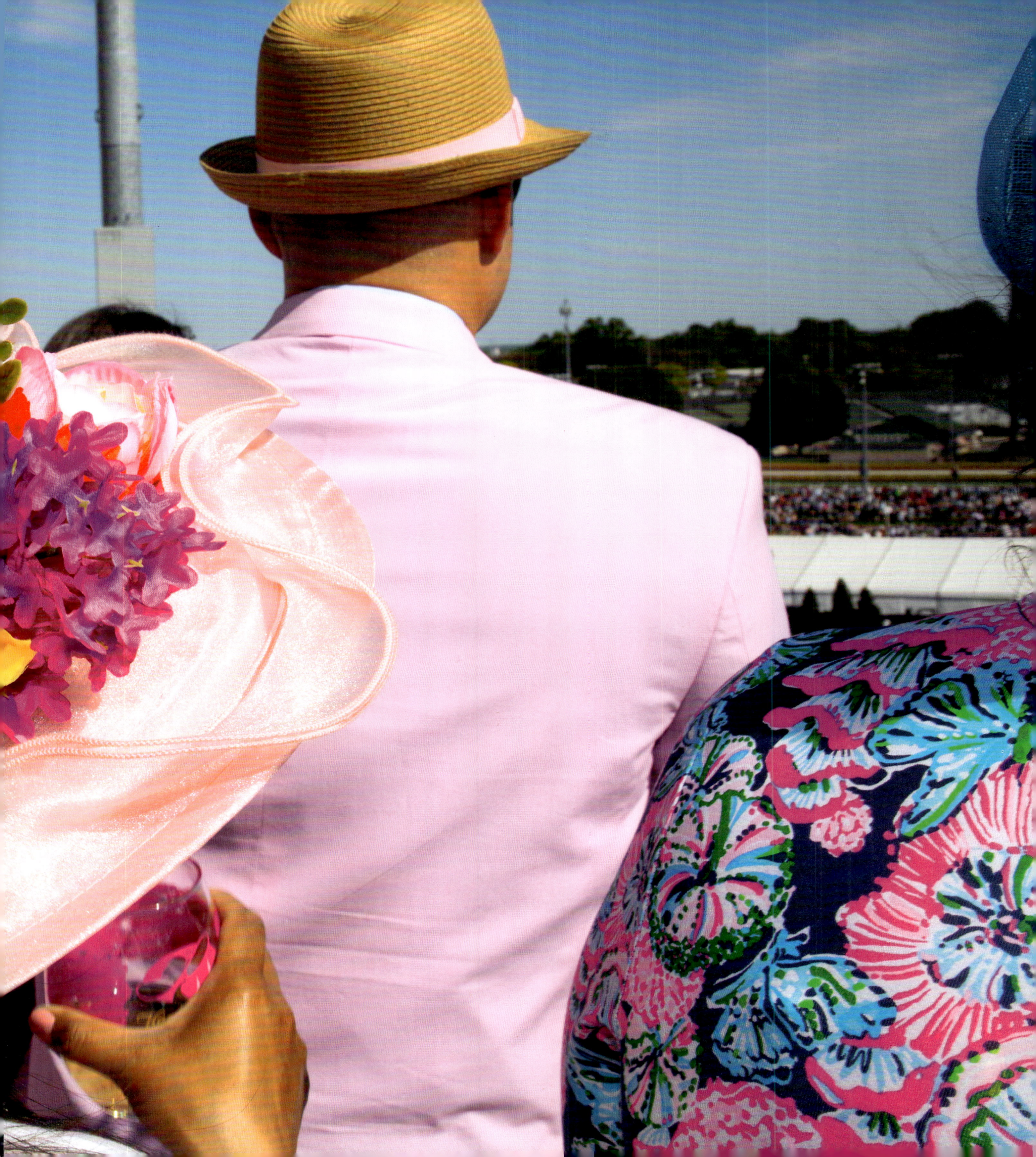

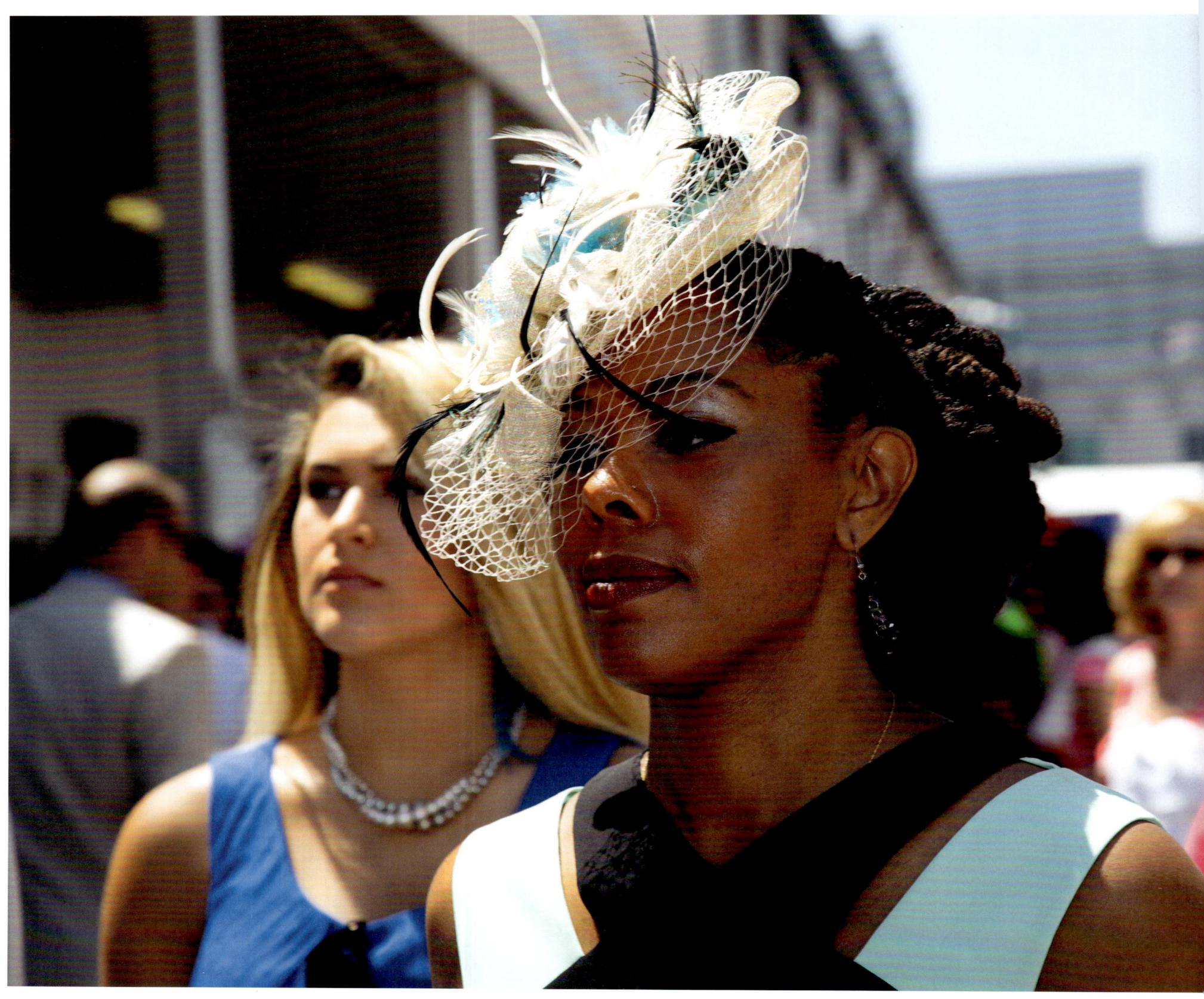

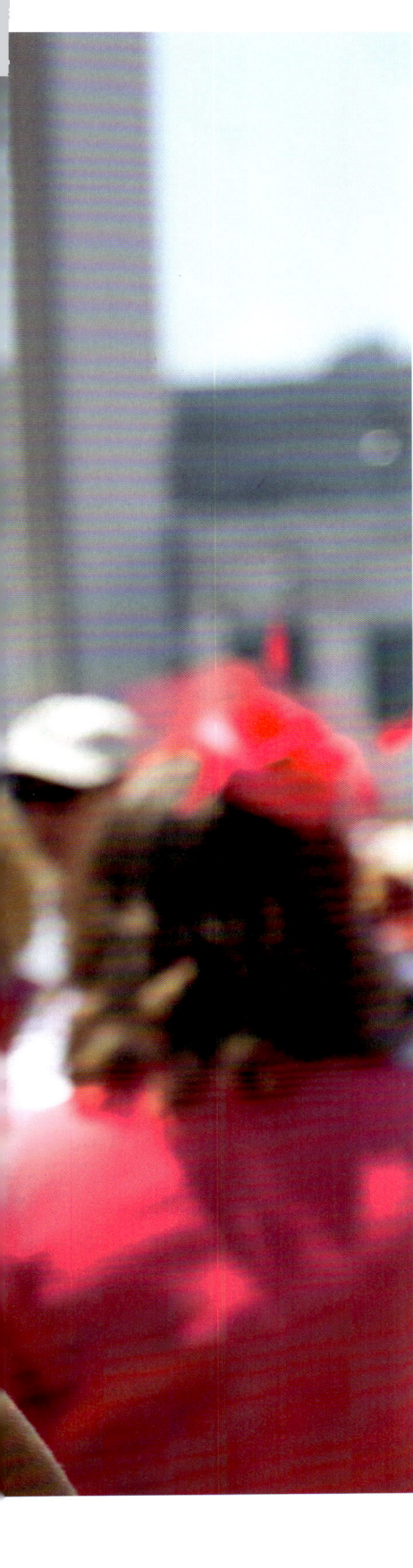

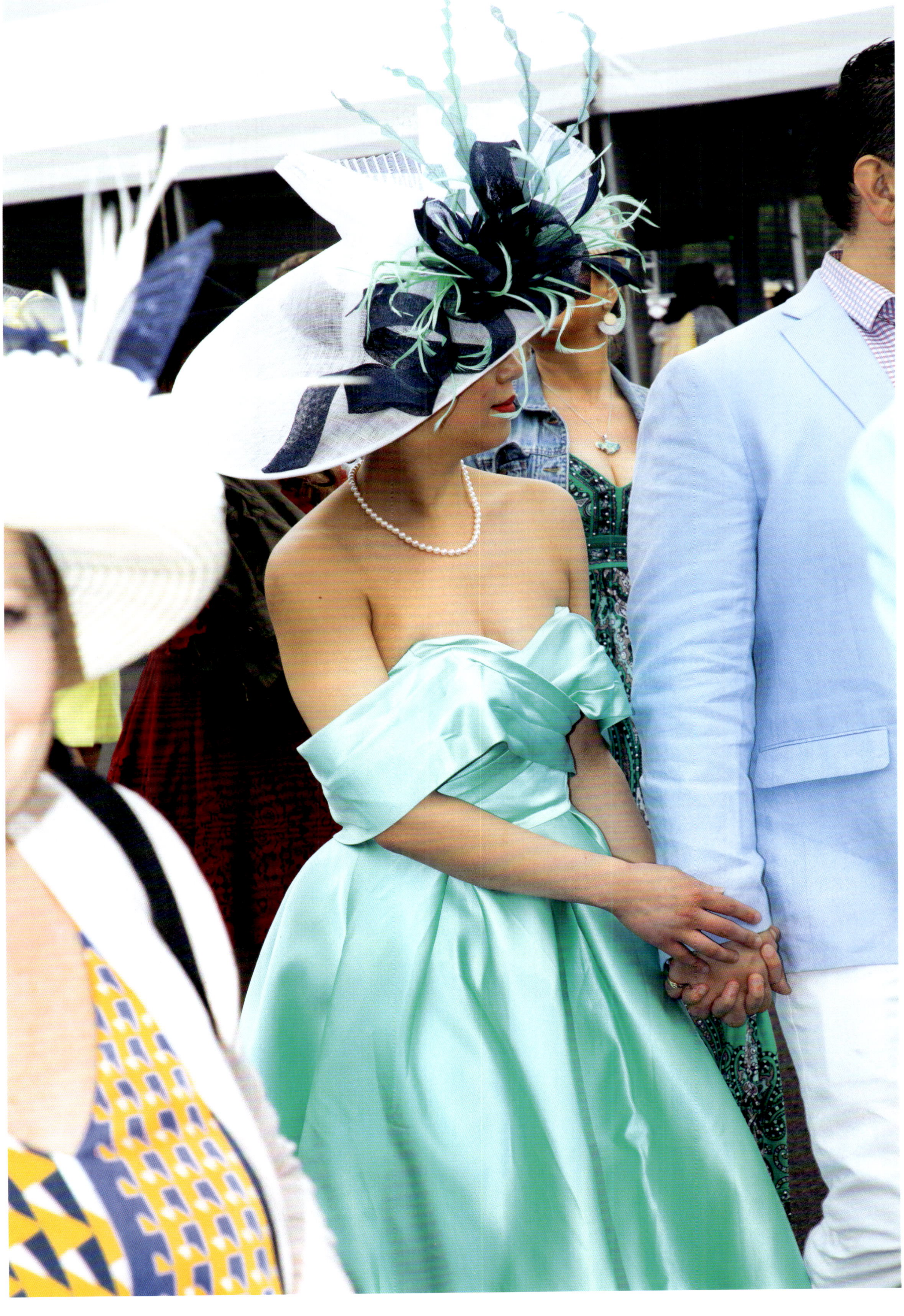

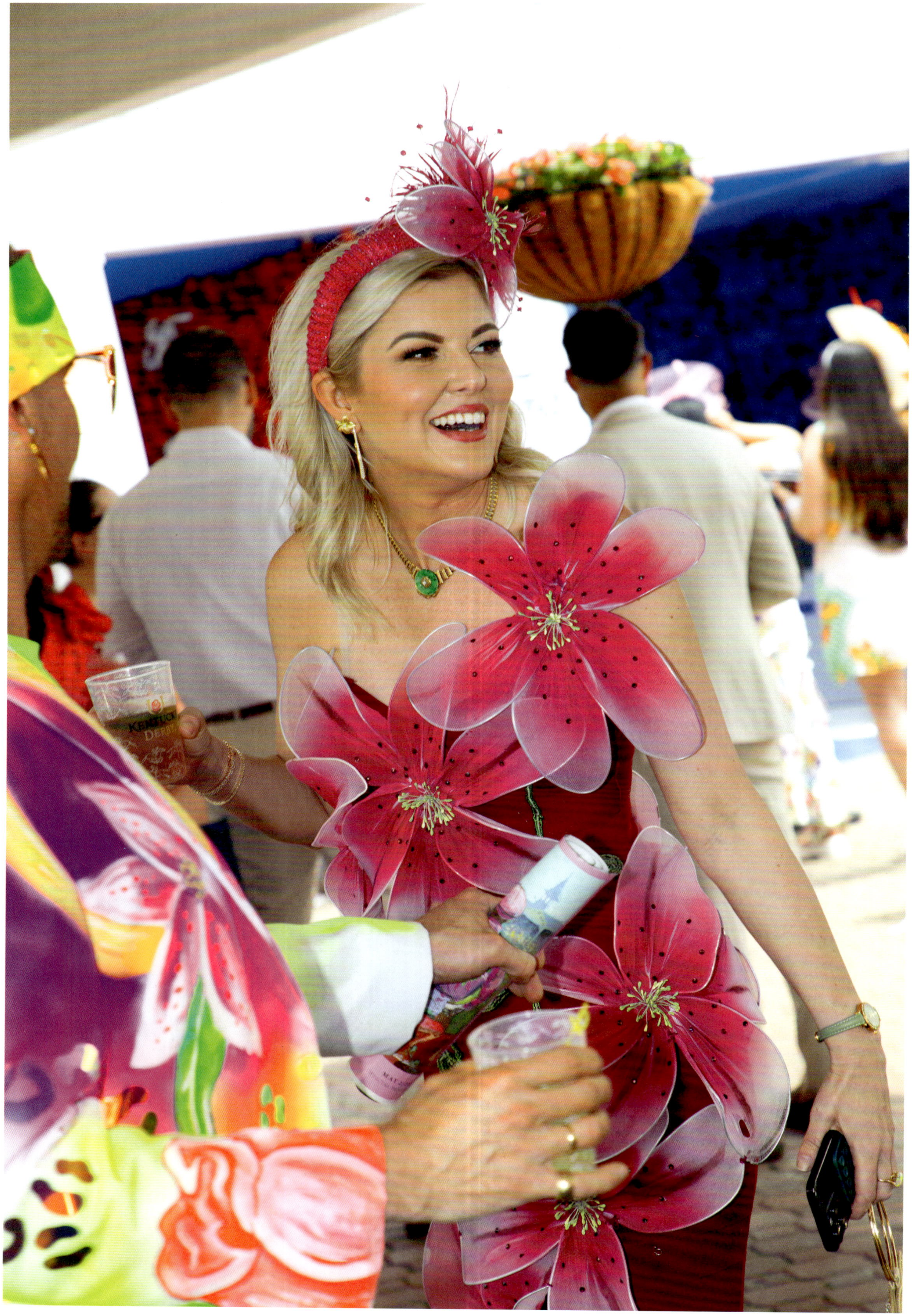

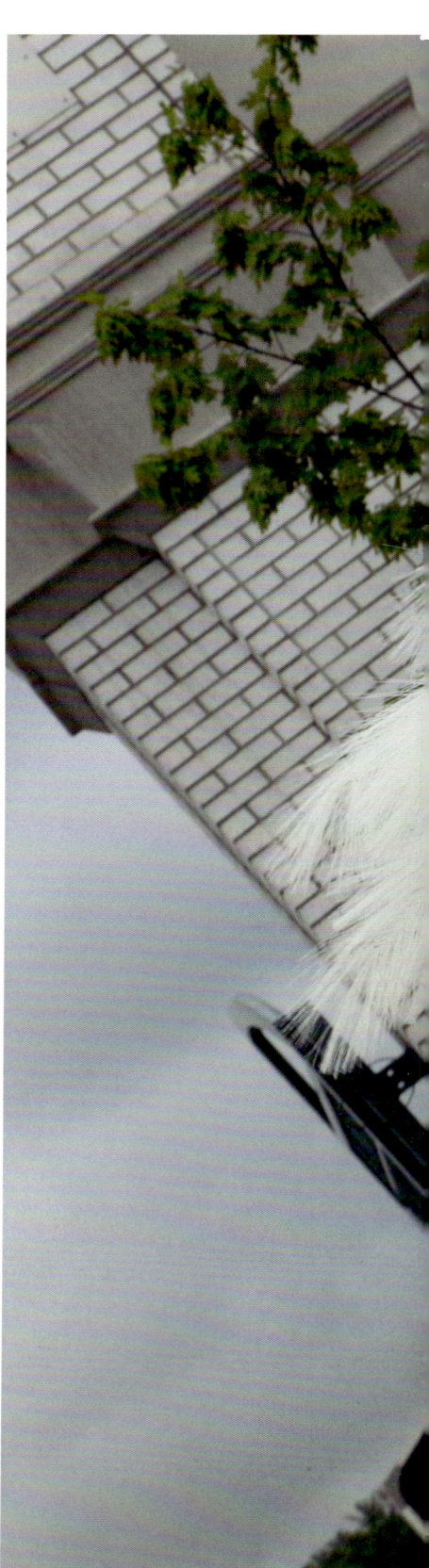

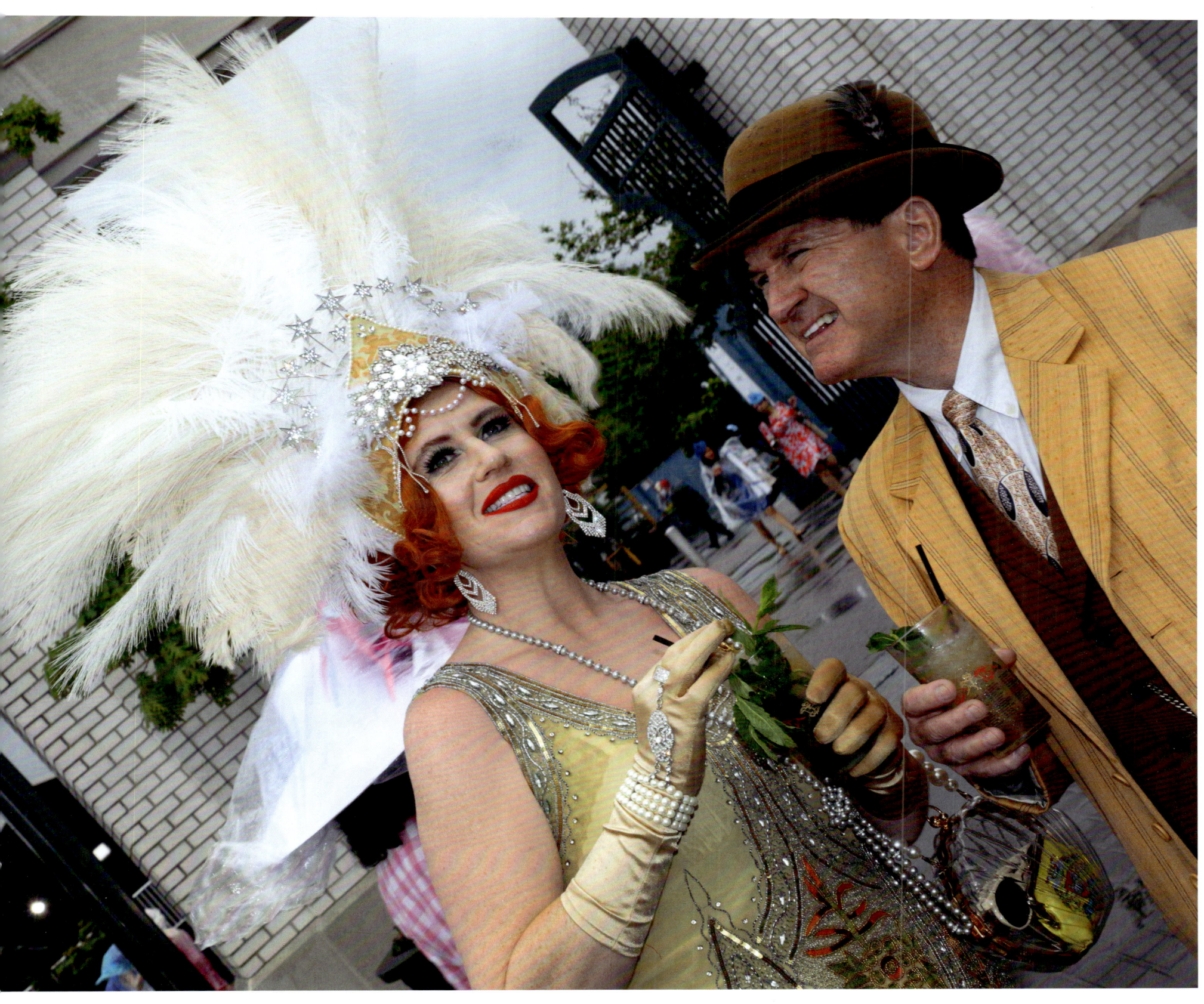

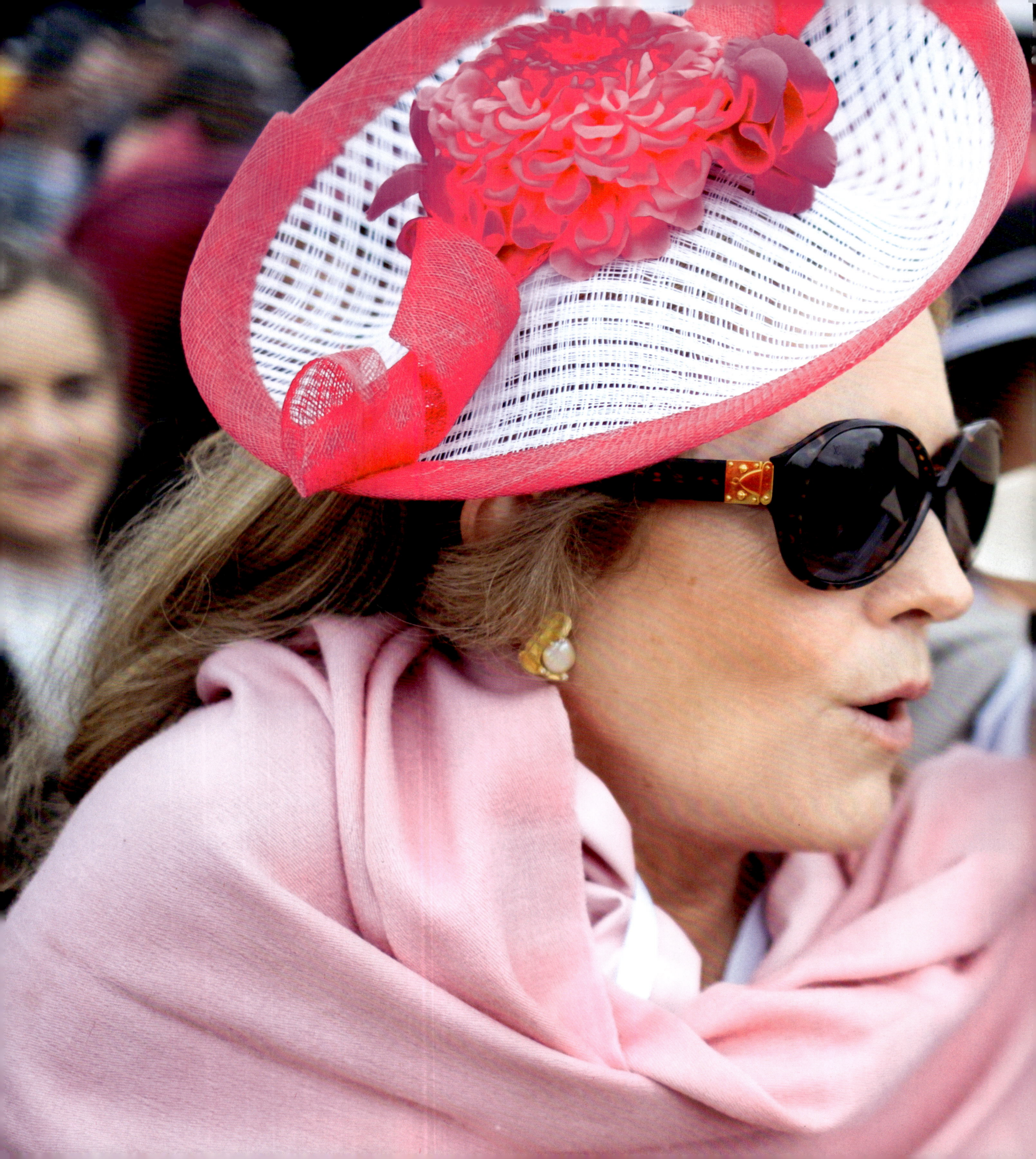

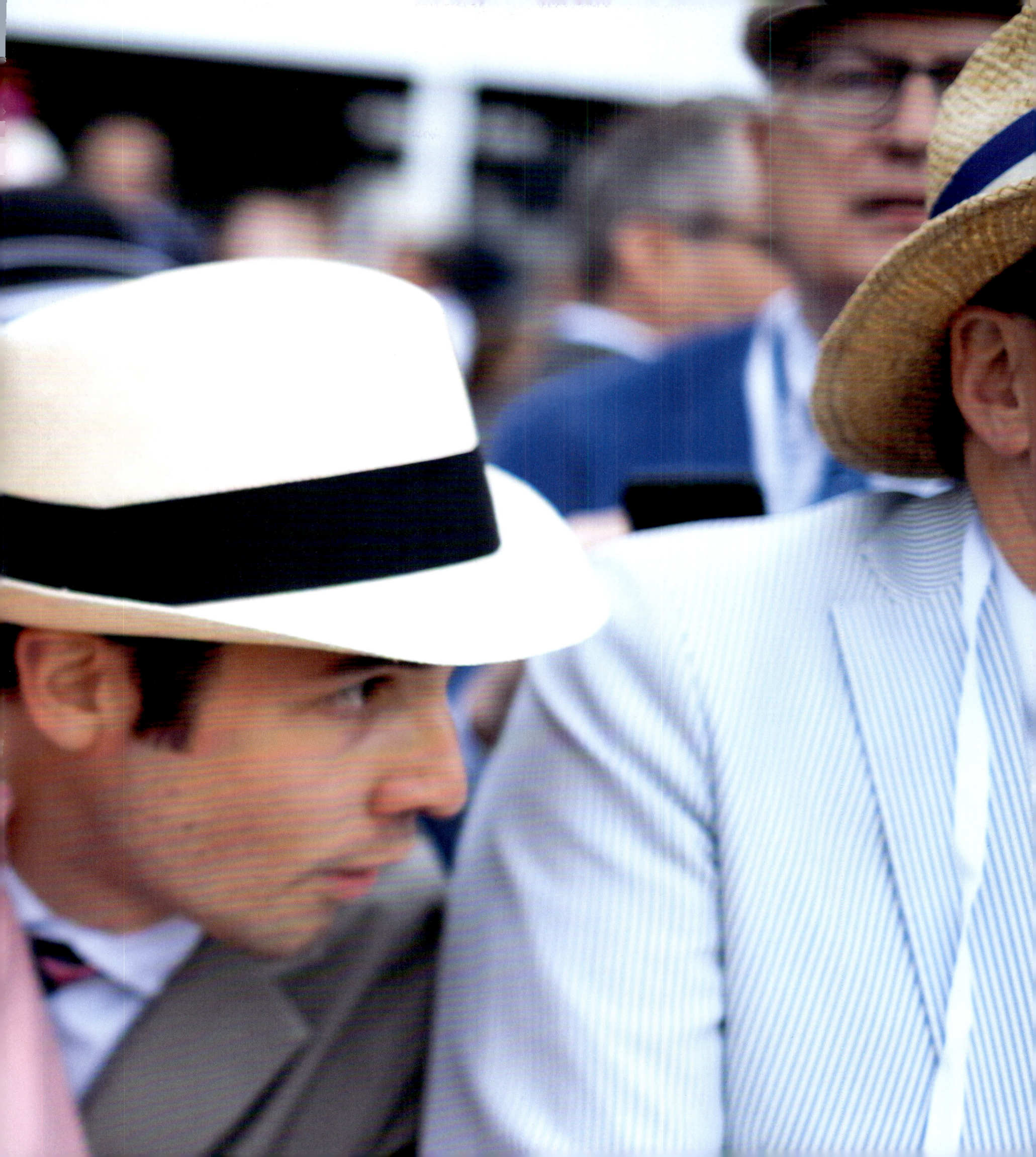

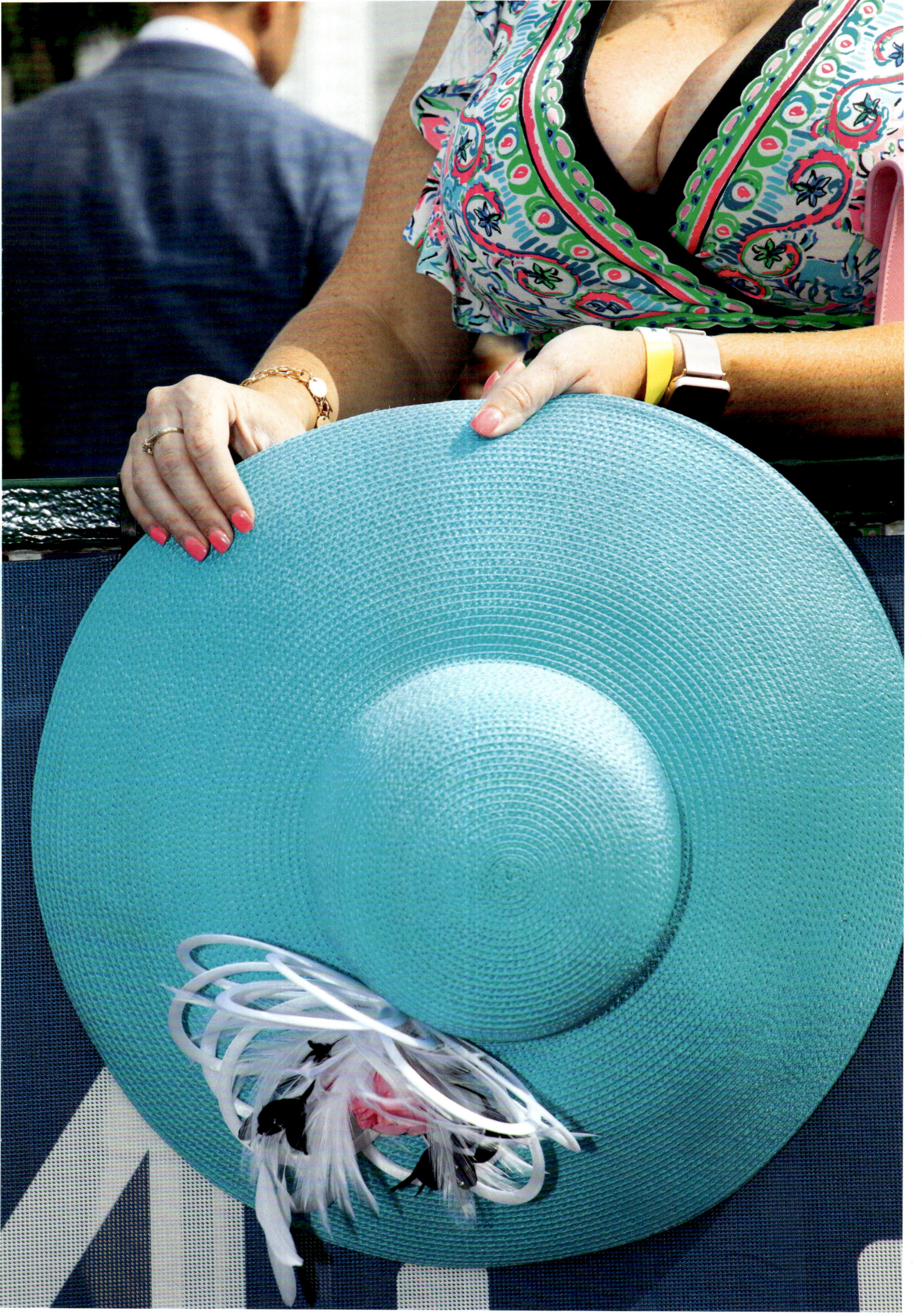

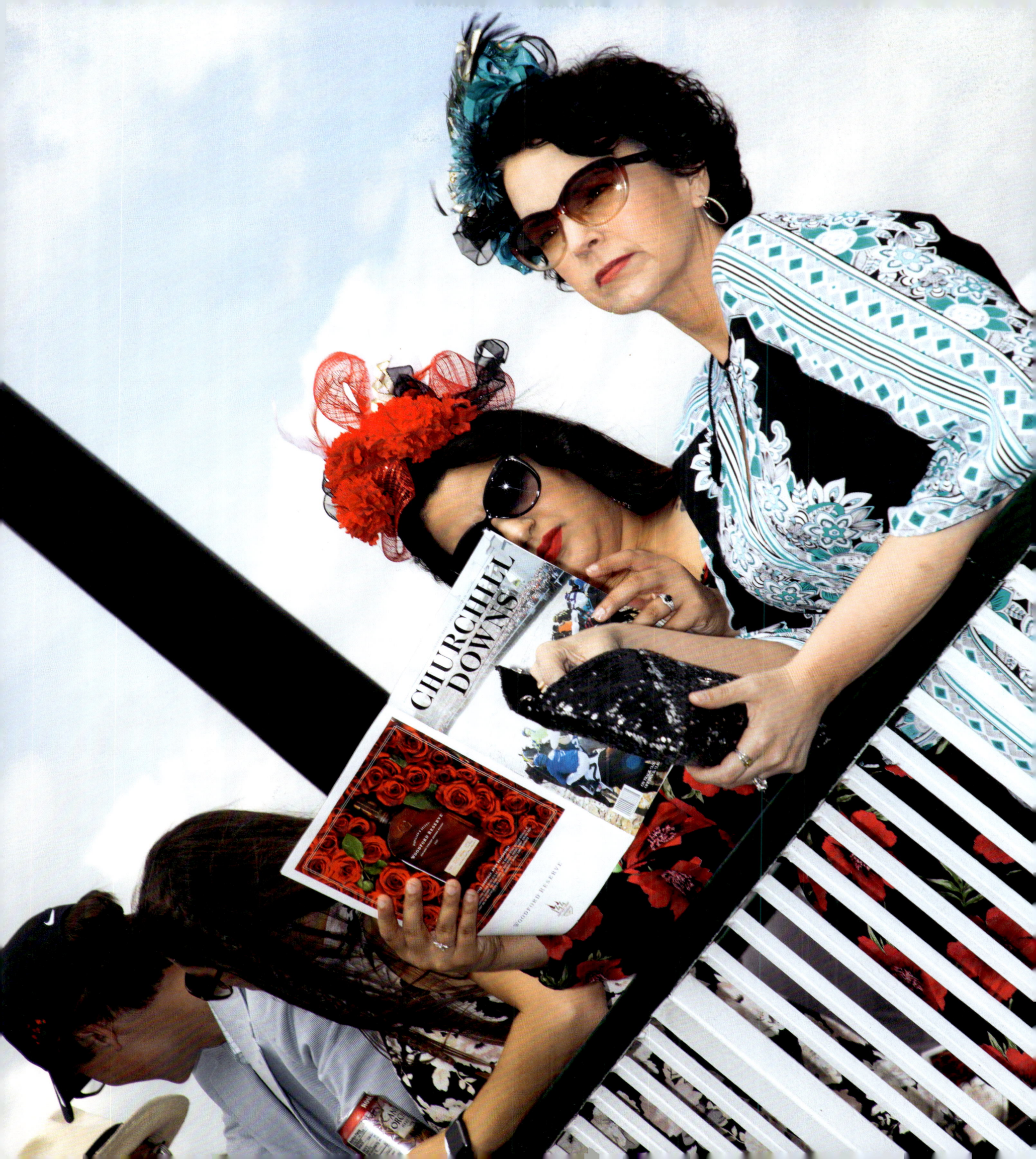

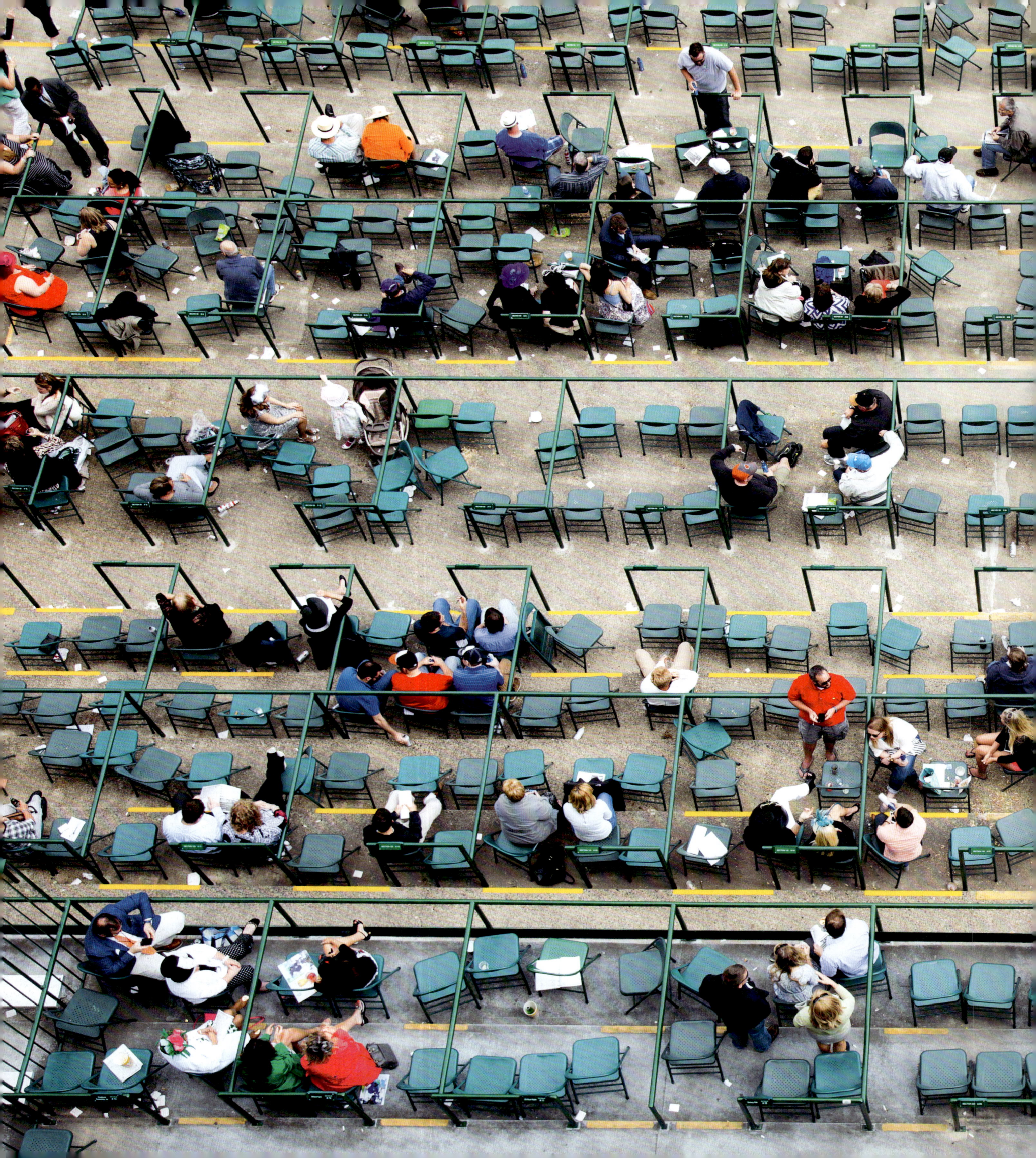

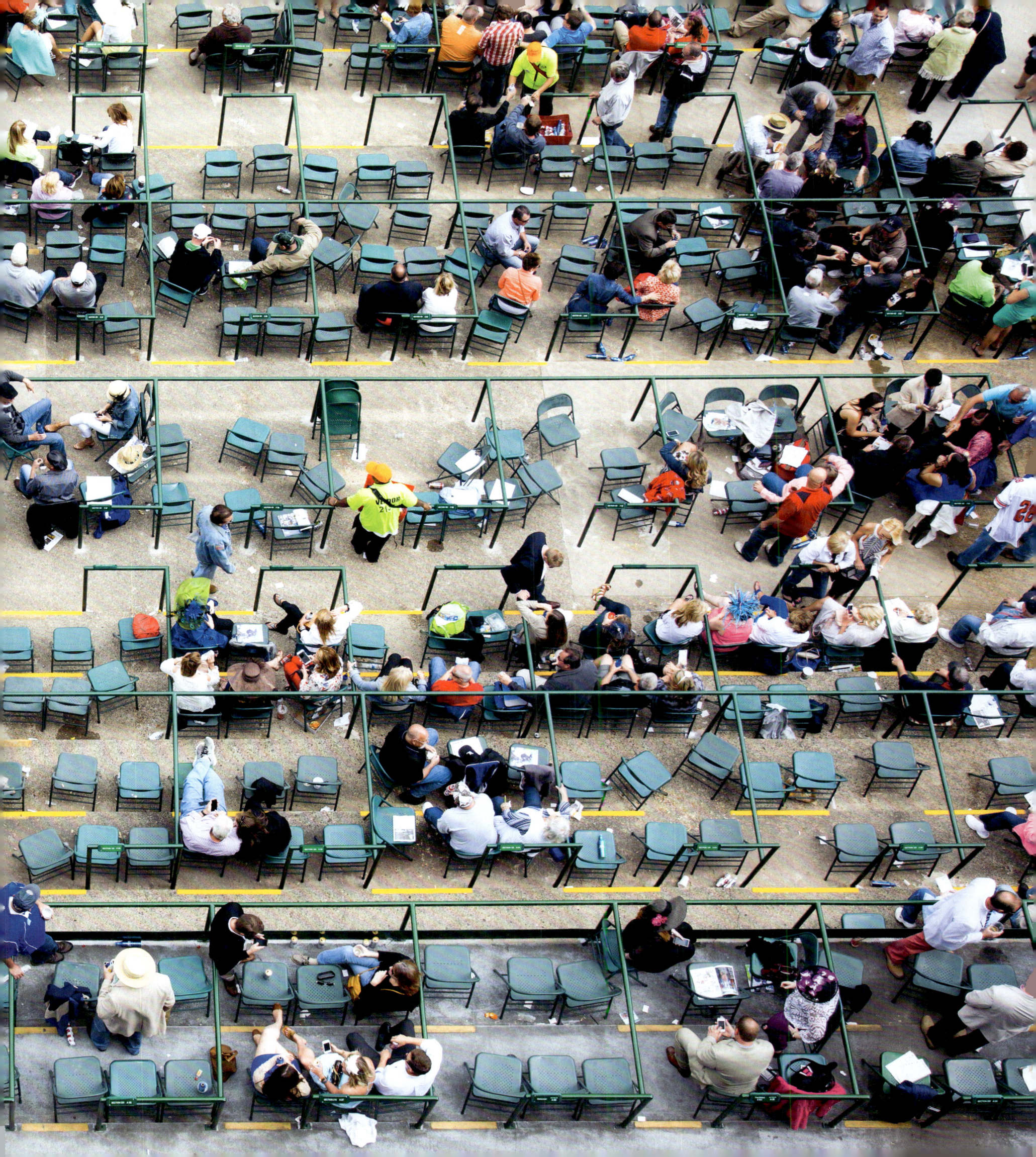

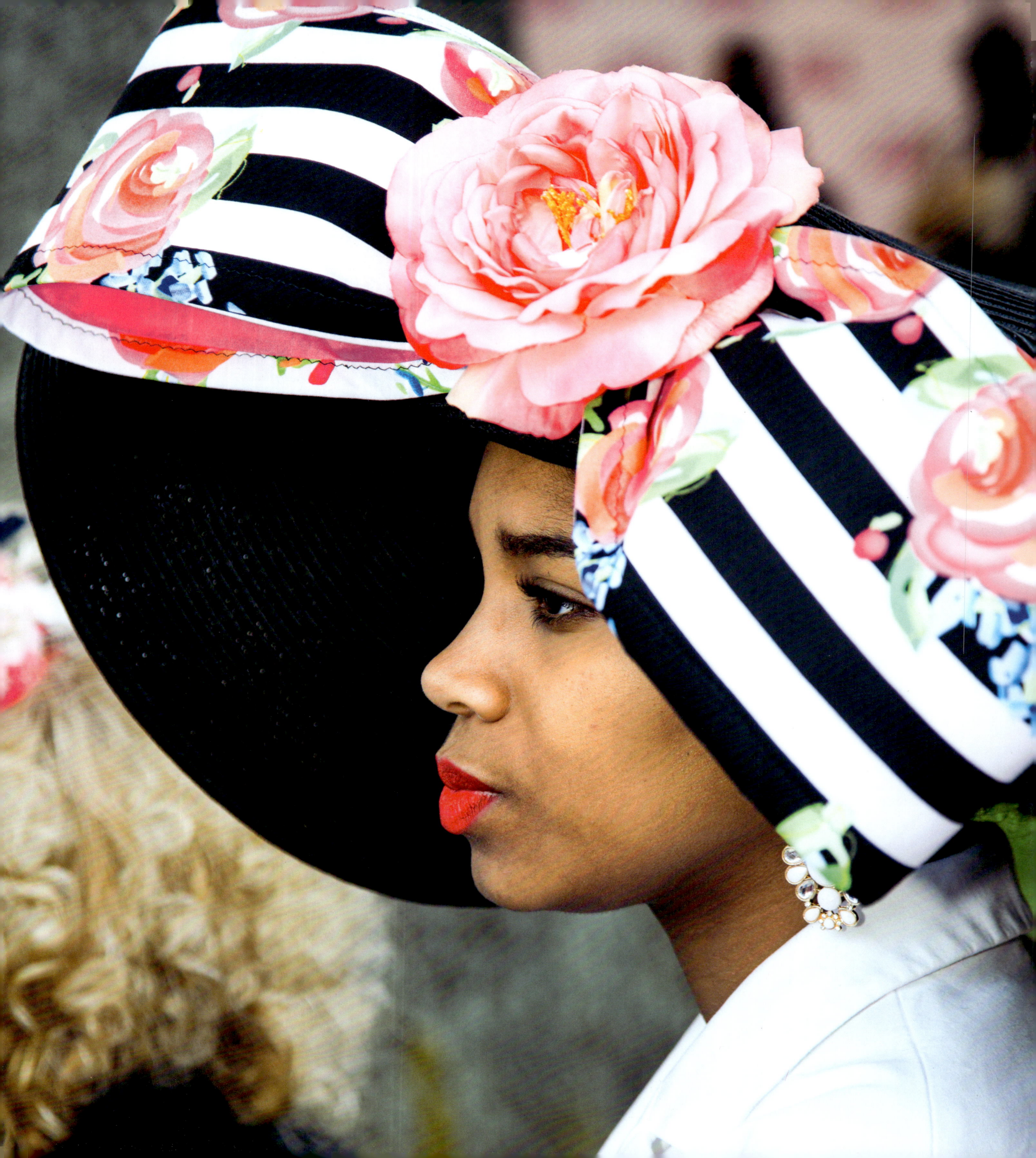

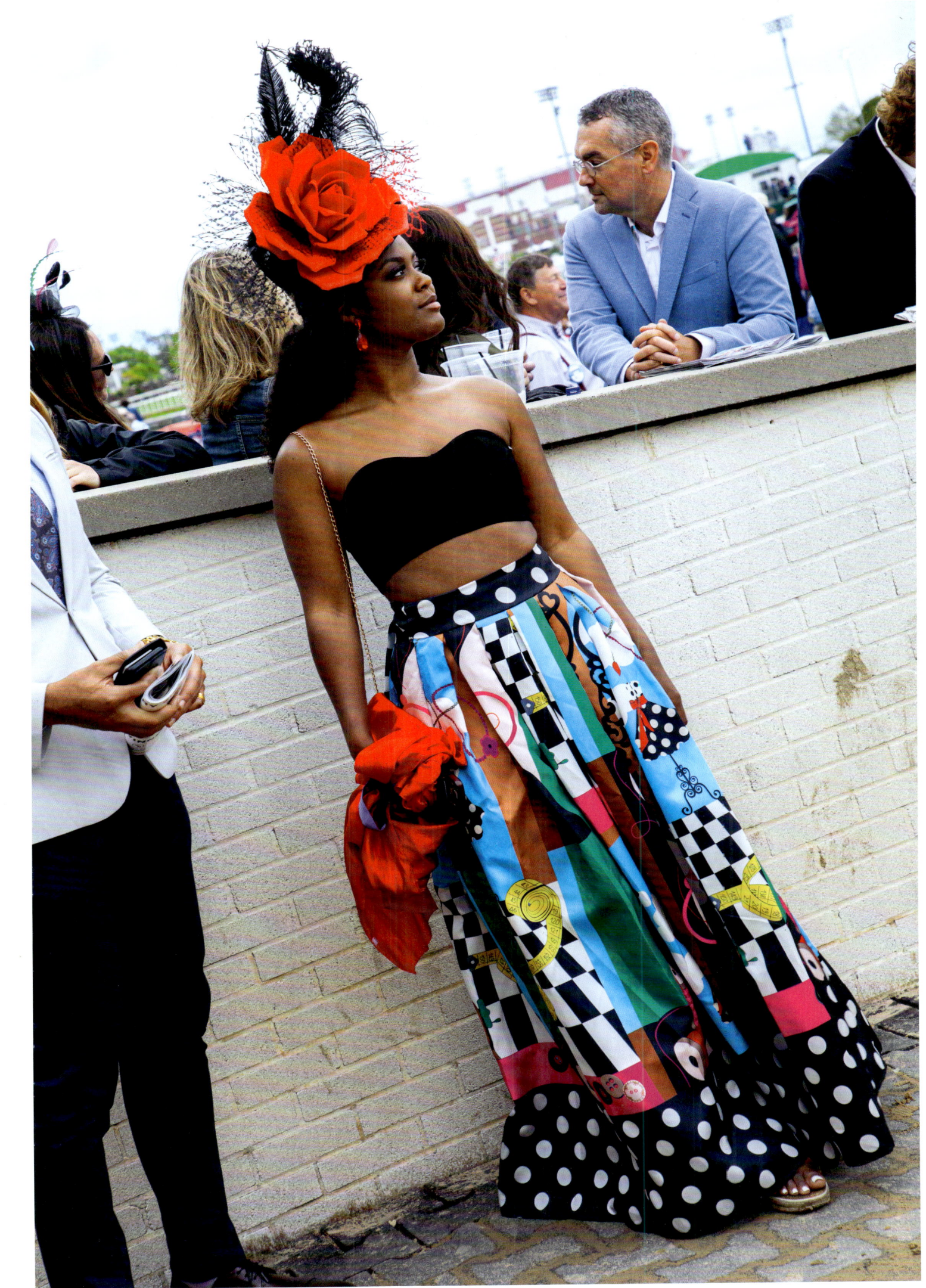

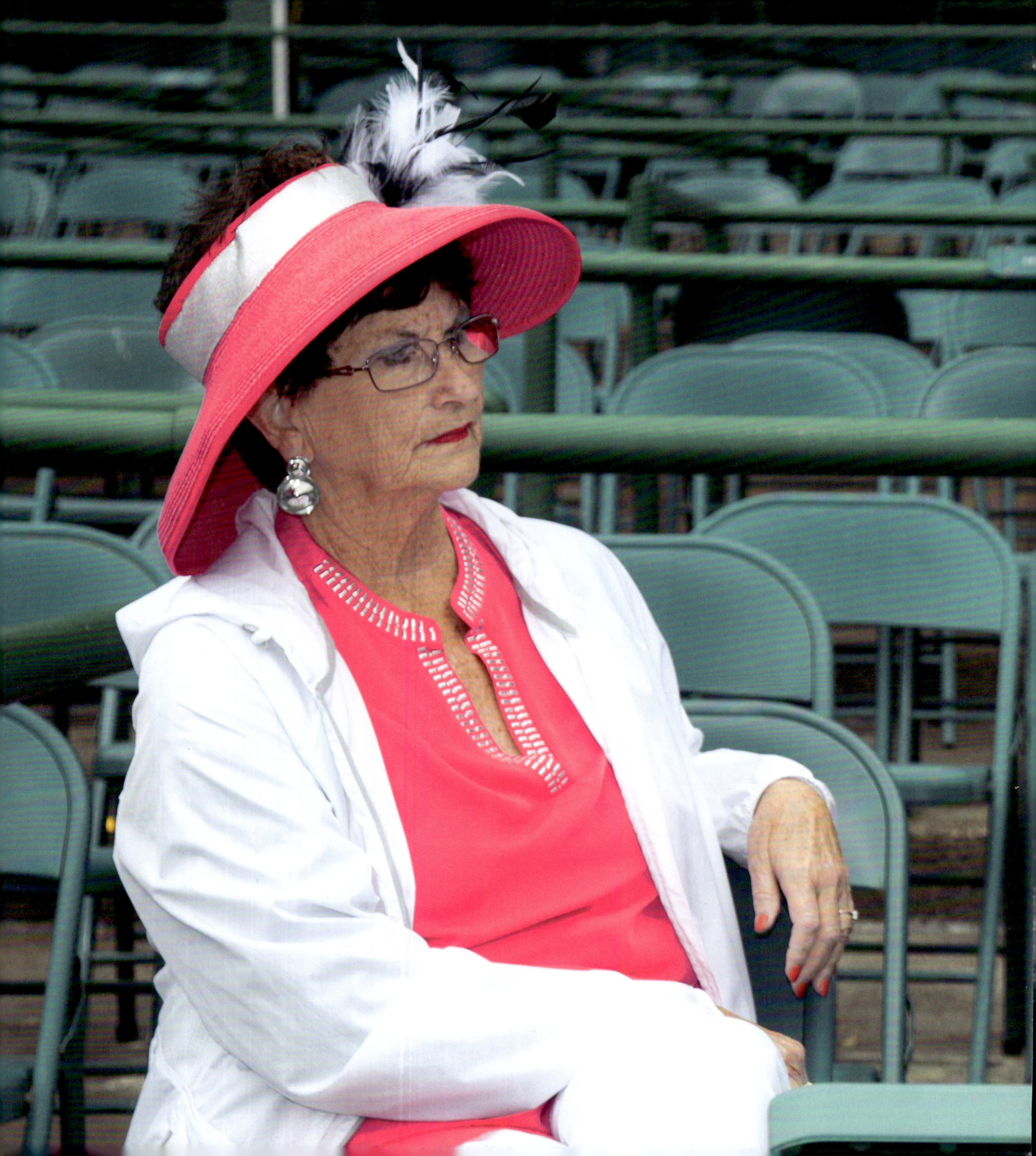

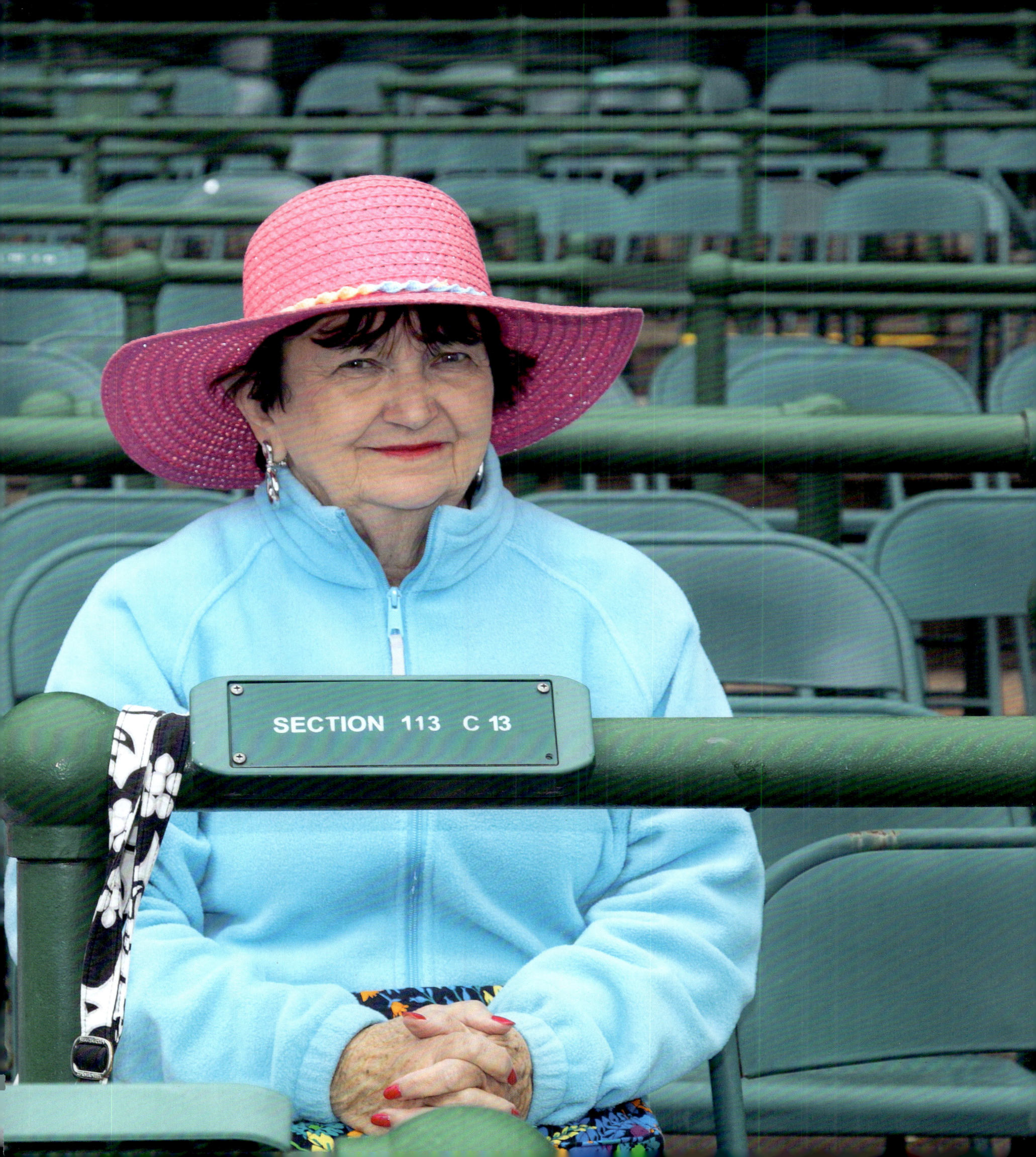

SECTION 113 C 13

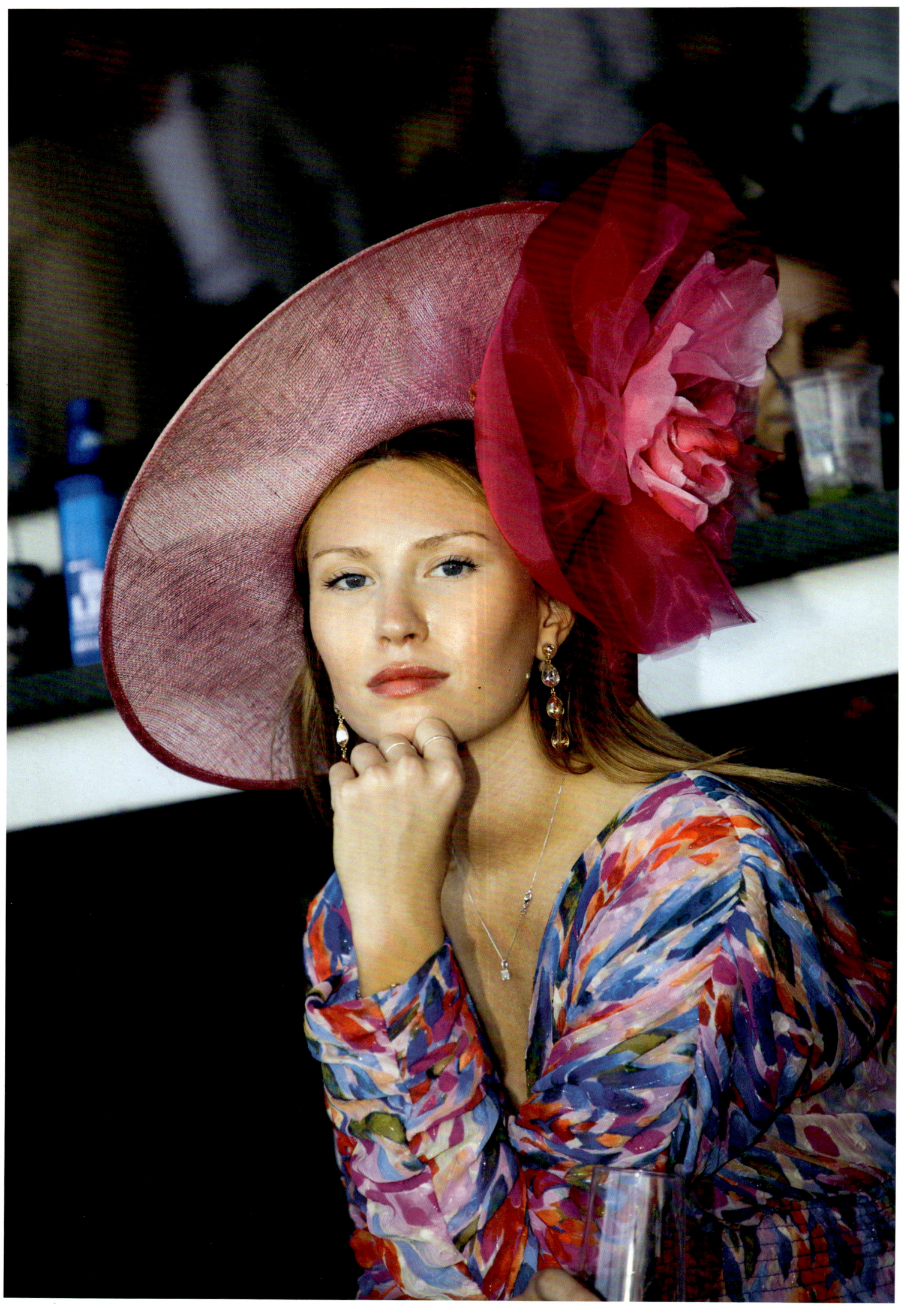

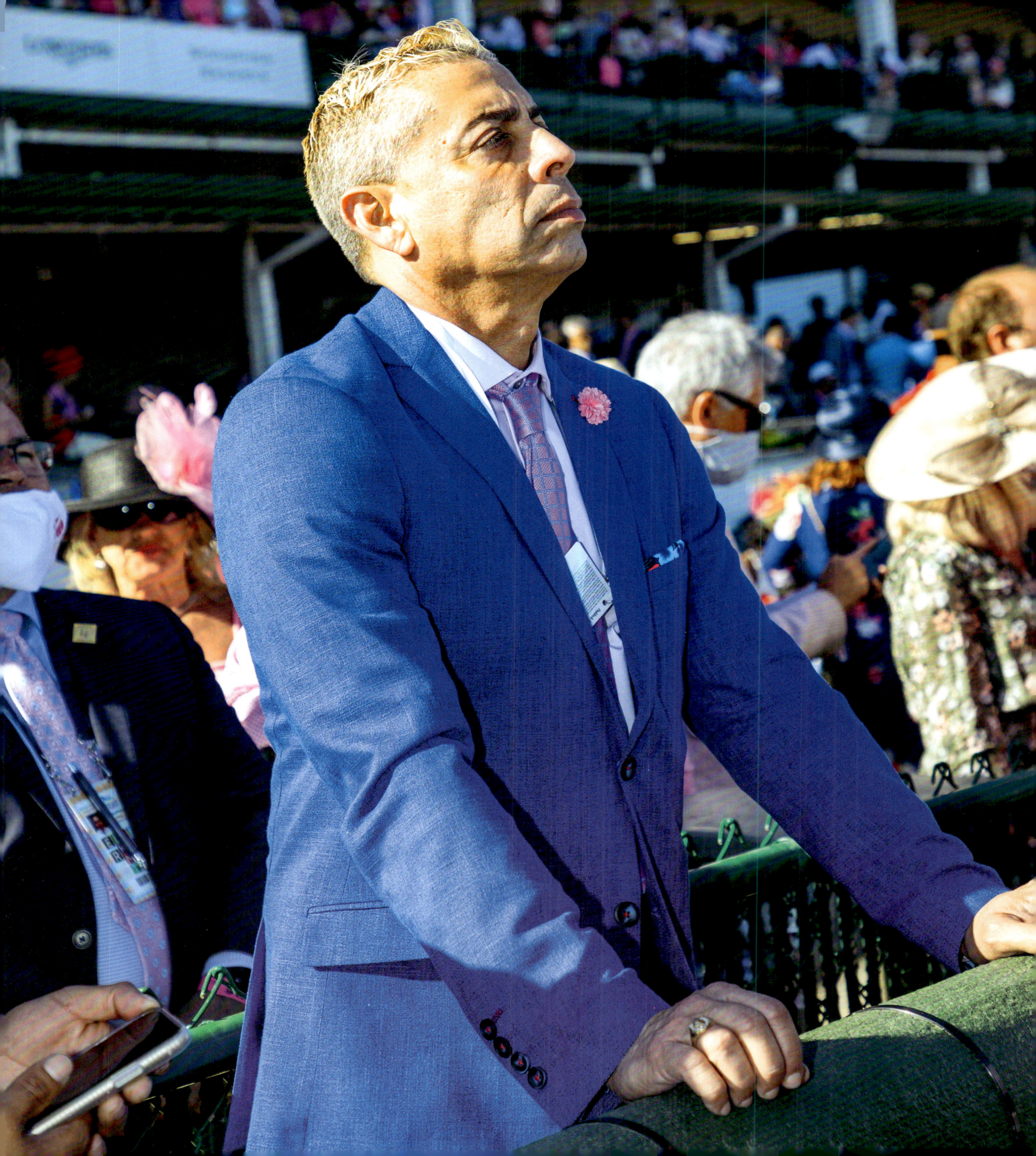

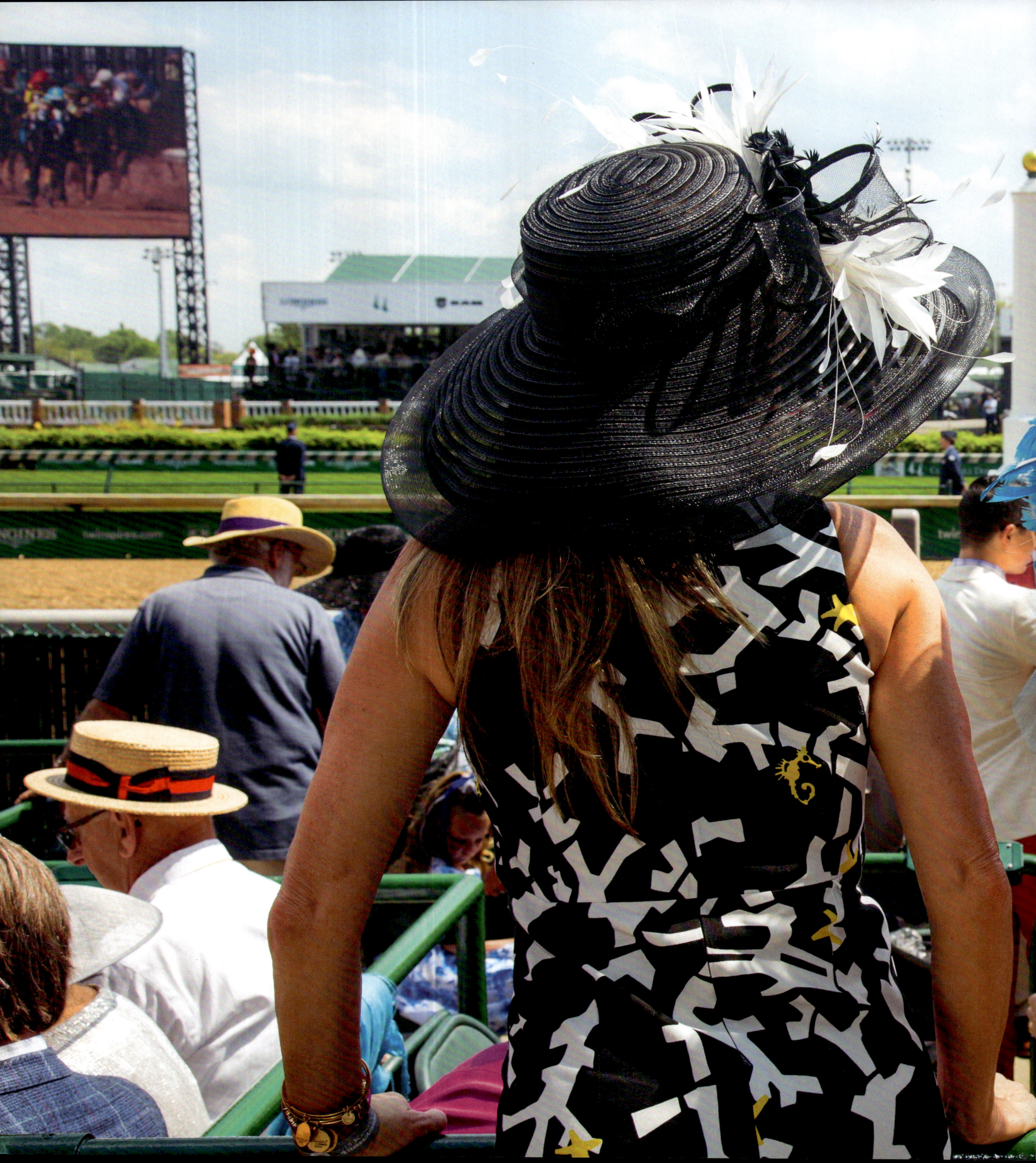

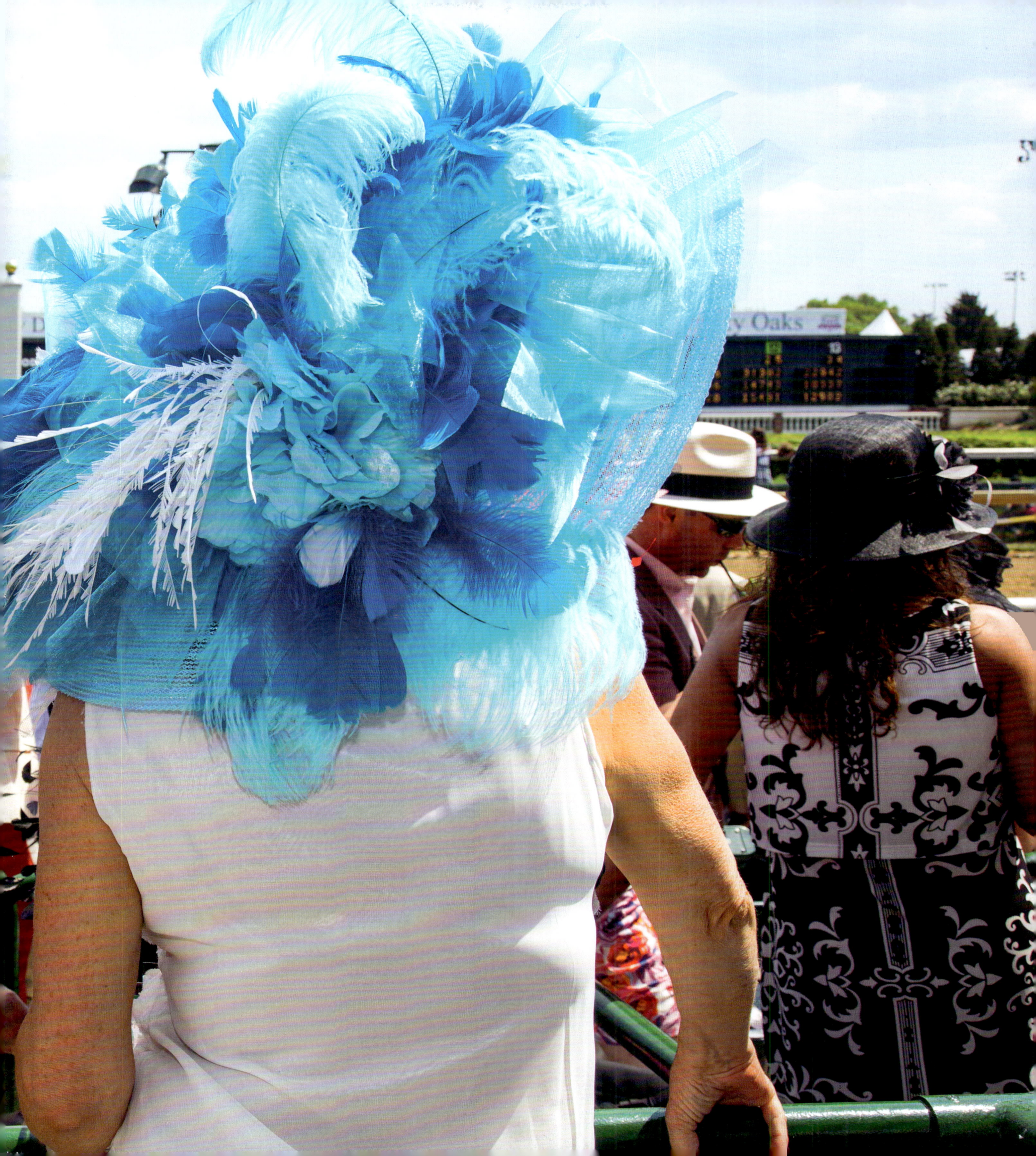

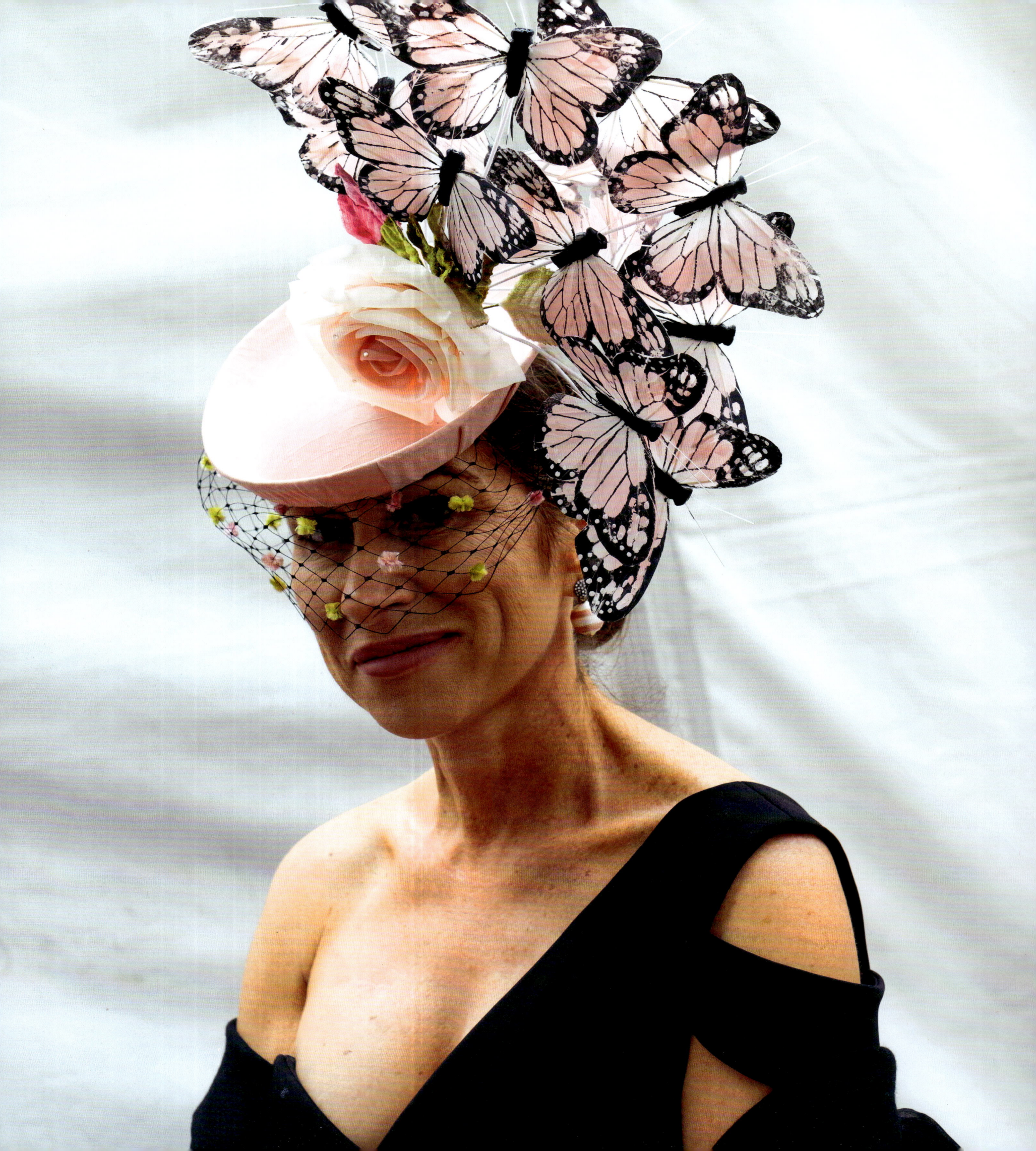

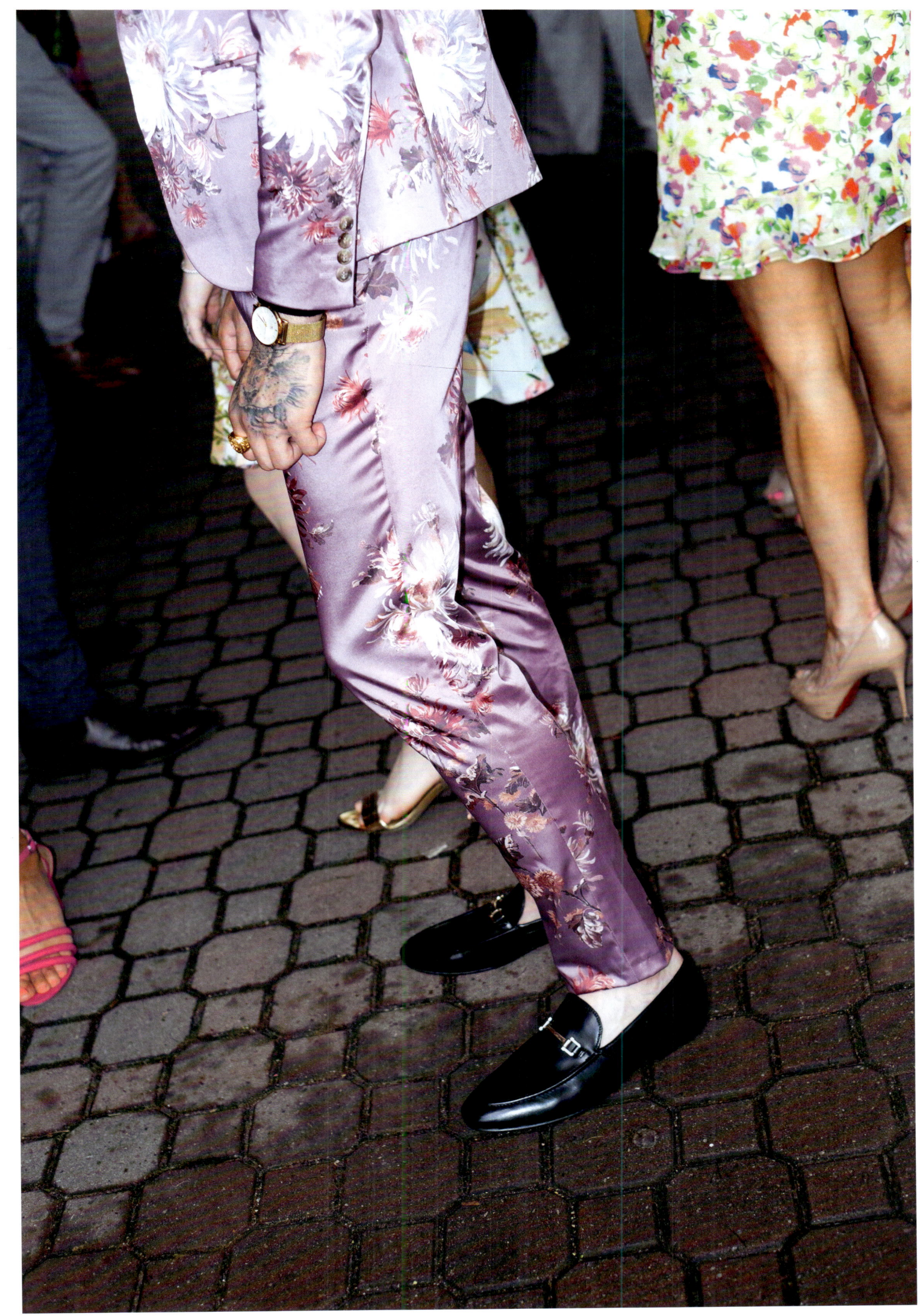

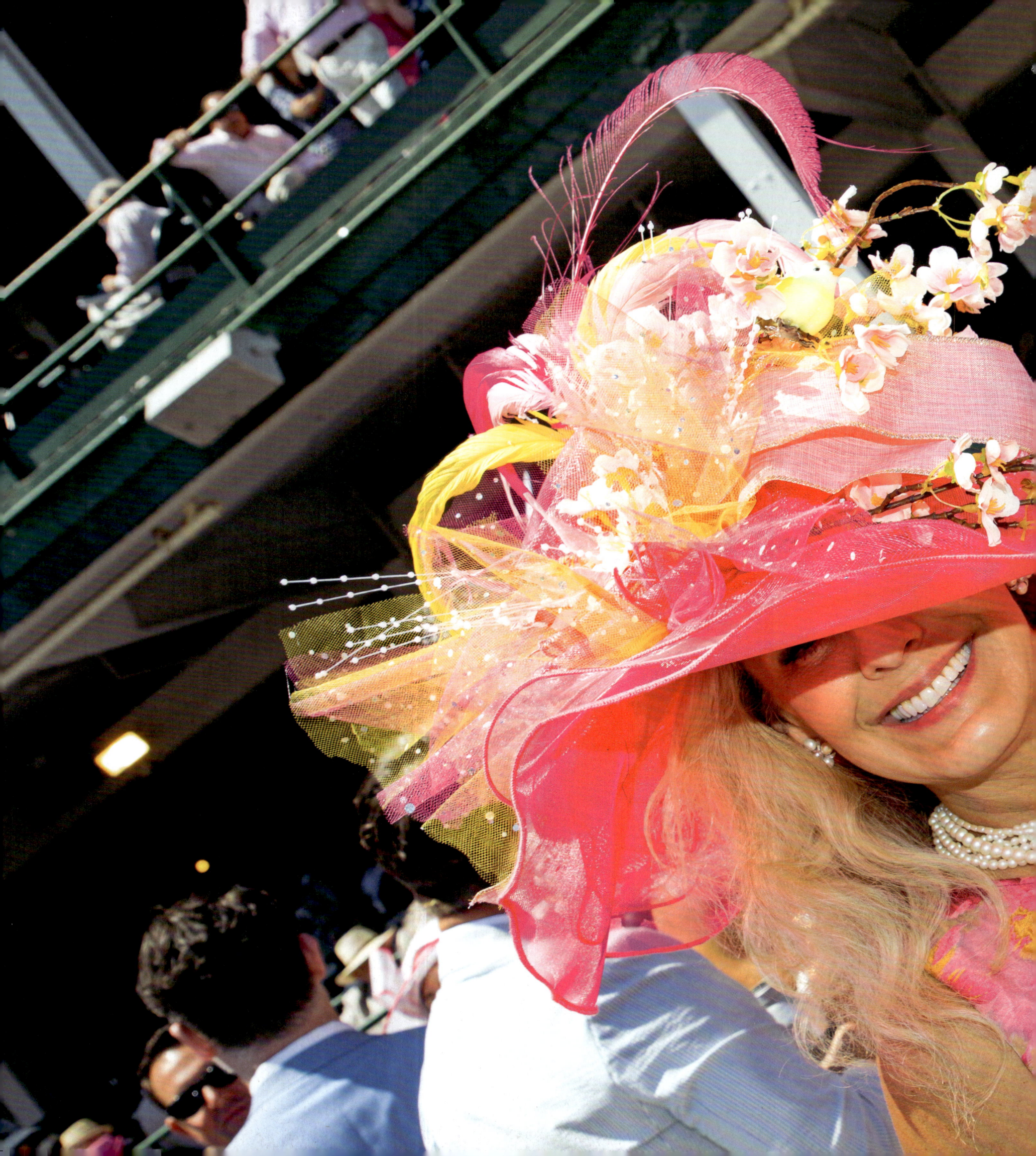

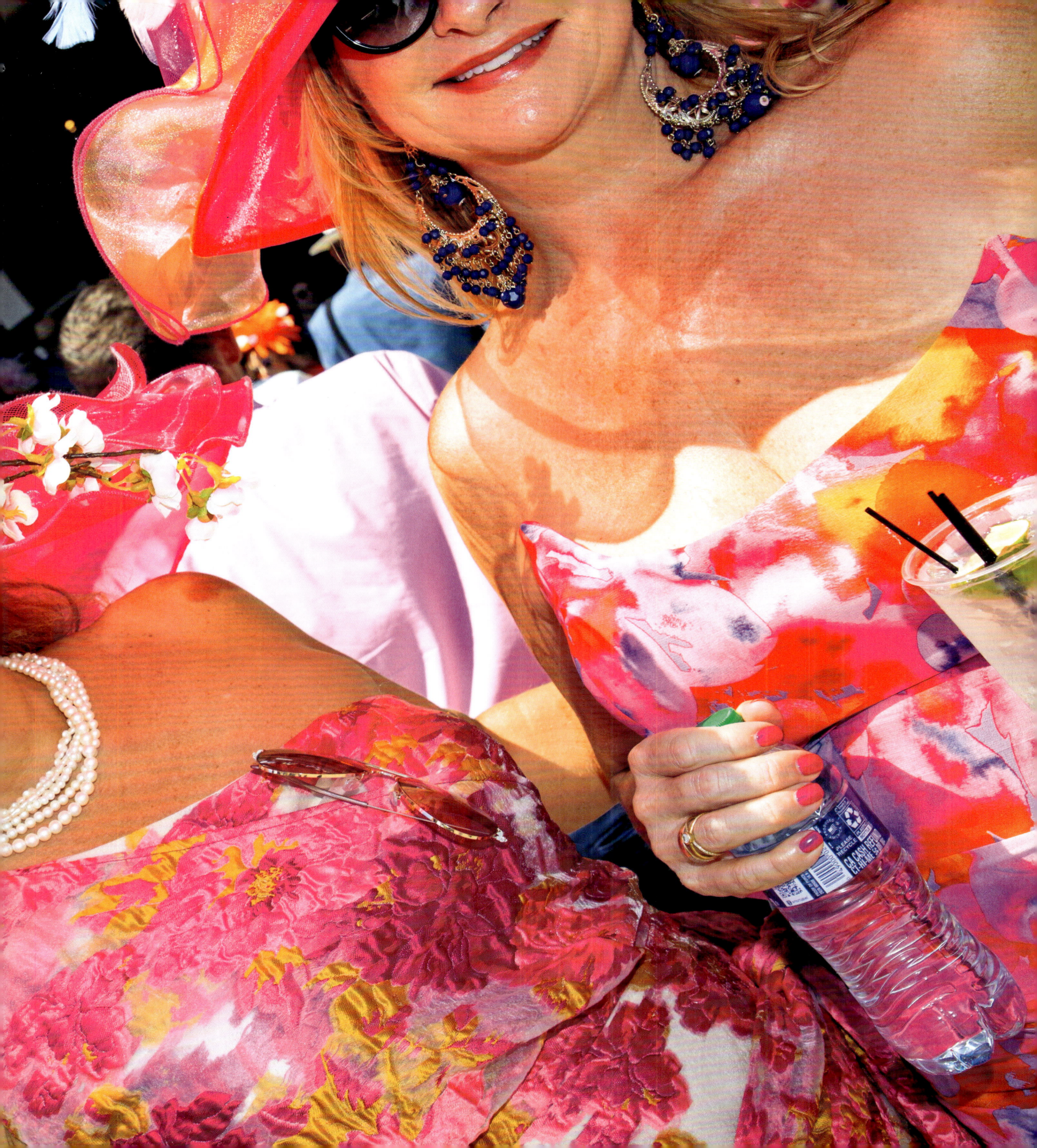

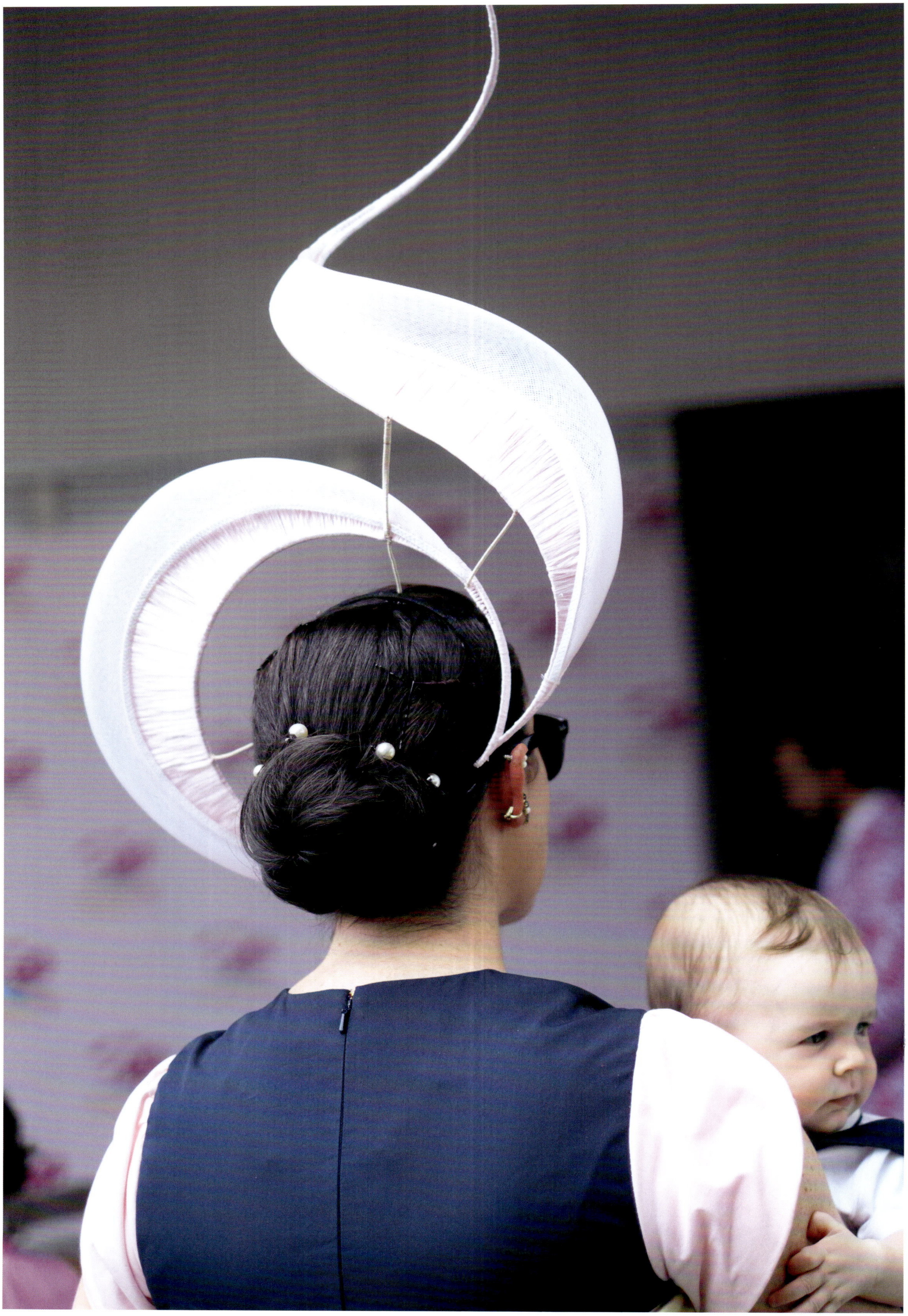

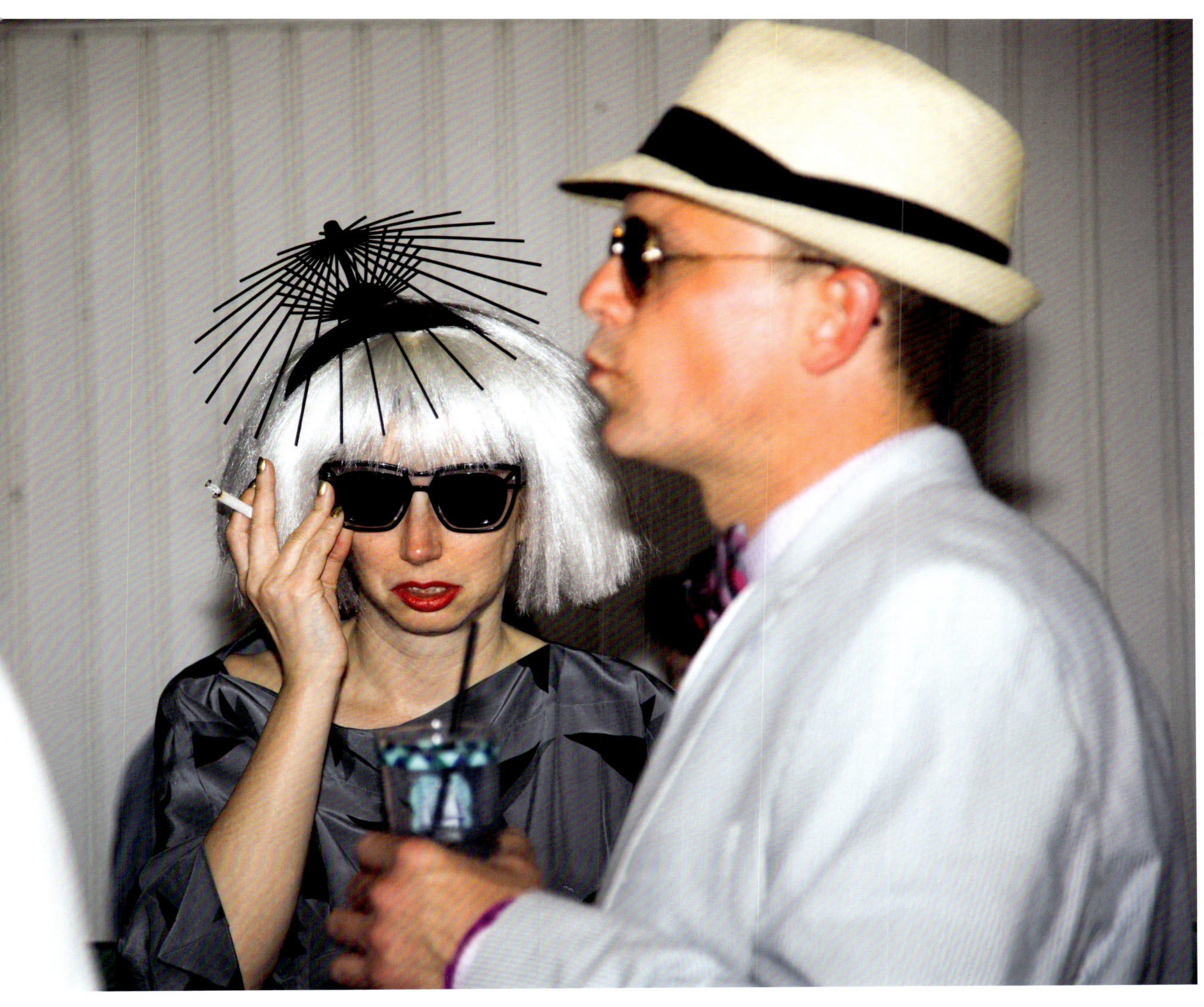

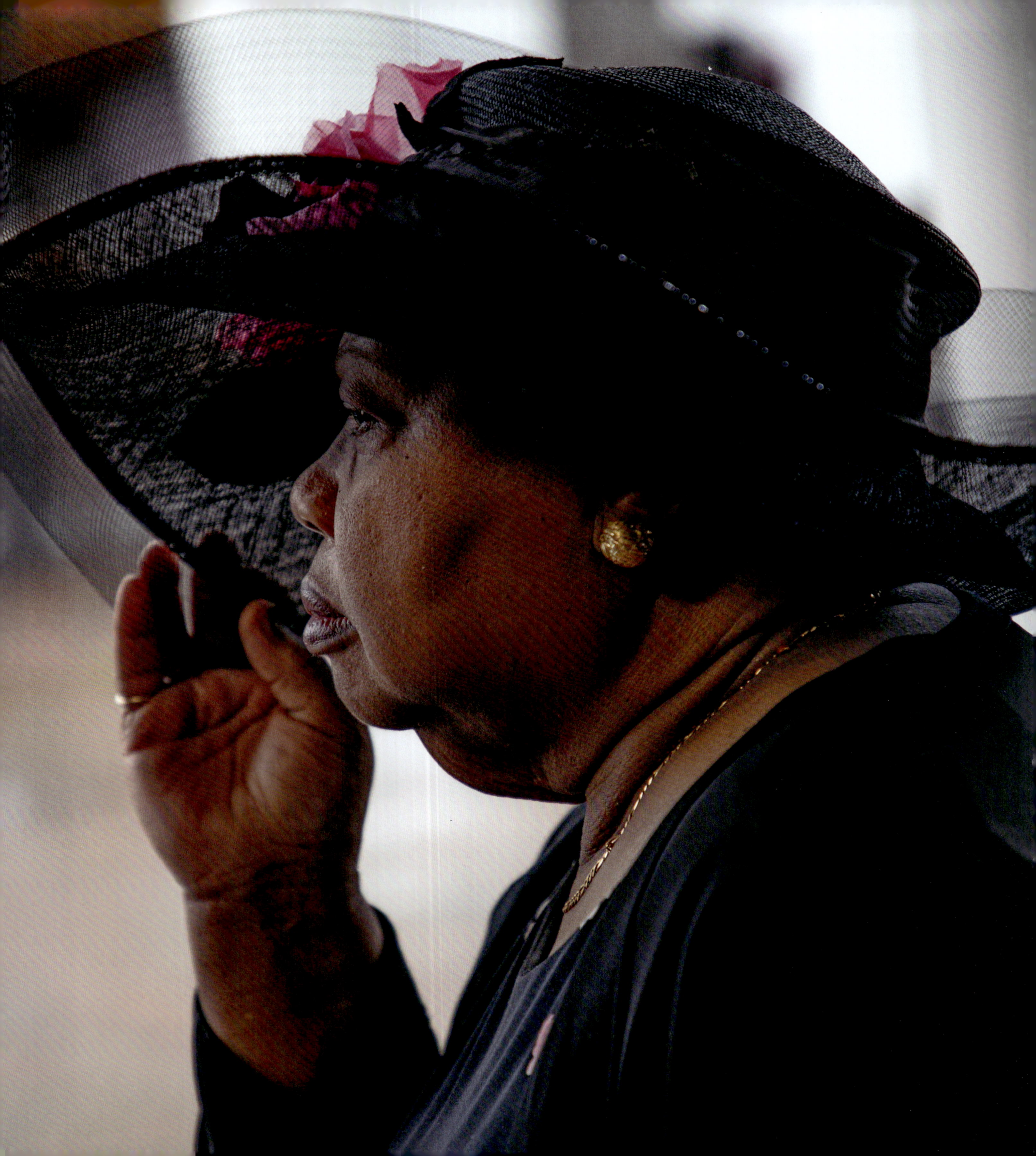

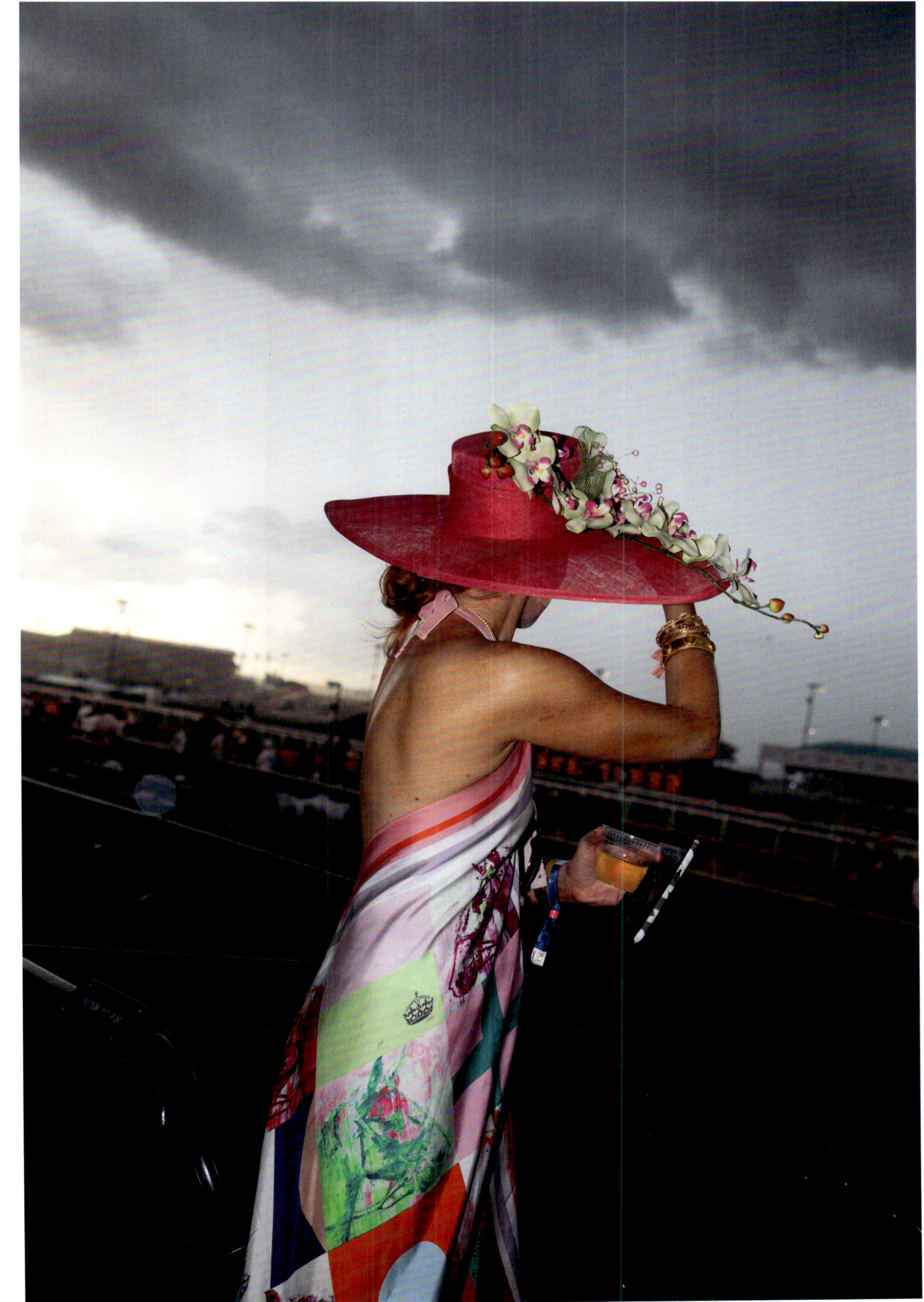

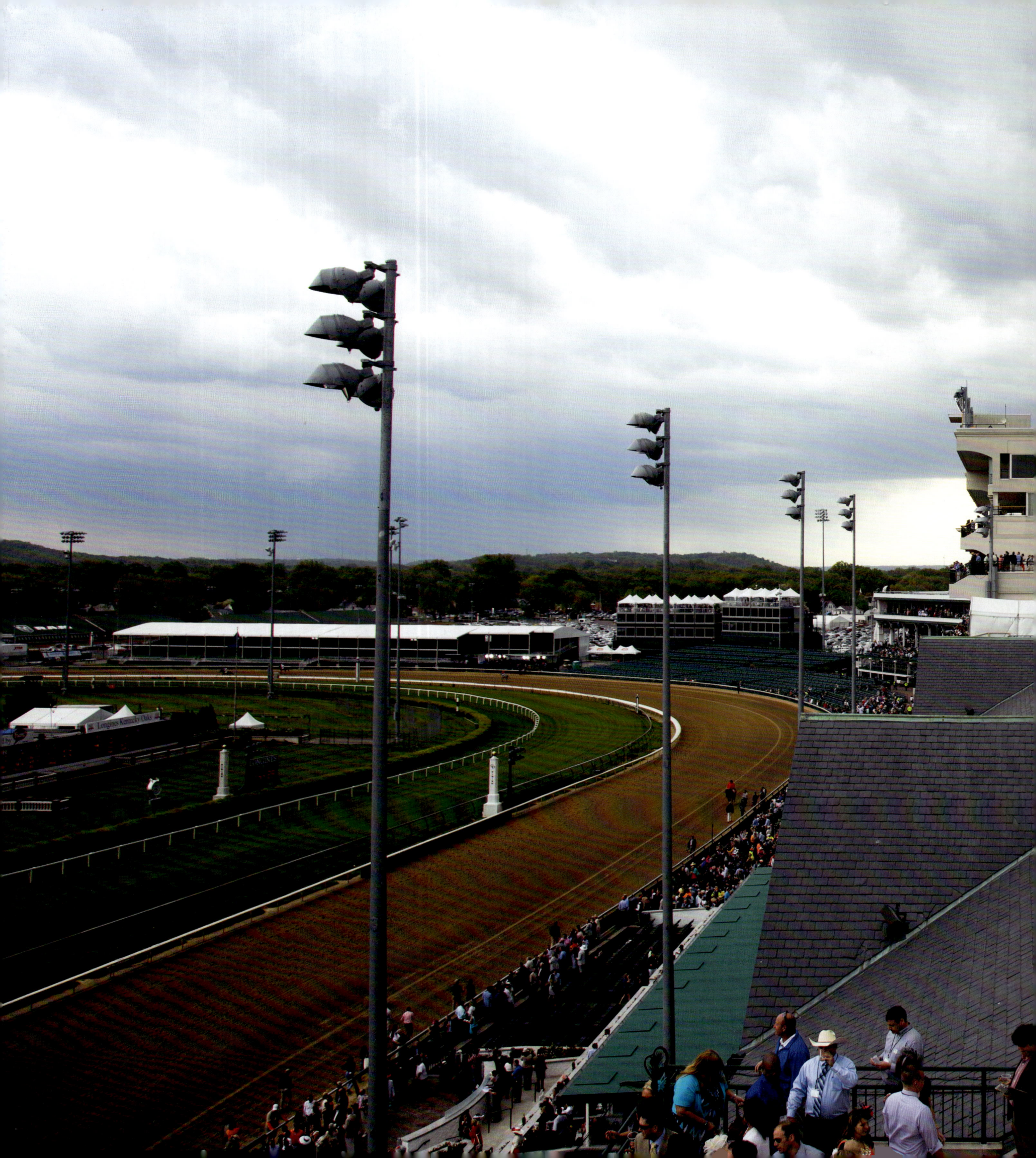

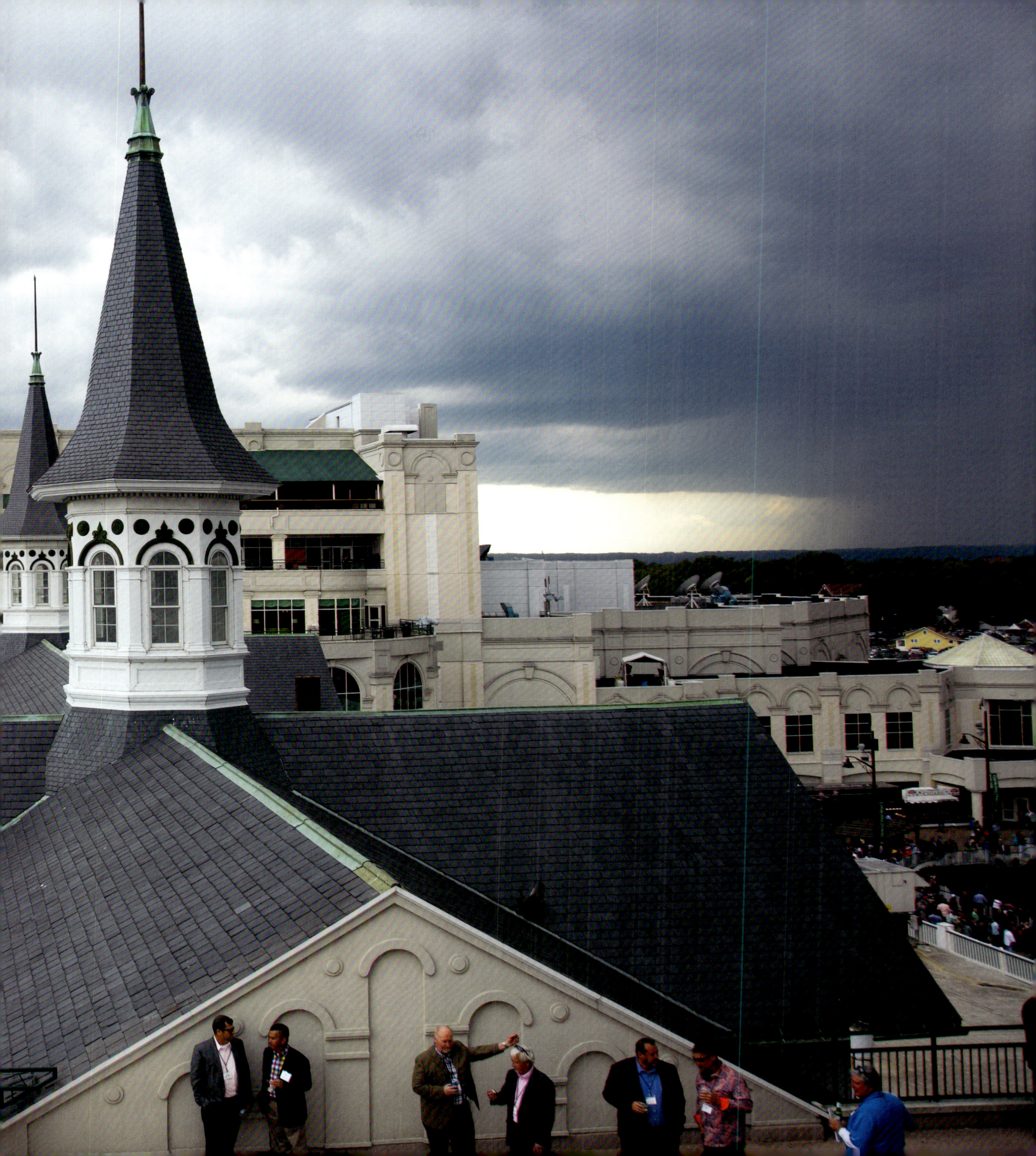

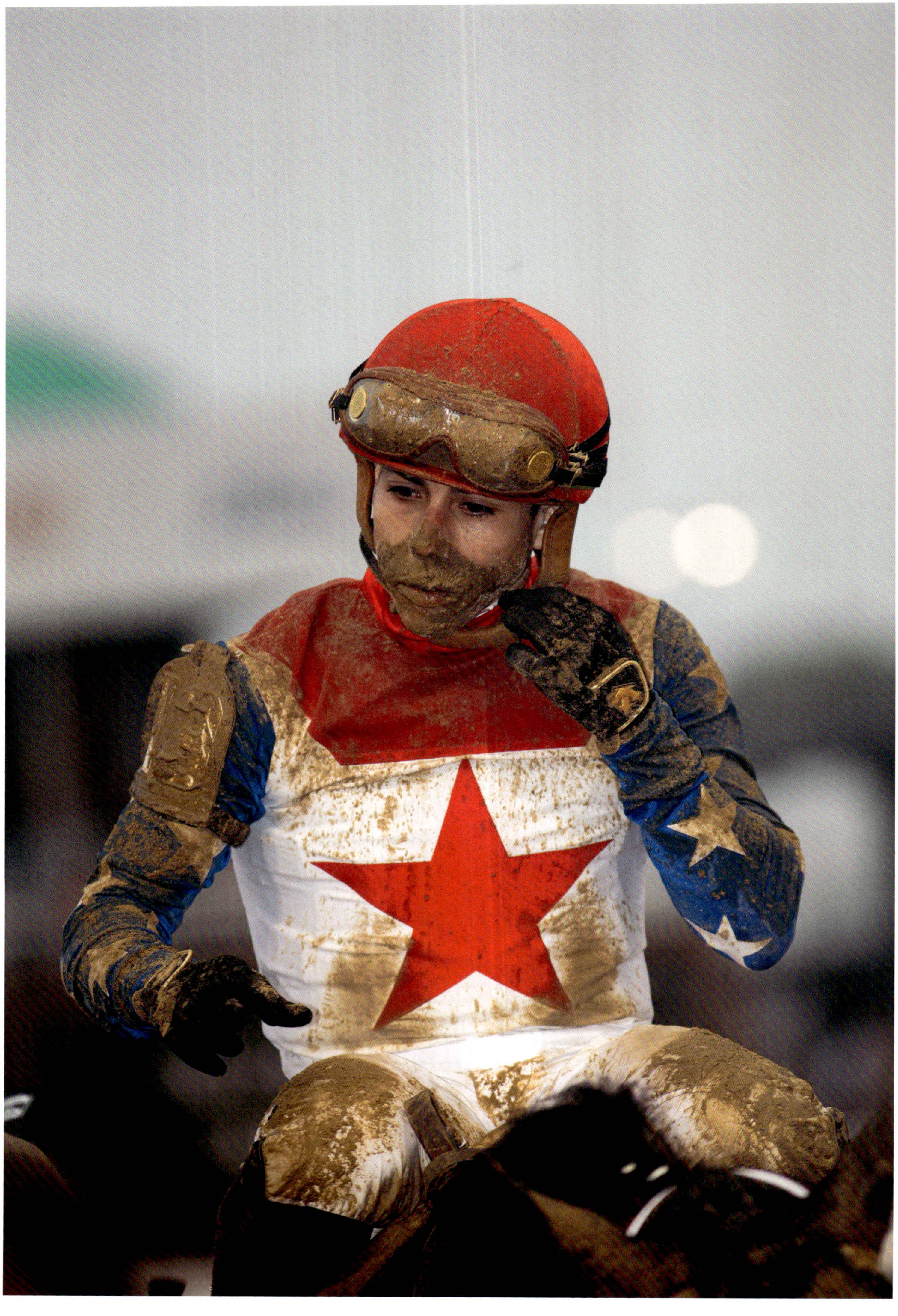

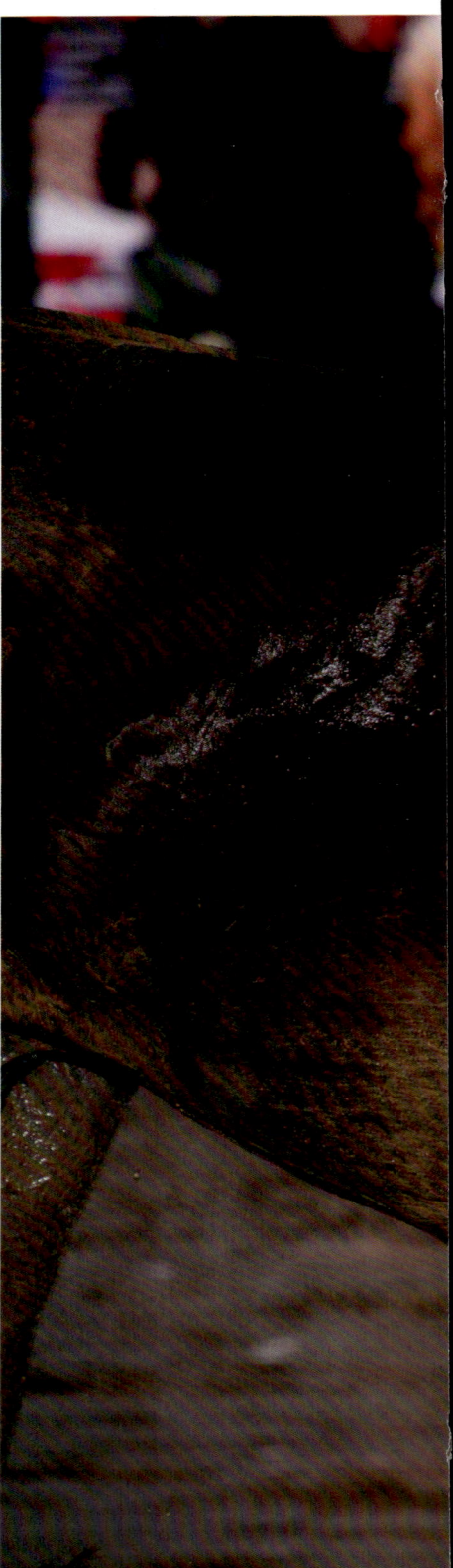

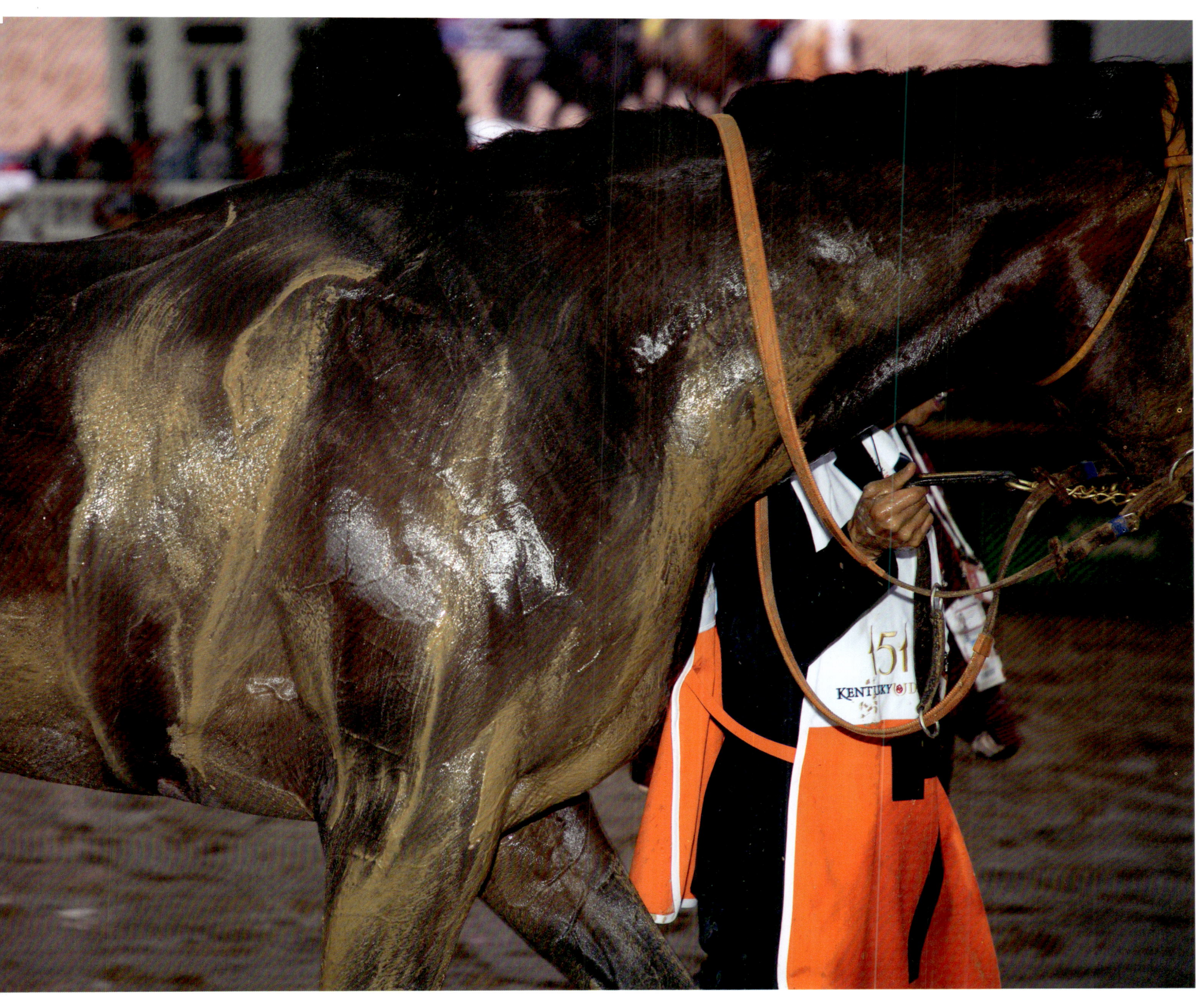

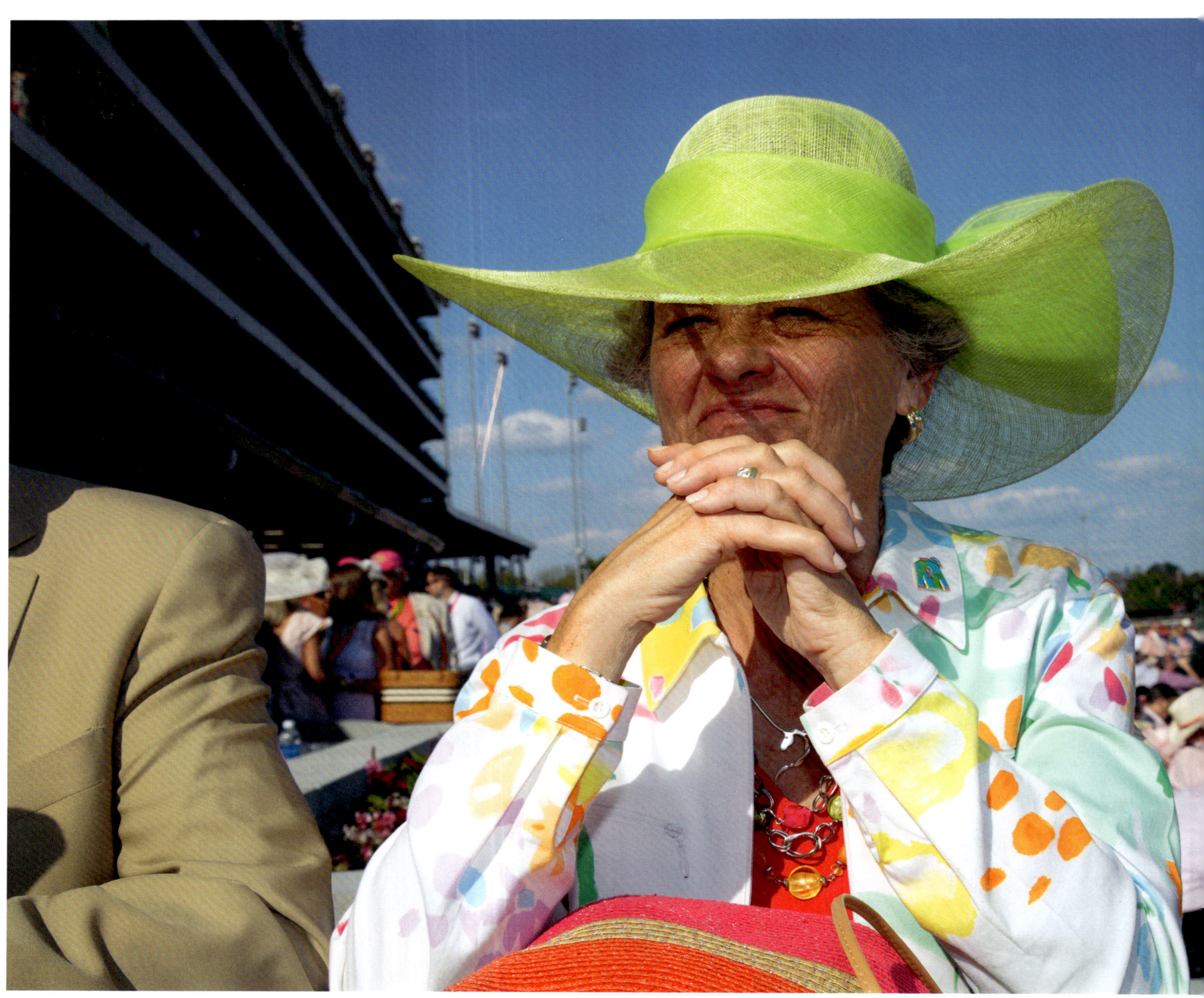

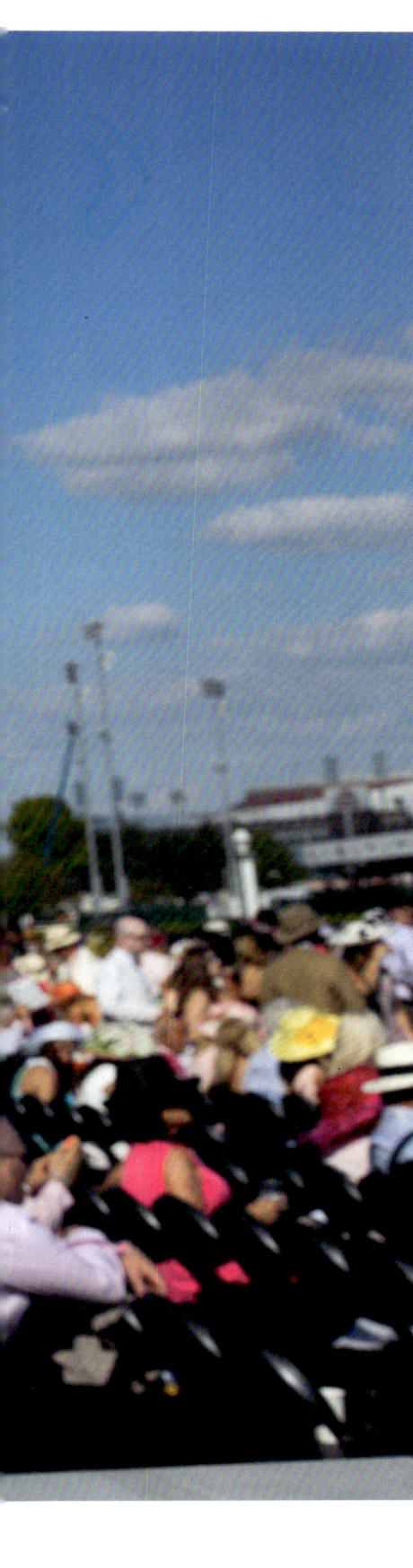

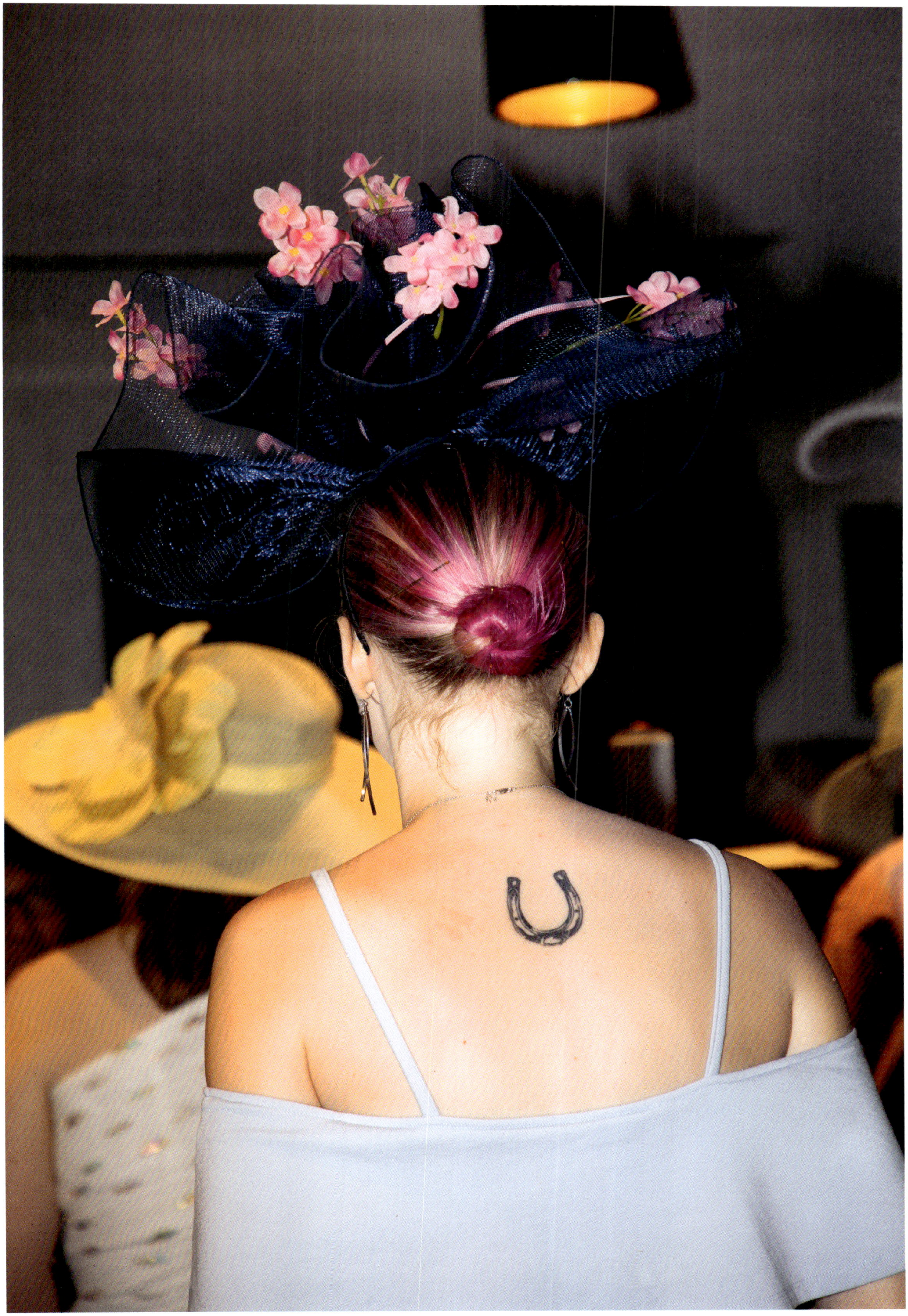

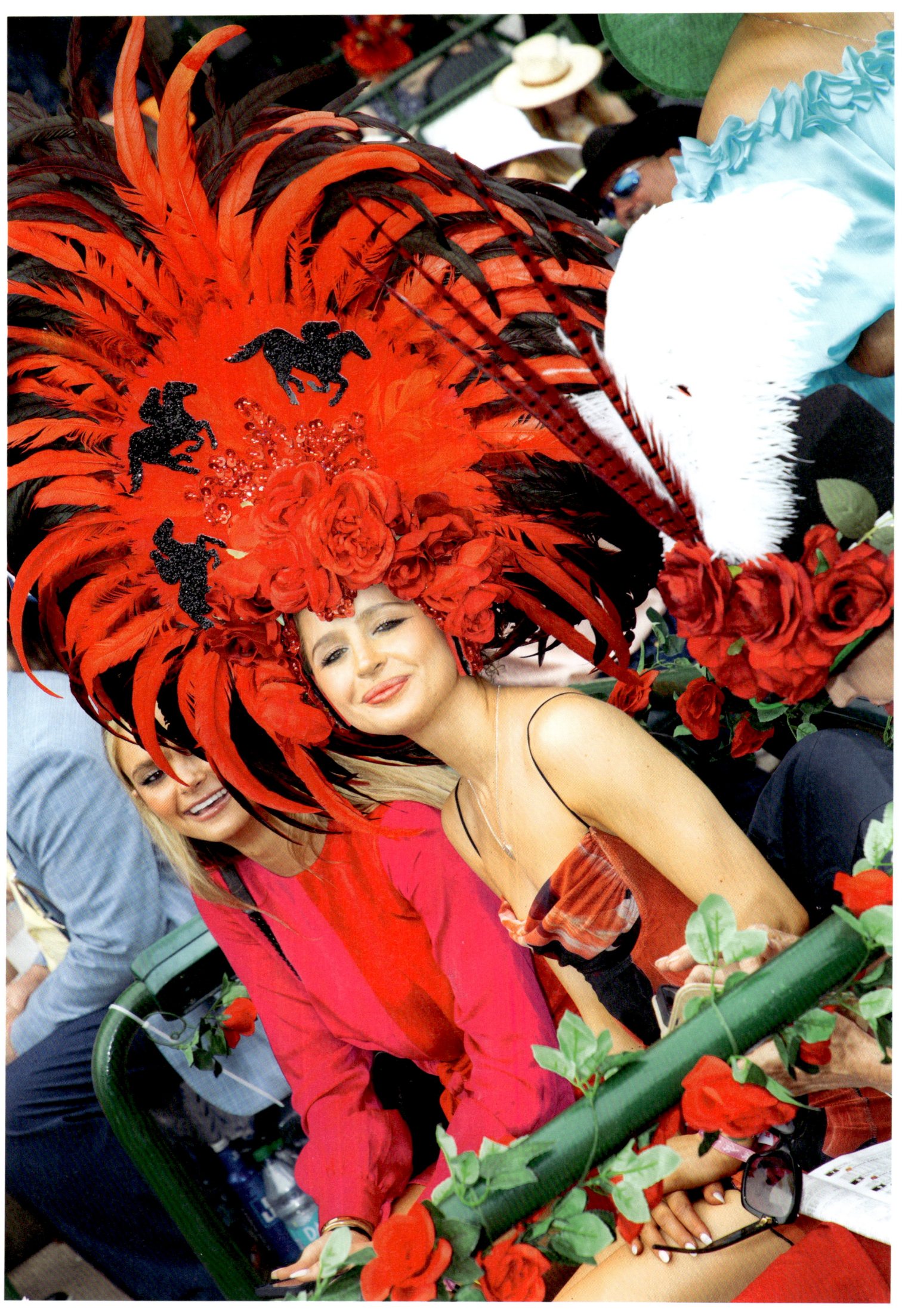

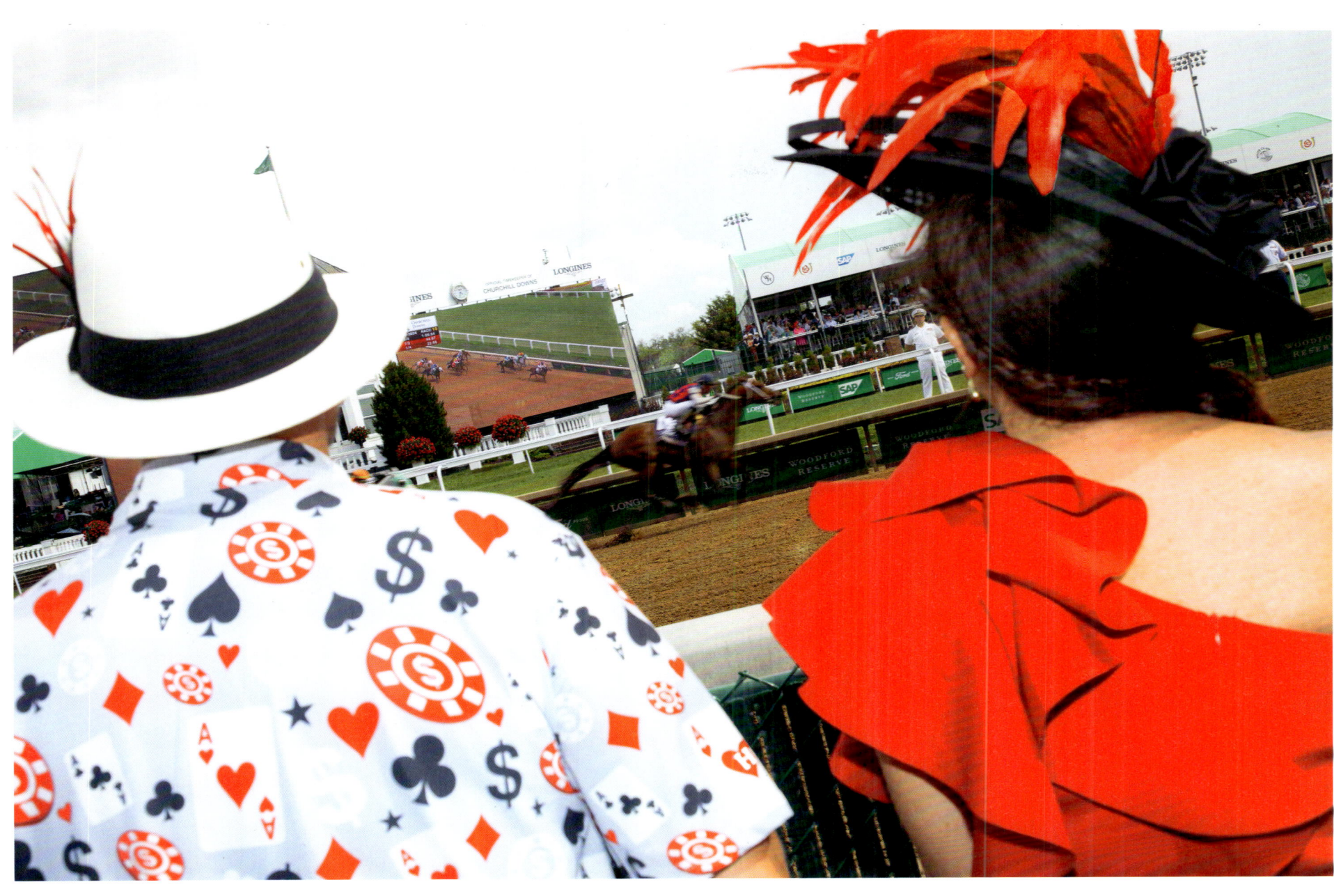

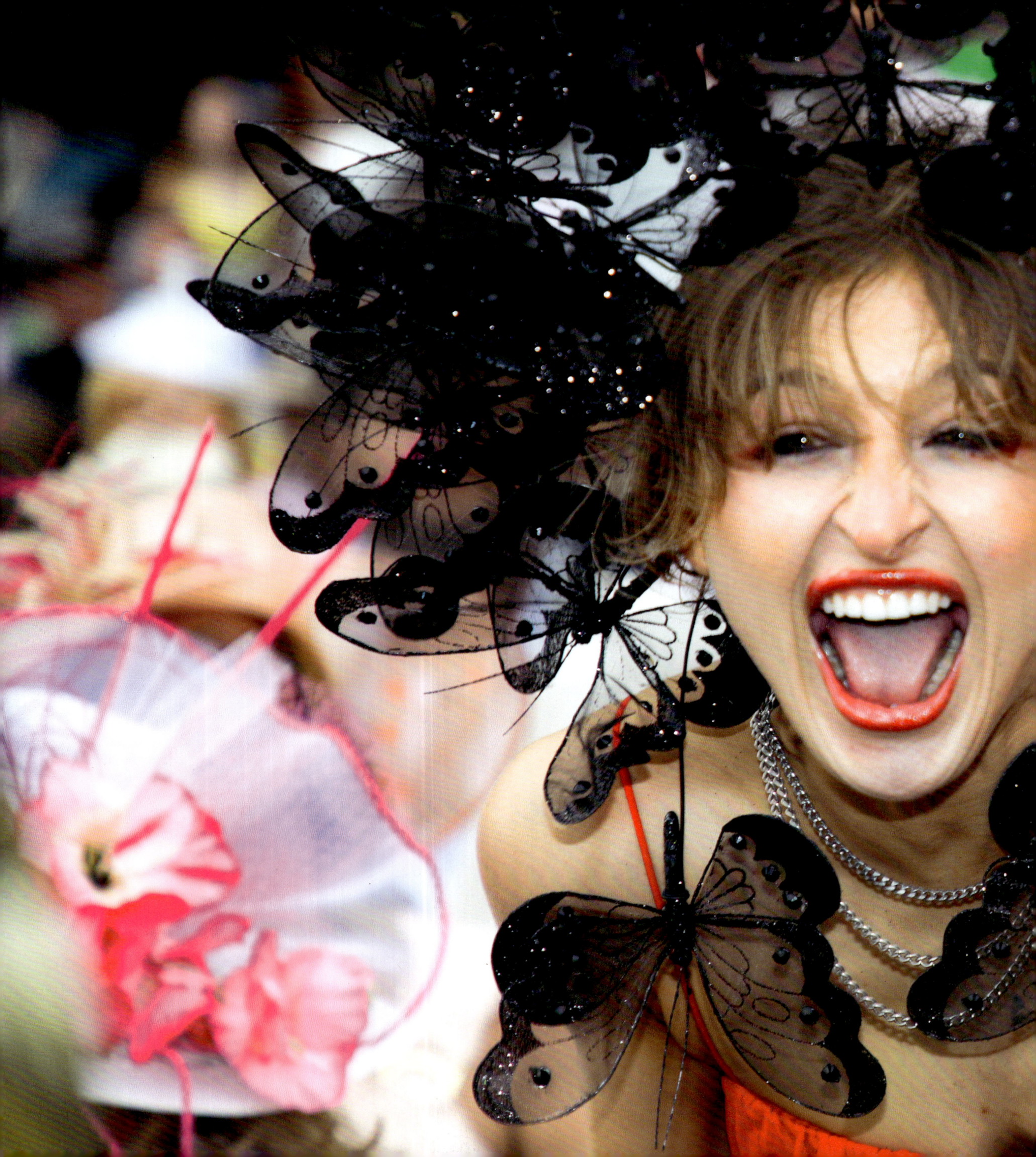

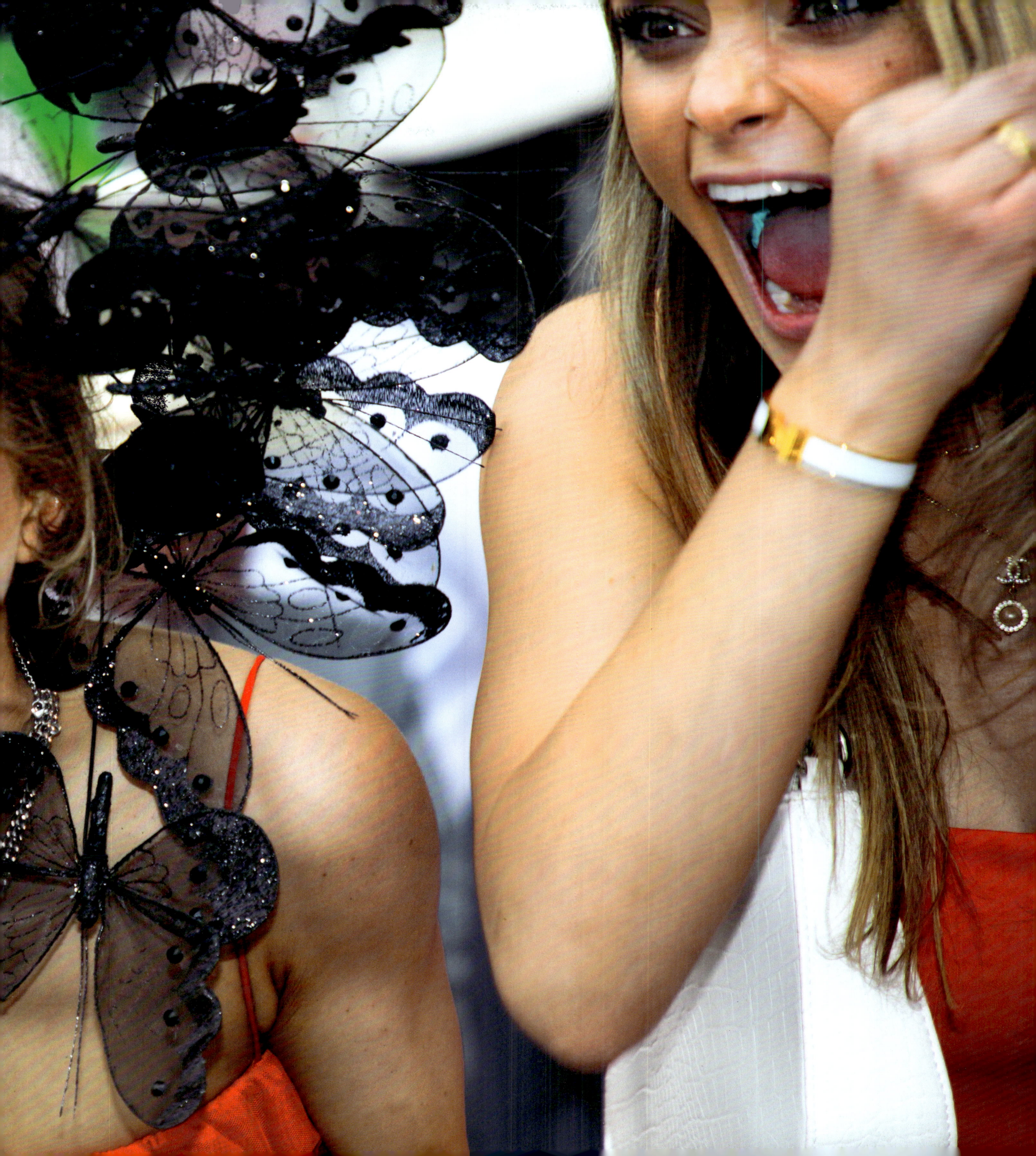

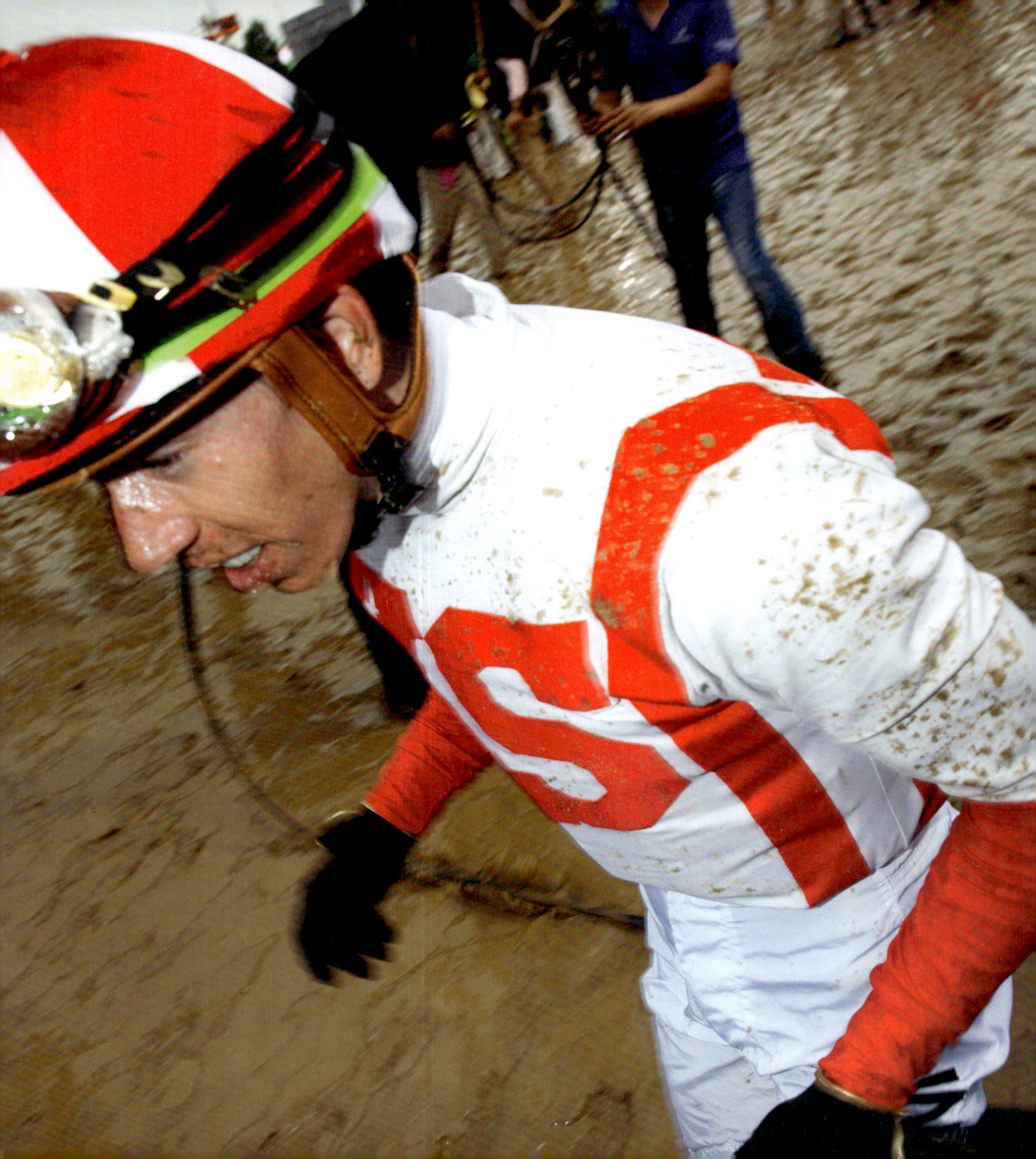

And They're off...   by Lili Kobielski

I was on horseback before I could walk—a little white pony named Andy who toted me through evenings of fireflies and a lonely childhood made sweeter by his friendship. My mother was raised on the back of a horse, as was her mother and grandmother, horses connecting four generations of women. The feeling when your stomach drops while gripping a sprinting thoroughbred, the long hours caring for them as foals, and the thrill of watching them race. I grew up close to Saratoga Racetrack, knowing the absolute delight of holding my mother's hand as the horses danced in the paddock with braided manes and rainbow saddle cloths.

I moved to New York City to study photography, inevitably finding myself homesick on the A train to Aqueduct Racetrack in Queens to catch a few races, to hear the familiar chatter of the horsemen and gamblers. I started photographing for *Vogue* soon after finishing school, collaborating with the brilliant editor, Suzanne Shaheen, who was hired to create visuals to invigorate *Vogue*'s new digital platform. She encouraged me to conceptualize and pitch my own stories in addition to taking assignment work, and when I noticed that *Vogue* historically had very little coverage of The Kentucky Derby, I begged for the assignment. I remember sitting at Suzy's kitchen table a few days before my first Derby, pouring over the mood board she'd made for the shoot: the brilliant colors and poppy flash of Martin Parr's hilarious and alternately cutting and kind social commentary and Tina Barney's subtle photographs of class, clothes, and manners. Both these geniuses of photography were rattling around my head every year while shooting the Derby, along with a healthy dose of the irreverent and luminary street photographer Daniel Arnold.

Navigating Louisville on Derby week is an illogical mess of road closures and flashing lights, a national holiday for the depressed stretch of town holding the racetrack. Rows of slightly sagged shotgun houses, barbeque joints, and liquor stores with bulletproof glass, lots of folks sitting on their porches watching the ladies teetering by in massive hats and too-high heels, their boyfriends rowdy and drinking before noon. A buzzing economy outside the track selling water, flip flops, racing programs, lawn parking, and homemade ribs to go. The crush of hats and brilliant colors are nearly blinding as tens of thousands approach the grandstand, mimicking the old-world elegance of London and Paris's racetracks, with a particularly American show of garishness and swagger. And that's the beautiful thing about the Derby—there is true elegance there. But this is not Royal Ascot; this is a messy, gorgeous, flaunting-everything affair, a time for pageantry, to prance, to feel fancy and seen. Racegoers make their own hats from cardboard, glue guns, beads, feathers—the bigger the better. They gamble, they drink and burn in the sun all day; they plop their little ones on the racetrack rail and pet the soft noses of the outriders' horses—the next generation of the horse-obsessed.

California Chrome, a cheap, long-shot Cinderella story won my first Derby. I remember the crushing rush of 100,000 people screaming, stomping, and crying as the horses flew by the finish line. For a moment, I felt the familiar drop in your stomach at imagining the speed. Nearly every Derby, I sat under the outside rail on the racetrack, smashed between AP and Getty photographers with their telescope-like lenses, so close to the horses that dirt from their hooves occasionally hurtled at us as they flew by. It's a great place to sit to view the races, but even better for viewing the colorful masses streaming through the grandstand. Every year, I would pace the length of the stretch and the first turn, the crowd's noise a wall of sound almost meditative. It's a joy as a photographer to be lost in a crowd and so utterly ignored. No one saw me, or if they did, they didn't care when I raised my camera, except for the few dozen who called me over to them, wanting a photo of their biggest hat yet, or their kids, or their best friends, or their lover. The more I photographed, the more I found spectacular details popping through the wall of humanity: goldfish ensconced in the resin heel of a shoe, a mohawk of roses, two startlingly Arbus-like twins in matching Chanel.

A few months ago, at my tenth and probably last Derby, I was watching the crowd, bemused and tired, waiting for the big race to go off. I thought how grateful I am to have reconciled my lifelong love of photography and horses with the people who go along with horses at this spectacular pageant for nearly a third of my life. As a dapple-gray horse danced by, I thought of my little white pony who meandered with me through the complicated fields of growing up, and of the generations of my family tied to these magnificent beasts and all the money, fun, speed, culture, and fashion that spirals from them. I turned back to face the crowd when hundred-dollar bills started fluttering down from "Millionaire's Row" at the top of the grandstand. People below were jumping and scrambling for the money, and, in the scuffle, rose petals glued to a giant hat exploded in the air as the announcer boomed, "And they're off in the Kentucky Derby!"

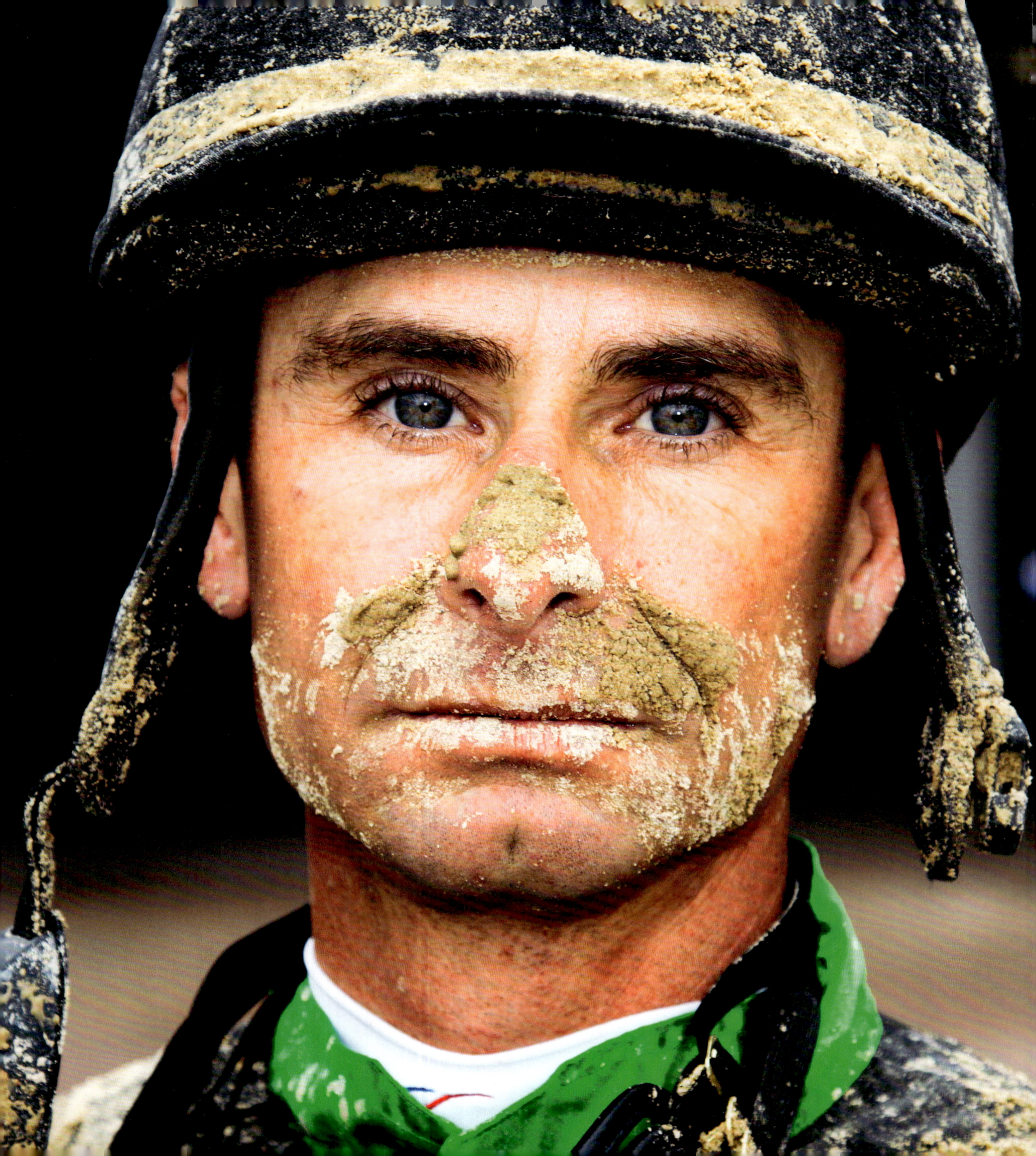

Thank you to...

My wonderful, wild boys, Cyprien and Henry, you make me better every day, and I am always trying to make you proud. My brilliant, unwavering, hardest-working husband, Maciek, for always loving us and supporting the next adventure. My parents, Mike and Jenny, I would be nothing without your spectacular talent, support, and love my whole life. My nearly life-long friend, Suzy, I am humbled by your accomplishments and I am the luckiest to have you in my life as a friend and editor, thank you for believing in and being the first ever to publish this work. Olivia, you are a splendid editor and friend and I am eternally grateful for your invaluable contributions to this body of work. Matthew and Sam, you are geniuses, kind, funny, and smart, and I am so incredibly lucky to have you both in my corner, championing this work. What a beautiful book you have made! Anthony, thank you for believing in me and this project, I am in awe of all that you do and eternally grateful that these photos will be memorialized by the finest of publishers. Helmut, how could I be so lucky? You are unmatched in talent, brilliance, kindness, and generosity. Thank you for sharing your light.

First published in the United States of America in 2026 by
Rizzoli International Publications, Inc.
49 West 27th Street
New York, NY 10001
www.rizzoliusa.com

Publisher: Charles Miers
Associate Publisher: Anthony Petrillose
Senior Editor: Gisela Aguilar
Production Director: Colin Hough Trapp
Managing Editor: Lynn Scrabis
Design Coordinator: Tim Biddick

Art Direction and Book Design by Sam Shahid & Matthew Kraus, Shahid/Kraus & Company

2026 2027 2028 2029 2030 / 10 9 8 7 6 5 4 3 2 1

ISBN: 978-0-8478-4224-7

Library of Congress Control Number: 2025946243

Printed in Singapore

This book is neither authorized by nor affiliated with Churchill Downs.

The authorized representative in the EU for product safety and compliance is
Mondadori Libri S.p.A., via Gian Battista Vico 42, Milan, Italy, 20123
www.mondadori.it

Visit us online:
Instagram: @RizzoliBooks
Facebook.com/RizzoliNewYork
Youtube.com/user/RizzoliNY

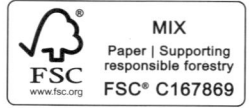

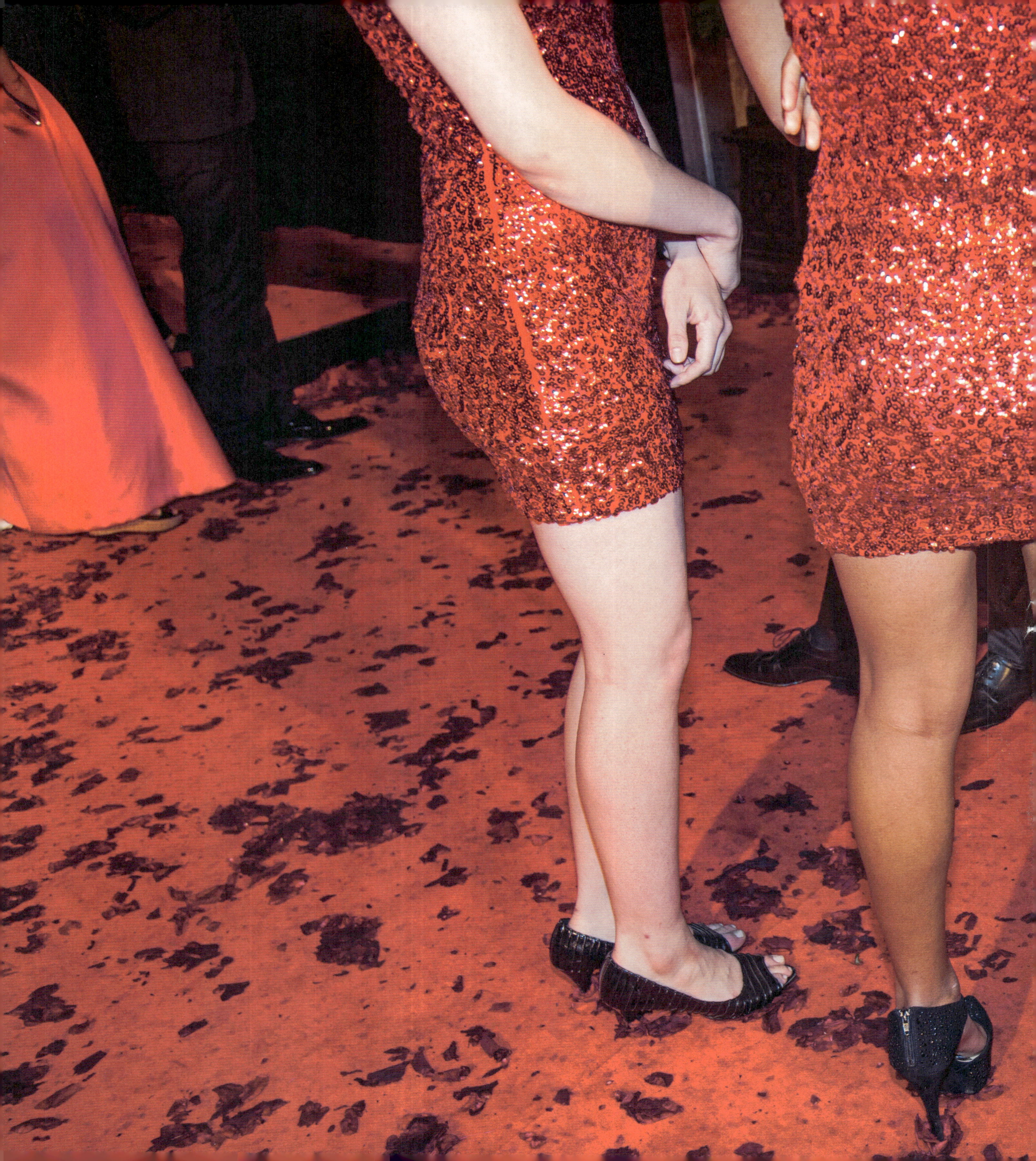